SOURCES
of the
WESTERN
TRADITION

Sources of the Western Tradition

TENTH EDITION

VOLUME II: FROM THE RENAISSANCE TO THE PRESENT

Marvin Perry

Baruch College, City University of New York

Howard E. Negrin, Editorial Associate

Australia • Brazil • Mexico • Singapore • United Kingdom • United States

***Sources of the Western Tradition
Volume II: From the Renaissance to the
Present, Tenth Edition***
Marvin Perry

Product Manager: Richard Lena

Project Manager: Julia Giannotti

Content Developer: Matt Gervais

Product Assistant: Alex Shore

Marketing Manager: Valerie Hartman

Content Project Manager: Dan Saabye

Manufacturing Planner: Fola Orekoya

IP Analyst: Alex Ricciardi

IP Project Manager: Betsy Hathaway

Production Service:
    Lumina Datamatics, Inc.

Compositor: Lumina Datamatics, Inc.

Senior Art Director: Cate Barr

Cover Designer: Lisa Devenish,
    Devenish Design

Cover Image: The Discord, 1855
    (colour litho)/Heppenheimer, F.
    (19th century)/NEW YORK HISTORICAL
    SOCIETY/Collection of the New-York
    Historical Society, USA/Bridgeman
    Images

For product information and technology assistance, contact us at Cengage Customer & Sales Support, 1-800-354-9706.
For permission to use material from this text or product, submit all requests online at **www.cengage.com/permissions**. Further permissions questions can be emailed to **permissionrequest@cengage.com**.

Library of Congress Control Number: 2012949049

ISBN: 978-1-337-39761-2

Cengage
20 Channel Center Street
Boston, MA 02210
USA

Cengage is a leading provider of customized learning solutions with employees residing in nearly 40 different countries and sales in more than 125 countries around the world. Find your local representative at **www.cengage.com**.

Cengage products are represented in Canada by Nelson Education, Ltd.

To learn more about Cengage platforms and services, visit **www.cengage.com**.
To register or access your online learning solution or purchase materials for your course, visit **www.cengagebrain.com**.

Printed in the United States of America
Print Number: 01   Print Year: 2017

Contents

Preface xiii
Prologue xvii
Introduction: The Middle Ages
    and the Modern World xix

PART ONE: EARLY MODERN EUROPE 1

CHAPTER 1 *The Rise of Modernity* 1

1. The Humanists' Fascination with
   Antiquity 3
      Petrarch, The Father of Humanism 4
      Leonardo Bruni, Study of Greek
         Literature and a Humanist Educational
         Program 5
2. Break with Medieval Political
   Theory 7
      Niccolò Machiavelli, *The Prince* 8
3. The Lutheran Reformation 11
      Martin Luther, Critique of Church
         Doctrines 11
4. European Expansion 15
      William Carr, The Dutch East India
         Company 15
5. The Atlantic Slave Trade 16
      John Newton, *Thoughts upon the African
         Slave Trade* 17
      Malachy Postlethwayt, Slavery
         Defended 19
      John Wesley, Slavery Attacked 20
6. A Secular Defense of Absolutism 23
      Thomas Hobbes, *Leviathan* 23
7. The Triumph of Constitutional Monarchy
   in England: The Glorious Revolution 26
      The English Declaration of Rights 27

CHAPTER 2 *The Scientific Revolution* 30

1. Galileo: Confirming the Copernican
   System 33
      Galileo Condemned by the
         Inquisition 34
2. Advocacy of Experimental Science 36
      Francis Bacon, Prophet of Modern
         Experimental Science 36
      William Harvey, The Circulation
         of the Blood 38
      Herman Boerhaave, *A New Method of
         Chemistry* 39
3. The Autonomy of the Mind 40
      René Descartes, *Discourse on Method* 41
4. The Mechanical Universe 44
      Isaac Newton, *Principia Mathematica* 44
5. The Limitations of Science 47
      Blaise Pascal, *Pensées* 47

CHAPTER 3 *The Enlightenment* 49

1. The Enlightenment Outlook 51
      Immanuel Kant, "What Is
         Enlightenment?" 51
2. Enlightenment Political Thought 53
      John Locke, *Second Treatise on
         Government* 54
      Thomas Jefferson, Declaration of
         Independence 56
      Montesquieu, *The Spirit of the Laws* 57
      Jean Jacques Rousseau, *The Social
         Contract* 59
      Thomas Paine, "The Absurdity of
         Hereditary Government" 62
3. Attack on Religion 63
      Voltaire, A Plea for Tolerance and
         Reason 63

Thomas Paine, *The Age of Reason*   67
Baron d'Holbach, "Religion Is a Mere
  Castle in the Air"   68

4. Epistemology   71
   John Locke, *Essay Concerning Human
     Understanding*   71
   Claude-Adrien Helvétius, *Essays on the
     Mind* and *A Treatise on Man*   73

5. Compendium of Knowledge   74
   Denis Diderot, *Encyclopedia*   75

6. Humanitarianism   77
   Caesare Beccaria, Condemning
     Torture   77
   John Howard, *State of the Prisons in
     England and Wales*   79
   Denis Diderot, *Encyclopedia*: "Men and
     Their Liberty Are Not Objects of
     Commerce. . . ."   80

7. Literature as Satire: Critiques of European
   Society   82
   Voltaire, *Candide*   82
   Montesquieu, *The Persian
     Letters*   84

8. Madame du Châtelet: A Woman of
   Brilliance   85
   Madame du Châtelet, An Appeal for
     Female Education   86

9. On the Progress of Humanity   87
   Marquis de Condorcet, Progress of the
     Human Mind   87

PART TWO: MODERN EUROPE   91

CHAPTER 4 *Era of the French Revolution*   91

1. Abuses of the Old Regime   94
   Arthur Young, Plight of the French
     Peasants   94
   Emmanuel Sieyès, *What Is the Third
     Estate?*   96

2. The Role of the Philosophes   97
   Alexis de Tocqueville, Critique of the
     Old Regime   97

3. Liberty, Equality, Fraternity   99
   *Declaration of the Rights of Man and of the
     Citizen*   100

4. Expansion of Human Rights   101
   Olympe de Gouges, *Declaration of the
     Rights of Woman and of the Female
     Citizen*   102
   Society of the Friends of Blacks, *Address
     to the National Assembly in Favor of the
     Abolition of the Slave Trade*   103
   *Petition of the Jews of Paris, Alsace,
     and Lorraine to the National Assembly,
     January 28, 1790*   105

5. The Jacobin Regime   107
   Maximilien Robespierre, Republic of
     Virtue   108
   General Louis de Lignières Turreau,
     Uprising in the Vendée   110
   The District of Saint-Quentin,
     De-Christianization   111

6. Napoleon: Destroyer and Preserver of the
   Revolution   112
   Napoleon Bonaparte, Leader, General,
     Tyrant, Reformer   113
   Madame de Staël, Critic of
     Napoleon   117

CHAPTER 5 *The Industrial Revolution*   119

1. Early Industrialization   121
   Edward Baines, Britain's Industrial
     Advantages and the Factory
     System   121
   Adam Smith, The Division of Labor   124

2. The New Science of Political
   Economy   125
   Adam Smith, Against Government
     Intervention in the Economy   126
   Thomas R. Malthus, *On the Principle of
     Population*   127

3. The Dark Side of Industrialization   130
   Sadler Commission, Report on Child
     Labor   130
   James Phillips Kay, Moral and Physical
     Dissipation   132
   Friedrich Engels, *The Condition of the
     Working Class in England*   134
4. Factory Discipline   135
   Factory Rules   136
5. The Capitalist Ethic   138
   Samuel Smiles, *Self-Help* and *Thrift*   138
6. Reformers   140
   Robert Owen, Ameliorating the Plight of
     the Poor   141

CHAPTER 6 *Romanticism, Reaction, Revolution*   144

1. Romanticism   146
   William Wordsworth, *Tables
     Turned*   146
   William Blake, *Milton*   147
2. Conservatism   148
   Edmund Burke, *Reflections on the Revolution
     in France*   149
   Klemens von Metternich, The Odious
     Ideas of the Philosophes   151
   Joseph de Maistre, Errors of the
     Enlightenment   152
3. Liberalism   153
   Benjamin Constant, On the Limits of
     Popular Sovereignty   153
   John Stuart Mill, *On Liberty*   154
4. Rise of Modern Nationalism   156
   Ernst Moritz Arndt, The War of
     Liberation   156
   Giuseppe Mazzini, Young Italy   158
5. Repression   160
   Karlsbad Decrees   160
6. 1848: The Year of Revolutions   161
   Flora Tristan, "Workers, Your Condition . . .
     Is Miserable and Distressing"   162
   Alexis de Tocqueville, The June Days   165
   Carl Schurz, Revolution Spreads to the
     German States   167

CHAPTER 7 *Thought and Culture in an Age of Science and Industry*   171

1. Realism in Literature   172
   Charles Dickens, *Hard Times*   173
   Henrik Ibsen, *A Doll's House*   174
2. Theory of Evolution   179
   Charles Darwin, Natural Selection   179
3. The Socialist Revolution   183
   Karl Marx and Friedrich Engels,
     Communist Manifesto   184
4. The Evolution of Liberalism   189
   L. T. Hobhouse, Justification for State
     Intervention   190
   Herbert Spencer, *The Man Versus the
     State*   191

CHAPTER 8 *Politics and Society, 1845–1914*   193

1. The Irish Potato Famine   194
   Poulett Scrope, Evictions   196
   Nicholas Cummins, The Famine in
     Skibbereen   197
2. The Lower Classes   198
   William Booth, *In Darkest England and the
     Way Out*   199
   Henry Mayhew, Prostitution in Victorian
     London   201
   M. I. Pokrovskaya, Working Conditions
     for Women in Russian Factories   204
3. Feminism and Antifeminism   205
   John Stuart Mill, *The Subjection
     of Women*   206
   Emmeline Pankhurst, "Why We Are
     Militant"   209
   The Goncourt Brothers, On Female
     Inferiority   212
   Almroth E. Wright, *The Unexpurgated Case
     Against Woman Suffrage*   213
4. German Racial Nationalism   216
   Houston Stewart Chamberlain,
     The Importance of Race   217

Pan-German League, "There Are Dominant Races and Subordinate Races"   219

5. Anti-Semitism: Regression to the Irrational   220
Theodor Fritsch, Rules to Follow Regarding Jews   221
The Dreyfus Affair: The Henry Memorial   222
The Kishinev Pogrom, 1903   223
Theodor Herzl, *The Jewish State*   226

CHAPTER 9 *European Imperialism*   229

1. The Spirit of British Imperialism   232
Joseph Chamberlain, The British Empire: Colonial Commerce and "The White Man's Burden"   232
Karl Pearson, Social Darwinism: Imperialism Justified by Nature   234

2. European Rule in Africa   236
Cecil Rhodes and Lo Bengula, "I Had Signed Away the Mineral Rights of My Whole Country"   237
Edmund Morel, *The Black Man's Burden*   239
Richard Meinertzhagen, An Embattled Colonial Officer in East Africa   241
German Brutality in Southwest Africa: Exterminating the Herero   244

3. Chinese Resentment of Western Imperialism   247
The Boxer Rebellion   247

4. British Rule in India   249
Lord Lytton, Speech to the Calcutta Legislature, 1878   249
Jawaharlal Nehru, India's Resentment of the British   250

5. Imperialism Debated   251
The Edinburgh Review, "We . . . Can Restore Order Where There Is Chaos, and Fertility Where There Is Sterility"   252
John Atkinson Hobson, An Early Critique of Imperialism   253

CHAPTER 10 *Modern Consciousness*   256

1. The Overman and the Will to Power   257
Friedrich Nietzsche, *The Will to Power* and *The Antichrist*   258

2. The Unconscious   262
Sigmund Freud, *Civilization and Its Discontents*   263

3. The Political Potential of the Irrational   264
Gustave Le Bon, Mass Psychology   264
Vilfredo Pareto, Politics and the Nonrational   267

4. Human Irrationality in the Modernist Novel   269
Joseph Conrad, *Heart of Darkness*   270

PART THREE: WESTERN CIVILIZATION IN CRISIS   275

CHAPTER 11 *World War I*   275

1. Militarism   277
Heinrich von Treitschke, The Greatness of War   277
Friedrich von Bernhardi, *Germany and the Next War*   278
Henri Massis and Alfred de Tarde, *The Young People of Today*   279

2. Pan-Serbism: Nationalism and Terrorism   281
The Black Hand   281
Baron von Giesl, Austrian Response to the Assassination   283

3. War as Celebration: The Mood in European Capitals   285
Roland Dorgelès, Paris: "That Fabulous Day"   285

Stefan Zweig, Vienna: "The Rushing
Feeling of Fraternity"   287

Philipp Scheidemann, Berlin: "The Hour
We Yearned For"   288

Bertrand Russell, London: "Average Men
and Women Were Delighted at the
Prospect of War"   289

4. The Horror of Trench Warfare   290
British and German Combatants,
The Battle of the Somme   291
Siegfried Sassoon, "Base Details"   293
Wilfred Owen, "Disabled"   293

5. Women at War   294
Naomi Loughnan, Genteel Women in the
Factories   294
Magda Trott, Opposition to Female
Employment   296
Russian Women in Combat   298

6. The Ethnic Cleansing of Turkey's Armenian
Minority   300
Takhoui Levonian and Yevnig Adrouni,
The Survivors Remember   301

7. The Paris Peace Conference   303
Woodrow Wilson, The Idealistic
View   303
Georges Clemenceau, French Demands for
Security and Revenge   305

8. The Bolshevik Revolution   307
V. I. Lenin, *What Is to Be Done?*   307
V. I. Lenin, The Call to Power   308

9. The War and European Consciousness   309
D. H. Lawrence, Disillusionment   310
Ernst von Salomon, Brutalization of the
Individual   311
Friedrich Wilhelm Heinz, The Persistent
War Spirit   312
Erich Maria Remarque, The Lost
Generation   313

CHAPTER 12 *Era of Totalitarianism*   314

1. Socialist Condemnation of the
Bolsheviks   318
Proclamation of the Kronstadt Rebels   318

Karl Kautsky, "Socialism Has Already
Suffered a Defeat"   319

2. Modernize or Perish   320
Joseph Stalin, The Hard Line   320

3. Forced Collectivization   321
Lev Kopelev, Terror in the
Countryside   322
Miron Dolot, Famine in Ukraine   323
Execution by Hunger   324

4. Shaping a New Society and a
"New Man"   325
A. O. Avdienko, The Cult of Stalin   325
Yevgeny Yevtushenko, Literature as
Propaganda   326

5. Stalin's Terror   327
Lev Razgon, *True Stories*   328
Anatoly Zhigulin, A "Cannibalistic
Sport"   329

6. The Rise of Italian Fascism   330
Benito Mussolini, Fascist Doctrines   331

7. The Fledgling Weimar Republic   333
Friedrich Jünger, Antidemocratic
Thought in the Weimar
Republic   334
Konrad Heiden, The Ruinous Inflation,
1923   337
Heinrich Hauser, "With Germany's
Unemployed"   338

8. The Rise of Nazism   342
Adolf Hitler, *Mein Kampf*   342
Kurt G. W. Ludecke, The Demagogic
Orator   347

9. The Leader-State   348
Ernst Rudolf Huber, "The Authority of
the Führer Is . . . All-Inclusive and
Unlimited"   349

10. The Nazification of Culture and Society   350
Jakob Graf, *Heredity and Racial Biology For
Students*   350
Louis P. Lochner, Book Burning   351
Stephen H. Roberts, The Nuremberg
Rally, 1936   352

11. Persecution of the Jews   354
The Nuremberg Laws: Depriving Jews of
Civil Liberties   355

Ernst Heimer, Jew-Hatred in School
Books   356

David H. Buffum, Night of the Broken
Glass (*Kristallnacht*)   357

12. The Anguish of the Intellectuals   359
Johan Huizinga, *In the Shadow of
Tomorrow*   359
Nicolas Berdyaev, Modern Ideologies at
Variance with Christianity   360

CHAPTER 13 *World War II*   363

1. Prescient Observers of Nazi
Germany   364
Horace Rumbold, "Pacifism Is the
Deadliest of Sins"   365
George S. Messersmith, "The Nazis
Were after . . . Unlimited Territorial
Expansion"   366

2. Remilitarization of the Rhineland   368
William L. Shirer, *Berlin Diary*   368

3. The Anschluss, March 1938   369
Stefan Zweig, *The World of Yesterday*   370

4. The Munich Agreement   372
Neville Chamberlain, In Defense of
Appeasement   372
Winston Churchill, "A Disaster of the
First Magnitude"   374

5. World War II Begins   376
Adolf Hitler, "Poland Will Be Depopulated
and Settled with Germans"   376

6. The Fall of France   378
Heinz Guderian, "French Leadership . . .
Could Not Grasp the Significance of the
Tank in Mobile Warfare"   379

7. Battle of Britain   380
Winston Churchill, "Blood Toil, Tears,
and Sweat"   381

8. Nazi Ideology and the German Military: The
Indoctrination of the German Solider   382
Nazi Tracts, Generals' Memorandums,
Letters Home, Bolsheviks and Jews as
Devils   383

Heinrich Himmler, The Racial
Empire   386

9. Stalingrad: A Turning Point   387
Anton Kuzmich Dragan, A Soviet Veteran
Recalls   387
Joachim Wieder, *Memories and
Reassessments*   389

10. The Holocaust   391
Hermann Graebe, Slaughter of Jews in
Ukraine   392
Rudolf Hoess, *Commandant of
Auschwitz*   394
Survivors, Concentration Camp Life and
Death   396
Joseph Freeman, The Death
March   397

11. Resistance in Warsaw   398
Marek Edelman, The Warsaw Ghetto
Uprising, 1943   399
Tadeusz Bor-Komorowski, The Warsaw
Uprising, 1944   402

12. D-Day, June 6, 1944   406
Historical Division, U.S. War
Department, *Omaha Beachhead*   406

13. The End of the Third Reich   409
Nerin E. Gun, The Liberation of
Dachau   409
Margaret Freyer, The Fire Bombing of
Dresden   411
Adolf Hitler, Political Testament   412

14. The Defeat of Japan   414
Veterans, The Battle of Iwo
Jima   415

CHAPTER 14 *Europe: A New
Era*   418

1. The Aftermath in Germany   420
Theodore H. White, Germany in
Ruins   420
A German Expellee from Czechoslovakia,
"Germans Were Driven Out of Their
Homeland Like Dogs"   421

The Nuremberg Trials of Nazi War
Criminals   422
Justice Robert H. Jackson, Closing
Arguments for Convicting Nazi War
Criminals   424

2. The Cold War   426
George F. Kennan, The Policy of
Containment   427

3. Communist Oppression   429
Fens Jicai, China's Cultural Revolution:
Communist Fanaticism   430
Teeda Butt Mam, Genocide in Cambodia:
"It Takes a River of Ink to Write Our
Stories"   433

4. Resistance and Dissidence in the
Communist World   435
Milovan Djilas, *The New Class: An
Analysis of the Communist
System*   435
Andor Heller, The Hungarian Revolution,
1956   436

5. The New Germany: Confronting the
Past   439
Hannah Vogt, *The Burden of
Guilt*   440
Richard von Weizsäcker, "We Seek
Reconciliation"   441

6. The Twilight of Imperialism   443
Mahatma Gandhi, The Partition of
India   444
Patrice Lumumba, Congo Independence
Day   446
Ho Chi Minh, Declaration of Independence
for the Republic of Vietnam, September 2,
1945   448

PART FOUR: THE CONTEMPORARY WORLD   451

CHAPTER 15 *The West in an Age of Globalism*   451

1. The Collapse of Communism   453
Vaclav Havel, The Failure of
Communism   454

2. Transplanting Western Democracy in
Non-Western Lands   456
Fareed Zakaria, "Democracy Has Its Dark
Sides"   457

3. The Editors, The European Union: An
Uncertain Future   458

4. The Editors, ISIS: Ideology, Appeal,
Terrorism   462

5. The Editors, Islam in Europe: Failure of
Assimilation   470

6. Female Oppression   473
U.N. Secretary-General, *Ending Violence
against Women:* "The Systematic
Domination of Women by Men"   474

7. The Taliban's War on Women   477
A Persecuted Afghan Woman, "You Come
from a Family of Infidels"   477

8. U.S. Department of State, Human
Trafficking   479

9. Resurgence of Anti-Semitism   482
U.S. State Department, *Contemporary
Global Anti-Semitism*   483

10. In Defense of European Values   488
Jacques Ellul, *The Betrayal of the
West*   489

Preface

Teachers of the Western Civilization survey course have long recognized the pedagogical value of primary sources, which are the raw materials of history. The tenth edition of *Sources of the Western Tradition* contains a wide assortment of documents—over 400 in total, principally primary sources—that have been carefully selected and edited to fit the needs of the survey and to supplement standard texts.

I have based my choice of documents for the two volumes on several criteria. To introduce students to those ideas and values that characterize the Western tradition, *Sources of the Western Tradition* emphasizes the works of the great thinkers. While focusing on the great ideas that have shaped the Western heritage, however, the volumes also provide a balanced treatment of political, economic, and social history. I have tried to select documents that capture the characteristic outlook of an age and provide a sense of the movement and development of Western history. The readings are of sufficient length to convey their essential meaning, and I have carefully extracted those passages that focus on the documents' main ideas.

An important feature of the compilation is the grouping of several documents that illuminate a single theme; such a constellation of related readings reinforces understanding of important themes and invites comparison, analysis, and interpretation. For example, in volume I, the section "The Humanists' Fascination with Antiquity" (see chapter 9), concerning the Renaissance, contains three interrelated readings: in the first, Petrarch shows his enthusiasm for ancient Greek and Roman culture; in the second, Leonardo Bruni discusses the value of studying Greek literature and proposes a humanist educational program; in the third, Lorenzo de' Medici expresses a quest for fame and glory in the manner of the ancients. In volume II, the section "The Twilight of Imperialism" (see chapter 14), contains three interrelated readings: in the first, Mahatma Gandhi warns against sectarian violence between Hindus and Muslims after India gained independence from Great Britain; in the second, Patrice Lumumba expresses deep resentment of the suffering and indignities experienced by the Congolese under colonialism and offers an inspiring vision of the future of an independent Congo; the third selection, expressing Vietnamese aspirations for independence at the end of World War II, is resonant with American and French revolutionary principles of the late-eighteenth century.

An overriding concern of mine in preparing this compilation was to make the documents accessible—to enable students to comprehend and to interpret historical documents on their own. I have provided several pedagogical features to facilitate this aim. Introductions of three types explain the historical setting, the authors' intent, and the meaning and significance of the readings. First, introductions to each chapter—thirteen in volume I and fifteen in volume II—provide comprehensive overviews of periods. Second, introductions to each numbered section or grouping treat the historical background for the reading(s) that follow(s). Third, each reading has a brief headnote that provides specific details about that reading.

Within some readings, interlinear notes, clearly set off from the text of the document, serve as transitions and suggest the main themes of the passages that follow. Used primarily in longer extracts of the great thinkers, these interlinear notes help to guide students through the readings.

To aid students' comprehension, brief editorial definitions or notes that explain unfamiliar or foreign terms are inserted into the running text. When terms or concepts in the documents require fuller explanations, these appear at the bottom of pages as footnotes. Where helpful,

I have retained the footnotes of authors, translators, or editors from whose works the documents were acquired. (Within the running text, original author or editor notes appear in parentheses, while my insertions appear in brackets. Within footnotes, my explanatory notes are distinguished by "—Eds." at the end of each one.) The review questions that appear at the ends of sections enable students to check their understanding of the documents; sometimes the questions ask for comparisons with other readings, linking or contrasting key concepts.

In the tenth edition, volume I contains thirty-three new documents. Among the chapters concerning the ancient world, in chapter 1 new selections have been added to the treatment of Mesopotamian literature and Near-Eastern mythical thought. Plato's misgivings about the political situation of his day, the famous *Epistle VII,* has been added to chapter 3. Accompanying Polybius's analysis of the Roman army in chapter 4 is a brief selection by a Roman official describing Roman discipline in the army. Livy's description of Hannibal's character enriches the selection on the Second Punic War. Dio Cassius's defense of Julius Caesar is also now included in chapter 4. Quintilian's astute insights into the learning process enhances the discussion of Roman culture in chapter 5. Josephus explains how the mighty Roman army was able to conquer and rule its vast empire. Added to the section on Christianity and Society in chapter 6 is a bishop's sermon on girls who took a vow of virginity in order to become "brides of Christ."

Turning to the Middle Ages, inserted into chapter 7 is a passage by Rhazes, a renowned Muslim physician, on the dangers of alcoholism. Also added is a medieval account of the administration of justice on an English manor. Chapter 8 has been reworked more than any of the other chapters. A new section, "The Lure of Combat," contains a poem by a nobleman capturing the excitement and appeal of combat. The second selection is drawn from a nobleman's book describing the honor a knight gained from success in tournaments

and battle. Another new section, "Medieval Entertainment," depicts sports in medieval London. Inserted into the section on Religious Dissent is Emperor Frederick II's account of the need to hunt down and exterminate heretics. A document revealing the questioning spirit of Adelard of Bath has been added to the section on medieval learning. Added to the treatment of medieval universities are examples of vagabond student poetry and an account of the ethnic hostility that prevailed in universities. New samples of troubadour love songs are now provided. Also new is Giovanni Boccaccio's famous description of the suffering caused by the Black Death.

The chapters dealing with Early Modern Europe have been somewhat altered. In chapter 9, Giorgio Vasari's assessment of Michelangelo's genius has been added to the section on Renaissance Art; passages illustrating Shakespeare's brilliant insights into human nature conclude the chapter. Added to chapter 10 are excerpts from *The Imitation of Christ,* Thomas à Kempis's great work of practical Christian spirituality, and The Twelve Articles illustrating the grievances of the peasants. In chapter 11, I have expanded the section on witchcraft with Friedrich Spee's sensitive account of the ordeal faced by a helpless woman indicted for witchcraft. The chapter also contains two new selections dealing with political thought: one, James I's insistence that kings derive their power from God; the other, a Huguenot noble's argument that resistance to royal absolutism was legitimate. To the selection from Francis Bacon in chapter 12, two other selections have been added under a new head, "Advocacy of Experimental Science." The new selections are William Harvey's account of his discovery of the circulation of the blood and chemist Herman Boerhaave's insistence that scientific truth requires the support of experimental evidence. A new section, "Enlightenment Political Thought," has been created for chapter 13. Supplementing the selections from John Locke, the Declaration of Independence, and Jean Jacques Rousseau, are excerpts from Montesquieu's *Spirit of the Laws,* discussing separation of powers, and Thomas Paine's *Rights of Man*, advocating a republican form of government over hereditary monarchy. Another new selection is Baron d'Holbach's critique of religion.

Volume II contains 53 new selections. Chapter 1, "The Rise of Modernity," has a new selection illustrating European expansion and the embryo of a world economy. The new additions to chapter 2, "The Scientific Revolution," and chapter 3, "The Enlightenment," are listed above in chapters 12 and 13 of volume I.

In the chapters concerning Modern Europe, chapter 4 has gained Olympe de Gouges's famous "Declaration of the Rights of Women and the Female Citizen." Chapter 6 now features Benjamin Constant's warning of the danger of unlimited popular sovereignty and Carl Schurz's eyewitness account of the enthusiasm that gripped German liberal-nationalists at the news of the February 1848 Revolution in Paris. An excerpt from Charles Dickens's *Hard Times,* illustrating realism in literature, has been inserted in chapter 7. Added to chapter 8 are two accounts of the horrific Irish Potato Famine and a female Russian doctor's description of the mistreatment of Russian women in factories. Added to chapter 9 are two opposing views of British rule in India, one by Lord Lytton, the other by Jawaharlal Nehru. Joseph Conrad's compelling *Heart of Darkness,* which explores human depravity, is a worthy addition to chapter 10.

All chapters in the third part of volume II, "Western Civilization in Crisis," have been altered. In chapter 11, three accounts by British and German combatants at the Battle of the Somme illustrate the horrors of trench warfare. A description of Russian women in combat complements the section "Women at War." The ethnic cleansing of Turkey's Armenian minority, which is often called genocide, is a fitting addition to a chapter on World War I. A passage from Lenin's *What Is to Be Done* provides insight into the Bolshevik Revolution. Two brief excerpts enrich the chapter's concluding section, "The War and European Con-

sciousness." Chapter 12 now includes two early attacks on the Soviet dictatorship, one the proclamation of the sailors at the Kronstadt naval base who revolted in 1921, the other by Karl Kautsky, a leading German Social Democrat. An excerpt from *Precocious Autobiography*, by a Russian poet, published after Stalin's death, describes the raw days of intellectual repression under Stalin. Two new selections deal with the persecution of the Jews in Nazi Germany prior to World War II; one is the Nuremberg Laws which deprived Jews of civil rights, while the other is a school book that depicts the Jew as the "devil in human form." The chapter now ends with a passage from *The Fate of Man in the Modern World* (1935) by Nicholas Berdyaev, a Russian Christian philosopher who argues that Communism and Nazism were modern forms of idolatry. Introducing chapter 13 are two analyses of the dangers posed by Hitler, written by British and American diplomats. Their warnings, written shortly after Hitler took power, provided astute insight into the dangers of the Third Reich. A virtually new and comprehensive section on Nazi ideology has also been added to the chapter. It contains excerpts from German generals, soldiers, and Nazi propaganda tracts depicting Jews and Communists as devils. Memorandums from Heinrich Himmler call for the Germans to regard subjugated peoples as slaves. Enriching the section on the Holocaust are several accounts by Jewish survivors depicting the cruel treatment of Jewish prisoners by SS guards. Several graphic accounts by American veterans describe the brutal campaign of the Pacific island of Iwo Jima in the last year of the war with Japan.

The final part, concerning the recent past and the contemporary world, has undergone considerable revision. Added to the first section, "The Aftermath in Germany," is Justice Robert H. Jackson's closing arguments at the Nuremberg trial of Nazi war criminals. George F. Kennan's influential article advising a policy of containment to deal with the Soviet threat defines the early days of the Cold War. A new section, "Communist Oppression in Asia" contains statements by victims of the Chinese Cultural Revolution and genocide in Cambodia. Another new section, "The Twilight of Imperialism," contains three selections: Mahatma Gandhi's plea for an end to the violence between Hindus and Muslims that engulfed India after the British departure; a speech by Patrice Lumumba, prime minister of the new Congo state on the day the Congo gained independence from Belgium; and a document proclaiming Vietnam's independence from France, a document that was disregarded by the French rulers of their Asian colony. In chapter 15, the concluding chapter, we had to deal with the problem of treating contemporary events that rapidly change. This holds true particularly for ISIS, Muslim migrants in Europe, and the European Union. To deal with this dilemma, my colleague Howard Negrin and I decided to write essays on these topics that were as up-to-date as possible and could be revised just prior to publication. The remaining new selections are a description of the Taliban's war on women by a young Afghan woman who lived through it and the testimonies of victims of human trafficking prepared by the U.S. Department of State.

I wish to thank the following instructors for their critical reading of the manuscript: Kelly DeVries, Loyola University Maryland; Don Schwegler, Elmira College; Paula Allen, Southeastern Oklahoma State University; Tobias Brinkmann, Penn State University Park; Andrew Aberdein, Florida Institute of Technology; Harvey Solganick, Southwestern Baptist Theological Seminary; and Donna Donald, Liberty University.

I am grateful to the staff of Wadsworth /Cengage Learning who lent their talents to the project. Nancy Blaine, who served as senior sponsoring editor for several editions, is no longer with the company but her contribution is still felt. Scott Greenan, though no longer with Cengage, made several significant recommendations and Julia Giannotti, senior development editor, effectively helped to resolve problems. A special thanks to Matt Gervais, development editor, who conscientiously and efficiently prepared the revision for production. I thank also Bridget Leahy who skillfully copyedited the manuscript and Mathew Rohit who ably guided it through production. Also deserving of my gratitude are Alexandra Ricciardi, Betsy Hathaway, and Kristine Janssens, who managed the difficult task of obtaining permissions smoothly; and Cate Rickard Barr, senior art director, who managed the design of the cover.

It is of course gratifying to do a tenth edition of *Sources of the Western Tradition*, which was first published in 1987. As always, I thank my wife, Phyllis Perry, for her encouragement and computer expertise, which saved me time and aggravation. The death several years ago of George Bock, my good friend and valuable assistant over many editions, still saddens me. He had insightfully evaluated proposed selections and introductions and diligently proofread. I am fortunate that Howard Negrin, another old and good friend who has replaced George, has demonstrated the same talent and diligence. Also deserving of thanks is my friend and neighbor, Herbert Beyenbach, for his excellent translation of an important German document. Finally I remain grateful to T. H. Von Laue, who collaborated with me on several editions until his death, to Angela Von Laue, who replaced her husband until retiring from the project, and to Joseph Peden, who died after the third edition.

M.P.

Prologue
Examining Primary Sources

When historians try to reconstruct and apprehend past events, they rely on primary or original sources—official documents prepared by institutions and eyewitness reports. Similarly, when they attempt to describe the essential outlook or worldview of a given era, people, or movement, historians examine other types of primary sources—the literature, art, philosophy, and religious expressions of the time. These original sources differ from secondary or derivative sources—accounts of events and times written at a later date by people who may or may not have had access to primary sources. *Sources of the Western Tradition* consists principally of primary sources, which are the raw materials of history; they provide historians with the basic facts, details, and thinking needed for an accurate reconstruction of the past.

Historians have to examine a document with a critical spirit. The first question asked is: Is the document authentic and reliable? An early illustration of critical historical awareness was demonstrated by the Renaissance thinker Lorenzo Valla (c. 1407–1457) in *Declamation Concerning the False Decretals of Constantine*. The so-called Donation of Constantine, which was used by popes to support their claim to temporal authority, stated that the fourth-century Roman emperor Constantine had given the papacy dominion over the western Empire. By showing that some of the words in the document were unknown in Constantine's time and therefore could not have been used by the emperor, Valla proved that the document was forged by church officials several hundred years after Constantine's death. A more recent example of the need for caution is shown by the discovery of the "Hitler Diaries" in the mid-1980s. Several prominent historians "authenticated" the manuscript before it was exposed as a forgery—the paper dated from the 1950s

and Hitler died in 1945. Nor can all eyewitness accounts be trusted, something Thucydides, the great Greek historian, noted 2,400 years ago.

> [E]ither I was present myself at the events which I have described or else I heard of them from eye-witnesses whose reports I have checked with as much thoroughness as possible. Not that even so the truth was easy to discover: different eye-witnesses give different accounts of the same events, speaking out of partiality for one side or the other or else from imperfect memories.

An eyewitness's personal bias can render a document worthless. For example, in *The Auschwitz Lie* (1973), Thies Christophersen, a former SS guard at Auschwitz-Birkenau, denied the existence of gas chambers and mass killings in the notorious Nazi death camp, which he described as a sort of resort where prisoners, after work, could swim, listen to music in their rooms, or visit a brothel. Years later he was captured on videotape—he mistakenly thought the interviewers were fellow Nazis—confessing that he had lied about the gas chambers because of loyalty to the SS and his desire to protect Germany's honor.

After examining the relevant primary sources and deciding on their usefulness, historians have to construct a consistent narrative and provide a plausible interpretation. Ideally, this requires that they examine documentary evidence in a wholly neutral, detached, and objective way. But is it possible to write history without being influenced by one's own particular viewpoint and personal biases?

No doubt several historians examining the same material might draw differing conclusions, and each could argue his or her position persuasively. This is not surprising, for history is not an exact science, and historians, like all individuals, are influenced by their upbringing and education, by their thoughts and feelings. Conflicting interpretations of historical events and periods are expected and acceptable features of historiography. But what is not acceptable is the deliberate distortion and suppression of evidence in order to substantiate one's own prejudices.

A flagrant example of writers of history misusing sources and distorting evidence in order to fortify their own prejudices is the recent case of British historian David Irving, author of numerous books on World War II, several of them well reviewed. Increasingly Irving revealed an undisguised admiration for Hitler and an antipathy toward Jews, which led him to minimize and disguise atrocities committed by the Third Reich. Addressing neo-Nazi audiences in several lands, he asserted that the Holocaust is "a major fraud. . . . There were no gas chambers. They were fakes and frauds." In *Lying About Hitler: History, Holocaust and the David Irving Trial* (2001), Richard J. Evans, a specialist in modern German history with a broad background in archival research, exposed instance after instance of how Irving, in his attempt to whitewash Hitler, misquoted sources, "misrepresented data, . . . skewed documents [and] ignored or deliberately suppressed material when it ran counter to his arguments. . . . [When I] followed Irving's claims and statements back to the original documents on which they purported to rest . . . Irving's work in this respect was revealed as a house of cards, a vast apparatus of deception and deceit."

The sources in this anthology can be read on several levels. First, they enhance understanding of the historical period in which they were written, shedding light on how people lived and thought and the chief concerns of the time. Several of the sources, written by some of humanity's greatest minds, have broader implications. They are founts of wisdom, providing insights of enduring value into human nature and the human condition. The documents also reveal the evolution of those core ideas and values—reason, freedom, and respect for human dignity—that constitute the Western heritage. Equally important, several documents reveal the precariousness of these values and the threats to them. It is the hope of the editors that an understanding of the evolution of the Western tradition will foster a renewed commitment to its essential ideals.

The documents in these volumes often represent human beings struggling with the vital questions of their day. As such they invite the reader to react actively and imaginatively to the times in which they were produced and to the individuals who produced them. The documents should also be approached with a critical eye. The reader has always to raise several pointed questions regarding the author's motivation, objectivity, logic, and accuracy. In addition, depending on the content of a particular document, the reader should consider the following questions: What does the document reveal about the times in which it was written? About the author? About the nature, evolution, and meaning of the Western tradition? About human nature and human relations? About good and evil? About progress? About war and peace? About gender relations? About life and death? Doubtless other questions will come to mind. In many instances, no doubt, the documents will impel readers to reflect on current issues and their own lives.

Introduction
The Middle Ages and the Modern World

Historians have traditionally divided Western history into three broad periods: ancient, medieval, and modern. What is meant by modernity? What has the modern world inherited from the Middle Ages? How does the modern West differ fundamentally from the Middle Ages?[1]

Medieval civilization began to decline in the fourteenth century, but no dark age comparable to the three centuries following Rome's fall descended on Europe; its economic and political institutions and technological skills had grown too strong. Instead, the waning of the Middle Ages opened up possibilities for another stage in Western civilization: the modern age.

The modern world is linked to the Middle Ages in innumerable ways. European cities, the middle class, the state system, English common law, universities—all had their origins in the Middle Ages. During medieval times, important advances were made in business practices, including partnerships, systematic bookkeeping, and the bill of exchange. By translating and commenting on the writings of Greek and Arabic thinkers, medieval scholars preserved a priceless intellectual heritage, without which the modern mind could never have evolved. Medieval thinkers established a tradition of critical thinking that in future centuries would nurture thought in areas other than theology.

Feudal traditions lasted long after the Middle Ages. Up to the French Revolution, for instance, French aristocrats enjoyed special privileges and exercised power over local government. In England, the aristocracy controlled local government until the Industrial Revolution transformed English society in the nineteenth century. Retaining the medieval ideal of the noble warrior, aristocrats continued to dominate the officer corps of European armies through the nineteenth century and even into the twentieth. Aristocratic notions of duty, honor, loyalty, and courtly love had endured into the twentieth century.

During the Middle Ages, Europeans began to take the lead over the Muslims, the Byzantines, the Chinese, and all the other peoples in the use of technology. Medieval technology and inventiveness stemmed in part from Christianity, which taught that God had created the world specifically for human beings to subdue and exploit. Consequently, medieval people employed animal power and labor-saving machinery to relieve human drudgery. Moreover, Christianity taught that God was above nature, not within it, so the Christian had no spiritual obstacle to exploiting nature—unlike, for instance, the Hindu. In contrast to classical humanism, the Christian outlook did not consider manual work degrading; even monks combined it with study.

The Christian stress on the sacred worth of the individual (each person had an immortal soul that was God's concern), on human equality (differences in rank and birth were of no account to God on Judgment Day), and on the higher law of God (divine precepts had a greater pull on conscience than did the state's laws) has never ceased to influence Western civilization. Even though in modern times the various Christian churches have not often taken the lead in political and social reform, the ideals identified with the Judeo-Christian tradition have become part of the Western heritage. As such, they have inspired social reformers who may no longer identify with their ancestral religion. In structuring canon (church) law into a coherent and rational system, church jurists provided a model for legal systems in emerging European states. Moreover, specific elements of

---

[1]Material for this introduction is taken from Marvin Perry et al., *Western Civilization*, 11th ed. (Boston: Cengage, 2009), pp. 282–287.

canon law have become an integral part of modern Western law. Medieval jurists, for example, argued for a replacement of trials by ordeals of fire or water, which were central to ancient Germanic folk law, with rational trial procedures, and insisted that marriages based on fraud or duress could be invalidated.

Believing that God's law was superior to state or national decrees, medieval philosophers provided a theoretical basis for opposing tyrannical kings who violated Christian principles. The idea that both the ruler and the ruled are bound by a higher law would, in a secularized form, become a principal element of modern liberal thought.

Feudalism also contributed to the history of liberty. According to feudal theory, the king, as a member of the feudal community, was duty-bound to honor agreements made with his vassals. Lords possessed personal rights, which the king was obliged to respect. Resentful of a king who ran roughshod over customary feudal rights, lords also negotiated contracts with the crown, such as the famous Magna Carta (1215), to define and guard their customary liberties. To protect themselves from the arbitrary behavior of a king, feudal lords initiated what came to be called *government by consent* and the *rule of law*.

During the Middle Ages, then, there gradually emerged the idea that law was not imposed on inferiors by an absolute monarch but required the collaboration of the king and his subjects; that the king, too, was bound by the law; and that lords had the right to resist a monarch who violated agreements. A related phenomenon was the rise of representative institutions, with which the king was expected to consult on the realm's affairs. The most notable such institution was the British Parliament; although subordinate to the king, it became a permanent part of the state. Later, in the seventeenth century, Parliament would successfully challenge royal authority. Thus, continuity exists between the feudal tradition of a king bound by law and the modern practice of limiting the authority of the head of state.

Although the elements of continuity are clear, the characteristic outlook of the Middle Ages is as different from that of the modern age as it was from the outlook of the ancient world. Religion was the integrating feature of the Middle Ages, whereas science and secularism—a preoccupation with worldly life—determine the modern outlook. The period from the Italian Renaissance of the fifteenth century through the eighteenth-century Age of Enlightenment constituted a gradual breaking away from the medieval world-view—a rejection of the medieval conception of nature, the individual, and the purpose of life. The transition from medieval to modern was neither sudden nor complete, for there are no sharp demarcation lines separating historical periods. While many distinctively medieval ways endured in the sixteenth, seventeenth, and even eighteenth centuries, these centuries saw as well the rise of new intellectual, political, and economic forms, which marked the emergence of modernity.

Medieval thought began with the existence of God and the truth of his revelation as interpreted by the church, which set the standards and defined the purposes for human endeavor. The medieval mind rejected the fundamental principle of Greek philosophy: the autonomy of reason. Without the guidance of revealed truth, reason was seen as feeble. Philosophical inquiry was not permissible if the mind arrived at ideas that the church considered heretical.

Scholastics engaged in genuine philosophical speculation, but they did not allow philosophy to challenge the basic premises of their faith. Unlike either ancient or modern thinkers, medieval scholars ultimately believed that reason alone could not provide a unified view of nature or society. A rational soul had to be guided by a divine light. For all medieval philosophers, the natural order depended on a supernatural order for its origin and purpose. To understand the natural world properly, it was necessary to know its relationship to the higher world. The discoveries of reason had to accord with Scripture as interpreted by the church. In medieval thought, says historian-philosopher Ernst Cassirer,

[n]either science nor morality, neither law nor state, can be erected on its own foundations. Supernatural assistance is always needed to bring them to true perfection. . . . Reason is and remains the servant of revelation; within the sphere of natural intellectual and psychological forces, reason leads toward, and prepares the ground for, revelation.[2]

In the modern view, both nature and the human intellect are self-sufficient. Nature is a mechanical system that operates without miracles or any other form of divine intervention. To comprehend nature and society, the mind needs no divine assistance; it accepts no authority above reason. The modern mentality finds it unacceptable to reject the conclusions of science on the basis of clerical authority and revelation or to ground politics, law, or economics on religious dogma. It refuses to settle public issues by appeals to religious belief, which is now seen as a strictly private concern.

The medieval philosopher understood both nature and society to be a hierarchical order. God was the source of moral values, and the church was responsible for teaching and upholding these ethical norms. Kings acquired their right to rule from God. The entire social structure constituted a hierarchy: The clergy guided society according to Christian standards; lords defended Christian society from its enemies; and serfs, lowest in the social order, toiled for the good of all. In the hierarchy of knowledge, a lower form of knowledge derived from the senses, and the highest type of knowledge, theology, dealt with God's revelation. The world beyond the moon, because it was closer to God, constituted a higher realm of existence; heavenly objects were made of a substance too pure, too spiritual to be found on earth. To the medieval mind, the cosmos was a giant ladder, a qualitative order, ascending toward heaven. God was at the summit of this hierarchical universe and the earth, base and vile, stood just above hell.

The hierarchical ordering of nature, society, and knowledge had a divine sanction.

Rejecting the medieval division of the universe into higher and lower realms and superior and inferior substances, the modern view postulated the uniformity of nature and nature's laws: the cosmos knows no privilege of rank; heavenly bodies follow the same laws of nature as earthly objects. Space is geometric and homogeneous, not hierarchical, heterogeneous, and qualitative. The universe was no longer conceived as finite and closed but as infinite, and the operations of the cosmos were explained mathematically. The modern thinker studies mathematical law and chemical composition, not grades of perfection. Spiritual meaning is not sought in an examination of the material world. Roger Bacon, for example, described seven coverings of the eye and then concluded that God had fashioned the eye in this manner in order to express the seven gifts of the Spirit. This way of thinking is alien to the modern scientific outlook. So, too, is the medieval belief that natural disasters, such as plagues and famines, are God's punishments for people's sins.

The outlook of the modern West also broke with the rigid division of medieval society into three orders: clergy, nobles, and commoners. The intellectual justification for this arrangement, as expressed by the English prelate John of Salisbury (c. 1115–1180), has been rejected by modern Westerners: "For inferiors owe it to their superiors to provide them with service, just as the superiors in their turn owe it to their inferiors to provide them with all things needful for their protection and succor."[3] Opposing the feudal principle that an individual's obligations and rights are a function of his or her rank in society, the modern view stressed equality of opportunity and equal treatment under the law. It rejected the idea that society should be guided by clergy, who were deemed to possess a special wisdom; by nobles, who were entitled to special privileges; and by monarchs, who were thought to receive their power from God.

[2]Ernst Cassirer, *The Philosophy of the Enlightenment* (Boston: Beacon, 1955), p. 40.

[3]John of Salisbury, *Policraticus*, trans. John Dickinson (New York: Russell & Russell, 1963), pp. 243–244.

The modern West also rejected the personal and customary character of feudal law. As the modern state developed, law assumed an impersonal and objective character. For example, if the lord demanded more than the customary forty days of military service, the vassal might refuse to comply, because he would see the lord's request as an unpardonable violation of custom and agreement, as well as an infringement on his liberties. In the modern state, with a constitution and a representative assembly, if a new law increasing the length of military service is passed, it merely replaces the old law. People do not refuse to obey it because the government has broken faith or violated custom.

In the modern world, the individual's relationship to the universe has been radically transformed. Medieval people lived in a geocentric universe that was finite in space and time. The universe was small, enclosed by a sphere of stars, beyond which were the heavens. The universe, it was believed, was some four thousand years old, and, in the not-too-distant future, Christ would return and human history would end. People in the Middle Ages knew why they were on earth and what was expected of them; they never doubted that heaven would be their reward for living a Christian life. Preparation for heaven was the ultimate aim of life. J. H. Randall, Jr., a historian of ideas, eloquently sums up the medieval view of a purposeful universe, in which the human being's position was clearly defined:

> The world was governed throughout by the omnipotent will and omniscient mind of God, whose sole interests were centered in man, his trial, his fall, his suffering and his glory. Worm of the dust as he was, man was yet the central object in the whole universe. . . . And when his destiny was completed, the heavens would be rolled up as a scroll and he would dwell with the Lord forever. Only those who rejected God's freely offered grace and with hardened hearts refused repentance would be cut off from this eternal life.[4]

This comforting medieval vision is alien to the modern outlook. Today, in a universe some 12 billion years old, in which the earth is a tiny speck floating in an endless cosmic ocean, where life evolved over tens of millions of years, many Westerners no longer believe that human beings are special children of God; that heaven is their ultimate goal; that under their feet is hell, where grotesque demons torment sinners; and that God is an active agent in human history. To many intellectuals, the universe seems unresponsive to the religious supplications of people, and life's purpose is sought within the limits of earthly existence. Science and secularism have driven Christianity and faith from their central position to the periphery of human concerns. In the nineteenth and twentieth centuries, Christian thinkers lamented the waning of faith. Distressed by all-consuming secularism, crude materialism, and vicious class and national antagonisms, these thinkers attributed the ills of the modern West to a diminishing commitment to Christianity and called for spiritual renewal. Some of them, looking back nostalgically to the Middle Ages, when life had an overriding religious purpose and few doubted the truth of Christian teachings, contended that the modern West would benefit from a reaffirmation of those Christian concerns and values that had energized medieval society.

The modern outlook developed gradually from the Renaissance to the eighteenth-century Age of Enlightenment. Mathematics rendered the universe comprehensible. Economic and political thought broke free of the religious frame of reference. Science became the great hope of the future. The thinkers of the Enlightenment wanted to liberate humanity from superstition, ignorance, and traditions that could not pass the test of reason. They saw themselves as emancipating culture from theological dogma and clerical authority. Rejecting the Christian idea of a person's inherent sinfulness, they held that the individual was basically good and that evil resulted from faulty institutions, poor education, and bad leadership. Thus, the concept of a rational and free society in which individuals could realize their potential slowly emerged.

---

[4]J. H. Randall, Jr., *The Making of the Modern Mind* (Boston: Houghton Mifflin, 1940), p. 34.

CHAPTER 1

The Rise of Modernity

THE TRIUMPH OF GALATEA, by Raphael, 1513. This fresco from the Palazzo della Farnesina in Rome exemplifies the Renaissance artist's elevation of the human form. The mythological subject is also humanistic in its evocation of the ancient Greek tradition. *(Villa Farnesina, Rome, Italy/Bridgeman Images)*

From the fifteenth through the seventeenth centuries, medieval attitudes and institutions broke down, and distinctly modern cultural, economic, and political forms emerged. For many historians, the Renaissance, which originated in the city-states of Italy, marks the starting point of the modern era. The Renaissance was characterized by a rebirth of interest in the humanist culture and outlook of ancient Greece and Rome. Although Renaissance individuals did not repudiate Christianity, they valued worldly activities and interests to a much greater degree than did the people of the Middle Ages, whose outlook was dominated by Christian otherworldliness. Renaissance individuals were fascinated by this world and by life's possibilities; they aspired to live a rich and creative life on earth and to fulfill themselves through artistic and literary activity.

Individualism was a hallmark of the Renaissance. The urban elite sought to demonstrate their unique talents, to assert their own individuality, and to gain recognition for their accomplishments. The most admired person during the Renaissance was the multi-talented individual, the "universal man," who distinguished himself as a writer, artist, linguist, athlete. Disdaining Christian humility, Renaissance individuals took pride in their talents and worldly accomplishments—"I can work miracles," said the great Leonardo da Vinci.

During the High Middle Ages there had been a revival of Greek and Roman learning. Yet there were two important differences between the period called the Twelfth-Century Awakening and the Renaissance. First, many more ancient works were restored to circulation during the Renaissance than during the cultural revival of the Middle Ages. Second, medieval scholastics had tried to fit the ideas of the ancients into a Christian framework; they used Greek philosophy to explain and demonstrate the truth of Christian teachings. Renaissance scholars, on the other hand, valued ancient works for their own sake, believing that Greek and Roman authors could teach much about the art of living.

A distinguishing feature of the Renaissance period was the humanist movement, an educational and cultural program based on the study of ancient Greek and Latin literature. By studying the humanities—history, literature, rhetoric, moral and political philosophy—humanists aimed to revive the worldly spirit of the ancient Greeks and Romans, which they believed had been lost in the Middle Ages.

Humanists were thus fascinated by the writings of the ancients. From the works of Thucydides, Plato, Cicero, Seneca, and other ancient authors, humanists sought guidelines for living life well in this world and looked for stylistic models for their own literary efforts. To the humanists, the ancients had written brilliantly, in an incomparable literary style, on friendship, citizenship, love, bravery, statesmanship, beauty, excellence, and every other topic devoted to the enrichment of human life.

Like the humanist movement, Renaissance art also marked a break with medieval culture. The art of the Middle Ages had served a religious function; its purpose was to lift the mind to God. It depicted a spiritual universe in which the supernatural was the supreme reality. The Gothic cathedral, with its flying buttresses, soared toward heaven, rising in ascending tiers; it reflected the medieval conception of a hierarchical universe with God at its apex. Painting also expressed gradations of spiritual values. Traditionally, the left side of a painting portrayed the damned, the right side the saved; dark colors expressed evil, light colors good. Spatial proportion was relative to spirituality—the less spiritually valuable a thing was, the less form it had (or the more deformed it was). Medieval art perfectly expressed the Christian view of the universe and the individual. The Renaissance shattered the dominance of religion over art, shifting attention from heaven to the natural world and to the human being; Renaissance artists often dealt with religious themes, but they placed their subjects in a naturalistic setting. Renaissance art also developed a new concept of visual space—perspective—that was defined from the standpoint of the individual observer. It was a quantitative space in which the artist, employing reason and mathematics, portrayed the essential form of the object as it appeared in three dimensions to the human eye: that is, it depicted the object in perspective.

The Renaissance began in the late fourteenth century in the northern Italian city-states, which had grown prosperous from the revival of trade in the Middle Ages. Italian merchants and bankers had the wealth to acquire libraries and fine works of art and to support art, literature, and scholarship. Surrounded by reminders of ancient Rome—amphitheaters, monuments, and sculpture—the well-to-do took an interest in classical culture and thought. In the late fifteenth and the sixteenth centuries, Renaissance ideas spread to Germany, France, Spain, and England through books available in great numbers due to the invention of the printing press in Germany in the mid-fifteenth century.

1   The Humanists' Fascination with Antiquity

Humanists believed that a refined person must know the literature of Greece and Rome. They strove to imitate the style of the ancients, to speak and write as eloquently as the Greeks and Romans. Toward these ends, they sought to read, print, and restore to circulation every scrap of ancient literature that could still be found.

Petrarch
THE FATHER OF HUMANISM

During his lifetime, Francesco Petrarca, or Petrarch (1304–1374), had an astounding reputation as a poet and scholar. Often called the "father of humanism," he inspired other humanists through his love for classical learning; for his criticism of medieval Latin as barbaric in contrast to the style of Cicero, Seneca, and other Romans; and for his literary works based on classical models. Petrarch saw his own age as a restoration of classical brilliance after an interval of medieval darkness.

A distinctly modern element in Petrarch's thought is the subjective and individualistic character of his writing. In talking about himself and probing his own feelings, Petrarch demonstrates a self-consciousness characteristic of the modern outlook.

Like many other humanists, Petrarch remained devoted to Christianity: "When it comes to thinking or speaking of religion, that is, of the highest truth, of true happiness and eternal salvation," he declared, "I certainly am not a Ciceronian or a Platonist but a Christian." Petrarch was a forerunner of the Christian humanism best represented by Erasmus (see pages 304–306). Christian humanists combined an intense devotion to Christianity with a great love for classical literature, which they much preferred to the dull and turgid treatises written by scholastic philosophers and theologians. In the following passage, Petrarch criticizes his contemporaries for their ignorance of ancient writers and shows his commitment to classical learning.

. . . O inglorious age! that scorns antiquity, its mother, to whom it owes every noble art—that dares to declare itself not only equal but superior to the glorious past. I say nothing of the vulgar, the dregs of mankind, whose sayings and opinions may raise a laugh but hardly merit serious censure. . . .

. . . But what can be said in defense of men of education who ought not to be ignorant of antiquity and yet are plunged in this same darkness and delusion?

You see that I cannot speak of these matters without the greatest irritation and indignation. There has arisen of late a set of dialecticians

[experts in logical argument], who are not only ignorant but demented. Like a black army of ants from some old rotten oak, they swarm forth from their hiding places and devastate the fields of sound learning. They condemn Plato and Aristotle, and laugh at Socrates and Pythagoras {all Greek philosophers}. And, good God! under what silly and incompetent leaders these opinions are put forth. . . . What shall we say of men who scorn Marcus Tullius Cicero, the bright sun of eloquence? Of those who scoff at Varro and Seneca [Roman philosophers] and are scandalized at what they choose to call the crude, unfinished style of Livy and Sallust [Roman historians]? . . .

Such are the times, my friend, upon which we have fallen; such is the period in which we live and are growing old. Such are the critics of

Petrarch: The First Modern Scholar and Man of Letters, trans. H. J. Robinson and H. W. Rolfe (New York: G. P. Putnam's Sons, 1909), pp. 208, 210, 213.

today, as I so often have occasion to lament and complain—men who are innocent of knowledge and virtue, and yet harbour the most exalted opinion of themselves. Not content with losing the words of the ancients, they must attack their genius and their ashes. They rejoice in their ignorance, as if what they did not know were not worth knowing. They give full rein to their license and conceit, and freely introduce among us new authors and outlandish teachings.

Leonardo Bruni
STUDY OF GREEK LITERATURE AND A HUMANIST EDUCATIONAL PROGRAM

Leonardo Bruni (1374–1444) was a Florentine humanist who extolled both intellectual study and active involvement in public affairs, an outlook called civic humanism. In the first reading from his *History of His Own Times in Italy*, **Bruni expresses the humanist's love for ancient Greek literature and language.**

Then first came a knowledge of Greek, which had not been in use among us for seven hundred years. Chrysoloras the Byzantine,[1] a man of noble birth and well versed in Greek letters, brought Greek learning to us. When his country was invaded by the Turks, he came by sea, first to Venice. The report of him soon spread, and he was cordially invited and besought and promised a public stipend to come to Florence and open his store of riches to the youth. I was then studying Civil Law,[2] but . . . I burned with love of academic studies, and had spent no little pains on dialectic and rhetoric. At the coming of Chrysoloras I was torn in mind, deeming it shameful to desert the law, and yet a crime to lose such a chance of studying Greek literature; and often with youthful impulse I would say to myself: "Thou, when it is permitted thee to gaze on Homer, Plato and Demosthenes,[3] and the other [Greek] poets, philosophers, orators, of whom such glorious things are spread abroad, and speak with them and be instructed in their admirable teaching, wilt thou desert and rob thyself? Wilt thou neglect this opportunity so divinely offered? For seven hundred years, no one in Italy has possessed Greek letters; and yet we confess that all knowledge is derived from them. How great advantage to your knowledge, enhancement of your fame, increase of your pleasure, will come from an understanding of this tongue? There are doctors of civil law everywhere; and the chance of learning will not fail thee. But if this one and only doctor of Greek letters disappears, no one can be found to teach thee." Overcome at length by these reasons, I gave myself to Chrysoloras,

Leonardo Bruni, *History of His Own Times in Italy* and *De Studiis a Literis* in Henry Osborn Taylor, *Thought and Expression in the Sixteenth Century*, 2nd rev. ed., vol. 1 (New York: Frederick Unger, 1930; republished 1959), pp. 36–37.
[1]Chrysoloras (c. 1355–1415), a Byzantine writer and teacher, introduced the study of Greek literature to the Italians, helping to open a new age of Western humanistic learning.—Eds.

[2]Civil law refers to the Roman law as codified by Emperor Justinian in the early sixth century a.d. and studied in medieval law schools.—Eds.
[3]Demosthenes (384–322 b.c.) was an Athenian statesman and orator whose oratorical style was much admired by Renaissance humanists.—Eds.

with such zeal to learn, that what through the wakeful day I gathered, I followed after in the night, even when asleep.

In a treatise, *De Studiis et Literis* (On Learning and Literature), written around 1405 and addressed to the noble lady Baptista di Montefeltro (1383–1450) daughter of the count of Urbino, Bruni outlines the basic course of studies that the humanists recommended as the best preparation for a life of wisdom and virtue. In addition to the study of Christian literature, Bruni encourages a wide familiarity with the best minds and stylists of ancient Greek and Latin cultures.

. . . The foundations of all true learning must be laid in the sound and thorough knowledge of Latin: which implies study marked by a broad spirit, accurate scholarship, and careful attention to details. Unless this solid basis be secured it is useless to attempt to rear an enduring edifice. Without it the great monuments of literature are unintelligible, and the art of composition impossible. To attain this essential knowledge we must never relax our careful attention to the grammar of the language, but perpetually confirm and extend our acquaintance with it until it is thoroughly our own. . . . To this end we must be supremely careful in our choice of authors, lest an inartistic and debased style infect our own writing and degrade our taste; which danger is best avoided by bringing a keen, critical sense to bear upon select works, observing the sense of each passage, the structure of the sentence, the force of every word down to the least important particle. In this way our reading reacts directly upon our style. . . .

But we must not forget that true distinction is to be gained by a wide and varied range of such studies as conduce to the profitable enjoyment of life, in which, however, we must observe due proportion in the attention and time we devote to them.

First amongst such studies I place History: a subject which must not on any account be neglected by one who aspires to true cultivation. For it is our duty to understand the origins of our own history and its development; and the achievements of Peoples and of Kings.

For the careful study of the past enlarges our foresight in contemporary affairs and affords to citizens and to monarchs lessons of incitement or warning in the ordering of public policy. From History, also, we draw our store of examples of moral precepts.

In the monuments of ancient literature which have come down to us History holds a position of great distinction. We specially prize such [Roman] authors as Livy, Sallust and Curtius;[4] and, perhaps even above these, Julius Caesar; the style of whose Commentaries, so elegant and so [clear], entitles them to our warm admiration. . . .

The great Orators of antiquity must by all means be included. Nowhere do we find the virtues more warmly extolled, the vices so fiercely decried. From them we may learn, also, how to express consolation, encouragement, dissuasion or advice. If the principles which orators set forth are portrayed for us by philosophers, it is from the former that we learn how to employ the emotions—such as indignation, or pity—in driving home their application in individual cases. Further, from oratory we derive our store of those elegant or striking turns of expression which are used with so much effect in literary compositions. Lastly, in oratory we find that wealth of vocabulary, that clear easy-flowing style, that verve and force, which are invaluable to us both in writing and in conversation.

I come now to Poetry and the Poets. . . . For we cannot point to any great mind of the past for whom the Poets had not a powerful attraction. Aristotle, in constantly quoting Homer, Hesiod, Pindar, Euripides and other [Greek] poets, proves that he knew their works hardly less intimately than those of the philosophers. Plato, also, frequently appeals to them, and in

---

[4]Q. Curtius Rufus, a Roman historian and rhetorician of the mid-first century A.D., composed a biography of Alexander the Great.—Eds.

this way covers them with his approval. If we turn to Cicero, we find him not content with quoting Ennius, Accius,[7] and others of the Latins, but rendering poems from the Greek and employing them habitually. . . . Hence my view that familiarity with the great poets of antiquity is essential to any claim to true education. For in their writings we find deep speculations upon Nature, and upon the Causes and Origins of things, which must carry weight with us both from their antiquity and from their authorship. Besides these, many important truths upon matters of daily life are suggested or illustrated. All this is expressed with such grace and dignity as demands our admiration. . . . To sum up what I have endeavoured to set forth. That high standard of education to which I referred at the outset is only to be reached by one who has seen many things and read much. Poet, Orator, Historian, and the rest, all must

be studied, each must contribute a share. Our learning thus becomes full, ready, varied and elegant, available for action or for discourse in all subjects. But to enable, us to make effectual use of what we know we must add to our knowledge the power of expression. These two sides of learning, indeed, should not be separated: they afford mutual aid and distinction. Proficiency in literary form, not accompanied by broad acquaintance with facts and truths, is a barren attainment; whilst information, however vast, which lacks all grace of expression, would seem to be put under a bushel or partly thrown away. Indeed, one may fairly ask what advantage it is to possess profound and varied learning if one cannot convey it in language worthy of the subject. Where, however, this double capacity exists—breadth of learning and grace of style— we allow the highest title to distinction and to abiding fame. If we review the great names of ancient [Greek and Roman] literature, Plato, Democritus, Aristotle, Theophrastus, Varro, Cicero, Seneca, Augustine, Jerome, Lactantius, we shall find it hard to say whether we admire more their attainments or their literary power.

---

[7]Ennius (239–169 B.C.) wrote the first great Latin epic poem, which was based on the legends of Rome's founding and its early history. Accius (c. 170–c. 90 B.C.), also a Roman, authored a history of Greek and Latin literature.—Eds.

REVIEW QUESTIONS

1. What do historians mean by the term "Renaissance humanism"?
2. What made Petrarch aware that a *renaissance*, or rebirth, of classical learning was necessary in his time?
3. Why did Leonardo Bruni abandon his earlier course of studies to pursue the study of Greek literature?
4. What subjects made up the basic course of studies advocated by Bruni?

---

2 Break with Medieval Political Theory

Turning away from the religious orientation of the Middle Ages, Renaissance thinkers discussed the human condition in secular terms and opened up possibilities for thinking about moral and political problems in new ways. Thus, Niccolò Machiavelli (1469–1527), a Florentine statesman and political theorist, broke with medieval political theory. Medieval political thinkers held that the ruler derived power from God and had a religious obligation to rule in accordance with God's precepts. Machiavelli, though, ascribed no divine origin to kingship, nor did he attribute events to the mysterious will of God; and he explicitly rejected the principle that kings should adhere to Christian moral teachings. For Machiavelli, the state was a purely human creation. Successful kings or princes, he asserted, should be concerned only with preserving and strengthening the state's power and must ignore questions of good and evil, morality and immorality. Machiavelli did not assert that religion was supernatural in origin and rejected the prevailing belief that Christian morality should guide political life. For him, religion's value derived from other factors: a ruler could utilize religion to unite his subjects and to foster obedience to law.

Niccolò Machiavelli
THE PRINCE

In contrast to medieval thinkers, Machiavelli did not seek to construct an ideal Christian community but to discover how politics was *really* conducted. In *The Prince*, written in 1513 and published posthumously in 1532, he studied politics in the cold light of reason, as the following passage illustrates.

It now remains for us to consider what ought to be the conduct and bearing of a Prince in relation to his subjects and friends. And since I know that many have written on this subject, I fear it may be thought presumptuous in me to write of it also; the more so, because in my treatment of it I depart widely from the views that others have taken.

But since it is my object to write what shall be useful to whosoever understands it, it seems to me better to follow the real truth of things than an imaginary view of them. For many Republics and Princedoms have been imagined that were never seen or known to exist in reality. And there is a great gulf between the manner in which we actually live and the way we ought to live.

Machiavelli removed ethics from political thinking. A successful ruler, he contended, is indifferent to moral and religious considerations. But will not the prince be punished on the Day of Judgment for violating Christian teachings? in startling contrast to medieval theorists, Machiavelli simply ignored the question. The action of a prince, he said, should be governed solely by necessity.

He that abandons reality for some fanciful ideal, is more likely to destroy rather than save himself, for anyone who would attempt to realize a high standard of goodness in everything, most be ruined among so many who are not good. It is essential, therefore, for a Prince who would maintain his position, to have learned how to be other than good, and to use or not to use his goodness as necessity requires.

Laying aside, therefore, all fanciful notions concerning a Prince, and considering those only that are true, I say that all men when they are

Adapted from Niccolò Machiavelli, *The Prince*, trans. Nina Hill Thomson (Oxford: The Clarendon Press, 1913), 3rd ed., pp. 109–110, 120–122, 125–130.

spoken of, and Princes more than others from their being set so high, are noted for certain of those qualities which attach either praise or blame. Thus one is accounted giving, another miserly; one is generous, another greedy; one cruel, another tenderhearted; one is faithless, another true to his word; one effeminate and cowardly, another high-spirited and courageous; one is courteous, another haughty; one lewd, another chaste; one upright, another crafty; one firm, another facile; one grave, another frivolous; one devout, another unbelieving; and the like. Everyone, I know, will admit that it would be most laudable for a Prince to be endowed with all of the above qualities that are reckoned good; but since it is impossible for him to possess or constantly practise them all, the conditions of human nature not allowing it, he must be discreet enough to know how to avoid the disapproval of those vices that would deprive him of his government, and, if possible, be on his guard also against those which might not deprive him of it; though if he cannot wholly restrain himself, he may with less scruple indulge in the latter. But he need never hesitate to incur the disapproval of those vices without which his authority can hardly be preserved. . . .

Machiavelli's rigorous investigation of politics led him to view human nature from the standpoint of its limitations and imperfections. The astute prince, he said, recognizes that human beings are by nature selfish, cowardly, and dishonest, and regulates his political strategy accordingly.

And here comes in the question whether it is better to be loved rather than feared, or feared rather than loved. It might be answered that we should wish to be both; but since love and fear can hardly exist together, if we must choose between them, it is far safer to be feared than loved. For of men it may generally be affirmed that they are thankless, fickle, false, studious to avoid danger, greedy of gain, devoted to you while you confer benefits upon them, and ready, as I said before, while the need is remote, to shed their blood, and sacrifice their property, their lives, and their children for you; but when it comes near they turn against you. The Prince, therefore, who without otherwise securing himself builds wholly on their pledges is undone.

Moreover, men are more likely to offend someone who seeks to make himself loved than someone who is feared.

For love is held by the tie of obligation, which, because men are a sorry breed, is broken on every prompting of self-interest; but fear is bound by the apprehension of punishment which never loosens its grasp.

Nevertheless a Prince should inspire fear in such ways that if he do not win love he may escape hate. For a man may very well be feared and yet not hated, as will always be the case so long as he does not intermeddle with the property or with the women of his citizens and subjects. And if constrained to put anyone to death, he should do so only when there is manifest cause or reasonable justification. But, above all, he must abstain from taking the property of others. For men will sooner forget the death of their father than the loss of their inheritance. . . .

Returning to the question of being loved or feared, I sum up by saying, that since his being loved depends upon his subjects, while his being feared depends upon himself, a wise Prince should build on what is his own, and not on what rests with others. Only, as I have said, he must do his best to escape hatred.

Everyone recognises how praiseworthy it is in a Prince to keep faith, and to act uprightly and not craftily. Nevertheless, we see from what has happened in our own days that Princes who have set little store by their word, but have known how to get the better of others by their cunning, have accomplished great things, and in the end had the better of those who trusted to honest dealing.

Be it known, then, that there are two ways of contending, one in accordance with the laws, the other by force; the first of which is proper to men, the second to beasts. But since the first method is often ineffectual, it becomes necessary to resort to the second. A Prince should, therefore, understand how to use well both the man and the beast. . . .

A prudent Prince neither can nor ought to keep his word when to keep it is hurtful to him and the causes which led him to pledge it are removed. If all men were good, this would not be good advice, but since they are dishonest and do not keep faith with you, you, in return, need not keep faith with them; and no Prince was ever at a loss for plausible reasons to cloak a breach of faith. Of this numberless recent instances could be given, and it might be shown how many solemn treaties and engagements have been rendered inoperative and idle through want of faith in Princes, and that he who has best known to play the fox has had the best success.

It is necessary, indeed, to put a good colour on this nature, and to be skilful in feigning and dissembling. But men are so simple, and governed so absolutely by their present needs, that he who wishes to deceive will never fail in finding willing dupes. . . .

It is not essential, then, that a Prince should have all the good qualities I have enumerated above, but it is most essential that he should seem to have them. Nay, I will venture to affirm that if he has and invariably practises them all, they are hurtful, whereas the appearance of having them is useful. Thus, it is well to seem merciful, faithful, humane, religious, and upright, and also to be so; but the mind should remain so balanced that were it needful not to be so,

you should be able and know how to change to the contrary.

And you are to understand that a Prince, and most of all a new Prince, cannot observe all those rules of conduct in respect whereof men are accounted good, being often forced, in order to preserve his Princedom, to act in opposition to good faith, charity, humanity, and religion. He must therefore keep his mind ready to shift as the winds and tides of Fortune turn, and, as I have already said, ought not to quit good courses if he can help it, but should know how to follow evil if he must.

A Prince should therefore be very careful that nothing ever escapes his lips which is not replete with the five qualities above named, so that to see and hear him, one would think him the embodiment of mercy, good faith, integrity, kindliness, and religion. And there is no virtue which it is more necessary for him to seem to possess than this last. . . .

Moreover, in the actions of all men, most of all Princes, the ends justify the means. Wherefore if a Prince succeeds in establishing and maintaining his authority, the means will always be judged honourable and be approved by everyone. For the vulgar are always taken by appearances and by results, and the world is made up of the vulgar, the few remain isolated when the many embrace the Prince.

A certain Prince of our own days, whom it is as well not to name, is always preaching peace and good faith, although the mortal enemy of both; and both, had he practised as he preaches, would, more often than once, have cost him his kingdom and authority.

REVIEW QUESTIONS

1. In what ways was Niccolò Machiavelli's advice to princes a break from the teachings of medieval political and moral philosophers?
2. Would Machiavelli's political advice help or hurt a politician in a modern democratic society?

3   The Lutheran Reformation

The reformation of the Western Christian church in the sixteenth century was precipitated by Martin Luther (1483–1546). A pious German Augustinian monk and theologian, Luther had no intention of founding a new church or overthrowing the political and ecclesiastical order of late medieval Europe. He was educated in the tradition of the New Devotion, which called for spiritual renewal, and as a theology professor at the university in Wittenberg, Germany, he opposed rationalistic, scholastic theology. Sympathetic at first to the ideas of Christian humanists like Erasmus, Luther too sought a reform of morals and an end to abusive practices within the church. But a visit to the papal court in Rome in 1510 left him profoundly shocked at its worldliness and disillusioned with the papacy's role in the church's governance.

Martin Luther
CRITIQUE OF CHURCH DOCTRINES

To finance the rebuilding of the church of St. Peter in Rome, the papacy in 1515 offered indulgences to those who gave alms for this pious work. An indulgence was a mitigation or remission of the penance imposed by a priest in absolving a penitent who confessed a sin and indicated remorse. Indulgences were granted by papal decrees for those who agreed to perform some act of charity, alms giving, prayer, pilgrimage, or other pious work. Some preachers of this particular papal indulgence deceived people into believing that a "purchase" of this indulgence would win them, or even the dead, a secure place in heaven.

In 1517, Luther tacked on the door of the Wittenberg castle church his *Ninety-five Theses* in which he denounced the abuses connected with the preaching of papal indulgences. The quarrel led quickly to other and more profound theological issues. His opponents defended the use of indulgences on the basis of papal authority, shifting the debate to questions about the nature of papal power within the church. Luther responded with a vigorous attack on the whole system of papal governance. The principal points of his criticism were set out in his *Address to the Christian Nobility of the German Nation Concerning the Reform of the Christian Estate*, published in August 1520. In the first excerpt that follows, Luther argued that the papacy was blocking any reform of the church and appealed to the nobility of Germany to intervene by summoning a "free council" to reform the church.

A central point of contention between Luther and Catholic critics was his theological teaching on justification (salvation) by faith and on the role of good works in the scheme of salvation. Luther had suffered anguish about his unworthiness before God. Then, during a mystical experience, Luther suddenly perceived that his salvation came not because of his good works but as a free gift from God due to Luther's faith in Jesus Christ.

Thus, while never denying that a Christian was obliged to perform good works, Luther argued that such pious acts were not helpful in achieving salvation. His claim that salvation, or justification, was attained through faith in Jesus Christ as Lord and Savior, and through that act of faith alone, became the rallying point of the Protestant reformers.

The Catholic position, not authoritatively clarified until the Council of Trent (1545–1563), argued that justification came not only through faith, but through hope and love as well, obeying God's commandments and doing good works. In *The Freedom of a Christian*, published in 1520, Luther outlined his teaching on justification by faith and on the inefficacy of good works; the second excerpt is from this work.

Another dispute between Luther and papal theologians was the question of interpretation of the Bible. In the medieval church, the final authority in any dispute over the meaning of scriptural texts or church doctrine was ordinarily the pope alone, speaking as supreme head of the church or in concert with the bishops in an ecumenical council. The doctrine of papal infallibility (that the pope could not err in teaching matters of faith and morals) was already well known, but belief in this doctrine had not been formally required. Luther argued that the literal text of scripture was alone the foundation of Christian truth, not the teaching of popes or councils. Moreover, Luther said that all believers were priests, and the clergy did not hold any power beyond that of the laity; therefore the special privileges of the clergy were unjustified. The third excerpt contains Luther's views on the interpretation of scripture and the nature of priestly offices.

ON PAPAL POWER

The Romanists [traditional Catholics loyal to the papacy] have very cleverly built three walls around themselves. Hitherto they have protected themselves by these walls in such a way that no one has been able to reform them. As

a result, the whole of Christendom has fallen abominably.

In the first place, when pressed by the temporal power they have made decrees and declared that the temporal power had no jurisdiction over them, but that, on the contrary, the spiritual power is above the temporal. In the second place, when the attempt is made to reprove them with the scriptures, they raise the objection that only the pope may interpret the scriptures. In the third place, if threatened with a council, their story is that no one may summon a council but the pope.

In this way they have cunningly stolen our three rods from us, that they may go unpunished. They have [settled] themselves within the safe stronghold of these three walls so that they can practice all the knavery and wickedness which we see today. Even when they have been compelled to hold a council they have weakened its power in advance by putting the princes under oath to let them remain as they were. In addition, they have given the pope full authority over all decisions of a council, so that it is all the same whether there are many councils or no councils. They only deceive us with puppet shows and sham fights. They fear terribly for their skin in a really free council! They have so intimidated kings and princes with this technique that they believe it would be an offense against God not to be obedient to the Romanists in all their knavish and ghoulish deceits. . . .

The Romanists have no basis in scripture for their claim that the pope alone has the right to call or confirm a council. This is just their own ruling, and it is only valid as long as it is not harmful to Christendom or contrary to the laws of God. Now when the pope deserves punishment, this ruling no longer obtains, for not to punish him by authority of a council is harmful to Christendom. . . .

Therefore, when necessity demands it, and the pope is an offense to Christendom, the first man who is able should, as a true member of the whole body, do what he can to bring about a truly free council. No one can do this so well as the temporal authorities, especially since they are also fellow-Christians, fellow-priests, fellow-members of the spiritual estate, fellow-lords over all things. Whenever it is necessary or profitable they ought to exercise the office and work which they have received from God over everyone.

JUSTIFICATION BY FAITH

You may ask, "What then is the Word of God, and how shall it be used, since there are so many words of God?" I answer: The Apostle explains this in Romans 1. The Word is the gospel of God concerning his Son, who was made flesh, suffered, rose from the dead, and was glorified through the Spirit who sanctifies. To preach Christ means to feed the soul, make it righteous,

set it free, and save it, provided it believes the preaching. Faith alone is the saving and efficacious use of the Word of God, according to Rom. 10[:9]: "If you confess with your lips that Jesus is Lord and believe in your heart that God raised him from the dead, you will be saved." Furthermore, "Christ is the end of the law, that everyone who has faith may be justified" [Rom. 10:4], Again, in Rom. 1[:17], "He who through faith is righteous shall live." The Word of God cannot be received and cherished by any works whatever but only by faith. Therefore it is clear that, as the soul needs only the Word of God for its life and righteousness, so it is justified by faith alone and not any works; for if it could be justified by anything else, it would not need the Word, and consequently it would not need faith.

This faith, cannot exist in connection with works—that is to say, if you at the same time claim to be justified by works, whatever their character. . . . Therefore the moment you begin to have faith you learn that all things in you are altogether blameworthy, sinful, and damnable, as the Apostle says in Rom. 3[:23], "Since all have sinned and fall short of the glory of God," and, "None is righteous no, not one: . . . all have turned aside, together they have gone wrong" [Rom. 3:10–12]. When you have learned this you. will know that you need Christ, who suffered and rose again for you so that, if you believe in him, you may through this faith become a new man in so far as your sins are forgiven and you are justified by the merits of another, namely, of Christ alone.

Since, therefore, this faith can rule only in the inner man, as Rom. 10[:10] says, "For man believes with his heart and so is justified," and since faith alone justifies, it is clear that the inner man cannot be justified, freed, or saved by any outer work or action at all, and that these works, whatever their character, have nothing to do with this inner man. . . .

Wherefore it ought to be the first concern of every Christian to lay aside all confidence in works and increasingly to strengthen faith alone and through faith to grow in the knowledge, not of works, but of Christ Jesus, who suffered and rose for him, as Peter teaches in the last chapter of his first Epistle [1 Pet. 5:10]. No other work makes a Christian. . . .

Our faith in Christ does not free us from works but from false opinions concerning works, that is, from the foolish presumption that justification is acquired by works. Faith redeems, corrects, and preserves our consciences so that we know that righteousness does not consist in works, although works neither can nor ought to be wanting. . . .

Thus what we do, live, and are in works and ceremonies, we do because of the necessities of this life and of the effort to rule our body. Nevertheless we are righteous, not in these, but in the faith of the Son of God.

THE INTERPRETATION OF THE BIBLE AND THE NATURE OF THE CLERGY

They (the Roman Catholic Popes) want to be the only masters of scriptures. . . . They assume sole authority for themselves and would persuade us with insolent juggling of words that the Pope, whether he be bad or good, cannot err in matters of faith. . . .

>. . . They cannot produce a letter to prove that the interpretation of scripture . . . belongs to the Pope alone. They themselves have usurped this power . . . and though they allege that this power was conferred on Peter when the keys were given to him, it is plain enough that the keys were not given to Peter alone but to the entire body of Christians [Matt. 16:19; 18:18]. . . .

. . . Every baptized Christian is a priest already, not by appointment or ordination from the Pope or any other man, but because Christ Himself has begotten him as a priest . . . in baptism . . . .

The Pope has usurped the term "priest" for his anointed and tonsured hordes [clergy and monks]. By this means they have separated themselves from the ordinary Christians and have called themselves uniquely the "clergy of God," God's heritage and chosen people who must help other Christians by their sacrifice and worship. . . . Therefore the Pope argues that he alone has the right and power to ordain and do what he will. . . .

[But] the preaching office is no more than a public service which happens to be conferred on someone by the entire congregation all the members of which are priests. . . .

. . . The fact that a pope or bishop anoints, makes tonsures, ordains, consecrates makes holy], and prescribes garb different from those of the laity . . . nevermore makes a Christian and a spiritual man. Accordingly, through baptism all of us are consecrated to the priesthood, as St. Peter says. . . [1 Pet. 2:9].

To make it still clearer, if a small group of pious Christian laymen were taken captive and settled in a wilderness and had among them no priest consecrated by a bishop, if they were to agree to choose one from their midst married or unmarried, and were to charge him with the office of baptizing, saying Mass, absolving [forgiving of sins], and preaching, such a man would be as truly a priest as he would if all bishops and popes had consecrated him.

What Luther Says: An Anthology, compiled by Ewald M. Plass (3 volumes), Saint Louis, MO: Concordia Publishing House, 1959), vol. 2, pp. 1062, 1063; vol. 3, pp. 1139–1140; vol. 2, p. 943.

REVIEW QUESTIONS

1. Why did Martin Luther see the papacy as the crucial block to any meaningful reform of the church?
2. How did Luther's teaching undermine the power of the clergy and traditional forms of piety?

4 European Expansion

During the period from 1450 to 1750, Western Europe entered an era of overseas exploration and commercial expansion that transformed society. European explorers and adventurers discovered a new way to reach the rich trading centers of India by sailing around Africa. They also conquered, colonized, and exploited a new world across the Atlantic. These discoveries and conquests brought about an extraordinary increase in business activity and the supply of money, which stimulated the growth of capitalism. A world economy was emerging in which European economic life depended on the market in Eastern spices, African slaves, and American silver. A dynamic Western Europe came to dominate many lands throughout the globe and served as the banker and profit taker in an emerging world economy.

William Carr
THE DUTCH EAST INDIA COMPANY

In 1693, William Carr, the English consul at Amsterdam, wrote a travelers' guide to the leading cities of Holland, Flanders, northern Germany, and Scandinavia. Of these, the largest and wealthiest was Amsterdam in Holland. In less than a century, this once small medieval city had grown to become the most important commercial port in the West and the center of European financial capitalism. In the following selection, Carr describes the commercial trading system of the famous Dutch East India Company, which established trading posts in South Africa, the Persian Gulf area, India, Ceylon, Bangladesh, Indonesia, China, and Japan. Although not mentioned by Carr, the Dutch West India Company conducted similar operations in the Caribbean and North America. The Dutch trading post of New Amsterdam at the mouth of the Hudson River would become the city of New York, the world center of finance capitalism in the twentieth century.

. . . The East India Company of the Netherlands is said to be a commonwealth within a commonwealth, and this is true when you consider the sovereign power and privileges the company has been granted by the States General [the ruling council of the Dutch Republic] and also consider its riches and vast number of subjects, and the many territories and colonies

it possesses in the East Indies. The company is said to have 30,000 men in its constant employ and more than 200 capital ships, in addition to its sloops, ketches, and yachts. The company possesses many colonies formerly belonging to Spain, Portugal, and various Indian princes, and as good Christians, company members have spread the Gospel of Christ in these lands, printing the Bible, prayer books, and catechisms in Indian languages and maintaining ministers and teachers to instruct those that are converted to the faith. Having said that this company is so extensive—as it were

William Carr, *Travels Through Holland, Germany, Sweden and Denmark by an English Gentleman* (London: Randal Taylor, 1693), see especially pages 14–18, 33–34, 60–64.

a commonwealth apart—I will demonstrate that it is a commonwealth first by its power, riches, and strength in the East Indies, and second, by its position in Europe. . . . But I will begin at the Cape of Good Hope [Africa] where the company has built a fort where it maintains a garrison to defend its ships when they stop there for fresh water. From there let us view the company on the island of Java, where it has built a fair city called Batavia and fortified it with bastions like those in Amsterdam. This city is the residence of the company's grand minister of state, called the General of the Indies. He has six privy counsellors (ordinary) and two extraordinary; they oversee the concerns of the company throughout the Indies, including matters of war and peace. . . . The General of the Indies has horse and foot soldiers, officers, and servants—as if he were a sovereign prince—all paid for by the company. . . . So formidable is the company in the East

Indies that it looks as though it aims to rule the South Seas. It also has a great trade with China and Japan. . . . With Persia also it has great commerce and is so confident that it wages war with the Persian monarch if he wrongs it in trade. It also has several colonies on the coast of Malabar and Coromandel [west coast of India] and in the country of the Great Mogul. . . . But especially let us examine the company on the rich island of Ceylon [Sri Lanka] where it controls the plains, so the king of the island is forced to live in the mountains while the company possesses the city of Colombo. . . . I will say no more of the company's power in the Indies, but let us examine its position in Europe. To begin with, in Amsterdam the company has two large stately palaces, one being in the old part of the city, and the other in the new; in the old part it keeps its court—where the Resident Committee of the company sits—and sells the company's goods.

REVIEW QUESTION

What evidence of the Dutch East India Company's power does Carr provide?

---

5 The Atlantic Slave Trade

As the first Portuguese merchants began to penetrate southward along the coast of Western Africa, they soon made deals with African tribes to provide them with slaves, generally prisoners of war and kidnap victims. From coastal slave markets, slave traders shipped their human cargo to the Portuguese colony of Brazil and the Spanish colonies in the West Indies. In addition, Arabs and Portuguese competed in conveying slaves from East Africa to the markets of the Middle East. The widespread use of African slaves marked a new stage in the history of slavery. In the Western world slavery became identified with race; the myth emerged that blacks were slaves by nature.

In the seventeenth century, the Dutch and English entered the West African slave trade, ousting the Portuguese as the principal slave traders to the West Indies and North America. The supply of laborers from Africa was essential to the New World's successful economic development. The Africans proved themselves to be skilled farmers and artisans who could endure the heavy labor of plantation life without the high rate of sickness and death that afflicted the local Native American populations. The Atlantic slave trade continued for more than three hundred years until finally suppressed by European governments in the nineteenth century. During that period, it is estimated that between 9.5 and 12 million African men, women, and children were shipped to the New World as slaves.

John Newton
THOUGHTS UPON THE AFRICAN SLAVE TRADE

For several years in the mid-eighteenth century, Englishman John Newton was involved in the forcible transporting of Africans to the New World. In time he began to question the morality of slavery. Ordained as a minister—he wrote the words to "Amazing Grace," the famous Christian hymn—Newton came to support abolitionism. In *Thoughts upon the African Slave Trade* (1788), he resolutely condemned the slave trade: "I know no method of getting money, not even that of robbing for it upon the highway, which has so direct a tendency to efface the moral sense, to rob the heart of every gentle and humane disposition, and to harden it, like steel, against all impressions of sensibility."

   In the following excerpts from this pamphlet, Newton tells of Africans attacking the ship's crew in a desperate bid for freedom and recalls the abuse of female captives by "white savages."

Usually, about two-thirds of a cargo of slaves are males. When a hundred and fifty or two hundred stout men, torn from their native land, many of whom never saw the sea, much less a ship, till a short space before they had embarked; who have, probably, the same natural prejudice against a white man, as we have against a black; and who often bring with them an apprehension they are bought to be eaten: I say, when thus circumstanced, it is not to be expected that they will tamely resign themselves to their situation. It is always taken for granted, that they will attempt to gain their liberty if possible. Accordingly, as we dare not trust them, we receive them on board, from the first as enemies; and, before their number exceeds, perhaps, ten or fifteen, they are all put in irons; in most ships, two and two together. . . .

   . . . One unguarded hour, or minute, is sufficient to give the slaves the opportunity they are always waiting for. An attempt to rise upon the ship's company, brings on instantaneous and horrid war: for, when they are once in motion, they are desperate; and where they do not conquer, they are seldom quelled without much mischief and bloodshed on both sides. . . .

John Newton, *Thoughts Upon the African Slave Trade* (London: J. Buckland, 1788), pp. 103–106.

. . . The captives, who formed and animated the plan, if they can be found out, must be treated as villains, and punished, to intimidate the rest. These punishments, in their nature and degree, depend upon the sovereign will of the captain. Some are content with inflicting such moderate punishment as may suffice for an example. But unlimited power, instigated by revenge, and where the heart, by a long familiarity with the sufferings of slaves is become callous, and insensible to the pleadings of humanity, is terrible!

I have seen them sentenced to unmerciful whippings, continued till the poor creatures have not had power to groan under their misery, and hardly a sign of life has remained. I have seen them agonizing for hours, I believe for days together, under the torture of the thumbscrews; a dreadful engine, which, if the screw be turned by an unrelenting hand, can give intolerable anguish. There have been instances in which cruelty has proceeded still further; but, as I hope they are few, and I can mention but one from my own knowledge, I shall but mention it.

I have often heard a captain, who has been long since been dead, boast of his conduct in a former voyage, when his slaves attempted to rise upon him. After he had suppressed the insurrection, he sat in judgment upon the insurgents; and not only, in cold blood, adjudged several of them, I know not how many, to die, but studied, with no small attention, how to make death as excruciating as possible. For my reader's sake, I suppress the recital of particulars.

. . . When the women and girls are taken on board a ship, naked, trembling, terrified, perhaps almost exhausted with cold, fatigue, and hunger, they are often exposed to the wanton rudeness of white savages. The poor creatures cannot understand the language they hear, but the looks and manner of the speakers are sufficiently intelligible. In imagination, the prey is divided, upon the spot, and only reserved till opportunity offers. Where resistance or refusal, would be utterly in vain, even the solicitation of consent is seldom thought of. But I forbear.— This is not a subject for declamation. Facts like these, so certain and so numerous, speak for themselves. Surely, if the advocates for the Slave Trade attempt to plead for it, before the wives and daughters of our happy land, or before those who have wives or daughters of their own, they must lose their cause.

Perhaps some hard-hearted pleader may suggest, that such treatment would indeed be cruel, in Europe: but the African women are negroes, savages, who have no idea of the nicer sensations which obtain among civilized people. I dare contradict them in the strongest terms. I have lived long, and conversed much, amongst these supposed savages. I have often slept in their towns, in a house filled with goods for trade, with no person in the house but myself, and with no other door than a mat; in that security, which no man in his senses would expect in this civilized nation, especially in this metropolis, without the precaution of having strong doors, strongly locked and bolted. And with regard to the women, in Sherbro [island off the coast of West Africa], where I was most acquainted, I have seen many instances of modesty, and even delicacy, which would not disgrace an English woman. Yet, such is the treatment which I have known permitted, if not encouraged, in many of our ships—they have been abandoned, without restraint, to the lawless will of the first comer.

Malachy Postlethwayt
SLAVERY DEFENDED

While some people attacked African bondage as morally repugnant, its proponents argued that it was a boon to shipping and manufacturing and also benefited Africans by liberating them from oppressive African rulers, who had captured and enslaved them, and placing them in the care of more humane Christian masters, who instructed them in Christian ideals. Malachy Postlethwayt (c. 1707–1767), an English economist, defended slavery in the following excerpt written in 1746.

The most approved judges of the commercial interests of these Kingdoms have ever been of the opinion, that our West-India and African trades are the most nationally beneficial of any we carry on. It is also allowed on all hands, that the trade to Africa is the Branch which renders our American colonies and plantations so advantageous to Great Britain, that traffic only affording our planters a constant supply of negro servants for the culture of their lands in the produce of sugars, tobacco, rice, rum, cotton, pimento, and all other our plantation-produce: so that the extensive employment of our shipping in, to, and from America, the great brood of Seamen consequent thereupon, and the daily bread of the most considerable part of our British manufactures, are owing primarily to the labours of Negroes; who, as they were the first happy instruments of raising our plantations; so their labour only can support and preserve them, and render them still more and more profitable to their mother-kingdom.

Malachy Postlethwayt, *The Nature and Private Advantages of the African Trade Considered: Being an Enquiry How Far It Concerns the Trading Interest of Great Britain, Effectually to Support and Maintain the Forts and Settlements in Africa Belonging to the Royal African Company of England* (London: John and Paul Knapton, 1746), pp. 1–6, 40–41.

The negro-trade, therefore, and the national consequences resulting from it, may be justly esteemed an inexhaustible fund of wealth and naval power to this nation. And by the surplus of negroes above what have served our own plantations, we have drawn likewise no inconsiderable quantities of treasure from the Spaniards, who are settled on the continent of America, . . . for Negroes furnished them from Jamaica. . . .

What renders the negro trade still more estimable and important, is, that near nine-tenths of those negroes are paid for in Africa with British produce and manufactures only; and the remainder with East-India commodities. We send no specie or bullion [coined money] to pay for the products of Africa but, 'tis certain, we bring from thence very large quantities of gold. . . .

And it may be worth consideration that while our plantations depend only on planting by negro servants, they will neither depopulate our own country, become independent of her dominion, or any way interfere with the interests of the British manufacturer, merchant, or landed gentleman; whereas were we under the necessity of supplying our colonies with white-men instead of blacks, they could not fail being in a capacity to interfere with the manufactures of this nation, in time to shake off their dependency thereon, and prove as injurious to the landed, and trading interests as ever they have hitherto been beneficial.

Many are prepossessed against this trade, thinking it a barbarous, inhuman and unlawful traffic for a Christian country to trade in Blacks; to which I would beg leave to observe; that though the odious appellation of slaves is annexed to this trade, it being called by some the slave-trade, yet it does not appear from the best enquiry I have been able to make, that the state of those people is changed for the worse, by being servants to our British planters in America; they are certainly treated with great [kindness] and humanity: and as the improvement of the planter's estates depends upon due care being taken of their healths and lives, I cannot but think their condition is much bettered to what it was in their own country.

Besides, the negro princes in Africa, 'tis well known, are in perpetual war with each other, and since before they had this method of disposing of their prisoners of war to Christian merchants, they were wont not only to be applied to inhuman sacrifices, but to extreme torture and barbarity, their transportation must certainly be a melioration [improvement] of their condition; provided living in a civilized Christian country,

is better than living among savages: Nay, if life be preferable to torment and cruel death, their state cannot, with any color of reason, be presumed to be worsened. . . .

As the present prosperity and splendor of the British colonies have been owing to negro labor, so not only their future advancement, but even their very being depends [on it]. That our colonies are capable of very great improvements, by the proper application of the labour of blacks, has been urged by the most experienced judges of commerce.

The negro princes and chiefs in Africa are generally at war with each other on the continent; and the prisoners of war, instead of being slain, or applied to inhuman sacrifices, are carefully preserved and sold to those Europeans only, who have established interest and power among the natives, by means of forts and settlements; or to such who are admitted to traffic with the natives, by virtue, and under the sanction and protection of such European settlements; which is the case of all the British merchants who trade to Africa at present, at full liberty, under the authority and protection of our Royal African Company's rights and privileges, interest and power among the natives. . . .

John Wesley
SLAVERY ATTACKED

John Wesley (1703–1791) was, with his brother Charles, the founder of the evangelical Methodist movement in England. Inspired by the Great Awakening in the American colonies, he launched a successful revival of Christianity in England in 1739. The rest of his long life was devoted to leadership of the Methodist movement.

Wesley's eyes were opened to the evils of slavery by reading an indictment of the slave trade by a French Quaker, Anthony Benezet. In 1774 Wesley published the tract *Thoughts Upon Slavery*, from which the extracts below are taken. Wesley drew heavily on Benezet's writings for his facts, but in warning participants in the slave trade of divine retribution, he spoke in the cadences of the inspired evangelical preacher.

Wesley became one of the leaders in the movement against slavery and his pioneering work, in which he was supported by the Methodist movement, helped bring about the abolition of slavery in England in 1807.

I would inquire whether [the abuses of slavery] can be defended on the principles of even heathen honesty, whether they can be reconciled (setting the Bible out of question) with any degree of either justice or mercy.

The grand plea is, "They are authorized by law." But can law, human law, change the nature of things? Can it turn darkness into light or evil into good? By no means. Notwithstanding ten thousand laws, right is right, and wrong is wrong still. There must still remain an essential [difference] between justice and injustice, cruelty and mercy. So that I still ask, who can reconcile this treatment of the Negroes first and last, with either mercy or justice? . . . Yea, where is the justice of taking away the lives of innocent, inoffensive men, murdering thousands of them in their own land, by the hands of their own countrymen, many thousands year after year on shipboard, and then casting them like dung into the sea and tens of thousands in that cruel slavery to which they are so unjustly reduced? . . .

But if this manner of procuring and treating Negroes is not consistent either with mercy or justice, yet there is a plea for it which every man of business will acknowledge to be quite sufficient. . . . "D—n justice, it is necessity. . . . It is necessary that we should procure slaves, and when we have procured them, it is necessary to use them with severity, considering their stupidity, stubbornness and wickedness."

I answer you stumble at the threshold. I deny that villainy is ever necessary. It is impossible that it should ever be necessary for any reasonable creature to violate all the laws of justice, mercy, and truth. No circumstances can make it necessary for a man to burst in sunder all the ties of humanity. It can never be necessary for a rational being to sink himself below a brute. A man can be under no necessity of degrading himself into a wolf. The absurdity of the supposition is so glaring that one would wonder anyone can help seeing it. . . .

"But the furnishing us with slaves is necessary for the trade, and wealth, and glory of our nation." Here are several mistakes. For first wealth is not necessary to the glory of any nation, but wisdom, virtue, justice, mercy, generosity, public spirit, love of our country. These are necessary to the real glory of a nation, but abundance of wealth is not.

. . . But, secondly, it is not clear that we should have either less money or trade (only less of that detestable trade of man-stealing), if there was not a Negro in all our islands or in all English America. It is demonstrable, white men inured to it by degrees can work as well as they, and they would do it, were Negroes out of the way, and proper encouragement given them. However, thirdly, I come back to the same point: Better no trade than trade procured by villainy. It is far better to have no wealth than to gain wealth at the expense of virtue. Better is honest poverty than all the riches bought by the tears, and sweat, and blood of our fellow creatures.

"However this be, it is necessary, when we have slaves, to use them with severity." What, to whip them for every petty offence, till they are all in gore blood? To take that opportunity of rubbing pepper and salt into their raw flesh? To drop burning wax upon their skin? To castrate them? To cut off half their foot with an axe? To hang them on gibbets, that they may die by inches with heat, and hunger, and thirst? To pin them down to the ground, and then burn them by degrees from the feet to the head? To roast them alive? When did a Turk or heathen find it necessary to use a fellow-creature thus?

John Wesley, *Thoughts Upon Slavery* (London: R. Hawes, 1774), pp. 29–53 passim.

I pray, to what end is this usage necessary? "Why to prevent their running away, and to keep them constantly to their labour, that they may not idle away their time. So miserably stupid is this race of men, yea, so stupid and so wicked." Allowing them to be as stupid as you say, to whom is that stupidity owing? Without question it lies at the door of their inhuman masters who give them no means, no opportunity of improving their understanding. . . . Consequently it is not their fault but yours: you must answer for it before God and man. . . .

And what pains have you taken, what method have you used, to reclaim them from their wickedness? Have you carefully taught them, "That there is a God, a wise, powerful, merciful being, the creator and governor of heaven and earth? That he has appointed a day wherein he will judge the world, will take account of all our thoughts, words and actions? That in that day he will reward every child of man according to his works: that 'Then the righteous shall inherit the kingdom prepared for them from the foundation of the world: and the wicked shall be cast into everlasting fire, prepared for the devil and his angels.'" If you have not done this, if you have taken no pains or thought about the matter, can you wonder at their wickedness? What wonder if they should cut your throat? And if they did, whom could you thank for it but yourself? You first acted the villain in making them slaves (whether you stole them or bought them). You kept them stupid and wicked by cutting them off from all opportunities of improving either in knowledge or virtue. And now you assign their want of wisdom and goodness as the reason for using them worse than brute beasts. . . .

It remains only to make a little application of the preceding observations . . . I therefore add a few words to those who are more immediately concerned, . . . and first to the captains employed in this trade. . . .

Is there a God? You know there is. Is he a just God? Then there must be a state of retribution; a state wherein the just God will reward every man according to his works. Then what reward will he render to you? O think betimes! Before you drop into eternity! Think now: he shall have judgment without mercy, that showed no mercy.

Are you a man? . . . Have you no sympathy? No sense of human woe? No pity for the miserable? . . . When you squeezed the agonizing creatures down in the ship, or when you threw their poor mangled remains into the sea, had you no relenting compassion? Did not one tear drop from your eye, one sigh escape from your breast? Do you feel no relenting now? If you do not, you must go on till the measure of your iniquities is full. Then will the great God deal with *you*, as you have dealt with *them*, and require all their blood at your hands. . . .

Today resolve, God being your helper, to escape for your life. Regard not money! All that a man hath will he give for his life! Whatever you lose, lose not your soul; nothing can countervail that loss. Immediately quit the horrid trade. At all events, be an honest man.

This equally concerns every merchant who is engaged in the slave-trade. It is you that induce the African villain, to sell his countrymen, and in order thereto, to steal, rob, murder men, women and children without number. . . .

And this equally concerns every gentleman that has an estate in our African plantations. Yea, all slave-holders of whatever rank and degree, seeing men-buyers are exactly at a level with men-sellers. Indeed you say, "I pay honestly for my goods, and am not concerned to know how they are come by." Nay, but . . . you know they are not honestly come by. . . .

If therefore you have any regard to justice (to say nothing of mercy, nor of the revealed law of God) render unto all their due. Give liberty to whom liberty is due, that is, to every child of man, to every partaker of human nature. Let none serve you but by his own act and deed, by his own voluntary choice. Away with all whips, all chains, all compulsion.

Be gentle toward all men. And see that you invariably do unto everyone, as you would he should do unto you.

REVIEW QUESTIONS

1. According to John Newton, what kind of treatment was given to Africans on slave ships? What did Newton think of this treatment?
2. What was Malachy Postlethwayt's argument in defense of slavery? How would John Newton respond to it? What is your response?
3. To whom did John Wesley address his arguments against the slave trade?
4. What were the commercial justifications for slavery that Wesley disputed? How did he account for the seeming inferiority of the slaves?

---

6 A Secular Defense of Absolutism

Thomas Hobbes (1588–1679), a British philosopher and political theorist, witnessed the agonies of the English civil war, including the execution of Charles I in 1649. These developments fortified Hobbes's conviction that absolutism was the most desirable and logical form of government. Only the unlimited power of a sovereign, said Hobbes, could contain human passions that disrupt the social order and threaten civilized life; only absolute rule could provide an environment secure enough for people to pursue their individual interests.

Leviathan (1651), Hobbes's principal work of political thought, broke with medieval political theory. Medieval thinkers assigned each group of people—clergy, lords, serfs, guildsmen—a place in a fixed social order; an individual's social duties were set by ancient traditions believed to have been ordained by God. During early modern times, the great expansion of commerce and capitalism spurred the new individualism already pronounced in Renaissance culture; group ties were shattered by competition and accelerating social mobility. Hobbes gave expression to a society where people confronted each other as competing individuals.

Thomas Hobbes
LEVIATHAN

Hobbes was influenced by the new scientific thought that saw mathematical knowledge as the avenue to truth. Using geometry as a model, Hobbes began with what he believed were self-evident axioms regarding human nature, from which he deduced other truths. He aimed at constructing political philosophy on a scientific foundation and rejected the authority of tradition and religion as inconsistent with a science of politics. Thus, although Hobbes supported absolutism, he dismissed the idea advanced by other theorists of absolutism that the monarch's power derived from God. He also rejected the idea that the state should not be obeyed when it violated God's law. *Leviathan* is a rational and secular political statement. In this modern approach, rather than in Hobbes's justification of absolutism, lies the work's larger significance.

Hobbes had a pessimistic view of human nature. Believing that people are innately selfish and grasping, he maintained that competition and dissension, rather than cooperation, characterize human relations. Even when reason teaches that cooperation is more advantageous than competition, Hobbes observed that people are reluctant to alter their ways, because passion, not reason, governs their behavior. In the following passages from *Leviathan*, Hobbes describes the causes of human conflicts.

Nature hath made men so equall, in the faculties of body, and mind; as that though there bee found one man sometimes manifestly stronger in body, or of quicker mind than another; yet when all is reckoned together, the difference between man, and man, is not so considerable, as that one man can thereupon claim to himselfe any benefit, to which another may not pretend, as well as he. For as to the strength of body, the weakest has strength enough to kill the strongest, either by secret machination, or by confederacy with others, that are in the same danger with himselfe. . . .

And as to the faculties of the mind . . . men are . . . [more] equall than unequall. . . .

From this equality of ability, ariseth equality of hope in the attaining of our Ends. And therefore if any two men desire the same thing, which neverthelesse they cannot both enjoy, they become enemies; and in the way to their End, . . . endeavour to destroy, or subdue one another. . . . If one plant, sow, build, or possesse a convenient Seat, others may probably be expected to come prepared with forces united, to dispossesse, and deprive him, not only of the fruit of his labour, but also of his life, or liberty. . . .

So that in the nature of man, we find three principall causes of quarrell. First, Competition; Secondly, Diffidence [insecurity], Thirdly, Glory.

The English Works of Thomas Hobbes of Malmesbury, vol. 3, *Leviathan*, ed. William Molesworth (London: J. Bohn, 1839), pp. 110–113, 116–117, 154, 157–158, 160–161.

The first, maketh men invade for Gain; the second, for Safety; and the third, for Reputation. The first use Violence, to make themselves Masters of other men's persons, wives, children, and cattell; the second, to defend them; the third, for trifles, as a word, a smile, a different opinion, and any other signe of undervalue, either direct in their Persons, or by reflexion in their Kindred, their Friends, their Nation, their Profession, or their Name.

Hereby it is manifest, that during the time men live without a common Power to keep them all in awe, they are in that condition which is called Warre; and such a warre, as is of every man, against every man. . . .

Hobbes then describes a state of nature—the hypothetical condition of humanity prior to the formation of the state—as a war of all against all. For Hobbes, the state of nature is a logical abstraction, a device employed to make his point. Only a strong ruling entity—the state—will end the perpetual strife and provide security. For Hobbes, the state is merely a useful arrangement that permits individuals to exchange goods and services in a secure environment. The ruling authority in the state, the sovereign, must have supreme power, or society will collapse and the anarchy of the state of nature will return.

Whatsoever therefore is [a consequence] of time of Warre, where every man is Enemy to every man; the same [results when] men live without other security, than what their own strength, and their own invention shall furnish them withall. In such condition, there is no place for Industry; because the fruit thereof is uncertain: and consequently no Culture of the Earth; no Navigation, nor use of the commodities that may be imported by Sea; no commodious Building; no Instruments of moving, and removing such things as require much force; no Knowledge of the face of the Earth; no account of Time; no Arts; no Letters; no Society; and which is worst of all, continuall feare, and danger of violent death; And the life of man, solitary, poore, nasty, brutish, and short. . . .

The Passions that encline men to Peace, are Feare of Death; Desire of such things as are necessary to commodious living; and a Hope by their Industry to obtain them. And Reason suggesteth convenient Articles of Peace, upon which men may be drawn to agreement. . . .

And because the condition of Man, (as hath been declared in the precedent Chapter) is a condition of Warre of everyone against everyone; in which case everyone is governed by his own Reason; and there is nothing he can make use of, that may not be a help unto him, in preserving his life against his enemyes; It followeth, that in such a condition, every man has a Right to every thing; even to one another's body. And therefore, as long as this naturall Right of every man to every thing endureth, there can be no security to any man, (how strong or wise soever he be,) of living out the time, which Nature ordinarily alloweth men to live. . . .

. . . If there be no Power erected, or not great enough for our security; every man will and may lawfully rely on his own strength and art, for caution against all other men. . . .

The only way to erect . . . a Common Power, as may be able to defend them from the invasion of [foreigners] and the injuries of one another, and thereby to secure them in such sort, as that by their owne industrie, and by the fruites of the Earth, they may nourish themselves and live

contentedly; is to conferre all their power and strength upon one Man, or upon one Assembly of men, that may reduce all their Wills, by plurality of voices, unto one Will . . . and therein to submit their Wills, everyone to his Will, and their Judgements, to his Judgment. This is more than Consent, or Concord; it is a reall Unitie of them all, in one and the same Person, made by Covenant of every man with every man, in such manner, as if every man should say to every man, *I Authorise and give up my Right of Governing my selfe, to this Man, or to this Assembly of men, on this condition, that thou give up thy Right to him, and Authorise all his Actions in like manner.* This done, the Multitude so united in one Person, is called a Common-wealth. . . . For by this Authorite, given him by every particular man in the Common-wealth, he hath the use of so much Power and Strength . . . conferred on him, that by terror thereof, he is in-abled to forme the wills of them all, to Peace at home, and mutuall [aid] against their enemies abroad. And in him consisteth the Essence of the Common-wealth; which (to define it,) is *One Person, of whose Acts a great Multitude, by mutuall Covenants one with another, have made themselves everyone the Author, to the end he may use the strength and means of them all, as he shall think expedient, for their Peace and Common Defence.*

And he that carryeth this Person, is called Soveraigne, and said to have *Soveraigne Power;* and everyone besides, his Subject. . . .

. . . They that have already Instituted a Common-wealth, being thereby bound by Covenant . . . cannot lawfully make a new Covenant, amongst themselves, to be obedient to any other, in any thing whatsoever, without his permission. And therefore, they that are subjects to a Monarch, cannot without his leave cast off Monarchy, and return to the confusion of a disunited Multitude; nor transferre their [obedience to the sovereign] to another Man, or other Assembly of men: for they . . . are bound, every man to every man, to [acknowledge] . . . that he that already is their Soveraigne, shall do, and judge fit to be done; so that [those who do not obey] break their Covenant made to that man, which is injustice: and they have also every man given the Soveraignty to him that beareth their Person; and therefore if they depose him, they take from him that which is his own, and so again it is injustice. . . . And whereas some men have pretended for their disobedience to their Soveraign, a new Covenant, made, not with men, but with God; this also is unjust: for there is no Covenant with God, but by mediation of some body that represenceth God's Person; which none doth but God's Lieutenant, who hath the Soveraignty under God. But this pretence of Covenant with God, is so evident a [lie], even in the pretenders own consciences, that it is not onely an act of an unjust, but also of a vile, and unmanly disposition. . . .

. . . Consequently none of [the sovereign's] Subjects, by any pretence of forfeiture, can be freed from his Subjection.

REVIEW QUESTIONS

1. What was Thomas Hobbes's view of human nature and what conclusions did he draw from it about the best form of government?
2. What has been the political legacy of Hobbes's notion of the state?

---

7 The Triumph of Constitutional Monarchy in England: The Glorious Revolution

Developments in England moved the country in a direction that was the opposite of the consolidation of royal power by Louis XIV in France. The struggle against absolute monarchy in England during the early seventeenth century reached a climax during the reign (ruled 1625–1649) of Charles I. Parliament raised its own army as civil war broke out between its supporters and those of the king. Captured by the Scottish Presbyterian rebels in 1646 and turned over to the English parliamentary army in 1647, Charles was held prisoner for two years until the Puritan parliamentary general Oliver Cromwell (1599–1658) decided to put him on trial for treason. The king was found guilty and executed in 1649.

The revolutionary parliamentary regime evolved into a military dictatorship headed by Cromwell. After Cromwell's death, Parliament in 1660 restored the monarchy and invited the late king's heir to end his exile and take the throne. Charles II (ruled 1660–1685), by discretion and skillful statesmanship, managed to evade many difficulties caused by the hostility of those who opposed his policies. He attempted to ease religious discrimination by ending the laws that penalized dissenters who rejected the official Church of England. But the religious prejudices of Parliament forced the king to desist, and the laws penalizing both Protestant dissenters and Roman Catholics remained in force. The king's motives for establishing religious toleration were suspect, since he himself was married to a French Catholic and his brother and heir James, duke of York, was also a staunch Catholic.

When James II succeeded to the throne in 1685, he tried unsuccessfully to get Parliament to repeal the Test Act, a law that forbade anyone to hold a civil or military office or to enter a university unless he was a member in good standing of the Church of England. This law effectively barred both Catholics and Protestant dissenters from serving in the king's government. When Parliament refused to act, James got the legal Court of the King's Bench to approve his decree suspending the Test Act. The court affirmed that the king, due to his sovereign authority, had absolute power to suspend any law at his sole discretion. The prerogatives claimed by the king were seen by many as an attempt to impose absolute monarchy on the English people.

King James further roused enemies by appointing many Catholics to high government posts and by issuing his Declaration of Indulgence for Liberty of Conscience on April 4, 1687. This declaration established complete freedom of worship for all Englishmen, ending all civil penalties and discriminations based on religious dissent. Instead of hailing the declaration as a step forward in solving the religious quarrels within the kingdom, many persons viewed suspension of these civil penalties as a further act of absolutism because James acted unilaterally without consulting Parliament. This act united the king's enemies and alienated his former supporters.

When the king's wife gave birth to a son in 1688, making the heir to the throne another Catholic, almost all factions (except the Catholics) abandoned James II and in 1689 invited the Dutch Protestant Prince William of Orange and his wife, Mary, James II's Protestant daughter, to come to England. James and his Catholic family and friends fled to France. Parliament declared the throne vacant and offered it to William and Mary as joint sovereigns. As a result of the "Glorious Revolution," the English monarchy became clearly limited by the will of Parliament.

THE ENGLISH DECLARATION OF RIGHTS

In depriving James II of the throne, Parliament had destroyed forever in Britain the theory of divine right as an operating principle of government and had firmly established a limited constitutional monarchy. The appointment of William and Mary was accompanied by a declaration of rights (later enacted as the Bill of Rights), which enumerated and declared illegal James II's arbitrary acts. The English Declaration of Rights, excerpted below, compelled William and Mary and future monarchs to recognize the right of the people's representatives to dispose of the royal office and to set limits on its powers. These rights were subsequently formulated into laws passed by Parliament. Prior to the American Revolution, colonists protested that British actions in the American colonies violated certain rights guaranteed in the English Bill of Rights. Several of these rights were later included in the Constitution of the United States.

And whereas the said late king James the Second having abdicated the government and the throne being thereby vacant, His Highness the prince of Orange (whom it hath pleased Almighty God to make the glorious instrument of delivering this kingdom from popery and arbitrary power) did (by the advice of the lords spiritual and temporal and divers principal persons of the commons)[1] cause letters to be written to the lords spiritual and temporal, being Protestants; and other letters to the several counties, cities, universities, boroughs and Cinque ports[2] for the choosing of such persons to represent them, as were of right to be sent to parliament, to meet and sit at Westminster upon the two and twentieth day of January in this year one thousand six hundred eighty and eight,[3] in order to [guarantee] . . . that their religion, laws and liberties might not again be in danger of being subverted; upon which letters elections having been accordingly made.

And thereupon the said lords spiritual and temporal and commons pursuant to their respective letters and elections being now assembled in a full and free representative of this nation, taking into their most serious consideration the best means for attaining the ends aforesaid, do in the first place (as their ancestors in like case have usually done) for the vindicating and asserting their ancient rights and liberties, declare:

That the pretended power of suspending of laws or the execution of laws by regal authority without consent of parliament is illegal.

That the pretended power of dispensing with laws or the execution of laws by regal authority as it hath been assumed and exercised of late is illegal.

That the commission for erecting the late court of commissioners for ecclesiastical causes and all other commissions and courts of like nature are illegal and pernicious.

That the levying money for or to the use of the crown by pretence of prerogative without grant of parliament for a longer time or in other manner than the same is or shall be granted is illegal.

That it is the right of the subjects to petition the king and all commitments and prosecutions for such petitioning are illegal.

That the raising or keeping a standing army within the kingdom in time of peace unless it be with consent of parliament is against the law.

That the subjects which are Protestants may have arms for their defence suitable to their conditions and as allowed by law.

That election of members of parliament ought to be free.

That the freedom of speech and debates or proceedings in parliament ought not to be impeached or questioned in any court or place out of parliament.

That excessive bail ought not to be required nor excessive fines imposed nor cruel and unusual punishments inflicted.

Select Documents of English Constitutional History, ed. George Burton Adams and H. Morse Stephen (London: Macmillan Co., 1902).
[1]"The lords spiritual" refers to the bishops of the Church of England who sat in the House of Lords, and "the lords temporal" refers to the nobility entitled to sit in the House of Lords. The commons refers to the elected representatives in the House of Commons.—Eds.
[2]The Cinque ports along England's southeastern coast (originally five in number) enjoyed special privileges because of their military duties in providing for coastal defense.—Eds.
[3]The year was in fact 1689 because until 1752, the English used March 25 as the beginning of the new year.—Eds.

That jurors ought to be duly impanelled and returned and jurors which pass upon men in trials for high treason ought to be freeholders.

That all grants and promises of fines and forfeitures of particular persons before conviction are illegal and void.

And that for redress of all grievances and for the amending, strengthening and preserving of the laws parliaments ought to be held frequently.

And they do claim, demand and insist upon all and singular the premises as their undoubted rights and liberties and that no declarations, judgments, doings or proceedings to the prejudice of the people in any of the said premises ought in any wise to be drawn hereafter into consequence or example.

REVIEW QUESTIONS

1. How did the English Declaration of Rights limit royal authority? With what result?
2. In what ways did the Glorious Revolution impact the American rebellion in the 1770s?

CHAPTER 2
The Scientific Revolution

GALILEO GALILEI, by Samuel Sartain, 1852. Galileo's support of the Copernican system and rejection of the medieval division of the universe into higher and lower realms make him a principal shaper of modern science. *(The Granger Collection, New York)*

The Scientific Revolution of the sixteenth and seventeenth centuries replaced the medieval view of the universe with a new cosmology and produced a new way of investigating nature. It overthrew the medieval conception of nature as a hierarchical order ascending toward a realm of perfection. Rejecting reliance on authority, the thinkers of the Scientific Revolution affirmed the individual's ability to know the natural world through the method of mathematical reasoning, the direct observation of nature, and carefully controlled experiments.

The medieval view of the universe had blended the theories of Aristotle and Ptolemy, two ancient Greek thinkers, with Christian teachings. In that view, a stationary earth stood in the center of the universe just above hell. Revolving around the earth were seven planets: the moon, Mercury, Venus, the sun, Mars, Jupiter, and Saturn. Because people believed that earth did not move, it was not considered a planet. Each planet was attached to a transparent sphere that turned around the earth. Encompassing the universe was a sphere of fixed stars; beyond the stars lay three heavenly spheres, the outermost of which was the abode of God. An earth-centered universe accorded with the Christian idea that God had created the universe for men and women and that salvation was the aim of life.

Also agreeable to the medieval Christian view was Aristotle's division of the universe into a lower, earthly realm and a higher realm beyond the moon. Two sets of laws operated in the universe, one on earth and the other in the celestial realm. Earthly objects were composed of four elements: earth, water, fire, and air; celestial objects were composed of the divine ether—a substance too pure, too clear, too fine, too spiritual to be found on earth. Celestial objects naturally moved in perfectly circular orbits around the earth; earthly objects, composed mainly of the heavy elements of earth and water, naturally fell downward, whereas objects made of the lighter elements of air and fire naturally flew upward toward the sky.

The destruction of the medieval world picture began with the publication in 1543 of *On the Revolutions of the Heavenly Spheres* by Nicolaus Copernicus, a Polish mathematician, astronomer, and clergyman. In Copernicus's system, the sun was in the center of the universe, and the earth was another planet that moved around the sun. Most thinkers of the time, committed to the Aristotelian–Ptolemaic system and to the biblical statements that seemed to support it, rejected Copernicus's heliocentric conclusions.

The work of Galileo Galilei, an Italian mathematician, astronomer, and physicist, was decisive in the shattering of the medieval cosmos and the shaping of the modern scientific outlook. Galileo advanced the modern view that knowledge of nature derives from direct observation and from mathematics. For Galileo, the universe was a "grand book which . . . is written in the language of mathematics, and its characters are triangles, circles, and other geometric figures without which it is humanly impossible to understand a single word of it." Galileo also pioneered experimental physics, advanced the modern idea that nature is uniform throughout the universe, and attacked reliance on scholastic authority rather than on experimentation in resolving scientific controversies.

Johannes Kepler (1571–1630), a German contemporary of Galileo, discovered three laws of planetary motion that greatly advanced astronomical knowledge. Kepler showed that the path of a planet was an ellipse, not a circle as Ptolemy (and Copernicus) had believed, and that planets do not move at uniform speed but accelerate as they near the sun. He devised formulas to calculate accurately both a planet's speed at each point in its orbit around the sun and a planet's location at a particular time. Kepler's laws provided further evidence that Copernicus had been right, for they made sense only in a sun-centered universe, but Kepler could not explain why planets stayed in their orbits rather than flying off into space or crashing into the sun. The resolution of that question was left to Sir Isaac Newton (1643–1727).

Newton's great achievement was integrating the findings of Copernicus, Galileo, and Kepler into a single theoretical system. In *Principia Mathematica* (1687), he formulated the mechanical laws of motion and attraction that govern celestial and terrestrial objects.

The creation of a new model of the universe was one great achievement of the Scientific Revolution; another accomplishment was the formulation of the scientific method. The scientific method encompasses two approaches to knowledge, which usually complement each other: the empirical (inductive) and the rational (deductive). Although all sciences use both approaches, the inductive method is generally more applicable in such descriptive sciences as biology, anatomy, and geology, which rely on the accumulation of data. In the inductive approach, general principles are derived from analyzing external experiences—observations and the results of experiments. In the deductive approach, used in mathematics and theoretical physics, truths are derived in successive steps from indubitable axioms. Whereas the inductive method builds its concepts from an analysis of sense experience, the deductive approach constructs its ideas from self-evident principles that are conceived by the mind itself without external experience. The deductive and inductive approaches to knowledge, and their interplay, have been a constantly recurring feature in Western intellectual history since the rationalism of Plato and the empiricism of Aristotle. The success of the scientific method in modern times arose from the skillful synchronization of induction and deduction by such giants as Leonardo da Vinci, Copernicus, Kepler, Galileo, and Newton.

The Scientific Revolution was instrumental in shaping the modern outlook. It destroyed the medieval conception of the universe and established the scientific method as the means for investigating nature and acquiring knowledge, even in areas having little to do with the study of the physical world. By demonstrating the powers of the human mind, the Scientific Revolution gave thinkers great confidence in reason and led eventually to a rejection of traditional beliefs in magic, astrology, and witches. In the eighteenth century, this growing skepticism led thinkers to question miracles and other Christian beliefs that seemed contrary to reason and natural law.

1 Galileo: Confirming the Copernican System

In proclaiming that the earth was not stationary but revolved around the sun, Nicolaus Copernicus (1473–1543) revolutionized the science of astronomy Fearing controversy and scorn, Copernicus long refused to publish his great work, *On the Revolutions of the Heavenly Spheres* (1543). However, persuaded by friends, he finally relented and permitted publication; a copy of his book reached him on his deathbed. As Copernicus anticipated, his ideas aroused the ire of many thinkers.

Both Catholic and Protestant philosophers and theologians including Martin Luther, attacked Copernicus for contradicting the Bible and Aristotle and Ptolemy, and they raised several specific objections. First, certain passages in the Bible imply a stationary earth and a sun that moves (for example, Psalm 93 says, "Yea, the world is established; it shall never be moved"; and in attacking Copernicus, Luther pointed out that "sacred scripture tells us that Joshua commanded the sun to stand still, and not the earth"). Second, a body as heavy as the earth cannot move through space at such speed as Copernicus suggested. Third, if the earth spins on its axis, why does a stone dropped from a height land directly below instead of at a point behind where it was dropped? Fourth, if the earth moved, objects would fly off it. And finally, the moon cannot orbit both the earth and the sun at the same time.

The brilliant Italian scientist Galileo Galilei (1564–1642) defended the Copernican theory, rejected the medieval division of the universe into higher and lower realms and proclaimed the modern idea of nature's uniformity. Learning that a telescope had been invented in Holland, Galileo built one for himself and used it to investigate the heavens. Through his telescope, Galileo saw craters and mountains on the moon; he concluded that celestial bodies were not pure, perfect, and immutable, as had been believed. There was no difference in quality between heavenly and earthly bodies; nature was the same throughout.

With his telescope, Galileo discovered four moons orbiting Jupiter, an observation that overcame a principal objection to the Copernican system.

Galileo showed that a celestial body could indeed move around a center other than the earth; that earth was not the common center for all celestial bodies; that a celestial body (earth's moon or Jupiter's moons) could orbit a planet at the same time that the planet revolved around another body (namely, the sun).

In 1615, in a letter addressed to Grand Duchess Christina of Tuscany, Galileo argued that passages from the Bible had no authority in matters of science:

> I think that in discussions of physical problems, we ought to begin not from the authority of scriptural passages but from sense-experience and necessary demonstrations. . . . I do not feel obliged to believe that the same God who has endowed us with senses, reason, and intellect has intended to forego their use and by some other means to give us knowledge which we can attain from them.

Galileo appealed to the Roman Catholic authorities asking them to halt their actions against the theories of Copernicus, but was unsuccessful. His support of Copernicus aroused the ire of both clergy and scholastic philosophers. In 1616, the church placed Copernicus's book on the index of forbidden books, and Galileo was ordered to cease his defense of the Copernican theory. In 1632, Galileo published *Dialogue Concerning the Two Chief World Systems* in which he upheld the Copernican view. Widely distributed and acclaimed, the book antagonized Galileo's enemies, who succeeded in halting further printing. Summoned to Rome, the aging and infirm scientist was put on trial by the Inquisition and ordered to renounce the Copernican theory. Galileo bowed to the Inquisition, which condemned the *Dialogue* and sentenced him to life imprisonment—largely house arrest at his own villa near Florence, where he was treated humanely.

GALILEO CONDEMNED BY THE INQUISITION

The following selection is drawn from the records of the Inquisition, which found Galileo guilty of teaching Copernicanism.

Whereas you, Galileo, son of the late Vincenzo Galilei, Florentine, aged seventy years, were in the year 1615 denounced to this Holy Office for holding as true the false doctrine taught by many, that the sun is the centre of the world and immovable, and that the earth moves, and also with a diurnal [daily] motion; for having

disciples to whom you taught the same doctrine; for holding correspondence with certain mathematicians of Germany concerning the same; for having printed certain letters, entitled "On the Solar Spots," wherein you developed the same doctrine as true; and for replying to the objections from the Holy Scriptures, which from time to time were urged against it, by glossing the said Scriptures according to your own meaning: and whereas there was thereupon produced the copy of a document in the form of

Karl von Gelber, *Galileo Galilei and the Roman curia, from Authentic Sources*, trans. Mrs. George Sturge (London: C. Kegan Paul and Co., 1879), pp. 231–234.

a letter, purporting to be written by you to one formerly your disciple, and in this divers propositions are set forth, following the hypothesis of Copernicus, which are contrary to the true sense and authority of Holy Scripture:

This Holy Tribunal being therefore desirous of proceeding against the disorder and mischief thence resulting, which went on increasing to the prejudice of the Holy Faith, by command of his Holiness and of the most eminent Lords Cardinals of this supreme and universal Inquisition, the two propositions of the stability of the sun and the motion of the earth were by the theological "Qualifiers" qualified as follows:

The proposition that the sun is the centre of the world and does not move from its place is absurd and false philosophically and formally heretical, because it is expressly contrary to the Holy Scripture.

The proposition that the earth is not the centre of the world and immovable, but that it moves, and also with a diurnal motion, is equally absurd and false philosophically, and theologically considered, at least erroneous in faith.

But whereas it was desired at that time to deal leniently with you, it was decreed at the Holy Congregation held before his Holiness on the 25th February, 1616, that his Eminence the Lord Cardinal Bellarmine should order you to abandon altogether the said false doctrine, and, in the event of your refusal, that an injunction should be imposed upon you by the Commissary of the Holy Office, to give up the said doctrine, and not to teach it to others, nor to defend it, nor even discuss it; and failing your acquiescence in this injunction, that you should be imprisoned.

And in order that a doctrine so pernicious might be wholly rooted out and not insinuate itself further to the grave prejudice of Catholic truth, a decree was issued by the Holy Congregation of the Index, prohibiting the books which treat of this doctrine, and declaring the doctrine itself to be false and wholly contrary to sacred and divine Scripture.

And whereas a book appeared here recently, printed last year at Florence, the title of which

shows that you were the author, this title being: "Dialogue of Galileo Galilei on the Two Principal Systems of the World, the Ptolemaic and the Copernican"; and whereas the Holy Congregation was afterwards informed that through the publication of the said book, the false opinion of the motion of the earth and the stability of the sun was daily gaining ground; the said book was taken into careful consideration, and in it there was discovered a patent violation of the aforesaid injunction that had been imposed upon you, for in this book you have defended the said opinion previously condemned and to your face declared to be so, although in the said book you strive by various devices to produce the impression that you leave it undecided, and in express terms as probable: which however is a most grievous error, as an opinion can in no wise be probable which has been declared and defined to be contrary to Divine Scripture:

Therefore by our order you were cited before this Holy Office, where, being examined upon your oath, you acknowledged the book to be written and published by you. You confessed that you began to write the said book about ten or twelve years ago, after the command had been imposed upon you as above; that you requested licence to print it, without however intimating to those who granted you this licence that you had been commanded not to hold, defend, or teach in any way whatever the doctrine in question. . . .

Invoking, therefore, the most holy name of our Lord Jesus Christ . . . . we say, pronounce, sentence, declare, that you, the said Galileo, by reason of the matters adduced in process, and by you confessed as above, have rendered yourself in the judgment of this Holy Office vehemently suspected of heresy, namely, of having believed and held the doctrine—which is false and contrary to the sacred and divine Scriptures—that the sun is the centre of the world and does not move from east to west, and that the earth moves and is not the centre of the world; and that an opinion may be held and defended as probable after it has been declared and defined to be contrary to Holy Scripture; and that consequently you have incurred all the censures and penalties imposed and promulgated in the sacred canons and other constitutions, general and particular, against such delinquents. From which we are content that you be absolved, provided that first, with a sincere heart, and unfeigned faith, you abjure, curse, and detest the aforesaid errors and heresies, and every other error and heresy contrary to the Catholic and Apostolic Roman Church in the form to be prescribed by us.

And in order that this your grave and pernicious error and transgression may not remain altogether unpunished, and that you may be more cautious for the future, and an example to others, that they may abstain from similar delinquencies—we ordain that the book of the *"Dialogues" of Galileo Galilei"* be prohibited by public edict.

We condemn you to the formal prison of this Holy Office during our pleasure, and by way of salutary penance, we enjoin that for three years to come you repeat once a week the seven penitential Psalms.

REVIEW QUESTIONS

1. What was Galileo Galilei's objection to using the Bible as a source of knowledge of physical things? According to him, how did one acquire knowledge of nature?
2. Why did the Inquisition regard the teaching of Copernicanism as dangerous?

---

2   Advocacy of Experimental Science

During the seventeenth and eighteenth centuries, the experimental method was increasingly employed in the various sciences. For example, experimenting with bodies in motion, Galileo formulated a law of falling bodies that he expressed mathematically. By "having frequent recourse to vivisections employing a variety of animals . . . and collating numerous observations," wrote the British physician William Harvey in 1628, he was able to demonstrate that all blood passes through a central organ, the heart, flowing away from the heart through the arteries and back to it through the veins, and that this constant, rotating circulation is caused by the rhythmic contractions of the heart muscle acting as a pump.

Francis Bacon
PROPHET OF MODERN EXPERIMENTAL SCIENCE

Sir Francis Bacon (1561–1626), an English statesman and philosopher, vigorously supported the advancement of science and the scientific method. He believed that increased comprehension and mastery of nature would improve living conditions for people and therefore wanted science to encompass systematic research; toward this end, he urged the state to fund scientific institutions.

Bacon denounced universities for merely repeating Aristotelian concepts and discussing abstruse problems—Is matter formless? Are all natural substances composed of matter?—that did not increase understanding of nature or contribute to human betterment. The webs spun by these scholastics, he said, were ingenious but valueless. Bacon wanted an educational program that stressed direct contact with nature and fostered new discoveries.

Bacon was among the first to appreciate the new science's value and to explain its method clearly. Like Leonardo da Vinci, Bacon gave supreme value to the direct observation of nature; for this reason he is one of the founders of the empirical tradition in modern philosophy. Bacon upheld the inductive approach—careful investigation of nature, accumulation of data, and experimentation—as the way to truth and useful knowledge. Because he wanted science to serve a practical function, Bacon praised artisans and technicians who improved technology.

Bacon was not himself a scientist; he made no discoveries and had no laboratory. Nevertheless, for his advocacy of the scientific method, Bacon is deservedly regarded as a prophet of modern science.

In these excerpts from the *Novum Organum* (New System of Logic) in 1620, Bacon criticizes contemporary methods used to inquire into nature. He expresses his ideas in the form of aphorisms—concise statements of principles or general truths.

I.   Man, being the servant and interpreter of Nature, can do and understand so much and so much only as he has observed in fact or in thought of the course of nature: beyond this he neither knows anything nor can do anything.

VIII.   . . . The sciences we now possess are merely systems for the nice ordering and setting forth of things already invented; not methods of invention or directions for new works.

XII.   The logic now in use serves rather to fix and give stability to the errors which have their foundation in commonly received notions than to help the search after truth. So it does more harm than good.

XIX.   There are and can be only two ways of searching into and discovering truth. The one [begins with] the . . . most general axioms, and from these principles, the truth of which it takes for settled and immoveable, proceeds to judgment and to the discovery of middle axioms. And this way is now in fashion. The other derives axioms from the senses and particulars, rising by a gradual and unbroken ascent, so that it arrives at the most general axioms last of all. This is the true way, but as yet untried.

XXIII.   There is a great difference between . . . certain empty dogmas, and the true signatures and marks set upon the works of creation as they are found in nature.

XXIV.   It cannot be that axioms established by argumentation should avail for the discovery of new works; since the subtlety of nature is greater many times over than the subtlety of argument. But axioms duly and orderly formed from particulars easily discover the way to new particulars, and thus render sciences active.

XXXI.   It is idle to expect any great advancement in science from the superinducing [adding] and engrafting of new things upon old. We must begin anew from the very foundations,

Novum Organum, ix, in *The Works of Francis Bacon,* vol. III, coll., ed., and trans. by James Spedding, Robert Leslie Ellis, and Douglas Dennon Heath (Boston: Taggard and Thompson, 1863), pp. 67–69, 71–72, 135–142.

unless we would revolve forever in a circle with mean and contemptible progress.

CIX.   There is therefore much ground for hoping that there are still laid up in the womb of nature many secrets of excellent use, having no affinity or parallelism with anything that is now known, but lying entirely out of the beat of the imagination, which have not yet been found out. They too no doubt will sometime or other, in the course and revolution of many ages, come to light of themselves, just as the others did; only by the method of which we are now treating they can be speedily and suddenly and simultaneously presented and anticipated.

William Harvey
THE CIRCULATION OF THE BLOOD

William Harvey (1578–1657), a British physician, showed that blood circulates in the body because of the pumping action of the heart muscle. Previous belief derived from Galen's theories. Galen (c. 138–c. 201), a Greco-Roman physician, claimed that there were two centers of blood, with the liver being the source of blood in the veins, and the heart being the source of arterial blood. In contrast, Harvey demonstrated that all blood passes through a single central organ, the heart, flowing away from the heart through the arteries and back to it through the veins, and that this constant, rotating circulation is caused by the rhythmic contractions of the heart muscle acting as a pump.

   This discovery of the circulation of blood marked a break with medieval medical ideas (inherited from the ancient world) and signified the emergence of modern physiology. Harvey employed the inductive method championed by Sir Francis Bacon; he drew conclusions after carefully observing and experimenting with living animals.

   In *The Motion of the Heart and Blood in Animals* (1628), Harvey described the heart as a mechanical pump, a description that corresponded to Newton's later view that the universe was a mechanical system. In this reading, Harvey discussed his reasons for writing the book and provided insights into his method.

When I first gave my mind to vivisections [cutting live animals open for experimentation], as a means of discovering the motions and uses of the heart, and sought to discover these from actual inspection, and not from the writings of others, I found the task so truly arduous, so full of difficulties, that I was almost tempted to think . . . that the motion of the heart was only to be comprehended by God. For I could neither rightly perceive at first when the systole and when the diastole took place, nor when and where dilatation and contraction occurred,[1] by reason of the rapidity of the motion, which in many animals is accomplished in the twinkling of an eye, coming and going like a flash of lightning; so that the systole presented itself to me now from this point, now from that; the diastole the same; and then everything was reversed, the motions

---

William Harvey, "The Motion of the Heart and Blood in Animals," in *The Works of William Harvey*, trans. Robert Willis (London: Sydenham Society, 1847), pp. 19–20, 48–49.

[1]In dilatation, the heart muscle is relaxed, creating the diastole, or expansion of the heart's chambers, during which they fill with blood. The heart's contraction, or systole, pumps the blood out of the chambers.—Eds.

occurring, as it seemed, variously and confusedly together. My mind was therefore greatly unsettled, nor did I know what I should myself conclude, nor what believe from others. . . .

At length, and by using greater and daily diligence, having frequent recourse to vivisections, employing a variety of animals for the purpose, and collating numerous observations, I thought that I had attained to the truth, that I should extricate myself and escape from this labyrinth [a maze, a confused state], and that I had discovered what I so much desired, both the motion and the use of the heart and arteries; since which time I have not hesitated to expose my views upon these subjects, not only in private to my friends, but also in public, in my anatomical lectures, after the manner of the Academy[2] of old.

These views, as usual, pleased some more, others less; some [criticized and slandered] me, and laid it to me as a crime that I had dared to depart from the precepts and opinion of all anatomists; others desired further explanations of the novelties, which they said were both worthy of consideration, and might perchance be found of signal use. At length, yielding to the requests of my friends, that all might be made participators in my labours, and partly moved by the envy of others, who, receiving my views with un-candid minds and understanding them indifferently, have [tried to denigrate] me

publicly, I have been moved to commit these things to the press, in order that all may be enabled to form an opinion both of me and my labours. . . .

But lest anyone should say that we give them words only, and make mere specious assertions without any foundation, and desire to innovate without sufficient cause, three points present themselves for confirmation, which being stated, I conceive that the truth I contend for will follow necessarily, and appear as a thing obvious to all. First, —the blood is incessantly transmitted by the action of the heart from the vena cava to the arteries in such quantity, that it cannot be supplied from the ingesta,[3] and in such wise that the whole mass must very quickly pass through the organ; Second, —the blood under the influence of the arterial pulse enters and is impelled in a continuous, equable, and incessant stream through every part and member of the body, in much larger quantity than were sufficient for nutrition, or than the whole mass of fluids could supply; Third, —the veins in like manner return this blood incessantly to the heart from all parts and members of the body. These points proved, I conceive it will be manifest that the blood circulates, revolves, propelled and then returning, from the heart to the extremities, from the extremities to the heart, and thus that it performs a kind of circular motion.

---

[2]The Academy refers to the Athens school founded by Plato at which public lectures were given.—Eds.

[3]The vena cava is the major vein that carries blood returning from the body into the heart. Ingesta refers to solid or liquid nutrients taken into the body.—Eds.

Herman Boerhaave
A NEW METHOD OF CHEMISTRY

Herman Boerhaave (1688–1738), a Dutch physician, transformed chemistry into an experimental discipline in which theoretical knowledge derived from systematic investigation. Rejecting mythical explanations of illness, he also aspired to make medicine a science concerned with the natural cause of disease. In his great work, *A New Method of Chemistry*, excerpted below, he argued that the science of chemistry does not derive simply from reasoning and deduction. Rather it depends on drawing uniform results from numerous experiments. He insisted that scientific truth requires the support of experimental and mathematical evidence.

The second part will deliver certain theorems, or principles of chemistry; wherein all the physical truths which have hitherto been discovered by chemists, are accurately comprised. . . . We allow of no other theory in chemistry, except what is built on general laws; which must originally have been deduced from a multitude of common incontestable facts, always happening in the same manner so as to authorize the enacting them into a general rule. Nor is it allowable to extend even such rule, however true it may prove, but only to apply it to single cases, where the same common reason is found to obtain. For certain bodies have peculiar powers, from whence effects arise, that do not come within the compass of any general theorem; but depend on a certain constitution peculiar perhaps to some one body.

Herman, Boerhaave *A New Method of Chemistry*, second edition (London: Printed for T. Longman at the Ship, 1741), pp. 2–3. Reprinted by Ecco. Spelling modernized.

REVIEW QUESTIONS

1. What intellectual attitude did Francis Bacon believe obstructed new scientific discoveries in his time?
2. What method of scientific inquiry did Bacon advocate?
3. What evidence led William Harvey to conclude that blood constantly circulates through the heart?
4. What method did he use to reach his conclusions?
5. Why did some of Harvey's colleagues refuse to believe his conclusions?
6. What did Herman Boerhaave mean by general laws?

3 The Autonomy of the Mind

René Descartes (1596–1650), a French mathematician and philosopher, united the new currents of thought initiated during the Renaissance and the Scientific Revolution. Descartes said that the universe was a mechanical system whose inner laws could be discovered through mathematical thinking and formulated in mathematical terms. With Descartes' assertions on the power of thought, human beings became fully aware of their capacity to comprehend the world through their mental powers. Because of his stated willingness to reject past systems and begin anew without any presuppositions and trusting to the mind's capacity for thought, Descartes is regarded as the founder of modern philosophy.

The deductive approach stressed by Descartes presumes that inherent in the mind are mathematical principles, logical relationships, the principle of cause and effect, concepts of size and motion, and so on—ideas that exist independently of human experience with the external world. Descartes, for example, would say that the properties of a right-angle triangle ($a^2 + b^2 = c^2$) are implicit in human consciousness prior to any experience one might have with a triangle. These innate ideas, said Descartes, permit the mind to give order and coherence to the physical world. Descartes held that the mind arrives at truth when it "intuits" or comprehends the logical necessity of its own ideas and expresses these ideas with clarity, certainty, and precision.

René Descartes
DISCOURSE ON METHOD

In the *Discourse on Method* (1637), Descartes proclaimed the mind's autonomy and importance, and its ability and right to comprehend truth. In this work he offered a method whereby one could achieve certainty and thereby produce a comprehensive understanding of nature and human culture. In the following passage from the *Discourse on Method*, he explained the purpose of his inquiry. How he did so is almost as revolutionary as the ideas he wished to express. He spoke in the first person, autobiographically, as an individual employing his own reason, and he addressed himself to other individuals, inviting them to use their reason. He brought to his narrative an unprecedented confidence in the power of his own judgment and a deep disenchantment with the learning of his times.

PART I

From my childhood, I have been familiar with books; and as I was given to believe that by their help a clear and certain knowledge of all that is useful in life might be acquired, I was ardently desirous of instruction. But as soon as I had finished the entire course of study, at the close of which it is customary to be admitted into the order of the learned, I completely changed my opinion. For I found myself involved in so many doubts and errors, that I was convinced I had advanced no farther in all my attempts at learning than the discovery at every turn of my own ignorance. And yet I was studying in one of the most celebrated schools in Europe, in which

Adapted from René Descartes, *The Methods, Meditations, and Philosophy of Descartes*, trans. John Vietch (Washington, D.C.: Walter Dunne, 1901), pp. 151–155, 157–161, 163, 170–171.

I thought there must be learned men, if such were anywhere to be found. I had been taught all that others learned there; and not contented with the sciences actually taught us, I had, in addition, read all the books that had fallen into my hands. . . .

And our age appeared to me as flourishing, and as fertile in powerful minds as any preceding one. I was thus led to take the liberty of judging of all other men by myself, and of concluding that there was no wisdom in existence that was of such a nature as I had previously been given to believe.

I still continued, however, to hold in esteem the studies of the schools—literature, languages, history, oratory, mathematics, science, theology, and philosophy. . . .

I revered our theology, and aspired as much as anyone to reach heaven: but being given assuredly to understand that . . . the revealed truths which lead to heaven are above our comprehension, I did not presume to subject them to the impotency of my reason; and I thought that in order competently to undertake their examination, there was need of some special help from heaven, and of being more than man.

Of Philosophy I will say nothing, except that when I saw that it had been cultivated for many ages by the most distinguished men, and that yet there is not a single matter within its sphere which is not still in dispute, and nothing, therefore, which is above doubt, I did not presume to anticipate that my success would be greater in it than that of others; and further, when I considered the number of conflicting opinions touching a single matter that may be upheld by learned men, while there can be but one true, I reckoned as well-nigh false all that was only probable. . . .

For these reasons, as soon as my age permitted me to pass from under the control of my instructors, I entirely abandoned the study of letters, and resolved no longer to seek any other science than the knowledge of myself, or of the great book of the world. I spent the remainder of my youth in traveling, in visiting courts and armies, in holding intercourse with men of different dispositions and ranks, in collecting varied experience, in proving myself in the different situations into which fortune threw me, and, above all, in making such reflection on the matter of my experience as to secure my improvement. For it occurred to me that I should find much more truth in the reasonings of each individual with reference to the affairs in which he is personally interested, and the issue of which must presently punish him if he has judged amiss, than in those conducted by a man of letters in his study engaging in speculative matters that are of no practical value to him. . . .

I had always a most earnest desire to know how to distinguish the true from the false, in order that I might be able clearly to discriminate the right path in life, and proceed in it with confidence. . . . But after I had been occupied several years in thus studying the book of the world, and in essaying to gather some experience, I at length resolved to make myself an object of study, and to employ all the powers of my mind in choosing the paths I ought to follow; an undertaking which was accompanied with greater success than it would have been had I never quitted my country or my books.

PART II

As for the opinions which up to that time I had embraced, I thought that I could not do better than resolve at once to reject them completely, that I might afterward be in a position to admit either others more correct, or even perhaps the same when they had undergone the scrutiny of reason. I firmly believed that in this way I should much better succeed in the conduct of my life than if I built only upon old foundations, and leaned upon principles which, in my youth, I had taken upon trust. . . .

I have never contemplated anything higher than the reformation of my own opinions, and basing them on a foundation wholly my own. . . .

I had become aware, even so early as during my college life, that no opinion, however absurd and incredible, can be imagined, which has not been maintained by some one of the philosophers; and afterward in the course of my travels I remarked that all those whose opinions are decidedly repugnant to ours are not on that account barbarians and savages, but on the contrary that many of these nations make an equally good, if not a better, use of their reason than we do. I took into account also the very different character which a person brought up from infancy in France or Germany exhibits, from that which, with the same mind originally, this individual would have possessed had he lived always among the Chinese or with savages. . . . I was thus led to infer that the ground of our opinions is far more custom and example than any certain knowledge. And, finally, although such be the ground of our opinions, I remarked that the opinion of the majority is no guarantee of truth. . . .

And thus I found myself constrained, as it were, to use my own reason in the conduct of my life. But like one walking alone and in the dark, I resolved to proceed so slowly and with such circumspection, that if I did not advance far, I would at least guard against falling. I did not even choose to dismiss summarily any of the opinions that had crept into my belief system unsupported by reason. . . .

Descartes' method consists of four principles that place the capacity to arrive at truth entirely within the province of the human mind. One finds a self-evident principle, such as a geometric axiom. From this general principle, other truths are deduced through logical reasoning. This is accomplished by breaking a problem down into its elementary components and then, step by step, moving toward more complex knowledge.

I was induced to seek some other method besides that of logic, algebra, and geometry which would comprise the advantages of these three and avoid their defects. Instead of the great number of precepts of which logic is composed, I believed that the four following would prove perfectly sufficient for me, provided I took the firm and unwavering resolution never in a single instance to fail in observing them.

The FIRST was never to accept anything for true which I did not clearly know to be such; that is to say, carefully to avoid haste and prejudice, and to comprise nothing more in my judgment than what was presented to my mind so clearly and distinctly as to exclude all ground of doubt.

The SECOND, to divide each of the difficulties under examination into as many parts as possible, and as might be necessary for its adequate solution.

The THIRD, to conduct my thoughts in such order that, by commencing with objects the simplest and easiest to know, I might ascend by

little and little, and, as it were, step by step, to the knowledge of the more complex; assigning in thought a certain order even to those objects which in their own nature are not orderly.

The LAST was in every case to make enumerations so complete, and reviews so general, that I might be assured that nothing was omitted. . . .

Descartes was searching for an incontrovertible truth that could serve as the first principle of philosophy. His arrival at the famous dictum "I think, therefore I am" marks the beginning of modern philosophy.

PART IV

As I desired to give my attention solely to the search after truth, I thought I ought to reject as absolutely false all opinions to which I had the least doubt in order to ascertain, after this procedure, those opinions that could be called wholly certain. Accordingly, seeing that our senses sometimes deceive us, I was willing to suppose that nothing was really the way our senses represented it. And because some men err even on the simplest matters of geometry, I was convinced that I too was open to error as any other. Hence, I rejected as false all the reasoning I had hitherto taken as true. Finally, when I considered that the very same thoughts which we experience when awake may also be experienced when we are asleep without their being true, I supposed that all objects that had ever entered into my mind when awake, had in them no more truth than the illusions of my dreams. But I immediately observed that while I wished to think all was false, it was absolutely necessary that it was I who did the thinking was something. And since this truth, *I think therefore I am*, was so certain and assured that all the elaborate arguments of sceptics were not capable of shaking it, I concluded that without reservation I could accept it as the first principle of the philosophy of which I was in search.

REVIEW QUESTIONS

1. Why was René Descartes critical of the learning of his day?
2. What are the implications of Descartes' famous words: "I think, therefore I am"?
3. Compare Descartes' method with the approach advocated by Francis Bacon.

---

4 The Mechanical Universe

By demonstrating that all bodies in the universe—earthly objects as well as moons, planets, and stars—obey the same laws of motion and gravitation, Sir Isaac Newton (1646–1723) completed the destruction of the medieval view of the universe. The idea that the same laws governed the movement of earthly and heavenly bodies was completely foreign to medieval thinkers, who drew a sharp division between a higher celestial world and a lower terrestrial one. In the *Principia Mathematica* (1687), Newton showed that the same forces that hold celestial bodies in their orbits around the sun make apples fall to the ground. For Newton, the universe was like a giant clock, all of whose parts obeyed strict mechanical principles and worked together in perfect precision. To Newton's contemporaries, it seemed as if mystery had been banished from the universe.

Isaac Newton
PRINCIPIA MATHEMATICA

In the first of the following passages from *Principia Mathematica*, Newton states the principle of universal law and lauds the experimental method as the means of acquiring knowledge.

RULES OF REASONING
IN PHILOSOPHY

Rule I. We are to admit no more causes of natural things than such as are both true and sufficient to explain their appearances.

To this purpose the philosophers say that Nature does nothing in vain, and more is in vain when less will serve; for Nature is pleased with simplicity, and affects not the pomp of superfluous causes.

Rule II.   Therefore to the same natural effects we must, as far as possible, assign the same causes.

As to respiration in a man and in a beast; the descent of stones in *Europe* and in *America*; the light of our culinary fire and of the sun; the reflection of light in the earth, and in the planets.

Rule III.   The qualities of bodies, which . . . are found to belong to all bodies within the

Sir Isaac Newton, *The Mathematical Principles of Natural Philosophy*, Book III, trans. Andre Motte (London: H. D. Symonds, 1803), II, pp. 160–162, 310–314.

reach of our experiments, are to be esteemed the universal qualities of all bodies whatsoever.

For since the qualities of bodies are only known to us by experiments, we are to hold for universal all such as universally agree with experiments. . . . We are certainly not to relinquish the evidence of experiments for the sake of dreams and vain fictions of our own devising; nor are we to recede from the analogy of Nature, which [is] . . . simple, and always consonant to itself. We no other way know the extension of bodies than by our senses, nor do these reach it in all bodies; but because we perceive extension in all that are sensible, therefore, we ascribe it universally to all others also. That abundance of bodies are hard, we learn by experience; and because the hardness of the whole arises from the hardness of the parts, we, therefore, justly infer the hardness of the undivided particles not only of the bodies we feel but of all others. That all bodies are impenetrable, we gather not from reason, but from sensation. The bodies which we handle we find impenetrable, and thence, conclude impenetrability to be an universal property of all bodies whatsoever. That all bodies are moveable, and endowed with certain powers (which we call. . . [*inertia*]) of persevering in their motion, or in their rest, we only infer from the like properties observed in the bodies which we have seen. The extension, hardness, impenetrability, mobility, . . . of the whole, result from the extension, hardness, impenetrability, mobility, . . . of the parts; and thence we conclude the least particles of all bodies to be also all extended, and hard and impenetrable, and moveable, . . . And this is the foundation of all philosophy. . . .

Lastly, if it universally appears, by experiments and astronomical observations, that all bodies about the earth gravitate towards the earth, and that in proportion to the quantity of matter which they severally contain; that the moon likewise, according to the quantity of its matter, gravitates towards the earth; that, on the other hand, our sea gravitates towards the moon; and all the planets mutually one towards another;

and the comets in like manner towards the sun; we must, in consequence of this rule, universally allow that all bodies whatsoever are endowed with a principle of mutual gravitation. . . .

Rule IV. In experimental philosophy we are to look upon propositions collected by general induction from phenomena as accurately or very nearly true, notwithstanding any contrary hypotheses that may be imagined, till such time as other phenomena occur, by which they may either be made more accurate, or liable to exceptions.

This rule we must follow, that the argument of induction may not be evaded by hypotheses.

Newton describes further his concepts of gravity and scientific methodology.

GRAVITY

Hitherto, we have explained the phenomena of the heavens and of our sea by the power of gravity, but have not yet assigned the cause of this power. This is certain, that it must proceed from a cause that penetrates to the very centres of the sun and planets, without suffering the least diminution of its force; that operates not according to the quantity of the surfaces of the particles upon which it acts (as mechanical causes used to do) but according to the quantity of the solid matter which they contain, and propagates its virtue on all sides to immense distances, decreasing always in the duplicate portion of the distances. . . .

Hitherto I have not been able to discover the cause of those properties of gravity from the phenomena, and I frame no hypothesis; for whatever is not deduced from the phenomena is to be called an hypothesis; and hypotheses, whether metaphysical or physical, whether of occult qualities or mechanical, have no place in experimental philosophy. In this philosophy particular propositions are inferred from the phenomena, and afterward rendered general by induction. Thus it was the impenetrability, the mobility, and the impulsive forces of bodies, and the laws of motion and of gravitation were discovered. And to us it is enough that gravity does really exist, and acts according to the laws which we have explained, and abundantly serves to account for all the motions of the celestial bodies, and of our sea.

A devout Anglican, Newton believed that God had created this superbly organized universe.

GOD AND THE UNIVERSE

This most beautiful system of the sun, planets, and comets could only proceed from the counsel and dominion of an intelligent and powerful Being. And if the fixed stars are the centers of other like systems, these, being formed by the like wise counsel, must be all subject to the dominion of One, especially since the light of the fixed stars is of the same nature with the light of the sun and from every system light passes into all the other systems; and lest the systems of the fixed stars should, by their gravity, fall on each other mutually, he hath placed those systems at immense distances from one another.

This Being governs all things not as the soul of the world, but as Lord over all; and on account of his dominion he is wont to be called "Lord God" . . . or "Universal Ruler." . . . It is the dominion of a spiritual being which constitutes a God. . . . And from his true dominion it

follows that the true God is a living, intelligent and powerful Being. . . . he governs all things, and knows all things that are or can be done. . . . He endures forever, and is everywhere present; and by existing always and everywhere, he constitutes duration and space. . . .

In him are all things contained and moved; yet neither affects the other: God suffers nothing from the motion of bodies; bodies find no resistance from the omnipresence of God. . . . As a blind man has no idea of colors so we have no idea of the manner by which the all-wise God preserves and understands all things. He is utterly void of all body and bodily figure, and can therefore neither be seen, nor heard, nor touched; nor ought to be worshipped under the representation of any corporeal thing. We have ideas of his attributes, but what the real substance of any thing is we know not. . . . Much less, then, have we any idea of the substance of God. We know him only by his most wise and excellent contrivances of things. . . . [W]e reverence and adore him as his servants; and a god without dominion, providence [divine intervention], and final causes, is nothing else but Fate and Nature. Blind metaphysical necessity, which is certainly the same always and everywhere, could produce no variety of things. All that diversity of natural things which we find suited to different times and places could arise from nothing but the ideas and will of a Being necessarily existing. . . . And thus much concerning God; to discourse of whom from the appearances of things does certainly belong to Natural Philosophy.

REVIEW QUESTIONS

1. What did Isaac Newton mean by universal law? What examples of universal law did he provide?
2. What method for investigating nature did Newton advocate?
3. Summarize Newton's arguments for God's existence.
4. For Newton, what is God's relationship to the universe?

5 The Limitations of Science

Most seventeenth- and eighteenth-century thinkers regarded the discoveries of Newton and others as a great triumph for civilization. These discoveries uncovered nature's mysteries, provided a method for exploring nature further, and demonstrated the capacity of the human mind.

In later centuries, further implications of the new cosmology caused great anguish. The conviction that God had created the universe for them, that the earth was fixed beneath their feet, and that God had given the earth the central position in his creation had brought medieval people a profound sense of security. They knew why they were here, and they never doubted that heaven was the final resting place for the faithful. Copernican astronomy dethroned the earth, expelled human beings from their central position, and implied an infinite universe. In the sixteenth and seventeenth centuries, few thinkers grasped the full significance of this displacement. However, in succeeding centuries, this radical cosmological transformation proved as traumatic for the modern mind as did Adam and Eve's expulsion from the Garden of Eden for the medieval mind. Today we know that the earth is one of billions and billions of celestial bodies, a tiny speck in an endless cosmic ocean, and that the universe is some twelve billion years old. Could such a universe have been created just for human beings? Could it contain a heaven that assures eternal life for the faithful and a hell with eternal fires and torments for sinners?

Blaise Pascal
PENSÉES

Few people at the time were aware of the full implications of the new cosmology. One who did understand was Blaise Pascal (1623–1662), a great French scientist and mathematician. A devout Catholic, Pascal was frightened by what he called "the eternal silence of these infinite spaces" and realized that the new science could stir doubt, uncertainty, and anxiety, which threatened belief.

It is true, wrote Pascal, that reason cannot prove that "God is or He is not." But if we were compelled to choose between God's existence or non-existence, we should "wager without hesitation that He is." If we are wrong, we "lose nothing," but if we are right "an eternity of life and happiness" awaits us.

The following excerpts from his *Pensées* illustrate Pascal's concerns about where science is taking us.

67.   *The vanity of the sciences.*—Physical science will not console me for the ignorance of morality in the time of affliction. But the science of ethics will always console me for the ignorance of the physical sciences.

76.   To write against those who made too profound a study of science: Descartes.

Pascal's Pensées, introduction by T. S. Eliot (New York: E. P. Dutton & Co., 1958), pp. 15, 23, 27, 55, 61.

77.   I cannot forgive Descartes. In all his philosophy he would have been quite willing to dispense with God. But he had to make Him give a fillip to set the world in motion; beyond this he has no further need of God.

83.   *We must thus begin the chapter on the deceptive powers.* Man is only a subject full of error, natural and ineffaceable, without grace. Nothing shows him the truth. Everything deceives him. These two sources of truth, reason and the senses, besides being both wanting in sincerity, deceive each other in turn. The senses mislead the reason with false appearances, and receive from reason in their turn the same trickery which they apply to her; reason has her revenge. The passions of the soul trouble the senses, and make false impressions upon them. They rival each other in falsehood and deception.

194.   I see those frightful spaces of the universe which surround me, and I find myself tied to one corner of this vast expanse, without knowing why I am put in this place rather than in another, nor why the short time which is given me to live is assigned to me at this point rather than at another of the whole eternity which was before me or which shall come after me. I see nothing but infinites on all sides, which surround me as an atom, and as a shadow which endures only for an instant and returns no more. All I know is that I must soon die, but what I know least is this very death which I cannot escape.

205.   When I consider the short duration of my life, swallowed up in the eternity before and after, the little space which I fill, and even can see, engulfed in the infinite immensity of spaces of which I am ignorant, and which know me not, I am frightened, and am astonished at being here rather than there; for there is no reason why here rather than there, why now rather than then. Who has put me here? By whose order and direction have this place and time been allotted to me?

206.   The eternal silence of these infinite spaces frightens me.

REVIEW QUESTIONS

1. What was Pascal's reaction to the new directions in science?
2. In today's world, what developments in science and technology cause great concern?

CHAPTER 3

The Enlightenment

ISAAC NEWTON AND VOLTAIRE, frontispiece to *Elémens de la philosophie de Neuton*, Voltaire's interpretation of Newton's work, 1738. The philosophe sits translating the inspired work of Newton; Voltaire's manuscript is illuminated by seemingly divine light coming from Newton himself, reflected down to Voltaire by a muse, representing Voltaire's lover Émilie du Châtelet—who actually translated Newton and collaborated with Voltaire to make sense of Newton's work. *(Marie Arouet de Voltaire)*

The Enlightenment of the eighteenth century culminated the movement toward modernity that started in the Renaissance era. The thinkers of the Enlightenment, called *philosophes*, attacked medieval otherworldliness, dethroned theology from its once-proud position as queen of the sciences, and based their understanding of nature and society on reason alone, unaided by revelation or priestly authority.

From the broad spectrum of Western history, several traditions flowed into the Enlightenment: the rational spirit born in classical Greece, the Stoic emphasis on natural law that applies to all human beings, and the Christian belief that all individuals are equal in God's eyes. A more immediate influence on the Enlightenment was Renaissance humanism, which focused on the individual and worldly human accomplishments and which criticized medieval theology-philosophy for its preoccupation with questions that seemed unrelated to the human condition. In many ways, the Enlightenment grew directly out of the Scientific Revolution. The philosophes praised both Newton's discovery of the mechanical laws that govern the universe and the scientific method that made this discovery possible. They wanted to transfer the scientific method—the reliance on experience and the critical use of the intellect—to the realm of society. They maintained that independent of clerical authority, human beings through reason could grasp the natural laws that govern the social world, just as Newton had uncovered the laws of nature that operate in the physical world. The philosophes said that those institutions and traditions that could not meet the test of reason, because they were based on authority, ignorance, or superstition, had to be reformed or dispensed with.

For medieval philosophers, reason had been subordinate to revelation; the Christian outlook determined the medieval concept of nature, morality, government, law, and life's purpose. During the Renaissance and Scientific Revolution, reason increasingly asserted its autonomy. For example, Machiavelli rejected the principle that politics should be based on Christian teachings that religious-moral principles derived from a higher world should determine a ruler's thinking and actions. Galileo held that on questions regarding nature, one should trust to observation, experimentation, and mathematical reasoning and should not rely on scripture. Descartes rejected reliance on past authority and maintained that through thought alone one could attain knowledge that has absolute certainty. Agreeing with Descartes that the mind is self-sufficient, the philosophes rejected the guidance of revelation and its priestly interpreters. They believed that through the use of reason, individuals could comprehend and reform society.

The Enlightenment philosophes articulated basic principles of the modern outlook: confidence in the self-sufficiency of the human mind, belief that individuals possess natural rights that governments should not violate, and the desire to reform society in accordance with rational principles. Their views influenced the reformers of the French Revolution, the Founding Fathers of the United States, and modern liberalism.

---

1 The Enlightenment Outlook

The critical use of the intellect was the central principle of the Enlightenment. The philosophes rejected beliefs and traditions that seemed to conflict with reason and attacked clerical and political authorities for interfering with the free use of the intellect.

Immanuel Kant
"WHAT IS ENLIGHTENMENT?"

The German philosopher Immanuel Kant (1724–1804) is a giant in the history of modern philosophy. Several twentieth-century philosophic movements have their origins in Kantian thought, and many issues raised by Kant still retain their importance. For example, in *Metaphysical Foundations of Morals* (1785), Kant set forth the categorical imperative that remains a crucial principle in moral philosophy. Kant asserted that when confronted with a moral choice, people should ask themselves: "Canst thou also will that thy maxim should be a universal law?" By this, Kant meant that people should ponder whether they would want the moral principle underlying their action to be elevated to a universal law that would govern others in similar circumstances. If they concluded that it should not, then the principle should be rejected as a universal maxim and the action avoided.

Kant valued the essential ideals of the Enlightenment and viewed the French Revolution, which put these ideals into law, as the triumph of liberty over despotism. In an essay entitled "What Is Enlightenment?" (1784), he contended that the Enlightenment marked a new way of thinking and eloquently affirmed the Enlightenment's confidence in and commitment to reason.

Enlightenment is man's leaving his self-caused immaturity. Immaturity is the incapacity to use one's intelligence without the guidance of another. Such immaturity is self-caused if it is not caused by lack of intelligence, but by lack of determination and courage to use one's intelligence without being guided by another. *Sapere Aude!* [Dare to know!] Have the courage to use your own intelligence! is therefore the motto of the enlightenment.

Through laziness and cowardice a large part of mankind, even after nature has freed them from alien guidance, gladly remain immature. It is because of laziness and cowardice that it is so easy for others to usurp the role of guardians. It is so comfortable to be a minor! If I have a book which provides meaning for me, a pastor who has conscience for me, a doctor who will judge my diet for me, and so on, then I do not need to exert myself. I do not have any need to think; if I can pay, others will take over the tedious job for me. The guardians who have kindly undertaken the supervision will see to it that by far the largest part of mankind, including the entire "beautiful sex," should consider the step into maturity, not only as difficult but as very dangerous.

After having made their domestic animals dumb and having carefully prevented these quiet creatures from daring to take any step beyond the lead-strings to which they have fastened them, these guardians then show them the danger which threatens them, should they attempt to walk alone. Now this danger is not really so very great; for they would presumably learn to walk after some stumbling. However, an example of this kind intimidates and frightens people out of all further attempts.

It is difficult for the isolated individual to work himself out of the immaturity which has become almost natural for him. He has even become fond of it and for the time being is incapable of employing his own intelligence, because he has never been allowed to make the attempt. Statutes and formulas, these mechanical tools of a serviceable use, or rather misuse, of his natural faculties, are the ankle-chains of a continuous immaturity. Whoever threw it off would make an uncertain jump over the smallest trench because he is not accustomed to such free movement. Therefore there are only a few who have pursued a firm path and have succeeded in escaping from immaturity by their own cultivation of the mind.

But it is more nearly possible for a public to enlighten itself: this is even inescapable if only the public is given its freedom. For there will always be some people who think for themselves, even among the self-appointed guardians of the great mass who, after having thrown off the yoke of immaturity themselves, will spread about them the spirit of a reasonable estimate of their own value and of the need for every man to think for himself. . . . [A] public can only arrive at enlightenment slowly. Through revolution, the abandonment of personal despotism may be engendered and the end of profit-seeking and domineering oppression may occur, but never a true reform of the state of mind. Instead, new prejudices, just like the old ones, will serve as the guiding reins of the great, unthinking mass. . . .

All that is required for this enlightenment is *freedom*; and particularly the least harmful of all that may be called freedom, namely, the freedom for man to make *public use* of his reason in all matters. But I hear people clamor on all sides: Don't argue! The officer says: Don't argue, drill! The tax collector: Don't argue, pay! The pastor: Don't argue, believe! . . . Here we have restrictions on freedom everywhere. Which restriction is hampering enlightenment, and which does not, or even promotes it? I answer: The *public use* of a man's reason must be free at all times, and this alone can bring enlightenment among men. . . .

I mean by the public use of one's reason, the use which a scholar makes of it before the entire reading public. . . .

The question may now be put: Do we live at present in an enlightened age? The answer is: No, but in an age of enlightenment. Much still prevents men from being placed in a position . . . to use their own minds securely and well in matters of religion. But we do have very definite indications that this field of endeavor is being opened up for men to work freely and reduce gradually the hindrances preventing a general enlightenment and an escape from self-caused immaturity.

REVIEW QUESTIONS

1. What did Immanuel Kant mean by the terms *enlightenment* and *freedom?*
2. In Kant's view, what factors delayed the progress of human enlightenment?
3. What are the political implications of Kant's views?

2 Enlightenment Political Thought

For the philosophes, established religion was one source of the ills that afflicted humanity; another source was despotism. If human beings were to achieve well-being and happiness, they had to contain the power of both priests and rulers. Eighteenth-century political thought is characterized by a thoroughgoing secularism; an indictment of despotism, the divine right of kings, and the special privileges of the aristocracy and the clergy; a respect for English constitutionalism because it enshrined the rule of law; and an affirmation of John Locke's theory that government had an obligation to protect the natural rights of its citizens. Central to the political outlook of the philosophes was the conviction that political solutions could be found for the ills that afflicted society.

Several entries in the *Encyclopedia* (published in twenty-eight volumes between 1751 and 1772) expressed essential elements of the philosophes' political thought. In his article "Political Authority," Diderot held that the monarch's authority "is limited by the laws of nature and the state." Although the king may inherit the throne, the government "is not private property, but public property that consequently can never be taken from the people, to whom it belongs exclusively, fundamentally, and as a freehold."

In general, the philosophes favored constitutional government that protected citizens from the abuse of power. With the notable exception of Rousseau, the philosophes' concern for liberty did not lead them to embrace democracy, for they placed little trust in the masses. Several philosophes, notably Voltaire, placed their confidence in reforming despots, like Frederick II of Prussia, who were sympathetic to enlightened ideas. However, the philosophes were less concerned with the form of government—monarchy or republic—than they were with preventing the authorities from abusing their power.

John Locke
SECOND TREATISE ON GOVERNMENT

John Locke (1632–1704), a British statesman, philosopher, and political theorist, was a principal source of the Enlightenment. Eighteenth-century thinkers were particularly influenced by Locke's advocacy of religious toleration, his reliance on experience as the source of knowledge, and his concern for liberty. In his first *Letter Concerning Toleration* (1689), Locke declared that Christians who persecute others in the name of religion vitiate Christ's teachings. Locke's political philosophy as formulated in the *Two Treatises on Government* (1690) complements his theory of knowledge (see page 71); both were rational and secular attempts to understand and improve the human condition. The Lockean spirit pervades the American Declaration of Independence and the U.S. Constitution and Bill of Rights; it is the basis of the liberal tradition that aims to protect individual liberty from despotic state authority.

Viewing human beings as brutish and selfish, Thomas Hobbes (see page 23) in *Leviathan* (1651) had prescribed a state with unlimited power; only in this way, he said, could people be protected from each other and civilized life preserved. Locke, regarding people as essentially good and humane, developed a conception of the state differing fundamentally from Hobbes's. Locke held that human beings are born with natural rights of life, liberty, and property; they establish the state to protect these rights. Consequently, neither executive nor legislature, neither king nor assembly has the authority to deprive individuals of their natural rights. Whereas Hobbes justified absolute monarchy, Locke explicitly endorsed constitutional government in which the power to govern derives from the consent of the governed and the state's authority is limited by agreement.

Locke said that originally, in establishing a government, human beings had never agreed to surrender their natural rights to any state authority. The state's founders intended the new polity to preserve these natural rights and to implement the people's will. Therefore, as the following passage from Locke's *Second Treatise on Government* illustrates, the power exercised by magistrates cannot be absolute or arbitrary.

. . . *Political power* is that power, which every man having in the state of nature, has given up into the hands of the society, and therein to the governors, whom the society hath set over itself, with this express or tacit trust, that it shall be employed for their good, and the preservation of their property; now this *power*, which every man

---

John Locke, *Two Treatises on Civil Government* (London: 1688, 7th reprinting by J. Whiston et al., 1772), pp. 292, 315–316, 354–355, 358–359, 361–362.

has *in the state of nature*, and which he parts with to the society in all such cases where the society can secure him, is to use such means, for the preserving of his own property, as he thinks good and nature allows him; and to punish the breach of the law of nature in others, so as (according to the best of his reason) may most conduce to the preservation of himself, and the rest of mankind. So that the *end and measure of this power*, when in every man's hands in the state of nature, being the preservation of all of his society, that is, all mankind in general, it can have no other *end or measure*, when in the hands of the magistrate, but to preserve the members of that society in their lives, liberties, and possessions; and so cannot be an absolute, arbitrary power over their lives and fortunes, which are as much as possible to be preserved; but a *power to make laws*, and annex such *penalties* to them, as may tend to the preservation of the whole, by cutting off those parts, and those only, which are so corrupt, that they threaten the sound and healthy, without which no severity is lawful. And this *power has its original only from compact*, and agreement, and the mutual consent of those who make up the community. . . .

These are the *bounds*, which the trust, that is put in them by the society, and the law of God and nature, have *set to the legislative* power of every common-wealth, in all forms of government.

First, They are to govern *by promulgated established laws*, not to be varied in particular cases, but to have one rule for rich and poor, for the favourite at court, and the country man at plough.

Secondly, These *laws* also ought to be designed *for* no other end ultimately, but *the good of the people.*

Thirdly, They must *not raise taxes* on *the property of the people, without the consent of the people*, given by themselves, or their deputies. And this properly concerns only such governments, where the *legislative* is always in being, or at least where the people have not reserved any part of the legislative to deputies, to be from time to time chosen by themselves.

Fourthly, The *legislative* neither must *nor can transfer the power of making laws* to any body else, or place it any where, but where the people [have placed it].

If government fails to fulfill the end for which it was established—the preservation of the individual's right to life, liberty, and property—the people have a right to dissolve that government.

. . . The *legislative acts against the trust* reposed in them, when they endeavour to invade the property of the subject, and to make themselves, or any part of the community, masters, or arbitrary disposers of the lives, liberties, or fortunes of the people.

The reason why men enter into society, is the preservation of their property; and the end why they chuse and authorize a legislative, *is*, that there may be laws made, and rules set, as guards and fences to the properties of all the members of the society, to limit the power, and moderate the dominion of every part and member of the society: for since it can never be supposed to be the will of the society, that the legislative should have a power to destroy that which every one designs to secure, by entering into society, and for which the people submitted themselves to legislators of their own making; whenever the *legislators endeavour to take away, and destroy the property of the people*, or to reduce them to slavery under arbitrary power, they put themselves into a state of war with the people, who are thereupon absolved from any farther obedience, and are left to the common refuge, which God hath provided for all men, against force and violence. Whensoever therefore the *legislative* shall transgress this fundamental rule of society; and either by ambition, fear, folly or corruption, *endeavour to grasp* themselves, *or put into the hands of any other, an absolute power* over the lives, liberties, and estates of the people; by this breach of trust they *forfeit the power* the people had put into their hands for quite contrary ends, and it devolves to the people, who have a right to resume their original liberty, and, by the establishment of a new legislative, (such as they shall think fit) provide for their own safety and security, which is the end for which they are in society. What I have said here, concerning the legislative in general, holds true also concerning the supreme executor, who having a double trust put in him, both to have a part in the legislative, and the supreme execution of the law, acts against both, when he goes about to set up his own arbitrary will as the law of the society. He *acts* also *contrary to his trust*, when he either employs the force, treasure, and offices of the society, to corrupt the *representatives*, and gain them to his purposes; or openly pre-engages the *electors*, and prescribes to their choice, such, whom he has, by sollicitations, threats, promises, or otherwise, won to his designs; and employs them to bring in such, who have promised beforehand what to vote, and what to enact. . . .

Locke responds to the charge that his theory will produce "frequent rebellion." Indeed, says Locke, the true rebels are the magistrates who, acting contrary to the trust granted them, violate the people's rights.

. . . Such *revolutions happen* not upon every little mismanagement in public affairs. *Great mistakes* in the ruling part, many wrong and inconvenient laws, and all the *slips* of human frailty, will be *borne by the people* without mutiny or murmur. But if a long train of abuses, prevarications and artifices, all tending the same way, make the design visible to the people, and they cannot but feel what they lie under, and see whither they are going; it is not to be wondered at, that they should then rouze themselves, and endeavour to put the rule into such hands which may secure to them the ends for which government was at first erected. . . .

. . . I answer, that *this doctrine* of a power in the people of providing for their safety a new, by a new legislative, when their legislators have acted contrary to their trust, by invading their property, is *the best defence against rebellion*, and the probablest means to hinder it: for *rebellion* being an opposition, not to persons, but authority, which is founded only in the constitutions and laws of the government; those, whoever they be, who by force break through, and by force justify their violation of them, are truly and properly *rebels*: for when men, by entering into society and civil government, have excluded force, and introduced laws for the preservation of property, peace, and unity amongst themselves, those who set up force again in opposition to the laws, do [rebel], that is, bring back again the state of war, and are properly rebels: which they who are in power, (by the pretence they have to authority, the temptation of force they have in their hands, and the flattery of those about them) being likeliest to do; the properest way to prevent the evil, is to shew them the danger and injustice of it, who are under the greatest temptation to run into it.

The end of government is the good of mankind; and which is *best for mankind*, that the people should always be exposed to the boundless will of tyranny, or that the rulers should be sometimes liable to be opposed, when they grow exorbitant in the use of their power, and employ it for the destruction, and not the preservation of the properties of their people?

Thomas Jefferson
DECLARATION OF INDEPENDENCE

Written in 1776 by Thomas Jefferson (1743–1826) to justify the American colonists' break with Britain, the Declaration of Independence enumerated principles that were quite familiar to English statesmen and intellectuals. The preamble to the Declaration, excerpted below, articulated clearly Locke's philosophy of natural rights. Locke had viewed life, liberty, and property as the individual's essential natural rights; Jefferson substituted the "pursuit of happiness" for property.

A DECLARATION BY THE REPRESENTATIVES OF THE UNITED STATES OF AMERICA, IN GENERAL CONGRESS ASSEMBLED

When in the Course of human Events, it becomes necessary for one People to dissolve the Political Bands which have connected them with another, and to assume among the Powers of the Earth, the separate and equal Station to which the Laws of Nature and of Nature's God entitle them, a decent Respect to the Opinions of Mankind requires that they should declare the causes which impel them to the Separation.

We hold these Truths to be self-evident, that all Men are created equal, that they are endowed by their Creator with certain unalienable Rights, that among these are Life, Liberty, and the Pursuit of Happiness—That to secure these Rights, Governments are instituted among Men, deriving their just Powers from the Consent of the Governed, That whenever any Form of Government becomes

destructive of these Ends, it is the Right of the People to alter or to abolish it, and to institute new Government, laying its Foundation on such Principles, and organizing its Powers in such Form, as to them shall seem most likely to effect their Safety and Happiness. Prudence, indeed, will dictate that Governments long established should not be changed for light and transient Causes; and accordingly all Experience hath shewn, that Mankind are more disposed to suffer, while Evils are sufferable, than to right themselves by abolishing the Forms to which they are accustomed. But when a long Train of Abuses and Usurpations, pursuing invariably the same Object, evinces a Design to reduce them under absolute Despotism, it is their right, it is their duty, to throw off such Government, and to provide new Guards for their future Security. Such has been the patient Sufferance of these Colonies; and such is now the Necessity which constrains them to alter their former Systems of Government. The History of the present King of Great-Britain is a History of repeated Injuries and Usurpations, all having in direct Object the Establishment of an absolute Tyranny over these States. . . .

First printing of the Declaration of Independence, July 4, 1776, Papers of the Continental Congress No. 1, Rough Journal of Congress, III.

Montesquieu
THE SPIRIT OF THE LAWS

Like other philosophes, Charles Louis de Secondat, Baron de la Brede et de Montesquieu (1689–1755), was an ardent reformer who used learning, logic, and wit to denounce the abuses of his day. His principal work, *The Spirit of the Laws* (1748), was a contribution to political liberty.

Montesquieu regarded despotism as a pernicious form of government, corrupt by its very nature. Ruling as he wishes and unchecked by law, the despot knows nothing of moderation and institutionalizes cruelty and violence; the slavelike subjects know only servitude, fear, and misery. Driven by predatory instincts, wrote Montesquieu, the despotic ruler involves his state in wars of conquest and personal glory, caring not at all about the suffering this causes his people.

To safeguard liberty from the abuse of power, Montesquieu advocated the principle of separation of powers. In every government, said Montesquieu, there are three sorts of powers: legislative, executive, and judiciary. When one person or one body exercises all three powers—if the same body both prosecutes and judges, for example—liberty cannot be preserved. Where sovereignty is monopolized by one person or body, power is abused and political liberty is denied. In a good government, one power balances and checks another power, and argument that impressed the framers of the U. S. Constitution. Following is Montesquieu's discussion of the principle of separation of powers.

It is true that in democracies the people seem to act as they please; but political liberty does not consist in an unlimited freedom. . . .

Liberty is a right of doing whatever the laws permit. If a citizen could do what [the laws] forbid, he would no longer be possessed of liberty, because all of his fellow-citizens would have the same power.

Democratic and aristocratic states are not in their own nature free. Political liberty is to be found only in moderate governments; and even in these it is not always found. It is there only when there is no abuse of power. But constant experience shows us that every man [given] power *is* apt to abuse it, and to carry his authority as far as it will go. . . .

To prevent this abuse, it is necessary from the very nature of things that power should be a check to power. A government may be so constituted that no man shall be compelled to do things to which the law does not oblige him, nor forced to abstain from things which the law permits. . . .

In every government there are three sorts of power. . . . By virtue of the first [legislative power], the prince or magistrate enacts temporary or perpetual laws and amends or [repeals] those that have already been enacted. By the second [executive power], he makes peace or war, sends or receives embassies, establishes the public security, and provides against invasions. By the third [judicial power], he punishes

criminals, or determines the disputes that arise between individuals. . . .

When the legislative and executive powers are united in the same person, or in the same body of magistrates, there can be no liberty, because apprehensions may arise lest the same monarch or senate should enact tyrannical laws [that he may] execute them in a tyrannical manner.

Again there is no liberty if the judiciary power be not separated from the legislative and the executive. Were it joined with the legislative, the life and liberty of the subject would be exposed to arbitrary control; for the judge would then be the legislator. Were it joined to the executive power, the judge might behave with violence and oppression.

There would be the end of everything were the same man or the same body . . . to exercise those three powers, that of enacting laws, that of executing the public resolutions, and that of trying the cases of individuals. . . .

In . . . a state there are always persons distinguished by their birth, riches, or honors: but were they to be confounded with the common people, and to have only the weight of a single vote like the rest, the common liberty would be their slavery, and they would have no interest in supporting it, as most of the [laws favored by the common people] would be against them. The share they have, therefore, in the legislature ought to be proportioned to their other advantages in the state; which happens only when they form a body that has a right to check the [follies] of the people, as the people have a right to oppose any [intrusion upon] theirs.

Montesquieu, *The Spirit of the Laws*, trans. Thomas Nugent (Cincinnati: Robert Clarke and Co., 1873), Bk. XI, Chs. 3, 4, 6, pp. 172, 173, 174, 178, 179.

The legislative power is therefore committed to the body of nobles and to that which represents the people, each having their assemblies and deliberations apart, each their separate views and interests. . . .

The executive power ought to be in the hands of a monarch because this branch of government, having need of [prompt action], is better administered by one than by many. On the other hand, whatever depends on the legislative power is oftentimes better regulated by many than by a single person.

But if there were no monarch, and the executive power [were] committed to a certain number of persons selected from the legislative body, there would be an end then of liberty; . . . the two powers would be united, [because] the same persons would sometimes possess, and would always be able to possess, a share in both.

Jean Jacques Rousseau
THE SOCIAL CONTRACT

To the philosophes, advances in the arts were hallmarks of progress. However, Jean Jacques Rousseau argued that the accumulation of knowledge improved human understanding but corrupted the morals of human beings. In *A Discourse on the Arts and Sciences* (1750) and *A Discourse on the Origin of Inequality* (1755), Rousseau diagnosed the illnesses of modern civilization. He said that human nature, which was originally good, had been corrupted by society. As a result, he stated at the beginning of *The Social Contract* (1762), "Man is born free; and everywhere he is in chains." How can humanity be made moral and free again? In *The Social Contract*, Rousseau suggested one cure: reforming the political system. He argued that in the existing civil society the rich and powerful who controlled the state oppressed the majority. Rousseau admired the small, ancient Greek city-state (polis), where citizens participated actively and directly in public affairs. A small state modeled after the ancient Greek polis, said Rousseau, would be best able to resolve the tensions between individual freedom and the requirements of the collective community.

In the opening chapters of *The Social Contract*, Rousseau rejected the principle that one person has a natural authority over others. All legitimate authority, he said, stemmed from human traditions, not from nature. Rousseau had only contempt for absolute monarchy and in *The Social Contract* sought to provide a theoretical foundation for political liberty. Like Hobbes and Locke, Rousseau refers to an original social contract that terminates the state of nature and establishes the civil state. The clash of particular interests in the state of nature necessitates the creation of civil authority.

I suppose men to have reached the point at which the obstacles in the way of their

Jean Jacques Rousseau, *The Social Contract and Discourses*, trans. G. D. H. Cole, Everyman's Library (London: J. H. Dent, 1991), pp. 13–15, 13–19, 23, and 26–28.

preservation in the state of nature [are] greater than the resources at the disposal of each individual for his maintenance in that state. That primitive condition can then subsist no longer; and the human race would perish unless it changed its manner of existence. . . .

This sum of forces can arise only where several persons come together: but, as the force and liberty of each man are the chief instruments of his self-preservation, how can he pledge them without harming his own interests, and neglecting the care he owes to himself? This difficulty, in its bearing on my present subject, may be stated in the following terms:

"The problem is to find a form of association which will defend and protect with the whole common force the person and goods of each associate, and in which each, while uniting himself with all, may still obey himself alone, and remain as free as before." This is the fundamental problem of which the *Social Contract* provides the solution.

In entering into the social contract, the individual surrenders his rights to the community as a whole, which governs in accordance with the general will—an underlying principle that expresses what is best for the community. The general will is a plainly visible truth that is easily discerned by reason and common sense purged of self-interest and unworthy motives. For Rousseau, the general will by definition is always right and always works to the community's advantage. True freedom consists of obedience to laws that coincide with the general will. Obedience to the general will transforms an individual motivated by self-interest, appetites, and passions into a higher type of person—a citizen committed to the general good. What happens, however, if a person's private will—that is, expressions of particular, selfish interests—clashes with the general will? As private interests could ruin the body politic, says Rousseau, "whoever refuses to obey the general will shall be compelled to do so by the whole body." Thus Rousseau rejects entirely the Lockean principle that citizens possess rights independently of and against the state. Because Rousseau grants the sovereign (the people constituted as a corporate body) virtually unlimited authority over the citizenry, some critics view him as a precursor of modern dictatorship.

The clauses of this contract . . . properly understood, may be reduced to one—the total [transference] of each associate, together with all his rights, to the whole community; for, in the first place, as each gives himself absolutely, the conditions are the same for all; and, this being so, no one has any interest in making them burdensome to others. . . .

If then we discard from the social compact what is not of its essence, we shall find that it reduces itself to the following terms:

"Each of us puts his person and all his power in common under the supreme direction of the general will, and, in our corporate capacity, we receive each member as an indivisible part of the whole."

At once, in place of the individual personality of each contracting party, this act of association creates a moral and collective body, composed of as many members as the assembly contains voters, and receiving from this act its unity, its common identity, its life, and its will. . . .

In order then that the social compact may not be an empty formula, it tacitly includes the undertaking, which alone can give force to the rest, that whoever refuses to obey the general will shall be compelled to do so by the whole body. This means nothing less than that he will be forced to be free; for this is the condition which, by giving each citizen to his country, secures him against all personal dependence. In this lies the key to the working of the political machine; this alone legitimizes civil undertakings, which, without it, would be absurd, tyrannical, and liable to the most frightful abuses.

The passage from the state of nature to the civil state produces a very remarkable change in man, by substituting justice for instinct in his conduct, and giving his actions the morality they had formerly lacked. Then only, when the voice of duty takes the place of physical impulses and right of appetite, does man, who so far had considered only himself, find that he is forced to act on different principles, and to consult his reason before listening to his inclinations. Although, in this state, he deprives himself of some advantages which he got from nature, he gains in return others so great, his faculties are so stimulated and developed, his ideas so extended, his feelings so ennobled, and his whole soul so uplifted, that, did not the abuses of this new condition often degrade him below that which he left, he would be bound to bless continually the happy moment which took him from it forever, and, instead of a stupid and unimaginative animal, made him an intelligent being and a man.

Let us draw up the whole account in terms easily commensurable. What man loses by the social contract is his natural liberty and an unlimited right to everything he tries to get and succeeds in getting; what he gains is civil liberty and the proprietorship of all he possesses. If we are to avoid mistake in weighing one against the other, we must clearly distinguish natural liberty, which is bounded only by the strength of the individual, from civil liberty, which is limited by the general will; and possession, which is merely the effect of force or the right of the first occupier, from property, which can be founded only on a positive title.

We might, over and above all this, add, to what man acquires in the civil state, moral liberty, which alone makes him truly master of himself; for the mere impulse of appetite is slavery, while obedience to a law which we prescribe to ourselves is liberty. . . .

The first and most important deduction from the principles we have so far laid down is that the general will alone can direct the State according to the object for which it was instituted, i.e. the common good: for if the clashing of particular interests made the establishment of societies necessary, the agreement of these very interests made it possible. The common element in these different interests is what forms the social tie; and, were there no point of agreement between them all, no society could exist. It is solely on the basis of this common interest that every society should be governed. . . .

It follows from what has gone before that the general will is always right and tends to the public advantage; but it does not follow that the deliberations of the people are always equally correct. Our will is always for our own good, but we do not always see what that is; the people is never corrupted, but it is often deceived, and on such occasions only does it seem to will what is bad.

There is often a great deal of difference between the will of all and the general will; the latter considers only the common interest, while the former takes private interest into account, and is no more than a sum of particular wills: but take away from these same wills the pluses and minuses that cancel one another, and the general will remains as the sum of the differences.

If, when the people, being furnished with adequate information, held its deliberations, the citizen's had no communication one with another, the grand total of the small differences would always give the general will, and the decision would always be good. But when factions arise, and partial associations are formed at the expense of the great association, the will of each of these associations becomes general in relation to its members, while it remains particular in relation to the State: it may then be said that there are no longer as many votes as there are men, but only as many as there are associations. The differences become less numerous and give a less general result. Lastly, when one of these associations is so great as to prevail over all the rest, the result is no longer a sum of small differences, but a single difference; in this case there is no longer a general will, and the opinion which prevails is purely particular.

It is therefore essential, if the general will is to be able to express itself, that there should be no partial society [factions] within the State, and that each citizen should think only his own thoughts. . . . But if there are partial societies, it is best to have as many as possible and to prevent them from being unequal. . . . These precautions are the only ones that can guarantee that the general will shall be always enlightened, and that the people shall in no way deceive itself.

Thomas Paine
"THE ABSURDITY OF HEREDITARY GOVERNMENT"

Thomas Paine (1737–1809), an Englishman who moved to America in 1774, was a prominent figure in both the American and the French Revolutions. His stirring appeals for separation of the colonies from Great Britain inspired the American colonists. Back in England in 1787, Paine became intrigued by events in France and supported the French Revolution, which began in 1789. In reply to Edmund Burke's attack on the Revolution, he wrote the *Rights of Man* (1791). Paine's pamphlet supporting the principles of the French Revolution aroused opposition in England, and he was forced to flee to France, where he was chosen a member of the National Convention. During the Reign of Terror he was imprisoned and narrowly escaped execution.

In this selection from the *Rights of Man*, Paine asserts that the republican form of government which the Revolution had brought to France is superior to hereditary monarchy and aristocracy. Many contemporaries viewed Paine as a dangerous radical.

All hereditary government is in its nature a tyranny. An heritable crown, or an heritable throne, or by what other fanciful name such things may be called, [has] no other significant explanation than that mankind are heritable property. To inherit a government is to inherit the people, as if they were flocks and herds. . . .

Kings succeed each other, not as [thinking persons], but as animals. It signifies not what their mental or moral characters are. . . .

Could it be made a decree in nature, or an edict registered in heaven, . . . that virtue and wisdom should invariably [be assured by] hereditary succession, the objections to it would be removed; but when we see that nature acts as if she disowned . . . the hereditary system; that the mental characters of successors, in all countries, are below the average of human understanding; that one is a tyrant, another an idiot,

a third insane, and some all three together, it is impossible to attach confidence to [hereditary succession]. . . .

Would we make any office hereditary that required wisdom and abilities to fill it? . . .

It requires some talents to be a common mechanic; but to be a king requires only . . . a sort of breathing [robot]. This sort of superstition may last a few years more, but it cannot long resist the awakened reason . . . of man. . . .

As the republic of letters brings forward the best literary productions by giving to genius a fair and universal chance; so the representative system of government is calculated to produce the wisest laws, by collecting wisdom where it can be found. I smile to myself when I contemplate the ridiculous insignificance into which literature and all the sciences would sink were they made hereditary; and I carry the same idea into governments. An hereditary governor as inconsistent as an hereditary author. I know not whether Homer or Euclid had sons; but I will

Thomas Paine, *Rights of Man* (New York: Peter Eckler, Publisher, 1892), pp. 162–167.

venture an opinion that if they had, and had left their works unfinished, those sons could not have completed them.

Do we need a stronger evidence of the absurdity of hereditary government than is seen in the descendants of those men, in any line of life, who once were famous? Is there scarcely an instance in which there is not a total reverse of the character? It appears as if the tide of mental faculties flowed as far as it could in certain channels, and then [reversed] its course. . . . How irrational then is the hereditary system which establishes channels of power, in company with which wisdom refuses to flow! By continuing this absurdity, man is perpetually in contradiction with himself; he accepts, for a king, or a chief magistrate, or a legislator, a person whom he would not elect for a constable.

REVIEW QUESTIONS

1. Compare the views of John Locke with those of Thomas Hobbes regarding the character of human nature, political authority, and the right of rebellion.
2. How did the U.S. Constitution implement Montesquieu's Major principle?
3. What did Jean Jacques Rousseau mean by the "general will"? What fraction did it serve on his political theory?
4. Why do some thinkers view Rousseau as a champion of democracy, whereas others see him as a spiritual precursor of totalitarianism?
5. Why was Thomas Paine viewed as a dangerous radical by some of his contemporaries?

---

3 Attack on Religion

Christianity came under severe attack during the eighteenth century. The philosophes rejected Christian doctrines that seemed contrary to reason. Deism, the dominant religious outlook of the philosophes, taught that religion should accord with reason and natural law. To deists, it seemed reasonable to believe in God, for this superbly constructed universe required a creator in the same manner that a watch required a watchmaker. But, said the deists, after God had constructed the universe, he did not interfere in its operations; the universe was governed by mechanical laws. Deists denied that the Bible was God's work, rejected clerical authority, and dismissed miracles—like Jesus walking on water—as incompatible with natural law. To them, Jesus was not divine but an inspired teacher of morality. Many deists still considered themselves Christians; the clergy, however, viewed the deists' religious views with horror.

Voltaire
A PLEA FOR TOLERANCE AND REASON

François Marie Arouet (1694–1778), known to the world as Voltaire, was the recognized leader of the French Enlightenment. Few of the philosophes had a better mind, and none had a sharper wit. A relentless critic of the Old Regime (the social structure in prerevolutionary France), Voltaire attacked superstition, religious fanaticism and persecution, censorship, and other abuses of eighteenth-century French society. Spending more than two years in Great Britain, Voltaire acquired a great admiration for English liberty, toleration, commerce, and science. In *Letters Concerning the English Nation* (1733), he drew unfavorable comparisons between a progressive Britain and a reactionary France.

Voltaire's angriest words were directed against established Christianity, to which he attributed many of the ills of modern society. Voltaire regarded Christianity as "the Christ-worshiping superstition" that someday would be destroyed "by the weapons of reason." He rejected revelation and the church hierarchy and was repulsed by Christian intolerance, but he accepted Christian morality and believed in God as the prime mover who set the universe in motion.

The following passages compiled from Voltaire's works—grouped according to topic—provide insight into the outlook of the philosophes. The excerpts come from sources that include his *Treatise on Tolerance* (1763), *The Philosophical Dictionary* (1764), and *Commentary on the Book of Crime and Punishments* (1766).

TOLERANCE

It does not require any great art or studied elocution to prove that Christians ought to tolerate one another. I will go even further and say that we ought to look upon all men as our brothers. What! call a Turk, a Jew, and a Siamese, my brother? Yes, of course; for are we not all children of the same father, and the creatures of the same God?

———

What is tolerance? . . . We are all full of weakness and errors; let us mutually pardon our follies. This is the last law of nature. . . .

It is clear that every private individual who persecutes a man, his brother, because he is not of the same opinion, is a monster. . . .

Of all religions, the Christian ought doubtless to inspire the most tolerance, although hitherto the Christians have been the most intolerant of all men.

———

I shall never cease, my dear sir, to preach tolerance from the housetops, despite the complaints of your priests and the outcries of ours, until persecution is no more. The progress of reason is slow, the roots of prejudice lie deep. Doubtless, I shall never see the fruits of my efforts, but they are seeds which may one day germinate.

. . . Tolerance has never brought civil war; intolerance has covered the earth with carnage. . . .

What! Is each citizen to be permitted to believe and to think that which his reason rightly or wrongly dictates? He should indeed, provided that he does not disturb the public order; for it is not contingent on man to believe or not to believe; but it is contingent on him to respect the usages of his country; and if you say that it is a crime not to believe in the dominant religion, you accuse then the first Christians, your ancestors[who rejected Roman religion], and you justify [Romans] whom you accuse of having martyred them.

You reply that there is a great difference, that all religions are the work of men, and

———

Voltaire, *Candide and Other Writings*, ed. Haskell M. Block (New York: Random House, 1956), pp. 374–375, 385, 406–407, 428–429, 443–444, 525, *passim*.

The section above that begins ". . . Tolerance has never brought. . ." is from E. L. Higgins, ed., *The French Revolution as Told by Contemporaries* (Boston: Houghton Mifflin, 1938), pp. 35–36. All other sections in this reading are from the Block text referenced at left.—Eds.

that the Apostolic Roman Catholic Church is alone the work of God. But in good faith, ought our religion because it is divine reign through hate, violence, exiles, usurpation of property, prisons, tortures, murders, and thanksgivings to God for these murders? The more the Christian religion is divine, the less it pertains to man to require it; if God made it, God will sustain it without you. You know that intolerance produces only hypocrites or rebels; what distressing alternatives! In short, do you want to sustain through executioners the religion of a God whom executioners have put to death and who taught only gentleness and patience?

———

DOGMA

. . . Is Jesus the Word? If He be the Word, did He emanate from God in time or before time? If He emanated from God, is He co-eternal and consubstantial with Him, or is He of a similar substance? Is He distinct from Him, or is He not? Is He made or begotten? Can He beget in His turn? Has He paternity? or productive virtue without paternity? Is the Holy Ghost made? or begotten? or produced? or proceeding from the Father? or proceeding from the Son? or proceeding from both? Can He beget? can He produce? is His hypostasis consubstantial with the hypostasis of the Father and the Son? and how is it that, having the same nature—the same essence as the Father and the Son, He cannot do the same things done by these persons who are Himself?

Assuredly, I understand nothing of this; no one has ever understood any of it, and that is why we have slaughtered one another.

The Christians tricked, cavilled, hated, and excommunicated one another, for some of these dogmas inaccessible to human intellect.

FANATICISM

Fanaticism is to superstition what delirium is to fever, what rage is to anger. He who has ecstasies and visions, who takes dreams for realities, and his own imaginations for prophecies is an enthusiast; he who reinforces his madness by murder is a fanatic. . . .

The most detestable example of fanaticism is that exhibited on the night of St. Bartholomew,[1] when the people of Paris rushed from house to house to stab, slaughter, throw out of the window, and tear in pieces their fellow citizens who did not go to mass.

There are some cold-blooded fanatics; such as those judges who sentence men to death for no other crime than that of thinking differently from themselves. . . .

Once fanaticism has infected a brain, the disease is almost incurable. I have seen convulsionaries who, while speaking of the miracles of Saint Paris [a fourth-century Italian bishop], gradually grew heated in spite of themselves. Their eyes became inflamed, their limbs shook, fury disfigured their face, and they would have killed anyone who contradicted them.

There is no other remedy for this epidemic malady than that philosophical spirit which, extending itself from one to another, at length softens the manners of men and prevents the access of the disease. For when the disorder has made any progress, we should, without loss of time, flee from it, and wait till the air has become purified.

PERSECUTION

What is a persecutor? He whose wounded pride and furious fanaticism arouse princes and magistrates against innocent men, whose only crime

———

[1]"St. Bartholomew" refers to the day of August 24, 1572, when the populace of Paris, instigated by King Charles IX at his mother's urging, began a week-long slaughter of Protestants. —Eds.

is that of being of a different opinion. "Impudent man! you have worshipped God; you have preached and practiced virtue; you have served man; you have protected the orphan, have helped the poor; you have changed deserts, in which slaves dragged on a miserable existence, into fertile lands peopled by happy families; but I have discovered that you despise me, and have never read my controversial work. You know that I am a rogue; that I have forged G[od]'s signature, that I have stolen. You might tell these things; I must anticipate you. I will, therefore, go to the confessor [spiritual counselor] of the prime minister, or the magistrate; I will show them, with outstretched neck and twisted mouth, that you hold an erroneous opinion in relation to the cells in which the Septuagint was studied; that you have even spoken disrespectfully ten years ago of Tobit's dog,[2] which you asserted to have been a spaniel, while I proved that it was a greyhound. I will denounce you as the enemy of God and man!" Such is the language of the persecutor; and if precisely these words do not issue from his lips, they are engraven on his heart with the pointed steel of fanaticism steeped in the bitterness of envy. . . .

O God of mercy! If any man can resemble that evil being who is described as ceaselessly employed in the destruction of your works, is it not the persecutor?

SUPERSTITION

In 1749 a woman was burned in the Bishopric of Würzburg [a city in central Germany], convicted of being a witch. This is an extraordinary phenomenon in the age in which we live. Is it possible that people who boast of their reformation and of trampling superstition under foot, who indeed supposed that they had reached the perfection of reason, could nevertheless believe in witchcraft, and this more than a hundred years after the so-called reformation of their reason?

In 1652 a peasant woman named Michelle Chaudron, living in the little territory of Geneva [now a city in Switzerland], met the devil going out of the city. The devil gave her a kiss, received her homage, and imprinted on her upper lip and right breast the mark that he customarily bestows on all whom he recognizes as his favorites. This seal of the devil is a little mark which makes the skin insensitive, as all the demonographical jurists of those times affirm.

The devil ordered Michelle Chaudron to bewitch two girls. She obeyed her master punctually. The girls' parents accused her of witchcraft before the law. The girls were questioned and confronted with the accused. They declared that they felt a continual pricking in certain parts of their bodies and that they were possessed. Doctors were called, or at least, those who passed for doctors at that time. They examined the girls. They looked for the devil's seal on Michelle's body—what the statement of the case called *satanic marks*. Into them they drove a long needle, already a painful torture. Blood flowed out, and Michelle made it known, by her cries, that satanic marks certainly do not make one insensitive. The judges, seeing no definite proof that Michelle Chaudron was a witch, proceeded to torture her, a method that infallibly produces the necessary proofs: this wretched woman, yielding to the violence of torture, at last confessed every thing they desired.

The doctors again looked for the satanic mark. They found a little black spot on one of her thighs. They drove in the needle. The torment of the torture had been so horrible that the poor creature hardly felt the needle; thus the crime was established. But as customs were becoming somewhat mild at that time, she was burned only after being hanged and strangled.

---

[2]The Septuagint, the version of the Hebrew scriptures used by Saint Paul and other early Christians, was a Greek translation done by Hellenized Jews in Alexandria sometime in the late third or the second century B.C. *Tobit's dog* appears in the book of Tobit, a Hebrew book contained in the Catholic version of the Bible.——Eds.

In those days every tribunal of Christian Europe resounded with similar arrests. The [twigs] were lit everywhere for witches, as for heretics. People reproached the Turks most for having neither witches nor demons among them. This absence of demons was considered an infallible proof of the falseness of a religion.

A zealous friend of public welfare, of humanity, of true religion, has stated in one of his writings on behalf of innocence, that Christian tribunals have condemned to death over a hundred thousand accused witches. If to these judicial murders are added the infinitely superior number of massacred heretics, that part of the world will seem to be nothing but a vast scaffold covered with torturers and victims, surrounded by judges, guards and spectators.

Thomas Paine
THE AGE OF REASON

Exemplifying the deist outlook was Thomas Paine. Paine's *Common Sense* (1776) was an eloquent appeal for American independence. Paine is also famous for *Rights of Man* (1791–1792), in which he defended the French Revolution, In *Age of Reason* (1794–1796), he denounced Christian mysteries, miracles, and prophecies as superstition and called for a natural religion that accorded with reason and science.

I believe in one God, and no more; and I hope for happiness beyond this life.

I believe in the equality of man; and I believe that religious duties consist in doing justice, loving mercy, and endeavoring to make our fellow-creatures happy.

But, lest it should be supposed that I believe many other things in addition to these, I shall, in the progress of this work, declare the things I do not believe, and my reasons for not believing them.

I do not believe in the creed professed by the Jewish church, by the Roman church, by the Greek church, by the Turkish church, by the Protestant church, nor by any church that I know of. My own mind is my own church. . . .

When Moses told the children of Israel that he received the two tablets of the [Ten] commandments from the hands of God, they were not obliged to believe him, because they had no other authority for it than his telling them so; and I have no other authority for it than some historian telling me so. The commandments carry no internal evidence of divinity with them; they contain some good moral precepts, such as any man qualified to be a lawgiver, or a legislator, could produce himself, without having recourse to supernatural intervention. . . .

When also I am told that a woman called the Virgin Mary, said, or gave out, that she was with child without any cohabitation with a man, and that her betrothed husband, Joseph, said that an angel told him so, I have a right to believe them or not; such a circumstance required a much stronger evidence than their bare word for it; but we have not even this—for neither Joseph nor Mary wrote any such matter themselves; it is only reported by others that *they said so*—it is hearsay upon hearsay, and I do not choose to rest my belief upon such evidence.

It is, however, not difficult to account for the credit that was given to the story of Jesus Christ

Thomas Paine, *Age of Reason Being an Investigation of the True and Fabulous Theology* (New York: Peter Eckler, 1892), pp. 5–11.

being the son of God. He was born when the heathen mythology had still some fashion and repute in the world, and that mythology had prepared the people for the belief of such a story. Almost all the extraordinary men that lived under the heathen mythology were reputed to be the sons of some of their gods. It was not a new thing, at that time, to believe a man to have been celestially begotten; the intercourse of gods with women was then a matter of familiar opinion. Their Jupiter [chief Roman god], according to their accounts, had cohabited with hundreds: the story, therefore, had nothing in it either new, wonderful, or obscene; it was conformable to the opinions that then prevailed among the people called Gentiles, or Mythologists, and it was those people only that believed it. The Jews who had kept strictly to the belief of one God, and no more, and who had always rejected the heathen mythology, never credited the story. . . .

Nothing that is here said can apply, even with the most distant disrespect, to the real character of Jesus Christ. He was a virtuous and an amiable man. The morality that he preached and practised was of the most benevolent kind; and though similar systems of morality had been preached by Confucius [Chinese philosopher], and by some of the Greek philosophers, many years before; by the Quakers [members of the Society of Friends] since; and by many good men in all ages, it has not been exceeded by any. . . .

. . . The resurrection and ascension [of Jesus Christ], supposing them to have taken place, admitted of public and ocular demonstration, like that of the ascension of a balloon, or the sun at noon-day, to all Jerusalem at least. A thing which everybody is required to believe, requires that the proof and evidence of it should be equal to all, and universal; and as the public visibility of this last related act was the only evidence that could give sanction to the former part, the whole of it falls to the ground, because that evidence never was given. Instead of this, a small number of persons, not more than eight or nine, are introduced as proxies for the whole world, to say they saw it, and all the rest of the world are called upon to believe it. But it appears that Thomas [one of Jesus's disciples] did not believe the resurrection, and, as they say, would not believe without having ocular and manual demonstration himself. *So neither will I*, and the reason is equally as good for me, and for every other person, as for Thomas.

It is in vain to attempt to palliate or disguise this matter. The story, so far as relates to the supernatural part, has every mark of fraud and imposition stamped upon the face of it. Who were the authors of it is as impossible for us now to know, as it is for us to be assured that the books in which the account is related were written by the persons whose names they bear; the best surviving evidence we now have respecting this affair is the Jews. They are regularly descended from the people who lived in the times this resurrection and ascension is said to have happened, and they say, *it is not true.*

Baron d'Holbach
"RELIGION IS A MERE CASTLE IN THE AIR"

More extreme than the deists were the atheists, who denied God's existence altogether. The foremost exponent of atheism was Paul-Henri Thiry, Baron d'Holbach (1723–1789), a prominent contributor to the *Encyclopedia*. Holbach hosted many leading intellectuals, including Diderot, Rousseau, and Condorcet (all represented in this chapter), at his country estate outside of Paris. He regarded the idea of God as a product of ignorance, fear, and superstition and said that terrified by natural phenomena—storms, fire, floods—humanity's primitive ancestors attributed these occurrences to unseen spirits, whom they tried to appease through rituals. In denouncing religion, Holbach was also affirming core Enlightenment ideals—reason and freedom—as the following passage from *Good Sense* (1772) reveals.

In a word, whoever will deign to consult common sense upon religious opinions, and will bestow on this inquiry the attention that is commonly given to any objects we presume interesting, will easily perceive that those opinions have no foundation; that Religion is a mere castle in the air. Theology is but the ignorance of natural causes reduced to a system; a long tissue of fallacies and contradictions. In every country, it presents us with romances void of probability. . . .

Savage and furious nations, perpetually at war, adore, under divers names, some God, conformable to their ideas, that is to say, cruel, carnivorous, selfish, bloodthirsty. We find, in all the religions of the earth, "a God of armies," a "jealous God," an "avenging God," a "destroying God," a "God," who is pleased with carnage, and whom his worshippers consider it as a duty to serve to his taste. Lambs, bulls, children, men, heretics, infidels, kings, whole nations, are sacrificed to him. Do not the zealous servants of this barbarous God think themselves obliged even to offer up themselves as a sacrifice to him? Madmen may everywhere be seen who, after meditating upon their terrible God, imagine that to please him they must do themselves all possible injury, and inflict on themselves, for this honour, the most exquisite torments. The gloomy ideas more usefully formed of the Deity, far from consoling them

under the evils of life, have every where disquieted their minds, and produced follies destructive to their happiness.

How could the human mind make any considerable progress, while tormented with frightful phantoms, and guided by men, interested in perpetuating its ignorance and fears? Man has been forced to vegetate in his primitive stupidity: he has been taught nothing but stories about invisible powers upon whom his happiness was supposed to depend. Occupied solely by his fears, and by unintelligible reveries, he has always been at the mercy of his priests, who have reserved to themselves the right of thinking for him, and directing his actions.

Thus man has remained a child without experience, a slave without courage, fearing to reason, and unable to extricate himself from the labyrinth, in which he has so long been wandering. He believes himself forced to bend under the yoke of his gods, known to him only by the fabulous accounts given by his ministers, who, after binding each unhappy mortal in the chains of his prejudice, remain his masters, or else abandon him defenceless to the absolute power of tyrants, no less terrible than the gods, of whom they are the representatives upon earth.

Oppressed by the double yoke of spiritual and temporal power, it has been impossible for the people to know and pursue their happiness. As Religion, so Politics and Morality became sacred things, which the profane were not permitted to handle. Men have had no other Morality, than what their legislators and priests

---

Paul Heinrich Dietrich Baron d'Holbach, *Good Sense or Natural Ideas Opposed to Ideas That Are Supernatural* (New York: G. Vale, 1856), pp. vii–xi.

brought down from the unknown regions of heaven. The human mind, confused by its theological opinions ceased to know its own powers, mistrusted experience, feared truth and disdained reason, in order to follow authority. Man has been a mere machine in the hands of tyrants and priests, who alone have had the right of directing his actions. Always treated as a slave, he has contracted the vices of a slave.

Such are the true causes of the corruption of morals, to which Religion opposes only ideal and ineffectual barriers. Ignorance and servitude are calculated to make men wicked and unhappy. Knowledge, Reason, and Liberty, can alone reform them, and make them happier. But every thing conspires to blind them and to confirm them in their errors. Priests cheat them, tyrants corrupt, the better to enslave them. Tyranny ever was, and ever will be, the true cause of man's depravity, and also of his habitual calamities. Almost always fascinated by religious fiction, poor mortals turn not their eyes to the natural and obvious causes of their misery; but attribute their vices to the imperfection of their natures, and their unhappiness to the anger of the gods. They offer up to heaven vows, sacrifices, and presents, to obtain the end of their sufferings, which in reality, are attributable only to the negligence, ignorance, and perversity of their guides, to the folly of their customs, to the unreasonableness of their laws, and above all, to the general want of knowledge. Let men's minds be filled with true ideas;

let their reason be cultivated; let justice govern them; and there will be no need of opposing to the passions, such a feeble barrier, as the fear of the gods. Men will be good, when they are well instructed, well governed, and when they are punished or despised for the evil, and justly rewarded for the good, which they do to their fellow citizens.

To discover the true principles of Morality, men have no need of theology, of revelation, or of gods: They have need only of common sense. They have only to commune with themselves, to reflect upon their own nature, to consult their visible interests, to consider the objects of society, and of the individuals who compose it; and they will easily perceive, that virtue is advantageous, and vice disadvantageous to such beings as themselves. Let us persuade men to be just, beneficent, moderate, sociable; not because such conduct is demanded by the gods, but, because it is pleasure to men. Let us advise them to abstain from vice and crime; not because they will be punished in the other world, but because they will suffer for it in this.—*There are*, says a great man [Montesquieu], *means to prevent crimes, and these means are punishments; there are means to reform manners, and these means are good examples. . . .*

. . . Men are unhappy, only because they are ignorant; they are ignorant, only because every thing conspires to prevent their being enlightened; they are wicked, only because their reason is not sufficiently developed

REVIEW QUESTIONS

1. What arguments did Voltaire offer in favor of religious toleration?
2. Why did Voltaire ridicule Christian theological disputation?
3. What did Voltaire mean by the term *fanaticism*? What examples did he provide? How was it to be cured?
4. What Christian beliefs did Thomas Paine reject? Why?
5. How did Baron d'Holbach's critique of religion affirm basic Enlightenment ideals?

4 Epistemology

The philosophes sought a naturalistic understanding of the human condition, one that examined human nature and society without reference to God's will. Toward this end, they sought to explain how the mind acquires knowledge; and as reformers, they stressed the importance of education in shaping a better person and a better society.

John Locke
ESSAY CONCERNING HUMAN UNDERSTANDING

In his *Essay Concerning Human Understanding* (1690), a work of immense significance in the history of philosophy, John Locke argued that human beings are not born with innate ideas (the idea of God and principles of good and evil, for example) divinely implanted in their minds. Rather, said Locke, the human mind at birth is a blank slate upon which are imprinted sensations derived from contact with the world. These sensations, combined with the mind's reflections on them, are the source of ideas. In effect, knowledge is derived from experience. In the tradition of Francis Bacon, Locke's epistemology (theory of knowledge) implied that people should not dwell on insoluble questions, particularly sterile theological issues, but should seek practical knowledge that promotes human happiness and enlightens human beings and gives them control over their environment.

Locke's empiricism, which aspired to useful knowledge and stimulated an interest in political and ethical questions that focused on human concerns, helped to mold the utilitarian and reformist spirit of the Enlightenment. If there are no innate ideas, said the philosophes, then human beings are not born with original sin, contrary to what Christians believed. All that individuals are derives from their particular experiences. If people are provided with a proper environment and education, they will become intelligent and productive citizens. "[O]f all the Men we meet with," wrote Locke, "Nine Parts of Ten are what they are, Good or Evil, useful or not, by their Education." 'Tis that which makes the great Difference in Mankind." This was how the reform-minded philosophes interpreted Locke. They preferred to believe that evil stemmed from faulty institutions and poor education, both of which could be remedied, rather than from a defective human nature. Excerpts from *Essay Concerning Human Understanding* follow.

Let us then suppose the mind to be, as we say, white paper, void of all characters, without

John Locke, *An Essay Concerning Human Understanding*, vol. 1, ed. Alexander Campbell Fraser (Oxford: Clarendon Press, 1894), pp. 121–125.

any ideas:—How comes it to be furnished? Whence comes it by that vast store which the busy and boundless fancy of man has painted on it with an almost endless variety? Whence has it all the *materials* of reason and knowledge? To this I answer, in one word, from

EXPERIENCE. In that all our knowledge is founded; and from that it ultimately derives itself. Our observation employed either, about external sensible objects or about the internal operations of our minds perceived and reflected on by ourselves, is that which supplies our understandings with all the *materials* of thinking. These two are the fountains of knowledge, from whence all the ideas we have, or can naturally have, do spring.

First, our Senses, conversant about particular sensible objects, do convey into the mind several distinct perceptions of things, according to those various ways wherein those objects do affect them. And thus we come by those *ideas* we have of *yellow, white, heat, cold, soft, hard, bitter, sweet*, and all those which we call sensible qualities; which when I say the senses convey into the mind, I mean, they from external objects convey into the mind what produces there those perceptions. This great source of most of the ideas we have, depending wholly upon our senses, and derived by them to the understanding, I call SENSATION.

Secondly, the other fountain from which experience furnisheth the understanding with ideas is,—the perception of the operations of our own mind within us, as it is employed about the ideas it has got. . . .

And such are *perception, thinking, doubting, believing, reasoning, knowing, willing*, and all the different actings of our own minds;—which we being conscious of, and observing in ourselves, do from these receive into our understandings as distinct ideas as we do from bodies affecting our senses. This source of ideas every man has wholly in himself; and though it be not sense, as having nothing to do with external objects, yet it is very like it, and might properly enough be called *internal sense.* But as I call the other Sensation, so I call this REFLECTION, the ideas it affords being such only as the mind gets by reflecting on its own operations within itself. By

reflection then, in the following part of this discourse, I would be understood to mean, that notice which the mind takes of its own operations, and the manner of them, by reason whereof there come to be ideas of these operations in the understanding. These two, I say, viz. external material things, as the objects of SENSATION, and the operations of our own minds within, as the objects of REFLECTION, are to me the only originals from whence all our ideas take their beginnings. . . .

The understanding seems to me not to have the least glimmering of any ideas which it doth not receive from one of these two. *External objects* furnish the mind with the ideas of sensible qualities, which are all those different perceptions they produce in us; and *the mind* furnishes the understanding with ideas of its own operations.

These, when we have taken a full survey of them, and their several modes (combinations, and relations), we shall find to contain all our whole stock of ideas; and that we have nothing in our minds which did not come in one of these two ways. Let any one examine his own thoughts, and thoroughly search into his understanding; and then let him tell me, whether all the original ideas he has there, are any other than of the objects of his senses, or of the operations of his mind, considered as objects of his reflection. And how great a mass of knowledge soever he imagines to be lodged there, he will, upon taking a strict view, see that he has not any idea in his mind but what one of these two have imprinted;—though perhaps, with infinite variety compounded and enlarged by the understanding, as we shall see hereafter.

He that attentively considers the state of a child, at his first coming into the world, will have little reason to think him stored with plenty of ideas, that are to be the matter of his future knowledge. It is *by degrees* he comes to be furnished with them.

Claude-Adrien Helvétius
ESSAYS ON THE MIND AND *A TREATISE ON MAN*

Even more than did Locke, Claude-Adrien Helvétius (1715–1777) emphasized the importance of the environment in shaping the human mind. Disparities in intelligence and talent, said Helvétius, are due entirely to environmental conditions and not to inborn qualities. Since human beings are malleable and perfectible, their moral and intellectual growth depends on proper conditioning. For this reason he called for political reforms, particularly the implementation of a program of enlightened public education.

In 1758 Helvétius published *Essays on the Mind*, which treated ethics in a purely naturalistic way. Shocked by his separation of morality from God's commands and from fear of divine punishment as well as by his attacks on the clergy, the authorities suppressed the book. His second major work, *A Treatise on Man*, was published posthumously in 1777. Apparently Helvétius wanted to avoid another controversy. The following passages from both works illustrate Helvétius's belief that "education makes us what we are."

ESSAYS ON THE MIND

The general conclusion of this discourse is, that genius is common, and the circumstances, proper to unfold it, very extraordinary. If we may compare what is profane to what is sacred, we may say in this respect, Many are called, but few are chosen.

The inequality observable among men, therefore, depends on the government under which they lie; on the greater or less happiness of the age in which they are born; on their education; on their desire of improvement, and on the importance of the ideas that are the subject of their contemplations.

The man of genius is then only produced by the circumstances in which he is placed.[1] Thus all the art of education consists in placing young men in such a concurrence of circumstances as are proper to unfold the buds of genius and virtue. [I am led to this conclusion by] the desire of promoting the happiness of mankind. I am convinced that a good education would diffuse light, virtue, and consequently, happiness in society; and that the opinion, that geniuses and virtue are merely gifts of nature, is a great obstacle to making any farther progress in the science of education, and in this respect is the great favourer of idleness and negligence. With this view, examining the effects which nature and

---

Claude Helvétius, *Essay on the Mind and Its Several Facilities*, translated from the French (London: J. M. Richardson, 1809).

---

[1] The opinion I advance must appear very pleasing to the vanity of the greatest part of mankind, and therefore, ought to meet with a favourable reception. According to my principles, they ought not to attribute the inferiority of their abilities to the humbling cause of a less perfect [endowment], but to the education they have received, as well as to the circumstances in which they have been placed. Every man of moderate abilities, in conformity with my principles, has a right to think, that if he had been more favoured by fortune, if he had been born in a certain age or country, he [would have] himself been like the great men whose genius he is forced to admire.

education may have upon us, I have perceived that education makes us what we are; in consequence of which I have thought that it was the duty of a citizen to make known a truth proper to awaken the attention, with respect to the means of carrying this education to perfection.

A TREATISE ON MAN

Some maintain that, *The understanding is the effect of a certain sort of interior temperament and organization.*

Locke and I say: *The inequality in minds or understandings, is the effect of a known cause, and this cause is the difference of education. . . .*

Among the great number of questions treated of in this work, one of the most important was to determine whether *genius, virtue,* and *talents,* to which nations owe their grandeur and felicity, were the effect of the difference of . . . the organs of the five senses [that is, differences due to birth] . . . or if the same genius, the same virtues, and the same talents were the effect of education, over which the laws and the form of government are all powerful.

If I have proved the truth of the latter assertion, it must be allowed that the happiness of nations is in their own hands, and that it entirely depends on the greater or less interest they take in improving the science of education.

REVIEW QUESTIONS

1. According to John Locke, knowledge originates in experience and has two sources—sensation and reflection. What does this mean, and what makes this view of knowledge so revolutionary?
2. How does Locke's view of the origin of knowledge compare to that of René Descartes (see Chapter 2)? Which view do you favor, or can you suggest another alternative?
3. What is the relationship between Locke's theory of knowledge and his conceptions of human nature and politics?
4. In what way may Claude Helvétius be regarded as a disciple of John Locke, and how did he expand the significance of Locke's ideas?

---

5 Compendium of Knowledge

The 28-volume *Encyclopedia,* whose 150 of more contributors included leading Enlightenment thinkers, was undertaken in Paris during the 1740s as a monumental effort to bring together all human knowledge and to propagate Enlightenment ideas. The *Encyclopedia's* numerous articles on science and technology and its limited coverage of theological questions attest to the new interests of eighteenth-century intellectuals. Serving as principal editor, Denis Diderot (1713–1784) steered the project through difficult periods, including the suspension of publication by French authorities. After the first two volumes were published, the authorities denounced the work for containing "maxims that would tend to destroy royal authority, foment a spirit of independence and revolt, . . . and lay the foundations for the corruption of morals and religion." In 1759, Pope Clement XIII condemned the *Encyclopedia* for having "scandalous doctrines [and] inducing scorn for religion." It required careful diplomacy and clever ruses to finish the project and still incorporate ideas considered dangerous by religious and governmental authorities. With the project's completion in 1772, Diderot and Enlightenment opinion triumphed over clerical censors and powerful elements at the French court.

Denis Diderot
ENCYCLOPEDIA

The *Encyclopedia* was a monument to the Enlightenment, as Diderot himself recognized. "This work will surely produce in time a revolution in the minds of man, and I hope that tyrants, oppressors, fanatics, and the intolerant will not gain thereby. We shall have served humanity." Some articles from the *Encyclopedia* follow.

ENCYCLOPEDIA   . . . In truth, the aim of an *encyclopedia* is to collect all the knowledge scattered over the face of the earth, to present its general outlines and structure to the men with whom we live, and to transmit this to those who will come after us, so that the work of past centuries may be useful to the following centuries, that our children, by becoming more educated, may at the same time become more virtuous and happier, and that we may not die without having deserved well of the human race. . . .

. . . We have seen that our *Encyclopedia* could only have been the endeavor of a philosophical century. . . .

I have said that it could only belong to a philosophical age to attempt an *encyclopedia*; and I have said this because such a work constantly demands more intellectual daring than is commonly found in [less courageous periods]. All things must be examined, debated, investigated without exception and without regard for anyone's feelings. . . . We must ride roughshod over all these ancient puerilities, overturn the barriers that reason never erected, give back to the arts and sciences the liberty that is so precious to

them. . . . We have for quite some time needed a reasoning age when men would no longer seek the rules in classical authors but in nature. . . .

FANATICISM   . . . is blind and passionate zeal born of superstitious opinions, causing people to commit ridiculous, unjust, and cruel actions, not only without any shame or remorse, but even with a kind of joy and comfort. *Fanaticism*, therefore, is only superstition put into practice. . . .

Fanaticism has done much more harm to the world than impiety. What do impious people claim? To free themselves of a yoke, while *fanatics* want to extend their chains over all the earth. Infernal zealomania! . . .

GOVERNMENT   . . . The good of the people must be the great purpose of the *government*. The governors are appointed to fulfill it; and the civil constitution that invests them with this power is bound therein by the laws of nature and by the law of reason, which has determined that purpose in any form of *government* as the cause of its welfare. The greatest good of the people is its liberty. Liberty is to the body of the state what health is to each individual; without health man cannot enjoy pleasure; without liberty the state of welfare is excluded from nations. A patriotic governor will therefore see that the right to defend and to maintain liberty is the most sacred of his duties. . . .

If it happens that those who hold the reins of *government* find some resistance when they use their power for the destruction and not the conservation of things that rightfully belong to the people, they must blame themselves, because the public good and the advantage of society are the purposes of establishing a *government*. Hence it necessarily follows that power cannot be arbitrary and that it must be exercised according to the established-laws so that the people may know its duty and be secure within the shelter of laws, and so that governors at the same time should be held within just limits and not be tempted to employ the power they have in hand to do harmful things to the body politic. . . .

HISTORY   . . . *On the usefullness of history.* The advantage consists of the comparison that a statesman or a citizen can make of foreign laws, morals, and customs with those of his country. This is what stimulates modern nations to surpass one another in the arts, in commerce, and in agriculture. The great mistakes of the past are useful in all areas. We cannot describe too often the crimes and misfortunes caused by absurd quarrels. It is certain that by refreshing our memory of these quarrels, we prevent a repetition of them. . . .

HUMANITY   . . . is a benevolent feeling for all men, which hardly inflames anyone without a great and sensitive soul. This sublime and noble enthusiasm is troubled by the pains of other people and by the necessity to alleviate them. With these sentiments an individual would wish to cover the entire universe in order to abolish slavery, superstition, vice, and misfortune. . . .

INTOLERANCE   . . . Any method that would tend to stir up men, to arm nations, and to soak the earth with blood is impious.

It is impious to want to impose laws upon man's conscience: this is a universal rule of conduct. People must be enlightened and not constrained. . . .

What did Christ recommend to his disciples when he sent them among the Gentiles? Was it to kill or to die? Was it to persecute or to suffer? . . .

Which is the true voice of humanity, the persecutor who strikes or the persecuted who moans?

PEACE   . . . War is the fruit of man's depravity; it is a convulsive and violent sickness of the body politic. . . .

If reason governed men and had the influence over the heads of nations that it deserves, we would never see them inconsiderately surrender themselves to the fury of war; they would not show that ferocity that characterizes wild beasts. . . .

POLITICAL AUTHORITY   No man has received from nature the right to command others. Liberty is a gift from heaven, and each individual of the same species has the right to enjoy it as soon as he enjoys the use of reason. . . .

The prince owes to his very subjects the *authority* that he has over them; and this *authority* is limited by the laws of nature and the state. The laws of nature and the state are the conditions under which they have submitted or are supposed to have submitted to its government. . . .

Moreover the government, although hereditary in a family and placed in the hands of one person, is not private property, but public property that consequently can never be taken from the people, to whom it belongs exclusively, fundamentally, and as a freehold. Consequently it is always the people who make the lease or the agreement: they always intervene in the contract that adjudges its exercise. It is not the state that belongs to the prince, it is the prince who belongs to the state: but it does rest with the prince to govern in the state, because the state has chosen him for that purpose: he has bound himself to the people and the administration of affairs, and they in their turn are bound to obey him according to the laws. . . .

THE PRESS [which includes newspapers, magazines, books, and so forth] . . . People ask if freedom of the *press* is advantageous or prejudicial to a state. The answer is not difficult. It is of the greatest importance to conserve this practice in all states founded on liberty. I would even say that the disadvantages of this liberty are so inconsiderable compared to its advantages that this ought to be the common right of the universe, and it is certainly advisable to authorize its practice in all governments. . . .

REVIEW QUESTIONS

1. Why was the publication of the *Encyclopedia* a vital step in the philosopher' hopes for reform?
2. To what extent were John Locke's political ideals reflected in the *Encyclopedia?*
3. Why was freedom of the press of such significance to the philosophes?

6 Humanitarianism

A humanitarian spirit pervaded the philosophes' outlook. Showing a warm concern for humanity, they attacked militarism, slavery, religious persecution, torture, and other violations of human dignity, as can be seen in passages from the *Encyclopedia* and Voltaire's works earlier in this chapter. Through reasoned arguments they sought to make humankind recognize and renounce its own barbarity. In the following selections, other eighteenth-century reformers denounce judicial torture, the abuse of prisoners, and slavery.

Caesare Beccaria
CONDEMNING TORTURE

In *Essay on Crimes and Punishments* (1764), Caesare Beccaria (1738–1794), an Italian economist and criminologist, faulted the powerful and thinkers for permitting the cruelty of punishments, and the irregularity of proceedings in criminal cases.

Surely, the groans of the weak, sacrificed to the cruel ignorance and indolence of the powerful, the barbarous torments lavished, and multiplied with useless severity, for crimes either not proved, or in their nature impossible, the filth and horrors of prison, increased by the most cruel tormentor of the miserable ought to have roused the attention of those whose business is to direct the opinions of mankind.

In the following passage, Beccaria condemns torture, commonly used to obtain confessions in many European countries, as irrational and inhuman.

The torture of a criminal during the course of his trial is a cruelty consecrated by custom in most nations. It is used with an intent either to make him confess his crime, or to explain some contradictions into which he had been led during his examination, or in order to discover his accomplices or in order finally to discover other crimes of which he is not accused, but of which he may be guilty.

No man can be judged a criminal until he be found guilty; nor can society take from him the public protection until it have been proved that he has violated the conditions on which it was granted. What right, then, but that of power, can authorise the punishment of a citizen so long as there remains any doubt of his guilt? This dilemma is frequent. Either he is guilty, or not guilty. If guilty, he should only suffer the punishment ordained by the laws, and torture becomes useless, as his confession is unnecessary. If he be not guilty, you torture the innocent; for, in the eye of the law, every man is innocent whose crime has not been proved. Besides, it is confounding all relations . . . to expect . . . that pain should be the test of truth, as if truth resided in the muscles and fibres of a wretch in torture. By this method the robust will escape, and the feeble be condemned. These are the inconveniencies of this pretended test of truth, worthy only of a cannibal, and which the Romans, in many respects barbarous, and whose savage virtue has been too much admired, reserved for the slaves alone. . . .

It would be superfluous to confirm these reflections by examples of innocent persons who, from the agony of torture, have confessed themselves guilty: innumerable instances may be found in all nations, and in every age. How amazing that mankind have always neglected to draw the natural conclusion!

The result of torture, then, is a matter of calculation, and depends on the constitution, which differs in every individual, and it is in proportion to his strength and sensibility; so that to discover truth by this method, is a problem which may be better solved by a mathematician than by a judge, and may be thus stated: *The force of the muscles and the sensibility of the nerves of an innocent person being given, it is required to find the degree of pain necessary to make him confess himself guilty of a given crime.*

The examination of the accused is intended to find out the truth. . . . [But] of two men equally innocent, or equally guilty, the most robust and resolute will be acquitted, and the weakest and most pusillanimous will be condemned, in consequence of the following excellent mode of reasoning. *I, the judge, must find some one guilty. Thou, who art a strong fellow, hast been able to resist the force of torment; therefore I acquit thee. Thou, being weaker, hast yielded to it; I therefore condemn thee. I am sensible, that the confession which was extorted from thee has no weight; but if thou dost not confirm by oath what thou hast already confessed, I will have thee tormented again.*

A very strange but necessary consequence of the use of torture is, that the case of the innocent is worse than that of the guilty. With regard to the first, either he confesses the crime which he has not committed, and is condemned, or he is acquitted, and has suffered a punishment he did not deserve. On the contrary, the person who is really guilty has the most favourable side of the question; for, if he supports the torture with firmness and resolution, he is acquitted, and has gained, having exchanged a greater punishment for a less.

Caesare Beccaria, *Essay on Crimes and Punishments*, trans. Edward D. Ingraham (Philadelphia, PA: Philip H. Nicklin, 1819), pp. 59–60, 64, 67.

John Howard
STATE OF THE PRISONS IN ENGLAND AND WALES

In 1777 John Howard (1726–1790), a British philanthropist, published *State of the Prisons in England and Wales.* Howard's publicizing of the terrible conditions in prisons led Parliament to enact penal reforms. Following are excerpts from Howard's influential book.

There are prisons, into which whoever looks will, at first sight of the people confined there, be convinced, that there is some great error in the management of them: the sallow meagre countenances declare, without words, that they are very miserable: many who went in healthy, are in a few months changed to emaciated dejected objects. Some are seen pining under diseases, *"sick and in prison;"* expiring on the floors, in loathsome cells, of pestilential fevers, and . . . smallpox: victims, I must not say to the cruelty, but I will say to the inattention, of sheriffs, and gentlemen in the commission of the peace.

The cause of this distress is, that many prisons are scantily supplied, and some almost totally unprovided with the necessaries of life.

There are several Bridewells [prisons for those convicted of lesser crimes such as vagrancy and disorderly conduct] (to begin with them) in which prisoners have no allowance of food at all. In some, the keeper farms what little is allowed them: and where he engages to supply each prisoner with one or two pennyworth of bread a day, I have known this shrunk to half, sometimes less than half the quantity, cut or broken from his own loaf.

It will perhaps be asked, does not their work maintain them? for every one knows that those offenders are committed to *hard labour.* The answer to that question, though true, will hardly be believed. There are very few Bridewells in which any work is done, or can be done. The prisoners have neither tools, nor materials of any kind; but spend their time in sloth, profaneness and debauchery, to a degree which, in some of those houses that I have seen, is extremely shocking. . . .

I have asked some keepers, since the late act for preserving the health of prisoners, why no care is taken of their sick: and have been answered, that the magistrates tell them *the act does not extend to Bridewells.*

In consequence of this, at the quarter sessions you see prisoners, covered (hardly covered) with rags; almost famished; and sick of diseases, which the discharged spread wherever they go, and with which those who are sent to the County-Gaols infect these prisons. . . .

Felons have in some Gaols two pennyworth of bread a day; in some three halfpennyworth; in some a pennyworth; in some a shilling a week. . . . I often weighed the bread in different prisons, and found the penny loaf 7½ to 8½ ounces, the other loaves in proportion. It is probable that when this allowance was fixed by its value, near double the quantity that the money will now purchase, might be bought for it: yet the allowance continues unaltered. . . .

This allowance being so far short of the cravings of nature, and in some prisons lessened by farming to the gaoler, many criminals are half starved: such of them as at their commitment were in health, come out almost famished, scarce able to move, and for weeks incapable of any labour.

Many prisons have NO WATER. This defect is frequent in Bridewells, and Town-Gaols. In the

John Howard, *The State of Prisons in England and Wales with Preliminary Observations and an Account of Some Foreign Prisons* (London: Warrington, 1777).

felons courts of some County-Gaols there is no water: in some places where there is water, prisoners are always locked up within doors, and have no more than the keeper or his servants think fit to bring them: in one place they are limited to three pints a day each—a scanty provision for drink and cleanliness! . . .

From hence any one may judge of the probability there is against the health and life of prisoners, crowded in close rooms, cells, and subterraneous dungeons, for fourteen or sixteen hours out of the four and twenty. In some of those caverns the floor is very damp: in others there is sometimes an inch or two of water; and the straw, or bedding is laid on such floors, seldom on barrack bedsteads. . . . Some Gaols have no SEWERS; and in those that have, if they be not properly attended to, they are, even to a visitant, offensive beyond expression: how noxious then to people constantly confined in those prisons!

In many Gaols, and in most Bridewells, there is no allowance of STRAW for prisoners to sleep on; and if by any means they get a little, it is not changed for months together, so that it is almost worn to dust. Some lie upon rags, others upon the bare floors. When I have complained of this to the keepers, their justification has been, "The county allows no straw; the prisoners have none but at my cost."

The evils mentioned hitherto affect the *health* and *life* of prisoners: I have now to complain of what is pernicious to their MORALS; and that

is, the confining all sorts of prisoners together: debtors and felons; men and women; the young beginner and the old offender: and with all these, in some counties, such as are guilty of misdemeanors only. . . .

In some Gaols you see (and who can see it without pain?) boys of twelve or fourteen eagerly listening to the stories told by practised and experienced criminals, of their adventures, successes, stratagems, and escapes.

I must here add, that in sorrier few Gaols are confined idiots and lunatics. . . . The insane, where they are not kept separate, disturb and terrify other prisoners. No care is taken of them, although it is probable that by medicines, and proper regimen, some of them might be restored to their senses, and to usefulness in life. . . .

A cruel custom obtains in most of our Gaols, which is that of the prisoners demanding of a new comer GARNISH, FOOTING, or (as it is called in some London Gaols) CHUMMAGE. "Pay or strip," are the fatal words. I say *fatal*, for they are so to some; who having no money, are obliged to give up part of their scanty apparel; and if they have no bedding or straw to sleep on, contract diseases, which I have known to prove mortal.

Loading prisoners with HEAVY IRONS, which make their walking, and even lying down to sleep, difficult and painful, is another custom which I cannot but condemn. In some County-Gaols the *women* do not escape this severity.

Denis Diderot
ENCYCLOPEDIA
"MEN AND THEIR LIBERTY ARE NOT OBJECTS OF COMMERCE. . . ."

Montesquieu, Voltaire, David Hume, Benjamin Franklin, Thomas Paine, and several other philosophes condemned slavery and the slave trade. In Book 15 of *The Spirit of the Laws* (1748), Montesquieu scornfully refuted all justifications for slavery. Ultimately, he said, slavery, which violates the fundamental principle of justice underlying the universe, derived from base human desires to dominate and exploit other human beings. In 1780, Paine helped draft the act abolishing slavery in Pennsylvania. Five years earlier, he wrote:

> Our Traders in Men . . . must know the wickedness of that slavetrade, if they attend to reasoning, or the dictates of their own hearts, and [those who] shun and stifle all these willfully sacrifice Conscience, and the character of integrity to that Golden Idol. . . . Most shocking of all is the alleging the sacred scriptures to favour this wicked practice.

The Encyclopedia denounced slavery as a violation of the individual's natural rights.

[This trade] is the buying of unfortunate Negroes by Europeans on the coast of Africa to use as slaves in their colonies. This buying of Negroes, to reduce them to slavery, is one business that violates religion, morality, natural laws, and all the rights of human nature.

Negroes, says a modern Englishman full of enlightenment and humanity, have not become slaves by the right of war; neither do they deliver themselves voluntarily into bondage, and consequently their children are not born slaves. Nobody is unaware that they are bought from their own princes, who claim to have the right to dispose of their liberty, and that traders have them transported in the same way as their other goods, either in their colonies or in America, where they are displayed for sale.

If commerce of this kind can be justified by a moral principle, there is no crime, however atrocious it may be, that cannot be made legitimate. Kings, princes, and magistrates are not the proprietors of their subjects: they do not,

therefore, have the right to dispose of their liberty and to sell them as slaves.

On the other hand, no man has the right to buy them or to make himself their master. Men and their liberty are not objects of commerce; they can be neither sold nor bought not paid for at any price. We must conclude from this that a man whose slave has run away should only blame himself, since he had acquired for money illicit goods whose acquisition is prohibited by all the laws of humanity and equity.

There is not, therefore, a single one of these unfortunate people regarded only as slaves who does not have the right to be declared free, since he has never lost his freedom, which he could not lose and which his prince, his father, and any person whatsoever in the world had not the power to dispose of. Consequently the sale that has been completed is invalid in itself. This Negro does not divest himself and can never divest himself of his natural right; he carries it everywhere with him, and he can demand everywhere that he be allowed to enjoy it. It is, therefore, patent inhumanity on the part of judges in free countries where he is transported, not to emancipate him immediately by declaring him free, since he is their fellow man, having a soul like them.

Denis Diderot, *The Encyclopedia: Selections*, ed. and trans. Stephen J. Gendzier (New York: Harper & Row, 1967), pp. 229–231. Copyright © 1967 by Harper & Row. Used by permission of the author.

REVIEW QUESTIONS

1. What were Caesare Beccaria's arguments against the use of torture in judicial proceedings? In your opinion, can torture ever be justified?

2. What ideals of the Enlightenment philosophes are reflected in Beccaria's arguments?
3. List the abuses in British jails that John Howard disclosed.
4. Why did the author of the *Encyclopedia* article regard slavery as a crime? How did he react to the argument that slaves are property?

---

7 Literature as Satire: Critiques of European Society

The French philosophes, particularly Voltaire, Diderot, and Montesquieu (all discussed earlier in this chapter), often used the medium of literature to decry the ills of their society and advance Enlightenment values. In the process, they wrote satires that are still read and admired for their literary merits and insights into human nature and society. The eighteenth century also saw the publication of Jonathan Swift's *Gulliver's Travels* (1726), one of the greatest satirical works written in English.

Voltaire
CANDIDE

In *Candide* (1759), Voltaire's most important work of fiction, he explored the question: Why do the innocent suffer? And because Voltaire delved into this mystery with wit, irony, satire, and wisdom, the work continues to be hailed as a literary masterpiece.

The illegitimate Candide (son of the sister of the baron in whose castle he lives in Westphalia) is tutored by the philosopher Pangloss, a teacher of "metaphysi-co-theologo-cosmolonigology": that is, a person who speaks nonsense. The naive Pangloss clings steadfastly to the belief that all that happens, even the worst misfortunes, are for the best.

Candide falls in love with Cunegund, the beautiful daughter of the baron of the castle; but the baron forcibly removes Candide from the castle when he discovers their love. Candide subsequently suffers a series of disastrous misfortunes, but he continues to adhere to the belief firmly instilled in him by Pangloss, that everything happens for the best and that this is the best of all possible worlds. Later, he meets an old beggar, who turns out to be his former teacher, Pangloss, who tells Candide that the Bulgarians have destroyed the castle and killed Cunegund and her family. Candide and Pangloss then travel together to Lisbon, where they survive the terrible earthquake,[1] only to have Pangloss hanged (but he escapes death) by the Inquisition. Soon thereafter, Candide is reunited with Cunegund, who, despite having been raped and sold into prostitution, has not been killed. Following further adventures and misfortunes, the lovers are again separated when Cunegund is captured by pirates.

After experiencing more episodes of human wickedness and natural disasters, Candide abandons the philosophy of optimism, declaring "that we must cultivate our gardens." By this Voltaire meant that we can never achieve utopia, but neither should we descend to the level of brutes. Through purposeful and honest work, and the deliberate pursuit of virtue, we can improve, however modestly, the quality of human existence.

The following excerpt from Candide starts with Candide's first misfortune after being driven out of the castle at Westphalia. Two men dressed in blue that he just met abduct him then force him to serve in the Bulgarian army. In addition to ridiculing philosophical optimism, Voltaire expresses his revulsion for militarism.

CHAPTER II

What befell Candide among the Bulgarians

"Have you not a great affection for—" "Oh, yes!" he replied. "I have a great affection for the lovely Miss Cunegund." "Maybe so," replied one of the men, "but that is not the question! We are asking you whether you have not a great affection for the King of the Bulgarians?"[2] "For the King of the Bulgarians?" said Candide. "Not at all. Why, I never saw him in my life." "Is it possible! Oh, he is a most charming king! Come, we must drink his health." "With all my heart, gentlemen." Candide said, and he tossed off his glass. "Bravo!" cried the blues. "You are now the support, the defender, the hero of the Bulgerians; your fortune is made; you are on the high road to glory." So saying, they put him in irons and carried him away to the regiment. There he was made to wheel about to the right, to the left, to draw his ramrod, to return his ramrod, to present, to fire, to march, and they gave him thirty blows with a cane. [When he did the drill better, he] was looked upon as a young fellow of surprising genius by all his comrades.

Candide was struck with amazement and could not for the soul of him conceive how he came to be a hero. One fine spring morning, he took it into his head to take a walk, and he marched straight forward, conceiving it to be a privilege of the human species, as well as of the brute creation, to make use of their legs how and when they pleased. He had not gone above two leagues when he was overtaken by four other heroes, six feet high, who bound him neck and heels, and carried him to a dungeon. A court-martial sat upon him, and he was asked which he liked best, either to run the gauntlet six and thirty times though the whole regiment, or to have his brains blown out with a dozen of musket balls. In vain did he remonstrate to them that the human will is free, and that he chose neither. They obliged him to make a choice, and he determined, in virtue of that divine gift called free will, to run the gauntlet six and thirty times. He had gone through his discipline twice, and the regiment being composed of two thousand men, they composed for him exactly four thousand strokes, which laid bare all his muscles and nerves, from the nape of his neck to his rump. As they were preparing to make him set out the third time, our young hero, unable to support it any longer, begged as a favour they would be so obliging as to shoot him through the head. The favour being granted, a bandage was tied over his eyes, and he was made to kneel down. At that very instant, his Bulgarian Majesty, happening to pass by, inquired into the delinquent's

---

Voltaire, *Candide or the Optimist*, reprinted from 1888 translation by Henry Morley (London: G. Routledge, 1922), pp. 5–9.
[1]The 1755 Lisbon earthquake and its aftermath of fire and flood almost totally destroyed Lisbon and killed thousands of people. —Eds.
[2]I.e., Prussians.

crime, and being a prince of great penetration, he found, from what he heard of Candide, that he was a young meta-physician, entirely ignorant of the world. And, therefore, out of his great clemency, he condescended to pardon him, for which his name will be celebrated in every journal, and every age. A skillful surgeon made a cure of Candide in three weeks by means of emollient unguents prescribed by Dioscorides. His sores were now skinned over, and he was able to march when the King of the Bulgarians gave battle to the King of the Abares.[3]

CHAPTER III

How Candide escaped from the Bulgarians, and what befell him afterwards

Never was anything so gallant, so well accoutered, so brilliant, and so finely disposed as the two armies. The trumpets, fifes, hautboys, [oboes], drums, and cannon, made such harmony as never was heard in hell itself. The entertainment began by a discharge of cannon, which, in the twinkling of an eye, laid flat about six thousand men on each side. The musket bullets swept away, out of the best of all possible worlds, nine or ten thousand scoundrels that infected its surface. The bayonet was next the sufficient reason for the deaths of several thousands. The whole might amount to thirty thousand souls.

Candide trembled like a philosopher and concealed himself as well as he could during this heroic butchery.

At length, while the two kings were causing *Te Deum*[4] to be sung in each of their camps, Candide took a resolution to go and reason somewhere else upon causes and effects. After passing over heaps of dead or dying men, the first place he came to was a neighbouring village, in the Abarian territories, which had been burned to the ground by the Bulgarians in accordance with international law. Here lay a number of old men covered with wounds, who beheld their wives dying with their throats cut, and hugging their children to their breasts all stained with blood. There several young virgins, whose bodies had been ripped open after they had satisfied the natural necessities of the Bulgarian heroes, breathed their last; while others, half burned in the flames, begged to be dispatched out of the world. The ground about them was covered with the brains, arms, and legs of dead men.

Candide made all the haste he could to another village, which belonged to the Bulgarians, and there he found that heroic Abares had treated it in the same fashion. From thence continuing to walk over palpitating limbs or through ruined buildings, at length he arrived beyond the theater of war, with a little provision in his pouch, and Miss Cunegund's image in his heart.

---

[3]I.e., French. The Seven Years' War had begun in 1756.

[4]A Te Deum ("We praise thee, God") is a special liturgical hymn praising and thanking God for granting some special favor, like a military victory or the end of a war.—Eds.

Montesquieu
THE PERSIAN LETTERS

Like other philosophes, Charles Louis de Secondat, Baron de la Brède et de Montesquieu (1689–1755), was an ardent reformer who used learning, logic, and wit to denounce the abuses of his day. His principal work, *The Spirit of the Laws* (1748), was a contribution to political liberty (see page 57). To safeguard liberty from despotism, which he regarded as a pernicious form of government that institutionalizes cruelty and violence, Montesquieu advocated the principle of separation of powers—that is, the legislative, executive, and judiciary should not be in the hands of one person or body. Montesquieu's hurnanitarianism and tolerant spirit are also seen in an earlier work, *The Persian Letters* (1721), published anonymously in Holland. In the guise of letters written by imaginary Persian travelers in Europe, Montesquieu makes a statement: He denounces French absolutism, praises English parliamentary government, and attacks religious persecution, as in this comment on the Spanish Inquisition, excerpted below.

LETTER XXIX

Rica to Ibben, at Smyrna

. . . I have heard that in Spain and Portugal there are dervishes who do not understand a joke, and who have a man burned as if he were straw. Whoever falls into the hands of these men is fortunate only if he has always prayed to God with little bits of wood in hand, has worn two bits of cloth attached to two ribbons, and has sometimes been in a province called Galicia![1] Otherwise, the poor devil is really in trouble. Even though he swears like a pagan that he is orthodox, they may not agree, and burn him for a heretic. It is useless for him to submit distinctions, for he will be in ashes before they even consider giving him a hearing.

Other judges presume the innocence of the accused; these always presume him guilty. In doubt they hold to the rule of inclining to severity, evidently because they consider mankind as evil. On the other hand, however, they hold such a high opinion of men that they judge them incapable of lying, for they accept testimony from deadly enemies, notorious women, and people living by some infamous profession. In passing sentence, the judges pay those condemned a little compliment, telling them that they are sorry to see them so poorly dressed in their brimstone shirts,[2] that the judges themselves are gentle men who abhor bloodletting, and are in despair at having to condemn them. Then, to console themselves, they confiscate to their own profit all the possessions of these poor wretches.

Happy the land inhabited by the children of the prophets! There these sad spectacles are unknown.[3] The holy religion brought by the angels trusts truth alone for its defense, and does not need these violent means for its preservation.

PARIS, THE 4TH OF THE MOON OF CHALVAL, 1712

Montesquieu, *The Persian Letters* (Indianapolis, IA: Bobbs-Merrill, 1964), pp. 53–54.

[1]The references are to a rosary, a scapular, and the pilgrimage shrine of St. James of Campostello in the Spanish province of Galicia.

---

[2]Those condemned by the Inquisition appeared for sentencing dressed in shirts colored to suggest the flames of their presumed postmortem destination.

[3]The Persians are the most tolerant of all the [Muslims].

REVIEW QUESTIONS

1. What does *Candide* reveal about Voltaire's general outlook?
2. How did Montesquieu characterize Spanish and Portuguese inquisitors?

8 Madame du Châtelet: A Woman of Brilliance

Gabrielle Emilie Le Tonnelier de Breteuil du Châtelet (1706–1749), known simply as Madame du Châtelet, was the daughter of a Parisian nobleman. She early showed signs of a superior intelligence, and her father provided tutors for the young Gabrielle Emilie. Since females were excluded from a university education, her husband, Marquis Florent-Claude Chastellet, later supported Emilie du Châtelet's love of learning by arranging for university professors of physics and mathematics to tutor her at home.

Madame du Châtelet
AN APPEAL FOR FEMALE EDUCATION

In her lifetime Madame du Châtelet learned Latin, Italian, German, and English and read and translated works in these languages. She collaborated with Voltaire, who was both her intellectual companion and lover, in writing *Elements of the Philosophy of Newton*, an attempt to explain Newton's theories to nonmathematicians. And she translated Newton's *Principia Mathematica* from the Latin into French.

In the following passage, drawn from the introduction of her translation of Bernard Mandeville's *The Fable of the Bees*, Madame du Châtelet makes a fervent appeal for educating women.

. . . Thus, while it is true to say that a good translation requires application and labor, it is, nonetheless, at best, a very mediocre work.

However mediocre this kind of work, it may be thought that it is audacious for a woman to aspire to do it.

I feel the full weight of prejudice that excludes us [women] so universally from the sciences, this being one of the contradictions of this world, which has always astonished me, as there are great countries whose laws allow us to decide their destiny, but none where we are brought up to think.

Another observation that one can make about this prejudice, which is odd enough, is that acting is the only occupation requiring some study and a trained mind to which women are admitted, and it is at the same time the only one that regards its professionals as infamous.

Let us reflect briefly on why for so many centuries, not one good tragedy, one good poem, one esteemed history, one beautiful painting, one good book of physics, has come from the hands of women. Why do these creatures whose understanding appears in all things equal to that of men, seem, for all that, to be stopped by an invincible force on this side of a barrier, let someone give me some explanation, if there is one. I leave it to naturalists to find a physical explanation, but until that happens, women will be entitled to protest against their education. As for me, I confess that if I were king I would wish to make this scientific experiment. I would reform an abuse that cuts out, so to speak, half of humanity. I would allow women to share in all the rights of humanity, and most of all those of the mind. Women seem to have been born to deceive, and their soul is scarcely allowed any other exercise. This new system of education that I propose would in all respects be beneficial to the human species. Women would be more valuable beings, men would thereby gain a new object of emulation, and our social interchanges which, in refining women's minds in the past, too often weakened and narrowed them, would now only serve to extend their knowledge. Some will probably recommend

Emilie du Châtelet, *Selected Philosophical and Scientific Writings*, ed. Judith P. Zinsser, trans. Isabelle Bout and Judith P. Zinsser (Chicago: The University of Chicago Press, 2009), pp. 48–49. Reprinted by permission of The University of Chicago Press.

that I ask M. the abbé of St. Pierre to combine this project with his.[1] Mine will perhaps seem as difficult to put into practice, even though it may be more reasonable.

I am convinced that many women are either ignorant of their talents, because of the flaws in their education, or bury them out of prejudice and for lack of a bold spirit. What I have experienced myself confirms me in this opinion. Chance led me to become acquainted with men of letters, I gained their friendship, and I saw with extreme surprise that they valued this amity.[2]

I began to believe that I was a thinking creature. But I only glimpsed this, and the world for which alone I believed I had been born [was one of dissipation that] carried away all my time and all my soul. I only believed in earnest in my capacity to think at an age when there was still time to become reasonable, but when it was too late to acquire talents.

Being aware of that has not discouraged me at all. I hold myself quite fortunate to have renounced in mid-course frivolous things that occupy most women all their lives, and I want to use what time remains to cultivate my soul. Feeling that nature has refused me the creative genius that discovers new truths, I have done justice to myself, and I am content to render with clarity the truths others have discovered, and which the diversity of languages renders useless for most readers.

---

[1]Charles-Irénée Castel, Abbé de St. Pierre (1658–1743), wrote a number of well-known treatises on education, including one that advocated *colleges* for girls with a course of study similar to that for boys.

[2]*L'amitié*, the French word used here, means more than simple friendship and carries the connotation of affection and concern.

REVIEW QUESTION

Why did Madame du Châtelet advocate a new system of education?

---

9 On the Progress of Humanity

During the French Revolution, the Marquis de Condorcet attracted the enmity of the dominant Jacobin party and in 1793 was forced to go into hiding. Secluded in Paris, he wrote *Sketch for a Historical Picture of the Progress of the Human Mind*. Arrested in 1794, Condorcet died during his first night in prison from either exhaustion or self-inflicted poison.

Marquis de Condorcet
PROGRESS OF THE HUMAN MIND

Sharing the philosophes' confidence in human goodness and in reason, Condorcet was optimistic about humanity's future progress. Superstition, prejudice, intolerance, and tyranny—all barriers to progress in the past—would gradually be eliminated, and humanity would enter a golden age. The following excerpts are from Condorcet's *Sketch*.

. . . The aim of the work that I have under-taken, and its result will be to show by appeal to reason and fact that nature has set no term to the perfection of human faculties; that the perfectibility of man is truly indefinite; and that the progress of this perfectibility, from now onwards independent of any power that might wish to halt it, has no other limit than the duration of the globe upon which nature has cast us. This progress will doubtless vary in speed, but it will never be reversed as long as the earth occupies its present place in the system of the universe, and as long as the general laws of this system produce neither a general cataclysm nor such changes as will deprive the human race of its present faculties and its present resources. . . .

. . . It will be necessary to indicate by what stages what must appear to us today a fantastic hope ought in time to become possible, and even likely; to show why, in spite of the transitory successes of prejudice and the support that it receives from the corruption of governments or peoples, truth alone will obtain a lasting victory; we shall demonstrate how nature has joined together indissolubly the progress of knowledge and that of liberty, virtue and respect for the natural rights of man. . . .

After long periods of error, after being led astray by vague or incomplete theories, publicists have at last discovered the true rights of man and how they can all be deduced from the single truth, that *man is a sentient being, capable of reasoning and of acquiring moral ideas.* . . .

At last man could proclaim aloud his right, which for so long had been ignored, to submit all opinions to his own reason and to use in the search for truth the only instrument for its recognition that he has been given. Every man learnt with a sort of pride that nature had not forever condemned him to base his beliefs on the opinions of others; the superstitions of antiquity and the abasement of reason before the [deception] of supernatural religion [had] disappeared from society as from philosophy.

Thus an understanding of the natural rights of man, the belief that these rights are inalienable and [cannot be forfeited], a strongly expressed desire for liberty of thought and letters, of trade and industry, and for the alleviation of the people's suffering, for the [elimination] of all penal laws against religious dissenters and the abolition of torture and barbarous punishments, the desire for a milder system of criminal legislation and jurisprudence which should give complete security to the innocent, and for a simpler civil code, more in conformance with reason and nature, indifference in all matters of religion which now were relegated to the status of superstitions and political [deception], a hatred of hypocrisy and fanaticism, a contempt for prejudice, zeal for the propagation of enlightenment: all these principles, gradually filtering down from philosophical works to every class of society whose education went beyond the catechism and the alphabet, became the common faith . . . [of enlightened people]. In some countries these principles formed a public opinion sufficiently widespread for even the mass of the people to show a willingness to be guided by it and to obey it. . . .

Force or persuasion on the part of governments, priestly intolerance, and even national prejudices, had all lost their deadly power to smother the voice of truth, and nothing could now protect the enemies of reason or the oppressors of freedom from a sentence to which the whole of Europe would soon subscribe. . . .

Our hopes for the future condition of the human race can be subsumed under three important heads: the abolition of inequality between nations, the progress of equality within each nation, and the true perfection of mankind. Will all nations one day attain that state

Antoine-Nicolas de Condorcet, *Sketch for a Historical Picture of the Progress of the Human Mind*, trans. June Barraclough, pp. 4–5, 9–10, 128, 136, 140–142, 173–175, 179. Copyright © 1955 Weidenfeld & Nicolson, an imprint of The Orion Publishing Group.

of civilization which the most enlightened, the freest and the least burdened by prejudices, such as the French and the Anglo-Americans [by virtue of their revolutions], have attained already? Will the vast gulf that separates these peoples from the slavery of nations under the rule of monarchs, from the barbarism of African tribes, from the ignorance of savages, little by little disappear? . . .

Is the human race to better itself, either by discoveries in the sciences and the arts, and so in the means to individual welfare and general prosperity; or by progress in the principles of conduct or practical morality; or by a true perfection of the intellectual, moral, or physical faculties of man, an improvement which may result from a perfection either of the instruments used to heighten the intensity of these faculties and to direct their use or of the natural constitution of man?

In answering these three questions we shall find in the experience of the past, in the observation of the progress that the sciences and civilization have already made, in the analysis of the progress of the human mind and of the development of its faculties, the strongest reasons for believing that nature has set no limit to the realization of our hopes. . . .

The time will therefore come when the sun will shine only on free men who know no other master but their reason; when tyrants and slaves, priests and their stupid or hypocritical instruments will exist only in works of history and on the stage; and when we shall think of them only to pity their victims and their dupes; to maintain ourselves in a state of vigilance by thinking on their excesses; and to learn how to recognize and so to destroy, by force of reason, the first seeds of tyranny and superstition, should they ever dare to reappear amongst us.

REVIEW QUESTIONS

1. According to Condorcet, what economic, political, and cultural policies were taught by the philosophes?
2. What image of human nature underlies Condorcet's theory of human progress?

CHAPTER 4

Era of the French Revolution

THE STORMING OF THE BASTILLE, JULY 14, 1789, by Jean-Pierre Houel, 1789. The fall of the Bastille, a symbol of the Old Regime's darkness and despotism, furthered the cause of reform. *(© akg-images)*

In 1789, many participants and observers viewed the revolutionary developments in France as the fulfillment of the Enlightenment's promise—the triumph of reason over tradition and ignorance, of liberty over despotism. It seemed that the French reformers were eliminating the abuses of an unjust system and creating a new society founded on the ideals of the philosophes.

Eighteenth-century French society, the Old Regime, was divided into three orders, or estates. The First Estate (the clergy) and the Second Estate (the nobility) enjoyed special privileges sanctioned by law and custom. The church collected tithes (taxes on the land), censored books regarded as a threat to religion and morality, and paid no taxes to the state (although the church did make a "free gift" to the royal treasury). Nobles were exempt from most taxes, collected manorial dues from peasants (even from free peasants), and held the highest positions in the church, the army, and the government.

Opinion among the aristocrats was divided. Some nobles, influenced by the liberal ideals of the philosophes, sought to reform France; they wanted to end royal despotism and establish a constitutional government. To this extent, the liberal nobility had a great deal in common with the bourgeoisie. These liberal nobles saw the king's financial difficulties in 1788 as an opportunity to regenerate the nation under enlightened leadership. When they resisted the king's policies, they claimed that they were opposing royal despotism. But at the same time, many nobles remained hostile to liberal ideals and opposed reforms that threatened their privileges and honorific status.

Peasants, urban workers, and members of the bourgeoisie belonged to the Third Estate, which comprised about 96 percent of the population. The bourgeoisie—which included merchants, bankers, professionals, and government officials below the top ranks—provided the leadership and ideology for the French Revolution. For most of the eighteenth century, the bourgeoisie did not challenge the existing social structure, including the special privileges of the nobility. But by 1789 the bourgeoisie wanted to abolish those privileges and to open prestigious positions to men of talent regardless of their birth; it wanted to give France a constitution that limited the monarch's power, established a parliament, and protected the rights of the individual.

The immediate cause of the French Revolution was a financial crisis. The wars of Louis XIV and subsequent foreign adventures, including French aid to the American colonists during their revolution, had emptied the royal treasury. The refusal of the clergy and the nobles to surrender their tax exemptions compelled Louis XVI to call a meeting of the Estates General—a medieval assembly that had last met in 1614—to deal with impending bankruptcy. Many nobles intended to use the Estates General to weaken the French throne and regain powers lost a century earlier under the absolute rule of Louis XIV. But the nobility's plans were unrealized; their revolt against the crown paved the way for the Third Estate's eventual destruction of the Old Regime.

Between June and November 1789 the bourgeoisie, aided by uprisings of the common people of Paris and the peasants in the countryside, gained control over the state and instituted reforms. During this opening and moderate phase of the Revolution (1789–1791), the newly created National Assembly abolished the special privileges of the aristocracy and clergy, formulated a declaration of human rights, subordinated the church to the state, reformed the country's administrative and judicial systems, and drew up a constitution creating a parliament and limiting the king's power.

Between 1792 and 1794 came a radical stage. Three principal factors propelled the Revolution in a radical direction: pressure from the urban poor, the *sans-culottes*, who wanted the government to do something about their poverty; a counterrevolution led by clergy and aristocrats who wanted to undo the reforms of the Revolution; and war with the European powers that sought to check French expansion and to stifle the revolutionary ideals of liberty and equality.

The dethronement of Louis XVI, the establishment of the Republic in September 1792, and the king's execution in January 1793 were all signs of growing radicalism. As the new Republic tottered under the twin blows of internal insurrection and foreign invasion, the revolutionary leadership grew more extreme. In June 1793 the radical Jacobins took power. Tightly organized, disciplined, and fiercely devoted to the Republic, the Jacobins mobilized the nation's material and human resources to defend it against the invading foreign armies. To deal with counterrevolutionaries, the Jacobins unleashed the Reign of Terror. Of the 500,000 people imprisoned for crimes against the Republic, some 16,000 were sentenced to death and executed by guillotine and another 20,000 perished in prison before they could be tried. More than 200,000 died in the civil war in the provinces, and 40,000 were summarily executed by firing squad, guillotine, and mass drownings ordered by military courts authorized by the National Convention (1792–1795). Although the Jacobins succeeded in saving the Revolution, their extreme measures aroused opposition. In the last part of 1794, power again passed into the hands of the moderate bourgeoisie, who wanted no part of Jacobin radicalism.

In 1799, Napoleon Bonaparte, a popular general with an inexhaustible yearning for power, helped to overthrow the Directory, which governed France from 1795 to 1799, and pushed the Revolution in still another direction, toward military dictatorship. Although Napoleon subverted the revolutionary ideal of liberty, he preserved the social gains of the Revolution—the abolition of the special privileges of the nobility and the clergy.

The era of French Revolution was a decisive period in the shaping of the modern West. By destroying aristocratic privileges and opening careers to talent, it advanced the cause of equality under the law. By weakening the power of the clergy, it promoted the secularization of society. By abolishing the divine right of monarchy, drafting a constitution, and establishing a parliament, it accelerated the growth of the liberal-democratic state. By eliminating the remnants of serfdom and the sale of government offices and by reforming the tax system, it fostered a rational approach to administration. In the nineteenth century, the ideals and reforms of the French Revolution spread in shock waves across Europe; in country after country, the old order was challenged by the ideals of liberty and equality.

1 Abuses of the Old Regime

The roots of the French Revolution lay in the aristocratic structure of French society. The Third Estate resented the special privileges of the aristocracy, a legacy of the Middle Ages, and the inefficient and corrupt methods of government. To many French people influenced by the ideas of the philosophes, French society seemed an affront to reason. By 1789, reformers sought a new social order based on rationality and equality.

Arthur Young
PLIGHT OF THE FRENCH PEASANTS

French peasants in the late eighteenth century were better off than the peasants of Eastern and Central Europe, where serfdom predominated. The great majority of France's 21 million peasants were free; many owned their own land, and some were prosperous. Yet the countryside was burdened with severe problems, which sparked a spontaneous revolution in 1789.

A rising birthrate led to the continual subdivision of French farms among peasant sons; on the resulting small holdings, peasants struggled to squeeze out a living. Many landless peasants, who were forced to work as day laborers, were also hurt by the soaring population. An oversupply of rural day laborers reduced many of the landless to beggary. An unjust and corrupt tax system also contributed to the peasants' poverty. Peasants paid excessive taxes to the state, church, and lords; taxes and obligations due the lords were particularly onerous medieval vestiges, as most peasants were no longer serfs. A poor harvest in 1788–1789 and inflation worsened conditions.

Arthur Young (1741–1820), an English agricultural expert with a keen eye for detail, traveled through France just prior to the Revolution. In *Travels During the Years 1787, 1788, and 1789*, he reported on conditions in the countryside.

. . . The abuses attending the levy of taxes were heavy and universal. The kingdom was parceled into generalities [administrative units], with an intendant at the head of each, into whose hands the whole power of the crown was delegated for everything except the military authority; but particularly for all affairs of finance. The generalities were subdivided into sections, at the head of which was a representative appointed by the intendant. The rolls of the *taille*, capitation, *vingtièmes*,[1] and other taxes, were distributed among districts, parishes, and individuals, at the pleasure of the intendant, who could exempt, change, add, or diminish at pleasure. Such an enormous power, constantly acting, and from which no man was free, must, in the nature of things, degenerate in many cases into absolute tyranny. It must be obvious that the friends, acquaintances, and dependents of the intendant, and of all his representatives, and the friends of these friends, to a long chain of dependence, might be favoured in taxation at the expense of their miserable neighbours; and that noblemen in favour at court, to whose protection the intendant himself would naturally look up, could find little difficulty in throwing much of the weight of their taxes on others, without a similar support. Instances, and even gross ones, have been reported to me in many parts of the kingdom, that made me shudder at the oppression to which people have been subjected by the undue favours granted to such crooked influence. But, without recurring to such cases, what must have been the state of the poor people paying heavy taxes, from which the nobility and clergy were exempted? A cruel aggravation of their misery, to see those who could best afford to pay,

exempted because able! . . . The *corvées* [taxes paid in labor, often road building], or police of the roads, were annually the ruin of many hundreds of farmers; more than 300 were reduced to beggary in filling up one vale in Lorraine: all these oppressions fell on the *tiers etat* [Third Estate] only; the nobility and clergy having been equally exempted from *tailles*, militia and *corvées*. The penal code of finance makes one shudder at the horrors of punishment inadequate to the crime. . . .

1. Smugglers of salt, armed and assembled to the number of five, in Provence, a fine of 500 liv. [*livres*, French coins] and nine years galleys [sentenced to backbreaking labor—rowing sea vessels], in all the rest of the kingdom, death.

2. Smugglers, armed, assembled, but in number under five, a fine of 300 liv. and three years galleys. Second offense, death. . . .

10. Buying smuggled salt, to resell it, the same punishments as for smuggling. . . .

The *capitaineries* [lords' exclusive hunting rights] were a dreadful scourge on all the occupiers of land. By this term is to be understood the paramountship of certain districts, granted by the king to princes of the blood, by which they were put in possession of the property of all game, even on lands not belonging to them. . . . In speaking of the preservation of the game in these *capitaineries*, it must be observed that by game must be understood whole droves of wild boars, and herds of deer not confined by any wall or pale, but wandering at pleasure over the whole country, to the destruction of crops; and to the peopling of the galleys by the wretched peasants, who presumed to kill them in order to save that food which was to support their helpless children. . . . Such were the exertions of arbitrary power which the lower orders felt directly from the royal authority; but, heavy as they were, it is a question whether the abuses, suffered indirectly through the nobility and the clergy, were not yet more oppressive. Nothing can exceed the complaints made in the *cahiers* (lists of Third Estate grievances drawn up in

---

Adapted from Arthur Young, *Travels During the Years 1787, 1788, and 1789* (London: Printed for W. Richardson, 1792), pp. 533–540.

[1]A *taille* was a tax levied on the value of a peasant's land or wealth. A capitation was a head or poll tax paid for each person. A *vingtième* was a tax on income and was paid chiefly by peasants. —Eds.

1789) under this head. They speak of the dispensation of justice in the manorial courts, as comprising every species of despotism . . . . The judges, commonly ignorant pretenders. who hold hold their courts in taverns . . . are absolutely dependent on the lords. Nothing can exceed the force of expression used in painting the oppressions of the seigneurs, in consequence of their feudal powers. . . . The countryman is tyrannically enslaved by it. . . . In passing through many of the French provinces, I was struck with the various and heavy complaints of the farmers and little proprietors of the feudal grievances, with the weight of which their industry was burdened; but I could not then conceive the multiplicity of the shackles which kept them poor and depressed. I understood it better afterwards.

[handwritten note: oppression of a system that does not allow mobility?]

Emmanuel Sieyès
WHAT IS THE THIRD ESTATE?

In a series of pamphlets, including *The Essay on Privileges* (1788) and *What Is the Third Estate?* (1789), Abbé Emmanuel Sieyès (1748–1836) expressed the bourgeoisie's disdain for the nobility. Although educated at Jesuit schools to become a priest, Sieyès had come under the influence of Enlightenment ideas. In *What Is the Third Estate?* he denounced the special privileges of the nobility, asserted that the people are the source of political authority, and maintained that national unity stands above estate or local interests. The ideals of the Revolution—liberty, equality, and fraternity—are found in Sieyès's pamphlet, excerpts of which follow.

[handwritten note: Nation - not estates or local interest]

Everywhere the Third Estate attends to nineteen-twentieths of [public functions] with this distinction; that it is laden with all that which is really painful, with all the burdens which the privileged classes refuse to carry. Do we give the Third Estate credit for this? . . . The facts are well known. Meanwhile the privileged have dared to impose a prohibition upon the order of the Third Estate. They have said to it: "Whatsoever may be your services to the country, whatever may be your abilities, you shall go thus far; you may not pass beyond!"

If this exclusion is a social crime against the Third Estate, if it is a veritable act of hostility, could it be said that it is useful to the public good? . . . If it discourages the Third Estate whom it rejects, is it not well known that it tends to render less able the higher order whom it favors? . . . Is it not to be remarked that since the government has become the patrimony of a particular class . . . positions have been created not on account of the necessities of the governed, but in the interests of the governing class. . . .

It suffices here to have made it clear that the pretended usefulness of a privileged order for the public service is nothing more than an illusion; that all that is burdensome in public service is

---

Adapted from Emmanuel Joseph Sieyès, *What Is the Third Estate?* The Department of History, University of Pennsylvania, translations and reprints from the original *Sources of European History* (1899), Vol. VI, no.1, pp. 33–35.

performed by the Third Estate; that without the privileged order the superior places would be infinitely better filled; that they naturally ought to be the responsibility and the reward of ability and recognized services, and that if privileged persons have come to usurp all the lucrative and honorable posts, it is a hateful injustice to the rank and file of citizens and at the same time a treason to the public good.

Who then shall dare to say that the Third Estate has not within itself all that is necessary for the formation of a complete nation? It is the strong and robust man who has one arm still shackled. If the privileged order should be abolished, the nation would be nothing less, but something more. Therefore, what is the Third Estate? Everything; but an everything shackled and oppressed. What would it be without the privileged order? Everything, but an everything

free and flourishing. Nothing can succeed without it, everything would be infinitely better without the others.

It is not sufficient to show that privileged persons, far from being useful to the nation, cannot but enfeeble and injure it; it is necessary to prove further that the noble order does not enter at all into the social organization; that it may indeed be a burden upon the nation, but that it cannot of itself constitute a nation.

Is it not evident that the noble order has privileges and expenditures which it dares to call its right, but which are apart from the rights of the great body of citizens?

The Third Estate embraces then all that which belongs to the nation; and all that which is not the Third Estate, cannot be regarded as being of the nation. What is the Third Estate? It is the whole.

REVIEW QUESTIONS

1. What abuse did Arthur Young see in the French system of taxation and justice?
2. Why did Young consider the *capitaineries* to be a particularly "dreadful scourge" on the peasants?
3. How important did Emmanuel Sieyès say the nobility (the privileged order) was to the life of the nation?
4. What importance did Sieyès attach to the contribution of the Third Estate to the life of the nation?

2 The Role of the Philosophes

The Enlightenment thinkers were not themselves revolutionaries. However, by subjecting the institutions and values of the Old Regime to critical scrutiny and by offering the hope that society could be reformed, the philosophes created the intellectual precondition for revolution.

Alexis de Tocqueville
CRITIQUE OF THE OLD REGIME

Born of a noble family, Alexis de Tocqueville (1805–1859) was active in French politics in the first half of the nineteenth century. After traveling in the United

States, he wrote *Democracy in America* (1835), a great work of historical literature. In 1856, he published *The Old Regime and the French Revolution*, which explored the causes of the French Revolution. In the following passage from *The Old Regime and the French Revolution*, de Tocqueville treats the role of the philosophes in undermining the Old Regime.

. . . [The thinkers of the Enlightenment] all agreed that it was expedient to substitute simple and elementary rules, deduced from reason and natural law, for the complicated traditional customs which governed the society of their time. Upon a strict scrutiny it may be seen that what might be called the political philosophy of the eighteenth century consisted, properly speaking, in this one notion.

These opinions were by no means novel; for three thousand years they had unceasingly traversed the imaginations of mankind, though without being able to stamp themselves there. How came they at last to take possession of the minds of all the writers of this period? Why, instead of progressing no farther than the heads of a few philosophers, as had frequently been the case, had they at last reached the masses, and assumed the strength and the fervour of a political passion to such a degree, that general and abstract theories upon the nature of society became daily topics of conversation, and even inflamed the imaginations of women and of the peasantry? How was it that literary men, possessing neither rank, nor honours, nor fortune, nor responsibility, nor power, became, in fact, the principal political men of the day? . . .

It was not by chance that the philosophers of the 18th century . . . coincided in entertaining notions so opposed to those which still served as bases to the society of their time: these ideas had been naturally suggested to them by the aspects of the society which they had all before their eyes. The sight of so many unjust or absurd privileges, the [burden] of which was more and

more felt whilst their cause was less and less understood, urged, or rather precipitated the minds of one and all to the idea of the natural equality of man's condition. Whilst they looked upon so many strange and irregular institutions, born of other times, which no one had attempted either to bring into harmony with each other or to adapt to modern wants, and which appeared likely to perpetuate their existence though they had lost their worth, they learned to abhor what was ancient and traditional, and naturally became desirous of re-constructing the social edifice of their day upon an entirely new plan—a plan which each one traced solely by the light of his reason. . . .

Had [the French] been able, like the English, gradually to modify the spirit of their ancient institutions by practical experience without destroying them, they would perhaps have been less inclined to invent new ones. But there was not a man who did not daily feel himself injured in his fortune, in his person, in his comfort, or his pride by some old law, some ancient political custom, or some other remnant of former authority, without perceiving at hand any remedy that he could himself apply to his own particular hardship. It appeared that the whole constitution of the country must either be endured or destroyed.

The French, however, had still preserved one liberty amidst the ruin of every other: they were still free to philosophize almost without restraint upon the origin of society, the essential nature of governments, and the primordial rights of mankind.

All those who felt themselves aggrieved by the daily application of existing laws were soon enamoured of these literary politics. The same taste soon reached even those who by nature or by their

Alexis de Toqueville, *On the State of the Society in France Before the Revolution of 1789,* trans. Henry Reeve (London: John Murray, 1856), pp. 255–257, 259–260, 267–269.

condition of life seemed the farthest removed from abstract speculations. Every taxpayer wronged by the unequal distribution of the *taille*[1] was fired by the idea that all men ought to be equal; every little landowner devoured by the rabbits of his noble neighbour was delighted to be told that all privileges were without distinction contrary to reason. Every public passion thus assumed the disguise of philosophy; all political action was violently driven back into the domain of literature; and the writers of the day, undertaking the guidance of public opinion, found themselves at one time in that position which the heads of parties commonly hold in free countries. No one in fact was any longer in a condition to contend with them for the part they had assumed. . . .

. . . [T]he writers of the time became a great political power, and ended by being the first power in the country.

------

[1]For an explanation of taxes, see footnote 1 on page 95.

Above the actual state of society—the constitution of which was still traditional, confused, and irregular, and in which the laws remained conflicting and contradictory, ranks sharply sundered, the conditions of the different classes fixed whilst their burdens were unequal—an imaginary state of society was thus springing up, in which everything appeared simple and co-ordinate, uniform, equitable, and agreeable to reason. The imagination of the people gradually deserted the former state of things in order to seek refuge in the latter. Interest was lost in what was, to foster dreams of what might be; and men thus dwelt in fancy in this ideal city, which was the work of literary invention. . . .

This circumstance, so novel in history, of the whole political education of a great people being formed by its literary men, contributed more than anything perhaps to bestow upon the French Revolution its peculiar stamp, and to cause those results which are still perceptible.

REVIEW QUESTIONS

1. According to Alexis de Tocqueville, how did the philosophes undermine the Old Regime?
2. Why did de Tocqueville believe the French people were receptive to the philosophes' ideas?

---

3 Liberty, Equality, Fraternity

In August 1789 the newly created National Assembly adopted the Declaration of the Rights of Man and of the Citizen, which expressed the liberal and universal ideals of the Enlightenment. The Declaration proclaimed that sovereignty derives from the people: that is, that the people are the source of political power; that men are born free and equal in rights; and that it is the purpose of government to protect the natural rights of the individual. Because these ideals contrasted markedly with the outlook of an absolute monarchy, a privileged aristocracy, and an intolerant clergy, some historians view the Declaration of Rights as the death knell of the Old Regime. Its affirmation of liberty, reason, and natural rights inspired liberal reformers in other lands.

DECLARATION OF THE RIGHTS OF MAN AND OF THE CITIZEN

Together with John Locke's *Second Treatise on Government*, the American Declaration of Independence, and the Constitution of the United States, the Declaration of the Rights of Man and of the Citizen, which follows, is a pivotal document in the development of modern liberalism.

The Representatives of the people of France, formed into a NATIONAL ASSEMBLY, considering that ignorance, neglect, or contempt of human rights, are the sole causes of public misfortunes and corruptions of Government, have resolved to set forth in a solemn declaration, these natural, imprescriptible, and unalienable rights: that this declaration, being constantly present to the minds of the members of the body social, they may be ever kept attentive to their rights and their duties: that the acts of the legislative and executive powers of Government, being capable of being every moment compared with the end of political institutions, may be more respected: and also, that the future claims of the citizens, being directed by simple and incontestible principles, may always tend to the maintenance of the Constitution, and the general happiness.

For these reasons the NATIONAL ASSEMBLY doth recognize and declare, in the presence of the Supreme Being, and with the hope of his blessing and favor, the following *sacred* rights of men and of citizens:

I. *Men are born, and always continue, free, and equal in respect of their rights. Civil distinctions, therefore, can be founded only on public utility.*

II. *The end of all political associations, is, the preservation of the natural and imprescriptible rights of man; and these rights are liberty, property, security, and resistance of oppression.*

III. *The nation is essentially the source of all sovereignty; nor can any* INDIVIDUAL *or* ANY BODY OF MEN*, be entitled to any authority which is not expressly derived from it.*

IV. Political Liberty consists in the power of doing whatever does not injure another. The exercise of the natural rights of every man, has no other limits than those which are necessary to secure to every *other* man the free exercise of the same rights; and these limits are determinable only by the law.

V. The law ought to prohibit only actions hurtful to society. What is not prohibited by the law, should not be hindered; nor should any one be compelled to that which the law does not require.

VI. The law is an expression of the will of the community. All citizens have a right to concur, either personally, or by their representatives, in its formation. It should be the same to all, whether it protects or punishes; and *all being equal in its sight, are equally eligible to all honors, places, and employments, according to their different abilities, without any other distinction than that created by their virtues and talents.*

VII. No man should be accused, arrested, or held in confinement, except in cases determined by the law, and according to the forms which it has prescribed. All who promote, solicit, execute, or cause to be executed, arbitrary orders, ought to be punished; and every citizen called upon or apprehended by virtue of the law, ought

---

Thomas Paine, *The Rights of Man* (New York: Peter Eckler, 1892), pp. 94–96.

immediately to obey, and renders himself culpable by resistance.

VIII. The law ought to impose no other penalties but such as are absolutely and evidently necessary; and no one ought to be punished, but in virtue of a law promulgated before the offence, and legally applied.

IX. Every man being presumed innocent till he has been convicted, whenever his detention becomes indispensable, all rigor [harshness] to him, more than is necessary to secure his person, ought to be provided against by the law.

X. No man ought to be molested on account of his opinions, not even on account of his *religious* opinions, provided his avowal of them does not disturb the public order established by the law.

XI. The unrestrained communication of thoughts and opinions being one of the most precious rights of man, every citizen may speak, write, and publish freely, provided he is responsible for the abuse of this liberty in cases determined by the law.

XII. A public force being necessary to give security to the rights of men and of citizens, that force is instituted for the benefit of the community, and not for the particular benefit of the persons with whom it is entrusted.

XIII. A common contribution being necessary for the support of the public force, and for defraying the other expenses of government, it ought to be divided equally among the members of the community, according to their abilities.

XIV. Every citizen has a right, either by himself or his representative, to a free voice in determining the necessity of public contributions, the appropriation of them, and their amount, mode of assessment, and duration.

XV. Every community has a right to demand of all its agents, an account of their conduct.

XVI. Every community in which a separation of powers and a security of rights is not provided for, wants a constitution.

XVII. The rights to property being inviolable and sacred, no one ought to be deprived of it, except in cases of evident public necessity, legally ascertained, and on condition of a previous just indemnity.

REVIEW QUESTIONS

1. What does the Declaration say about the nature of political liberty? What are its limits, and how are they determined?
2. How does the Declaration show the influence of John Locke (see chapter 3)?
3. The ideals of the Declaration have become deeply embedded in the Western outlook. Discuss this statement.

---

4 Expansion of Human Rights

The abolition of the special privileges of the aristocracy and the ideals proclaimed by the Declaration of the Rights of Man and of the Citizen aroused the hopes of reformers in several areas: in what was considered radicalism, even by the framers of the Declaration of the Rights of Man, some women began to press for equal rights; humanitarians called for the abolition of the slave trade; and Jews, who for centuries had suffered disabilities and degradation, petitioned for full citizenship.

Olympe de Gouges
DECLARATION OF THE RIGHTS OF WOMAN AND OF THE FEMALE CITIZEN

The daughter of working class parents—her father was a butcher and her mother was the daughter of a cloth merchant—Olympe de Gouges (1745–1793) educated herself and became a prominent woman of letters. Her fame rested principally on her plays, but she also wrote essays denouncing slavery and advocating women's rights. After 1789 she wrote numerous pamphlets in support of the Revolution. Maintaining that the Revolution had scorned women, de Gouges wrote the Declaration of the Rights of Woman and of the Female Citizen (1791), which demanded that women be granted the same rights as men. She was executed during the Reign of Terror by the Jacobin regime, ostensibly for royalist sympathies. Following is the core of the Declaration of the Rights of Woman.

The sex that is superior in beauty, as well as courage in maternal suffering, recognizes and declares, in the presence of and under the auspices of the Supreme Being, the following rights of woman and citizeness.

Article I. Woman is born free and remains equal in rights to man. Social distinctions can only be founded on the common utility.

Article II. The goal of all political association is the maintenance of the natural and inalienable rights of woman and of man: these rights are liberty, property, security, and above all resistance to oppression.

Article III. The principle of all sovereignty resides essentially in the Nation, which is only the joining of woman and man; no body, no individual, who does not clearly emanate from it can exercise authority.

Article IV. Freedom and justice consist of restoring all that belongs to others; thus the exercise of the natural rights of woman is only limited by a permanent tyranny that man himself opposes; these limits should be reformed by the laws of nature and reason.

Article V. The laws of nature and of reason prohibit all actions harmful to society: all that is not prohibited by these wise and holy laws can not be prevented, and no one can be forced to do what they do not require.

Article VI. The law must be the expression of the general will; all female and male citizens must concur personally or through their representatives in its enactment; it must be the same for every one: all female and male citizens being equal before its eyes must be equally eligible for all honors, positions, and public employments according to their abilities, without any distinctions but those based on their virtues and talents.

Article VII. No woman is excluded; she is accused, arrested, and detained in cases determined by the law. Women, like men, obey this rigorous law.

Article VIII. The law must only establish penalties that are strictly and obviously necessary, and no one can be punished except by virtue of

Shannon Hartigan, Rea McKay, and Marie-Therese Sequin (eds.), *Femmes au pouvoir, re'flexions autour d'Olympe de Gouges* (Moncton, N.B.: Editions d'Acadie, 1995), pp. 278–281. Translated by Howard E. Negrin.

a law established and promulgated prior to the infraction and legally applied to women.

Article IX. For all women who are found guilty, all the rigor of the law is applied.

Article X. No one can be disturbed for even basic opinions; woman has the right to mount the scaffold [to be executed]; she must equally have the right to mount the tribune [and present her views]: provided that her appearances do not trouble the public order established by law.

Article XI. The free communication of thoughts and opinions is one of the most precious rights of woman, since this freedom assures fathers the right to acknowledge the legitimacy of their children. Every citizeness can freely state I am the mother of a child that is yours, without a barbarous prejudice forcing her to hide the truth; except [when she must] answer for an abuse of this freedom in cases determined by law.

Article XII. The guarantee of the rights of woman and citizeness should be of general utility; this guarantee must be instituted for the advantage of all, and not for the particular utility of those to whom it has been entrusted.

Article XIII. For the maintenance of the public power and for administrative expenses, the taxes of woman and man are equal; she shares in all demanding duties, in all painful tasks; she must therefore have an equal share in the distribution of positions, employments, responsibilities, honors, and trades.

Article XIV. The female citizens and male citizens have the right to acknowledge by themselves or through their representatives the necessity of public taxation. The female citizens can only agree to public administration, and in the determination of the apportionment, basis, collection, and duration of the tax.

Article XV. The mass of women, joined for taxes with that of men, has a right to demand an accounting of their administration from all public agents.

Article XVI. All societies in which the guarantee of rights is not assured, nor the separation of powers determined, have no constitutions; the constitution is null if the majority of citizens who constitute the nation have not collaborated in its writing.

Article XVII. Property belongs to both sexes, whether united or separated: it is an inviolable and sacred right for each one; as a true patrimony of nature, no one can be deprived of it, unless a public necessity, legally certified, requires it, and under condition of a fair and prior indemnification.

Society of the Friends of Blacks
ADDRESS TO THE NATIONAL ASSEMBLY IN FAVOR OF THE ABOLITION OF THE SLAVE TRADE

Planters in the French West Indies and shipbuilding and sugar refining interests opposed any attempts to eliminate slavery or the slave trade since they profited handsomely from these institutions. On February 5, 1790, the Society of the Friends of Blacks addressed the National Assembly and, using the language of the Declaration of the Rights of Man, called for the abolition of the slave trade.

Recognizing the power of proslavery forces, the society made it clear that it was not proposing the abolition of slavery itself. In 1791, the slaves of Saint Domingue in the Caribbean revolted, and in 1794, the Jacobins in the National Convention abolished slavery in the French colonies. The island's white planters resisted the decree, and in 1801 Napoleon sent twenty thousand troops to Saint Domingue in an unsuccessful attempt to restore slavery. In 1804, the black revolutionaries established the independent state of Haiti.

Following are excerpts from the Society of the Friends of Blacks' address to the National Assembly.

The humanity, justice, and generosity that you have directed to the reform of the most deeply rooted abuses, cause the Society of the Friends of Blacks to hope that you will welcome with benevolence its demand in favor of this numerous portion of humanity so cruelly oppressed for two centuries.

This Society, so cowardly and unjustly slandered, only derives its mission from the humanity that has brought it to defend the blacks, even under the former despotism. Oh! Can there be a more respectable title in the eyes of this august Assembly, which has so often avenged in its decrees the rights of man?

You have declared these rights; you have engraved them on an immortal monument, that all men are born and live free and equal in rights; you have returned these rights to the French people, which a despotism had for so long a time stolen from them . . . you have broken the bonds of feudalism that still degraded a portion of our fellow citizens; you have announced the destruction of all stigmatizing distinctions that religious or political prejudices had introduced into the great family of humanity.

The men, whose cause we defend, don't have such elevated pretentions, although citizens of the same empire and men like us, they have the same rights as us. We don't at all demand that you restore to the French blacks these political rights, which alone attest to and maintain the

dignity of man; we don't even demand their freedom. No, the slander, paid for no doubt by the greed of the ship-owners, has attributed this intention to us and spread it everywhere; it is designed to provoke people against us, to provoke the planters and their numerous creditors, who are alarmed by even a gradual emancipation. It is designed to alarm all French people, for whom one paints an image of the prosperity of the colonies as inseparable from the slave trade and the perpetuity of slavery.

No, never has such an idea entered our minds; we have said it, printed it at the founding of our Society, and we repeat it in order to destroy this basic argument blindly adopted by all the maritime cities, basic argument on which rests almost all their addresses [to the National Assembly]. The immediate liberation of the blacks would not only be a fatal move for the colonies; it would even be a fatal gift for the blacks in the state of abjection and incompetence to which greed has reduced them. This would be like abandoning to themselves and without help babies in the cradle, or crippled and powerless beings.

It is therefore not yet time to demand it, this freedom; we only demand that one stop regularly slaughtering every year thousands of blacks in order to take hundreds captive; we demand that from this time forward one stop prostituting, profaning the French name, in order to authorize these thefts, these appalling murders; we demand in a word the abolition of the slave trade, and we implore you to promptly consider this important subject. . . .

Finally, one will say to you, in order to turn you away from so pressing an issue, that to abolish the

Adresse a l'Assemblée Nationale, pour l'abolition de la traite des noirs, par la Société de Amis des Noirs de Paris, trans. Howard E. Negrin (Paris: Imp. L. Potier de Lille, 1790) pp. 1–4, 18–20, 22.

slave trade, that even to consider the resolution, would spark a revolution among the blacks.

Such was also the language spoken in the past to prevent reform of abuses among us. Is it with benevolent acts that one inflames men? Ah! If the oppressors of the blacks, cause, by torments and humiliations, almost all feelings to be extinguished in their souls, they have not yet extinguished that of gratitude; a thousand striking facts attest to this. And with what gratitude will they not be filled when they will learn that the first Assembly of France wishes to soften their fate, to prevent forever the murder of their fellow-beings; their chains will seem less heavy to them because perhaps one day their children will no longer be crushed by them. They will no longer bury their posterity in nothingness. Better treated, they will wait patiently for the moment when their slavery will have to end, and sedition will be far from their souls. Is one seditious in the bosom of good treatment?

If, on the contrary, some reason can lead them to insurrection, would it not be the indifference of the National Assembly to their fate? Would it not be the persistence in weighing them down with chains when one has consecrated everywhere this eternal axiom: that all men are born free and equal in rights. Oh what then, there would be only for the blacks fetters and gallows when happiness shines for whites alone. Let us not doubt it, our happy revolution should re-ignite the blacks, whose vengeance and resentment have been ignited for a long time; and it's not at all with punishments that this upheaval will be repressed. From an unappeased insurrection twenty others will be born, one of which alone can forever ruin the colonists. There is only one way to prevent it; that is the abolition of the slave trade; at least a resolution by this Assembly to consider it without delay. The news of a decree, even a preliminary one, will produce two good effects at the same time; it will calm the agitation of the blacks, it will force the planters, who will no longer soon expect new African recruits, to treat their blacks better. Thus you will stop, with a single word, the bloodshed on the African coasts, the barbarous treatment [of blacks] on our islands, and you will prepare for an enduring prosperity of our colonies by another arrangement of things. . . .

We beseech you, even in the name of the colonies, which only such a declaration can calm, in the name of your glory, in the name of justice, in the name of humanity, for which a delay of one month, one day costs streams of blood. We beseech you finally in the name of heaven, who no doubt contemplates with joy the revolution that you have carried out, who will bless it, who will more strongly protect it when seeing you use your power to dry the tears of these unfortunates against whom European greed has conspired for so long a time.

PETITION OF THE JEWS OF PARIS, ALSACE, AND LORRAINE TO THE NATIONAL ASSEMBLY, JANUARY 28, 1790

After several heated debates, the National Assembly granted full citizenship to the Jews on September 27, 1791. Influenced by the French example, almost all European states in the nineteenth century would also emancipate the Jews dwelling within their borders. In the following Petition of the Jews of Paris, Alsace, and Lorraine to the National Assembly, January 28, 1790, the Jews pointed to historic wrongs and invoked the ideals of the Revolution as they called for equal rights.

A great question is pending before the supreme tribunal of France. *Will the Jews be citizens or not?*

Already, this question has been debated in the National Assembly; and the orators, whose intentions were equally patriotic, did not agree at all on the result of their discussion. Some wanted Jews admitted to civil status. Others found this admission dangerous. A third opinion consisted of preparing the complete improvement of the lot of the Jews by gradual reforms.

In the midst of all these debates, the national assembly believed that it ought to adjourn the question. . . .

It was also said that the adjournment was based on the necessity of knowing with assurance what were the true desires of the Jews; given, it was added, the disadvantages of according to this class of men rights more extensive than those they want.

But it is impossible that such a motive could have determined the decree of the national assembly.

First, the wish of the Jews is perfectly well-known, and cannot be equivocal. They have presented it clearly in their addresses of 26 and 31 August, 1789. The Jews of Paris repeated it in a *new address* of 24 December. They ask that all the degrading distinctions that they have suffered to this day be abolished and that they be declared CITIZENS. . . .

Their desires, moreover, as we have just said, are well known; and we will repeat them here. They ask to be CITIZENS. . . .

In truth, [the Jews] are of a religion that is condemned by the one that predominates in France. But the time has passed when one could say that it was only the dominant religion that could grant access to advantages, to prerogatives, to the lucrative and honorable posts in society. For a long time they confronted the Protestants with this maxim, worthy of the Inquisition, and the Protestants had no civil

standing in France. Today, they have just been reestablished in the possession of this status; they are assimilated to the Catholics in everything; the intolerant maxim that we have just recalled can no longer be used against them. Why would they continue to use it as an argument against the Jews?

In general, civil rights are entirely independent from religious principles. And all men of whatever religion, whatever sect they belong to, whatever creed they practice, provided that their creed, their sect, their religion does not offend the principles of a pure and severe morality, all these men, we say, equally able to serve the fatherland, defend its interests, contribute to its splendor, should all equally have the title and the rights of citizen. . . .

[The Jews] are reproached at the same time for the vices that make them unworthy of civil status and the principles which render them at once unworthy and incompetent. A rapid glance at the bizarre as well as cruel destiny of these unfortunate individuals will perhaps remove the disfavor with which some seek to cover them. . . .

Always persecuted since the destruction of Jerusalem [by the Romans], pursued at times by fanaticism and at others by superstition, by turn chased from the kingdoms that gave them an asylum and then called back to these same kingdoms, excluded from all the professions and arts and crafts, deprived even of the right to be heard as witnesses against a Christian, relegated to separate districts [ghettos] like another species of man with whom one fears having communication, pushed out of certain cities which have the privilege of not receiving them, obligated in others to pay for the air that they breathe as in Augsburg where they pay a *florin* an hour or in Bremen a *ducat* a day, subject in several places to shameful tolls. Here is the list of a part of the harassment still practiced today against the Jews.

And [critics of the Jews] would dare to complain of the state of degradation into which some of them can be plunged! They would dare to complain of their ignorance and their vices! Oh! Do not accuse the Jews, for that would only

Excerpted from *The French Revolution and Human Rights*, Lynn Hunt, editor and translator, pp. 93–97. Copyright © 1996 by Bedford/St. martin's. Used by permission of the translator.

precipitate onto the Christians themselves all the weight of these accusations. . . .

Let us now enter into more details. The Jews have been accused of the crime of usury. But first of all, all of them are not usurers; and it would be as unjust to punish them all for the offense of some as to punish all the Christians for the usury committed by some of them and the speculation of many. . . .

Reflect, then, on the condition of the Jews. Excluded from all the professions, ineligible for all the positions, deprived even of the capacity to acquire property, not daring and not being able to sell openly the merchandise of their commerce, to what extremity are you reducing them? You do not want them to die, and yet you refuse them the means to live: you refuse them the means, and you crush them with taxes. You leave them therefore really no other resource than usury. . . .

Everything that one would not have dared to undertake, moreover, or what one would only have dared to undertake with an infinity of precautions a long time ago, can now be done

and one must dare to undertake it in this moment of universal regeneration, when all ideas and all sentiments take a new direction; and we must hasten to do so. Could one still fear the influence of a prejudice against which reason has appealed for such a long time, when all the former abuses are destroyed and all the former prejudices overturned? Will not the numerous changes effected in the political machine uproot from the people's minds most of the ideas that dominated them? Everything is changing; the lot of the Jews must change at the same time; and the people will not be more surprised by this particular change than by all those which they see around them every day. This is therefore the moment, the true moment to make justice triumph: attach the improvement of the lot of the Jews to the revolution; amalgamate, so to speak, this partial revolution to the general revolution. Your efforts will be crowned with success, and the people will not protest, and time will consolidate your work and render it unshakable.

REVIEW QUESTIONS

1. What did the demands of Olympe de Gouges, the Society of the Friends of Blacks, and the Jews of Paris, Alsace, and Lorraine have to do with the French Revolution and the ideas of the Enlightenment, and how did they exemplify the expansion of human rights?
2. In proposing the abolition of the slave trade, what did the Society of the Friends of Blacks petition the National Assembly to do? Was it feasible? Do you feel it was adequate? Explain.
3. On what grounds did the Jews of Paris, Alsace, and Lorraine petition the National Assembly to grant the Jews citizenship? What historic wrongs did they decry? What views of religion and politics did they uphold?

---

5 The Jacobin Regime

In the summer of 1793 the French Republic was threatened with internal insurrection and foreign invasion. During this period of acute crisis, the Jacobins provided strong leadership. They organized a large national army of citizen soldiers who, imbued with love for the nation, routed the invaders on the northern frontier. To deal with internal enemies, the Jacobins instituted the Reign of Terror, in which Maximilien Robespierre (1758–1794) played a pivotal role. In the early stage of the Revolution, as a member of the National Assembly, Robespierre had strongly supported liberal reforms. He attacked, at times with great fervor, slavery, capital punishment, and censorship; he favored civil rights for Jews; and, in what was considered a radical measure, he supported giving all men the right to vote regardless of how much property they owned.

Maximilien Robespierre
REPUBLIC OF VIRTUE

It was not because they were bloodthirsty or power mad that many Jacobins, including Robespierre, supported the use of terror. Rather, they were idealists who believed that terror was necessary to rescue the Republic and the Revolution from destruction. Deeply committed to republican democracy, Robespierre saw himself as the bearer of a higher faith, molding a new society founded on reason, good citizenship, patriotism, and virtue. Robespierre viewed those who prevented the implementation of this new society as traitors and sinners who had to be killed for the good of humanity.

In his speech of February 5, 1794, Robespierre provided a comprehensive statement of his political theory, in which he equated democracy with virtue and justified the use of terror in defending democracy.

What is the end of our revolution? The tranquil enjoyment of liberty and equality; the reign of that eternal justice whose laws are graven not on marble or stone but in the hearts of all men, even in the heart of the slave who has forgotten them or of the tyrant who disowns them.

We wish an order of things where all the low and cruel passions are enchained, all the beneficent and generous passions awakened by the laws; where ambition subsists in a desire to deserve glory and serve the country; where distinctions grow out of the system of equality; where the citizen submits to the authority of the magistrate. The magistrate obeys that of the people, and the people are governed by a love of justice; where the country secures the comfort of each individual, and where each individ-

ual prides himself on the prosperity and glory of the country; where every soul expands by a free communication of republican sentiments, and by the necessity of deserving the esteem of a great people; where the hearts serve to embellish that liberty which gives them value and support, and commerce is a source of public wealth and not merely of the immense riches of a few individuals.

We wish in our country [to substitute] . . . all the virtues and miracles of a Republic [for] all the vices and absurdities of the Monarchy.

We wish, in a word to fulfill the intentions of nature and the destiny of man, realize the promises of philosophy, and acquit providence of a long reign of crime and tyranny. [We wish] that France, once illustrious among enslaved nations, may, by eclipsing the glory of all the free countries that ever existed, become a model to nations, a terror to oppressors, a consolation to the oppressed, an ornament of the universe; and that, by sealing the work with our blood,

National Convention, *Report upon the Principles of Political Morality . . . Second Year of the Republic* [February 6, 1794], *by Maximilien Robespierre* (Philadelphia: Benjamin Franklin Bache, 1794), pp. 3–7, 10.

we may at least witness the dawn of the bright day of universal happiness. This is our ambition, this is our aim.

What kind of government can realize these [wonders]? A democratic or republican government only; these two terms are synonymous notwithstanding the abuse of common language; for aristocracy is no more republic than monarchy is. A democracy is not a state where the people, always assembled, regulate by themselves all public affairs, much less one where one hundred thousand portions of the people, by measures that are insulated, [hasty], and contradictory, should decide the fate of the whole nation: such a government has never existed except to bring back the people [to] the yolk of despotism.

A democratic government is that in which the sovereign people, guided by laws of their own enactment, do for themselves everything that they can do well, and by means of delegates all which they cannot do for themselves. It is therefore in the principles of democratic government that you are to seek the rules of your political conduct.

But in order to found and consolidate democracy among us, to reach the peaceful reign of constitutional laws, we must terminate the war of liberty against tyranny. . . . This is the end of the revolutionary government that you have framed. . . .

But the French are the first people in the world that have established democracy in its purity by holding out to all men equality and a full enjoyment of the rights of citizen; and this is, in my opinion, the true reason why all tyrants leagued against the republic will be vanquished.

From this time great conclusions [are] to be drawn from the principles that we have just laid down.

Since virtue and equality are the soul of the republic, and your aim is to found, to consolidate the republic, it follows that the first rule of your political conduct should be, to let all your measures tend to maintain equality and encourage virtue; for the first care of the legislator

should be to strengthen the principles on which the government rests. Hence all that tends to excite a love of country, to purify manners, to exalt the mind, to direct the passions of the human heart toward the public good, you should adopt and establish. All that tends to concentrate and debase them into selfish egotism, to awaken an infatuation for littleness, and a disregard for greatness, you should reject and repress. In the system of the French revolution, that which is immoral is impolitic, and that which tends to corrupt is counter-revolutionary. Weakness, vices, prejudices are the road to monarchy. . . .

. . . Externally all the despots surround you; internally all the friends of tyranny conspire: they will conspire until crime is deprived of all hope. It is necessary to annihilate both the internal and external enemies of the republic or perish with its fall; then in this situation, your first political maxim should be, that the people are guided by reason, the enemies of the people driven by terror alone.

If virtue be the spring of popular government in times of peace, the spring of that government during a revolution is virtue combined with terrorism: virtue, without which terror is destructive; terror, without which virtue is impotent. Terror is only justice, prompt, severe, and inflexible; it is then an emanation of virtue; it is less a distinct principle than a natural consequence of the general principle of democracy, applied to the most pressing needs of the country.

In notes written in the style of a Catholic catechism, Robespierre advocated terror against the enemies of the Revolution.

THE NECESSITY FOR TERROR

What is our goal? The enforcement of the constitution for the benefit of the people.

E. L. Higgins, ed., The French Revolution as Told by Contemporaries (Boston: Houghton Mifflin, 1938), p. 301.

Who will our enemies be? The vicious and the rich.

What means will they employ? Slander and hypocrisy.

What things may be favorable for the employment of these? The ignorance of the *sans-culottes*.[1]

The people must therefore be enlightened. But what are the obstacles to the enlightenment of the people? Mercenary writers who daily mislead them with impudent falsehoods.

What conclusions may be drawn from this? 1. These writers must be proscribed as the most dangerous enemies of the people. 2. Right-minded literature must be scattered about in profusion.

_____

[1] *Sans-culottes* literally means without the fancy breeches worn by the aristocracy. The term refers generally to a poor city dweller (who wore simple trousers). Champions of equality, the *sans-culottes* hated the aristocracy and the rich bourgeoisie.

What are the other obstacles to the establishment of liberty? Foreign war and civil war.

How can foreign war be ended? By putting republican generals in command of our armies and punishing those who have betrayed us.

How can civil war be ended? By punishing traitors and conspirators, particularly if they are deputies or administrators; by sending loyal troops under patriotic leaders to subdue the aristocrats of Lyon, Marseille, Toulon, the Vendée, the Jura, and all other regions in which the standards of rebellion and royalism have been raised; and by making frightful examples of all scoundrels who have outraged liberty and spilled the blood of patriots.

1. Proscription of perfidious and counterrevolutionary writers and propagation of proper literature.

2. Punishment of traitors and conspirators, particularly deputies and administrators.

3. Appointment of patriotic generals; dismissal and punishment of others.

4. Sustenance and laws for the people.

General Louis de Ligniéres Turreau
UPRISING IN THE VENDÉE

In the Vendée, in western France, peasants loyal to the monarchy, to their priests, and to Catholic tradition (all of which the Revolution had attacked) and led by nobles waged war against the Republic. It was a merciless conflict. Republican authorities executed, generally without a trial, thousands of suspects by firing squad and mass drowning. Frenzied republican soldiers, under orders from their superiors, burned villages, slaughtered livestock, and indiscriminately killed tens of thousands of peasants. Following is a letter from General Turreau to the minister of war on January 19, 1794, in which he describes the brutal campaign his troops waged against the peasants in the Vendée.

My purpose is to burn everything, to leave nothing but what is essential to establish the neces-

_____

Claude Petitfrere, ed., *La Vendée et les Vendéens*, pp. 59–60.

sary quarters for exterminating the rebels. This great measure is one which you should prescribe; you should also make an advance statement as to the fate of the women and children we will come across in this rebellious countryside. If they are all to be put to the sword, I cannot undertake such action without authorization.

All brigands caught bearing arms, or convicted of having taken up arms to revolt against their country, will be bayoneted. The same will apply to girls, women, and children in the same circumstances. Those who are merely under suspicion will not be spared either, but no execution may be carried out except by previous order of the general.

All villages, farms, woods, heathlands, generally anything which will burn, will be set on fire, although not until any perishable supplies found there have been removed. But, it must be repeated, these executions must not take place until so ordered by the general.

I hasten to describe to you the measures which I have just put in hand for the extermination of all remaining rebels scattered about the interior of the Vendée. I was convinced that the only way to do this was by deploying a sufficient number of columns to spread right across the countryside and effect a general sweep, which would completely purge the cantons as they passed. Tomorrow, therefore, these twelve columns will set out simultaneously, moving from east to west. Each column commander has orders to search and burn forests, villages, market towns and farms, omitting, however those places which I consider important posts and those which are essential for establishing communications.

In a letter dated December 26, 1793, a high government official describes mass drowning.

I am writing to you about the more than twelve hundred brigands shot at Savenay; but, according to the intelligence that I have since been given and that I do not doubt, it seems that more than two thousand were shot. They call that "sending to the hospital." Here, an entirely different method is used to get rid of this bad element. These criminals are put into boats which are then sunk. This is called "sending to the water tower." In truth, if the brigands have sometimes complained about dying of hunger, they cannot at least complain about dying of thirst. About twelve hundred were made to drink today. I do not know who thought up this kind of punishment, but it is much more speedy than the guillotine which henceforth seems destined to cut off the heads of nobles, priests and all those who, according to the rank which they formerly occupied, had a great influence over the common people.

The District of Saint-Quentin
DE-CHRISTIANIZATION

Anticlericalism reinforced by the exigencies of war fostered a phenomenon known as de-Christianization. Removed from churches were valuables that could be channeled into the war effort. In many regions, priests were dismissed and churches were closed, policies supported by the belief that the clergy supported the counterrevolution. To purge the Republic of religion, the Convention drew up a republican calendar in which the year one started, not with Christ's birth, but with the founding of the French Republic on September 22, 1792. On November 10, 1793, a celebration honoring the goddess Reason took place in the cathedral of Notre Dame de Paris. The initiative for de-Christianization came from deputies sent to the provinces by the National Convention and by local anticlericalism.

Maintaining that belief in God fostered civic order and that attacking the church drove people to support the counterrevolution, Robespierre was a staunch opponent of de-Christianization. The following edict was issued by the general council of the District of Saint-Quentin in northeastern France.

[T]he permanent and general council of the District of Saint-Quentin,

considering that the time has come when fanaticism and religious superstition must disappear for ever from the soil of liberty;

that it is urgent that the throne of error and falsehood be overthrown at the same time as that of the tyrant, to be replaced by the eternal reign of reason and philosophy;

that all individuals hitherto known under the general name of priests or ministers of public worship, disavowing the errors and prejudices to which they have been subjugated until now, and with the aid of which they have blinded and tyrannised the people for too long, must finally take in the social order the place which nature has assigned them . . .

that all churches and chapels, for too long the theatre of imposture, become today temples of reason and schools of republican virtue decrees . . . the following:

Article 1. All municipalities, within twenty-four hours of receiving the present decree, will pull down and remove all crosses, whether in iron, copper, lead or other metal, which are to be found on or in churches, chapels, cemeteries or other public places in their municipality.

Article 2. In the place of crosses on churches, the municipalities will have flown the national colours, surmounted with the bonnet of liberty.

Article 3. In the next twenty-four hours, they will proceed with a detailed inventory of all objects in silver, copper, lead, iron and other metals; of all vestments in linen, surplices, chasubles and so on which were in their commune for the former use of public worship.

Philip G. Dwyer and Peter mcPhee, eds., *The French Revolution and Napoleon: a sourcebook* (London: Routledge, 2002), p. 88.

REVIEW QUESTIONS

1. Compare and contrast Maximilien Robespierre's vision of the Republic of Virtue with the ideals of the Declaration of the Rights of Man and of the Citizen (see page 100). What did Robespierre mean by virtue?
2. On what grounds did Robespierre justify terror?
3. Like medieval inquisitors, Robespierre regarded people with different views not as opponents but as sinners. Discuss this statement.
4. How did the Jacobins justify their ruthless policies in the Vendée?
5. The philosophes would have been ambivalent toward de-Christianization. Discuss.

---

6 Napoleon: Destroyer and Preserver of the Revolution

In 1799, a group of conspirators that included Napoleon Bonaparte (1769–1821), an ambitious and popular general, staged a successful coup d'état. Within a short time, Napoleon became a one-man ruler, and in 1804 he crowned himself Emperor of the French. Under Napoleon's military dictatorship, political freedom (a principal goal of the French Revolution) was suppressed. Nevertheless, Napoleon preserved, strengthened, and spread to other lands many of the Revolution's reforms. He supported religious tolerance, secular education, and access to positions according to ability; he would not restore the privileges of the aristocracy and church.

Napoleon Bonaparte
LEADER, GENERAL, TYRANT, REFORMER

Napoleon was a brilliant military commander who carefully planned each campaign, using speed, deception, and surprise to confuse and demoralize his opponents. By rapid marches, Napoleon would concentrate a superior force against a segment of the enemy's strung-out forces. Recognizing the importance of good morale, he sought to inspire his troops by appealing to their honor, their vanity, and their love of France.

In 1796, Napoleon, then a young officer, was given command of the French army in Italy. In the Italian campaign, he demonstrated a genius for propaganda and psychological warfare, as the following proclamations to his troops indicate.

LEADER AND GENERAL

March 27, 1796

Soldiers, you are naked, ill fed! The Government owes you much; it can give you nothing. Your patience, the courage you display in the midst of these rocks, are admirable; but they procure you no glory, no fame is reflected upon you. I seek to lead you into the most fertile plains in the world. Rich provinces, great cities will be in your power. There you will find honor, glory, and riches. Soldiers of Italy, would you be lacking in courage or constancy?

April 26, 1796

Soldiers:

In a fortnight you have won six victories, taken twenty-one [flags], fifty-five pieces of artil-

lery, several strong positions, and conquered the richest part of Piedmont [a region in northern Italy]; you have captured 15,000 prisoners and killed or wounded more than 10,000 men. . . .

. . . You have won battles without cannon, crossed rivers without bridges, made forced marches without shoes, camped without brandy and often without bread. Soldiers of liberty, only republican phalanxes [infantry troops] could have endured what you have endured. Soldiers, you have our thanks! The grateful *Patrie* [nation] will owe its prosperity to you. . . .

The two armies which but recently attacked you with audacity are fleeing before you in terror; the wicked men who laughed at your misery and rejoiced at the thought of the triumphs of your enemies are confounded and trembling.

But, soldiers, as yet you have done nothing compared with what remains to be done. . . .

. . . Undoubtedly the greatest obstacles have been overcome; but you still have battles to fight, cities to capture, rivers to cross. Is there one among you whose courage is abating? . . . No. . . . All of you are consumed with a desire to

Diary passages from *The Corsican: A Diary of Napoleon's Life in His Own Words,* ed. R. M. Johnson (Boston and New York: Houghton Mifflin, The Riverside Press, Cambridge, 1910), pp. 140–143, 145, 166, 189, 322.

extend the glory of the French people; all of you long to humiliate those arrogant kings who dare to contemplate placing us in fetters; all of you desire to dictate a glorious peace, one which will indemnify the *Patrie* for the immense sacrifices it has made; all of you wish to be able to say with pride as you return to your villages, "I was with the victorious army of Italy!"

Friends, I promise you this conquest; but there is one condition you must swear to fulfill—to respect the people whom you liberate, to repress the horrible pillaging committed by scoundrels incited by our enemies. Otherwise you would not be the liberators of the people; you would be their scourge. . . . Plunderers will be shot without mercy; already, several have been. . . .

Peoples of Italy, the French army comes to break your chains; the French people is the friend of all peoples; approach it with confidence; your property, your religion, and your customs will be respected.

We are waging war as generous enemies, and we wish only to crush the tyrants who enslave you.

The following passages from Napoleon's diary shed light on his generalship, ambition, and leadership qualities.

1800

What a thing is imagination! Here are men who don't know me, who have never seen me, but who only knew of me, and they are moved by my presence, they would do anything for me! And this same incident arises in all centuries and in all countries! Such is fanaticism! Yes, imagination rules the world. The defect of our modern institutions is that they do not speak to the imagination. By that alone can man be governed; without it he is but a brute.

1800

The impact of an army, like the total of mechanical coefficients, is equal to the mass multiplied by the velocity.

A battle is a dramatic action which has its beginning, its middle, and its conclusion. The result of a battle depends on the instantaneous flash of an idea. When you are about to give battle concentrate all your strength, neglect nothing; a battalion often decides the day.

In warfare every opportunity must be seized; for fortune is a woman: if you miss her today, you need not expect to find her tomorrow.

There is nothing in the military profession I cannot do for myself. If there is no one to make gunpowder, I know how to make it; gun carriages, I know how to construct them; if it is founding a cannon, I know that; or if the details of tactics must be taught, I can teach them.

The presence of a general is necessary: he is the head, he is the all in all of an army. It was not the Roman army that conquered Gaul, but Cæsar; it was not the Carthaginians that made the armies of the Republic tremble at the very gates of Rome, but Hannibal; it was not the Macedonian army that marched to the Indus [River], but Alexander; . . . it was not the Prussian army that defended Prussia during seven years against the three strongest Powers of Europe, but Frederick the Great.

Concentration of forces, activity, activity with the firm resolve to die gloriously: these are the three great principles of the military art that have always made fortune favourable in all my operations. Death is nothing; but to live defeated and ingloriously, is to die every day.

I am a soldier, because that is the special faculty I was born with; that is my life, my habit. I have commanded wherever I have been. I commanded, when twenty-three years old, at the siege of Toulon; . . . I carried the soldiers of the army of Italy with me as soon as I appeared among them; I was born that way. . . .

It was by becoming a Catholic that I pacified the Vendée [region in western France], and a [Muslim] that I established myself in Egypt;

it was by becoming ultramontane[1] that I won over public opinion in Italy. If I ruled a people of Jews, I would rebuild the temple of Solomon!

1802

My power proceeds from my reputation, and my reputation from the victories I have won. My power would fall if I were not to support it with more glory and more victories. Conquest has made me what I am; only conquest can maintain me. . . .

1804

My mistress is power; I have done too much to conquer her to let her be snatched away from me. Although it may be said that power came to me of its own accord, yet I know what labour, what sleepless nights, what scheming, it has involved. . . .

1809

Again I repeat that in war morale and opinion are half the battle. The art of the great captain has always been to make his troops appear very numerous to the enemy, and the enemy's very few to his own. So that today, in spite of the long time we have spent in Germany, the enemy do not know my real strength. We are constantly striving to magnify our numbers. Far from confessing that I had only 100,000 men at Wagram [French victory over Austria in 1809] I am constantly suggesting that I had 220,000. In my Italian campaigns, in which I had only a handful of troops, I always exaggerated my numbers. It served my purpose, and has not lessened my glory. My generals and practised soldiers could always perceive, after the event, all the skilfulness of my operations, even that of having exaggerated the numbers of my troops.

In several ways, Napoleon anticipated the strategies of twentieth-century dictators. He concentrated power in his own hands, suppressed opposition, and sought to mold public opinion by controlling the press and education. The following Imperial Catechism of 1806, which schoolchildren were required to memorize and recite, is a pointed example of Napoleonic indoctrination.

TYRANT

Lesson VII. Continuation of the Fourth Commandment.

Q. What are the duties of Christians with respect to the princes who govern them, and what in particular are our duties towards Napoleon I, our Emperor?

A. Christians owe to the princes who govern them, and we owe in particular to Napoleon I, our Emperor, *love, respect, obedience, fidelity, military service* and the tributes laid for the preservation and defence of the Empire and of his throne; we also owe to him fervent prayers for his safety and the spiritual and temporal prosperity of the state.

Q. Why are we bound to all these duties towards our Emperor?

A. First of all, because God, who creates empires and distributes them according to His will, in loading our Emperor with gifts, both in peace and in war, has established him as our sovereign and has made him the minister of His power and His image upon the earth. *To honor and to serve our Emperor is then to honor and to serve God himself.* Secondly, because our Lord Jesus Christ by His doctrine as well as by His example, has Himself taught us what we owe to our sovereign: He was born the subject of Caesar Augustus;[2] He paid the prescribed [tax]; and just as He ordered to

---

[1]Favoring the pope over competing authorities.—Eds.

Frank Malloy Anderson, ed., *The Constitutions and Other Select Documents Illustrative of the History of France, 1789–1907* (Minneapolis: H. W. Wilson, 1908), pp. 312–313.

[2]Caesar Augustus (27 B.C.–A.D. 14) was the Roman emperor at the time that Jesus was born.—Eds.

render to God that which belongs to God, so He ordered to render to Caesar that which belongs to Caesar.

Q. Are there not particular reasons which ought to attach us more strongly to Napoleon I, our Emperor?

A. Yes; for it is he whom God has raised up under difficult circumstances to re-establish the public worship of the holy religion of our fathers and to be the protector of it. He has restored and preserved public order by his profound and active wisdom; he defends the state by his powerful arm; he has become the anointed of the Lord through the consecration which he received from the sovereign pontiff, head of the universal church.

Q. What ought to be thought of those who may be lacking in their duty towards our Emperor?

A. According to the apostle Saint Paul, they would be resisting the order established by God himself and would render themselves *worthy of eternal damnation.*

Q. Will the duties which are required of us towards our Emperor be equally binding with respect to his lawful successors in the order established by the constitutions of the Empire?

A. Yes, without doubt; for we read in the holy scriptures, that God, Lord of heaven and earth, by an order of His supreme will and through His providence, gives empires not only to one person in particular, but also to his family.

In the following letter (April 22, 1805) to Joseph Fouché, minister of police, Napoleon reveals his intention to regulate public opinion.

Repress the journals a little; make them produce wholesome articles. I want you to write to the editors of the . . . newspapers that are most widely read in order to let them know that the time is not far away when, seeing that they are no longer of service to me, I shall suppress them

along with all the others. . . . Tell them that the . . . Revolution is over, and that there is now only one party in France; that I shall never allow the newspapers to say anything contrary to my interests; that they may publish a few little articles with just a bit of poison in them, but that one fine day somebody will shut their mouths.

With varying degrees of success, Napoleon's administrators in conquered lands provided positions based on talent, equalized taxes, and abolished serfdom and the courts of the nobility. They promoted freedom of religion, fought clerical interference with secular authority, and promoted secular education. By undermining the power of European clergy and aristocrats, Napoleon weakened the Old Regime irreparably in much of Europe. A letter from Napoleon to his brother Jérôme, king of Westphalia, illustrates Napoleon's desire for enlightened rule.

REFORMER

Fontainebleau, November 15, 1807
To Jérôme Napoléon, King of Westphalia

I enclose the Constitution for your Kingdom. It embodies the conditions on which I renounce all my rights of conquest, and all the claims I have acquired over your state. You must faithfully observe it. I am concerned for the happiness of your subjects, not only as it affects your reputation, and my own, but also for its influence on the whole European situation. Don't listen to those who say that your subjects are so accustomed to slavery that they will feel no gratitude for the benefits you give them. There is more intelligence in the Kingdom of Westphalia than they would have you believe; and your throne will never be firmly established except upon the trust and affection of the common people. What German opinion impatiently demands is that men of no rank, but of marked ability, shall

---

David L. Dowd, *Napoleon: Was He the Heir of the Revolution?* (New York: Holt, Rinehart and Winston, 1966), p. 41.

Letters of Napoleon, trans. and ed. J. M. Thompson (Oxford: Basil Blackwell, 1934), pp. 207–208.

have an equal claim upon your favour and your employment, and that every trace of serfdom, or of a feudal hierarchy between the sovereign and the lowest class of his subjects, shall be done away. The benefits of the Code Napoléon [legal code introduced by Napoleon], public trial, and the introduction of juries, will be the leading features of your government. And to tell you the truth, I count more upon their effects, for the extension and consolidation of your rule, than upon the most resounding victories. I want your subjects to enjoy a degree of liberty, equality, and prosperity hitherto unknown to the German people. I want this liberal regime to produce, one way or another, changes which will be of the utmost benefit to the system of the Confederation, and to the strength of your monarchy.

Such a method of government will be a stronger barrier between you and Prussia than the Elbe [River], the fortresses, and the protection of France. What people will want to return under the arbitrary Prussian rule, once it has tasted the benefits of a wise and liberal administration? In Germany, as in France, Italy, and Spain, people long for equality and liberalism. I have been managing the affairs of Europe long enough now to know that the burden of the privileged classes was resented everywhere. Rule constitutionally. Even if reason, and the enlightenment of the age, were not sufficient cause, it would be good policy for one in your position; and you will find that the backing of public opinion gives you a great natural advantage over the absolute Kings who are your neighbours.

Madame de Staël
CRITIC OF NAPOLEON

While large numbers of the French were enthralled by Napoleon's military exploits and welcomed his rule, some were repelled by his tyrannical policies and actions. One of his severest critics was Madame de Staël (1766–1817), a prominent French intellectual. A political moderate, de Staël advocated both political liberty and intellectual freedom. Refusing to support Napoleon's one-man rule, she angered the tyrant who, in 1804, banished her from Paris and later from all of France. During her years in exile, primarily in Switzerland, Madame de Staël wrote extensively on politics and literature.

Following is an excerpt from *Consideration on the Principal Events of the French Revolution*, published posthumously in 1818. The selection focuses on Napoleon's tyrannical ways in his early years as First Consul.

General Bonaparte decreed a constitution in which there were no safeguards. Besides, he took great care to leave in existence the laws announced during the Revolution, in order to select from this detestable arsenal the weapon that suited him. The special commissions, deportations, exiles, the bondage of the press—these steps unfortunately taken in the name of liberty— were very useful to tyranny. To adopt them, he sometimes advanced reasons of state, sometimes the need of the times, sometimes the acts of his

---

Madame de staël on Politics, Literature and National Character, trans. and ed. morroe berger (Garden City, New York: Doubleday & Company, Inc., 1965), pp. 93–96.

opponents, sometimes the need to maintain tranquillity. Such is the artillery of phrases that supports absolute power, for "emergencies" never end, and the more one seeks to repress by illegal measures the more one creates disaffected people who justify new injustices. The establishment of the rule of law is always put off till tomorrow. . . .

The many newspapers in France were soon subjected to the most rigorous but cleverly devised censorship. . . . So Bonaparte established that prattling tyranny from which he later derived so much benefit. All the press repeated the same thing each day, without any one being allowed to contradict them. Just as regular troops are a greater threat than militias to the independence of nations, so hired writers make public opinion much more depraved than it would be if people communicated only by speech and thus based their judgments only upon facts. . . .

Among all the prerogatives of authority, one of the most favorable to tyranny is the power to exile without trial. The *lettres de cachet* of the Old Regime have been justly advanced as one of the most urgent grounds for making a revolution in France. But it was Bonaparte, the people's choice, who, trampling under foot all the principles for which the people had risen up, arrogated the power to exile anyone who displeased him a little and to imprison, without any meddling from the courts, anyone who displeased him more. I can understand, I admit, how most of the former courtiers [aristocrats] rallied to Bonaparte's political system. They needed to make only one concession to it: to change masters. But the republicans, who must have been shocked by every word, every act, every decree, of Napoleon's regime—how could they lend themselves to his tyranny?

REVIEW QUESTIONS

1. In his proclamations how did Napoleon Bonaparte try to raise the morale of his troops?
2. How did Napoleon use propaganda to achieve his goals?
3. For what purpose was religious authority cited in the catechism of 1806? What would Machiavelli (see chapter 1) have thought of this device?
4. How seriously did Napoleon adhere to the ideals of the Enlightenment and French Revolution? Show how Napoleon spread the reforms of the French Revolution.
5. In her critique of Napoleon, Madame de Staël demonstrates an astute awareness of politics and human nature. Discuss this statement.

CHAPTER 5
The Industrial Revolution

LAMBETH GASWORKS, by Gustave Doré, 1872. This engraving, from Blanchard Jerold and Doré's *London: A Pilgrimage* (1872), shows the harsh conditions within industry during the latter half of the nineteenth century. At the time of this scene, most of the lighting in major cities like London was provided by gas. (*Central Saint Martins College of Art and Design, London/Bridgeman Images*)

In the last part of the eighteenth century, as a revolution for liberty and equality swept across France and sent shock waves across Europe, a different kind of revolution, a revolution in industry, was transforming life in Great Britain. In the nineteenth century, the Industrial Revolution spread to the United States and to the European continent. Today, it encompasses virtually the entire world; everywhere the drive to substitute technology for human labor continues at a rapid pace.

After 1760, dramatic changes occurred in Britain in the way goods were produced and labor organized. New forms of power, particularly steam, replaced animal strength and human muscle. Better ways of obtaining and using raw materials were discovered, and a new form of organizing production and workers—the factory—came into common use. In the nineteenth century, technology moved from triumph to triumph with, at the time, a momentum unprecedented in human history. The resulting explosion in economic production and productivity transformed society.

Rapid industrialization caused hardships for the new class of industrial workers, many of them recent arrivals from the countryside. Arduous and monotonous, factory labor was geared to the strict discipline of the clock, the machine, and the production schedule. Employment was never secure. Sick workers received no pay and were often fired; aged workers suffered pay cuts or lost their jobs. During business slumps, employers lowered wages with impunity, and laid-off workers had nowhere to turn for assistance. Because factory owners did not consider safety an important concern, accidents were frequent. Yet the Industrial Revolution was also a great force for human betterment. Ultimately it raised the standard of living, even for the lowest classes, lengthened life expectancy, and provided more leisure time and more possibilities for people to fulfill their potential.

The Industrial Revolution dramatically altered political and social life at all levels, but especially for the middle class, whose engagement in capitalist ventures brought greater political power and social recognition. During the course of the nineteenth century, the bourgeoisie came to hold many of the highest offices in Western European states, continuing a trend that had been fostered by the French Revolution.

Cities grew in size, number, and importance. Municipal authorities were unable to cope with the rapid pace of urbanization, and without adequate housing, sanitation, or recreational facilities, the exploding urban centers became another source of working-class misery. In pre-industrial Britain, most people had lived in small villages. They knew where their roots were; relatives, friends, and the village church gave them a sense of belonging. The industrial centers separated people from nature and from their places of origin, shattering traditional ways of life that had given men and women a sense of security.

The plight of the working class created a demand for reform, but the British government, committed to *laissez-faire* economic principles that militated against state involvement, was slow to act. In the last part of the nineteenth century, however, the development of labor unions, the rising political voice of the working class, and the growing recognition that the problems created by industrialization required government intervention speeded up the pace of reform. Rejecting the road of reform, Karl Marx (see chapter 7) called for a working-class revolution that would destroy the capitalist system.

1 Early Industrialization

Several factors help to explain why the Industrial Revolution began in Great Britain. That country had an abundant labor supply, large deposits of coal and iron ore, and capital available for investing in new industries. A large domestic middle class and overseas colonies provided markets for manufactured goods. Colonies were also a source for raw materials, particularly cotton for the textile industry. The Scientific Revolution and an enthusiasm for engineering fostered a spirit of curiosity and inventiveness. Britain had enterprising and daring entrepreneurs who organized new businesses and discovered new methods of production.

Edward Baines
BRITAIN'S INDUSTRIAL ADVANTAGES AND THE FACTORY SYSTEM

In 1835, Edward Baines (1800–1890), an early student of industrialization, wrote *The History of the Cotton Manufacture in Great Britain*—about one of the leading industries in the early days of the Industrial Revolution. In the passages that follow, Baines discusses the reasons for Britain's industrial transformation and the advantages of the factory system.

Three things may be regarded as of primary importance for the successful prosecution of manufactures, namely, water-power, fuel, and iron. Wherever these exist in combination, and where they are abundant and cheap, machinery may be manufactured and put in motion at small cost; and most of the processes of making and finishing cloth, whether chemical or mechanical, depending, as they do, mainly on the two great agents of water and heat, may likewise be performed with advantage.

Edward Baines, *The History of the Cotton Manufacture in Great Britain* (London: Fisher and Jackson, 1835), pp. 84–89.

. . . A great number of streams . . . furnish water-power adequate to turn many hundred mills: they afford the element of water, indispensable for scouring, bleaching, printing, dyeing, and other processes of manufacture: and when collected in their larger channels, or employed to feed canals, they supply a superior inland navigation, so important for the transit of raw materials and merchandise.

Not less important for manufactures than the copious supply of good water, is the great abundance of coal. . . . This mineral fuel animates the thousand arms of the steam-engine, and furnishes the most powerful agent in all chemical and mechanical operations.

In mentioning the advantages which Lancashire [the major cotton manufacturing area] possesses as a seat of manufactures, we must not omit its ready communication with the sea by means of its well-situated port, Liverpool, through the medium of which it receives, from Ireland, a large proportion of the food that supports its population, and whose commerce brings from distant shores the raw materials of its manufactures, and again distributes them, converted into useful and elegant clothing, amongst all the nations of the earth. Through the same means a plentiful supply of timber is obtained, so needful for building purposes.

To the above natural advantages, we must add, the acquired advantage of a canal communication, which ramifies itself through all the populous parts of this country, and connects it with the inland counties, the seats of other flourishing manufactures, and the sources whence iron, lime, salt, stone, and other articles in which Lancashire is deficient, are obtained. By this means Lancashire, being already possessed of the primary requisites for manufactures, is enabled, at a very small expense, to command things of secondary importance, and to appropriate to its use the natural advantages of the whole kingdom. The canals, having been accomplished by individual enterprise, not by national funds, were constructed to supply a want already existing: they were not, therefore,

original sources of the manufactures, but have extended together with them, and are to be considered as having essentially aided and accelerated that prosperity from whose beginnings they themselves arose. The recent introduction of railways will have a great effect in making the operations of trade more intensely active, and perfecting the division of labour, already carried to so high a point. By the railway and the locomotive engine, the extremities of the land will, for every beneficial purpose, be united.

In comparing the advantages of England for manufactures with those of other countries, we can by no means overlook the excellent commercial position of the country—intermediate between the north and south of Europe; and its insular situation, which, combined with the command of the seas, secures our territory from invasion or annoyance. The German ocean, the Baltic, and the Mediterranean are the regular highways for our ships; and our western ports command an unobstructed passage to the Atlantic, and to every quarter of the world.

A temperate climate, and a hardy race of men, have also greatly contributed to promote the manufacturing industry of England.

The political and moral advantages of this country, as a seat of manufactures, are not less remarkable than its physical advantages. The arts are the daughters of peace and liberty. In no country have these blessings been enjoyed in so high a degree, or for so long a continuance, as in England. Under the reign of just laws, personal liberty and property have been secure; mercantile enterprise has been allowed to reap its reward; capital has accumulated in safety; the workman has "gone forth to his work and to his labour until the evening;" and, thus protected and favoured, the manufacturing prosperity of the country has struck its roots deep, and spread forth its branches to the ends of the earth.

England has also gained by the calamities of other countries, and the intolerance of other governments. At different periods, the Flemish and French protestants, expelled from their native lands, have taken refuge in England, and have

Was a Religion Still.
Protestants = more progressive?

repaid the protection given them by practising and teaching branches of industry, in which the English were then less expert than their neighbours. The wars which have at different times desolated the rest of Europe, and especially those which followed the French revolution, (when mechanical invention was producing the most wonderful effects in England) checked the progress of manufacturing improvement on the continent, and left England for many years without a competitor. At the same time, the English navy held the sovereignty of the ocean, and under its protection the commerce of this country extended beyond all former bounds, and established a firm connexion between the manufacturers of Lancashire and their customers in the most distant lands.

When the natural, political, and [external] causes, thus enumerated, are viewed together, it cannot be [a] matter of surprise that England has obtained a preeminence over the rest of the world in manufactures.

A crucial feature of the Industrial Revolution was a new production system—the making of goods in factories. By bringing all the operations of manufacturing under one roof, industrialists made the process of production more efficient. Baines describes the factory system's advantages over former methods.

. . . Hitherto the cotton manufacture had been carried on almost entirely in the houses of the workmen: the hand or stock cards,[1] the spinning wheel, and the loom required no larger apartment than that of a cottage. A spinning jenny[2] of small size might also be used in a cottage, and in many instances was so used: when the number of spindles was considerably increased, adjacent work-shops were used. But

---

[1]Prior to spinning, raw fibers had to be carded with a brushlike tool that cleaned and separated them.—Eds.
[2]The spinning jenny, which was hand-powered, was the first machine that spun fiber onto multiple spindles at the same time; that is, it produced more thread or yarn in less time than the single-thread spinning wheel.—Eds.

the water-frame, the carding engine, and the other machines which [Richard] Arkwright brought out in a finished state, required both more space than could be found in a cottage, and more power than could be applied by the human arm. Their weight also rendered it necessary to place them in strongly-built mills, and they could not be advantageously turned by any power then known but that of water.

The use of machinery was accompanied by a greater division of labour than existed in the primitive state of the manufacture; the material went through many more processes; and of course the loss of time and the risk of waste would have been much increased, if its removal from house to house at every stage of the manufacture had been necessary. It became obvious that there were several important advantages in carrying on the numerous operations of an extensive manufacture in the same building. Where water power was required, it was economical to build one mill, and put up one water-wheel, rather than several. This arrangement also enabled the master spinner himself to superintend every stage of the manufacture: it gave him a greater security against the wasteful or fraudulent consumption of the material: it saved time in the transference of the work from hand to hand: and it prevented the extreme inconvenience which would have resulted from the failure of one class of workmen to perform their part, when several other classes of workmen were dependent upon them. Another circumstance which made it advantageous to have a large number of machines in one manufactory was, that mechanics must be employed on the spot, to construct and repair the machinery, and that their time could not be fully occupied with only a few machines.

All these considerations drove the cotton spinners to that important change in the economy of English manufactures, the introduction of the factory system; and when that system had once been adopted, such were its pecuniary advantages, that mercantile competition would have rendered it impossible, even had it been desirable, to abandon it.

Adam Smith
THE DIVISION OF LABOR

Baines's emphasis on the division of labor in the expanding use of machinery can be traced to Adam Smith, who in the eighteenth century pioneered the study of economics. Adam Smith (1723–1790) was a bright and thoughtful academic who had attended Glasgow University in his native Scotland and then Oxford University in England before being appointed professor of logic at Glasgow at age twenty-eight and professor of moral philosophy a year later. After some years of travel on the Continent, Smith wrote over a span of years his masterpiece, *An Inquiry into the Nature and Causes of the Wealth of Nations*. This work (see also next section), published in 1776, made him instantly famous. He began *The Wealth of Nations* by analyzing the benefits of the division of labor—the system in which each worker performs a single set task or a single step in the manufacturing process.

The greatest improvement in the productive powers of Labour, and the greater skill, dexterity, and judgment with which it is anywhere directed, or applied, seem to have been the effects of the division of labour. . . .

This great increase of the quantity of work, which, in consequence of the division of labour, the same number of people are capable of performing, is owing to three different circumstances; first, to the increase of dexterity in every particular workman; secondly, to the saving of the time which is commonly lost in passing from one species of work to another; and lastly, to the invention of a great number of machines which facilitate and abridge labour, and enable one man to do the work of many. . . .

To take an example, therefore, from a very trifling manufacture; but one in which the division of labour has been very often taken notice of, the trade of the pin-maker; a workman not educated to this business (which the division of labour has rendered a distinct trade), nor acquainted with the use of the machinery

employed in it (to the invention of which the same division of labour has probably given occasion), could scarce, perhaps, with his utmost industry, make one pin in a day, and certainly could not make twenty. But in the way in which this business is now carried on, not only the whole work is a peculiar trade, but it is divided into a number of branches, of which the greater part are likewise peculiar trades. One man draws out the wire, another straightens it, a third cuts it, a fourth points it, a fifth grinds it at the top for receiving the head: to make the head requires two or three distinct operations; to put it on is a peculiar business; to whiten the pins is another; it is even a trade by itself to put them into the paper; and the important business of making a pin is, in this manner, divided into about eighteen distinct operations, which, in some manufactories, are all performed by distinct hands, though in others the same man will sometimes perform two or three of them. I have seen a small manufactory of this kind where ten men only were employed, and where some of them consequently performed two or three distinct operations. But though they were very poor [craftsmen], and therefore but indifferently accommodated with the necessary

---

Adam Smith, *An Inquiry into the Nature and Causes of the Wealth of Nations*, ed. J. R. McCulloch (London: Ward and Lock, 1813), pp. 19, 20, 22.

machinery, they could, when they exerted themselves, make among them about twelve pounds of pins in a day. There are in a pound upwards of four thousand pins of a middling size. Those ten persons, therefore, could make among them upwards of forty-eight thousand pins in a day. Each person, therefore, making a tenth part of forty-eight thousand pins, might be considered as making four thousand eight hundred pins in a day. But if they had all wrought separately and independently, and without any of them having been educated to this peculiar business, they certainly could not each of them have made twenty, perhaps not one pin in a day; that is, certainly, not the two hundred and fortieth, perhaps not the four thousand eight hundredth part of what they are at present capable of performing, in consequence of a proper division and combination of their different operations. . . .

REVIEW QUESTIONS

1. Apart from its natural resources, what other assets for industrial development did England possess?
2. What were the factory system's advantages over the domestic system of production?
3. How, according to Adam Smith, did the division of labor lead to increased productivity?

2 The New Science of Political Economy

The new spirit of scientific inquiry manifest in the seventeenth and eighteenth centuries extended also into the economic field, creating the new science of political economy. Its pioneer was Adam Smith, author of the classic book *The Wealth of Nations* (see also previous section). Smith was an optimist, in favor of leaving individuals' economic activities to their own devices. For that reason he condemned government interference in the economy—so common in his day under the protectionist government's mercantilism policy, which sought to increase the nation's wealth by expanding exports while minimizing imports. The "invisible hand," which according to Smith turned individual gain into social advantage, also favored free trade among nations, based on an international division of labor.

Adam Smith's optimistic assumptions were soon called into question by Thomas Robert Malthus (1766–1834). A Church of England clergyman and professor of history and political economy at a small college run by the East India Company, Malthus gave the study of political economy not only a moral but also a pessimistic twist, for he stressed the immutable poverty of nations. He contributed two books to the science of political economy. The first, *An Essay on the Principle of Population, as It Affects the Future Improvement of Society*, was published in 1798. It was followed in 1803 by a second and enlarged edition entitled *An Essay on the Principle of Population, or, a View of Its Past and Present Effects on Human Happiness.* In these works Malthus argued that population growth was the true reason for the misery of the poor.

Adam Smith
AGAINST GOVERNMENT INTERVENTION IN THE ECONOMY

The Wealth of Nations carries the important message of *laissez-faire*, which means that the government should intervene as little as possible in economic affairs and leave the market to its own devices. It advocates the liberation of economic production from all limiting regulation in order to benefit "the people and the sovereign," not only in Great Britain but also in the community of countries. Admittedly, in his advocacy of free trade Smith made allowance for the national interest, justifying "certain public works and certain public institutions," including the government and the state. He defended, for instance, the Navigation Acts, which stipulated that goods brought from its overseas colonies into England be carried in British ships. Neither did he want to ruin established industries by introducing free trade too suddenly. Adam Smith was an eighteenth-century cosmopolitan who viewed political economy as an international system. His preference was clearly for economic cooperation among nations as a source of peace. In the passage that follows, Smith argues that economic activity unrestricted by government best serves the individual and society.

Every individual is continually exerting himself to find out the most advantageous employment for whatever capital he can command. It is his own advantage, indeed, and not that of the society, which he has in view. But the study of his own advantage, naturally, or rather necessarily, leads him to prefer that employment which is most advantageous to the society. . . .

. . . As every individual, therefore, endeavours as much as he can both to employ his capital in the support of domestic industry, and so to direct that industry that its produce may be of the greatest value, every individual necessarily labours to render the annual revenue of the society as great as he can. He generally, indeed, neither intends to promote the public interest, nor knows how much he is promoting it. By preferring the support of domestic to that of foreign industry, he intends only his own security; and by directing that industry in such a manner as its produce may be of the greatest value, he intends only his own gain, and he is in this, as in many other cases, led by an invisible hand to promote an end which was no part of his intention. Nor is it always the worse for the society that it was no part of it. By pursuing his own interest he frequently promotes that of the society more effectually than when he really intends to promote it. I have never known much good done by those who affected to trade for the public good. . . .

. . . The statesman who should attempt to direct private people in what manner they ought to employ their capitals, would not only load himself with a most unnecessary attention, but assume an authority which could safely be trusted, not only to no single person, but to no council or senate whatever, and which would nowhere be so dangerous as in the hands of a man who had folly and presumption enough to fancy himself fit to exercise it. . . .

Adam Smith, *An Inquiry into the Nature and Causes of the Wealth of Nations,* ed. J. R. McCulloch (London: Ward and Lock, 1813), pp. 352, 354, 544–545.

It is thus that every system which endeavours, either by extraordinary encouragements to draw towards a particular species of industry a greater share of the capital of the society than would naturally go to it, or, by extraordinary restraints, force from a particular species of industry some share of the capital which would otherwise be employed in it, is in reality subversive to the great purpose which it means to promote. It retards, instead of accelerating, the progress of the society towards real wealth and greatness; and diminishes, instead of increasing, the real value of the annual produce of its land and labour.

All systems either of preference or of restraint, therefore, being thus completely taken away, the obvious and simple system of natural liberty establishes itself of its own accord. Every man, as long as he does not violate the laws of justice, is left perfectly free to pursue his own interest his own way, and to bring both his industry and capital into competition with those of any other man, or order of men. The sovereign is completely discharged from a duty, in the attempting to perform which he must always be exposed to innumerable delusions, and for the proper performance of which no human wisdom or knowledge could ever be sufficient: the duty of superintending the industry of private people, and of directing it towards the employments most suitable to the interest of the society. According to the system of natural liberty, the sovereign has only three duties to attend to; three duties of great importance, indeed, but plain and intelligible to common understandings: first, the duty of protecting the society from the violence and invasion of other independent societies; secondly, the duty of protecting, as far as possible, every member of the society from the injustice or oppression of every other member of it, or the duty of establishing an exact administration of justice; and, thirdly, the duty of erecting and maintaining certain public works and certain public institutions which it can never be for the interest of any individual, or small number of individuals, to erect and maintain; because the profit could never repay the expense to any individual or small number of individuals, though it may frequently do much more than repay it to a great society.

Why should the sovereign not interfere?

Thomas R. Malthus
ON THE PRINCIPLE OF POPULATION

Malthus assumed that population tended forever to outgrow the resources needed to sustain it. The balance between population and its life-sustaining resources was elementally maintained, he gloomily argued, by famine, war, and other fatal calamities. As a clergyman, he believed in sexual abstinence as the means of limiting population growth. He also saw little need to better the condition of the poor, whom he considered the most licentious part of the population, because he believed that they would then breed faster and, by upsetting the population/ resource balance, bring misery to all. This view—that poverty was an iron law of nature—buttressed supporters of strict *laissez-faire* who opposed government action to aid the poor.

POPULATION'S EFFECTS ON SOCIETY

I have read some of the speculations on the perfectibility of man and of society with great pleasure. I have been warmed and delighted with the enchanting picture which they hold forth. I ardently wish for such happy improvements. But I see great and, to my understanding, unconquerable difficulties in the way to them. These difficulties it is my present purpose to state, declaring, at the same time, that so far from exulting in them, as a cause of triumphing over the friends of innovation, nothing would give me greater pleasure than to see them completely removed. . . .

[These difficulties are]

First, That food is necessary to the existence of man.

Secondly, That the passion between the sexes is necessary and will remain nearly in its present state.

These two laws, ever since we have had any knowledge of mankind, appear to have been fixed laws of our nature; and as we have not hitherto seen any alteration in them, we have no right to conclude that they will ever cease to be what they are now, without an immediate act of power in that Being who first arranged the system of the universe, and for the advantage of His creatures, still executes, according to fixed laws, all its various operations. . . .

Assuming, then, my postulata as granted, I say that the power of population is indefinitely greater than the power in the earth to produce subsistence for man.

Population, when unchecked, increases in a geometrical ratio. Subsistence only increases in an arithmetical ratio. A slight acquaintance with numbers will show the immensity of the first power in comparison of the second.

By that law of our nature which makes food necessary to the life of man, the effects of these two unequal powers must be kept equal.

This implies a strong and constantly operating check on population from the difficulty of subsistence. This difficulty must fall somewhere and must necessarily be severely felt by a large portion of mankind. . . .

This natural inequality of the two powers of population and of production in the earth, and that great law of our nature which must constantly keep their efforts equal, form the great difficulty that to me appears insurmountable in the way to perfectibility of society. . . .

Consequently, if the premises are just, the argument is conclusive against the perfectibility of the mass of mankind.

POPULATION'S EFFECTS ON HUMAN HAPPINESS

The ultimate check to population appears then to be a want of food, arising necessarily from the different ratios according to which population and food increase. But this ultimate check is never the immediate check, except in cases of actual famine.

The immediate check may be stated to consist in all those customs, and all those diseases, which seem to be generated by a scarcity of the means of subsistence; and all those causes, independent of this scarcity, which tend prematurely to weaken and destroy the human frame.

These checks to population, which are constantly operating with more or less force in every society, and keep down the number to the level of the means of subsistence, may be classed under two general heads—the preventive and the positive checks.

Thomas Robert Malthus, *First Essay on Population* (1789; reprinted for the Royal Economic Society, London: Macmillan & Co. Ltd., 1926), pp. 7, 11–14, 16–17.

This and subsequent excerpt are from Thomas Robert Malthus, *An Essay on the Principles of Population, or, a View of Its Past and Present Effects on Human Happiness,* 7th ed. (1798; London: Reeves and Turner, 1872), pp. 6–8.

The preventive check, as far as it is voluntary, is peculiar to man, and arises from that distinctive superiority in his reasoning faculties which enables him to calculate distant consequences. Man cannot look around him and see the distress which frequently presses upon those who have large families; he cannot contemplate his present possessions or earnings which he now nearly consumes himself, and calculate the amount of each share, when with a little addition they must be divided, perhaps, among seven or eight, without feeling a doubt whether, if he follow the bent of his inclinations, he may be able to support the offspring which he will probably bring into the world. . . .

The conditions are calculated to prevent, and certainly do prevent, a great number of persons in all civilized nations from pursuing the dictate of nature in an early attachment to one woman. . . .

The positive checks to population are extremely various, and include every cause, whether arising from vice or misery, which in any degree contributes to shorten the natural duration of human life. Under this head, therefore, may be enumerated all unwholesome occupations, severe labor and exposure to the seasons, extreme poverty, bad nursing of children, great towns, excesses of all kinds, the whole train of common diseases and epidemics, wars, plague, and famine. . . .

POPULATION AND POVERTY

Almost everything that has been hitherto done for the poor, has tended, as if with solicitous care, to throw a veil of obscurity over this subject and to hide from them the true cause of their poverty. When the wages of labour are hardly sufficient to maintain two children, a man marries and has five or six. He of course finds himself miserably distressed. . . . He accuses his parish. . . . He accuses the avarice of the rich. . . . He accuses the partial and unjust institutions of society. . . . In searching for objects of accusation, he never [alludes] to the quarter from which all his misfortunes originate. The last person that he would think of accusing is himself. . . .

We cannot justly accuse them [the common people] of improvidence [thriftlessness] and want of industry, till . . . after it has been brought home to their comprehensions, that they are themselves the cause of their own poverty; that the means of redress are in their own hands, and in the hands of no other persons whatever; that the society in which they live and the government which presides over it, are totally without power in this respect; and however ardently they [government] may desire to relieve them, and whatever attempts they may make to do so, they are really and truly unable to execute what they benevolently wish, but unjustly promise.

REVIEW QUESTIONS

1. What did Adam Smith say were the results of a *laissez-faire* policy?
2. What, according to Smith, were the duties of the sovereign under the system of natural liberty? Do you think there are other duties that should be added?
3. What are the "fixed laws" of human nature according to Thomas Malthus? For Malthus, how did the power of population growth compare with that of the means to increase food?
4. What distinction did Malthus draw between preventive and positive checks to population growth?
5. Why is Malthus considered to have been a pessimist?
6. Do any of Malthus's arguments apply to our world today?

3   The Dark Side of Industrialization

Among the numerous problems caused by rapid industrialization, none aroused greater concern among humanitarians than child labor in factories and mines. In preindustrial times, children had always been part of the labor force, indoors and out, a practice that was continued during the early days of the Industrial Revolution. In the cotton industry, for instance, the proportion of children and adolescents under eighteen was around 40–45 percent of the labor force; in some large firms the proportion was even greater. Employers discovered early that youngsters adapted more easily to machines and factory discipline than did adults, who were used to traditional handicraft routines. Child labor took children away from their parents, undermined family life, and deprived children of schooling. Factory routines dulled their minds, and the long hours spent in often unsanitary environments endangered their health.

Sadler Commission
REPORT ON CHILD LABOR

Due to concern about child labor, in 1832 a parliamentary committee chaired by Michael Thomas Sadler investigated the situation of children employed in British factories. The following testimony is drawn from the records of the Sadler Commission.

May 18, 1832

Michael Thomas Sadler, Esquire, in the chair.
Mr. Matthew Crabtree, called in; and Examined.

What age are you?—Twenty-two.[1]

What is your occupation?—A blanket manufacturer.

Have you ever been employed in a factory?—Yes.

At what age did you first go to work in one?—Eight.

How long did you continue in that occupation?—Four years.

Will you state the hours of labour at the period when you first went to the factory, in ordinary times?—From 6 in the morning to 8 at night.

Fourteen hours?—Yes.

With what intervals for refreshment and rest?—An hour at noon.

Then you had no resting time allowed in which to take your breakfast, or what is in Yorkshire called your "drinking"?—No.

When trade was brisk what were your hours?—From 5 in the morning to 9 in the evening.

Sixteen hours?—Yes.

With what intervals at dinner?—An hour.

Report from the Committee on the Bill to Regulate the Labour of Children in the Mills and Factories of the United Kingdom, British Sessional Papers, 1831–1832, House of Commons, XV, pp. 95–96, 99–100.

[1]In the original source, each paragraph was numbered; this reading includes paragraphs 2481–2519 and 2597–2604.—Eds.

How far did you live from the mill?—About two miles.

Was there any time allowed for you to get your breakfast in the mill?—No.

Did you take it before you left home?—Generally.

During those long hours of labour could you be punctual, how did you awake?—I seldom did awake spontaneously. I was most generally awoke or lifted out of bed, sometimes asleep, by my parents.

Were you always in time?—No.

What was the consequence if you had been too late?—I was most commonly beaten.

Severely?—Very severely, I thought.

In whose factory was this?—Messrs. Hague & Cook's, of Dewsbury.

Will you state the effect that those long hours had upon the state of your health and feelings?—I was, when working those long hours, commonly very much fatigued at night, when I left my work, so much so that I sometimes should have slept as I walked if I had not stumbled and started awake again, and so sick often that I could not eat, and what I did eat I vomited.

Did this labour destroy your appetite?—It did.

In what situation were you in that mill?—I was a piecener [see following].

Will you state to the Committee whether piecening is a very laborious employment for children, or not?—It is a very laborious employment. Pieceners are continually running to and fro, and on their feet the whole day.

The duty of the piecener is to take the cardings[2] from one part of the machinery, and to place them on another?—Yes.

So that the labour is not only continual, but it is unabated to the last?—It is unabated to the last.

Do you not think, from your own experience, that the speed of the machinery is so calculated as to demand the utmost exertions of a child, supposing the hours were moderate?—It is as much as they could do at the best; they are always upon the stretch, and it is commonly very difficult to keep up with their work.

State the condition of the children towards the latter part of the day, who have thus to keep up with the machinery?—It is as much as they can do when they are not very much fatigued to keep up with their work, and towards the close of the day, when they come to be more fatigued, they cannot keep up with it very well, and the consequence is that they are beaten to spur them on.

Were you beaten under those circumstances?—Yes.

Frequently?—Very frequently.

And principally at the latter end of the day?—Yes.

And is it your belief that if you had not been so beaten, you should not have got through the work?—I should not if I had not been kept up to it by some means.

Does beating then principally occur at the latter end of the day, when the children are exceedingly fatigued?—It does at the latter end of the day, and in the morning sometimes, when they are very drowsy, and have not got rid of the fatigue of the day before.

What were you beaten with principally?—A strap.

Any thing else?—Yes, a stick sometimes; and there is a kind of roller which runs on the top of the machine called a billy, perhaps two or three yards in length, and perhaps an inch and a half, or more, in diameter; the circumference would be four or five inches, I cannot speak exactly.

Were you beaten with that instrument?—Yes.

Have you yourself been beaten, and have you seen other children struck severely with that roller?—I have been struck very severely with it myself, so much so as to knock me down, and I have seen other children have their heads broken with it.

---

[2]*Cardings* were woolen fibers that had been combed in preparation for spinning and weaving. —Eds.

You think that it is a general practice to beat the children with the roller?—It is.

You do not think then that you were worse treated than other children in the mill?—No, I was not, perhaps not so bad as some were. . . .

Can you speak as to the effect of this labour in the mills and factories on the morals of the children, as far as you have observed?—As far as I have observed with regard to morals in the mills, there is every thing about them that is disgusting to everyone conscious of correct morality.

Do you find that the children, the females especially, are very early demoralized in them?—They are.

Is their language indecent?—Very indecent; and both sexes take great familiarities with each other in the mills, without at all being ashamed of their conduct.

Do you connect their immorality of language and conduct with their excessive labour?—It may be somewhat connected with it, for it is to be observed that most of that goes on towards night, when they begin to be drowsy; it is a kind of stimulus which they use to keep them awake; they say some pert thing or other to keep themselves from drowsiness, and it generally happens to be some obscene language.

Have not a considerable number of the females employed in mills illegitimate children very early in life?—I believe there are; I have known some of them have illegitimate children when they were between 16 and 17 years of age.

How many grown up females had you in the mill?—I cannot speak to the exact number that were grown up; perhaps there might be thirty-four or so that worked in the mill at that time.

How many of those had illegitimate children?—A great many of them, eighteen or nineteen of them, I think.

Did they generally marry the men by whom they had the children?—No, it sometimes happens that young women have children by married men, and I have known an instance, a few weeks since, where one of the young women had a child by a married man.

James Phillips Kay
MORAL AND PHYSICAL DISSIPATION

Rapid industrialization produced a drastic change of environment for workers, who moved from the casual, slow-paced English villages and small towns to large, congested, and impersonal industrial cities. The familiar social patterns and cherished values by which preindustrial people had oriented themselves grew weak or disappeared, for these patterns and values clashed with the requirements of the new industrial age. Many people in England, from the highest to the lowest classes, still felt wedded to the old ways and hated the congested industrial centers. In 1832 James Phillips Kay, a physician, published a pamphlet describing the moral and physical condition of the working class in Manchester. His study, excerpted below, provided additional evidence of the painful effects industrialization had on factory workers and their families.

The township of Manchester chiefly consists of dense masses of houses, inhabited by the population engaged in the great manufactories of the cotton trade. . . . Prolonged and exhausting labour, continued from day to day, and from year to year, is not calculated to develop the intellectual or moral faculties of man. The dull routine of a ceaseless drudgery, in which the same mechanical process is incessantly repeated, resembles the torment of Sisyphus[1]—the toil, like the rock, recoils perpetually on the wearied operative. The mind gathers neither stores nor strength from the constant extension and retraction of the same muscles. The intellect slumbers, in supine inertness; but the grosser parts of our nature attain a rank development. To condemn man to such severity of toil is, in some measure, to cultivate in him the habits of an animal. He becomes reckless. He disregards the distinguishing appetites and habits of his species. He neglects the comforts and delicacies of life. He lives in squalid wretchedness, on meagre food, and expends his superfluous gains in debauchery. . . .

[T]he population. . . . is crowded into one dense mass, in cottages separated by narrow, unpaved, and almost pestilential streets; in an atmosphere loaded with the smoke and exhalations of a large manufacturing city. The operatives are congregated in rooms and workshops during twelve hours in the day, in an enervating, heated atmosphere, which is frequently loaded with dust or filaments of cotton, or impure from constant respiration, or from other causes. They are engaged in an employment which absorbs their attention, and unremittingly employs their physical energies. They are drudges who watch the movements, and assist the operations, of a mighty material force, which toils with an energy ever unconscious of fatigue. The persevering labour of the operative must rival the mathematical precision, the incessant motion, and the exhaustless power of the machine.

Hence, besides the negative results—the total abstraction of every moral and intellectual stimulus—the absence of variety—banishment from the grateful air and the cheering influences of light, the physical energies are exhausted by incessant toil, and imperfect nutrition. Having been subjected to the prolonged labour of an animal—his physical energy wasted—his mind in supine inaction—the artizan has neither moral dignity nor intellectual nor organic strength to resist the seductions of appetite. His wife and children, too frequently subjected to the same process, are unable to cheer his remaining moments of leisure. Domestic economy is neglected, domestic comforts are unknown. A meal of the coarsest food is prepared with heedless haste, and devoured with equal precipitation. Home has no other relation to him than that of shelter—few pleasures are there—it chiefly presents to him a scene of physical exhaustion, from which he is glad to escape. Himself impotent of all the distinguishing aims of his species, he sinks into sensual sloth, or revels in more degrading licentiousness. His house is ill furnished, uncleanly, often ill ventilated, perhaps damp; his food, from want of forethought and domestic economy, is meagre and innutritious; he is debilitated and hypochondriacal, and falls the victim of dissipation. . . .

The absence of religious feeling, the neglect of all religious ordinances, we conceive to afford substantive evidence of so great a moral degradation of the community, as generally to ensure a concomitant civic debasement. . . .

James Phillips Kay, M. D., *Moral and Physical Condition of the Working Classes Employed in the Cotton Manufacture in Manchester* (London: James Ridgway, 1832), pp. 6–8, 10–11, 39.

[1]This refers to the myth of Sisyphus, a cruel king of Corinth, who was condemned in Hades to forever push a big rock up to the top of a hill, only to have it roll back down again. —Eds.

Friedrich Engels
THE CONDITION OF THE WORKING CLASS IN ENGLAND

The miseries of the industrial towns distressed Friedrich Engels (1820–1895), a well-to-do German intellectual and son of a prosperous German manufacturer. In the early 1840s, Engels moved to Manchester, a great English industrial center, where he eventually established himself in business. In that decade, he also entered into a lifelong collaboration with Karl Marx, the founder of modern socialism (see chapter 7). Engels yearned for the fellowship and the pleasures of nature that he had experienced in preindustrial Germany. In the new urban centers, he found only alienation and human degradation—even in cosmopolitan London in 1844. The following passage is from his *The Condition of the Working Class in England*.

. . . It is only when [a person] has visited the slums of this great city that it dawns upon him that the inhabitants of modern London have had to sacrifice so much that is best in human nature in order to create those wonders of civilisation with which their city teems. The vast majority of Londoners have had to let so many of their potential creative faculties lie dormant, stunted and unused in order that a small, closely-knit group of their fellow citizens could develop to the full the qualities with which nature has endowed them. The restless and noisy activity of the crowded streets is highly distasteful, and it is surely abhorrent to human nature itself. Hundreds of thousands of men and women drawn from all classes and ranks of society pack the streets of London. Are they not all human beings with the same innate characteristics and potentialities? Are they not all equally interested in the pursuit of happiness? And do they not all aim at happiness by following similar methods? Yet they rush past

each other as if they had nothing in common. They are tacitly agreed on one thing only—that everyone should keep to the right of the pavement so as not to collide with the stream of people moving in the opposite direction. No one even thinks of sparing a glance for his neighbour in the streets. The more that Londoners are packed into a tiny space, the more repulsive and disgraceful becomes the brutal indifference with which they ignore their neighbours and selfishly concentrate upon their private affairs. We know well enough that this isolation of the individual—this narrow-minded egotism—is everywhere the fundamental principle of modern society. But nowhere is this selfish egotism so blatantly evident as in the frantic bustle of the great city. The disintegration of society into individuals, each guided by his private principles and each pursuing his own aims has been pushed to its furthest limits in London. Here indeed human society has been split into its component atoms.

From this it follows that the social conflict—the war of all against all—is fought in the open. . . . Here men regard their fellows not as human beings, but as pawns in the struggle for

Friedrich Engels, *The Condition of the Working Class in England, in 1844*, ed. and trans. W. O. Henderson and W. H. Chaloner (London: Blackwell, 1958), pp. 30–31, 33.

existence. Everyone exploits his neighbour with the result that the stronger tramples the weaker under foot. The strongest of all, a tiny group of capitalists, monopolise everything, while the weakest, who are in the vast majority, succumb to the most abject poverty.

What is true of London, is true also of all the great towns, such as Manchester, Birmingham and Leeds. Everywhere one finds on the one hand the most barbarous indifference and selfish egotism and on the other the most distressing scenes of misery and poverty. . . .

Every great town has one or more slum areas into which the working classes are packed. Sometimes, of course, poverty is to be found hidden away in alleys close to the stately homes of the wealthy. Generally, however, the workers are segregated in separate districts where they struggle through life as best they can out of sight of the more fortunate classes of society.

The slums of the English towns have much in common—the worst houses in a town being found in the worst districts. They are generally unplanned wildernesses of one- or two-storied terrace houses built of brick. Wherever possible these have cellars which are also used as dwellings. These little houses of three or four rooms and a kitchen are called cottages, and throughout England, except for some parts of London, are where the working classes normally live. The streets themselves are usually unpaved and full of holes. They are filthy and strewn with animal and vegetable refuse. Since they have neither gutters nor drains the refuse accumulates in stagnant, stinking puddles. Ventilation in the slums is inadequate owing to the hopelessly unplanned nature of these areas. A great many people live huddled together in a very small area, and so it is easy to imagine the nature of the air in these workers' quarters.

REVIEW QUESTIONS

1. According to the testimony given in the Sadler Commission, how young were the children employed in the factories? How many hours and at what times of day did they work?
2. What do you think were the reasons for the employment of children from the employers' point of view? From the parents' point of view?
3. What measures were employed in the factories to keep children alert at their tasks?
4. According to James Phillips Kay, what harmful effects did industrialization have on factory workers and their families?
5. According to Friedrich Engels, how had the industrial city caused deterioration in the quality of human relationships? What did he mean by the statement that "human society has been split into its component atoms"?

4 Factory Discipline

For the new industries to succeed, workers needed to adopt the rigorous discipline exercised by the new industrial capitalists themselves. But adapting to labor with machines in factories proved traumatic for the poor, uneducated, and often unruly folk, who previously had toiled on farms and in village workshops and were used to a less demanding pace.

FACTORY RULES

The problem of adapting a preindustrial labor force to the discipline needed for coordinating large numbers of workers in the factory was common to all industrializing countries. The Foundry and Engineering Works of the Royal Overseas Trading Company, in the Moabit section of Berlin, issued the following rules in 1844. The rules aimed at instilling obedience and honesty as well as "good order and harmony" among the factory's workers. The rules not only stressed time-keeping (with appropriate fines for latecomers), but also proper conduct in all aspects of life and work in the factory.

In every large works, and in the co-ordination of any large number of workmen, good order and harmony must be looked upon as the fundamentals of success, and therefore the following rules shall be strictly observed.

Every man employed in the concern . . . shall receive a copy of these rules, so that no one can plead ignorance. Its acceptance shall be deemed to mean consent to submit to its regulations.

(1) The normal working day begins at all seasons at 6 A.M. precisely and ends, after the usual break of half an hour for breakfast, an hour for dinner and half an hour for tea, at 7 P.M., and it shall be strictly observed.

Five minutes before the beginning of the stated hours of work until their actual commencement, a bell shall ring and indicate that every worker employed in the concern has to proceed to his place of work, in order to start as soon as the bell stops.

The doorkeeper shall lock the door punctually at 6 A.M., 8:30 A.M., 1 P.M. and 4:30 P.M.

Workers arriving 2 minutes late shall lose half an hour's wages; whoever is more than 2 minutes late may not start work until after the next break, or at least shall lose his wages until then. Any disputes about the correct time shall be settled by the clock mounted above the gate-keeper's lodge.

These rules are valid both for time and for piece-workers, and in cases of breaches of these rules, workmen shall be fined in proportion to their earnings. The deductions from the wage shall be entered in the wage-book of the gatekeeper whose duty they are; they shall be unconditionally accepted as it will not be possible to enter into any discussions about them.

(2) When the bell is rung to denote the end of the working day, every workman, both on piece and on day-wage, shall leave his workshop and the yard, but is not allowed to make preparations for his departure before the bell rings. Every breach of this rule shall lead to a fine of five silver groschen [pennies] to the sick fund. Only those who have obtained special permission by the overseer may stay on in the workshop in order to work.—If a workman has worked beyond the closing bell, he must give his name to the gatekeeper on leaving, on pain of losing his payment for the overtime.

(3) No workman, whether employed by time or piece, may leave before the end of the working day, without having first received permission from the overseer and having given his name to the gatekeeper. Omission of these two actions shall lead to a fine of ten silver groschen payable to the sick fund.

(4) Repeated irregular arrival at work shall lead to dismissal. This shall also apply to those

From A. Schroter and Walter Becker, *Die deutsche Maschinenbau industrie in der industriellen Revolution* in S. Polland and C. Holmes, *Documents of European Economic History*, pp. 534–536.

who are found idling by an official or overseer, and refuse to obey their order to resume work.

(5) Entry to the firm's property by any but the designated gateway, and exit by any prohibited route, e.g. by climbing fences or walls, or by crossing the Spree [River], shall be punished by a fine of fifteen silver groschen to the sick fund for the first offences, and dismissal for the second.

(6) No worker may leave his place of work otherwise than for reasons connected with his work.

(7) All conversation with fellow-workers is prohibited; if any worker requires information about his work, he must turn to the overseer, or to the particular fellow-worker designated for the purpose.

(8) Smoking in the workshops or in the yard is prohibited during working hours; anyone caught smoking shall be fined five silver groschen for the sick fund for every such offence.

(9) Every worker is responsible for cleaning up his space in the workshop, and if in doubt, he is to turn to his overseer.—All tools must always be kept in good condition, and must be cleaned after use. This applies particularly to the turner, regarding his lathe.

(10) Natural functions must be performed at the appropriate places, and whoever is found soiling walls, fences, squares, etc., and similarly, whoever is found washing his face and hands in the workshop and not in the places assigned for the purpose, shall be fined five silver groschen for the sick fund.

(11) On completion of his piece of work, every workman must hand it over at once to his foreman or superior, in order to receive a fresh piece of work. Pattern makers must on no account hand over their patterns to the foundry without express order of their supervisors. No workman may take over work from his fellow-workman without instruction to that effect by the foreman.

(12) It goes without saying that all over-seers and officials of the firm shall be obeyed without question, and shall be treated with due deference. Disobedience will be punished by dismissal.

(13) Immediate dismissal shall also be the fate of anyone found drunk in any of the workshops.

(14) Untrue allegations against superiors or officials of the concern shall lead to stern reprimand, and may lead to dismissal. The same punishment shall be meted out to those who knowingly allow errors to slip through when supervising or stocktaking.

(15) Every workman is obliged to report to his superiors any acts of dishonesty or embezzlement on the part of his fellow work-men. If he omits to do so, and it is shown after subsequent discovery of a misdemeanour that he knew about it at the time, he shall be liable to be taken to court as an accessory after the fact and the wage due to him shall be retained as punishment. Conversely, anyone denouncing a theft in such a way as to allow conviction of the thief shall receive a reward of two Thaler [dollar equivalent], and, if necessary, his name shall be kept confidential.—Further, the gatekeeper and the watchman, as well as every official, are entitled to search the baskets, parcels, aprons etc. of the women and children who are taking the dinners into the works, on their departure, as well as search any worker suspected of stealing any article whatever. . . .

REVIEW QUESTIONS

1. Judging by the Berlin factory rules, what were the differences between preindustrial and industrial work routines?
2. How might these rules have affected the lives of families?

5 The Capitalist Ethic

The remarkable advance in industry and material prosperity in the nineteenth century has been hailed as the triumph of the middle class, or bourgeoisie, which included bankers, merchants, factory owners, professionals, and government officials. Unlike the upper classes, which lived on inherited wealth, middle-class people supported themselves by diligent, assiduous activity—what has been called "the capitalist (or bourgeois) ethic." A vigorous spirit of enterprise and the opportunity for men of ability to rise from common origins to riches and fame help explain the growth of industrialism in England. These industrial capitalists adopted the attitude of medieval monks that "idleness is the enemy of the soul," to which they added "time is money."

The ideal of dedicated and responsible hard work directed by an internal rather than an external discipline was seen as the ultimate source of human merit and was widely publicized in the nineteenth century. It encouraged upward mobility among the lower classes and sustained the morale of ambitious middle-class people immersed in the keen competition of private enterprise. By shaping highly motivated private citizens, the capitalist ethic, it was argued, also provided a vital source of national strength.

Samuel Smiles
SELF-HELP AND *THRIFT*

Samuel Smiles (1812–1904) was the most famous messenger of the capitalist ethic at its best. His father, a Scottish papermaker and general merchant, died early, leaving his eleven children to fend for themselves. Samuel was apprenticed to a medical office, in due time becoming a physician in general practice. Turned journalist, he edited the local newspaper in the English city of Leeds, hoping to cure the ills of society by promoting the social and intellectual development of the working classes. Leaving his editorial office, he stepped into railroad management as a friend of George Stephenson, the inventor of the locomotive and promoter of railroads, whose biography Smiles wrote in 1857. Two years later he published *Self-Help*, which had grown out of a lecture to a small mutual-improvement society in which people sought each other's help in bettering their condition. The book was an instant success and was translated into many languages, including Japanese. Having retired after twenty-one years as a railway administrator and prolific author, Smiles suffered a stroke. Recovered, he traveled widely, writing more books about deserving but often unknown achievers. All along, he practiced in his personal life the virtues that he preached. The following selections reveal not only Samuel Smiles's philosophy of life but also the values inspiring the achievements of capitalism.

SELF-HELP

"Heaven helps those who help themselves" is a well-tried maxim, embodying in a small compass the results of vast human experience. The spirit of self-help is the root of all genuine growth in the individual; and, exhibited in the lives of many, it constitutes the true source of national vigour and strength. Help from without is often enfeebling in its effects, but help from within invariably invigorates. Whatever is done *for* men or classes, to a certain extent takes away the stimulus and necessity of doing for themselves; and where men are subjected to over-guidance and over-government, the inevitable tendency is to render them comparatively helpless.

Even the best institutions can give a man no active help. Perhaps the most they can do is, to leave him free to develop himself and improve his individual condition. But in all times men have been prone to believe that their happiness and well-being were to be secured by means of institutions rather than by their own conduct. Hence the value of legislation as an agent in human advancement has usually been much over-estimated. . . . [N]o laws, however stringent, can make the idle industrious, the thriftless provident, or the drunken sober. Such reforms can only be effected by means of individual action, economy, and self-denial; by better habits, rather than by greater rights. . . .

National progress is the sum of individual industry, energy, and uprightness, as national decay is of individual idleness, selfishness, and vice. What we are accustomed to decry as great social evils, will, for the most part, be found to be but the outgrowth of man's own perverted life; and though we may endeavour to cut them down and extirpate them by means of Law, they will only spring up again with fresh luxuriance in some other form, unless the conditions of personal life and character are radically improved. If this view be correct, then it follows that the highest patriotism and philanthropy consist, not so much in altering laws and modifying institutions, as in helping and stimulating men to elevate and improve themselves by their own free and independent individual action.

It may be of comparatively little consequence how a man is governed from without, whilst everything depends upon how he governs himself from within. The greatest slave is not he who is ruled by a despot, great though that evil be, but he who is [enslaved by] his own moral ignorance, selfishness, and vice. . . .

Smiles's book *Thrift*, published in 1875, restates and expands on the themes stressed in *Self-Help*.

THRIFT

The object of this book is to induce men to employ their means for worthy purposes, and not to waste them upon selfish indulgences. Many enemies have to be encountered in accomplishing this object. There are idleness, thoughtlessness, vanity, vice, intemperance. The last is the worst enemy of all. Numerous cases are cited in the course of the following book, which show that one of the best methods of abating the curse of Drink is to induce old and young to practice the virtue of Thrift. . . .

It is the savings of individuals which compose the wealth—in other words, the well-being— of every nation. On the other hand, it is the wastefulness of individuals which occasions the impoverishment of states. So that every thrifty person may be regarded as a public benefactor, and every thriftless person as a public enemy. . . .

. . . All that is great in man comes of labor—greatness in art, in literature, in science. Knowledge—"the wing wherewith we fly to heaven"—is only acquired through labor. Genius is but a capability of laboring intensely: it is the power of making great and sustained

Samuel Smiles, *Self-Help; with Illustrations of Conduct and Perseverance* (London: John Murray, 1897), pp. 1–3.

Samuel Smiles, *Thrift* (New York: A. L. Burt, n.d.), pp. 6, 14, 18, 21.

efforts. Labor may be a chastisement, but it is indeed a glorious one. It is worship, duty, praise, and immortality—for those who labor with the highest aims and for the purest purposes. . . .

. . . Of all wretched men, surely the idle are the most so—those whose life is barren of utility, who have nothing to do except to gratify their senses. Are not such men the most [complaining], miserable, and dissatisfied of all, constantly in a state of *ennui* [boredom], alike useless to themselves and to others—mere cumberers [troublesome occupiers] of the earth, who, when removed, are missed by none, and whom none regret? Most wretched and ignoble lot, indeed, is the lot of the idlers.

Who have helped the world onward so much as the workers; men who have had to work from necessity or from choice? All that we call progress—civilization, well-being, and prosperity—depends upon industry, diligently applied—from the culture of a barley-stalk to the construction of a steamship; from the stitching of a collar to the sculpturing of "the statue that enchants the world."

All useful and beautiful thoughts, in like manner, are the issue of labor, of study, of observation, of research, of diligent elaboration. . . .

By the working-man we do not mean merely the man who labors with his muscles and sinews. A horse can do this. But *he* is pre-eminently the working-man who works with his brain also, and whose whole physical system is under the influence of his higher faculties. The man who paints a picture, who writes a book, who makes a law, who creates a poem, is a working-man of the highest order; not so necessary to the physical sustainment of the community as the plowman or the shepherd, but not less important as providing for society its highest intellectual nourishment. . . .

But a large proportion of men do not provide for the future. They do not remember the past. They think only of the present. They preserve nothing. They spend all that they earn. They do not provide for themselves; they do not provide for their families. They may make high wages, but eat and drink the whole of what they earn. Such people are constantly poor, and hanging on the verge of destitution. . . .

REVIEW QUESTIONS

1. What, according to Samuel Smiles, were the key values that should guide the individual?
2. How did Smiles define success in life?
3. What, in his opinion, were the enemies of individual and national achievement?
4. Do Smiles's writings offer good advice to the poor in the United States today? Explain why or why not.

6 Reformers

Rapid industrialization created numerous hardships for factory hands, including long hours, harsh discipline, unsafe working conditions, and child labor. The distress of workers, which was publicized by parliamentary investigating committees and enlightened intellectuals, spurred a demand for reform. Early socialists like Robert Owen proposed establishing model communities for workers and their families. Other reformers urged parliamentary reforms that would give workers a voice in the political process.

Robert Owen
AMELIORATING THE PLIGHT OF THE POOR

In 1799, Robert Owen (1771–1858) became part owner and manager of the New Lanark cotton mills in Scotland. Distressed by the widespread mistreatment of workers, Owen resolved to improve the lives of his employees and show that it was possible to do so without destroying profits. He raised wages, upgraded working conditions, refused to hire children under ten, and provided workers with neat homes, food, and clothing, all at reasonable prices. He set up schools for children and for adults. In every way, he demonstrated his belief that healthier, happier workers produced more than the less fortunate ones. Owen believed that industry and technology could and would enrich humankind if they were organized according to the proper principles. Visitors came from all over Europe to see Owen's factories.

Just like many philosophes during the Enlightenment, Owen was convinced that the environment was the principal shaper of character—that the ignorance, alcoholism, and crime of the poor derived from bad living conditions. Public education and factory reform, said Owen, would make better citizens of the poor. Owen came to believe that the entire social and economic order must be replaced by a new system based on harmonious group living rather than on competition. He established a model community at New Harmony, Indiana, but it was short-lived.

In the following selection, excerpts from a report communicated to a committee of the House of Commons in 1817, Owen proposes the establishment of a model community that would ameliorate the plight of the poor and unemployed.

Under the existing laws,[1] the unemployed working classes are maintained by, and consume part of, the property and produce of the wealthy and industrious, while their powers of body and mind remain unproductive. They frequently acquire the bad habits which ignorance and idleness never fail to produce; they amalgamate with the regular poor, and become a nuisance to society.

Most of the poor have received bad and vicious habits from their parents; and so long as their present treatment continues, those bad and vicious habits will be transmitted to their children and, through them, to succeeding generations.

Any plan, then, to ameliorate their condition, must prevent bad and vicious habits from being taught to their children, and provide the means by which only good and useful ones may be given to them. . . .

Under this view of the subject, any plan for the amelioration of the poor should combine means to prevent their children from

Robert Owen, *A New View of Society* (New York: Bliss & White, 1825), pp. 145–55.

[1]The Poor Law was established in 1601 and taxed all householders in each parish to provide relief to the aged, sick, and infant poor in the parish, as well as employing the able-bodied poor in the workhouse. The law was supplemented in the late eighteenth century to provide allowances to workers who received wages beneath subsistence level. This proved to be so expensive that in the Poor Law reform in 1834, pauperism was stigmatized as a moral failing, and the only relief provided was employment in the workhouse. —Eds.

acquiring bad habits, and to give them good ones—to provide useful training and instruction for them—to provide proper labour for the adults—to direct their labour and expenditure so as to produce the greatest benefit to themselves and to society; and to place them under such circumstances as shall remove them from unnecessary temptations, and closely unite their interest and duty.

The plan represented is on a scale considered to be sufficient to accommodate about 1,200 persons.

And these are to be supposed men, women, and children, of all ages, capacities, and dispositions; most of them very ignorant; many with bad and vicious habits, possessing only the ordinary bodily and mental faculties of human beings, and who require to be supported out of the funds appropriated to the maintenance of the poor—individuals who are at present not only useless and a direct burden on the public, but whose moral influence is highly pernicious, since they are the medium by which ignorance and certain classes of vicious habits and crimes are fostered and perpetuated in society.

It is evident that while the poor are suffered to remain under the circumstances in which they have hitherto existed, they and their children, with very few exceptions, will continue unaltered in succeeding generations.

In order to effect any radically beneficial change in their character, they must be removed from the influence of such circumstances, and placed under those which, being congenial to the natural constitution of man and the well-being of society, cannot fail to produce that amelioration in their condition which all classes have so great an interest in promoting. . . .

Each lodging-room within the squares is to accommodate a man, his wife, and two children under three years of age; and to be such as will permit them to have much more comforts than the dwellings of the poor usually afford.

It is intended that the children above three years of age should attend the school, eat in the mess-room, and sleep in the dormitories; the parents being, of course, permitted to see and converse with them at meals and all other proper times;—that before they leave school they shall be well instructed in all necessary and useful knowledge;—that every possible means shall be adopted to prevent the acquirement of bad habits from their parents or otherwise;—that no pains shall be spared to impress upon them such habits and dispositions as may be most conductive to their happiness through life, as well as render them useful and valuable members of the community to which they belong. . . .

The ignorance of the poor, their ill-training, and their want of a rational education make it necessary that those of the present generation should be actively and regularly occupied through the day in some essentially useful work; yet in such a manner as that their employment should be healthy and productive. The plan which has been described will most amply admit of this. . . .

It is impossible to find language sufficiently strong to express the inconsistency, as well as the injustice, of our present proceedings towards the poor and working classes. They are left in gross ignorance; they are permitted to be trained up in habits of vice, and in the commission of crimes; and, as if purposely to keep them in ignorance and vice, and goad them on to commit criminal acts, they are perpetually surrounded with temptations which cannot fail to produce all those effects. . . .

The poor and unemployed working classes, however, cannot, must not, be abandoned to their fate, lest the consequences entail misfortune on us all. Instead of being left, as they now are, to the dominion of ignorance, and to the influence of circumstances which are fatal to their industry and morals—a situation in which it is easy to perceive the inefficacy, or rather the injuriousness, of granting them a provision in a mere pecuniary shape—they should, on the contrary, be afforded the means of procuring a certain and comfortable subsistence by their labour, under a system which will not only direct that labour and its earnings to the best advantage, but, at the same time, place them under circumstances the most favourable to the growth of morals and of happiness. In short, instead of allowing their habits to proceed under the worst influence possible, or rather, as it were, to be left to chance, thus producing unintentionally crimes that render necessary the severities of our penal code, let a system for the prevention of pauperism and of crimes be adopted, and the operation of our penal code will soon be restricted to very narrow limits. . . .

If... the plan shall prove, on investigation, to be correct in principle, to be easy of practice, and that it can relieve the poor and unemployed of the working classes from the grievous distresses and degradation under which they suffer, it becomes equally the duty of all who profess to desire the amelioration of the lower orders, to exert themselves without further delay to carry it into execution, in order that another year of extensive and unnecessary suffering and demoralization, from the want of a sufficiency of wholesome food and proper training and instruction, may not uselessly pass away.

REVIEW QUESTION

What bad habits did Owen attribute to the poor? How did he propose to remedy the situation?

CHAPTER 6
Romanticism, Reaction, Revolution

LIBERTY LEADING THE PEOPLE, by Eugene Delacroix, oil on canvas, 1830. Combining Romantic style with political beliefs in this painting, Delacroix commemorates the French Revolution of 1830, when the reactionary Charles X was replaced by Louis Philippe. *(© Erich Lessing/Art Resource, NY)*

In 1815 the European scene had changed. Napoleon was exiled to the island of St. Helena, and a Bourbon king, in the person of Louis XVIII, again reigned in France. The Great Powers of Europe, meeting at Vienna, had drawn up a peace settlement that awarded territory to the states that had fought Napoleon and restored to power some rulers dethroned by the French emperor. The Congress of Vienna also organized the Concert of Europe, an alliance of leading European powers, to guard against a resurgence of the revolutionary spirit that had kept Europe in turmoil for some twenty-five years. The conservative leaders of Europe wanted no more Robespierres who resorted to terror and no more Napoleons who sought to dominate the Continent.

However, reactionary rulers' efforts to turn the clock back to the Old Regime could not contain the forces unleashed by the French Revolution. Between 1820 and 1848 a series of revolts rocked Europe. The principal causes were liberalism, which demanded constitutional government and the protection of the freedom and rights of the individual citizen, and nationalism, which called for the reawakening and unification of the nation and its liberation from foreign domination.

In the 1820s, the Concert of Europe crushed a quasi-liberal revolution in Spain and liberal uprisings in Italy, and Tsar Nicholas I of Russia subdued liberal officers who challenged tsarist autocracy. The Greeks, however, successfully fought for independence from the Ottoman Turks.

Between 1830 and 1832, another wave of revolutions swept over Europe. Italian liberals and nationalists failed to free Italy from foreign rule or to wrest reforms from autocratic princes, and the tsar's troops crushed a Polish bid for independence from Russian rule. But in France, rebels overthrew the reactionary Bourbon Charles X in 1830 and replaced him with a more moderate ruler, Louis Philippe; a little later Belgium gained its independence from Holland.

The year 1848 was decisive in the struggle for liberty and nationhood. In France, democrats overthrew Louis Philippe and established a republic that gave all men the right to vote. However, in Italy and Germany, revolutions attempting to unify each land failed, as did a bid in Hungary for independence from the Hapsburg Empire. After enjoying initial successes, the revolutionaries were crushed by superior might, and their liberal and nationalist objectives remained largely unfulfilled. By 1870, however, many nationalist aspirations had been realized. The Hapsburg Empire granted Hungary autonomy in 1867; and by 1870–1871, the period of the Franco-Prussian War, Germany and Italy became unified states. That authoritarian and militaristic Prussia unified Germany, rather than liberals like those who had fought in the revolutions of 1848, greatly affected the future of Europe.

In the early nineteenth century a new cultural orientation, Romanticism, emphasized the liberation of human emotions and the free expression of personality in artistic creations. The Romantics' attack on the rationalism of the Enlightenment and their veneration of the past influenced conservative thought, and their concern for a people's history and traditions contributed to the development of nationalism. By encouraging innovation in art, music, and literature, the Romantics greatly enriched European cultural life.

1 Romanticism

Romantics attacked the outlook of the Enlightenment, protesting that the philosophes' excessive intellectualizing and their mechanistic view of the physical world and human nature distorted and fettered the human spirit and thwarted cultural creativity. The rationalism of the philosophes, said the Romantics, had reduced human beings to soulless thinking machines, and vibrant nature to lifeless wheels, cogs, and pulleys. In contrast to the philosophes' scientific and analytic approach, the Romantics asserted the intrinsic value of emotions and imagination and extolled the spontaneity, richness, and uniqueness of the human spirit. To the philosophes, the emotions obstructed clear thinking.

For Romantics, feelings and imagination were the human essence, the source of cultural creativity, and the avenue to true understanding. Their beliefs led the Romantics to rebel against strict standards of aesthetics that governed artistic creations. They held that artists, musicians, and writers must trust their own sensibilities and inventiveness and must not be bound by textbook rules; the Romantics focused on the creative capacities inherent in the emotions and urged individuality and freedom of expression in the arts. In the age of Romanticism, the artist and poet succeeded the scientist as the exemplar of Western civilization.

William Wordsworth
TABLES TURNED

The works of the great English poet William Wordsworth (1770–1850) exemplify many tendencies of the Romantic movement. In the interval during which he tried to come to grips with his disenchantment with the French Revolution, Wordsworth's creativity reached its height. In the preface to *Lyrical Ballads* (1798), Wordsworth produced what has become known as the manifesto of Romanticism. He wanted poetry to express powerful feelings; he also contended that, because it is a vehicle for the imagination, poetry is the source of truth. Wordsworth thus represented a shift in perspective comparable to the shift made by Descartes in philosophy, but for Wordsworth imagination and feeling, not mathematics and logic, yielded highest truth.

The philosophes had regarded nature as a giant machine, all of whose parts worked in perfect precision and whose laws could be uncovered through the scientific method. The Romantics rejected this mechanical model. To them, nature was a living organism filled with beautiful forms whose inner meaning was grasped through the human imagination; they sought from nature a higher truth than mechanical law. In "Tables Turned" (1798), Wordsworth exalts nature as humanity's teacher.

Up! up! my Friend, and quit your books;
Or surely you'll grow double:
Up! up! my Friend, and clear your looks;
Why all this toil and trouble?

The sun, above the mountain's head,
A freshening lustre mellow
Through all the long green fields has spread,
His first sweet evening yellow.

Books! 'tis a dull and endless strife:
Come, hear the woodland linnet [Old World
    finch],
How sweet his music! on my life,
There's more of wisdom in it.

And hark! how blithe the throstle [thrush] sings!
He, too, is no mean preacher:

———
Williams Wordsworth, "Tables Turned," in *The Poetical Works of William Wordsworth* (London: Moxon, 1869), p. 361.

Come forth into the light of things,
Let Nature be your Teacher.
She has a world of ready wealth,
Our minds and hearts to bless—
Spontaneous wisdom breathed by health,
Truth breathed by cheerfulness.

One impulse from a vernal wood
May teach you more of man,
Of moral evil and of good,
Than all the sages can.

Sweet is the lore which Nature brings;
Our meddling intellect
Mis-shapes the beauteous forms of things:—
We murder to dissect.

Enough of Science and of Art;
Close up those barren leaves [book pages];
Come forth, and bring with you a heart
That watches and receives.

William Blake
MILTON

William Blake (1757–1827) was a British engraver, poet, and religious mystic. He also affirmed the creative potential of the imagination and expressed distaste for the rationalist-scientific outlook of the Enlightenment, as is clear from these lines in his poem "Milton," written in 1804.

. . . the Reasoning Power in Man:
This is a false Body; an Incrustation [scab] over
    my Immortal

———
William Blake, *Milton: A Poem in Two Books* (London: Printed by William Blake, 1804), pp. 42, 44.

Spirit; a Selfhood, which must be put off &
    annihilated always[s]
To cleanse the Face of my Spirit by
    Self-examination,
To bathe in the Waters of Life, to wash off the
    Not Human,

I come in Self-annihilation & the grandeur of
    Inspiration,
To cast off Rational Demonstration by Faith in
    the Saviour,
To cast off the rotten rags of Memory by
    Inspiration,
To cast off Bacon, Locke & Newton from
    Albion's covering,[1]
To take off his filthy garments & clothe him
    with Imagination,
To cast aside from Poetry all that is not
    Inspiration,
That it no longer shall dare to mock with the
    aspersion of Madness

. . .

To cast off the idiot Questioner who is always
    questioning

---

[1]Bacon, Locke, and Newton were British thinkers who valued reason and science, and Albion is an ancient name for England. —Eds.

But never capable of answering, who sits with
    a sly grin
Silent plotting when to question, like a thief in
    a cave,
Who publishes doubt & calls it knowledge,
    whose Science is Despair,
Whose pretence to knowledge is Envy, whose
    whole Science is
To destroy the wisdom of ages to gratify ravenous
    Envy
That rages round him like a Wolf day & night
    without rest:
He smiles with condescension, he talks of
    Benevolence & Virtue,
And those who act with Benevolence & Virtue
    they murder time on time.
These are the destroyers of Jerusalem, these are
    the murderers
Of Jesus, who deny the Faith & mock at Eternal Life. . . .

REVIEW QUESTIONS

1. In "Tables Turned," what connection did Wordsworth see between nature and the human mind? How did his idea of nature differ from that of the scientists? According to Wordsworth, what effect did nature have on the imagination?
2. Why did William Blake attack reason?
3. The Romantic movement was a reaction against the dominant ideas of the Enlightenment. Discuss this statement.

---

2   Conservatism

In the period after 1815, conservatism was the principal ideology of those who repudiated the Enlightenment and the French Revolution. Conservatives valued tradition over reason, aristocratic and clerical authority over equality, and the community over the individual. Edmund Burke (1729–1797), a leading Anglo-Irish statesman and political thinker, was instrumental in shaping the conservative outlook. His *Reflections on the Revolution in France* (1790) attacked the violence and fundamental principles of the Revolution. Another leading conservative was Joseph de Maistre (1753–1821), who fled his native Sardinia in 1792 (and again in 1793) after it was invaded by the armies of the new French

Republic. De Maistre denounced the Enlightenment for spawning the French Revolution, defended the church as a civilizing agent that made individuals aware of their social obligations, and affirmed tradition as a model more valuable than instant reforms embodied in "paper constitutions."

The symbol of conservatism in the first half of the nineteenth century was Prince Klemens von Metternich (1773–1859) of Austria. A bitter opponent of Jacobinism and Napoleon, he became the pivotal figure at the Congress of Vienna (1814–1815), where European powers met to redraw the map of Europe after their victory over France. Metternich said that the Jacobins had subverted the pillars of civilization and that Napoleon, by harnessing the forces of the Revolution, had destroyed the traditional European state system. No peace was possible with Napoleon, who championed revolutionary doctrines and dethroned kings, and whose rule rested not on legitimacy but on conquest and charisma. No balance of power could endure an adventurer who obliterated states and sought European domination.

Edmund Burke
REFLECTIONS ON THE REVOLUTION IN FRANCE

Burke regarded the revolutionaries as wild-eyed fanatics who had uprooted all established authority, tradition, and institutions, thereby plunging France into anarchy. Not sharing the faith of the philosophes in human goodness, Burke held that without the restraints of established authority, people revert to savagery. For Burke, monarchy, aristocracy, and Christianity represented civilizing forces that tamed the beast in human nature. By undermining venerable institutions, he said, the French revolutionaries had opened the door to anarchy and terror. Burke's *Reflections*, excerpts of which follow, was instrumental in the shaping of conservative thought.

Burke's position on the F.R. + why?

. . . You [revolutionaries] chose to act as if you had never been moulded into civil society, and had every thing to begin anew. You began ill, because you began by despising every thing that belonged to you. . . . If the last generations of your country appeared without much lustre in your eyes, you might have passed them by, and derived your claims from a more early race of ancestors. Under a pious predilection for those ancestors, your imaginations would have realized in them a standard of virtue and wisdom, beyond the vulgar practice of the hour: and you would have risen with the example to whose imitation you aspired. Respecting your forefathers, you would have been taught to respect yourselves. You would not have chosen to consider the French as a people of yesterday, as a nation of low-born servile wretches, until the emancipating year of 1789. . . . By following wise examples you would have given new

---

Edmund Burke, *Reflections on the Revolution in France* (London: Printed for J. Dodsley, 1791), pp. 51–55, 90–91, 116–117, 127, 129.

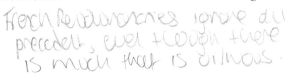

French Revolutionaries ignore all precedent, even though there is much that is virtuous.

examples of wisdom to the world. You would have rendered the cause of liberty venerable in the eyes of every worthy mind in every nation. . . . You would have had a free constitution; a potent monarchy; a disciplined army; a reformed and venerated clergy; a mitigated but spirited nobility, to lead your virtue. . . .

Compute your gains: see what is got by those extravagant and presumptuous speculations which have taught your leaders to despise all their predecessors, and all their contemporaries, and even to despise themselves, until the moment in which they became truly despicable. By following those false lights, France has bought undisguised calamities at a higher price than any nation has purchased the most unequivocal blessings! . . . France, when she let loose the reins of regal authority, doubled the licence, of a ferocious dissoluteness in manners, and of an insolent irreligion in opinions and practices; and has extended through all ranks of life. . . . all the unhappy corruptions that usually were the disease of wealth and power. This is one of the new principles of equality in France. . . .

. . . The science of government being therefore so practical in itself, and intended for such practical purposes, a matter which requires experience, and even more experience than any person can gain in his whole life, however sagacious and observing he may be, it is with infinite caution that any man ought to venture upon pulling down an edifice which has answered in any tolerable degree for ages the common purposes of society, or on building it up again, without having models and patterns of approved utility before his eyes. . . .

. . . The nature of man is intricate; the objects of society are of the greatest possible complexity; and therefore no simple disposition or direction of power can be suitable either to man's nature, or to the quality of his affairs.

When ancient opinions of life are taken away, the loss cannot possibly be estimated. From that moment we have no compass to govern us; nor can we know distinctly to what port we steer. . . .

. . . Nothing is more certain than that our manners, our civilization, and all the good things which are connected with manners and with civilization have, in this European world of ours, depended for ages upon two principles and were, indeed, the result of both combined: I mean the spirit of a gentleman and the spirit of religion. . . .

Burke next compares the English people with the French revolutionaries.

. . . Thanks to our sullen resistance to innovation, thanks to the cold sluggishness of our national character, we still bear the stamp of our forefathers. . . . We are not the converts of Rousseau; we are not the disciples of Voltaire; Helvetius has made no progress amongst us.[1] Atheists are not our preachers; madmen are not our lawgivers. We know that *we* have made no discoveries, and we think that no discoveries are to be made, in morality, nor many in the great principles of government. . . . We fear God; we look up with awe to kings, with affection to parliaments, with duty to magistrates, with reverence to priests, and with respect to nobility. . . .

. . . We are afraid to put men to live and trade each on his own private stock of reason, because we suspect that this stock in each man is small, and that the individuals would do better to avail themselves of the general bank and capital of nations and of ages.

---

[1]Rousseau, Voltaire, and Helvétius were French philosophes of the eighteenth century noted, respectively, for advocating democracy, attacking the abuses of the Old Regime, and applying scientific reasoning to moral principles (see chapter 3). —Eds.

Klemens von Metternich
THE ODIOUS IDEAS OF THE PHILOSOPHES

Two decades of revolutionary warfare had shaped Metternich's political thinking. After the fall of Napoleon, Metternich worked to restore the European balance of power and to suppress revolutionary movements. In the following memorandum to Tsar Alexander I, dated December 15, 1820, Metternich denounces the French philosophes for their "false systems" and "fatal errors" that weakened the social fabric and gave rise to the French Revolution. In their presumption, the philosophes forsook the experience and wisdom of the past, trusting only their own thoughts and inclinations.

The progress of the human mind has been extremely rapid in the course of the last three centuries. This progress having been accelerated more rapidly than the growth of wisdom (the only counterpoise to passions and to error); a revolution prepared by the false systems . . . has at last broken out. . . .

. . . There were . . . some men [the philosophes], unhappily endowed with great talents, who felt their own strength, and . . . who had the art to prepare and conduct men's minds to the triumph of their detestable enterprise—an enterprise all the more odious as it was pursued without regard to results, simply abandoning themselves to the one feeling of hatred of God and of His immutable moral laws.

France had the misfortune to produce the greatest number of these men. It is in her midst that religion and all that she holds sacred, that morality and authority, and all connected with them, have been attacked with a steady and systematic animosity, and it is there that the weapon of ridicule has been used with the most ease and success.

Drag through the mud the name of God and the powers instituted by His divine decrees, and the revolution will be prepared! Speak of a social contract,[1] and the revolution is accomplished! The revolution was already completed in the palaces of Kings, in the drawing-rooms and boudoirs of certain cities, while among the great mass of the people it was still only in a state of preparation. . . .

. . . The French Revolution broke out, and has gone through a complete revolutionary cycle in a very short period, which could only have appeared long to its victims and to its contemporaries. . . .

. . . The revolutionary seed had penetrated into every country. . . . It was greatly developed under the *régime* of the military despotism of Bonaparte. His conquests displaced a number of laws, institutions, and customs; broke through bonds sacred among all nations, strong enough to resist time itself; which is more than can be said of certain benefits conferred by these innovators.

Klemens von Metternich, *Memoirs of Prince Metternich*, trans. Mrs. Alexander Napier (London: Richard Bentley & Sons, 1881), pp. 461–463.

[1]The social contract theory consisted essentially of the following principles: (1) people voluntarily enter into an agreement to establish a political community; (2) government rests on the consent of the governed: (3) people possess natural freedom and equality, which they do not surrender to the state. These principles were used to challenge the divine right of kings and absolute monarchy. —Eds.

Joseph de Maistre
ERRORS OF THE ENLIGHTENMENT

The following critique of the philosophes, the French Revolution, and manufactured constitutions is taken from Joseph de Maistre's *Essay on the Generative Principle of Political Constitutions* (1808–1809).

One of the greatest errors of a century which professed them all was to believe that a political constitution could be created and written *a priori*, whereas reason and experience unite in proving that a constitution is a divine work and that precisely the most fundamental and essentially constitutional of a nation's laws could not possibly be written. . . .

. . . Was it not a common belief everywhere that a constitution was the work of the intellect, like an ode or a tragedy? Had not Thomas Paine declared, with a profundity that charmed the universities, that a constitution does not exist as long as one cannot put it in his pocket? The unsuspecting, overweening self-confidence of the eighteenth century balked at nothing, and I do not believe that it produced a single stripling of any talent who did not make three things when he left school: an educational system, a constitution, and a world. . . .

. . . I do not believe that the slightest doubt remains as to the unquestionable truth of the following propositions:

The fundamental principles of political constitutions exist prior to all written law.

Constitutional law *(loi)* is and can only be the development or sanction of a pre-existing and unwritten law *(droit)*. . . .

. . . [H]e who believes himself able by writing alone to establish a clear and lasting doctrine IS A GREAT FOOL. . . .

. . . [N]o real and great institution can be based on written law; . . . imperceptible growth is the true promise of durability in all things. . . .

Everything brings us back to the general rule. *Man cannot create a constitution, and no legitimate constitution can be written.* The collection of fundamental laws which necessarily constitute a civil or religious society never has been or will be written *a priori*.

De Maistre assails the philosophes for attacking religion. Without Christianity, he says, people become brutalized, and civilization degenerates into anarchy.

Religion alone civilizes nations. No other known force can influence the savage. . . . [W]hat shall we think of a generation which has thrown everything to the winds, including the very foundations of the structure of society, by making education exclusively scientific? It was impossible to err more frightfully. For every educational system which does not have religion as its basis will collapse in an instant, or else diffuse only poisons throughout the State. . . . [I]f the guidance of education is not returned to the priests, and if science is not uniformly relegated to a subordinate rank, incalculable evils await us. We shall become brutalized by science, and that is the worst sort of brutality. . . .

Not until the first half of the eighteenth century did impiety really become a force. We see it at first spreading in every direction with amazing energy. From palaces to hovels, it insinuates itself everywhere, infesting everything. . . .

Joseph de Maistre, *On God and Society: Essays on the Generative Principle of Political Constitutions,* ed. Elisha Greifer and trans. with the assistance of Laurence M. Porter, pp. 3, 12–14, 29, 30, 33, 40, 45, 51, 54, 86. (Regnery-Gateway, 1959).

REVIEW QUESTIONS

1. Why was Edmund Burke opposed to the French Revolution?
2. What was Klemens von Metternich's opinion of "the progress of the human mind . . . in the . . . last three centuries" and its effect upon the society of his time?
3. What did Metternich mean by, "Drag through the mud the name of God and the powers instituted by His divine decrees, and the revolution will be prepared!"?
4. Why did Joseph de Maistre believe that man cannot create a constitution and no legitimate constitution can be written?
5. What views of late eighteenth- and early nineteenth-century conservatives are valued by American conservatives today?

---

3 Liberalism

Conservatism was the ideology of the old order that was hostile to the Enlightenment and the French Revolution; in contrast, liberalism aspired to carry out the promise of the philosophes and the Revolution. Liberals called for a constitution and parliamentary government that protected individual liberty and denounced censorship, arbitrary arrest, and other forms of repression. They believed that through reason and education, social evils could be remedied. Liberals rejected an essential feature of the Old Regime—the special privileges of the aristocracy and the clergy—and held that the individual should be judged on the basis of achievement, not birth. At the core of the liberal outlook lay the conviction that the individual would develop into a good and productive human being and citizen if not coerced by governments and churches.

Benjamin Constant
ON THE LIMITS OF POPULAR SOVEREIGNTY

Benjamin Constant (1767–1830), a leading French liberal theorist, feared the danger posed to liberty by democratic revolutionaries like Robespierre and his fellow Jacobins, who would exercise unlimited authority to establish liberty. Constant embraced the principle of popular sovereignty (that government derives its legitimacy and authority from the people), but warned against the danger of unlimited popular sovereignty. Neither the people as a whole nor their delegated representatives, said Constant, should possess total authority over the lives of individuals. To limit sovereignty, Constant supported a system of separation of powers in which no branch of government can exceed the authority granted to it. The following passage is taken from his book *Principles of Politics*, published in 1815.

When you establish that the sovereignty of the people is unlimited, you create and toss random into human society a degree of power which is too large in itself, and which is bound to constitute evil, in whatever hands it is placed. Entrust it to one man, to several, to all, you will still find it is equally an evil. . . .

In a society founded upon the sovereignty of the people, it is certain that no individual, no class, are entitled to subject the rest to their particular will. But it is not true that society as a whole has unlimited authority over its members. . . .

There is, on the contrary, a part of human existence which by necessity remains individual and independent, and which is, by right, outside any [governmental authority]. Sovereignty has only a limited and relative existence. At the point where independence and individual existence begin, the jurisdiction of sovereignty ends. If society oversteps this line, it is as guilty as the despot who has, as his only title, his exterminating sword. . . .

Biancamaria Fontana, ed. and tr., Benjamin Constant *Political Writings* (New York: Cambridge University Press, 1988), pp. 176–177, 179–180, 182.

When sovereignty is unlimited, there is no means of sheltering individuals from governments . . . who declare themselves their representatives, nor that of the kings, by whatever title they reign, nor, finally, that of the law, which, being merely the expression of the will of the people or of the prince, according to the form of government, must be circumscribed within the same limits as the authority from which it emanates.

The citizens possess individual rights independently of all social and political authority, and any authority which violates these rights becomes illegitimate. The rights of the citizens are individual freedom, religious freedom, freedom of opinion, which includes the freedom to express oneself openly, the enjoyment of property, a guarantee against all arbitrary power. No authority can call these rights into question without destroying its own credentials. . . .

Let us now sum up the consequences of our principles. The sovereignty of the people is not unlimited: it is, on the contrary, circumscribed within the limits traced by justice and by the rights of individuals.

John Stuart Mill
ON LIBERTY

Freedom of thought and expression were principal concerns of nineteenth-century liberals. The classic defense of intellectual freedom is *On Liberty* (1859), written by John Stuart Mill (1806–1873), a prominent British philosopher. Mill argued that no individual or government has a monopoly on truth, for all human beings are fallible. Therefore, the government and the majority have no legitimate authority to suppress views, however unpopular; they have no right to interfere with a person's liberty so long as that person's actions do no injury to others. Nothing is more absolute, contended Mill, than the inviolable right of all adults to think and live as they please so long as they respect the rights of others. For Mill, toleration of opposing and unpopular viewpoints is a necessary trait in order for a person to become rational, moral, and civilized.

The object of this essay is to assert one very simple principle, as entitled to govern absolutely the dealings of society with the individual. . . . That principle is that the sole end for which mankind are warranted, individually or collectively, in interfering with the liberty of action of any of their number is self-protection. That the only purpose for which power can be rightfully exercised over any member of a civilized community, against his will, is to prevent harm to others. His own good, either physical or moral, is not a sufficient warrant. He cannot rightfully be compelled to do or forbear because it will be better for him to do so, because it will make him happier, because, in the opinions of others, to do so would be wise or even right. These are good reasons for remonstrating with him, or reasoning with him, or persuading him, or entreating him, but not for compelling him or visiting him with any evil in case he do otherwise. To justify that, the conduct from which it is desired to deter him must be calculated to produce evil to someone else. The only part of the conduct of anyone for which he is amenable to society is that which concerns others. In the part which merely concerns himself, his independence is, of right, absolute. Over himself, over his own body and mind, the individual is sovereign. . . .

. . . This, then, is the appropriate region of human liberty. It comprises, first, the inward domain of consciousness, demanding liberty of conscience in the most comprehensive sense, liberty of thought and feeling, absolute freedom of opinion and sentiment on all subjects, practical or speculative, scientific, moral, or theological. The liberty of expressing and publishing opinions may seem to fall under a different principle, since it belongs to that part of the conduct of an individual which concerns other people, but, being almost of as much importance as the liberty of thought itself and

resting in great part on the same reasons, is practically inseparable from it. Secondly, the principle requires liberty of tastes and pursuits, of framing the plan of our life to suit our own character, of doing as we like, subject to such consequences as may follow, without impediment from our fellow creatures, so long as what we do does not harm them, even though they should think our conduct foolish, perverse, or wrong. Thirdly, from this liberty of each individual follows the liberty, within the same limits, of combination among individuals; freedom to unite for any purpose not involving harm to others: the persons combining being supposed to be of full age and not forced or deceived.

No society in which these liberties are not, on the whole, respected is free, whatever may be its form of government; and none is completely free in which they do not exist absolute and unqualified. The only freedom which deserves the name is that of pursuing our own good in our own way, so long as we do not attempt to deprive others of theirs or impede their efforts to obtain it. Each is the proper guardian of his own health, whether bodily *or* mental and spiritual. Mankind are greater gainers by suffering each other to live as seems good to themselves than by compelling each to live as seems good to the rest. . . .

. . . Let us suppose, therefore, that the government is entirely at one with the people, and never thinks of exerting any power of coercion unless in agreement with what it conceives to be their voice. But I deny the right of the people to exercise such coercion, either by themselves or by their government. The power itself is illegitimate. The best government has no more title to it than the worst. It is as noxious, or more noxious, when exerted in accordance with public opinion than when in opposition to it. If all mankind minus one were of one opinion, mankind would be no more justified in silencing that one person than he, if he had the power, would be justified in silencing mankind. Were an opinion a personal possession of

---

John Stuart Mill, *On Liberty* (Boston: Ticknor and Fields, 1863), pp. 22–23, 27–29, 35–36.

no value except to the owner, if to be obstructed in the enjoyment of it were simply a private injury, it would make some difference whether the injury was inflicted only on a few persons or on many. But the peculiar evil of silencing the expression of an opinion is that it is robbing the human race, posterity as well as the existing generation—those who dissent from the opinion, still more than those who hold it. If the opinion is right, they are deprived of the opportunity of exchanging error for truth; if wrong, they lose, what is almost as great a benefit, the clearer perception and livelier impression of truth produced by its collision with error.

REVIEW QUESTIONS

1. Benjamin Constant held that the consent of the people cannot make legitimate what is illegitimate. What implications did his statement "the jurisdiction of sovereignty stops at the point where the independence of individual life starts" have for liberalism and the prevailing ideas about majority rule?
2. What was the purpose of John Stuart Mill's essay?
3. For Mill, what is the "peculiar evil of silencing the expression of an opinion," however unpopular?
4. On what grounds would Mill permit society to restrict individual liberty? Do you think it is ever legitimate for the state to restrain an individual from harming himself?

4 Rise of Modern Nationalism

Nationalism espoused the individual's allegiance to the national community and sought to unify divided nations and to liberate subject peoples. In the early nineteenth century, most nationalists were liberals who viewed the struggle for unification and freedom from foreign oppression as an extension of the struggle for individual rights. Few liberals recognized that nationalism was a potentially dangerous force that could threaten liberal ideals of freedom and equality.

Ernst Moritz Arndt
THE WAR OF LIBERATION

By glorifying a nation's language and ancient traditions and folkways, Romanticism contributed to the evolution of modern nationalism, particularly in Germany. German Romantics longed to create a true folk community in which the individual's soul would be immersed in the nation's soul. Through the national community, individuals could find the meaning in life for which they yearned. The Romantic veneration of the past produced a mythical way of thinking about politics and history, one that subordinated reason to powerful emotions. In particular, some German Romantics attacked the liberal–rational tradition of the Enlightenment and the French Revolution as hostile to the true German spirit.

The Napoleonic wars kindled nationalist sentiments in the German states. Hatred of the French occupier evoked a feeling of outrage and a desire for national unity among some Germans, who before the occupation had thought not of a German fatherland but of their own states and princes. These Germans called for a war of liberation against Napoleon. Attracting mostly intellectuals, the idea of political unification had limited impact on the rest of the people, who remained loyal to local princes and local territories. Nevertheless, the embryo of nationalism was conceived in the German uprising against Napoleon in 1813. The writings of Ernst Moritz Arndt (1769–1860), composed in the same year, vividly express the emerging nationalism. The following excerpts describe Arndt's view of the War of Liberation and present his appeal for German unity.

Fired with enthusiasm, the people rose, "with God for King and Fatherland." Among the Prussians there was only one voice, one feeling, one anger and one love, to save the Fatherland and to free Germany. The Prussians wanted war; war and death they wanted; peace they feared because they could hope for no honorable peace from Napoleon. War, war, sounded the cry from the Carpathians [mountains] to the Baltic [Sea], from the Niemen to the Elbe [rivers]. War! cried the nobleman and landed proprietor who had become impoverished. War! the peasant who was driving his last horse to death. . . . War! the citizen who was growing exhausted from quartering soldiers and paying taxes. War! the widow who was sending her only son to the front. War! the young girl who, with tears of pride and pain, was leaving her betrothed. Youths who were hardly able to bear arms, men with gray hair, officers who on account of wounds and mutilations had long ago been honorably discharged, rich landed proprietors and officials, fathers of large families and managers of extensive businesses—all were unwilling to remain behind. Even young women, under all sorts of disguises, rushed to arms; all wanted to drill, arm themselves and fight and die for the Fatherland. . . .

From Ernst Moritz Arndt, *The War of Liberation*, 1913.

The most beautiful thing about all this holy zeal and happy confusion was that all differences of position, class, and age were forgotten . . . that the one great feeling for the Fatherland, its freedom and honor, swallowed all other feelings, caused all other considerations and relationships to be forgotten.—

In another passage, Arndt appealed for German unity.

German man, feel again God, hear and fear the eternal, and you hear and fear also your *Volk* [folk, people, nation]; you feel again in God the honor and dignity of your fathers, their glorious history rejuvenates itself again in you, their firm and gallant virtue reblossoms in you, the whole German Fatherland stands again before you in the august halo of past centuries! Then, when you feel and fear and honor all this, then you cry, then you lament, then you wrathfully reproach yourself that you have become so miserable and evil: then starts your new life and your new history. . . . From the North Sea to the Carpathians, from the Baltic to the Alps, from the Vistula to the Schelde [rivers], one faith, one love, one courage, and one enthusiasm must gather again the whole German folk in brotherly

Where is Albht doing?

community; they must learn to feel how great, mighty, and happy their fathers were in obedience to one German emperor and one Reich, at a time when the many discords had not yet turned one against the other, when the many cowards and knaves had not yet betrayed them; . . . above the ruins and ashes of their destroyed Fatherland they must weepingly join hands and pray and swear all to stand like one man and to fight until the sacred land will be free. . . . Feel the infinite and sublime which slumbers hidden in the lap of the days, those light and mighty spirits which now glimmer in isolated meteors but which soon will shine in all suns and stars; feel the new birth of times, the higher, cleaner breath of spiritual life and do not longer be fooled and confused by the insignificant and small. No longer Catholics and Protestants, no longer Prussians and Austrians, Saxons and Bavarians, Silesians and Hanoverians, no longer of different faith, different mentality, and different will—be Germans, be one, will to be one by love and loyalty, and no devil will vanquish you.

Giuseppe Mazzini
YOUNG ITALY

In 1815, Italy was a fragmented nation. Hapsburg Austria ruled Lombardy and Venetia in the north, and a Bourbon king sat on the throne of the Kingdom of the Two Sicilies in the south. The duchies of Tuscany, Parma, and Modena were ruled by Hapsburg princes subservient to Austria. The papal states in central Italy were ruled by the pope. The House of Savoy, an Italian dynasty, ruled the Kingdom of Piedmont, which became the cornerstone of Italian unification. Inspired by past Italian glories—the Roman Empire and the Renaissance—Italian nationalists demanded an end to foreign occupation and the unification of the Italian peninsula. As in other lands, national revival and unification appealed principally to intellectuals and the middle class.

Who was Mazzini.

A leading figure in the *Risorgimento*—the struggle for Italian nationhood—was Giuseppe Mazzini (1805–1872). Often called the "soul of the Risorgimento," Mazzini devoted his life to the creation of a unified and republican Italy; he believed that a free and democratic Italy would serve as a model to the other nations of Europe. In 1831, he founded Young Italy, a society dedicated to the cause of Italian unity. The following reading includes the oath taken by members of Young Italy.

Young Italy is a brotherhood of Italians who believe in a law of Progress and Duty, and are convinced that Italy is destined to become one nation,—convinced also that she possesses sufficient strength within herself to become one, and that the ill success of her former efforts is to be attributed not to the weakness, but to the misdirection of the revolutionary elements within her—that the secret of force lies in constancy and unity of effort. They join this association in the firm intent of consecrating both thought and action to the great aim of

Joseph Mazzini: His Life, Writings, and Political Principles, trans. and ed. Emilie Ashurst Venturi, intro. William Lloyd Garrison (New York: Hurd and Houghton, 1872), pp. 62, 69, 71–74.

Unity of effort

reconstituting Italy as one independent sovereign nation of free men and equals. . . .

Young Italy is Republican. . . . Republican—because theoretically every nation is destined, by the law of God and humanity, to form a free and equal community of brothers; and the republican is the only form of government that insures this future. . . .

The means by which Young Italy proposes to reach its aim are—education and insurrection, to be adopted simultaneously, and made to harmonize with each other. Education must ever be directed to teach by example, word, and pen the necessity of insurrection. Insurrection, whenever it can be realized, must be so conducted as to render it a means of national education. . . .

Insurrection—by means of guerrilla bands—is the true method of warfare for all nations desirous of emancipating themselves from a foreign yoke. This method of warfare supplies the want—inevitable at the commencement of the insurrection—of a regular army; it calls the greatest number of elements into the field, and yet may be sustained by the smallest number. It forms the military education of the people, and consecrates every foot of the native soil by the memory of some warlike deed. . . .

Each member will, upon his initiation into the association of Young Italy, pronounce the following form of oath, in the presence of the initiator:

In the name of God and of Italy;

In the name of all the martyrs of the holy Italian cause who have fallen beneath foreign and domestic tyranny;

By the duties which bind me to the land wherein God has placed me, and to the brothers whom God has given me;

By the love—innate in all men—I bear to the country that gave my mother birth, and will be the home of my children;

By the hatred—innate in all men—I bear to evil, injustice, usurpation and arbitrary rule;

By the blush that rises to my brow when I stand before the citizens of other lands, to know that I have no rights of citizenship, no country, and no national flag;—

By the aspiration that thrills my soul towards that liberty for which it was created, and is impotent to exert; towards the good it was created to strive after, and is impotent to achieve in the silence and isolation of slavery;

By the memory of our former greatness, and the sense of our present degradation;

By the tears of Italian mothers for their sons dead on the scaffold, in prison, or in exile;

By the sufferings of the millions,—

I, . . . believing in the mission intrusted by God to Italy, and the duty of every Italian to strive to attempt its fulfillment; convinced that where God has ordained that a nation shall be, He has given the requisite power to create it; that the people are the depositaries of that power, and that in its right direction for the people, and by the people, lies the secret of victory; convinced that virtue consists in action and sacrifice, and strength in union and constancy of purpose: I give my name to Young Italy, an association of men holding the same faith, and swear:

To dedicate myself wholly and forever to the endeavor with them to constitute Italy one free, independent, republican nation; to promote by every means in my power—whether by written or spoken word, or by action—the education of my Italian brothers towards the aim of Young Italy; towards association, the sole means of its accomplishment, and to virtue, which alone can render the conquest lasting; to abstain from enrolling myself in any other association from this time forth; to obey all the instructions, in conformity with the spirit of Young Italy, given me by those who represent with me the union of my Italian brothers; and to keep the secret of these instructions, even at the cost of my life; to assist my brothers of the association both by action and counsel—

NOW AND FOREVER

This do I swear, invoking upon my head the wrath of God, the abhorrence of man, and the infamy of the perjurer, if I ever betray the whole or a part of this my oath.

REVIEW QUESTIONS

1. Ernst Moritz Arndt's writings show the interconnection between Romanticism and nationalism. Discuss this statement.
2. Why do you suppose many students were attracted to Young Italy?
3. Giuseppe Mazzini was a democrat, a nationalist, and a Romantic. Discuss this statement.

---

5 Repression

Russia, Austria, Prussia, and Great Britain agreed to act together to preserve the territorial settlement of the Congress of Vienna and the balance of power. After paying its indemnity, France was admitted into this Quadruple Alliance, also known as the Concert of Europe. Metternich intended to use the Concert of Europe to maintain harmony among nations and internal stability within nations. Toward this end, conservatives in their respective countries censored books and newspapers, imprisoned liberal activists, and suppressed nationalist uprisings.

KARLSBAD DECREES

In 1819, Metternich and representatives from other German states meeting at Karlsbad drew up several decrees designed to stifle liberalism and nationalism. The Karlsbad Decrees called for the dissolution of the *Burschenschaften* (German student fraternities), the censoring of books and newspapers, and the dismissal of professors who spread liberal doctrines.

Provisional Decree relative to the Measures to be taken concerning the Universities.

Sect. 1. The Sovereign shall make choice for each university of an extraordinary commissioner, furnished with suitable instructions and powers, residing in the place where the university is established. . . .

The duty of this commissioner shall be to . . . observe carefully the spirit with which the professors and tutors are guided in their public and private lectures; . . . and to devote a constant attention to every thing which may tend to the maintenance of morality, good order and decency among the youths.

Sect. 2. The governments of the states, members of the confederation, reciprocally engage to remove from their universities and other establishment of instruction, the professors and other public teachers, against whom it may be proved, that in departing from their duty, in overstepping the bounds of their duty, in abusing their legitimate influence over the minds of youth, by the propagation of pernicious dogmas, hostile to order and public tranquility, or in sapping

Reprinted from Great Britain, "Annual Register" (1819), pp. 159–160.

the foundation of existing establishments, they have shown themselves incapable of executing the important functions entrusted to them. . . .

A professor or tutor thus excluded, cannot be admitted in any other state of the confederation to any other establishment of public instruction.

Sect. 3. The laws long since made against secret or unauthorized associations at the universities, shall be maintained in all their force and rigour, and shall be particularly extended with so much the more severity against the well-known society formed some years ago under the name of the General Burschenschaft, as it has for its basis an idea, absolutely inadmissible, of community and continued correspondence between the different universities.

The governments shall mutually engage to admit to no public employment any individuals who may continue or enter into any of those associations after the publication of the present decree.

Decree relative to the Measures for preventing the Abuses of the Press.

Sect. 1. . . . No writing appearing in the form of a daily paper or periodical pamphlet . . . shall be issued from the press without the previous consent of the public authority. . . .

Sect. 7. The editor of a journal, or other periodical publication, that may be suppressed by command of the Diet, shall not be allowed, during the space of five years, to conduct any similar publication in any states of the confederation. . . .

Decree relative to the formation of a Central Commission, for the purpose of Ulterior Inquiry respecting Revolutionary Plots, discovered in some of the States of the Confederation.

Art. 1. In 15 days from the date of this decree, an extraordinary commission of inquiry, appointed by the Diet and composed of 7 members, including the President, shall assemble in the city of Mentz, a fortress of the confederation.

2. The object of this commission is, to make careful and detailed inquires respecting the facts, the origin and the multiplied ramifications of the secret revolutionary and demagogic associations, directed against the political constitution and internal repose, as well of the confederation in general, as of the individual members thereof.

REVIEW QUESTIONS

1. What was Metternich afraid of?
2. Draw parallels between the Karlsbad Decrees and the actions of certain regimes in the twentieth and twenty-first centuries.

6 1848: The Year of Revolutions

In 1848, revolutions for political liberty and nationhood broke out in many parts of Europe. An uprising in Paris set this revolutionary tidal wave in motion. In February 1848, democrats seeking to create a French republic and to institute universal manhood suffrage precipitated a crisis; the pursuant uprising in Paris forced King Louis Philippe to abdicate. The leaders of the new French Republic championed political democracy but, with some notable exceptions like Louis Blanc (1811–1882), had little concern for the plight of the laboring poor.

The publication of the *Organization of Labor* (1839) had established Blanc as a leading French social reformer. Blanc urged the government to finance national workshops—industrial corporations, in which the directors would be elected by the workers—to provide employment for the urban poor. The government responded to Blanc's insistence that all workers have the "right to work" by indeed establishing national workshops, but these provided jobs for only a fraction of the unemployed, and many workers were given wages for doing nothing. Property owners regarded the workshops as a waste of government funds and as nests of working-class radicalism. When the government closed the workshops in June 1848, Parisian workers revolted.

Flora Tristan
"WORKERS, YOUR CONDITION . . . IS MISERABLE AND DISTRESSING"

Flora Tristan (1803–1844) did not live to see the working-class revolution of 1848, but her appeals for social justice contributed to the unrest of French workers, which exploded in the June Days. Addressing audiences in several cities, Tristan urged workers to strengthen their cause by uniting in a national Workers' Union. In October 1848 eight thousand French workers expressed their gratitude to Tristan by witnessing the unveiling of a monument in her honor at her gravesite. As the following selections from her writings indicate, Tristan was also a pioneer French feminist.

Workers, your condition in present-day society is miserable and distressing: in good health, you have no right to work; in illness, weakness, injury, old age, you have no right to go to a hospital; in poverty, lacking everything, you have no right to beg because begging is against the law. This precarious situation reduces you to a state of savagery in which a man, like a forest dweller, is forced each morning to think up the means to provide himself with sustenance for the day ahead. Such an existence is a real torment. The lot of the animal that chews the cud in the cattle-shed is a thousand times better

Flora Tristan, *Union Ouvrière*, trans. Angela Von Laue (Paris: Edition d'Histoire Sociale, 1967, 1884), pp. 4–6, 51–59, 62–63, 69. Used with permission of Angela Von Laue.

than yours; he is certain to eat tomorrow; his master takes care of him in the barn, with straw and hay for winter. . . .

Workers, you are unhappy, yes, without a doubt; but what is the cause of your misery? . . . Why do you remain isolated? Isolated you are weak and exhausted under the burdens of all sorts of misery. So, come out of your isolation, unite! In unity is strength! There are so many of you.

I come to propose to you a general union between working men and working women, without distinction of trades, living in the same country; a union for and constituted by the working class, and which would construct several establishments (Palaces of the Workers' Union) distributed across France. There, children of both sexes from six to eighteen years old would be educated, and it would be a refuge for all ill, wounded, or old workers.

There are in France around five million working men and two million working women. Let these seven million workers unite themselves in thought and action to create a great commune for the benefit of all men and women. . . .

Tristan was determined that workingmen accept workingwomen as equals. She described the lives of workingwomen, showing how their lives were blighted by the lack of education and the ill-treatment of husbands, who were themselves scorned by the other classes in France. The footnotes are Tristan's.

In the life of the workers, the woman is everything. She is their sole providence [caregiver and controlling influence]. If she fails them, everything fails. It is said, "The woman makes or breaks the home," and that is the exact truth; that is why it has become a proverb. Yet what education, what instruction, what direction, what moral or physical development does the woman of the people receive? None. As a child she is left to the mercy of a mother or grandmother who, themselves, received no education; one of them, according to her nature, will be brutal and bad-tempered, will beat and ill-treat her without reason; the other will be weak and careless, and let her do just what she pleases. (In this, as in everything that I set down, I speak in general terms; of course I admit that there are numerous exceptions.) The poor child will grow up in the midst of bewildering contradictions. One day angered by blows and unjust treatment, the next day spoiled by indulgences no less pernicious.

Instead of going to school, she, rather than her brothers, will be kept at home, because she is better suited to household jobs, such as rocking babies, running errands, watching over the soup, etc. At age twelve she goes out

to domestic service; there she continues to be exploited by her employer, and often as ill-treated as she was at her parent's house.

Nothing embitters character, hardens the heart, nor results in a bad temper like the continual suffering that a child endures as a result of unjust and brutal treatment. . . .

Such will be the normal situation for a poor young girl of twenty. Then she will marry, without love, and only because it is necessary to marry in order to escape the tyranny of her parents. What happens next? I assume she will have children; in her turn she will be totally incapable of raising her sons and her daughters properly: she will be as brutal toward them as her mother and grandmother were to her.[1] . . . .

The majority of the women of the people are brutal, spiteful, at times harsh. It's true; but how is it that this state of affairs so little matches the gentle, sensitive, generous nature of women in general?

Poor working-class wives! They have so many causes of irritation! First the husband. (One must admit that there are few workers' households that are happy.) The husband, having received more education, being the head of the household by law, and also by the money that he brings into the household, thinks himself (and indeed he is) far superior to the wife who brings in only a small daily wage, and is only a very humble servant in the house.

The result of this is that the husband treats his wife with, at least, much disdain. The poor wife who feels humiliated by each word, each look that her husband gives her, revolts openly or within herself, according to her nature; from that come violent painful scenes, which lead

---

[1]The women of the people show themselves to be very tender mothers for little children up to the age of two to three years. Their womanly instinct understands that a child during its first two years needs continual care. But beyond this age they ill-treat them (save for exceptions).

to a constant state of irritation between the master and the servant (one can even say slave, because the wife is, so to speak, the property of the husband). This state becomes so upsetting that the husband, instead of staying home to chat with his wife, is in a hurry to flee, and as he has no other place to go, he goes to the tavern and drinks absinthe with other husbands as unhappy as he, in the hope of drowning his sorrows.[2]

These means of distraction make things worse. The wife, who has to wait for the money until Sunday in order to provide for her family during the week, is in despair at seeing her husband spend the greater part of it at the tavern. Then his irritation is filled to over-flowing, and his cruelty and spitefulness are redoubled. . . .

Then, after the bitter distress caused by the husband, come pregnancies, illnesses, loss of work and poverty, poverty that is always planted at the door like the head of Medusa.

---

[2]Why do workers go to the tavern? Egotism has struck the upper classes, those who rule, with complete blindness. They do not understand that their fortune, their happiness, and their security depend on the moral, intellectual, and material betterment of the working class. They abandon the worker to poverty and ignorance, reasoning according to the ancient maxim that the more brute-like the people are, the easier it is to muzzle them. All this was true before the *Declaration of the Rights of Man*. Since then it is a crassly ignorant anachronism, a grave mistake. Moreover, one should be at least consistent: if one believes that it is a good and wise policy to leave the poor in a brute condition, then why recriminate ceaselessly against their vices?

The rich accuse the workers of being lazy, debauched, drunken, and in order to support their accusations they say, "If the workers are poor, it is solely their own fault. Go to the . . . taverns, you will find them full of workers who are there to drink and waste their time." I believe that if the workers, instead of going to the tavern, assembled seven at a time (a number permitted by the September laws) in one room, to learn about their rights and consider what action to take in order to make them legally valid, the rich would be more unhappy than they are at seeing the taverns full.

In the present state of affairs the tavern is the worker's temple; it is the only place where he can go. He does not believe in the church, he understands nothing in the theater. That is why the taverns are always full. . . .

The taverns are not the cause of evil, but simply the effect. The cause of evil lies solely in the ignorance, the poverty, the brutalization into which the working class is plunged. . . .

Added to all this is the incessant strain caused by four or five crying, turbulent, annoying children who whirl around their mother, and all that in the cramped worker's dwelling where there is no place to move. Oh! One would have to be an angel on earth not to be irritated, brutal, and bad-tempered in such a situation. In the midst of such a family, however, what happens to the children? They see their father only in the evenings and on Sunday. This father, always in a state of irritation or inebriation, does not speak to them except in anger, and they receive from him only abuse and blows, hearing their mother plead with him continually, they acquire hatred and scorn for him. As for their mother, they fear her, they obey her, but they do not love her. One is made in such a way that one cannot love those who treat one badly. . . . Not having any reason to stay with his mother, the child will seek for any pretext to move away from home. Bad company is easy to get into, for girls as for boys. Idleness leads to vagrancy, and following vagrancy comes crime. . . .

Do you begin to understand, you, the men who exclaim in horror before trying to examine the question, why I claim rights for the women? It is because I wish that she were placed on an absolutely equal footing with the man, and that she enjoy it by virtue of the legal right that every person has at birth. . . .

All the evils of the working class are summed up in these two words: poverty and ignorance, ignorance and poverty. Now, in order to get out of this labyrinth, I see only one way: begin by educating women, because women are in charge of raising their children, male and female. . . .

Therefore it is up to you, workers, who are the victims of inequality in practice and of injustice—it is up to you to establish at last the reign of justice on earth and of absolute equality between men and women.

Give the world a great example, an example that will prove to your oppressors that it is by law that you wish to triumph and not by brute force; nevertheless, you, seven, ten, fifteen million proletarians [workers] have this brute force at your disposal!

While claiming justice for yourselves, prove that you are just and impartial; proclaim, you strong men, men with bare arms, that you recognize the woman as your equal, and because of this claim, you recognize her equal right to the benefits of the Universal Union of Workingmen and Workingwomen.

Alexis de Tocqueville
THE JUNE DAYS

The bourgeoisie who came to power in the February Revolution of 1848 were committed to political democracy, but only a few favored the social reforms demanded by the laboring poor. To the French workers, the June 1848 revolt was against poverty and for a fairer distribution of property (in contrast to the first revolt in February 1848, which concerned political change). Viewing this uprising as a threat to property and indeed to civilization, the rest of France rallied against the workers, who were crushed after several days of bitter street fighting.

In his *Recollections,* published posthumously in 1893, Alexis de Tocqueville (1805–1859), a leading statesman and political theorist (see chapter 4), included a speech he made on January 29, 1848, before the French Chamber of Deputies, in which he warned the officials about the mood of the laboring poor.

. . . I am told that there is no danger because there are no riots; I am told that, because there is no visible disorder on the surface of society, there is no revolution at hand.

Gentlemen, permit me to say that I believe you are deceived. True, there is no actual disorder; but it has entered deeply into men's minds. See what is passing in the breasts of the working classes, who, I grant, are at present quiet. No doubt they are not disturbed by political passion, properly so-called, to the same extent that they have been; but can you not see that their passions, instead of political, have become social? Do you not see that there are gradually forming in their breasts opinions and ideas which are destined not only to upset

The Recollections of Alexis de Tocqueville, trans. A. T. De Mattos (New York: Macmillan, 1896), pp. 14, 187–189, 197–200.

this or that law, ministry, or even form of government, but society itself, until it totters upon the foundations on which it rests today? Do you not listen to what they say to themselves each day? Do you not hear them repeating unceasingly that all that is above them is incapable and unworthy of governing them; that the present distribution of goods throughout the world is unjust; that property rests on a foundation which is not an equitable foundation? And do you not realize that when such opinions take root, when they spread in an almost universal manner, when they sink deeply into the masses, they are bound to bring with them sooner or later, I know not when nor how, a most formidable revolution?

This, gentlemen, is my profound conviction: I believe that we are at this moment sleeping on a volcano. I am profoundly convinced of it. . . .

Later in his Recollections, de Tocqueville describes the second uprising in 1848, called the June Days.

I come at last to the insurrection of June, the most extensive and the most singular that has occurred in our history, and perhaps in any other: the most extensive, because, during four days, more than a hundred thousand men were engaged in it; the most singular, because the insurgents fought without a war-cry, without leaders, without flags, and yet with a marvellous harmony and an amount of military experience that astonished the oldest officers.

What distinguished it also, among all the events of this kind which have succeeded one another in France for sixty years, is that it did not aim at changing the form of government, but at altering the order of society. It was not, strictly speaking, a political struggle, in the sense which until then we had given to the word, but a combat of class against class, a sort of Servile War [slave uprising in ancient Rome]. It represented the facts of the Revolution of February in the same manner as the theories of Socialism represented its ideas; or rather it issued naturally from these ideas, as a son does from his mother. We behold in it nothing more than a blind and rude, but powerful, effort on the part of the workmen to escape from the necessities of their condition, which had been depicted to them as one of unlawful oppression, and to open up by main force a road towards that imaginary comfort with which they had been deluded. It was this mixture of greed and false theory which first gave birth to the insurrection and then made it so formidable. These poor people had been told that the wealth of the rich was in some way the produce of a theft practised upon themselves. They had been assured that the inequality of fortunes was as opposed to morality and the welfare of society as it was to nature. Prompted by their needs and their

passions, many had believed this obscure and erroneous notion of right, which, mingled with brute force, imparted to the latter an energy, a tenacity and a power which it would never have possessed unaided.

It must also be observed that this formidable insurrection was not the enterprise of a certain number of conspirators, but the revolt of one whole section of the population against another. Women took part in it as well as men. While the latter fought, the former prepared and carried ammunition; and when at last the time had come to surrender, the women were the last to yield. These women went to battle with, as it were, a housewifely ardour: they looked to victory for the comfort of their husbands and the education of their children. . . .

As we know, it was the closing of the national workshops that occasioned the rising. Dreading to disband this formidable soldiery at one stroke, the Government had tried to disperse it by sending part of the workmen into the country. They refused to leave. On the 22nd of June, they marched through Paris in troops, singing in cadence, in a monotonous chant, "We won't be sent away, we won't be sent away. . . ."

. . . The spirit of insurrection circulated from one to the other of this immense class, and in each of its parts, as the blood does in the body; it filled the quarters where there was no fighting, as well as those which served as the scene of battle; it had penetrated into our houses, around, above, below us. The very places in which we thought ourselves the masters swarmed with domestic enemies; one might say that an atmosphere of civil war enveloped the whole of Paris, amid which, to whatever part we withdrew, we had to live. . . .

. . . It was easy to perceive through the multitude of contradictory reports that we had to do with the most universal, the best armed, and the most furious insurrection ever known in Paris. The national workshops and various revolutionary bands that had just been disbanded supplied it with trained and disciplined soldiers and with leaders. It was extending every moment, and it was difficult to believe that it would not end by being victorious, . . . all the great insurrections of the last sixty years had triumphed. . . .

Nevertheless, we succeeded in triumphing over this so formidable insurrection; nay more, it was just that which rendered it so terrible which saved us. . . . Had the revolt borne a less radical character and a less ferocious aspect, it is probable that the greater part of the middle class would have stayed at home; France would not have come to our aid; the National Assembly itself would perhaps have yielded, or at least a minority of its members would have advised it; and the energy of the whole body would have been greatly unnerved. But the insurrection was of such a nature that any understanding with it became at once impossible, and from the first it left us no alternative but to defeat it or to be destroyed ourselves.

Carl Schurz
REVOLUTION SPREADS TO THE GERMAN STATES

The February Revolution was eagerly received by German liberals and nationalists who yearned for a unified Germany governed by a national parliament and a constitution that guaranteed basic liberties. In his Reminiscences (posthumous, 1907–1908), Carl Schurz (1929–1906), a student at the University of Bonn in 1848-1849, recalled the excitement in Bonn:

> Such tidings rushed in upon us from all sides like a roaring hurricane. . . . A great multitude gathered for a solemn procession through the streets of the town. The most respectable citizens, not a few professors and a great number of students and people of all grades marched in close ranks. . . . Professor Kinkel. . . . spoke with a wonderful eloquence . . . depicting a resurrection of German unity and greatness and of the liberties and rights of the German people, which now must be conceded by the princes or won by force by the people. . . . People clapped their hands, they shouted, they embraced one another, they shed tears.

After the revolution failed, Schurz fled to Switzerland and eventually went to the United States, where he had a distinguished career as a senator, cabinet member, and journalist. In the following excerpt from his Reminiscences, Schurz tells of the hopes of German liberals and nationalists when hearing of what seemed a successful revolution in Paris.

One morning, toward the end of February, 1848, I sat quietly in my attic-chamber, working hard at my tragedy of "Ulrich von Hut- ten," when suddenly a friend rushed breathlessly into the room, exclaiming: "What, you sitting here! Do you not know what has happened?"

Carl Schurz, *The Reminiscences of Carl Schurz, vol. 1* (New York: The McClure Company, 1907), pp. 112–117.

"No; what?"

"The French have driven away Louis Philippe and proclaimed the republic."

I threw down my pen—and that was the end of "Ulrich von Hutten." I never touched the manuscript again. We tore down the stairs, into the street, to the market-square, the accustomed meeting-place for all the student societies after their midday dinner. Although it was still forenoon, the market was already crowded with young men talking excitedly. There was no shouting, no noise, only agitated conversation. What did we want there? This probably no one knew. But since the French had driven away Louis Philippe and proclaimed the republic, something of course must happen here, too. Some of the students had brought their rapiers along, as if it were necessary at once to make an attack or to defend ourselves. We were dominated by a vague feeling as if a great outbreak of elemental forces had begun, as if an earthquake was impending of which we had felt the first shock, and we instinctively crowded together. Thus we wandered about in numerous bands . . . [and] fell into conversation with all manner of strangers, to find in them the same confused, astonished and expectant state of mind; then back to the market-square, to see what might be going on there; then again somewhere else, and so on, without aim and end, until finally late in the night fatigue compelled us to find the way home.

The next morning there were the usual lectures to be attended. But how profitless! The voice of the professor sounded like a monotonous drone coming from far away. What he had to say did not seem to concern us. The pen that should have taken notes remained idle. At last we closed with a sigh the notebook and went away, impelled by a feeling that now we had something more important to do—to devote ourselves to the affairs of the fatherland. And this we did by seeking as quickly as possible again the company of our friends, in order to discuss what had happened and what was to come. In these conversations, excited as they were, certain ideas and catchwords worked themselves to the surface, which expressed more or less the feelings of the people. Now had arrived in Germany the day for the establishment of "German Unity,' and the founding of a great, powerful national German Empire. In the first line the convocation of a national parliament. Then the demands for civil rights and liberties, free speech, f;i;ee press, the right of free assembly, equality before the law, a freely elected representation of the people with legislative power, responsibility of ministers, self-government of the communes, the right of the people to carry arms, the formation of a civic guard with elective officers, and so on— in short, that which was called a "constitutional form of government on a broad democratic basis/' Republican ideas were at first only sparingly expressed. But the word democracy was soon on all tongues, and many, too, thought it a matter of course that if the princes should try to withhold from the people the rights and liberties demanded, force would take the place of mere petition. Of course the regeneration of the fatherland must, if possible, be accomplished by peaceable means. A few days after the outbreak of this commotion I reached my nineteenth birthday. I remember to have been so entirely absorbed by what was happening that I could hardly turn my thoughts to anything else. Like many of my friends, I was dominated b'y the feeling that at last the great opportunity had arrived for giving to the German people the liberty which was their birthright and to the German fatherland its unity and greatness, and that it was now the first duty of every German to do and to sacrifice everything for this sacred object. We were profoundly, solemnly in earnest ....

Exciting news came from all sides. In Cologne a threatening ferment prevailed. In the taverns and on the streets resounded the "Marseillaise" {French national anthem, symbol of the Revolution}, which at that time still passed in all Europe as the "hymn of liberty/' On the public places great meetings were held to consult about the demands to be made by the people. A large deputation, headed by the late lieutenant of artillery, August von Willich, forced its way into the hall of the city council, vehemently insisting that the municipality present as its own the demands of the people of Cologne to the king. The streets resounded with the military drumbeat; the soldiery marched upon the popular gatherings, and Willich, as well as another ex-artillery officer, Fritz Anneke, were arrested; whereupon increasing excitement....

. . . In Coblenz, Di.isseldorf, Aachen, Crefeld, Cleves and other cities on the Rhine similar demonstrations took place. In South Germany—in Baden, Hessen-on-the-Rhine, Nassau, Wi.irtemberg, Bavaria—the same revolutionary spirit burst forth like a prairie-fire. In Baden the Grand Duke acceded almost at once to what was asked of him, and so did the rulers of Wurtemberg, Nassau, and Hessen- Darmstadt....

Great news came from Vienna. There the students of the university were the first to assail the Emperor of Austria with the cry for liberty and citizens' rights. Blood flowed in the streets, and the downfall of Prince Metter- nich was the result. The students i organized themselves as the armed guard of liberty. In the great cities of Prussia there was a mighty commotion. Not only Cologne, Coblenz and Trier, but also Breslau, Konigsberg and Frank- furt-on-the-Oder, sent deputations to Berlin to entreat the king. In the Prussian capital the masses surged upon the streets, and everybody looked for events of great import.

While such tidings rushed in upon us from all sides like a roaring hurricane, we in the little university town of Bonn were also busy preparing addresses to the sovereign, to circulate them for signature and to send them to Berlin. On the 18th of March we too had our mass demonstration. A great multitude gathered for a solemn procession through the streets of the town. The most respectable citizens, not a few professors and a great number of students and people of all grades marched in close ranks. At the head of the procession Professor Kinkel bore the tricolor, black, red and gold, which so long had been prohibited as the revolutionary flag. Arrived on the market-square he mounted the steps of the city hall and spoke to the assembled throng. He spoke with wonderful eloquence, his voice ringing out in its most powerful tones as he depicted a resurrection of German unity and .greatness and of the liberties and rights of the German people, which now must be conceded by the princes or won by force by the people. And when at last he waved the black, red and gold banner, and predicted to a free German nation a magnificent future, enthusiasm without bounds broke forth. People clapped their hands, they shouted, they embraced one another, they shed tears. In a moment the city was covered with black, red and gold flags, and not only the Burschenschaft, but almost everybody wore a black-red-gold cockade on his hat. While on that 18th of March we were parading through the streets suddenly sinister rumors flew from mouth to mouth. It had been reported that the king of Prussia, after long hesitation, had finally concluded, like the other German princes, to concede the demands that were pouring upon him from all sides. But now a whispered report flew around that the soldiery had suddenly fired upon the people and that a bloody struggle was raging in the streets of Berlin.

REVIEW QUESTIONS

1. To what causes did Flora Tristan attribute the miseries of the working class in France? What remedies did she propose?
2. According to Alexis de Tocqueville, why did Parisian workers revolt in 1848?
3. How did the goals of Parisian workers who revolted in 1848 differ from those of members of Giuseppe Mazzini's Young Italy?
4. De Tocqueville observed that what distinguished this revolt was that it aimed to change the order of society, not the form of government. Explain.
5. What were the goals of Schurz and many of his colleagues? How did they seek to reconcile nationalism and liberalism?

CHAPTER 7

Thought and Culture in an Age of Science and Industry

A CARICATURE OF DARWIN, by Faustin Betbeder, 1874. Darwin's theory of evolution created much controversy and aroused considerable bitterness. In this caricature, the ape-like Darwin, holding a mirror, is explaining his theory of evolution to a fellow ape. (© *Hulton Archive/Getty Images*)

Romanticism dominated European art, literature, and music in the early nineteenth century. Stressing the feelings and the free expression of personality, the Romantic movement was a reaction against the rationalism of the Enlightenment. In the middle decades of the century, realism and its close auxiliary naturalism supplanted Romanticism as the chief norm of cultural expression. Rejecting religious, metaphysical, and Romantic interpretations of reality, realists aspired to an exact and accurate portrayal of the external world and daily life. Realist and naturalist writers used the empirical approach: the careful collection, ordering, and interpretation of facts employed in science, which was advancing steadily in the nineteenth century. Among the most important scientific theories formulated was Charles Darwin's theory of evolution, which revolutionized conceptions of time and the origins of the human species.

The principal currents of political thought, Marxism and liberalism, also reacted against Romantic, religious, and metaphysical interpretations of nature and society, focused on the empirical world, and strove for scientific accuracy. This emphasis on objective reality helped to stimulate a growing criticism of social ills, for despite unprecedented material progress, reality was often sordid, somber, and dehumanizing. In the last part of the century, reformers motivated by an expansive liberalism, revolutionary or evolutionary socialism, or a socially committed Christianity pressed for the alleviation of social injustice.

1 Realism in Literature

The middle decades of the nineteenth century were characterized by the growing importance of science and industrialization in European life. A movement known as positivism sought to apply the scientific method to the study of society. Rejecting theological and metaphysical theories as unscientific, positivists sought to arrive at the general laws that underlie society by carefully assembling and classifying data.

This stress on a rigorous observation of reality also characterized realism and naturalism, the dominant movements in art and literature. In several ways, realism differed from Romanticism, the dominant cultural movement in the first half of the century. Romantics were concerned with the inner life—with feelings, intuition, and imagination. They sought escape from the city into natural beauty, and they venerated the past, particularly the Middle Ages, which they viewed as noble, idyllic, and good in contrast to the spiritually impoverished present. Realists, on the other hand, shifted attention away from individual human feelings to the external world, which they investigated with the meticulous care of the scientist. Preoccupied with reality as it actually is, realist writers and artists depicted ordinary people, including the poor and humble, in ordinary circumstances. With a careful eye for detail and in a matter-of-fact way devoid of Romantic exuberance and exaggeration, realists described peasants, factory workers, laundresses, beggars, criminals, and prostitutes.

Realism quickly evolved into naturalism. Naturalist writers held that human behavior was determined by the social environment. They argued that certain social and economic conditions produced predictable traits in men and women and that cause and effect operated in society as well as in physical nature.

Charles Dickens
HARD TIMES

British novelist Charles Dickens (1812–1870) depicted in detail the squalor of English industrial cities, the drudgery of factory labor, and the hypocrisy of society. His novel *Hard Times* (1854) was his harshest indictment of the industrial system, and it offers a good example of the realist genre in literature.

It was a town of red brick, or of brick that would have been red if the smoke and ashes had allowed it; but as matters stood it was a town of unnatural red and black like the painted face of a savage. It was a town of machinery and tall chimneys, out of which interminable serpents of smoke trailed themselves for ever and ever, and never got uncoiled. It had a black canal in it, and a river that ran purple with ill-smelling dye, and vast piles of building full of windows where there was a rattling and a trembling all day long, and where the piston of the steam-engine worked monotonously up and down like the head of an elephant in a state of melancholy madness. It contained several large streets all very like one another, and many small streets still more like one another, inhabited by people equally like one another, who all went in and out at the same hours, with the same sound upon the same pavements, to do the same work, and to

whom every day was the same as yesterday and tomorrow, and every year the counterpart of the last and the next. . . .

In the hardest working part of Coketown; in the innermost fortifications of that ugly citadel, where Nature was as strongly bricked out as killing airs and gases were bricked in; at the heart of the labyrinth of narrow courts upon courts, and close streets upon streets, which had come into existence piecemeal, every piece in a violent hurry for some one man's purpose, and the whole an unnatural family, shouldering, and trampling, and pressing one another to death; in the last close nook of this great exhausted receiver, where the chimneys, for want of air to make a draught, were built in an immense variety of stunted and crooked shapes, as though every house put out a sign of the kind of people who might be expected to be born in it; among the multitude of Coketown, generically called 'the Hands,'—a race who would have found more favour with some people, if Providence had seen fit to make them only hands, or, like the lower creatures of the seashore, only hands and stomachs. . . .

Charles Dickens, *The Uncommercial Traveler; Hard Times: and the Mystery of Edwin Drood* (New York: Harper and Brothers, 1876), pp. 130, 144, 216.

As Coketown cast ashes not only on its own head but on the neighbourhood's too—after the manner of those pious persons who do penance for their own sins by putting other people into sackcloth—it was customary for those who now and then thirsted for a draught of pure air, which is not absolutely the most wicked among the vanities of life, to get a few miles away by the railroad, and then begin their walk, or their lounge in the fields. . . .

Though the green landscape was blotted here and there with heaps of coal, it was green elsewhere, and there were trees to see, and there were larks singing (though it was Sunday), and there were pleasant scents in the air, and all was over-arched by a bright blue sky. In the distance one way, Coketown showed as a black mist; in another distance hills began to rise; in a third, there was a faint change in the light of the horizon where it shone upon the far-off sea. Under their feet, the grass was fresh; beautiful shadows of branches flickered upon it, and speckled it; hedgerows were luxuriant; everything was at peace. Engines at pits' mouths, and lean old horses that had worn the circle of their daily labour into the ground, were alike quiet; wheels had ceased for a short space to turn; and the great wheel of earth seemed to revolve without the shocks and noises of another time.

Henrik Ibsen
A DOLL'S HOUSE

Realism was not restricted to the novel alone. The leading realist playwright, Henrik Ibsen (1828–1906), a Norwegian, examined with clinical precision the commercial and professional classes, their personal ambitions, business practices, and family relationships. In a period of less than ten years, Ibsen wrote four realist "problem plays"—*Pillars of Society* (1877), *A Doll's House* (1879), *Ghosts* (1881), and *An Enemy of the People* (1882)—that drew attention to bourgeois pretensions, hypocrisy, and social conventions that thwart individual growth. Thus, Ibsen's characters are typically torn between their sense of duty to others and their own selfish wants. Although Ibsen wrote about profound social issues, he viewed himself as a dramatist relating a piece of reality and not a social reformer agitating for reform.

In *A Doll's House,* Ibsen took up a theme that shocked bourgeois audiences in the late nineteenth century: a woman leaving her husband and children in search of self-realization. Nora Helmer resents being a submissive and dutiful wife to a husband who does not take her seriously, who treats her like a child, a doll.

In the following selection from *A Doll's House,* Nora tells her husband, Torvald, how she resents being treated like a child and why she is leaving him.

(She sits down at one side of the table.)

HELMER Nora—what is this?—this cold, set face?

NORA Sit down. It will take some time; I have a lot to talk over with you.

HELMER *(sits down at the opposite side of the table)* You alarm me, Nora!—and I don't understand you.

NORA No, that is just it. You don't understand me, and I have never understood you

---

Eleven Plays of Henrik Ibsen, intro. H. L. Mencken (New York: The Modern Library, n.d.), pp. 84–92.

either—before to-night. No, you mustn't interrupt me. You must simply listen to what I say. Torvald, this is a settling of accounts.

HELMER What do you mean by that?

NORA *(after a short silence)* Isn't there one thing that strikes you as strange in our sitting here like this?

HELMER What is that?

NORA We have been married now eight years. Does it not occur to you that this is the first time we two, you and I, husband and wife, have had a serious conversation?

HELMER What do you mean by serious?

NORA In all these eight years—longer than that—from the very beginning of our acquaintance, we have never exchanged a word on any serious subject.

HELMER Was it likely that I would be continually and for ever telling you about worries that you could not help me to bear?

NORA I am not speaking about business matters. I say that we have never sat down in earnest together to try and get at the bottom of anything.

HELMER But, dearest Nora, would it have been any good to you?

NORA That is just it; you have never understood me. I have been greatly wronged, Torvald—first by papa and then by you.

HELMER What! By us two—by us two, who have loved you better than anyone else in the world?

NORA *(shaking her head)* You have never loved me. You have only thought it pleasant to be in love with me.

HELMER Nora, what do I hear you saying?

NORA It is perfectly true, Torvald. When I was at home with papa, he told me his opinion about everything, and so I had the same opinions; and if I differed from him I concealed the fact, because he would not have liked it. He called me his doll-child, and he played with me just as I used to play with my dolls. And when I came to live with you—

HELMER What sort of an expression is that to use about our marriage?

NORA *(undisturbed)* I mean that I was simply transferred from papa's hands into yours. You arranged everything according to your own taste, and so I got the same tastes as you—or else I pretended to, I am really not quite sure which—I think sometimes the one and sometimes the other. When I look back on it, it seems to me as if I had been living here like a poor woman—just from hand to mouth. I have existed merely to perform tricks for you, Torvald. But you would have it so. You and papa have committed a great sin against me. It is your fault that I have made nothing of my life.

HELMER How unreasonable and how ungrateful you are, Nora! Have you not been happy here?

NORA No. I have never been happy. I thought I was, but it has never really been so.

HELMER Not—not happy!

NORA No, only merry. And you have always been so kind to me. But our home has been nothing but a playroom. I have been your doll-wife, just as at home I was papa's doll-child; and here the children have been my dolls. I thought it great fun when you played with me, just as they thought it great fun when I played with them. That is what our marriage has been, Torvald.

HELMER There is some truth in what you say—exaggerated and strained as your view of it is. But for the future it shall be different. Playtime shall be over, and lesson-time shall begin.

NORA Whose lessons? Mine, or the children's?

HELMER Both yours and the children's, my darling Nora.

NORA Alas, Torvald, you are not the man to educate me into being a proper wife for you.

HELMER And you can say that!

NORA And I—how am I fitted to bring up the children?

HELMER Nora!

NORA Didn't you say so yourself a little while ago—that you dare not trust me to bring them up?

HELMER In a moment of anger! Why do you pay any heed to that?

NORA Indeed, you were perfectly right. I am not fit for the task. There is another task I must undertake first. I must try and educate myself—you are not the man to help me in that. I must do that for myself. And that is why I am going to leave you now.

HELMER *(springing up)* What do you say?

NORA I must stand quite alone, if I am to understand myself and everything about me. It is for that reason that I cannot remain with you any longer.

HELMER Nora! Nora!

NORA I am going away from here now, at once. I am sure Christine will take me in for the night—

HELMER You are out of your mind! I won't allow it! I forbid you!

NORA It is no use forbidding me anything any longer. I will take with me what belongs to myself. I will take nothing from you, either now or later.

HELMER What sort of madness is this!

NORA To-morrow I shall go home—I mean, to my old home. It will be easiest for me to find something to do there.

HELMER You blind, foolish woman!

NORA I must try and get some sense, Torvald.

HELMER To desert your home, your husband and your children! And you don't consider what people will say!

NORA I cannot consider that at all. I only know that it is necessary for me.

HELMER It's shocking. This is how you would neglect your most sacred duties.

NORA What do you consider my most sacred duties?

HELMER Do I need to tell you that? Are they not your duties to your husband and your children?

NORA I have other duties just as sacred.

HELMER That you have not. What duties could those be?

NORA Duties to myself.

HELMER Before all else, you are a wife and a mother.

NORA I don't believe that any longer. I believe that before all else I am a reasonable human being, just as you are—or, at all events, that I must try and become one. I know quite well, Torvald, that most people would think you right, and that views of that kind are to be found in books; but I can no longer content myself with what most people say, or with what is found in books. I must think over things for myself and get to understand them.

HELMER Can you not understand your place in your own home? Have you not a reliable guide in such matters as that?—have you no religion?

NORA I am afraid, Torvald, I do not exactly know what religion is.

HELMER What are you saying?

NORA I know nothing but what the clergyman said, when I went to be confirmed. He told us that religion was this, and that, and the other. When I am away from all this, and am alone, I will look into that matter too. I will see if what the clergyman said is true, or at all events if it is true for me.

HELMER This is unheard of in a girl of your age! But if religion cannot lead you aright, let me try and awaken your conscience. I suppose you have some moral sense? or—answer me—am I to think you have none?

NORA I assure you, Torvald, that is not an easy question to answer. I really don't know. The thing perplexes me altogether. I only know that you and I look at it in quite a different light. . . .

HELMER You talk like a child. You don't understand the conditions of the world in which you live.

NORA No, I don't. But now I am going to try. I am going to see if I can make out who is right, the world or I.

HELMER You are ill, Nora; you are delirious; I almost think you are out of your mind.

NORA I have never felt my mind so clear and certain as tonight.

HELMER And is it with a clear and certain mind that you forsake your husband and your children.

NORA Yes, it is.

HELMER Then there is only one possible explanation.

NORA What is that?

HELMER You do not love me any more.

NORA No, that is just it.

HELMER Nora!—and you can say that!

NORA It gives me great pain, Torvald, for you have always been so kind to me, but I cannot help it. I do not love you any more.

HELMER *(regaining his composure)* Is that a clear and certain conviction too?

NORA Yes, absolutely clear and certain. That is the reason I will not stay here any longer.

HELMER And can you tell me what I have done to forfeit your love?

NORA Yes, indeed I can. It was to-night, when the wonderful thing did not happen; then I saw you were not the man I had thought you.

HELMER Explain yourself better—I don't understand you.

When Nora was a young wife, Torvald became dangerously ill; doctors told her (but not him) that the only way to save her husband's life was to live in a warmer climate. Nora tried tears and entreaties with Torvald, saying that he ought to be kind to her by taking her on an extended trip to Italy, even if it meant taking a loan. Unaware of Nora's true intent—she wanted to save his life—Torvald would not hear of it. When she said her father provided the money, Torvald agreed. In reality, she borrowed the money by forging her dying father's name, something Torvald never knew. She continues to pay off the loan by carefully managing the funds alloted to her by Torvald for running the house, and Torvald does not know her secret. Recently promoted to a top position in the bank, Torvald fires Krogstad, who happened to be the person from whom Nora had borrowed the money. On news that

he was fired, Krogstad delivers a letter to Torvald's home revealing the loan and the forgery. After reading the letter, Torvald hurls invectives at Nora: "miserable creature," "hypocrite," "liar," "criminal." "I shall not allow you to bring up the children; I dare not trust them to you."

NORA I have waited so patiently for eight years; for goodness knows, I knew very well that wonderful things don't happen every day. Then this horrible misfortune came upon me; and then I felt quite certain that the wonderful thing was going to happen at last. When Krogstad's letter was lying out there, never for a moment did I imagine that you would consent to accept this man's conditions. I was so absolutely certain that you would say to him: Publish the thing to the whole world. And when that was done—

HELMER Yes, what then—when I had exposed my wife to shame and disgrace?

NORA When that was done, I was so absolutely certain, you would come forward and take everything upon yourself, and say: I am the guilty one.

HELMER Nora—!

NORA You mean that I would never have accepted such a sacrifice on your part? No, of course not. But what would my assurances have been worth against yours? That was the wonderful thing which I hoped for and feared; and it was to prevent that, that I wanted to kill myself.

HELMER I would gladly work night and day for you, Nora—bear sorrow and want for your sake. But no man would sacrifice his honour for the one he loves.

NORA It is a thing hundreds of thousands of women have done.

HELMER Oh, you think and talk like a heedless child.

NORA Maybe. But you neither think nor talk like the man I could bind myself to. As soon as your fear was over—and it was not fear for what threatened me, but for what might happen to you—when the whole thing was past, as far as you were concerned it was exactly as if nothing at all had happened. Exactly as before, I was your little skylark, your doll, which you would in future treat with doubly gentle care, because it was so brittle and fragile. *(Getting up.)* Torvald—it was then it dawned upon me that for eight years I had been living here with a strange man, and had borne him three children—. Oh, I can't bear to think of it! I could tear myself into little bits!

HELMER *(sadly)* I see, I see. An abyss has opened between us—there is no denying it. But, Nora, would it not be possible to fill it up?

NORA As I am now, I am no wife for you.

HELMER I have it in me to become a different man.

NORA Perhaps—if your doll is taken away from you.

HELMER But to part!—to part from you! No, no. Nora, I can't understand that idea.

NORA *(going out to the right)* That makes it more certain that it must be done.

(She comes back with her cloak and hat and a small bag which she puts on a chair by the table)

HELMER Nora, Nora, not now! Wait till tomorrow.

NORA *(putting on her cloak)* I cannot spend the night in a strange man's room.

HELMER But can't we live here like brother and sister—?

NORA *(putting on her hat)* You know very well that would not last long. *(Puts the shawl round her.)* Good-bye, Torvald. I won't see the little ones. I know they are in better hands than mine. As I am now, I can be of no use to them.

HELMER But some day, Nora—some day?

NORA How can I tell? I have no idea what is going to become of me.

HELMER But you are my wife, whatever becomes of you.

NORA Listen, Torvald. I have heard that when a wife deserts her husband's house, as I am doing now, he is legally freed from all obligations towards her. In any case I set you free from all your obligations. You are not to feel yourself bound in the slightest way, any more than I shall. There must be perfect freedom on both sides. See, here is your ring back. Give me mine.

HELMER That too?

NORA That too.

HELMER Here it is.

NORA That's right. Now it is all over. I have put the keys here. The maids know all about everything in the house—better than I do. Tomorrow, after I have left her, Christine will come here and pack up my own things that I brought with me from home. I will have them sent after me.

HELMER All over! All over!—Nora, shall you never think of me again?

NORA I know I shall often think of you and the children and this house.

HELMER May I write to you, Nora?

NORA No—never. You must not do that.

HELMER But at least let me send you—

NORA Nothing—nothing—

HELMER Let me help you if you are in want.

NORA No. I can receive nothing from a stranger.

HELMER Nora—can I never be anything more than a stranger to you?

NORA *(taking her bag)* Ah, Torvald, the most wonderful thing of all would have to happen.

HELMER Tell me what that would be!

NORA Both you and I would have to be so changed that—Oh, Torvald, I don't believe any longer in wonderful things happening.

HELMER But I will believe in it. Tell me? So changed that—?

NORA That our life together would be a real wedlock. Good-bye.

(She goes out through the hall.)

HELMER *(sinks down on a chair at the door and buries his face in his hands)* Nora! Nora! *(looks round, and rises)* Empty. She is gone. *(A hope flashes across his mind.)* The most wonderful thing of all—?

(The sound of a door shutting is heard from below.)

REVIEW QUESTIONS

1. Select one sentence that, in your opinion, best exemplifies Dickens's talent for realism. Explain why.
2. What does *A Doll's House* tell you about middle-class life in the nineteenth century?
3. Do you agree with Nora's decision? Explain.

---

2 Theory of Evolution

In a century of outstanding scientific discoveries, none was more significant than the theory of evolution formulated by the English naturalist Charles Darwin (1809–1882). From December 1831 to 1836, Darwin had served as naturalist at sea on the *H.M.S. Beagle*, which surveyed parts of South America and some Pacific islands. He collected and classified many specimens of animal and plant life and from his investigations eventually drew several conclusions that startled the scientific community and enraged many members of the clergy.

Before Darwin's theory of evolution, most people adhered to the biblical account of creation found in Genesis, which said that God had created the universe, the various species of animal and plant life, and human beings, all in six days. The creation account also said that God had given each species of animal and plant a form that distinguished it from every other species. It was commonly held that the creation of the universe and of the first human beings had occurred some five or six thousand years earlier.

On the basis of his study, Darwin held that all life on earth had descended from earlier living forms; that human beings had evolved from lower, nonhuman species; and that the process had taken millions of years. Adopting the Malthusian idea that population reproduces faster than the food supply increases, Darwin held that within nature there is a continual struggle for existence. He said that the advantage lies with those living things that are stronger, faster, better camouflaged from their enemies, or better fitted in some way—such as adaptability—for survival than are other members of their species; those more fit to survive pass along the advantageous trait to offspring. This principle of natural selection explains why some members of a species survive and reproduce and why those less fit perish.

Charles Darwin
NATURAL SELECTION

According to Darwin, members of a species inherit variations that distinguish them from others in the species, and over many generations these variations become more pronounced. In time, a new variety of life evolves that can no longer breed with the species from which it descended. In this way, new species emerge and older ones die out. Human beings were also a product of natural selection, evolving from earlier, lower, nonhuman forms of life. In this first passage, from his autobiography, Darwin described his empirical method and his discovery of a general theory that coordinated and illuminated the data he found. Succeeding excerpts are from his *The Origin of Species* (1859) and *The Descent of Man* (1871).

DARWIN'S DESCRIPTION OF HIS METHOD AND DISCOVERY

From September 1854 I devoted my whole time to arranging my huge pile of notes, to observing, and to experimenting in relation to the transmutation of species. During the voyage of the *Beagle* I had been deeply impressed by discovering in the Pampean formation[1] great fossil animals covered with armour like that on the existing armadillos; secondly, by the manner in which closely allied animals replace one another in proceeding southwards over the Continent; and thirdly, by the South American character of most of the productions of the Galapagos archipelago,[2] and more especially by the manner in which they differ slightly on each island of the group; none of the islands appearing to be very ancient in a geological sense.

It was evident that such facts as these, as well as many others, could only be explained on the supposition that species gradually become modified; and the subject haunted me. But it was equally evident that neither the action of the surrounding conditions, nor the will of the organisms (especially in the case of plants) could account for the innumerable cases in which organisms of every kind are beautifully adapted to their habits of life—for instance, a woodpecker or a tree-frog to climb trees, or a seed for dispersal by hooks or plumes. I had always

been much struck by such adaptations, and until these could be explained it seemed to me almost useless to endeavour to prove by indirect evidence that species have been modified.

After my return to England it appeared to me that by following the example of Lyell[3] in Geology, and by collecting all facts which bore in any way on the variation of animals and plants under domestication and nature, some light might perhaps be thrown on the whole subject. My first note-book was opened in July 1837. I worked on true Baconian principles,[4] and without any theory collected facts on a wholesale scale, more especially with respect to domesticated productions, by printed enquiries, by conversation with skilful breeders and gardeners, and by extensive reading. When I see the list of books of all kinds which I read and abstracted, including whole series of Journals and Transactions, I am surprised at my industry. I soon perceived that selection was the keystone of man's success in making useful races of animals and plants. But how selection could be applied to organisms living in a state of nature remained for some time a mystery to me.

In October 1838, that is, fifteen months after I had begun my systematic enquiry, I happened to read for amusement Malthus[5] on *Population*, and being well prepared to appreciate the

---

Charles Darwin, *His Life Told in an Autobiographical Chapter and in a Selected Series of His Published Letters*, ed. Francis Darwin (New York: D. Appleton, 1893), pp. 41–43, 45, 49.

[1] The Pampean formation refers to the vast plain that stretches across Argentina, from the Atlantic Ocean to the foothills of the Andes Mountains.—Eds.

[2] The Galapagos Islands, a Pacific archipelago 650 miles west of Ecuador, are noted for their unusual wildlife, which Darwin observed.—Eds.

[3] Sir Charles Lyell (1797–1875) was a Scottish geologist whose work showed that the planet had evolved slowly over many ages. Like Lyell, Darwin sought to interpret natural history by observing processes still going on.—Eds.

[4] "Baconian principles" refers to Sir Francis Bacon (1561–1626), one of the first to insist that new knowledge should be acquired through experimentation and the accumulation of data. (See chapter 2.)—Eds.

[5] Thomas Malthus (1766–1834) was an English economist who maintained that population increases geometrically (2, 4, 8, 16, and so on) but the food supply increases arithmetically (1, 2, 3, 4, and so on). (See page 127.)—Eds.

struggle for existence which everywhere goes on from long-continued observation of the habits of animals and plants, it at once struck me that under these circumstances favourable variations would tend to be preserved and unfavourable ones to be destroyed. The result of this would be the formation of new species. Here, then, I had at last got a theory by which to work. . . .

My *Descent of Man* was published in February 1871. As soon as I had become, in the year of 1837 or 1838, convinced that species were mutable productions, I could not avoid the belief that man must come under the same law.

In the following excerpt from *The Origin of Species* (1859), Darwin explained the struggle for existence and the principle of natural selection.

THE ORIGIN OF SPECIES

. . . Owing to this struggle [for existence], variations, however slight . . . , if they be in any degree profitable to the individuals of a species, in their infinitely complex relations to other organic beings and to their physical conditions of life, will tend to the preservation of such individuals, and will generally be inherited by the offspring. The offspring, also, will thus have a better chance of surviving, for, of the many individuals of any species which are periodically born, but a small number can survive. I have called this principle, by which each slight variation, if useful, is preserved, by the term Natural Selection, in order to mark its relation to man's power of selection. But the expression often used by Mr. Herbert Spencer[6] of the Survival of the Fittest is more accurate, and is sometimes equally convenient. . . .

A struggle for existence inevitably follows from the high rate at which all organic beings

tend to increase. Every being, which during its natural lifetime produces several eggs or seeds, must suffer destruction during some period of its life, and during some season or occasional year, otherwise, on the principle of geometrical increase, its numbers would quickly become so inordinately great that no country could support the product. Hence, as more individuals are produced than can possibly survive, there must in every case be a struggle for existence, either one individual with another of the same species, or with the individuals of distinct species, or with the physical conditions of life. It is the doctrine of Malthus applied with manifold force to the whole animal and vegetable kingdoms; for in this case there can be no artificial increase of food, and no prudential restraint from marriage. Although some species may be now increasing, more or less rapidly, in numbers, all cannot do so, for the world would not hold them.

There is no exception to the rule that every organic being naturally increases at so high a rate, that, if not destroyed, the earth would soon be covered by the progeny of a single pair. Even slow-breeding man has doubled in twenty-five years, and at this rate, in less than a thousand years, there would literally not be standing-room for his progeny. . . . The elephant is reckoned the slowest breeder of all known animals, and I have taken some pains to estimate its probable minimum rate of natural increase; it will be safest to assume that it begins breeding when thirty years old, and goes on breeding till ninety years old, bringing forth six young in the interval, and surviving till one hundred years old; if this be so, after a period of from 740 to 750 years there would be nearly nineteen million elephants alive, descended from the first pair. . . .

. . . Can we doubt (remembering that many more individuals are born than can possibly survive) that individuals having any advantage, however slight, over others, would have the best chance of surviving and of procreating their kind? On the other hand, we may feel sure

Charles Darwin, *The Origin of Species*, vol. 1 (New York: D. Appleton, 1872), pp. 77, 79, 98, 133–134.
[6]The British philosopher Herbert Spencer (1820–1903) coined the term *survival of the fittest*. (See page 189.)—Eds.

that any variation in the least degree injurious would be rigidly destroyed. This preservation of favourable individual differences and variations, and the destruction of those which are injurious, I have called Natural Selection, or the Survival of the Fittest. . . .

. . . Natural Selection acts solely through the preservation of variations in some way advantageous, which consequently endure. Owing to the high geometrical rate of increase of all organic beings, each area is already fully stocked with inhabitants; and it follows from this, that as the favoured forms increase in number, so, generally, will the less favoured decrease and become rare. . . .

From these several considerations I think it inevitably follows, that as new species in the course of time are formed through natural selection, others will become rarer and rarer, and finally extinct. The forms which stand in closest competition with those undergoing modification and improvement will naturally suffer most. . . . [E]ach new variety or species, during the progress of its formation, will generally press hardest on its nearest kindred, and tend to exterminate them. We see the same process of extermination amongst our domesticated productions, through the selection of improved forms by man.

In *The Descent of Man* (1871), Darwin argued that human beings have evolved from lower forms of life.

THE DESCENT OF MAN

The main conclusion here arrived at, and now held by many naturalists who are well competent to form a sound judgment, is that man is descended from some less highly organised form. The grounds upon which this conclusion

---

Charles Darwin, *The Descent of Man* (New York: D. Appleton, 1876), pp. 606–607, 619.

rests will never be shaken, for the close similarity between man and the lower animals in embryonic development, as well as in innumerable points of structure and constitution . . . are facts which cannot be disputed. They have long been known, but until recently they told us nothing with respect to the origin of man. Now when viewed by the light of our knowledge of the whole organic world, their meaning is unmistakable. The great principle of evolution stands up clear and firm, when these groups of facts are considered in connection with others, such as the mutual affinities of the members of the same group, their geographical distribution in past and present times, and their geological succession. It is incredible that all these facts should speak falsely. He who is not content to look, like a savage, at the phenomena of nature as disconnected, cannot any longer believe that man is the work of a separate act of creation. He will be forced to admit that the close resemblance of the embryo of man to that, for instance, of a dog—the construction of his skull, limbs and whole frame on the same plan with that of other mammals, independently of the uses to which the parts may be put . . . and a crowd of analogous facts—all point in the plainest manner to the conclusion that man is the co-descendant with other mammals of a common progenitor.

We have seen that man incessantly presents individual differences in all parts of his body and in his mental faculties. These differences or variations seem to be induced by the same general causes, and to obey the same laws as with the lower animals. In both cases similar laws of inheritance prevail. Man tends to increase at a greater rate than his means of subsistence; consequently he is occasionally subjected to a severe struggle for existence, and natural selection will have effected whatever lies within its scope. A succession of strongly-marked variations of a similar nature is by no means requisite; slight fluctuating differences in the individual suffice for the work of natural selection. . . .

Man may be excused for feeling some pride at having risen, though not through his own exertions, to the very summit of the organic scale; and the fact of his having thus risen, instead of having been aboriginally placed there, may give him hope for a still higher destiny in the distant future. But we are not here concerned with hopes or fears, only with the truth as far as our reason permits us to discover it; and I have given the evidence to the best of my ability. We must, however, acknowledge, as it seems to me, that man with all his noble qualities, with sympathy which feels for the most debased, with benevolence which extends not only to other men but to the humblest living creature, with his god-like intellect which has penetrated into the movements and constitution of the solar system—with all these exalted powers—Man still bears in his bodily frame the indelible stamp of his lowly origin.

REVIEW QUESTIONS

1. How did Charles Darwin make use of Thomas Malthus's theory of population growth?
2. How did Darwin account for the extinction of old species and the emergence of new ones?
3. What did Darwin mean when he said that man "with his god-like intellect . . . still bears in his bodily frame the indelible stamp of his lowly origin"?

3 The Socialist Revolution

After completing a doctorate at the University of Jena in 1841, Karl Marx (1818–1883) edited a newspaper that was suppressed by the Prussian authorities for its radicalism and atheism. He left his native Rhineland for Paris, where he became friendly with Friedrich Engels (see chapter 5). Expelled from France at the request of Prussia, Marx went to Brussels. In 1848, Marx and Engels produced for the Communist League the *Communist Manifesto*, advocating the violent overthrow of capitalism and the creation of a socialist society. Marx returned to Prussia and participated in a minor way in the Revolutions of 1848 in Germany. Expelled from Prussia in 1849, he went to England. He spent the rest of his life there, writing and agitating for the cause of socialism.

The *Communist Manifesto* presented a philosophy of history and a theory of society that Marx expanded upon in his later works, particularly *Capital* (1867). In the tradition of the Enlightenment, he maintained that history, like the operations of nature, was governed by scientific law. To understand the past and the present and to predict the essential outlines of the future, said Marx, one must concentrate on economic forces, on how goods are produced and how wealth is distributed. Marx's call for a working-class revolution against capitalism and for the making of a classless society established the ideology of twentieth-century Communist revolutionaries.

Karl Marx and Friedrich Engels
COMMUNIST MANIFESTO

In the opening section of the *Manifesto*, the basic premise of the Marxian philosophy of history is advanced: class conflict—the idea that the social order is divided into classes based on conflicting economic interests.

BOURGEOIS AND PROLETARIANS

The history of all hitherto existing society is the history of class struggles.

Freeman and slave, patrician and plebeian [aristocrat and commoner, in the ancient world], lord and serf, guild-master [master craftsman] and journeyman [who worked for a guild-master], in a word, oppressor and oppressed, stood in constant opposition to one another, carried on an uninterrupted, now hidden, now open fight, that each time ended, either in a revolutionary reconstitution of society at large, or in the common ruin of the contending classes.

In the earlier epochs of history we find almost everywhere a complicated arrangement of society into various orders, a manifold gradation of social rank. In ancient Rome we have patricians, knights, plebeians, slaves; in the Middle Ages, feudal lords, vassals [landowners pledged to lords], guild-masters, journeymen, apprentices, serfs; in almost all of these classes, again, subordinate gradations.

The modern bourgeois society that has sprouted from the ruins of feudal society, has not done away with class antagonisms. It has but established new forms of struggle in place of the old ones.

Our epoch, the epoch of the bourgeoisie [capitalist class], possesses, however, this distinctive feature; it has simplified the class antagonisms. Society as a whole is more and more splitting up into two great hostile camps, into two great classes directly facing each other: Bourgeoisie and Proletariat [industrial workers].

From the serfs of the Middle Ages sprang the chartered burghers of the earliest towns. From these burgesses the first elements of the bourgeoisie were developed.

The discovery of America, the rounding of the Cape, opened up fresh ground for the rising bourgeoisie. The East-Indian and Chinese markets, the colonization of America, trade with the colonies, the increase in the means of exchange and in commodities generally, gave to commerce, to navigation, to industry, an impulse never before known, and thereby, to the revolutionary element in the tottering feudal society, a rapid development.

The feudal system of industry, under which industrial production was monopolized by closed guilds, now no longer sufficed for the growing wants of the new market. The manufacturing system took its place. The guild-masters were pushed on one side by the manufacturing middle class; division of labor between the different corporate guilds vanished in the face of division of labor in each single workshop.

Meantime the markets kept ever growing, the demand ever rising. . . . Thereupon steam and machinery revolutionized industrial production. The place of manufacture was taken by the giant, Modern Industry, the place of the industrial middle class, by industrial millionaires, the leaders of whole industrial armies, the modern bourgeois.

Modern Industry has established the world's market, for which the discovery of America paved the way. This market has given an immense development to commerce, to navigation, to

Karl Marx and Friedrich Engels, *Manifesto of the Communist Party*, authorized English translation, edited and annotated by Friedrich Engels (Chicago: Charles B. Kerr Publishing Company, 1912), pp. 8–48, passim.

communication by land. This development has, in its turn, reacted on the extension of industry; and in proportion, as industry, commerce, navigation, railways extended, in the same proportion, the bourgeoisie developed, increased its capital, and pushed into the background every class handed down from the Middle Ages.

We see, therefore, how the modern bourgeoisie is itself the product of a long course of development, of a series of revolutions in the modes of production and of exchange.

Each step in the development of the bourgeoisie was accompanied by a corresponding political advance of that class. An oppressed class under the sway of the feudal nobility, an armed and self-governing association in the mediaeval commune [town], . . . the bourgeoisie has at last, since the establishment of Modern Industry and of the world's market, conquered for itself, in the modern representative State, exclusive political sway. The executive of the modern State is but a committee for managing the common affairs of the whole bourgeoisie.

The bourgeoisie, historically, has played a most revolutionary part.

The bourgeoisie, wherever it has got the upper hand, has put an end to all feudal, patriarchal, idyllic relations. It has pitilessly torn asunder the motley feudal ties that bound man to his "natural superiors," and has left remaining no other nexus [link] between man and man than naked self-interest, than callous "cash payment." It has drowned the most heavenly ecstasies of religious fervor, of chivalrous enthusiasm, . . . in the icy water of egotistical calculation. It has resolved personal worth into exchange value, and in place of the numberless indefeasible chartered freedoms, has set up that single, unconscionable freedom—Free Trade. In one word, for exploitation, veiled by religious and political illusions, it has substituted naked, shameless, direct, brutal exploitation. . . .

The bourgeoisie, states the *Manifesto*, has subjected nature's forces to human control to an unprecedented degree and has

replaced feudal organization of agriculture (serfdom) and manufacturing (guild system) with capitalist free competition. But the capitalists cannot control these "gigantic means of production and exchange." Periodically, capitalist society is burdened by severe economic crises; capitalism is afflicted with overproduction—more goods are produced than the market will absorb. In all earlier epochs, which were afflicted with scarcity, the *Manifesto* declares, such a condition "would have seemed an absurdity." To deal with the crisis, the capitalists curtail production, thereby intensifying the poverty of the proletariat, who are now without work. In capitalist society, the exploited worker suffers from physical poverty (a result of low wages) and spiritual poverty (a result of the monotony, regimentation, and impersonal character of the capitalist factory system). For the proletariat, work is not the satisfaction of a need but a repulsive means for survival. The products they help make bring them no satisfaction; they are alienated from their labor.

In proportion as the bourgeoisie, *i.e.*, capital, is developed, in the same proportion is the proletariat, the modern working class, developed—a class of laborers, who live only so long as they find work, and who find work only so long as their labor increases capital. These laborers, who must sell themselves piecemeal, are a commodity, like every other article of commerce, and are consequently exposed to all the vicissitudes of competition, to all the fluctuations of the market.

Owing to the extensive use of machinery and to division of labor, the work of the proletarians has lost all individual character, and, consequently, all charm for the workman. He becomes an appendage of the machine, and it is only the most simple, most monotonous, and most easily acquired knack, that is required of him. Hence, the cost of production of a workman is restricted, almost entirely, to the means of subsistence that he requires for his maintenance, and for the propagation of his race. But the price of a commodity, and therefore also of labor, is equal to its cost of production. In proportion, therefore, as the repulsiveness of the work increases, the wage decreases. Nay more, in proportion as the use of machinery and division of labor increases, in the same proportion the burden of toil also increases, whether by prolongation of the working hours, by increase of the work exacted in a given time, or by increased speed of the machinery, etc.

Modern industry has converted the little workshop of the patriarchal master into the great factory of the industrial capitalist. Masses of laborers, crowded into the factory, are organized like soldiers. As privates of the industrial army they are placed under the command of a perfect hierarchy of officers and sergeants. Not only are they slaves of the bourgeois class, and of the bourgeois state; they are daily and hourly enslaved by the machine, by the overlooker, and, above all, by the individual bourgeois manufacturer himself. The more openly this despotism proclaims gain to be its end and aim, the more petty, the more hateful and the more embittering it is.

The less the skill and exertion of strength implied in manual labor, in other words, the more modern industry develops, the more is the labor of men superseded by that of women. Differences of age and sex have no longer any distinctive social validity for the working class. All are instruments of labor, more or less expensive to use, according to their age and sex.

No sooner has the laborer received his wages in cash, for the moment escaping exploitation by the manufacturer, than he is set upon by the other portions of the bourgeoisie, the landlord, the shop-keeper, the pawnbroker, etc. . . . .

The exploited workers organize to defend their interests against the capitalist oppressors.

But with the development of industry the proletariat not only increases in number; it becomes concentrated in greater masses, its strength grows, and it feels that strength more. The various interests and conditions of life within the ranks of the proletariat are more and more

equalized, in proportion as machinery obliterates all distinctions of labor and nearly everywhere reduces wages to the same low level. The growing competition among the bourgeois, and the resulting commercial crises, make the wages of the workers ever more fluctuating. The unceasing improvement of machinery, ever more rapidly developing, makes their livelihood more and more precarious: the collisions between individual workmen and individual bourgeois take more and more the character of collisions between two classes. Thereupon the workers begin to form combinations (trade unions) against the bourgeoisie; they club together in order to keep up the rate of wages; they found permanent associations in order to make provision beforehand for these occasional revolts. Here and there the contest breaks out into riots.

Now and then the workers are victorious, but only for a time. The real fruit of their battles lies, not in the immediate results, but in [their ever-expanding unity]. . . . .

Increasingly, the proletariat, no longer feeling part of the old society, seeks to destroy it.

The proletarian is without property; his relation to his wife and children has no longer anything in common with the bourgeois family relations. . . . Law, morality, religion, are to him so many bourgeois prejudices, behind which lurk in ambush just as many bourgeois interests.

All the preceding classes that got the upper hand sought to fortify their already acquired status by subjecting society at large to their conditions of appropriation. The proletarians . . . have nothing of their own to secure and to fortify; their mission is to destroy all previous securities for, and insurances of, individual property.

All previous historical movements were movements of minorities, or in the interest of minorities. The proletarian movement is the self-conscious, independent movement of the immense majority, in the interest of the immense majority. The proletariat, the lowest stratum of our present society, cannot stir, cannot raise itself up, without the whole super-incumbent [overlying] strata of official society being [shattered]. . . .

In depicting the most general phases of the development of the proletariat, we traced the more or less veiled civil war, raging within existing society, up to the point where that war breaks out into open revolution, and where the violent overthrow of the bourgeoisie lays the foundation for the sway of the proletariat. . . .

The modern laborer . . . instead of rising with the progress of industry, sinks deeper and deeper below the conditions of existence of his own class. He becomes a pauper, and pauperism develops more rapidly than population and wealth. And here it becomes evident that the bourgeoisie is unfit any longer to be the ruling class in society and to impose its conditions of existence upon society as an overriding law. It is unfit to rule because it is incompetent to assure an existence to its slave within his slavery, because it cannot help letting him sink into such a state that it has to feed him instead of being fed by him. Society can no longer live under this bourgeoisie, in other words its existence is no longer compatible with society.

The essential condition for the existence and for the sway of the bourgeois class, is the formation and augmentation of capital; the condition for capital is wage-labor. Wage—labor rests exclusively on competition between the laborers. The advance of industry, whose involuntary promoter is the bourgeoisie, replaces the isolation of the laborers, due to competition, by their revolutionary combination, due to association. The development of modern industry, therefore, cuts from under its feet the very foundation on which the bourgeoisie produces and appropriates products. What the bourgeoisie therefore produces above all, are its own gravediggers. Its fall and the victory of the proletariat are equally inevitable. . . .

Communists, says the *Manifesto*, are the most advanced and determined members of working-class parties. Among the aims of the Communists are organization of the working class into a revolutionary party; overthrow of bourgeois power and the assumption of political power by the proletariat; and an end to exploitation of one individual by another and the creation of a classless society. These aims will be achieved by the abolition of bourgeois private property (private ownership of the means of production) and the abolition of the bourgeoisie as a class.

The Communists, therefore, are on the one hand, practically, the most advanced and resolute section of the working class parties of every country, that section which pushes forward all others; on the other hand, theoretically, they have over the great mass of the proletariat the advantage of clearly understanding the line of march, the conditions, and the ultimate general results of the proletarian movement.

The immediate aim of the Communists is the same as that of all the other proletarian parties: formation of the proletariat into a class, overthrow of the bourgeois supremacy, conquest of political power by the proletariat. . . .

The distinguishing feature of Communism is not the abolition of property generally, but the abolition of bourgeois property. But modern bourgeois private property is the final and most complete expression of the system of producing and appropriating products, that is based on class antagonisms, on the exploitation of the many by the few.

In this sense the theory of the Communists may be summed up in the single sentence: Abolition of private property. . . .

One argument leveled against Communists by bourgeois critics, says the *Manifesto*, is that the destruction of the bourgeoisie would lead to the disappearance of bourgeois culture, which is "identical with the disappearance of all culture," and the loss of all moral and religious truths. Marx insists that these ethical and religious ideals lauded by the bourgeoisie are not universal truths at all but are common expressions of the ruling class at a particular stage in history.

___

That culture, the loss of which he [the bourgeois] laments, is for the enormous majority, a mere training to act as a machine.

But don't wrangle with us so long as you [the bourgeoisie] apply to our [the Communists'] intended abolition of bourgeois property, the standard of your bourgeois notions of freedom, culture, law, etc. Your very ideas are but the outgrowth of the conditions of your bourgeois production and bourgeois property, just as your jurisprudence is but the will of your class made into a law for all, a will, whose essential character and direction are determined by the economical conditions of existence of your class.

The selfish misconception that induces you to transform into eternal laws of nature and of reason, the social forms springing from your present mode of production and form of property—historical relations that rise and disappear in the progress of production—this misconception you share with every ruling class that has preceded you. . . .

Does it require deep intuition to comprehend that man's ideas, views, and conceptions, in one word, man's consciousness changes with every change in the conditions of his material existence, in his social relations and in his social life?

What else does the history of ideas prove than that intellectual production changes its character in proportion as material production is changed? The ruling ideas of each age have ever been the ideas of its ruling class. . . .

. . . The ideas of religious liberty and freedom of conscience [the much heralded values of the bourgeoisie] merely gave expression to the sway of free competition within the domain of knowledge.

"Undoubtedly," it will be said, "religious, moral, philosophical, and juridical ideas have been modified in the course of historic development. But religion, morality, philosophy,

political science, and law, constantly survived this change.

"There are besides, eternal truths, such as Freedom, Justice, etc., that are common to all states of society. But Communism abolishes eternal truths, it abolishes all religion and all morality, instead of constituting them on a new basis; it therefore acts as a contradiction to all past historical experience." . . .

The Communist revolution is the most radical rupture with traditional property relations; no wonder that its development involves the most radical rupture with traditional ideas. . . .

___

Aroused and united by Communist intellectuals, says the *Manifesto*, the proletariat will wrest power from the bourgeoisie and overthrow the capitalist system that has oppressed them. In the new society, people will be fully free.

___

We have seen above that the first step in the revolution by the working class is to raise the proletariat to the position of the ruling class, to win the battle of democracy.

The proletariat will use its political supremacy to wrest, by degrees, all capital from the bourgeoisie; to centralize all instruments of production in the hands of the State, *i.e.*, of the proletariat organized as the ruling class; and to increase the total of productive forces as rapidly as possible. . . .

When, in the course of development, class distinctions have disappeared and all production has been concentrated in the hands of a vast association of the whole nation, the public power will lose its political character. Political power, properly so called, is merely the organized power of one class for oppressing another. If the proletariat during its contest with the bourgeoisie is compelled, by the force of circumstances, to organize itself as a class, if, by means of a revolution, it makes itself the ruling class, and, as such, sweeps away by force the old conditions of production, then it will, along with these conditions, have swept away the conditions for the existence of class antagonism, and of classes generally, and will thereby have abolished its own supremacy as a class.

In place of the old bourgeois society with its classes and class antagonisms we shall have an association in which the free development of each is the condition for the free development of all. . . .

The Communists disdain to conceal their views and aims. They openly declare that their ends can be attained only by the forcible overthrow of all existing social conditions. Let the ruling classes tremble at a communistic revolution. The proletarians have nothing to lose but their chains. They have a world to win.

Working men of all countries, unite!

REVIEW QUESTIONS

1. What do Karl Marx and Friedrich Engels mean by the term *class struggle?* What historical examples of class conflict are provided?
2. According to the *Manifesto*, what role has the state played in the class conflict?
3. How does the *Manifesto* describe the condition of the working class under capitalism?
4. According to the *Manifesto*, why is capitalism doomed? What conditions will bring about the end of capitalism?
5. "The ruling ideas of each age have ever been the ideas of its ruling class." What is meant by this statement? Do you agree or disagree? Explain.
6. Have Marx's predictions proven accurate? Explain your answer.

4 The Evolution of Liberalism

The principal concern of early nineteenth-century liberalism was protecting the rights of the individual against the demands of the state. For this reason, liberals advocated a constitution that limited the state's authority and a bill of rights that stipulated the citizen's basic freedoms. Believing that state interference in the economy endangered individual liberty and private property, liberals were strong advocates of *laissez-faire*—leaving the market to its own devices. And convinced that the unpropertied and uneducated masses were not deeply committed to individual freedom, liberals approved property requirements for voting and office holding.

In the last part of the nineteenth century, however, liberalism changed substantially as many liberals came to support government reforms to deal with the problems created by unregulated industrialization. By the early twentieth century, liberalism—not without reservation and opposition on the part of some liberals—was planting the seed of social democracy, which maintains that government has an obligation to assist the needy.

L. T. Hobhouse
JUSTIFICATION FOR STATE INTERVENTION

L. T. Hobhouse (1864–1929), an academic who also wrote for the *Manchester Guardian*, expressed these views in *Liberalism* (1911).

[It was conceived by an earlier liberalism] that, however deplorable the condition of the working classes might be, the right way of raising them was to trust to individual enterprise and possibly, according to some thinkers, to voluntary combination. By these means the efficiency of labour might be enhanced and its regular remuneration raised. By sternly withholding all external supports we should teach the working classes to stand alone, and if there were pain in the disciplinary process there was yet hope in the future. They would come by degrees to a position of economic independence in which they would be able to face the risks of life, not in reliance upon the State, but by the force of their own brains and the strength of their own right arms.

These views no longer command the same measure of assent. On all sides we find the State making active provision for the poorer classes and not by any means for the destitute alone. We find it educating the children, providing medical inspection, authorizing the feeding of the [needy] at the expense of the rate-payers, helping them to obtain employment through free Labour Exchanges, seeking to organize the labour market with a view to the mitigation of unemployment, and providing old age pensions for all whose incomes fall below thirteen shillings a week, without exacting any contribution. Now, in all this, we may well ask, is the State going forward blindly on the paths of broad and generous but unconsidered charity?

Is it and can it remain indifferent to the effect on individual initiative and personal or parental responsibility? Or may we suppose that the wiser heads are well aware of what they are about, have looked at the matter on all sides, and are guided by a reasonable conception of the duty of the State and the responsibilities of the individual? Are we, in fact—for this is really the question—seeking charity or justice?

We said above that it was the function of the State to secure the conditions upon which mind and character may develop themselves. Similarly we may say now that the function of the State is to secure conditions upon which its citizens are able to win by their own efforts all that is necessary to a full civic efficiency. It is not for the State to feed, house, or clothe them. It is for the State to take care that the economic conditions are such that the normal man who is not defective in mind or body or will can by useful labour feed, house, and clothe himself and his family. The "right to work" and the right to a "living wage" are just as valid as the rights of person or property. That is to say, they are integral conditions of a good social order. A society in which a single honest man of normal capacity is definitely unable to find the means of maintaining himself by useful work is to that extent suffering from malorganization. There is somewhere a defect in the social system, a hitch in the economic machine. Now, the individual workman cannot put the machine straight. He is the last person to have any say in the control of the market. It is not his fault if there is overproduction in his industry, or if a new and cheaper process has been introduced

L. T. Hobhouse, *Liberalism* (Westport, CT: Greenwood Press, 1980), pp. 83–84.

which makes his particular skill, perhaps the product of years of application, [obsolete] in the market. He does not direct or regulate industry. He is not responsible for its ups and downs, but he has to pay for them. That is why it is not charity but justice for which he is asking. . . .

If this view of the duty of the State and the right of the workman is coming to prevail, it is owing partly to an enhanced sense of common responsibility, and partly to the teaching of experience. . . .

Herbert Spencer
THE MAN VERSUS THE STATE

Committed to a traditional *laissez-faire* policy, however, some liberals attacked state intervention as a threat to personal freedom and a betrayal of central liberal principles. In *The Man Versus the State* (1884), British philosopher Herbert Spencer (1820–1903) warned that increased government regulation would lead to socialism and slavery.

The extension of this policy . . . [of government legislation] fosters everywhere the tacit assumption that Government should step in whenever anything is not going right. "Surely you would not have this misery continue!" exclaims some one, if you hint . . . [an objection] to much that is now being said and done. Observe what is implied by this exclamation. It takes for granted . . . that every evil can be removed: the truth being that with the existing defects of human nature, many evils can only be thrust out of one place or form into another place or form—often being increased by the change. The exclamation also implies the unhesitating belief, here especially concerning us, that evils of all kinds should be dealt with by the State. . . . Obviously, the more numerous governmental interventions become, the more confirmed does this habit of thought grow, and the more loud and perpetual the demands for intervention.

Every extension of the regulative policy involves an addition to the regulative agents—a

further growth of officialism and an increasing power of the organization formed of officials. . . .

. . . Moreover, every additional State-interference strengthens the tacit assumption that it is the duty of the State to deal with all evils and secure all benefits. Increasing power of a growing administrative organization is accompanied by decreasing power of the rest of the society to resist its further growth and control. . . .

"But why is this change described as 'the coming slavery'?" is a question which many will still ask. The reply is simple. All socialism involves slavery. . . .

Evidently then, the changes made, the changes in progress, and the changes urged, will carry us not only towards State-ownership of land and dwellings and means of communication, all to be administered and worked by State-agents, but towards State-usurpation of all industries: the private forms of which, disadvantaged more and more in competition with the State, which can arrange everything for its own convenience, will more and more die away, just as many voluntary schools have, in presence

Herbert Spencer, *The Man Versus the State* (London: William & Norgate, 1884), pp. 28, 33–34, 38–39, 41, 107.

of Board-schools. And so will be brought about the desired ideal of the socialists. . . .

. . . It is a matter of common remark, often made when a marriage is impending, that those possessed by strong hopes habitually dwell on the promised pleasures and think nothing of the accompanying pains. A further exemplification of this truth is supplied by these political enthusiasts and fanatical revolutionists. Impressed with the miseries existing under our present social arrangements, and not regarding these miseries as caused by the ill-working of a human nature but partially adapted to the social state, they imagine them to be forthwith curable by this or that rearrangement. Yet, even did their plans succeed it could only be by substituting one kind of evil for another. A little deliberate thought would show that under their proposed arrangements, their liberties must be surrendered in proportion as their material welfares were cared for.

For no form of co-operation, small or great, can be carried on without regulation, and an implied submission to the regulating agencies. . . .

. . . So that each [individual] would stand toward the governing agency in the relation of slave to master.

"But the governing agency would be a master which he and others made and kept constantly in check; and one which therefore would not control him or others more than was needful for the benefit of each and all."

To which reply the first rejoinder is that, even if so, each member of the community as an individual would be a slave to the community as a whole. Such a relation has habitually existed in militant communities, even under quasi-popular forms of government. In ancient Greece the accepted principle was that the citizen belonged neither to himself nor to his family, but belonged to his city—the city being with the Greek equivalent to the community. And this doctrine, proper to a state of constant warfare, is a doctrine which socialism unawares re-introduces into a state intended to be purely industrial and [commercial]. The services of each will belong to the aggregate of all; and for these services, such returns will be given as the authorities think proper. So that even if the administration is of the beneficent kind intended to be secured, slavery, however mild, must be the outcome of the arrangement. . . .

The function of Liberalism in the past was that of putting a limit to the powers of kings. The function of true Liberalism in the future will be that of putting a limit to the powers of Parliaments.

REVIEW QUESTIONS

1. Why did L. T. Hobhouse believe that state intervention was needed to create "a good social order"?
2. What was Herbert Spencer's answer to the argument that government legislation is necessary to relieve human misery? Has history proven him correct?
3. What did Spencer mean by the dictum "All socialism involves slavery"?
4. According to Spencer, what was true liberalism? Compare his conception of liberalism with that of Hobhouse.

CHAPTER 8

Politics and Society, 1845–1914

HOMELESS CHILDREN, 1875. These boys have just arrived at the London orphanage of Dr. Barnardo. This orphanage represents the nineteenth-century spirit of reform that tried to address the evils and injustices of the industrial age that often afflicted children of the poor. *(Courtesy of Barnardo's, www.barnardos.org.uk)*

In the last half of the nineteenth century, the people of Europe, more numerous than ever and concentrated in ever-growing cities, interacted with each other in a busy exchange of goods, ideas, and services, which led to remarkable creativity in industry, science, and the arts. The physical sciences flourished; medical science advanced; the psychoanalytic method developed under Sigmund Freud. New technologies speeded communication and transportation, which intensified human contact and competition. Industrialization, promoted by capitalist enterprise, spread throughout Europe and the United States, raising the standard of living and advancing expectations among the poor for a better life. The new mobility and social interdependence provided greater opportunity for individual gain, but they also increased social tensions.

One source of tension arose from the growing demands among the lower classes for social justice and a share of political power; the misery of the poor and disenfranchised masses became a hot political issue. At the same time the agitation for women's rights mounted; women wanted to have rights equal to those of men in education and politics. Although women faced strenuous resistance with regard to suffrage, they continued to fight toward that goal. A third troublesome factor in European politics and society was nationalism, which was becoming more extreme, racist, aggressive, and dangerous. One expression of nationalism which exhibited these traits was anti-Semitism. Of long standing in European history, it became an active political force toward the end of the nineteenth century.

No country was more threatened by sociopolitical unrest than the Russian Empire. Contact with Western Europe convinced the tsarist government of the need to modernize their backward country and catch up with "the West," as Russians called the richer lands of Europe—a challenge beyond the resources of the tsarist regime. Increasing discontent among workers led to a revolution in 1905.

Despite the impressive achievements of European civilization and the domination of the globe by European states, the Continent was becoming more and more deeply divided by the early 1900s. The competition for wealth and power heightened international rivalries. Nationalist ambitions, backed in most countries by popular support, and an arms race further worsened international relations. Although few people at the time recognized it, Europe's period of peace and security was ending. World War I, which broke out in 1914, was on the horizon.

1 The Irish Potato Famine

The Act of Union that joined Ireland to England in 1801 was designed to subjugate the rebellious Irish, and was based on mutual distrust. The English regarded the Irish with contempt; to them the Irish were feckless, untrustworthy, Catholic, and prolific. The Irish, in turn, resented English domination.

Landowners in the predominantly rural country were English; the majority of them lived in England on the considerable rents from their lands. They leased their land to tenant farmers and rented out very small plots to landless laborers. A peasant family of six could feed itself all winter on the produce of one and a half acres planted solely with potatoes. In the summer they went hungry.

In 1845 potato blight destroyed a large part of the potato crop. Despite agitated reports from Ireland of impending famine, the British government was slow to provide food and employment on public works to cope with the disaster. The potato crop had failed before, but never more than two years running; between 1845 and 1848 it failed three times.

Charles Trevelyan, in charge of the British government relief effort, turned a deaf ear to constant appeals for extra food. He indeed stopped the food relief scheme "to prevent people from being habitually dependent on the government." When reports of mob violence and deaths from starvation could no longer be denied, the government opened soup kitchens, which distributed a watery soup to the starving millions. Reassured by a sound but small potato crop in 1847, the government assumed the crisis was over and closed the soup kitchens, leaving private organizations to feed the still starving people.

From the beginning, Trevelyan was determined that Ireland should pay for its own relief work by levying local rates—property taxes paid by landlords and tenants. Landlords were to pay all the rates for their poorest tenants and half for the more prosperous ones. Ironically this measure, intended to protect tenants, persuaded landlords to avoid payment by evicting their tenants. Some of the homeless wandered the roads in search of food or begged in the cities; others starved to death; the more fortunate emigrated to an uncertain future.

All along, aid came from private relief organizations in England, Ireland, and the United States. They acted swiftly and efficiently to raise money and provide clothing; the Quakers operated soup kitchens where need was greatest. Yet it was only a matter of time before fever broke out; this occurred in the middle of the winter of 1846–1847. Medical resources were limited. The overcrowded, underfunded workhouses took some patients; others were treated in new fever hospitals; and "fever sheds" and army tents housed the overflow.

An attempted rebellion against England by Irish patriots in the summer of 1848 stifled any remaining compassion for Ireland. In the fall of 1848 the potato crop failed again, and there was no help from the government. Farms were abandoned, and emigration to England, Canada, and America increased.

The English landlords, ruined by rates, their rental income depleted, sold bankrupt estates. Cholera devastated the masses of the poor. The depopulated, neglected countryside continued to decay.

The decennial census of 1851 reported a population decrease from 8.1 to 6.5 million in a period when the population should have risen to nine million. The number of deaths from famine and disease is usually estimated at around one million. The remainder of the decline was due to emigration. The economic distress of Ireland continued for years to come.

Poulett Scrope
EVICTIONS

The British government could hardly claim that it was ignorant of the treatment of tenants by landlords in Ireland. Evictions of tenants whose leases had expired, or who were unable to pay their rent, had long been a way for landlords to clear their land and turn it over to cattle or grain. Unlike England, Ireland had no growing industrial towns to absorb surplus labor. Eviction, especially in winter, was frequently a death sentence.

During the potato famine, the ruined crops and the consequent inability of tenants to pay their rent led to further evictions. Poulett Scrope (1797–1876), a member of Parliament, had for years prior to the famine advocated the recognition of tenants' rights in Ireland. In the speech below, delivered in the House of Commons in 1846, he clearly described what was happening in the Irish countryside.

Remember, life is destroyed in Ireland in other ways than by the bullet of the assassin. Life is taken in Ireland by the slow agonies of want, and disease engendered by want, where human beings are deprived (however legally) of the only means of living, and no resource afforded them in its place. When a landlord clears his estate by driving from their homes hundreds of poor tenants, who have no other possible source of refuge, does he not as effectually destroy their lives (at least, many of them) as if he shot them at once? It would be a mercy to do so in comparison.

Do you deny that the lives of the peasantry are unprotected by law—that they are obliged to protect themselves by these criminal outrages? I ask you if, since these very discussions began we have not had proofs—multiplied proofs—of the mode in which the landlords of Ireland are decimating the people of Ireland? Ay, in the midst of fever and famine, was not a whole village razed by Mr. Gerrard—400 souls turned out upon the highway—not allowed even to rest in the roadside ditches? Was not another village razed by the Marquis of Waterford? Another, I believe, by Mr. Clark, of Nenagh, who was murdered; another by Mr. Pierce Carrick, who was murdered for the same intention. All these, and numerous other facts of the same kind, are going on at this moment. Even in this morning's papers I see a fresh announcement of a clearance of 180 individuals. . . .

[L]andlords consider themselves justified in consolidating their estates, and ejecting the numerous families of tenantry who have occupied under the old leases. Now, I ask, what becomes of these ejected wretches, whose houses are pulled down, who are driven forth from the land where they were born and bred, hunted even out of the roadside ditches, when they take shelter there, as was literally the case in the Gerrard clearances? Where are they to go? How are they to live? . . . If they squat on another landlord's estate they are driven off again as nuisances, pests—as people, in one word, who have no right to exist. . . . I ask, what becomes of them? Why, we know on the best authority they wander to the big towns and try to live by beggary. . . . Is not an ejectment of this kind tantamount to a sentence of death on a small farmer or cottier, whose only chance of living and maintaining his family is the occupation of

From G. J. Shaw Lefevre, *Peel and O'Connell: A Review of the Irish Policy of Parliament from the Act of Union to the Death of Sir Robert Peel* (London: Kegan Paul, 1887), pp. 288–289.

a bit of land? Can you wonder at his retaliating on him whom he feels to be his oppressor? Or can you wonder that thousands, who know themselves to be exposed to this fate, every day contrive to save themselves from it by a system of outrage and intimidation?

Nicholas Cummins
THE FAMINE IN SKIBBEREEN

The south and west of Ireland suffered worst from famine. With poor soil fit for little more than potatoes, the area was in desperate straits by the fall of 1846.

Skibbereen, in the remote southwest of Ireland, lacked suitable people to form a relief committee, without which it was not eligible for government relief. Public works were the only employment and did not pay enough to feed a family. In December 1846, when hundreds had died of hunger, two Protestant clergymen from the town confronted Trevelyan in London and pleaded for food. But Trevelyan was determined to adhere to government policy and no food was sent.

Two weeks later Nicholas Cummins, a magistrate from Cork, visited the area and was horrified. He reported to the authorities without success and then wrote a letter to the Duke of Wellington, an Irishman, with a copy to *The Times*, the most influential newspaper in London. The letter was published on Christmas Eve, 1846, and Skibbereen became a symbol of the famine disaster.

His letter received a wider circulation when meetings were held all over the United States in 1847 to raise money for famine relief in Ireland. Speakers on several occasions read his letter as an eyewitness account of the famine.

I thought it right personally to investigate the truth of several lamentable accounts which had reached me, of the appalling state of misery to which that part of the country was reduced. . . . I was surprised to find the wretched hamlet apparently deserted. I entered some of the hovels to ascertain the cause, and the scenes which presented themselves were such as no tongue or pen can convey the slightest idea of. In the first, six famished and ghastly skeletons, to all appearances dead, were huddled in a corner on some filthy straw, their sole covering what seemed a ragged horsecloth, their wretched legs hanging about, naked above the knees. I approached with horror, and found by a low moaning they were alive—they were in fever, four children, a woman and what had once been a man. It is impossible to go through the detail. Suffice it to say, that in a few minutes I was surrounded by at least 200 such phantoms, such frightful spectres as no words can describe, either from famine or from fever. Their demoniac yells are still ringing in my ears, and their horrible images are fixed upon my brain. My heart sickens at the recital, but I must go on.

In another case, decency would forbid what follows, but it must be told. My clothes were nearly torn off in my endeavor to escape from the throng of pestilence around, when my

Cecil Woodham-Smith, *The Great Hunger: Ireland 1845–49* (London: Hamish Hamilton, 1962), pp. 162–163.

neckcloth was seized from behind by a grip which compelled me to turn, I found myself grasped by a woman with an infant just born in her arms and the remains of a filthy sack across her loins—the sole covering of herself and baby. The same morning the police opened a house on the adjoining lands, which was observed shut for many days, and two frozen corpses were found, lying upon the mud floor, half devoured by rats.

A mother, herself in a fever, was seen the same day to drag out the corpse of her child, a girl about twelve, perfectly naked, and leave it half covered with stones. In another house, within 50 yards of the cavalry station at Skibbereen, the dispensary doctor found seven wretches lying unable to move, under the same cloak. One had been dead many hours, but the others were unable to move either themselves or the corpse.

REVIEW QUESTIONS

1. How do you explain the failure of the British government to deal with the potato famine?
2. Apart from the British government, who else should bear responsibility for the lack of adequate relief?

---

2 The Lower Classes

The members of the upper and middle classes in European society looked down on "the lower classes"—industrial workers, domestic help, and peasants; and still further down, the street people, the mentally disturbed, the homeless, the unemployed, and vagrants; and at the bottom, the criminal underworld. These "lower classes" were most vulnerable to the vicissitudes of the business cycle and dependent on small and uncertain incomes; commonly they worked long hours under dehumanizing strain and were housed in urban slums under unsanitary conditions; they were hungry, illiterate, often reduced to outright destitution, and desperate to earn some money. In the slums of London's East End, one could see ragged men collect dog excrement for use in tanning leather; prostitution thrived.

In the economic progress of the nineteenth century, the overall material conditions of society improved remarkably, sharpening the social contrasts. Concerned people spoke of "two nations," the rich and the poor. The poor, however, were not entirely passive; workers began to rally, trying to improve their condition by political action, thereby scaring the upper classes into social awareness. At the same time, humanitarian concerns, often rising from religious inspiration, stirred some of the well-to-do. Toward the end of the nineteenth century, the misery of the poor caused lively public debate and heated political agitation.

William Booth
IN DARKEST ENGLAND AND THE WAY OUT

The poor were not without compassionate friends. One of them was William Booth (1829–1912), the founder of the Salvation Army. Growing up poor himself, he was apprenticed to a pawnbroker while still a boy. At fifteen, under Methodist influence, he experienced a religious conversion, which eventually turned him into a Methodist minister; his wife and helpmate was one of the first Methodist woman preachers. Settled in London, he combined work at a pawnshop with ministering to the poor in the slums of London's East End. Booth and his wife devoted themselves to rescuing and rehabilitating the homeless, the unemployed, and the sinners of the urban underworld. In 1879 the organization that they had created officially became the Salvation Army. William Booth was its general; ordained ministers were its officers; the soldiers were men and women dedicated to saving others from the misery from which they themselves had escaped. All wore the Salvation Army's special uniform. The Salvation Army grew rapidly, spreading over the world. It now serves in seventy-seven countries, with over 300,000 soldiers in the United States.

In 1890 General Booth published *In Darkest England and the Way Out*, describing the misery of the poor and outlining his methods of achieving spiritual salvation through social service. In the opening two chapters, Booth outlined the extent of poverty in England at the height of its imperial glory. He begins by comparing England with journalist-explorer Henry Stanley's description of the brutality, slavery, and disease in "Darkest Africa."

WHY "DARKEST ENGLAND"?

This summer the attention of the civilised world has been arrested by the story which Mr. Stanley has told of "Darkest Africa" and his journeyings across the heart of the Lost Continent. . . .

It is a terrible picture, and one that has engraved itself deep on the heart of civilisation. But while brooding over the awful presentation of life as it exists in the vast African forest, it seemed to me only too vivid a picture of

many parts of our own land. As there is a darkest Africa is there not also a darkest England? Civilisation, which can breed its own barbarians, does it not also breed its own pygmies? May we not find a parallel at our own doors, and discover within a stone's throw of our cathedrals and palaces similar horrors to those which Stanley has found existing in the great Equatorial forest?

The more the mind dwells upon the subject, the closer the analogy appears. The [Arab] ivory raiders who brutally traffic in the unfortunate denizens of the forest glades, what are they but the [exploiters] who flourish on the weakness of our poor? . . . As in Africa, it is

---

William Booth, *In Darkest England and the Way Out* (London: International Headquarters of the Salvation Army, 1890), pp. 9, 11–16, 18–20.

all trees, trees, trees with no other world conceivable; so is it here—it is all vice and poverty and crime. To many the world is all slum, with the Workhouse as an intermediate purgatory before the grave. . . . Who can battle against the ten thousand million trees? Who can hope to make headway against the innumerable adverse conditions which doom the dweller in Darkest England to eternal and immutable misery?

. . . Talk about Danté's Hell, and all the horrors and cruelties of the torture-chamber of the lost! The man who walks with open eyes and with bleeding heart through the shambles of our civilisation needs no such fantastic images of the poet to teach him horror. Often and often, when I have seen the young and the poor and the helpless go down before my eyes into the morass, trampled underfoot by beasts of prey in human shape that haunt these regions, it seemed as if God were no longer in His world, but that in His stead reigned a fiend, merciless as Hell, ruthless as the grave. Hard it is, no doubt, to read in Stanley's pages of the slave-traders coldly arranging for the surprise of a village, the capture of the inhabitants, the massacre of those who resist, and the violation of all the women; but the stony streets of London, if they could but speak, would tell of tragedies as awful, of ruin as complete, of ravishments as horrible, as if we were in Central Africa; only the ghastly devastation is covered, corpse-like, with the artificialities and hypocrisies of modern civilisation.

The lot of a negress in the Equatorial Forest is not, perhaps, a very happy one, but is it so very much worse than that of many a pretty orphan girl in our Christian capital? . . . A young penniless girl, if she be pretty, is often hunted from pillar to post by her employers, confronted always by the alternative—Starve or Sin. And when once the poor girl has consented to buy the right to earn her living by the sacrifice of her virtue, then she is treated as a slave and an outcast by the very men who have ruined her. . . . [A]nd she is swept downward. . . .

The blood boils with impotent rage at the sight of these enormities, callously inflicted, and silently borne by these miserable victims. Nor is it only women who are the victims, although their fate is the most tragic. Those firms which reduce sweating [hard labor at low wages] to a fine art, who systematically and deliberately defraud the workman of his pay, who grind the faces of the poor, and who rob the widow and the orphan, and who for a pretence make great professions of public-spirit and philanthropy, those men nowadays are sent to Parliament to make laws for the people. The old prophets sent them to Hell—but we have changed all that. They send their victims to Hell, and are rewarded by all that wealth can do to make their lives comfortable. Read the House of Lords' Report on the Sweating System, and ask if any African slave system, making due allowance for the superior civilisation, and therefore sensitiveness, of the victims, reveals more misery.

Darkest England, like Darkest Africa, reeks with malaria. The foul and fetid breath of our slums is almost as poisonous as that of the African swamp. Fever is almost as chronic there as on the Equator. Every year thousands of children are killed off by what is called defects of our sanitary system. They are in reality starved and poisoned, and all that can be said is that, in many cases, it is better for them that they were taken away from the trouble to come.

Just as in Darkest Africa it is only a part of the evil and misery that comes from the superior race who invade the forest to enslave and massacre its miserable inhabitants, so with us, much of the misery of those whose lot we are considering arises from their own habits. Drunkenness and all manner of uncleanness, moral and physical, abound. Have you ever watched by the bedside of a man in delirium tremens [trembling and delusions brought on by alcohol abuse]? Multiply the sufferings of that one drunkard by the hundred thousand, and you have some idea of what scenes are being witnessed in all our great cities at this moment. . . . A population sodden with drink, steeped in vice, eaten up by every social and physical malady, these are the denizens of Darkest England amidst whom my life has been spent, and to whose rescue I would now summon all that is best in the manhood and womanhood of our land. . . .

. . . [T]he grimmest social problems of our time should be sternly faced, not with a view to the generation of profitless emotion, but with a view to its solution. . . .

Relying on the statistics of Charles Booth (no relation), William Booth concluded that three million people, one-tenth of the population, were pauperized and degraded.

THE SUBMERGED TENTH

What, then, is Darkest England? For whom do we claim that "urgency" which gives their case priority over that of all other sections of their countrymen and countrywomen? . . .

. . . The [people] in Darkest England, for whom I appeal, are (1) those who, having no capital or income of their own, would in a month be dead from sheer starvation were they exclusively dependent upon the money earned by their own work; and (2) those who by their utmost exertions are unable to attain the regulation allowance of food which the law prescribes as indispensable even for the worst criminals in our gaols.

I sorrowfully admit that it would be Utopian in our present social arrangements to dream of attaining for every honest Englishman a gaol standard of all the necessaries of life. Some time, perhaps, we may venture to hope that every honest worker on English soil will always be as warmly clad, as healthily housed, and as regularly fed as our criminal convicts—but that is not yet.

Neither is it possible to hope for many years to come that human beings generally will be as well cared for as horses. Mr. Carlyle long ago remarked that the four-footed worker has already got all that this two-handed one is clamouring for. . . .

What, then, is the standard towards which we may venture to aim with some prospect of realisation in our time? It is a very humble one, but if realised it would solve the worst problems of modern Society.

It is the standard of the London Cab Horse. . . .

The first question, then, which confronts us is, what are the dimensions of the Evil? How many of our fellow-men dwell in this Darkest England? How can we take the census of those who have fallen below the Cab Horse standard to which it is our aim to elevate the most wretched of our countrymen? . . .

Henry Mayhew
PROSTITUTION IN VICTORIAN LONDON

The destitute poor often turned to crime and prostitution for survival. In *London Labour and the London Poor*, published in 1862, Henry Mayhew (1812–1887), who had cultivated friendly contacts with London street people, including criminals and prostitutes, reported his findings with compassionate detachment. Practicing sociology with a human face, Mayhew pioneered oral history in hundreds of case studies. He hoped "to give the rich a more intimate knowledge of the sufferings and frequent heroism under those sufferings, of the poor—that it may

. . . cause those who are in 'high places' and those of whom much is expected, to bestir themselves to improve the condition of a class of people whose misery, ignorance, and vice, amidst all the immense wealth and great knowledge of 'the first city in the world' is . . . a national disgrace. . . ." Below Mayhew records a young London prostitute's account of her squalid life.

STATEMENT OF A PROSTITUTE

The narrative which follows—that of a prostitute, sleeping in the low-lodging houses, where boys and girls are all huddled promiscuously together, discloses a system of depravity, atrocity, and enormity, which certainly cannot be paralleled in any nation, however barbarous, nor in any age, however "dark." The facts detailed, it will be seen, are gross enough to make us all blush for the land in which such scenes can be daily perpetrated. The circumstances, which it is impossible to publish, are of the most loathsome and revolting nature.

A good-looking girl of sixteen gave me the following awful statement:—

"I am an orphan. When I was ten I was sent to service as maid of all-work, in a small tradesman's family. It was a hard place, and my mistress used me very cruelly, beating me often. When I had been in place three weeks, my mother died; my father having died . . . years before. I stood my mistress's ill-treatment for about six months. She beat me with sticks as well as with her hands. I was black and blue, and at last I ran away. I got to Mrs.———, a low lodging-house. I didn't know before that there was such a place. I heard of it from some girls at the glasshouse [baths and washhouses], where I went for shelter. I went with them to have a halfpenny worth of coffee, and they took me to the lodging-house. I then had three shillings, and stayed about a month, and did nothing wrong, living on the three shillings and

what I pawned my clothes for, as I got some pretty good things away with me. In the lodging-house I saw nothing but what was bad, and heard nothing but what was bad. I was laughed at, and was told to swear. They said, 'Look at her for a d———modest fool'—sometimes worse than that, until by degrees I got to be as bad as they were. During this time I used to see boys and girls from ten and twelve years old sleeping together, but understood nothing wrong. I had never heard of such places before I ran away. I can neither read nor write. My mother was a good woman, and I wish I'd had her to run away to. I saw things between almost children that I can't describe to you—very often I saw them, and that shocked me. At the month's end, when I was beat out, I met with a young man of fifteen—I myself was going on to twelve years old—and he persuaded me to take up with him. I stayed with him three months in the same lodging-house, living with him as his wife, though we were mere children, and being true to him. At the three months' end he was taken up for picking pockets, and got six months. I was sorry, for he was kind to me; though I was made ill through him; so I broke some windows in St. Paul's-churchyard to get into prison to get cured. I had a month in the Compter [debtors' prison], and came out well. I was scolded very much in the Compter, on account of the state I was in, being so young. I had 2s. 6d. [two shillings and sixpence] given to me when I came out, and was forced to go into the streets for a living. I continued walking the streets for three years, sometimes making a good deal of money, sometimes none, feasting one day and starving the next. The bigger girls could persuade me to do anything they liked

Henry Mayhew, *London Labour and the London Poor*, vol. 1 (London: Charles Griffin and Company, 1862), pp. 458–460.

with my money. I was never happy all the time, but I could get no character [reference] and could not get out of the life. I lodged all this time at a lodging-house in Kent-street. They were all thieves and bad girls. I have known between three and four dozen boys and girls sleep in one room. The beds were horrid filthy and full of vermin. There was very wicked carryings on. The boys, if any difference, was the worst. We lay packed on a full night, a dozen boys and girls squeedged into one bed. That was very often the case—some at the foot and some at the top—boys and girls all mixed. I can't go into all the particulars, but whatever could take place in words or acts between boys and girls did take place, and in the midst of the others. I am sorry to say I took part in these bad ways myself, but I wasn't so bad as some of the others. There was only a candle burning all night, but in summer it was light great part of the night. Some boys and girls slept without any clothes, and would dance about the room that way. I have seen them, and, wicked as I was, felt ashamed. I have seen two dozen capering about the room that way; some mere children, the boys generally the youngest. . . .

"There were no men or women present. There were often fights. The deputy never interfered. This is carried on just the same as ever to this day, and is the same every night. I have heard young girls shout out to one another how often they had been obliged to go to the hospital, or the infirmary, or the workhouse. There was a great deal of boasting about what the boys and girls had stolen during the day. I have known boys and girls change their 'partners,' just for a night. At three years' end I stole a piece of beef from a butcher. I did it to get into prison. I was sick of the life I was leading, and didn't know how to get out of it. I had a month for stealing. When I got out I passed two days and a night in the streets doing nothing wrong, and then went and threatened to break Messrs.——— windows again. I did that to get into prison again; for when I lay quiet of a night in prison

I thought things over, and considered what a shocking life I was leading, and how my health might be ruined completely, and I thought I would stick to prison rather than go back to such a life. I got six months for threatening. When I got out I broke a lamp next morning for the same purpose, and had a fortnight. That was the last time I was in prison. I have since been leading the same life as I told you of for the three years, and lodging at the same houses, and seeing the same goings on. I hate such a life now more than ever. I am willing to do any work that I can in washing and cleaning. I can do a little at my needle. I could do hard work, for I have good health. I used to wash and clean in prison, and always behaved myself there. At the house where I am it is 3*d.* a night; but at Mrs.———'s it is 1*d.* and 2*d.* a night, and just the same goings on. Many a girl—nearly all of them—goes out into the streets from this penny and twopenny house, to get money for their favourite boys by prostitution. If the girl cannot get money she must steal something, or will be beaten by her 'chap' when she comes home. I have seen them beaten, often kicked and beaten until they were blind from bloodshot, and their teeth knocked out with kicks from boots as the girl lays on the ground. The boys, in their turn, are out thieving all day, and the lodging-house keeper will buy any stolen provisions of them, and sell them to the lodgers. I never saw the police in the house. If a boy comes to the house on a night without money or sawney [stolen cheese or bacon], or something to sell to the lodgers, a handkerchief or something of that kind, he is not admitted, but told very plainly, 'Go thieve it, then,' Girls are treated just the same. Any body may call in the daytime at this house and have a halfpenny worth of coffee and sit any length of time until evening. I have seen three dozen sitting there that way, all thieves and bad girls. There are no chairs, and only one form [bench] in front of the fire, on which a dozen can sit. The others sit on the floor all about the room, as near the fire as they can. Bad language goes on during the day, as I have told you it did during the night, and indecencies too, but nothing like so bad as at night. They talk about where there is good places to go and thieve. The missioners call sometimes, but they're laughed at often when they're talking, and always before the door's closed on them. If a decent girl goes there to get a ha'porth of coffee, seeing the board over the door, she is always shocked. Many a poor girl has been ruined in this house since I was, and boys have boasted about it. I never knew boy or girl do good, once get used there. Get used there, indeed, and you are life-ruined. I was an only child, and haven't a friend in the world. I have heard several girls say how they would like to get out of the life, and out of the place. From those I know, I think the cruel parents and mistresses cause many to be driven there. One lodging-house keeper, Mrs.———, goes out dressed respectable, and pawns any stolen property, or sells it at public-houses."

M. I. Pokrovskaya
WORKING CONDITIONS FOR WOMEN IN RUSSIAN FACTORIES

This report, describing how women were treated in Russian factories, was written by a female Russian doctor and published in an English suffragist magazine in 1914.

The matter of fines which are exacted from factory workers by their employers is a very serious one. Fines are imposed for: late arrival, work which is not found to be up to standard, for laughter, even for indisposition. At a certain well-known calendar factory in St. Petersburg the women workers receive 0.45 rbls. [rubles] a day, and the fines have been known to amount to 0.50 rbls. a day. At a weaving factory, also in St. Petersburg, women operatives may earn as much as 1.25 rbls. a day, but owing to deductions for various fines the earnings often sink to as low as 0.25 rbls. a day. If a worker is feeling unwell and sits down, a fine is incurred . . . . If an article is dropped, the fine is [levied and] . . . if the worker fails to "stand to attention" at the entrance of employer or foreman and until he leaves the room, she is fined. . . . At a well-known chocolate factory in Moscow the fine for laughing is 0.75 rbls. and if a worker is 15 minutes late she is dismissed for one week. At another old established and famous chocolate factory in case of sudden illness a woman employee is instantly discharged. In a certain cartridge factory the workers are searched before leaving, and those who persist in having pockets are fined. . . .

In the majority of factories where women are employed the working day is from 10 to 11½ hours, after deducting the dinner and breakfast intervals. On Saturday, in many factories . . . the work sometimes lasts 16 and 18 hours per day. The workers are forced to work overtime on pain of instant dismissal or of transference to inferior employment, and in the case of children actual physical force is used to make them continue in their places. Dining and lunch rooms are rarely provided, and in many places no definite time

M. I. Pokrovskaya, *Jus Suffragii,* (February 6, 1914). Translated by Sonia Lethers.

is allowed for meals. In one well-known factory one hour is allowed for meals, but there is no place where the workers can eat their food except in the work-rooms or in the lavatories.

The position of women workers on the tobacco plantations is the worst. According to a report published by the Sevastopol branch of the Women's Protective Union, young girls are sometimes kept at work during 22 hours in the day. Owing to the difficulties of carrying on the process of breaking the tobacco leaves in the daytime, the girl-workers are driven into the plantations at 4 A.M. where they work until 9 A.M. After that they are engaged in the processes of weighing and tying the packets of tobacco, which work is continued through practically the whole day, with the exception of short intervals for meals. At the same time the women workers are continually exposed to brutal and degrading treatment and assault. Not infrequently their earnings are not paid to them. . . .

It happens sometimes, as on April 25th, 1913, at a cotton spinning factory in St. Petersburg, that the workers strike as a protest against the dismissal of old workers and their replacement by girls between 14 and 16 years of age. The result of the strike was a wholesale dismissal of all the women, whose places were filled by young girls. Not infrequently the women strike on account of the rude treatment which they receive from the foreman, actual bodily ill-treatment not being unknown. Such strikes rarely accomplish anything.

The worst aspect of woman's factory labour is, however, the moral danger to which women are exposed from those in power over them.

Immoral proposals from foremen and from their assistants are of general occurrence, and women who resist are persecuted in every possible way, and sometimes actually violated.

In a large tobacco factory in St. Petersburg the women workers who were asking for raised pay were cynically informed that they could augment their income by prostitution.

All these hard conditions in connection with factory life have the result of driving a certain number of women workers into tolerated houses of prostitution or into the streets. This is directly encouraged by the management of some factories.

REVIEW QUESTIONS

1. What, according to William Booth, were the essential aspects of life in "Darkest England"? Why did he draw the comparison to "Darkest Africa"?
2. Do any of Booth's scathing criticisms apply to contemporary America?
3. How does the London prostitute's account of her life confirm the view that poverty was the underlying cause of prostitution? What circumstances prevented her from leaving the profession?
4. What did the working conditions and treatment of women workers indicate about the position of women in Russian working class society?

3 Feminism and Antifeminism

Inspired by the ideals of equality voiced in the Enlightenment and the French Revolution, women in nineteenth-century Europe and the United States began to demand equal rights, foremost the right to vote. In the United States, the women's suffrage movement held its first convention in 1848 in Seneca Falls, New

York. The women adopted a Declaration of Principles that said in part: "We hold these truths to be self-evident: that all men and women are created equal." The struggle for equal rights and voting privileges continued, and by the end of the century, women were voting in a few state elections. Finally, in 1920, the Nineteenth Amendment gave women voting privileges throughout the United States.

In England, having failed to persuade Parliament in the mid-1860s to give them the vote, women organized reform societies, drew up petitions, and protested unfair treatment. The Women's Social and Political Union (WSPU), organized by Emmeline Pankhurst, employed militant tactics, which increased the hostility of their opponents.

During World War I, women worked in offices, factories, and service industries at jobs formerly held by men. Their wartime service made it clear that women played an essential role in the economic life of nations, and many political leaders argued for the extension of the vote to them. In 1918, British women over the age of thirty gained the vote; in 1928, Parliament lowered the voting age for British women to twenty-one, the same as for men.

The first countries to permit women to vote were New Zealand in 1893 and Australia in 1902. In Europe, women were granted voting rights by stages, first for municipal elections, later for national ones. Finland extended voting rights to women in 1906; the other Scandinavian countries followed suit, but the majority of European countries did not allow women to vote until after World War I.

In their struggle for equal rights, women faced strong opposition. Opponents argued that feminist demands would threaten society by undermining marriage and the family. Thus in 1870, a member of the British House of Commons wondered "what would become, not merely of women's influence, but of her duties at home, her care of the household, her supervision of all those duties and surroundings which make a happy home . . . if we are to see women coming forward and taking part in the government of the country." This concern for the family was combined with a traditional biased view of woman's nature, as one writer for the *Saturday Review*, an English periodical, revealed:

> The power of reasoning is so small in women that they need [outside] help, and if they have not the guidance and check of a religious conscience, it is useless to expect from them self-control on abstract principles. They do not calculate consequences, and they are reckless when they once give way, hence they are to be kept straight only through their affections, the religious sentiment and a well educated moral sense.

John Stuart Mill
THE SUBJECTION OF WOMEN

John Stuart Mill (see also chapter 6), a British philosopher and a liberal, championed women's rights. His interest in the subject was awakened by Harriet Taylor, a long-time friend and an ardent feminist, whom he married in 1851. Mill and Taylor had an intense intellectual companionship both before and after their marriage, and Taylor helped shape his ideas on the position of women in society and the urgent need for reform. In 1867, Mill, as a Member of Parliament, proposed that the suffrage be extended to women (the proposal was rejected by a vote of 194 to 74). In *The Subjection of Women* (1869), Mill argued that male dominance of women constituted a flagrant abuse of power. He maintained that female inequality, "a single relic of an old world of thought and practice exploded in everything else," violated the principle of individual rights and hindered the progress of humanity. Excerpts from Mill's classic in the history of feminism follow.

The object of this Essay is to explain, as clearly as I am able, the grounds of an opinion which I have held from the very earliest period when I had formed any opinions at all on social or political matters, and which, instead of being weakened or modified, has been constantly growing stronger by the progress of reflection and the experience of life: That the principle which regulates the existing social relations between the two sexes—the legal subordination of one sex to the other—is wrong in itself, and now one of the chief hindrances to human improvement; and that it ought to be replaced by a principle of perfect equality, admitting no power or privilege on the one side, nor disability on the other. . . .

. . . The adoption of this system of inequality never was the result of deliberation, or forethought, or any social ideas, or any notion whatever of what conduced to the benefit of humanity or the good order of society. It arose simply from the fact that from the very earliest twilight of human society, every woman (owing to the value attached to her by men, combined with her inferiority in muscular strength) was found in a state of bondage to some man. . . .

But, it will be said, the rule of men over women differs from all these others in not being a rule of force: it is accepted voluntarily; women make no complaint, and are consenting parties to it. In the first place, a great number

of women do not accept it. Ever since there have been women able to make their sentiments known by their writings (the only mode of publicity which society permits to them), an increasing number of them have recorded protests against their present social condition: and recently many thousands of them, headed by the most eminent women known to the public, have petitioned Parliament for their admission to the parliamentary suffrage. The claim of women to be educated as solidly, and in the same branches of knowledge, as men, is urged with growing intensity, and with a great prospect of success; while the demand for their admission into professions and occupations hitherto closed against them becomes every year more urgent. Though there are not in this country, as there are in the United States, periodical Conventions and an organized party to agitate for the Rights of Women, there is a numerous and active Society organized and managed by women, for the more limited object of obtaining the political franchise. Nor is it only in our own country and in America that women are beginning to protest, more or less collectively, against the disabilities under which they labour. France, and Italy, and Switzerland, and Russia now afford examples of the same thing. How many more women there are who silently cherish similar aspirations, no one can possibly know; but there are abundant tokens how many *would* cherish them, were they not so strenuously taught to repress them as contrary to the proprieties of their sex. . . .

John Stuart Mill, *The Subjection of Women* (London: J. M. Dent and Sons, 1929), pp. 3–6, 10–12, 15, 60–61, 64, 73, 82, 161–162, 214–215.

Men do not want solely the obedience of women, they want their sentiments. All men, except the most brutish, desire to have, in the woman most nearly connected with them, not a forced slave but a willing one; not a slave merely, but a favourite. They have therefore put everything in practice to enslave their minds. The masters of all other slaves rely, for maintaining obedience, on fear; either fear of themselves, or religious fears. The masters of women wanted more than simple obedience, and they turned the whole force of education to effect their purpose. All women are brought up from the very earliest years in the belief that their ideal of character is the very opposite to that of men; not self-will, and government by self-control, but submission, and yielding to the control of others. All the moralities tell them that it is the duty of women, and all the current sentimentalities that it is their nature, to live for others; to make complete abnegation of themselves, and to have no life but in their affections. And by their affections are meant the only ones they are allowed to have—those to the men with whom they are connected, or to the children who constitute an additional and indefeasible tie between them and a man. When we put together three things—first, the natural attraction between opposite sexes; secondly, the wife's entire dependence on the husband, every privilege or pleasure she has being either his gift, or depending entirely on his will; and lastly, that the principal object of human pursuit, consideration, and all objects of social ambition, can in general be sought or obtained by her only through him—it would be a miracle if the object of being attractive to men had not become the polar star of feminine education and formation of character. And, this great means of influence over the minds of women having been acquired, an instinct of selfishness made men avail themselves of it to the utmost as a means of holding women in subjection, by representing to them meekness, submissiveness, and resignation of all individual will into the hands of a man, as an essential part of sexual attractiveness. Can it be doubted that any of the other yokes which mankind have succeeded in breaking would have subsisted till now if the same means had existed, and had been as sedulously [diligently] used to bow down their minds to it?

Mill argues that women should be able to participate in political life and should not be barred from entering the professions.

On the other point which is involved in the just equality of women, their admissibility to all the functions and occupations hitherto retained as the monopoly of the stronger sex. . . . I believe that their disabilities [in occupation and civil life] elsewhere are only clung to in order to maintain their subordination in domestic life; because the generality of the male sex cannot yet tolerate the idea of living with an equal. Were it not for that, I think that almost everyone, in the existing state of opinion in politics and political economy, would admit the injustice of excluding half the human race from the greater number of lucrative occupations, and from almost all high social functions; ordaining from their birth either that they are not, and cannot by any possibility become, fit for employments which are legally open to the stupidest and basest of the other sex, or else that however fit they may be, those employments shall be interdicted to them, in order to be preserved for the exclusive benefit of males. . . .

It will perhaps be sufficient if I confine myself, in the details of my argument, to functions of a public nature: since, if I am successful as to those, it probably will be readily granted that women should be admissible to all other occupations. . . .And here let me begin . . . [with] the suffrage, both parliamentary and municipal. . . .

. . . To have a voice in choosing those by whom one is to be governed, is a means of self-protection due to everyone, though he were to remain for ever excluded from the function of governing. . . . Under whatever conditions, and within whatever limits, men are admitted to the suffrage, there is not a shadow of justification for not admitting women under the same. The majority of the women of any class are not likely to differ in political opinion from the majority of the men of the same class, unless the question be one in which the interests of women, as such, are in some way involved; and if they are so, women require the suffrage, as their guarantee of just and equal consideration. . . .

With regard to the fitness of women, not only to participate in elections, but themselves to hold offices or practise professions involving important public responsibilities; I have already observed that this consideration is not essential to the practical question in dispute: since any woman, who succeeds in an open profession, proves by that very fact that she is qualified for it. And in the case of public offices, if the political system of the country is such as to exclude unfit men, it will equally exclude unfit women: while if it is not, there is no additional evil in the fact that the unfit persons whom it admits may be either women or men. . . .

. . . There is no country of Europe in which the ablest men have not frequently experienced, and keenly appreciated, the value of the advice and help of clever and experienced women of the world, in the attainment both of private and of public objects; and there are important matters of public administration to which few men are equally competent with such women; among others, the detailed control of expenditure. But what we are now discussing is not the need which society has of the services of women in public business, but the dull and hopeless life to which it so often condemns them, by forbidding them to exercise the practical abilities which many of them are conscious of, in any wider field than one which to some of them never was, and to others is no longer, open. If there is anything vitally important to the happiness of human beings, it is that they should relish their habitual pursuit [that is, they should be happy in their work]. This requisite of an enjoyable life is very imperfectly granted, or altogether denied, to a large part of mankind; and by its absence many a life is a failure, which is provided, in appearance, with every requisite of success.

Emmeline Pankhurst
"WHY WE ARE MILITANT"

Agitation in Great Britain for woman suffrage reached a peak during the turbulent years of parliamentary reform, 1909–1911. Under the leadership of Emmeline Pankhurst (1858–1928) and her daughter Christabel, women engaged in demonstrations; disrupted political meetings; and, when dragged off to jail, resorted to passive resistance and hunger strikes. Some hunger strikers were subjected to the cruelty of force feeding. In 1913 Emmeline Pankhurst carried her appeal to the United States, where she delivered the speech that follows.

I know that in your minds there are questions like these; you are saying, "Woman Suffrage is sure to come; the emancipation of humanity is an evolutionary process, and how is it that some

women, instead of trusting to that evolution, instead of educating the masses of people of their country, instead of educating their own sex to prepare them for citizenship, how is it that these militant women are using violence and upsetting the business arrangements of the country in their undue impatience to attain their end?"

Let me try to explain to you the situation. . . .

The extensions of the franchise to the men of my country have been preceded by very great violence, by something like a revolution, by something like civil war. In 1832, you know we were on the edge of a civil war and on the edge of revolution, and it was at the point of the sword—no, not at the point of the sword—it was after the practice of arson on so large a scale that half the city of Bristol was burned down in a single night, it was because more and greater violence and arson were feared that the Reform Bill of 1832 [which gave the vote to the middle class] was allowed to pass into law. In 1867, . . . rioting went on all over the country, and as the result of that rioting, as the result of that unrest, . . . as a result of the fear of more rioting and violence, the Reform Act of 1867 [which gave workers the vote] was put upon the statute books.

In 1884 . . . rioting was threatened and feared, and so the agricultural labourers got the vote.

Meanwhile, "during the '80s", women, like men, were asking for the franchise. Appeals, larger and more numerous than for any other reform, were presented in support of Woman's Suffrage. Meetings of the great corporations [group of principal officials in a town or city government], great town councils, and city councils, passed resolutions asking that women should have the vote. More meetings were held, and larger, for Woman Suffrage than were held for votes for men, and yet the women did not get it. Men got the vote because they were and would be violent. The women did not get it because they were constitutional and law-abiding. . . .

I believed, as many women still in England believe, that women could get their way in

Excerpts from a speech by Emmeline Pankhurst given October 21, 1913, in *Suffrage and the Pankhursts*, ed. Jane Marcus (New York: Routledge and Kegan Paul, 1987), pp. 153–157, 159–161.

some mysterious manner, by purely peaceful methods. We have been so accustomed, we women, to accept one standard for men and another standard for women, that we have even applied that variation of standard to the injury of our political welfare.

Having had better opportunities of education, and having had some training in politics, having in political life come so near to the "superior" being as to see that he was not altogether such a fount of wisdom as they had supposed, that he had his human weaknesses as we had, the twentieth century women began to say to themselves, "Is it not time, since our methods have failed and the men's have succeeded, that we should take a leaf out of their political book?". . .

Well, we in Great Britain, on the eve of the General Election of 1905, a mere handful of us—why, you could almost count us on the fingers of both hands—set out on the wonderful adventure of forcing the strongest Government of modern times to give the women the vote. . . .

The Suffrage movement was almost dead. The women had lost heart. You could not get a Suffrage meeting that was attended by members of the general public. . . .

Two women changed that in a twinkling of an eye at a great Liberal demonstration in Manchester, where a Liberal leader, Sir Edward Grey, was explaining the programme to be carried out during the Liberals' next turn of office. The two women put the fateful question, "When are you going to give votes to women?" and refused to sit down until they had been answered. These two women were sent to gaol, and from that day to this the women's movement, both militant and constitutional, has never looked back. We had little more than one moribund society for Woman Suffrage in those days. Now we have nearly 50 societies for Woman Suffrage, and they are large in membership, they are rich in money, and their ranks are swelling every day that passes. That is how militancy has put back the clock of Woman Suffrage in Great Britain. . . .

I want to say here and now that the only justification for violence, the only justification for damage to property, the only justification for risk to the comfort of other human beings is the fact that you have tried all other available means and have failed to secure justice, and as a law-abiding person—and I am by nature a law-abiding person, as one hating violence, hating disorder—I want to say that from the moment we began our militant agitation to this day I have felt absolutely guiltless in this matter.

I tell you that in Great Britain there is no other way. . . .

Well, I say the time is long past when it became necessary for women to revolt in order to maintain their self-respect in Great Britain. The women who are waging this war are women who would fight, if it were only for the idea of liberty—if it were only that they might be free citizens of a free country—I myself would fight for that idea alone. But we have, in addition to this love of freedom, intolerable grievances to redress. . . .

Those grievances are so pressing that, so far from it being a duty to be patient and to wait for evolution, in thinking of those grievances the idea of patience is intolerable. We feel that patience is something akin to crime when our patience involves continued suffering on the part of the oppressed.

We are fighting to get the power to alter bad laws; but some people say to us, "Go to the representatives in the House of Commons, point out to them that these laws are bad, and you will find them quite ready to alter them."

Ladies and gentlemen, there are women in my country who have spent long and useful lives trying to get reforms, and because of their voteless condition, they are unable even to get the ear of Members of Parliament, much less are they able to secure those reforms.

Our marriage and divorce laws are a disgrace to civilisation. I sometimes wonder, looking back from the serenity of past middle age, at the courage of women. I wonder that women have

the courage to take upon themselves the responsibilities of marriage and motherhood when I see how little protection the law of my country affords them. I wonder that a woman will face the ordeal of childbirth with the knowledge that after she has risked her life to bring a child into the world she has absolutely no parental rights over the future of that child. Think what trust women have in men when a woman will marry a man, knowing, if she has knowledge of the law, that if that man is not all she in her love for him thinks him, he may even bring a strange woman into the house, bring his mistress into the house to live with her, and she cannot get legal relief from such a marriage as that. . . .

. . . [W]e realise how political power, how political influence, which would enable us to get better laws, would make it possible for thousands upon thousands of unhappy women to live happier lives. . . .

Take the industrial side of the question: have men's wages for a hard day's work ever been so low and inadequate as are women's wages today? Have men ever had to suffer from the laws, more injustice than women suffer? Is there a single reason which men have had for demanding liberty that does not also apply to women?

Why, if you were talking to the *men* of any other nation you would not hesitate to reply in the affirmative. There is not a man in this meeting who has not felt sympathy with the uprising of the men of other lands when suffering from intolerable tyranny, when deprived of all representative rights. You are full of sympathy with men in Russia. You are full of sympathy with nations that rise against the domination of the Turk. You are full of sympathy with all struggling people striving for independence. How is it, then, that some of you have nothing but ridicule and contempt and [condemnation] for women who are fighting for exactly the same thing?

All my life I have tried to understand why it is that men who value their citizenship as their dearest possession seem to think citizenship ridiculous when it is to be applied to the women of their race. And I find an explanation, and it is the only one I can think of. It came to me when I was in a prison cell, remembering how I had seen men laugh at the idea of women going to prison. Why they would confess they could not bear a cell door to be shut upon themselves for a single hour without asking to be let out. A thought came to me in my prison cell, and it was this: that to men women are not human beings like themselves. Some men think we are superhuman; they put us on pedestals; they revere us; they think we are too fine and too delicate to come down into the hurly-burly of life. Other men think us sub-human; they think we are a strange species unfortunately having to exist for the perpetuation of the race. They think that we are fit for drudgery, but that in some strange way our minds are not like theirs, our love for great things is not like theirs, and so we are a sort of sub-human species.

We are neither superhuman nor are we sub-human. We are just human beings like yourselves.

Our hearts burn within us when we read the great mottoes which celebrate the liberty of your country; when we go to France and we read the words, liberty, fraternity and equality, don't you think that we appreciate the meaning of those words? And then when we wake to the knowledge that these things are not for us, they are only for our brothers, then there comes a sense of bitterness into the hearts of some women, and they say to themselves, "Will men never understand?" But so far as we in England are concerned, we have come to the conclusion that we are not going to leave men any illusions upon the question.

When we were patient, when we believed in argument and persuasion, they said, "You don't really want it because, if you did, you would do something unmistakable to show you were determined to have it." And then when we did something unmistakable they said, "You are behaving so badly that you show you are not fit for it."

Now, gentlemen, in your heart of hearts you do not believe that. You know perfectly well that there never was a thing worth having that was not worth fighting for. You know perfectly well that if the situation were reversed, if you had no constitutional rights and we had all of them, if you had the duty of paying and obeying and trying to look as pleasant, and we were the proud citizens who could decide our fate and yours, because we knew what was good for you better than you knew yourselves, you know perfectly well that you wouldn't stand it for a single day, and you would be perfectly justified in rebelling against such intolerable conditions.

The Goncourt Brothers
ON FEMALE INFERIORITY

The brothers Edmund (1822–1896) and Jules (1830–1870) Goncourt were French writers who produced in partnership novels, plays, and art and literary criticism. Starting in December 1851, they kept a journal in which they recorded, often insightfully, the doings of Parisian cultural and social life. In the following entries the Goncourts reveal an extreme bias against women. Even if these sentiments were not shared by all intellectuals, they do show the traditional prejudices confronting French feminists.

13 October, 1855

A conversation about woman, after a couple of tankards of beer at Binding's. Woman is an evil, stupid animal unless she is educated and civilized to a high degree. She is incapable of dreaming, thinking, or loving. Poetry in a woman is never natural but always a product of education. Only the woman of the world is a woman; the rest are females.

Inferiority of the feminine mind to the masculine mind. All the physical beauty, all the strength, and all the development of a woman is concentrated in and as it were directed towards the central and lower parts of the body: the pelvis, the buttocks, the thighs; the beauty of a man is to be found in the upper, nobler parts, the pectoral muscles, the broad shoulders, the high forehead. Venus has a narrow forehead. Dürer's *Three Graces* have flat heads at the back and little shoulders; only their hips are big and beautiful. As regards the inferiority of the feminine mind, consider the self-assurance of a woman, even when she is only a girl, which allows her to be extremely witty with nothing but a little vivacity and a touch of spontaneity. Only man is endowed with the modesty and timidity which woman lacks and which she uses only as weapons.

Woman: the most beautiful and most admirable of laying machines.

21 May, 1857

Men like ourselves need a woman of little breeding and education who is nothing but gaiety and natural wit, because a woman of that sort can charm and please us like an agreeable animal to which we may become quite attached. But if a mistress has acquired a veneer of breeding, art, or literature, and tries to talk to us on an equal footing about our thoughts and our feeling for beauty; if she wants to be a companion and partner in the cultivation of our tastes or the writing of our books, then she becomes for us as unbearable as a piano out of tune—and very soon an object of dislike.

Almroth E. Wright
THE UNEXPURGATED CASE AGAINST WOMAN SUFFRAGE

Sir Almroth Wright (1861–1947) was an eminent physician and one of the founders of modern immunology. He was also a thinker who attempted to construct "a system of Logic which searches for Truth," as he put it.

Wright's opposition to giving women the vote was expressed in letters to *The Times* of London and in a slender book, *The Unexpurgated Case Against Woman Suffrage* (1913). In the extracts below, he describes how the disabilities of women make female suffrage impossible, at one point dismissing the suffrage movement as the product of "sex-hostility" caused by the excess population of women without hope of marrying. All told, he found that women's suffrage would be a recipe for social disaster, resulting in unacceptable demands for economic and intellectual equality.

The primordial argument against giving woman the vote is that that vote would not represent physical force.

Now it is by physical force alone and by prestige—which represents physical force in the background—that a nation protects itself against foreign interference, upholds its rule over subject populations, and enforces its own laws. And nothing could in the end more certainly lead to war and revolt than the decline of the military spirit and loss of prestige which would inevitably follow if man admitted woman into political co-partnership. . . .

[A] virile and imperial race will not brook any attempt at forcible control by women. Again, no military foreign nation or native race would ever believe in the stamina and firmness of purpose of any nation that submitted even to the semblance of such control. . . .

The woman voter would be pernicious to the State not only because she could not back her vote by physical force, but also by reason of her intellectual defects.

Woman's mind . . . arrives at conclusions on incomplete evidence; has a very imperfect sense of proportion; accepts the congenial as true, and rejects the uncongenial as false; takes the imaginary which is desired for reality, and treats the undesired reality which is out of sight as nonexistent—building up for itself in this way, when biased by predilections and aversions, a very unreal picture of the external world.

The explanation of this is to be found in all the physiological attachments of woman's mind: in the fact that mental images are in her over-intimately linked up with emotional reflex responses; that yielding to such reflex responses gives gratification; that intellectual analysis and suspense of judgment involve an inhibition of reflex responses which is felt as neural distress; that precipitate judgment brings relief from this physiological strain; and that woman looks

upon her mind not as an implement for the pursuit of truth, but as an instrument for providing her with creature comforts in the form of agreeable mental images. . . .

In further illustration of what has been said above, it may be pointed out that woman, even intelligent woman, nurses all sorts of misconceptions about herself. She, for instance, is constantly picturing to herself that she can as a worker lay claim to the same all-round efficiency as a man—forgetting that woman is notoriously unadapted to tasks in which severe physical hardships have to be confronted; and that hardly anyone would, if other alternative offered, employ a woman in any work which imposed upon her a combined physical and mental strain, or in any work where emergencies might have to be faced. . . .

Yet a third point has to come into consideration in connexion with the woman voter. This is, that she would be pernicious to the State also by virtue of her defective moral equipment. . . .

It is only a very exceptional woman who would, when put to her election between the claims of a narrow and domestic and a wider or public morality, subordinate the former to the latter.

In ordinary life, at any rate, one finds her following in such a case the suggestions of domestic—I had almost called it animal—morality.

It would be difficult to find anyone who would trust a woman to be just to the rights of others in the case where the material interests of her children, or of a devoted husband, were involved. And even to consider the question of being in such a case intellectually just to anyone who came into competition with personal belongings like husband and child would, of course, lie quite beyond the moral horizon of ordinary woman. . . . In this matter one would not be very far from the truth if one alleged that there are no good women, but only women who have lived under the influence of good men. . . .

In countries, such as England, where an excess female population [of three million]

Almroth E. Wright, *The Unexpurgated Case Against Woman Suffrage* (London: Constable, 1913), section 5.

has made economic difficulties for woman, and where the severe sexual restrictions, which here obtain, have bred in her sex-hostility, the suffrage movement has as its avowed ulterior object the abrogation of all distinctions which depend upon sex; and the achievement of the economic independence of woman.

To secure this economic independence every post, occupation, and Government service is to be thrown open to woman; she is to receive everywhere the same wages as man; male and female are to work side by side; and they are indiscriminately to be put in command the one over the other. Furthermore, legal rights are to be secured to the wife over her husband's property and earnings. The programme is, in fact, to give to woman an economic independence out of the earnings and taxes of man.

Nor does feminist ambition stop short here. It demands that women shall be included in every advisory committee, every governing board, every jury, every judicial bench, every electorate, every parliament, and every ministerial cabinet; further, that every masculine foundation, university, school of learning, academy, trade union, professional corporation, and scientific society shall be converted into an epicene institution [including both male and female]—until we shall have everywhere one vast cock-and-hen show.

The proposal to bring man and woman together everywhere into extremely intimate relationships raises very grave questions. It brings up, first, the question of sexual complications; secondly, the question as to whether the tradition of modesty and reticence between the sexes is to be definitely sacrificed; and, most important of all, the question as to whether [bringing men and women together] would place obstacles in the way of intellectual work. . . .

The matter cannot so lightly be disposed of. It will be necessary for us to find out whether really intimate association with woman on the purely intellectual plane is realisable. And if it is, in fact, unrealisable, it will be necessary to consider whether it is the exclusion of women from masculine corporations; or the perpetual attempt of women to force their way into these, which would deserve to be characterised as *selfish*. . . .

What we have to ask is whether—even if we leave out of regard the whole system of attractions or, as the case may be, repulsions which comes into operation when the sexes are thrown together—purely intellectual intercourse between man and the typical unselected woman is not barred by the intellectual immoralities and limitations which appear to be secondary sexual characters of woman. . . .

Wherever we look we find aversion to compulsory intellectual co-operation with woman. We see it in the sullen attitude which the ordinary male student takes up towards the presence of women students in his classes. We see it in the fact that the older English universities, which have conceded everything else to women, have made a strong stand against making them actual members of the university; for this would impose them on men as intellectual associates. Again we see the aversion in the opposition to the admission of women to the bar.

But we need not look so far afield. Practically every man feels that there is in woman—patent, or hidden away—an element of unreason which, when you come upon it, summarily puts an end to purely intellectual intercourse. One may reflect, for example, upon the way the woman's suffrage controversy has been conducted.

But the feminist will want to argue. She will—taking it as always for granted that woman has a right to all that men's hands or brains have fashioned—argue that it is very important for the intellectual development of woman that she should have exactly the same opportunities as man. And she will, scouting the idea of any differences between the intelligences of man and woman, discourse to you of their intimate affinity. . . .

From these general questions, which affect only the woman with intellectual aspirations, we pass to consider what would be the effect of feminism upon the rank and file of women if it made of these co-partners with man in work. They would suffer, not only because woman's physiological disabilities and the restrictions which arise out of her sex place her at a great disadvantage when she has to enter into competition with man, but also because under feminism man would be less and less disposed to take off woman's shoulders a part of her burden.

And there can be no dispute that the most valuable financial asset of the ordinary woman is the possibility that a man may be willing—and may, if only woman is disposed to fulfil her part of the bargain, be not only willing but anxious—to support her, and to secure for her, if he can, a measure of that freedom which comes from the possession of money.

In view of this everyone who has a real fellow-feeling for woman, and who is concerned for her material welfare, as a father is concerned for his daughter's, will above everything else desire to nurture and encourage in man the sentiment of chivalry, and in woman that disposition of mind that makes chivalry possible.

And the woman workers who have to fight the battle of life for themselves would indirectly profit from this fostering of chivalry; for those women who are supported by men do not compete in the limited labour market which is open to the woman worker.

From every point of view, therefore, except perhaps that of the exceptional woman who would be able to hold her own against masculine competition—and men always issue informal letters of [admission] to such an exceptional woman—the woman suffrage which leads up to feminism would be a social disaster.

REVIEW QUESTIONS

1. In John Stuart Mill's view, what was the ultimate origin of the subjection of women?
2. According to Mill, what character qualities did men seek to instill in women? Why, according to Mill's argument, should women have the right to participate in politics and public affairs on equal terms with men?
3. Why did Emmeline Pankhurst think that violence was justified in fighting for women's rights?
4. Why, according to her, did men, who valued their citizenship as their dearest possession, feel it was ridiculous to grant it to women?
5. In what ways did the Goncourt brothers consider women inferior?
6. Why did Sir Almroth Wright think that women voters would be pernicious to the state?
7. In Wright's view, how were feminist reforms disadvantageous to women?

4 German Racial Nationalism

In the first half of the nineteenth century, nationalism and liberalism went hand in hand. Liberals sought both the rights of the individual and also national independence and unification. Liberals expected that nationalism would unite a people in freedom and fellowship and foster a cultural flowering. They did not anticipate the emergence of an extreme nationalism that would subvert liberal values. Placing the nation above everything, extreme nationalists rejected the liberal ideals of liberty, equality, and tolerance. The extreme nationalism of the late nineteenth and early twentieth centuries contributed to Word War I and the rise of Fascism. It was the seedbed of totalitarian nationalism. Extreme nationalism was a general European phenomenon, but it proved particularly dangerous in Germany.

German nationalists were especially attracted to racist doctrines. Racist thinkers held that race was the key to history and that not only physical features, but also moral, aesthetic, and intellectual qualities distinguished one race from another. In their view, a race retained its vigor and achieved greatness when it preserved its purity; intermarriage between races was contamination that would result in genetic, cultural, and military decline. Unlike liberals, who held that anyone who accepted German law was a member of the German nation, German racist thinkers argued that a person's nationality was a function of his or her "racial soul" or "blood." On the basis of this new conception of nationality, racists argued that Jews, no matter how many centuries their ancestors had dwelt in Germany, could never think and feel like Germans and should be deprived of citizenship. Like their Nazi successors, nineteenth-century German racists claimed that the German race was purer than, and therefore superior to, all other races; its superiority was revealed in such physical characteristics as blond hair, blue eyes, and fair skin—all signs of inner qualities lacking in other races.

Houston Stewart Chamberlain
THE IMPORTANCE OF RACE

German racist thinkers embraced the ideas of Houston Stewart Chamberlain (1855–1927), an Englishman whose devotion to Germanism led him to adopt German citizenship. In *Foundations of the Nineteenth Century* (1899), Chamberlain attempted to assert in scientific fashion that races differed not only physically but also morally, spiritually, and intellectually and that the struggle between races was the driving force of history. He held that the Germans, descendants of the ancient Aryans (see pages 216, ftn. and 219), were physically superior and bearers of a higher culture. He attributed Rome's decline to the dilution of its racial qualities through miscegenation. The blond, blue-eyed, long-skulled Germans, possessing the strongest strain of Aryan blood and distinguished by an inner spiritual depth, were the true shapers and guardians of high civilization.

Chamberlain's book was enormously popular in Germany. Nationalist organizations frequently cited it. Kaiser Wilhelm II called *Foundations* a "hymn to Germanism" and read it to his children. "Next to the national liberal historians like Heinrich von Treitschke and Heinrich von Sybel," concludes German historian Fritz Fischer, "Houston Stewart Chamberlain had the greatest influence upon the spiritual life of Wilhelmine Germany."

Chamberlain's racist and anti-Semitic views make him a spiritual forerunner of Nazism, and he was praised as such by Alfred Rosenberg, the leading Nazi racial theorist in the early days of Hitler's movement. Josef Goebbels, the Nazi propagandist, hailed Chamberlain as a "pathbreaker" and "pioneer" after meeting him in 1926.

Nothing is so convincing as the consciousness of the possession of Race. The man who belongs to a distinct, pure race, never loses the sense of it. . . . Race lifts a man above himself: it endows him with extraordinary—I might almost say supernatural—powers, so entirely does it distinguish him from the individual who springs from the chaotic jumble of peoples drawn from all parts of the world: and should this man of pure origin be perchance gifted above his fellows, then the fact of Race strengthens and elevates him on every hand, and he becomes a genius towering over the rest of mankind, not because he has been thrown upon the earth like a flaming meteor by a freak of nature, but because he soars heavenward like some strong and stately tree, nourished by thousands and thousands of roots—no solitary individual, but the living sum of untold souls striving for the same goal. . . .

. . . As far back as our glance can reach, we see human beings, we see that they differ essentially in their gifts and that some show more vigorous powers of growth than others. Only one thing can be asserted without leaving the basis of historical observation: a high state of excellence is only attained gradually and under particular circumstances, it is only forced activity that can bring it about; under other circumstances it may completely degenerate. The struggle which means destruction for the fundamentally weak race steels the strong; the same struggle, moreover, by eliminating the weaker elements, tends still further to strengthen the strong. Around the childhood of great races, as we observe, even in the case of the metaphysical Indians, the storm of war always rages. . . .

. . . Only quite definite, limited mixtures of blood contribute towards the ennoblement of a race, or, it may be, the origin of a new one. Here again the clearest and least ambiguous examples are furnished by animal breeding. The mixture of blood must be strictly limited as regards time, and it must, in addition, be appropriate; not all and any crossings, but only definite ones can form the basis of ennoblement. By time-limitation I mean that the influx of new blood must take place as quickly as possible and then cease; continual crossing ruins the stongest race. To take an extreme example, the most famous pack of greyhounds in England was crossed once only with bulldogs, whereby it gained in courage and endurance, but further experiments prove that when such a crossing is continued, the characters of both races disappear and quite characterless mongrels remain behind. . . .

. . . Marius and Sulla[1] had, by murdering the flower of the genuine Roman youth, dammed the source of noble blood and at the same time, by the freeing of slaves, brought into the nation perfect floods of African and Asiatic blood, thus transforming Rome into . . . the trysting-place of all the mongrels of the world. . . .

Let us attempt a glance into the depths of the soul. What are the specific intellectual and moral characteristics of this Germanic race? Certain anthropologists would fain teach us that all races are equally gifted; we point to history and answer: that is a lie! The races of mankind are markedly different in the nature and also in the extent of their gifts, and the Germanic races belong to the most highly gifted group, the group usually termed Aryan[2]. . . .

The civilisation and culture, which radiating from Northern Europe, to-day dominate (though in very varying degrees) a considerable

---

Houston Stewart Chamberlain, *Foundations of the Nineteenth Century* , trans. John Lees (1968; New York: Howard Fertig, 2005), vol. I, pp. 269, 276, 283–284, 286, 542; vol. II, pp. 228–229.

---

[1]In the prolonged civil war unleashed by Marius (157–86 B.C.) and Sulla (138–78 B.C.), both commanders resorted to terror against their opponent's supporters.—Eds.

[2]Most European languages derive from the Aryan language spoken by people who lived thousands of years ago in the region from the Caspian Sea to the Hindu Kush Mountains. Around 2000 B.C., some Aryan-speaking people migrated to Europe and India. Nineteenth-century racialist thinkers held that Europeans, descendants of the ancient Aryans, were racially superior to other peoples.—Eds.

part of the world, are the work of Teutonism[3]; what is not Teutonic consists either of alien elements not yet exorcised, which were formerly forcibly introduced and still, like baneful germs, circulate in the blood, or of alien wares sailing, to the disadvantage of our work and further development, under the Teutonic flag,

under Teutonic protection and privilege, and they will continue to sail thus, until we send these pirate ships to the bottom. This work of Teutonism is beyond question the greatest that has hitherto been accomplished by man. . . . As the youngest of races, we Teutons could profit by the achievements of former ones; but this is no proof of a universal progress of humanity, but solely of the pre-eminent capabilities of a definite human species, capabilities which have been proved to be gradually weakened by influx of non-Teutonic blood.

---

[3]Teutons were a Germanic tribe in ancient times. Teutonism refers to the special character of German society and culture. Nationalists used the term to express German superiority.—Eds.

Pan-German League
"THERE ARE DOMINANT RACES AND SUBORDINATE RACES"

Organized in 1894, the ultranationalist and imperialist Pan-German League called for German expansion both in Europe and overseas. It often expressed blatantly Social Darwinist and racist views as illustrated in the following article, which appeared in 1913 in the league's principal publication.

The historical view as to the biological evolution of races tells us that there are dominant races and subordinate races. Political history is nothing more than the history of the struggles between the dominant races. Conquest in particular is always a function of the dominant races. . . .

Where now in all the world does it stand written that conquering races are under obligations to grant after an interval political rights to the conquered? Is not the practice of political rights an advantage which biologically belongs to the dominant races? . . . In my opinion, the rights of men are, first, personal

freedom; secondly, the right of free expression of opinion—as well as freedom of the press; . . . and, finally, the right to work, in case one is without means. . . .

In like manner there is the school question. The man with political rights sets up schools, and the speech used in the instruction is his speech. . . . The purpose must be to crush the [individuality of the] conquered people and its political and lingual existence. . . .

The conquerors are acting only according to biological principles if they suppress alien languages and undertake to destroy strange popular customs. . . . Only the conquering race must be populous, so that it can overrun the territory it has won. Nations that are populous are, moreover, the only nations which have a moral claim to conquest, for it is wrong that in one

---

Conquest and Kultur, compiled by Wallace Notestein and Elmer E. Stoll (Washington, D.C.: Committee on Public Administration, 1918), pp. 90–91.

country there should be overpopulation while close at hand—and at the same time on better soil—a less numerous population stretches its limbs at ease.

[As to the inferior races:] From political life they are to be excluded. They are eligible only to positions of a non-political character, to commercial commissions, chambers of commerce, etc. . . . The principal thing for the conqueror is the outspoken will to rule and the will to destroy the political and national life of the conquered. . . .

REVIEW QUESTIONS

1. Why were many Germans attracted to Chamberlain's racial theories?
2. Why is Chamberlain regarded as a spiritual forerunner of Hitler?
3. Why is an ideology based on biological racism, as in the case of the Pan-Germanic League, particularly dangerous?

5 Anti-Semitism: Regression to the Irrational

Anti-Semitism, a European phenomenon of long standing, rose to new prominence in the late nineteenth century. Formerly segregated by law into ghettoes, Jews, under the aegis of the Enlightenment and the French Revolution, had gained legal equality in most European lands. In the nineteenth century, Jews participated in the economic and cultural progress of the times and often achieved distinction in business, the professions, and the arts and sciences. However, driven by irrational fears and mythical conceptions that had survived from the Middle Ages, many people regarded Jews as a dangerous race of international conspirators and foreign intruders who threatened their nations.

Throughout the nineteenth century, anti-Semitic outrages occurred in many European lands. Russian anti-Semitism assumed a particularly violent form in the infamous pogroms—murderous mob attacks on Jews—occasionally abetted by government officials. Even in highly civilized France, anti-Semitism proved a powerful force. At the time of the Dreyfus Affair (see page 220), Catholic and nationalist zealots demanded that Jews be deprived of their civil rights. In Germany, anti-Semitism became associated with the ideological defense of a distinctive German culture, the Volkish thought popular in the last part of the nineteenth century. After the foundation of the German Empire in 1871, the pace of economic and cultural change quickened, and with it the cultural disorientation that fanned anti-Semitism. Volkish thinkers, who valued traditional Germany—the landscape, the peasant, and the village—associated Jews with the changes brought about by rapid industrialization and modernization. Compounding the problem was the influx into Germany of Jewish immigrants from the Russian Empire, who were searching for a better life and brought with them their own distinctive culture and religion, which many Germans found offensive. Nationalists and conservatives used anti-Semitism in an effort to gain a mass following.

Racial-nationalist considerations were the decisive force behind modern anti-Semitism. Racists said that the Jews were a wicked race of Asiatics, condemned by their genes; they differed physically, intellectually, and spiritually from Europeans who were descendants of ancient Aryans. The Aryans emerged some 4,000 years ago, probably between the Caspian Sea and the Hindu Kush Mountains. Intermingling with others, the Aryans lost whatever identity as a people they might have had. After discovering similarities between core European languages (Greek, Latin, German) and ancient Persian and ancient Sanskrit (the language of the conquerors of India), nineteenth-century scholars believed that these languages all stemmed from a common tongue spoken by the Aryans. From there, some leaped to the conclusion that the Aryans constituted a distinct race endowed with superior racial qualities.

Houston Stewart Chamberlain (see previous section) pitted Aryans and Jews against each other in a struggle of world historical importance. As agents of a spiritually empty capitalism and divisive liberalism, the Jews, said Chamberlain, were the opposite of the idealistic, heroic, and faithful Germans. Chamberlain denied that Jesus was a Jew, hinting that he was of Aryan stock, and held that the goal of the Jew was "to put his foot upon the neck of all the nations of the world and be lord and possessor of the whole earth." Racial anti-Semitism became a powerful force in European intellectual life, especially in Germany. It was the seedbed of Hitler's movement.

Theodor Fritsch
RULES TO FOLLOW REGARDING JEWS

Theodor Fritsch (1852–1933), a prolific writer, editor, and publisher of anti-Semitic books, newspapers, and journals, did much to stir German public opinion against the Jews. The Nazis hailed him as a respected precursor of their movement.

In the following passage, Fritsch lists ten rules Germans should follow in order to protect themselves from their Jewish adversary.

- Be proud of the fact that you are a German and try seriously, hard and steadily to practice the virtues of our people, courage, fidelity and truthfulness, and to awaken and nurture them in your children.

- You should know that you have a common, unrelenting adversary, together with all your fellow Germans, without distinction of faith or political opinion. He is called Jew.

- You shall keep your blood uncontaminated. Consider it a crime to spoil your people's breed with Jewish breed. For you must know that the Jewish blood is indisputable, and preserves the body and the soul according to the Jewish way into the later generations.

- You shall help your fellow Germans, and be supportive in all things, which are not contrary to the German conscience, when the Jew oppresses him; but you shall at once report every offense or crime committed by the Jew, in deed, word or letter, as soon as you become

From Theodor Fritsch, *Antisemiten-Katechismus* (Liepzig: Herm. Beyer, 1893), translated by Herbert Beyenbach.

aware of it, to the courts, so that the Jew will not blaspheme the laws of our country with impunity.

- Divorce yourself from the Jews socially. You shall not have any contact or social interaction with the Jew, but shun him, and keep him away from you and your family, and especially your daughters, to protect them from bodily and mental harm.

- Divorce yourself from the Jew in all business matters. You shall not choose a Jew as a business partner, don't borrow from him, don't buy anything from him, and do not allow your wife to do it. You shall not sell to him, or use him as an intermediary in your business, so that you may remain free and do not become the Jew's servant, to prevent him from accumulating more money and power, which he only uses to enslave our people.

- You shall drive the Jew out of your mind, and shall not follow the example of his trickery and cheating, as you will never reach his level of deceit, but you will only earn the contempt of your fellow-Germans, and the punishment of the courts.

- You shall not entrust your legal rights to a Jewish advocate, your body to a Jewish physician, nor your children to a Jewish teacher, so that you are not harmed in honor, body, and soul.

- You shall not listen to the Jew, or believe him, and keep away all Jewish writings from your German home and hearth, so that this lingering poison shall not unnerve and corrupt you and your family.

- You shall not commit acts of violence against the Jews, for this is not worthy of you, and is against the law. But if a Jew attacks you, repel his Semitic insolence with German wrath.

THE DREYFUS AFFAIR: THE HENRY MEMORIAL

In 1894, on the basis of forged evidence in which army officers were complicit, Captain Alfred Dreyfus, the first Jewish officer to be appointed to the French general staff, was convicted of selling secrets to Germany and sentenced to prison for life on Devil's Island, the forbidding penal colony in South America. After five years of what amounted to solitary confinement, Dreyfus was granted a second trial. Again found guilty, but with extenuating circumstances, he was sentenced to ten years' detention. Finally, after a new inquiry, Dreyfus was vindicated and restored to the army.

The Dreyfus Affair tore France apart. The Right—nationalists, clergy, the army, royalists, and conservatives—believing that the honor of the army was at stake, insisted on Dreyfus' guilt despite the mounting evidence that he was framed. A torrent of anti-Semitic venom was unleashed and "Death to the Jews" became a rallying cry of the French Right.

Major Hubert-Joseph Henry, who had forged documents implicating Dreyfus, committed suicide when the forgery was discovered. The Right hailed Lieutenant Colonel Henry (he had been promoted posthumously) as a martyr who gave his life "for the honor of the army and the good of the country." Édouard Drumont's paper *La Libre Parole*, which had engaged in vile anti-Semitic invectives during the crisis, raised money for a memorial fund for Henry's widow. Donors to the fund often vented their hatred of Jews, as the following examples from a list of donors published in 1898–1899 illustrate.

A rural priest, who offers up the most ardent prayers for the extermination of the two enemies of France: the Jew and the Freemason.[1] 5 fr.

A teacher, sworn enemy of stateless people. 1.50 fr.

A teacher from the Jura, who does not fail to tell his students that Jews and their friends are the vampires of France. 1 fr.

A future medical student, already sharpening his scalpels to dissect the Maccabee Dreyfus, bored through by a dozen bullets of a firing squad. 0.25 fr.

A group of policemen who would be very happy to thump hard and fast on Dreyfusards and filthy Yids, while, *by command and under pain of dismissal*, they are compelled to protect these rogues. 12.50 fr.

A royalist widow who misses the old bygone days when Jews were kept in their place. 2 fr.

A widow, who raises her son for God and France and in hatred of Freemasons and Jews. 0.15 fr.

A woman with great admiration for Drumont, who would like to see him govern France with the power of a king or emperor. 0.15 fr.

Sabatier (Madame Achille). Saint Joan of Arc, patron of our Sweet France, deliver us from the Jews! 20 fr.

H. L., brother of an infantry lieutenant, for [French President] Felix Faure when he kills as many kikes as rabbits. 0.50 fr.

XXXX [the identification used by the donor]. Finding not enough Jews to massacre, I propose cutting them in two, in order to get twice as many. 0.50 fr.

When will the alarm bell sound to rid France of the evil Yids? 1 fr.

A lieutenant of the colonial infantry. For the shame of the Jews and the triumph of honest men. 3 fr.

L. M., ex-second lieutenant of the 159th infantry. Long live France! Down with the kikes and freemasons who insult the army! 5 fr.

An administrative officer, in retirement. For the expulsion of the Yids. 5 fr.

A superior officer who would be delighted to see France in the hands of the French. 5 fr.

A section of officers from a frontier fortress who await with impatience the order to try new cannon and new explosives on the 100,000 Jews [there were not more than 75,000 French Jews, half of them in Paris] who poison the country. 25 fr.

A veteran of 1870, who considers the Jews the ten plagues of Egypt reunited. 2 fr.

Galey (Abbot), for the defense of the eternal law against the Puritan quackery and Judeo-Huguenot swindling. 5 fr.

Michael Burns, *France and the Dreyfus Affair: A Documentary History* (New York: Bedford/St. Martin's, 1999), p. 130.

[1]The Freemasonry was a fraternal organization that arose in Europe in the late sixteenth and early seventeenth centuries. The Catholic Church condemned it as a secret society in opposition to the church and its teachings.—Eds.

THE KISHINEV POGROM, 1903

Between 1881 and 1921 there were three large-scale waves of pogroms (mob attacks against Jews) in Russia. The civil and military authorities generally made no attempt to stop the murderous rampages and, at times, provided support. The worst of the pogroms occurred during the Civil War, which followed the Bolshevik Revolution of 1917; some 60,000 Jews were slaughtered, particularly in the Ukraine, long a hotbed of anti-Semitism.

None of the numerous anti-Semitic outbreaks against Russian Jews in the years before World War I had a greater impact than that of the Kishinev pogrom, in southwestern Russia, in 1903. Its exceptional brutalities left a deep mark on Jewish consciousness. In 1903 almost half of Kishinev's population was Jewish; having achieved success in commerce and petty industry, Jews were the mainstay of the city's prosperity. This condition aroused the anti-Semitic feelings of their neighbors, already predisposed to hatred of Jews by a deeply embedded Christian bias.

After the assassination of Tsar Alexander II in 1881, the anti-Semitism of the Russian government gained ground. With influential support, a journalist named Pavolski Krushevan founded a newspaper in 1897 called *The Bessarabian,* which stirred up anti-Semitic sentiment. He accused the Jews of exploiting the Christian population and, worse, of ritual murder. In the course of five years, Krushevan stepped up his agitation, printing lurid stories designed to incite popular violence against Jews. He and his like-minded associates brought public indignation to the boiling point in the spring of 1903. Calling for "a bloody reckoning with the Jews," he prepared the attack for April 6. It was Easter Sunday for the Christians and part of the Passover week for the Jews. The details of what happened in Kishinev on April 6 and 7 are taken from a report entitled *Die Judenpogrome in Russland* (The Jewish Pogroms in Russia), prepared by a Zionist organization in London and published in Germany in 1910.

Sunday morning the weather cleared. The Jews were celebrating the last two days of Passover. Not anticipating trouble, they put on their holiday clothes and went to the synagogue. . . .

. . . Suddenly at about 3 P.M. a crowd of men appeared on the square Novyi Bazar, all dressed in red shirts. The men howled like madmen, incessantly shouting: "Death to the Jews. Beat the Jews." In front of the Moscow Tavern the crowd of some hundred split into 24 groups of 10–15 men each. There and then the systematic destruction, pillaging, and robbing of Jewish houses and shops began. At first they threw stones in great quantity and force, breaking windows and shutters. Then they tore open doors and windows, breaking into the Jewish houses and living quarters, smashing whatever furniture and equipment they found. The Jews had

to hand over to the robbers their jewelry, money, and whatever other valuables they possessed. If they offered the slightest resistance, they were beaten over the head with pieces of their broken furniture. The storerooms were ransacked with special fury. The goods were either carried away or thrown on the street and destroyed. A large crowd of Christians followed the rioters, members of the intelligentsia, officials, students in the theological school, and others. . . .

At 5 P.M. the first Jew was murdered. The robbers stormed a trolley car with a Jewish passenger on board, shouting "Throw out the Jew." The Jew was pushed out and from all sides beaten on his head until his skull cracked and his brains spilled out. At first the sight of a dead Jew seemed to momentarily scare the bandits, but when they saw that the police did not care, they dispersed in all directions, shouting "Kill the Jews!"

On those streets where the pillaging took place Jews had to give up all attempts at self-defense. . . . But on the square Novyi Bazar the Jewish butchers gathered to defend themselves

Die zur Erforschung der Pogrom Eingesetzten Kommission, Die Judenpogrome in Russland: Herausgegeben im Auftrage des Zionistischen Hilfsfonds in London, vol. 2, *Einzeldarstellungen,* trans. Theodore H. Von Laue (Köln: Judischer Verlag GmbH, 1910), pp. 11–24.

and their families. They bravely fought back and chased away the attackers, who were as cowardly as they were wild. Then the police came and arrested the Jews.

That was the final signal for the organizers of the mob. Until 10 P.M. the unleashed passions were vented in plunder, robbery, and destruction. Seven other murders took place. . . .

The Jews spent the night from Sunday to Monday in indescribable fear, yet hoping that the terror might be over.

During that night the leaders of the pogrom prepared further attacks, as in war. First the gangs which during the previous evening had arrived from the countryside were equipped with weapons. All weapons were of the same kind: axes, iron bars, and clubs, all strong enough to break doors and shutters, and even metal cabinets and safes. All men wore the same outfit: the red workshirts were worn by all members of the rabble, by peasants, workers, petty bourgeois, even seminary students and police. The second systematic action was the marking of all Jewish houses by the committee organizing the pogrom. During the night all Jewish houses and shops were painted with white chalk. Next came the organization of a permanent information and communication network among the various gangs. Several bicyclists were engaged, who subsequently played an important role. The bicyclists were high school students, theological students, and officials. The organization covered more than the city of Kishinev. Messengers were sent out to the nearest villages inviting the peasants: "Come to the city and help plunder the Jews. Bring big bags." Around 3 A.M. the preparations were finished. The signal for the attack was given.

The terror that now followed can hardly be described—orgies of loathsome savagery, blood-thirsty brutishness, and devilish lechery claimed their victims. Forty-nine Jews were murdered in Kishinev. When one hears about the excess of horror, one recognizes that only

a few victims were lucky enough to die a simple death. Most of them had to suffer a variety of unbelievable abuse and repulsive torture unusual even among barbarians.

From 3 A.M. to 8 P.M. on Monday the gangs raged through the ruins and rubble which they themselves had piled up. They plundered, robbed, destroyed Jewish property, stole it, burned it, devastated it. They chased, slew, raped, and martyred the Jews. Representatives of all layers of the population took part in this witches' sabbath; soldiers, policemen, officials, and priests; children and women; peasants, workers, and vagabonds.

Major streets resounded with the terrifying roar of murdering gangs and the heart rending cries of the unfortunate victims. . . . The storerooms and shops were robbed, as on the previous day, down to the last item. . . . In the Jewish houses, the gangs burst into the living quarters with murderous howls, demanding all money and valuables. . . . If, however, the Jews could offer nothing or did not respond quickly enough, or if the gangsters were in a murderous mood, the men were knocked down, badly wounded, or killed. The women were raped one after the other in front of their men and children. They tore the arms and legs off the children, or broke them; some children were carried to the top floor and thrown out of the window. . . .

Early Monday morning a Jewish deputation hurried to the governor of the province to plead for protection. He answered that he could do nothing, since he had no orders from St. Petersburg [the capital]. At the same time he refused to accept private telegrams from St. Petersburg.

The vain appeal of the Jews to the governor was followed by a catastrophic worsening of their fate. The gangs henceforth could count on the patronage of the highest authority. . . .

In ever-rising fury the robbery, murder, and desecration continued. Jews had their heads hacked off. Towels were soaked in their blood and then waved like red flags. The murderers wrote with Jewish blood on white flags in large letters: "Death to the Jews!" They slit open the bodies of men and women, ripped out their guts and filled the hollows with leathers. They jumped on the corpses and danced, roaring, and drunk with vodka—men and women of "the best society." Officials and policemen laughed at the spectacle and joined in the fun. They beat pregnant women on their stomachs until they bled to death. . . .

They cut off the breasts of women after raping them. . . . Nails were driven into Chaja Sarah Phonarji's nostrils until they penetrated her skull. They hacked off the upper jaw of David Chariton, with all his teeth and his upper lip. Another man, Jechiel Selzer, had his ears pulled off before being beaten on the head until he became insane. . . .

These are some of the inhumanities committed during the pogrom. They are certified as true by eyewitnesses and the testimony of Christian physicians and Russian newspapers, which had passed through the most anti-Semitic and despotic censorship.

The synagogues were stormed and plundered with special spite. In one synagogue the gabai [sexton] braved death in front of the holy ark holding the Torah. Dressed in the *tales* [prayer shawl] and with the *tephalin* [phylacteries] on his forehead, he prepared for the onslaught of the murderers in order to protect the sacred scroll. He was cut down in the foulest manner. Then they tore, here and elsewhere, the Torah from the holy ark and cut the parchment into small scraps (Christian children later sold them on the streets for a few kopeks as mementos of Kishinev). After that the mobsters demolished, here as elsewhere, the synagogue's interior.

The barbarism of these scenes was so shattering that no less than 13 Jews went out of their minds. . . .

It would be unjust and ungrateful not to mention those Christians who in those days of mad brutality proved themselves true human beings and illustrious exceptions. They deserve to be remembered with special esteem because they were so few. . . .

Theodor Herzl
THE JEWISH STATE

Theodor Herzl (1860–1904) was raised in a comfortable Jewish middle-class home. Moving from Budapest, where he was born, to Vienna, the capital of the Austro-Hungarian Empire, he started to practice law, but soon turned to journalism, writing from Paris for the leading Vienna newspaper. A keen observer of the contemporary scene, he vigorously agitated for the ideal of an independent Jewish state. It was not a new idea but one whose time had come. Nationalist ferment was rising everywhere, often combined with virulent anti-Semitism. Under the circumstances, Herzl argued, security for Jews could be guaranteed only by a separate national state for Jews, preferably in Palestine.

In 1896 he published his program in a book, *Der Judenstaat* (The Jewish State), in which he envisaged a glorious future for an independent Jewish state harmoniously cooperating with the local population. In the following year he presided over the first Congress of Zionist Organizations held in Basel (Switzerland), attended mostly by Jews from Central and Eastern Europe. In its program the congress called for "a publicly guaranteed homeland for the Jewish people in the land of Israel." Subsequently, Herzl negotiated with the German emperor, the British government, and the sultan of the Ottoman Empire (of which Palestine was a part) for diplomatic support. In 1901 the Jewish National Fund was created to help settlers purchase land in Palestine. At his death, Herzl firmly expected a Jewish state to arise sometime in the future. The following excerpts from his book express the main points in his plea for a Jewish state.

We are a people—one people.

We have honestly endeavored everywhere to merge ourselves in the social life of surrounding communities and to preserve the faith of our fathers. We are not permitted to do so. In vain are we loyal patriots, our loyalty in some places running to extremes; in vain do we make the same sacrifices of life and property as our fellow-citizens; in vain do we strive to increase the fame of our native land in science and art, or her wealth by trade and commerce. In countries where we have lived for centuries we are still cried down as strangers, and often by those whose ancestors were not yet domiciled in the land where Jews had already had experience of suffering. . . . I think we shall not be left in peace.

Oppression and persecution cannot exterminate us. No nation on earth has survived such struggles and sufferings as we have gone through. Jew-baiting has merely stripped off our weaklings; the strong among us were invariably true to their race when persecution broke out against them. . . .

. . . [O]ld prejudices against us still lie deep in the hearts of the people. He who would have proofs of this need only listen to the people where they speak with frankness and simplicity: proverb and fairy-tale are both Anti-Semitic. . . .

No one can deny the gravity of the situation of the Jews. Wherever they live in perceptible numbers, they are more or less persecuted. Their equality before the law, granted by statute,

has become practically a dead letter. They are debarred from filling even moderately high positions, either in the army, or in any public or private capacity. And attempts are made to thrust them out of business also: "Don't buy from Jews!"

Attacks in Parliaments, in assemblies, in the press, in the pulpit, in the street, on journeys—for example, their exclusion from certain hotels—even in places of recreation, become daily more numerous. The forms of persecutions varying according to the countries and social circles in which they occur. In Russia, imposts are levied on Jewish villages; in Rumania, a few persons are put to death; in Germany, they get a good beating occasionally; in Austria, Anti-Semites exercise terrorism over all public life; in Algeria, there are travelling agitators; in Paris, the Jews are shut out of the so-called best social circles and excluded from clubs. Shades of anti-Jewish feeling are innumerable. But this is not to be an attempt to make out a doleful category of Jewish hardships.

I do not intend to arouse sympathetic emotions on our behalf. That would be a foolish, futile, and undignified proceeding. I shall content myself with putting the following questions to the Jews: Is it not true that, in countries where we live in perceptible numbers, the position of Jewish lawyers, doctors, technicians, teachers, and employees of all descriptions becomes daily more intolerable? Is it not true, that the Jewish middle classes are seriously threatened? Is it not true, that the passions of the mob are incited against our wealthy people? Is it not true, that our poor endure greater sufferings than any other proletariat? I think that this external pressure makes itself felt

From Theodor Herzl, *The Jewish State: An Attempt at a Modern Solution of the Jewish Question* (New York: American Zionist Emergency Council, 1946), pp. 76–77, 85–86, 91–93, 96. Reprinted by permission of the American Zionist Federation.

everywhere. In our economically upper classes it causes discomfort, in our middle classes continual and grave anxieties, in our lower classes absolute despair.

Everything tends, in fact, to one and the same conclusion, which is clearly enunciated in that classic Berlin phrase: *"Juden Raus!"* (Out with the Jews!)

I shall now put the Question in the briefest possible form: Are we to "get out" now and where to?

Or, may we yet remain? And, how long?

Let us first settle the point of staying where we are. Can we hope for better days, can we possess our souls in patience, can we wait in pious resignation till the princes and peoples of this earth are more mercifully disposed towards us? I say that we cannot hope for a change in the current of feeling. . . . The nations in whose midst Jews live are all either covertly or openly Anti-Semitic. . . .

. . . We might perhaps be able to merge ourselves entirely into surrounding races, if these were to leave us in peace for a period of two generations. But they will not leave us in peace. For a little period they manage to tolerate us, and then their hostility breaks out again and again. . . .

Thus, whether we like it or not, we are now, and shall henceforth remain, a historic group with unmistakable characteristics common to us all.

We are one people—our enemies have made us one without our consent, as repeatedly happens in history. Distress binds us together, and, thus united, we suddenly discover our strength. Yes, we are strong enough to form a State, and, indeed, a model State. We possess all human and material resources necessary for the purpose. . . .

Let the sovereignty be granted us over a portion of the globe large enough to satisfy the rightful requirements of a nation; the rest we shall manage for ourselves.

The creation of a new State is neither ridiculous nor impossible. We have in our day witnessed the process in connection with nations which were not largely members of the middle class, but poorer, less educated, and consequently weaker than ourselves. . . .

Palestine is our ever-memorable historic home. The very name of Palestine would attract our people with a force of marvellous potency. If His Majesty the Sultan were to give us Palestine, we could in return undertake to regulate the whole finances of Turkey. We should there form a portion of a rampart of Europe against Asia, an outpost of civilization as opposed to barbarism. We should as a neutral State remain in contact with all Europe, which would have to guarantee our existence. The sanctuaries of Christendom would be safeguarded by assigning to them an extra-territorial status such as is well-known to the law of nations. We should form a guard of honor about these sanctuaries, answering for the fulfillment of this duty with our existence. This guard of honor would be the great symbol of the solution of the Jewish Question after eighteen centuries of Jewish suffering.

REVIEW QUESTIONS

1. What, according to Hermann Ahlwardt, were the racial characteristics of Jews? What, in contrast, were the racial characteristics of Germans?
2. What racist elements are evident in Fritsch's writing?
3. Do you see any common threads in the anti-Semitic sentiments voiced by the donors to the Henry Memorial?
4. What social groups in Kishinev took part in the attack on the Jews? What does the pogrom reveal about human nature? What role did government officials play?
5. Why did Theodor Herzl believe that the creation of a Jewish state was the only solution to the Jewish question?

CHAPTER 9
European Imperialism

THE SUBMISSION OF KING PREMPAH, 1896. Prempah, chief of the Ashanti tribe, disregarded treaties he signed with the British and faced military defeat. Here, he and his mother submit to the authority of the British governor of the Gold Coast (now Ghana) in 1896. *(Hulton Archive/Getty Images)*

Overseas territorial expansion has been part of European history since the fifteenth century. Portuguese and Spaniards explored maritime routes around Africa to India and East Asia; they crossed the Atlantic to the Western Hemisphere, soon followed by the English, Dutch, and French. All began to establish overseas colonies as bases for their ships and traders. Acquisition of colonies became part of the European power struggle. It was based on Europe's rapid progress in science, technology, economic skills, and political organization, enriched by ready assimilation of useful achievements from around the world. No other peoples could match Western Europe's power resources.

The Europeans established control over territory in India, East Asia, and coastal Africa; they populated North America with their immigrants and gained control over South America. In the late eighteenth century the English extended their seapower into the Pacific Ocean, claiming Australia and New Zealand. After achieving independence the United States also felt the expansionist urge, ultimately stretching from the Atlantic to the Pacific. In the nineteenth century the Spaniards and Portuguese in South America set up their own independent states; the Western Hemisphere became an extension of the European state system.

In the late nineteenth century, industrial growth and worldwide trade created among Europeans a new global competition for empire. The search for vital raw materials, markets, and investments intensified economic outreach, leading to ruthless exploitation and domination. The expenses of imperialism, usually greater than its economic benefits, were justified by rising nationalism, which fueled the quest for overseas possessions. What counted by the end of the century, as the traditional European rivalries expanded around the world, was global power; overseas possessions enhanced national prestige. Britain, thanks to its seapower, emerged as the colonial giant, claiming India as the core of the British Empire and provoking imitation by other ambitious European countries. Envious of the British Empire, other states did not want to be left behind.

Thus started a frantic race to occupy the last unclaimed parts of the world. The European powers began a "scramble for Africa." The Russians pressed into the Near East and Central Asia. Anti-foreign Japan, pried open to Western influence by Commodore Matthew Perry of the United States in 1854, quickly westernized itself without impairing its cultural continuity, a unique case in history; catching the imperialist fever, Japan looked toward neighboring China for possible conquests. In 1898 the United States moved across the Pacific, occupying Hawaii and the Philippines. In 1900, responding to the Boxer Rebellion, a massive outburst in China of anti-foreign violence, the major European powers plus the United States and Japan expanded their rule in that country, greatly limiting the power of its government and inflicting a ruinous blow to its age-old pride. In the Age of Imperialism the world had essentially fallen under European—or now more generally "Western"—domination.

Obviously, the imperialist impact varied, depending on local conditions. Because of its geographical obstacles (dense tropical rainforests, savannahs, and deserts) sub-Saharan Africa was penetrated by the Europeans only late in the nineteenth century, carved up by England, France, Germany, and Belgium, each imposing its own boundaries regardless of local loyalties. Once established, the imperialists began to dominate their helpless subjects; all resistance was ruthlessly suppressed with the aid of indigenous soldiers. Convinced of their superiority, the imperialists often viewed Africans with disdain, dismissing their culture as barbaric. Indigenous ways, uncomprehended by and generally repulsive to Europeans, provided a profound challenge to Western attitudes. Their reactions ranged from Social Darwinist racism (see page 232) to a patronizing conviction that they were obliged to civilize their subjects according to their own values. In Africa especially, Christian missionaries played an important role in this effort, at considerable personal risk; because of tropical diseases and lack of medical care, their death rate was painfully high. Only gradually, and sometimes with the missionaries' help, did the imperialist masters begin to open their minds to their subjects' cultures, even then never questioning their own superiority. Extending the benefits of imperial rule over "primitive" people was a source of deep patriotic pride.

The European masters never appreciated the devastating effects of their domination upon indigenous life and traditions in African and Asian lands. All peoples were now subject to profound cultural disorientation. Indigenous customary ways were discredited as inferior by the invaders, while Western ways remained alien and perplexing to the conquered. The cultural gap between indigenous and Western life became a source of much misery and violence. In Africa the Europeans encountered the sharpest cultural contrasts with their own ways, while in India the British confronted a high civilization that lacked political power. Here too the British imperialists faced a difficult task in imposing their own standards on their subjects. In many lands the clash between indigenous and Western ways continues to the present day.

The imperialists generally imposed their Western culture upon all other cultures, thereby also disseminating their own ideals of freedom and self-determination. After World War I these ideals began to impress the educated minority, as in India. After World War II all colonial countries struggled toward independence. Thus imperialism gave rise to the present unprecedented age of intense global interaction, in which all peoples, to a lesser or greater degree, have to adjust to each other largely on Western, now simply called "modern," terms.

1   The Spirit of British Imperialism

In 1872 the British statesman Benjamin Disraeli (1804–1881) delivered a famous speech at the Crystal Palace in London that posed a crucial choice for his country: it was either insignificance in world affairs or imperial power with prosperity and global prestige. His speech was soon followed by an outburst of speeches, lectures, and books in which imperialists made claims for British worldwide superiority, buttressed by arguments drawn from racist and Social Darwinist convictions popular at the time. Although public opinion was divided, these ideas found a receptive audience.

Joseph Chamberlain
THE BRITISH EMPIRE: COLONIAL COMMERCE AND "THE WHITE MAN'S BURDEN"

British imperialists like Joseph Chamberlain (1836–1914) argued that the welfare of Britain depended upon the preservation and extension of the Empire, because colonies fostered trade and served as a source of raw materials. In addition, Chamberlain asserted that the British Empire had a sacred duty to carry civilization, Christianity, and British law to the "backward" peoples of Africa and Asia. As a leading statesman, Chamberlain made many speeches, both in Parliament and before local political groups, that endorsed imperialist ventures. Excerpts from these speeches, later collected and published under the title *Foreign and Colonial Speeches* (1897), follow.

June 10, 1896

. . . The Empire, to parody a celebrated expression, is commerce. It was created by commerce, it is founded on commerce, and it could not exist a day without commerce. (Cheers.) . . . The fact is history teaches us that no nation has ever achieved real greatness without the aid of commerce, and the greatness of no nation has survived the decay of its trade. Well, then, gentlemen, we have reason to be proud of our

commerce and to be resolved to guard it from attack. (Cheers.) . . .

March 31, 1897

. . . We have suffered much in this country from depression of trade. We know how many of our fellow-subjects are at this moment unemployed. Is there any man in his senses who believes that the crowded population of these islands could exist for a single day if we were to cut adrift from us the great dependencies which now look to us for protection and assistance, and which are the natural markets for our trade? (Cheers.) The area of the United Kingdom is only 120,000 miles;

Joseph Chamberlain, *Foreign and Colonial Speeches* (London: G. Routledge and Sons, 1897), pp. 102, 131–133, 202, 244–246.

Small island -
vast empire.

the area of the British Empire is over 9,000,000 square miles, of which nearly 500,000 are to be found in the portion of Africa with which we have been dealing. If tomorrow it were possible, as some people apparently desire, to reduce by a stroke of the pen the British Empire to the dimensions of the United Kingdom, half at least of our population would be starved (cheers). . . .

January 22, 1894

We must look this matter in the face, and must recognise that in order that we may have more employment to give we must create more demand. (Hear, hear.) Give me the demand for more goods and then I will undertake to give plenty of employment in making the goods; and the only thing, in my opinion, that the Government can do in order to meet this great difficulty that we are considering, is so to arrange its policy that every inducement shall be given to the demand; that new markets shall be created, and that old markets shall be effectually developed. (Cheers.) . . . I am convinced that it is a necessity as well as a duty for us to uphold the dominion and empire which we now possess. (Loud cheers.) . . . I would never lose the hold which we now have over our great Indian dependency—(hear, hear)—by far the greatest and most valuable of all the customers we have or ever shall have in this country. For the same reasons I approve of the continued occupation of Egypt; and for the same reasons I have urged upon this Government, and upon previous Governments, the necessity for using every legitimate opportunity to extend our influence and control in that great African continent which is now being opened up to civilisation and to commerce; and, lastly, it is for the same reasons that I hold that our navy should be strengthened—(loud cheers)—until its supremacy is so assured that we cannot be shaken in any of the possessions which we hold or may hold hereafter.

Believe me, if in anyone of the places to which I have referred any change took place which deprived us of that control and influence of which I have been speaking, the first to suffer would be the working-men of this country. Then, indeed, we should see a distress which would not be temporary, but which would be chronic, and we should find that England was entirely unable to support the enormous population which is now maintained by the aid of her foreign trade. If the working-men of this country understand, as I believe they do—I am one of those who have had good reason through my life to rely upon their intelligence and shrewdness—if they understand their own interests, they will never lend any countenance to the doctrines of those politicians who never lose an opportunity of pouring contempt and abuse upon the brave Englishmen, who, even at this moment, in all parts of the world are carving out new dominions for Britain, and are opening up fresh markets for British commerce, and laying out fresh fields for British labour. (Applause.) . . .

March 31, 1897

. . . We feel now that our rule over these territories can only be justified if we can show that it adds to the happiness and prosperity of the people—(cheers)—and I maintain that our rule does, and has, brought security and peace and comparative prosperity to countries that never knew these blessings before. (Cheers.)

In carrying out this work of civilisation we are fulfilling what I believe to be our national mission, and we are finding scope for the exercise of those faculties and qualities which have made of us a great governing race. (Cheers.) I do not say that our success has been perfect in every case, I do not say that all our methods have been beyond reproach; but I do say that in almost every instance in which the rule of the Queen has been established and the great *Pax Britannica*[1] has been enforced, there has come

---

[1]*Pax Britannica* means "British Peace" in the tradition of the *Pax Romana*—the peace, stability, and prosperity that characterized the Roman Empire at its height in the first two centuries A.D. —Eds.

with it greater security to life and property, and a material improvement in the condition of the bulk of the population. (Cheers.) No doubt, in the first instance, when these conquests have been made, there has been bloodshed, there has been loss of life among the native populations, loss of still more precious lives among those who have been sent out to bring these countries into some kind of disciplined order, but it must be remembered that this is the condition of the mission we have to fulfil. . . .

. . . You cannot have omelettes without breaking eggs; you cannot destroy the practices of barbarism, of slavery, of superstition, which for centuries have desolated the interior of Africa, without the use of force; but if you will fairly contrast the gain to humanity with the price which we are bound to pay for it, I think you may well rejoice in the result of such expeditions as those which have recently been conducted with such signal success— (cheers)—in Nyassaland, Ashanti, Benin, and Nupé [regions in Africa]—expeditions which may have, and indeed have, cost valuable lives, but as to which we may rest assured that for one life lost a hundred will be gained, and the cause of civilisation and the prosperity of the people will in the long run be eminently advanced. (Cheers.) But no doubt such a state of things, such a mission as I have described, involve heavy responsibility . . . and it is a gigantic task that we have undertaken when we have determined to wield the sceptre of empire. Great is the task, great is the responsibility, but great is the honour—(cheers); and I am convinced that the conscience and the spirit of the country will rise to the height of its obligations, and that we shall have the strength to fulfil the mission which our history and our national character have imposed upon us. (Cheers.)

Karl Pearson
SOCIAL DARWINISM: IMPERIALISM JUSTIFIED BY NATURE

In the last part of the nineteenth century, the spirit of expansionism was buttressed by application of Darwin's theory of evolution to human society. Theorists called Social Darwinists argued that nations and races, like the species of animals, were locked in a struggle for existence in which only the fittest survived and deserved to survive. British and American imperialists employed the language of Social Darwinism to promote and justify Anglo-Saxon expansion and domination of other peoples. Social Darwinist ideas spread to Germany, which was inspired by the examples of British and American expansion. In a lecture given in 1900 and titled "National Life from the Standpoint of Science," Karl Pearson (1857–1936), a British professor of mathematics, expressed the beliefs of Social Darwinists.

What I have said about bad stock seems to me to hold for the lower races of man. How

many centuries, how many thousands of years, have the Kaffir [a tribe in southern Africa] or the negro held large districts in Africa undisturbed by the white man? Yet their intertribal struggles have not yet produced a civilization in the least comparable with the Aryan

Karl Pearson, *National Life from the Standpoint of Science* (London: Adam and Charles Black, 1905), pp. 21, 23–27, 36–37, 44, 46–47, 60–61, 64.

(see pages 216, ftn. and 219) [Western European]. Educate and nurture them as you will, I do not believe that you will succeed in modifying the stock. History shows me one way, and one way only, in which a high state of civilization has been produced, namely, the struggle of race with race, and the survival of the physically and mentally fitter race. . . .

. . . Let us suppose we could prevent the white man, if we liked, from going to lands of which the agricultural and mineral resources are not worked to the full; then I should say a thousand times better for him that he should not go than that he should settle down and live alongside the inferior race. The only healthy alternative is that he should go and completely drive out the inferior race. That is practically what the white man has done in North America. . . . But I venture to say that no man calmly judging will wish either that the whites had never gone to America, or would desire that whites and Red Indians were to-day living alongside each other as negro and white in the Southern States, as Kaffir and European in South Africa, still less that they had mixed their blood as Spaniard and Indian in South America. . . . I venture to assert, then, that the struggle for existence between white and red man, painful and even terrible as it was in its details, has given us a good far outbalancing its immediate evil. In place of the red man, contributing practically nothing to the work and thought of the world, we have a great nation, mistress of many arts, and able, with its youthful imagination and fresh, untrammelled impulses, to contribute much to the common stock of civilized man. . . .

But America is but one case in which we have to mark a masterful human progress following an inter-racial struggle. The Australian nation is another case of great civilization supplanting a lower race unable to work to the full the land and its resources. . . . The struggle means suffering, intense suffering, while it is in progress; but that struggle and that suffering have been the stages by which the white man has reached his present stage of development, and they account for the fact that he no longer lives in caves and feeds on roots and nuts. This dependence of progress on the survival of the fitter race, terribly black as it may seem to some of you, gives the struggle for existence its redeeming features; it is the fiery crucible out of which comes the finer metal. You may hope for a time when the sword shall be turned into the ploughshare, when American and German and English traders shall no longer compete in the markets of the world for their raw material and for their food supply, when the white man and the dark shall share the soil between them, and each till it as he lists [pleases]. But, believe me, when that day comes mankind will no longer progress; there will be nothing to check the fertility of inferior stock; the relentless law of heredity will not be controlled and guided by natural selection. Man will stagnate. . . .

The . . . great function of science in national life . . . is to show us what national life means, and how the nation is a vast organism subject . . . to the great forces of evolution. . . . There is a struggle of race against race and of nation against nation. In the early days of that struggle it was a blind, unconscious struggle of barbaric tribes. At the present day, in the case of the civilized white man, it has become more and more the conscious, carefully directed attempt of the nation to fit itself to a continuously changing environment. The nation has to foresee how and where the struggle will be carried on; the maintenance of national position is becoming more and more a conscious preparation for changing conditions, an insight into the needs of coming environments. . . .

. . . If a nation is to maintain its position in this struggle, it must be fully provided with trained brains in every department of national activity, from the government to the factory, and have, if possible, a *reserve of brain and physique* to fall back upon in times of national crisis. . . .

You will see that my view—and I think it may be called the scientific view of a nation—is that of an organized whole, kept up to a high pitch of internal efficiency by insuring that its numbers are substantially recruited from the better stocks, and kept up to a high pitch of external efficiency by contest, chiefly by way of war with inferior races, and with equal races by the struggle for trade-routes and for the sources of raw material and of food supply. This is the natural history view of mankind, and I do not think you can in its main features subvert it. . . .

. . . Is it not a fact that the daily bread of our millions of workers depends on their having somebody to work for? that if we give up the contest for trade-routes and for free markets and for waste lands, we indirectly give up our food-supply? Is it not a fact that our strength depends on these and upon our colonies, and that our colonies have been won by the ejection of inferior races, and are maintained against equal races only by respect for the present power of our empire? . . .

. . . We find that the law of the survival of the fitter is true of mankind, but that the struggle is that of the [social] animal. A community not knit together by strong social instincts, by sympathy between man and man, and class and class, cannot face the external contest, the

competition with other nations, by peace or by war, for the raw material of production and for its food supply. This struggle of tribe with tribe, and nation with nation, may have its mournful side; but we see as a result of it the gradual progress of mankind to higher intellectual and physical efficiency. It is idle to condemn it; we can only see that it exists and recognise what we have gained by it—civilization and social sympathy. But while the statesman has to watch this external struggle, . . . he must be very cautious that the nation is not silently rotting at its core. He must insure that the fertility of the inferior stocks is checked, and that of the superior stocks encouraged; he must regard with suspicion anything that tempts the physically and mentally fitter men and women to remain childless. . . .

. . . The path of progress is strewn with the wrecks of nations; traces are everywhere to be seen of the hecatombs [slaughtered remains] of inferior races, and of victims who found not the narrow way to perfection. Yet these dead people are, in very truth, the stepping stones on which mankind has arisen to the higher intellectual and deeper emotional life of today.

REVIEW QUESTIONS

1. How did Joseph Chamberlain define the national mission of the "great governing race"? What were the economic benefits of that mission?
2. How did Karl Pearson define the difference between "inferior" and "superior" races?
3. What measures did Pearson advocate for keeping a nation such as Britain at its highest potential?

2 European Rule in Africa

Africa, the world's second largest continent after Asia, posed a special challenge to European imperialists who penetrated its tropical depths. While African territories north of the Sahara desert had long been integrated into Mediterranean and Middle Eastern life, in sub-Saharan Africa the Europeans encountered harrowing conditions as nowhere else in the world. They were repelled by the debilitating climate, impenetrable rainforests, deadly diseases, and the great variety of dark-skinned peoples and their unfamiliar customs. Seen through European eyes, Africans were illiterate heathen barbarians, still trading in help-less slaves among themselves and with Arabs, decades after Western countries had banned slave trading with Africa.

Cultural differences conditioned by African geography and climate con-stituted an immense divide between Europeans and Africans. The profound inequality in military and political power provided the sharpest contrast. Afri-cans lived mostly in small communities divided by over one thousand languages; a few large states like Mali and "Songai" had grown under Muslim influence but then collapsed by the sixteenth century. Cut off from developments in the Far East and Western Europe that had long stimulated science, technology, and political power, sub-Saharan Africans, divided among themselves, helplessly faced the Europeans, who were equipped with superior weapons and backed up by powerful states. Inevitably, they fell victim to European imperialism. By the late nineteenth century Europeans had acquired sufficient resources, includ-ing medicines against tropical diseases, to explore the interior and establish their rule. Sub-Saharan Africa now became the focus of rivalry among England, France, and Germany; even the king of Belgium claimed a huge share in the much publicized "scramble for Africa."

At times the European conquerors proceeded with unrestrained brutality, proclaiming in the language of Social Darwinism that the "inferior" races of Africa had to be sacrificed to "progress."

Cecil Rhodes and Lo Bengula
"I HAD SIGNED AWAY THE MINERAL RIGHTS OF MY WHOLE COUNTRY"

A good example of how colonial expansion in Africa proceeded is furnished by Cecil Rhodes's dealings with Lo Bengula, king of Matabeleland, Mashonaland, and adjacent territories (now Zimbabwe). Raised in London, Rhodes migrated to southern Africa where he quickly made a fortune in the diamond industry. In his "Confession of Faith" of 1877 Rhodes had included hope for poor Africans: "just fancy those parts {of the world} that are at present inhabited by the most despicable specimens of human beings, what an alternative there would be if they were brought under Anglo-Saxon influence." Eleven years later, eager to expand his business, he arranged through three of his agents a contract with Lo Bengula, giving his agents "the complete and inclusive charge" of all the metals and minerals in the king's lands. In return, he pledged a financial subsidy and delivery of weapons. The illiterate Lo Bengula put his mark to the contract that follows.

Know all men by these presents, that whereas Charles Dunell Rudd, of Kimberley; Rochfort Maguire, of London; and Francis Robert Thompson, of Kimberley, have covenanted and agreed . . . to pay me, my heirs and successors, the sum of one hundred pounds sterling, British currency, on the first day of every lunar month: and further, to deliver at my royal kraal [village] one thousand Martini-Henry breech-loading rifles, together with one hundred thousand rounds of suitable ball cartridges . . . to be delivered with reasonable dispatch . . . and further to deliver on the Zambesi River a steamboat with guns suitable for defensive purposes, or in lieu of the said steamboat, should I [so] elect, to pay to me the sum of five hundred pounds sterling, British currency. On the execution of these presents, I, Lo Bengula, King of Matabeleland, Mashonaland, and other adjoining territories . . . do hereby grant and assign unto the said grantees . . . the complete and exclusive charge over all metals and minerals situated and contained in my kingdoms . . . together with full power to do all things that they may deem necessary to win and procure the same, and to hold, collect, and enjoy the profits and revenues, if any, derivable from the said metals and minerals, subject to the aforesaid payment; and whereas I have been much molested of late by divers persons seeking and desiring to obtain grants and concessions of land and mining rights in my territories, I do hereby authorize the said grantees . . . to exclude from my kingdom . . . all persons seeking land, metals, minerals, or mining rights therein, and I do hereby undertake to render them all such needful assistance as they may from time to time require for the exclusion of such persons, and to grant no concessions of land or mining rights . . . without their consent and concurrence. . . .

Sir Lewis Michell, *The Life and Times of the Right Honourable Cecil John Rhodes, 1853–1902*, vol. 1 (New York and London: Mitchell Kennerley, 1910), pp. 255–257.

This given under my hand this thirtieth day of October, in the year of our Lord 1888, at my royal kraal.

Lo Bengula X his mark
C. D. Rudd
Rochfort Maguire
F. R. Thompson

When the terms of the contract became known among Lo Bengula's subjects, they protested that their ruler had been tricked. After having his fears confirmed by friendly British missionaries, Lo Bengula executed his head counselor and sent a mission to Queen Victoria. After an unsatisfactory response, he sent a formal protest on April 23, 1889. This pathetic appeal from the untutored African ruler had no effect on the course of events. He was told by the Queen's advisor that it was "impossible for him to exclude white men." The advisor said that the Queen had made inquiries as to the persons concerned and was satisfied that they "may be trusted to carry out the working for gold in the chief's country without molesting his people, or in any way interfering with their kraals [villages], gardens [cultivated fields], or cattle." Thus Rhodes made Lo Bengula's territories his personal domain and part of the British Empire.   Following is Lo Bengula's futile appeal to Queen Victoria.

Some time ago a party of men came to my country, the principal one appearing to be a man called Rudd. They asked me for a place to dig for gold, and said they would give me certain things for the right to do so. I told them to bring what they could give and I would show them what I would give. A document was written and presented to me for signature. I asked what it contained, and was told that in it were my words and the words of those men. I put my hand to it. About three months afterwards I heard from other sources that I had given by that document the right to all the minerals of my country. I called a meeting of my *Indunas* [counselors], and also of the white men and demanded a copy of the document. It was proved to me that I had signed away the mineral rights of my whole country to Rudd and his friends. I have since had a meeting of my *Indunas* and they will not recognise the paper, as it contains neither my words nor the words of those who got it. . . . I write to you that you may know the truth about this thing.

E. D. Morel, *The Black Man's Burden* (New York: B. W. Huebsch, Inc., 1920), pp. 34–35.

Edmund Morel
THE BLACK MAN'S BURDEN

E. D. Morel (1873–1924), an English author and journalist with a keen sense of moral responsibility, was especially concerned with the colonial exploitation of Africa. The most extreme abuses of the nineteenth century took place in the Congo Free State established in 1885 under the personal rule of King Leopold II of Belgium. By 1904 the king's ruthless methods of enriching himself while destroying the native population had become a scandal widely publicized in England and the United States. Morel took a leading part in denouncing the selfish exploiters of the Congo system. As a result, in 1908 Leopold II was forced to turn over his colonial domain to the Belgian government, which initiated more humane policies.

After World War I, Morel, moved by "the desolation and misery into which Europe was plunged," foresaw a new era heralding the birth of "an international conscience in regard to Africa." In 1920 he published his book, *The Black Man's Burden: The White Man in Africa from the Fifteenth Century to World War I.* While recognizing the accomplishments of Europeans in Africa, "many of them worthy of admiration," he was foremost concerned with the immense suffering Europe had inflicted upon the peoples of that continent, pleading that "Africa is really helpless against the material goods of the white man, as embodied in the trinity of imperialism, capitalistic-exploitation, and militarism." He wanted to make the public aware of the evils that were still perpetrated in many African regions. As a left-wing intellectual and a Member of Parliament for the Labour Party, he thus helped to set off an anticolonial tide of compassion for the African people. The following passages are selected from Morel's description of the Congo system.

The Congo Free State—known since August, 1908, as the Belgian Congo—is roughly one million square miles in extent. When Stanley discovered the course of the Congo and observed its densely-populated river banks, he formed the, doubtless very much exaggerated, estimate that the total population amounted to forty millions. In the years that followed, when the country had been explored in every direction by travellers of diverse nationalities, estimates varied between twenty and thirty millions. No estimate fell below twenty millions. In 1911 an official census was taken. It was not published

E. D. Morel, *The Black Man's Burden* (New York: B. W. Huebsch, Inc., 1920), pp. 109, 112, 115–119.

in Belgium, but was reported in one of the British Consular dispatches. *It revealed that only eight and a half million people were left.* The Congo system lasted for the best part of twenty years. The loss of life can never be known with even approximate exactitude. But data, extending over successive periods, are procurable in respect of a number of regions, and a careful study of these suggests that a figure of ten million victims would be a very conservative estimate.

. . . It is very difficult for anyone who has not experienced in his person the sensations of the tropical African forest to realise the tremendous handicaps which man has to contend against whose lot is cast beneath its sombre shades; the extent to which nature, there seen in her most titanic and ruthless moods, presses upon man; the intellectual disabilities against which man must needs constantly struggle not to sink to the level of the brute; the incessant combat to preserve life and secure nourishment. Communities living in this environment who prove themselves capable of systematic agriculture and of industry; who are found to be possessed of keen commercial instincts; who are quick at learning, deft at working iron and copper, able to weave cloths of real artistic design; these are communities full of promise in which the divine spark burns brightly. To destroy these activities; to reduce all the varied, and picturesque, and stimulating episodes in savage life to a dull routine of endless toil for uncomprehended ends; to dislocate social ties and disrupt social institutions; to stifle nascent desires and crush mental development; to graft upon primitive passions the annihilating evils of scientific slavery, and the bestial imaginings of civilized man, unrestrained by convention or law; in fine, to kill the soul in a people—this is a crime which transcends physical murder. And this crime it was, which, for twenty dreadful years, white men perpetrated upon the Congo natives. . . .

From 1891 until 1912, the paramount object of European rule in the Congo was the pillaging of its natural wealth to enrich private interests in Belgium. To achieve this end a specific,

well-defined system was thought out in Brussels and applied on the Congo. . . .

The Policy was quite simple. Native rights in land were deemed to be confined to the actual sites of the town or village, and the areas under food cultivation around them. Beyond those areas no such rights would be admitted. The land was "vacant," *i.e.,* without owners. Consequently the "State" was owner. The "State" was Leopold II, not in his capacity of constitutional Monarch of Belgium, but as Sovereign of the "Congo Free State." Native rights in nine-tenths of the Congo territory being thus declared non-existent, it followed that the native population had no proprietary right in the plants and trees growing upon that territory, and which yielded rubber, resins, oils, dyes, etc.: no right, in short, to anything animal, vegetable, or mineral which the land contained. In making use of the produce of the land, either for internal or external trade or internal industry and social requirements, the native population would thus obviously be making use of that which did not belong to it, but which belonged to the "State," *i.e.,* Leopold II. It followed logically that any third person—European or other—acquiring, or attempting to acquire, such produce from the native population by purchase, in exchange for corresponding goods or services, would be guilty of robbery, or attempted robbery, of "State property." A "State" required revenue. Revenue implied taxation. The only articles in the Congo territory capable of producing revenue were the ivory, the rubber, the resinous gums and oils; which had become the property of the "State." The only medium through which these articles could be gathered, prepared and exported to Europe—where they would be sold and converted into revenue—was native labour. Native labour would be called upon to furnish those articles in the name of "taxation."

. . . Regulations were issued forbidding the natives to sell rubber or ivory to European merchants, and threatening the latter with prosecution if they bought these articles from the natives. In the second place, every official in the country had to be made a partner in the business of getting rubber and ivory out of the natives in the guise of "taxation." Circulars, which remained secret for many years, were sent out, to the effect that the paramount duty of Officials was to make their districts yield the greatest possible quantity of these articles; promotion would be reckoned on that basis. As a further stimulus to "energetic action" a system of sliding-scale bonuses was elaborated, whereby the less the native was "paid" for his *labour* in producing theses articles of "taxation," *i.e.,* the lower the outlay in obtaining them, the higher was the Official's commission. . . . "Concessionaire" Companies were created to which the King farmed out a large proportion of the total territory, retaining half the shares in each venture. These privileges were granted to business men, bankers, and others with whom the King thought it necessary to compound. They floated their companies on the stock exchange. The shares rose rapidly. . . .

These various measures at the European end were comparatively easy. The problem of dealing with the natives themselves was more complex. A native army was the pre-requisite. The five years . . . [from 1886 to 1891] were employed in raising the nucleus of a force of 5,000. It was successively increased to nearly 20,000 apart from the many thousands of "irregulars" employed by the Concessionaire Companies. This force was amply sufficient for the purpose, for a single native soldier armed with a rifle and with a plentiful supply of ball cartridge can terrorise a whole village. The same system of promotion and reward would apply to the native soldier as to the Official—the more rubber from the village, the greater the prospect of having a completely free hand to loot and rape. A systematic warfare upon the women and children would prove an excellent means of pressure. They would be converted into "hostages" for the good behaviour, in rubber collecting, of the men. "Hostage houses" would become an institution in the Congo. But in certain parts of the Congo the rubber vine did not grow. This peculiarity of nature was, in one way, all to the good. For the army of Officials and native soldiers, with their wives, and concubines, and camp-followers generally, required feeding. The non-rubber producing districts should feed them. Fishing tribes would be "taxed" in fish; agricultural tribes in foodstuffs. In this case, too, the women and children would answer for the men. Frequent military expeditions would probably be an unfortunate necessity. Such expeditions would demand in every case hundreds of carriers for the transport of loads, ammunition, and general [baggage]. Here, again, was an excellent school in which this idle people could learn the dignity of labour. The whole territory would thus become a busy hive of human activities, continuously and usefully engaged for the benefit of the "owners" of the soil thousands of miles away, and their crowned Head, whose intention, proclaimed on repeated occasions to an admiring world, was the "moral and material regeneration" of the natives of the Congo.

Such was the Leopoldian "system," briefly epitomised. It was conceived by a master brain.

Richard Meinertzhagen
AN EMBATTLED COLONIAL OFFICER IN EAST AFRICA

Richard Meinertzhagen (1878–1967) was stationed as a young soldier in Kenya from 1902 to 1906, serving on the raw frontier of British imperialism. Living under great hardships in the African wilderness, exposed to poisoned arrows, his sensibilities outraged by the practices of people the colonial conquerors called "niggers" and "savages," he participated in imposing British rule on the rebellious Nandi tribe. In his spare time he enjoyed shooting wild animals, while also appreciating as an ornithologist the exotic birds he observed. The entries in his diary reprinted below provide insight into the harrowing experiences and the anguish of an isolated young Englishman facing the strains of colonial service, where Western and indigenous ways clashed more sharply than anywhere else in the world.

August 20, 1902

News came in this evening that a policeman had been murdered by a village only a mile or so from the station, as a protest against the white men. . . . At midnight I sent a reliable native to the offending village to ascertain what was happening. He returned at 3 A.M. this morning, saying all the neighbouring villages had joined forces with the offending village and were at the moment conducting an orgy round the dead policeman's body, which had been badly mutilated. A council of war had been held by the natives and they had decided to march on Fort Hall at dawn. So we marched out of the station at 3.30 A.M., crossed the Mathyoia and reached our destination half an hour before dawn. The village had bonfires burning and the Wakikuyu were dancing round them in all their war-paint. It was really rather a weird sight. The alarm was given by a native who tried to break through our rather thin cordon. He refused to stop when challenged and was shot down. There was then a rush from the village into the surrounding bush, and we killed about 17 niggers. Two policemen and one of my men were killed. I narrowly escaped a spear which whizzed past my head. Then the fun began. We at once burned the village and captured the sheep and goats. After that we systematically cleared the valley in which the village was situated, burned all the huts, and

killed a few more niggers, who finally gave up the fight and cleared off, but not till 3 more of our men had been killed.

At 3 P.M. we returned to Fort Hall and told the chiefs who had assembled to meet us that they were to go out to the village at once, get into touch with the local chief, bring him in, and generally spread the news that our anger was by no means appeased. They returned just before dark with a deputation from the village, saying their chief was killed and they begged for mercy. McClean [a fellow official] fined them 50 head of cattle, at the same time intimating that half would be remitted if the murderers of the policeman were produced. This they promised to do tomorrow. We have told them that we are quite prepared to continue tomorrow what we began today, and I think they are impressed. Such nonsense as attacking the station is completely driven from their stupid heads. So order once more reigns in Kenya District.

September 8, 1902

I have performed a most unpleasant duty today. I made a night march to the village at the edge of forest where the white settler had been so brutally murdered the day before yesterday. Though the war drums were sounding throughout the night we reached the village without incident and surrounded it. By the light of fires we could see savages dancing in the village, and our guides assured me that they were dancing round the mutilated body of the white man.

From Colonel R. Meinertzhagen, *Kenya Diary, 1902–1906.*

I gave orders that every living thing except children should be killed without mercy. I hated the work and was anxious to get through with it. So soon as we could see to shoot we closed in. Several of the men tried to break out but were immediately shot. I then assaulted the place before any defence could be prepared. Every soul was either shot or bayoneted, and I am happy to say that no children were in the village. They, with the younger women, had already been removed by the villagers to the forest. We burned all the huts and razed the banana plantations to the ground.

In the open space in the centre of the village was a sight which horrified me—a naked white man pegged out on his back, mutilated and disembowelled, his body used as a latrine by all and sundry who passed by. We washed his corpse in a stream and buried him just outside the village. The whole of this affair took so short a time that the sun was barely up before we beat a retreat to our main camp.

My drastic action on this occasion haunted me for many years, and even now I am not sure whether I was right. My reason for killing all adults, including women, was that the latter had been the main instigators of not only the murder but the method of death, and it was the women who had befouled the corpse after death.

November 23, 1902

Meanwhile a Land Office under my friend Barton Wright has been started with a view to parcelling out land to settlers. Eliot thinks there is a great future for East Africa, transforming it into a huge white farming and stock area. Perhaps that is correct, but sooner or later it must lead to a clash between black and white. I cannot see millions of educated Africans—as there will be in a hundred years' time—submitting tamely to white domination. After all, it is an African country, and they will demand domination. Then blood will be spilled, and I have little doubt about the eventual outcome.

February 19, 1904

Before this expedition started I issued an order to my company and to the Masai Levies [African soldiers in the pay of the British authorities] that if any man was guilty of killing women or children he would be shot. My men are mere savages in the laws and customs of war, and the Masai are bloodthirsty villains to whom the killing of women and children means nothing.

Today we had occasion to rush a small village in which some of the enemy were concealed and from which they were firing arrows at the column. I quickly formed up 10 of my men and 30 Masai and rushed the place. The enemy ran, and we killed 4 of them. I formed up this party some 150 yards on the other side of the village before moving on, and then heard a woman shriek from the village, which I had presumed empty. I ran back to the village, where I saw two of my men and three Masai in the act of dragging a woman from a hut, and the body of a small boy on the ground, one of the Levies being in the act of withdrawing his spear from the little body. Another levy was leading a small girl by the hand and was about to knock her on the head with his knobkerrie [a short club with a knob at the end]. I yelled to him to stay his hand, but I suppose his blood was up, for he paid no attention to me and killed the child. Meanwhile one of my own men bayoneted the woman within 30 yards of me. Putting up my rifle I shot the man dead and then his companion, who I think contemplated having a pot shot at me. The Levies bolted, but I bagged them all three before they were clear of the village.

July 27, 1904

On reading through the first part of this record I am shocked by the account of taking human life and the constant slaughter of big game. I do not pretend to excuse it, but perhaps I may explain it. I have no belief in the sanctity of human life or in the dignity of the human race. Human life has never been sacred; nor has man, except in a few exceptional cases, been dignified. Moreover, in Kenya fifty years ago, when stationed with 100 soldiers amid an African population of some 300,000, in cases of emergency where local government was threatened we had to act, and act quickly. To do nothing in an emergency is to do something definitely wrong, and talking comes under the category of "nothing." There was no telegraph or telephone, no motor cars or wireless, and action was imperative for safety. Thank God there was no time or opportunity for talks, conferences and discussions.

I also regarded discipline in my company as paramount, more important when dealing with coloured troops than with one's own countrymen. What may appear to have been outrageous and cruel conduct on my part was an insistence on strict discipline—the obedience of orders. I have seen so many coloured troops rendered useless by inefficient discipline.

September 15, 1905

Living isolated in a savage country, rarely speaking my own language, and surrounded by a population whose civilisation is on a much lower plane than my own are conditions to which I have indeed grown accustomed, but which do not improve on acquaintance unless one lowers one's own plane to that of the savage, when perhaps one might be contented. . . .

. . . Others with greater strength of character than myself might suffer little from moral and intellectual starvation. To others, natural history or some object of unceasing pursuit is an effective barrier against complete isolation. But my experience shows me that it is but a small percentage of white men whose characters do not in one way or another undergo a subtle process of deterioration when they are compelled to live for any length of time among savage races and under such conditions as exist in tropical climates. It is hard to resist the savagery of Africa when one falls under its spell. One soon reverts to one's ancestral character, both mind and temperament becoming brutalised. I have seen so much of it out here and I have myself felt the magnetic power of the African climate drawing me lower and lower to the level of a savage. This is a condition which is accentuated by worry or mental depression, and which has to be combated with all the force in one's power. My love of home and my family, the dread of being eventually overcome by savage Africa, the horror of losing one's veneer of western civilisation and cutting adrift from all one holds good—these are the forces which help me to fight the temptation to drift down to the temporary luxury of the civilisation of the savage.

March 20, 1906

Natives are queer creatures and hold still queerer ideas. No European can fully understand the working of the black mind. Their morals, ideals and principles are all based on quite different models from ours. . . .

GERMAN BRUTALITY IN SOUTHWEST AFRICA: EXTERMINATING THE HERERO

In the 1880s Germany gained control over what became German Southwest Africa (modern-day Namibia). Hoping to profit from farming, cattle raising, and mining, Germans settled the new colony. The German settlers brutalized the native Herero people, exploiting their labor and flogging, murdering, and raping with impunity. "The missionary says that we are children of God like our white brothers," said a Herero to a German settler, "but just look at us. Dogs, slaves, worse than the baboons on the rocks. . . . That is how you treat us." In 1904, the Hereros attacked isolated German farms, torturing and killing settlers. Kaiser Wilhelm dispatched an army from Germany commanded by Lothar von Trotha to crush the rebellion. The German army drove the Hereros into the desert of Sandveld, beyond the colony's border, and sealed off water holes; von Trotha then ordered his soldiers to kill Hereros, including women and children, still remaining on German territory, and German patrols in the desert made a sport of hunting down and killing Herero stragglers dying of thirst and starvation. Prisoners were herded into forced labor camps where more than half died of malnutrition and mistreatment and women were subjected to constant rape. Those Hereros who managed to survive the desert found asylum in British-controlled Bechuanaland (modern-day Botswana). Between 1904 and 1907, 65,000 of the 80,000 Hereros perished in what some call the first genocide of the twentieth century. In the first part of this selection, a leader of German settlers explicitly reveals his racist attitude, shared by most of the settlers, toward the Herero.

The decision to colonize in South Africa means nothing else than that the Native tribes must withdraw from the lands on which they have pastured *their* cattle and so let the *White man* pasture *his* cattle on these self-same lands. If the moral right of this standpoint is questioned, the answer is that for people of the culture standard of the South African Natives, the loss of their free national barbarism and the development of a class of workers in the service of and dependent on the Whites is primarily a law of existence in the highest degree. For a people, as for an individual, an existence appears to be justified in the degree that it is useful in the progress of general development. By no argument in the world can it be shown that the preservation of any degree of national independence, national prosperity and political organisation by the races of South West Africa would be of greater or even of equal advantage for the development of mankind in general or the German people in particular than that these races should be made serviceable in the enjoyment of their former territories by the White races.

South West Africa and Its Human Issues by Wellington (1967) 197w from p.196. By permission of Oxford University Press.

Following is the proclamation that von Trotha read to his officers in October 1904 calling for the annihilation of the Herero.

I the great General of the German troops send this letter to the Herero people.

The Herero are no longer German subjects. They have murdered and stolen, they have cut off the ears, noses and other body parts of wounded soldiers, now out of cowardice they no longer wish to fight. I say to the people anyone who delivers a captain will receive 1000 Mark, whoever delivers Samuel will receive 5000 Mark. The Herero people must however leave the land. If the populace does not do this I will force them with the *Groot Rohr* [cannon]. Within the German borders every Herero, with or without a gun, with or without cattle, will be shot. I will no longer accept women and children, I will drive them back to their people or I will let them be shot at.

Jan-Bart Gewald, *Herero Heroes: A Socio-Political History of the Herero of Namibia, 1890–1923* (Athens: Ohio University Press, 1999), pp. 172–173, 174, 188. This material is used by permission of Ohio University Press, www.ohioswallow.com.

These are my words to the Herero people.

The great General of the mighty German Kaiser.

The following day von Trotha revealed further the implications of his proclamation.

Now I have to ask myself *how* to end the war with the Hereros. The views of the Governor and also a few old Africa hands on the one hand, and my views on the other, differ completely. They first wanted to negotiate for some time already and regard the Herero nation as necessary labour material for the future development of the country. I believe that the [Herero] nation as such should be annihilated, or, if this was not possible by tactical measures, have to be expelled from the country by operative means and further detailed treatment. This will be possible if the water-holes from Grootfontein to Gobabis are occupied. The constant movement of our troops will enable us to find the small groups of the nation who have moved back westwards and destroy them gradually. . . .

My intimate knowledge of many central African tribes (Bantu and others) has everywhere convinced me of the necessity that the Negro does not respect treaties but only brute force. . . .

I find it most appropriate that the nation perishes instead of infecting our soldiers and diminishing their supplies of water and food. Apart from that, mildness on my side would only be interpreted as weakness by the other side. They have to perish in the Sandveld or try to cross the Bechuanaland border.

A German officer described the results of von Trotha's policy.

. . . I followed their [trail] and found numerous wells which presented a terrifying sight.

Cattle which had died of thirst lay scattered around the wells. These cattle had reached the wells but there had not been enough time to water them. The Herero fled ahead of us into the Sandveld. Again and again this terrible scene kept repeating itself. With feverish energy the men had worked at opening the wells, however the water became ever sparser, and wells evermore rare. They fled from one well to the next and lost virtually all their cattle and a large number of their people. The people shrunk into small remnants who continually fell into our hands, sections of the people escaped now and later through the Sandveld into English territory. It was a policy which was equally gruesome as senseless, to hammer the people so much, we could have still saved many of them and their rich herds, if we had pardoned and taken them up again, they had been punished enough. I suggested this to General von Trotha but he wanted their total extermination.

A German missionary described the brutalization of Herero prisoners of war.

"When [. . .] [I] arrived in Swakopmund in 1905 there were very few Herero present. Shortly thereafter vast transports of prisoners of war arrived. They were placed behind double rows of barbed wire fencing, which surrounded all the buildings of the harbour department quarters, and housed in miserable structures constructed out of simple sacking and planks, in such a manner that in one structure 30–50 people were forced to stay without distinction as to age and sex. From early morning until late at night, on weekdays as well as on Sundays and holidays, they had to work under the clubs of brutal overseers until they broke down. Added to this the food was extremely scarce: the rice without any necessary additions was not enough to support their bodies, already weakened by life in the field [as refugees] and used to the hot sun of the interior, from the cold and the exertion without rest of all their powers in the prison conditions of Swakopmund. Like cattle hundreds were driven to death and like cattle they were buried. This opinion may appear hard or exaggerated, lots changed and became milder during the course of the imprisonment [. . .] but the chronicles are not permitted to suppress that such a remorseless brutality, randy sensuality, and brutish overlordship was to be found amongst the troops and civilians here that a full description is hardly possible."

REVIEW QUESTIONS

1. How did Cecil Rhodes gain control over the riches in Lo Bengula's land?
2. What were the effects of King Leopold's rule over the Congo people? How did he establish the "Leopoldian system"?
3. Describe Richard Meinertzhagen's attitude toward the Africans he encountered.
4. How did German settlers regard the Herero?
5. What was General von Trotha's policy toward the Hereros? How did he justify the policy?

3 Chinese Resentment of Western Imperialism

By the end of the nineteenth century, European powers had carved out spheres of influence in China. The Chinese were compelled to make humiliating trade and railway concessions to the imperialists. Resentment of foreign domination drew people to a secret religious society, the Society of Righteous and Harmonious Fists, so-called because its members engaged in the martial arts and rigorous calisthenics that, they believed, gave them supernatural power, including resistance to bullets. The "Boxers" were convinced that driving the "foreign devils" from China would improve the poor harvests and renew commitment to ancient Chinese traditions now threatened by foreign ways.

THE BOXER REBELLION

In 1900, the Boxers roamed the countryside burning churches and foreign residences and slaughtering missionaries and Chinese Christians; in June, the Boxers converged on Beijing. Western diplomats, their families and staff, and Chinese Christians sought refuge in the Legation quarters and a Roman Catholic cathedral. For almost two months the defenders, a small military force enhanced by the besieged civilians, withstood attacks until rescued by a multinational force.

The Western armies looted Beijing and later compelled the imperial government to pay a high indemnity and agree to the stationing of Western troops in the capital. The following wall posters reveal the Boxers' anti-Western and anti-Christian outlook.

"EXTERMINATE ALL FOREIGN DEVILS"

The will of heaven is that the telegraph wires be first cut, then the railways torn up and then shall the foreign devils be decapitated. On that day shall the hour of their calamities come. The time for rain to fall is yet far off, and all on account of these devils.

I thereby make known these commands to all you righteous folk that ye may strive with one accord to exterminate all foreign devils and to turn aside the path of heaven.

"CHINA YET REGARDS THEM AS BARBARIANS"

Foreign devils have come with their teaching, and converts to Christianity, Roman Catholic and Protestant, have become numerous. These (churches) have attracted all the greedy and grasping as converts, and to an unlimited degree they have practiced oppression, until every good official has been corrupted and has become their servant. So telegraphs and railways have been established, foreign rifles and guns have been manufactured. Locomotives, balloons, and electric lamps the foreign devils think excellent. Though they ride in sedans unbefitting their rank, China yet regards them as barbarians. The Volunteer Associated Fists will burn down the foreign houses and restore the temples. Foreign goods of every kind they will destroy. They will destroy the evil demons and establish right teaching. The purpose of heaven is fixed and a clean sweep is to be made. Within three years all will be accomplished.

Richard Allen, *The Siege of the Peking Legations* (London: Smith, Elder, 1901), p. 19.

Adapted from Rev. George T. Candlin, "The Associated Fists," in *Open Court* (London: September 1900), pp. 558–560.

"YOU'LL SEE THE DEVIL'S EYES / ARE ALL A SHINING BLUE"

Divinely aided Boxers,
United-in-Righteousness Corps
Arose because the Devils
Messed up the Empire of yore.

They proselytize their sect,
And believe in only one God,
The spirits and their own ancestors
Are not even given a nod.

Their men are all immoral;
Their women truly vile.
For the Devils it's mother-son sex
That serves as the breeding style.

And if you don't believe me,
Then have a careful view:
You'll see the Devils' eyes
Are all a shining blue.

No rain comes from Heaven.
The earth is parched and dry.
And all because the churches
Have bottled up the sky.

The gods are very angry.
The spirits seek revenge.
En masse they come from Heaven
To teach the Way to men.

The Way is not a heresy;
It's not the White Lotus Sect.
The chants and spells we utter,
Follow mantras, true and correct.

Raise up the yellow charm,
Bow to the incense glow.
Invite the gods and spirits
Down from the mountain grotto.

Reprinted with permission of The University of California Press, from Joseph W. Esherick, *The Origins of the Boxer Uprising*, 1987, pp. 299–300; permission conveyed through Copyright Clearance Center, Inc.

Spirits emerge from the grottos;
Gods come down from the hills,
Possessing the bodies of men,
Transmitting their boxing skills.

When their martial and magic techniques
Are all learned by each one of you,
Suppressing the Foreign Devils
Will not be a tough thing to do.

Rip up the railroad tracks!
Pull down the telegraph lines!

Quickly! Hurry up! Smash them—
The boats and the steamship combines.

The mighty nation of France
Quivers in abject fear,
While from England, America, Russia
And from Germany nought do we hear.

When at last all the Foreign Devils
Are expelled to the very last man,
The Great Qing, united, together,
Will bring peace to this our land.

REVIEW QUESTIONS

1. What reasons did the Boxers give for hating the West?
2. What were their demands?

---

4 British Rule in India

Feeling a moral obligation to improve the quality of life for Indian peoples, British rulers advanced railway construction, irrigation, public education, and religious tolerance. Some British policies also aroused enmity. For example, the British rigorously curtailed Indian manufacturing in order to force Indians to buy British goods, a policy that decimated the Indian textile industry. Despite their efforts, including imprisonment, Britain could not contain demands for Indian independence, which was achieved in 1947.

Lord Lytton
SPEECH TO THE CALCUTTA LEGISLATURE, 1878

Lord Lytton (1831–1891) came from an aristocratic family. He gained recognition as a poet, while also serving in diplomatic posts at European capitals. In 1876, he was appointed viceroy of India, facing war on the Afghan frontier and trouble with Russia, as well as a major famine. He organized famine relief, promoted internal free trade in India, and decentralized the British administration, hoping to benefit the Indian masses. In 1877 he designed a triumphal pageant to celebrate the proclamation of Queen Victoria as empress of India.

Lord Lytton felt warmly about the Indians, and he tried to practice tolerance toward the native people while protecting the supremacy of British rule. However, his artistic temperament and lack of experience made him an ineffective administrator and his rule was unpopular. Yet he was also a man of unusual sensibility, and in a speech delivered in 1878, Lytton provided great insight into the revolutionary impact of British imperialism upon India. Excerpts from this speech follow.

We have endeavored to base our rule in India on justice, uprightness, progressive enlightenment, and good government, as these are understood in England; and it is at least a plausible postulate, which at first sight appears to be a sound one, that, so long as these are the characteristics of our rule, we need fear no disaffection on the part of the masses.

It must, however, be remembered that the problem undertaken by the British rulers of India (a political problem more perplexing in its conditions and, as regards the results of its solution, more far-reaching than any which, since the dissolution of the Pax Romana,[1] has been undertaken by a conquering race) is the application of the most refined principles of European government, and some of the . . . institutions of European society, to a vast Oriental population, in whose history, habits, and traditions they have had no previous existence.

Such phrases as "Religious toleration," "Liberty of the press," "Personal freedom of the subject," "Social supremacy of the Law," and others, which in England have long been the mere catchwords of ideas common to the whole race, and deeply impressed upon its character by all the events of its history, and all the most cherished recollections of its earlier life, are here in India, to the vast mass of our native subjects, the mysterious formulas of a foreign, and more or less uncongenial system of administration, which is scarcely, if at all, intelligible to the greater number of those for whose benefit it is maintained. It is a fact which, when I first came to India, was strongly impressed on my attention by one of India's wisest and most thoughtful administrators; it is a fact which there is no disguising; and it is also one which cannot be too constantly or too anxiously recognised, that by enforcing these principles, and establishing these institutions, we have placed, and must permanently maintain ourselves at the head of a gradual but gigantic revolution—the greatest and most momentous social, moral, and religious, as well as political, revolution which, perhaps, the world has ever witnessed.

Excerpted from Betty Balfour, ed., *The History of Lord Lytton's Indian Administration, 1876–1880: Compiled from Letters and Official Papers* (London: Longmans, Green Co., 1899), pp. 510–511.

[1]Covering the period 27 B.C. to A.D. 180, the Pax Romans (the Roman Peace) was the high point of Roman rule.—Eds.

Jawaharlal Nehru
INDIA'S RESENTMENT OF THE BRITISH

Born into a wealthy Indian family, Jawaharlal Nehru (1889–1964) received a privileged education and legal training in England, practicing law on his return to India in 1912. Participating in organized resistance to British rule, Nehru was frequently arrested and jailed. During his longest prison term (August 1942–March 1945) he wrote *The Discovery of India*, in which he expressed admiration for Western culture and recognized India's backwardness. He also blamed British arrogance and economic exploitation for his country's continued poverty. In the following passage from this work, Nehru expresses his disdain for British racism.

I remember that when I was a boy the British-owned newspapers in India were full of official news and utterances; of service news, transfers, and promotions; of the doings of English society, of polo, races, dances, and amateur theatricals. There was hardly a word about the people of India, about their political, cultural, social, or economic life. Reading them, one would hardly suspect that they existed. . . . English clubs in India usually have territorial names—the Bengal Club, the Allahabad Club, etc. They are confined to Britishers, or rather to Europeans. There need be no objection to territorial designation or even to a group of persons having a club for themselves and not approving of outsiders joining it. But this designation is derived from the old British habit of considering that they are the real India that counts, the real Bengal, the real Allahabad. Others are just excrescences, useful in their own way, if they know their place, but otherwise a nuisance. The exclusion of non-Europeans is far more a

racial affair than a thoroughly justifiable way for people having cultural affinities meeting together in their leisure moments for play and social intercourse, and disliking the intrusion of other elements. For my part I have no objection to exclusive English or European clubs, and very few Indians would care to join them. But when this social exclusiveness is clearly based on racialism and on a ruling class always exhibiting its superiority and unapproachability, it bears another aspect. In Bombay there is a well-known club which did not allow, and so far as I know, does not allow, an Indian (except as a servant) even in its visitors' room, even though he might be a ruling prince or a captain of industry.

Racialism in India is not so much English versus Indian. It is European as opposed to Asiatic. In India every European, be he German or Pole or Rumanian, is automatically a member of the ruling race. Railway carriages, station retiring rooms, benches in parks, are marked "For Europeans Only." This is bad enough in South Africa or elsewhere, but to have to put up with it in one's own country is a humiliating and exasperating reminder of our enslaved condition.

Jawaharlal Nehru, *The Discovery of India* (New York: The John Day Company, 1946), pp. 293–294.

REVIEW QUESTIONS

1. Why did Lord Lytton consider the British impact on India as the most "momentous revolution the world has ever witnessed?"
2. According to Nehru, what were the features of British racism in India?

5 Imperialism Debated

Imperialist ventures aroused considerable debate. Advocates of overseas empires often argued in moral terms—Europeans were bringing the advantages of a higher civilization to African and Asian lands, many of which were steeped in barbarism. Rejecting this position, opponents of imperialism maintained that colonial ventures were motivated by capitalist greed and resulted in exploitation and bloodshed.

The Edinburgh Review
"WE . . . CAN RESTORE ORDER WHERE THERE IS CHAOS, AND FERTILITY WHERE THERE IS STERILITY"

The author of the following article published in 1907 in *The Edinburgh Review* praises imperialist powers for serving as "the missionaries of civilization."

[L]et us in the first place say boldly that the modern European movement of expansion is not purely, nor even primarily, a colonising movement. It is not a movement merely in favour of annexing territory, of opening up new countries, of settling on the soil and bringing backwoods and prairies under cultivation. It is much more a movement towards organising, directing and controlling where organisation, direction and control are needed and are lacking. What pushes us on in Egypt, and France on in Morocco, is not so much the lust of dominion and desire for acquiring fresh possessions, as the sense that we, England or France, can restore order where there is chaos, and fertility where there is sterility. Our Cromers and Willcockses and Garstins[1] act not from narrowly selfish motives of personal or even national aggrandisement. They act because they are charged with certain ideas and capacities which, in the sphere where they are called upon to work, are precisely the ideas and capacities of which there is most urgent need. The triumph of Lord Cromer has been the triumph of certain principles of good government and administration, the triumph of continuity, consistency, strength of purpose and honesty, in a land where society was falling to pieces for the lack of these

things. The triumph of Sir W. Willcocks and Sir W. Garstin has been the triumph of practical science and skill in a region where there existed wonderful opportunities for their display, and where they were entirely ignored. But at the same time these ideas of government and these applications of science not only are not the especial property of our Cromers and Willcockses and Garstins, but they are not the especial property of the English nation. They are not individual, and they are not national; but neither are they universal or world-wide. The idea of a Government and administration honestly devoted to the welfare of society, which has proved such a blessing to the Egyptian people, the idea of a scientific knowledge and skill applied to the practical affairs of life, which has so marvellously extended the productivity of the Nile Valley, are in truth European ideas. They are ideas which the Western races have spent centuries in testing, analysing and perfecting, and they in fact constitute the main elements in what we call in the lump European civilisation.

Europe had absorbed these political and scientific ideas until she was full to bursting with them when the greatly increased facilities in locomotion resulting from her own practical science brought her into contact with regions where these ideas had never been heard of, and where life in consequence was lived under conditions of anarchy, with none of its possibilities realised and resources developed. The result of this contact has been a lively recognition on the part of Europe of the field for effective action

---

The Edinburgh Review 206 (October 1907), pp. 373–376.

[1]Evelyn Baring, 1st Earl of Cromer (1841–1917), British consul-general in Egypt from 1883 to 1907. Sir William Willcocks (1852–1932) and Sir William Garstin (1849–1925) were instrumental in the design and construction of the first Aswan Dam in Egypt. Built between 1898 and 1902, the dam was valuable for flood control and irrigation. —Eds.

social anarchy +
wasted opportunity.

thus opened to her, and an overmastering desire to bring her political and scientific ideas to bear on these new scenes of social anarchy and wasted opportunity. Nothing is easier than, in the way this desire has been carried out, to see only shallow and selfish motives at work; but there could be no more infallible proof of intellectual inferiority and second-rateness than is implied in . . . such explanations. Under the selfish rivalries and jealousies which are apt to distort and colour a national application of European ideas there has always been the deeper motive at work, the consciousness of possessing the powers and the knowledge most needed and which could be most favourably exercised. This deeper European motive has been stronger than the selfish national motive. We have profited by the work we have done in India, and shall profit perhaps by the work we are doing in Egypt. France has on the whole profited by the work she has done in Algeria and Tunisia, and will probably profit some day by the work that awaits her in Morocco. But the work was not done for the profit, nevertheless. It was done on the same impulse as prompts any man of firm will and strong purpose to intervene on the side of order amidst anarchy, or as prompts a man who knows how a thing should be done to instruct those who do not know and are making a bungle of it. It was done, in a word, because those who did it, no matter what others may have thought, or what they may have thought themselves, were acting, not on behalf

you often the while who has profited?

of England or on behalf of France, but on behalf of European ideas and European science. If the reader doubts this, let him ask himself with what thoughts Englishmen receive the news of barrages and dams built on the Nile, of deserts fertilised and a peasantry emancipated. Is it the case that our thoughts turn primarily to the chances of national benefits and advantages; or is it not rather true that we should still be proud of our work in Egypt even if we were out of pocket by it, and that no part of Lord Cromer's policy has been more generally approved than that which was directed to thwarting the selfish aims of those who saw in the new improvements a chance of money-making? . . .

Most of us, probably, are ready enough to admit our own disinterestedness. We are no greedy landgrabbers, but the apostles of an idea, the missionaries of Western civilisation. We make that claim for ourselves, and we make it also for those with whom we are in friendship and sympathy. We make it for France. France, introducing order into chaos, transforming a pirates' den into a beautiful and prosperous city, and reviving by her wells and springs the date palms of a thousand perishing oases, is also a missionary of Western civilisation. Her action, like ours, is to be accounted for, not by selfish and sordid motives, but by an appreciation of the great opportunities that have been set before her for bringing European ideas and European science to bear upon regions which most need their influence. . . .

sacred ethics or this word?

John Atkinson Hobson
AN EARLY CRITIQUE OF IMPERIALISM

One of the early English critics of imperialism was the social reformer and economist John Atkinson Hobson (1858–1940). Hobson's primary interest was social reform, and he turned to economics to try to solve the problem of poverty. Serving as a reporter in South Africa, Hobson concluded that capitalist mine owners had dragged Britain into an unnecessary war. As an economist, he argued that the unequal distribution of income made capitalism unproductive and unstable. It could not maintain itself except through investing in less developed countries on an increasing scale, thus fostering colonial expansion. Lenin, leader of the Russian Revolution, later adopted this thesis. Hobson's stress upon the economic causes of imperialism has been disputed by some historians who see the desire for national power and glory as a far more important cause. Hobson attacked imperialism in the following passages from his book *Imperialism* (1902).

. . . The decades of Imperialism have been prolific in wars; most of these wars have been directly motivated by aggression of white races upon "lower races," and have issued in the forcible seizure of territory. Every one of the steps of expansion in Africa, Asia, and the Pacific has been accompanied by bloodshed; each imperialist Power keeps an increasing army available for foreign service; rectification of frontiers, punitive expeditions, and other euphemisms for war are in incessant progress. The *pax Britannica*, always an impudent falsehood, has become of recent years a grotesque monster of hypocrisy; along our Indian frontiers, in West Africa, in the Soudan, in Uganda, in Rhodesia fighting has been well-nigh incessant. . . . Peace as a national policy is antagonised not merely by war, but by militarism, an even graver injury. Apart from the enmity of France and Germany, the main cause of the vast armaments which are draining the resources of most European countries is their conflicting interests in territorial and commercial expansion. . . .

Our economic analysis has disclosed the fact that it is only the interests of competing cliques of business men—investors, contractors, export manufacturers, and certain professional classes—that are antagonistic; that these cliques, usurping the authority and voice of the people, use the public resources to push their private businesses, and spend the blood and money of the people in this vast and disastrous military game, feigning national antagonisms which have no basis in reality. It is not to the interest of the British people, either as producers of wealth or as tax-payers, to risk a war with Russia and France in order to join Japan in preventing Russia from seizing [K]orea; but it may serve the interests of a group of commercial politicians to promote this dangerous policy. The South African war [the Boer War, 1899–1902], openly fomented by gold speculators for their private purposes, will rank in history as a leading case of this usurpation of nationalism. . . .

. . . So long as this competitive expansion for territory and foreign markets is permitted to misrepresent itself as "national policy" the antagonism of interests seems real, and the peoples must sweat and bleed and toil to keep up an ever more expensive machinery of war. . . .

. . . The industrial and financial forces of Imperialism, operating through the party, the press, the church, the school, mould public opinion and public policy by the false idealisation of those primitive lusts of struggle, domination, and acquisitiveness which have survived throughout the eras of peaceful industrial order and whose stimulation is needed once again for the work of imperial aggression, expansion, and the forceful exploitation of lower races. For these business politicians biology and sociology weave thin convenient theories of a race struggle for the subjugation of the inferior peoples, in order that we, the Anglo-Saxon, may take their lands and live upon their labours; while economics buttresses the argument by representing our work in conquering and ruling them as our share in the division of labour among nations, and history devises reasons why the lessons of past empire do not apply to ours, while social ethics paints the motive of "Imperialism" as

J. A. Hobson, *Imperialism* (London: Adam and Charles Black, 1905), pp. 21, 23–27, 36–37, 44, 46–47, 60–61, 64.

the desire to bear the "burden" of educating and elevating races of "children." Thus are the "cultured" or semi-cultured classes indoctrinated with the intellectual and moral grandeur of Imperialism. For the masses there is a cruder appeal to hero-worship and sensational glory, adventure and the sporting spirit: current history falsified in coarse flaring colours, for the direct stimulation of the combative instincts. But while various methods are employed, some delicate and indirect, others coarse and flamboyant, the operation everywhere resolves itself into an incitation and direction of the brute lusts of human domination which are everywhere latent in civilised humanity, for the pursuance of a policy fraught with material gain to a minority of co-operative vested interests which usurp the title of the commonwealth. . . .

. . . The presence of a scattering of white officials, missionaries, traders, mining or plantation overseers, a dominant male caste with little knowledge of or sympathy for the institutions of the people, is ill-calculated to give to these lower races even such gains as Western civilisation might be capable of giving.

The condition of the white rulers of these lower races is distinctively parasitic; they live upon these natives, their chief work being that of organising native labour for their support. The normal state of such a country is one in which the most fertile lands and the mineral resources are owned by white aliens and worked by natives under their direction, primarily for their gain: they do not identify themselves with the interests of the nation or its people, but remain an alien body of sojourners, a "parasite" upon the carcass of its "host," destined to extract wealth from the country and retire to consume it at home. All the hard manual or other severe routine work is done by natives. . . .

Nowhere under such conditions is the theory of white government as a trust for civilisation made valid; nowhere is there any provision to secure the predominance of the interests, either of the world at large or of the governed people, over those of the encroaching nation, or more commonly a section of that nation. The relations subsisting between the superior and the inferior nations, commonly established by pure force, and resting on that basis, are such as preclude the genuine sympathy essential to the operation of the best civilising influences, and usually resolve themselves into the maintenance of external good order so as to forward the profitable development of certain natural resources of the land, under "forced" native labour, primarily for the benefit of white traders and investors, and secondarily for the benefit of the world of white Western consumers.

This failure to justify by results the forcible rule over alien peoples is attributable to no special defect of the British or other modern European nations. It is inherent in the nature of such domination. . . .

REVIEW QUESTIONS

1. According to the author of the article in *The Edinburgh Review*, what specific benefits did Europeans bring to their overseas possessions?
2. Why, in Hobson's opinion, was the *pax Britannica* an "impudent falsehood"?
3. One ideal of imperialists was to spread civilizing influences among native populations. How did Hobson interpret this sense of mission?

CHAPTER 10

Modern Consciousness

SIGMUND FREUD, the father of psychoanalysis, penetrated the world of the unconscious. He concluded that powerful drives govern human behavior more than reason does. His explorations of the unconscious produced an image of the human being that broke with the Enlightenment's view of the individual's essential goodness and rationality. (Hans Casparius/Hulton Archive/Getty Images).

The closing decades of the nineteenth century and the opening of the twentieth witnessed a crisis in Western thought. Rejecting the Enlightenment belief in the essential rationality of human beings, thinkers such as Friedrich Nietzsche and Sigmund Freud stressed the immense power of the nonrational in individual and social life. They held that subconscious drives, impulses, and instincts lay at the core of human nature, that people were moved more by religious-mythic images and symbols than by logical thought, that feelings determine human conduct more than reason does. This new image of the individual led to unsettling conclusions. If human beings are not fundamentally rational, then what are the prospects of resolving the immense problems of modern industrial civilization? Although most thinkers shared the Enlightenment's visions of the rational reform of society and humanity's future progress, doubters were also heard.

At the same time that Nietzsche, Freud, and other thinkers were breaking with the Enlightenment view of human nature and society, artists and writers were rebelling against traditional forms of artistic and literary expression that had governed European cultural life since the Renaissance. Rejecting both classical and realist models, they subordinated form and objective reality to the inner life—to feelings, imagination, and the creative process. These avant-garde writers and artists found new and creative ways to express those explosive forces within the human psyche that increasingly had become the subject of contemporary thinkers. Their experimentations produced a great cultural revolution called *modernism*, which still profoundly influences the arts. Like Freud, modernist artists and writers probed beyond surface appearances for a more profound reality—impulses, instincts, and drives—hidden in the human psyche. Artists like Pablo Picasso and writers like James Joyce and Franz Kafka exhibited a growing fascination with the nonrational—with dreams, fantasies, sexual conflicts, and guilt, with tortured, fragmented, and dislocated inner lives. In the process, they rejected traditional aesthetic standards established during the Renaissance and the Enlightenment and experimented with new forms of artistic and literary representation.

These developments in thought and culture produced insights into human nature and society and opened up new possibilities in art and literature. But such changes also contributed to the disorientation and insecurity that characterized the twentieth century.

1   The Overman and the Will to Power

Few modern thinkers have aroused more controversy than the German philosopher Friedrich Nietzsche (1844–1900). Although scholars pay tribute to Nietzsche's originality and genius, they are often in sharp disagreement over the meaning and influence of his work. Nietzsche was a relentless critic of modern society. He attacked democracy, universal suffrage, equality, and socialism for suppressing a higher type of human existence. Nietzsche was also critical of the Western rational tradition. The theoretical outlook, the excessive intellectualizing of philosophers, he said, smothers the will, thereby stifling creativity and nobility; reason also falsifies life through the claim that it allows apprehension of universal truth, for no such truth exists. Nietzsche was not opposed to the critical use of the intellect, but like the Romantics, he focused on the immense vitality of the emotions. He also held that life is a senseless flux devoid of any overarching purpose. There are no moral values revealed by God. Indeed, Nietzsche proclaimed that God is dead. Nor are values and certainties woven into the fabric of nature that can be apprehended by reason—the "natural rights of man," for example. All the values taught by Christian and bourgeois thinkers are without foundation, said Nietzsche. There is only naked man living in a godless and absurd world.

Nietzsche called for the emergence of the *overman* or *superman*, a higher type of man who asserts his will, gives order to chaotic passions, makes great demands on himself, and lives life with a fierce joy. The overman aspires to self-perfection. Without fear or guilt, he creates his own values and defines his own life. In this way, he overcomes nihilism—the belief that there is nothing of ultimate value. It is such rare individuals, the highest specimens of humanity, that concern Nietzsche, not the herdlike masses.

The overman grasps the central reality of human existence—that people instinctively, uncompromisingly, ceaselessly, strive for power. The will to exert power is the determining factor in domestic politics, personal relations, and international affairs. Life is a contest in which the enhancement of power is the ultimate purpose of our actions; it brings supreme enjoyment: "the love of power is the demon of men. Let them have everything—health, food, a place to live, entertainment—they are and remain unhappy and low-spirited: for the demon waits and waits and will be satisfied. Take everything from them and satisfy this and they are almost happy—as happy as men and demons can be."

Friedrich Nietzsche
THE WILL TO POWER AND *THE ANTICHRIST*

Two of Nietzsche's works—*The Will to Power* and *The Antichrist*—are represented in the following readings. First published in 1901, one year after Nietzsche's death, *The Will to Power* consists of the author's notes written in the years 1883 to 1888. The following passages from this work show Nietzsche's contempt for democracy and socialism and proclaim the will to power.

THE WILL TO POWER 720 (1886–1887)

The most fearful and fundamental desire in man, his drive for power—this drive is called "freedom"—must be held in check the longest. This is why ethics . . . has hitherto aimed at holding the desire for power in check: it disparages the tyrannical individual and with its glorification of social welfare and patriotism emphasizes the power-instinct of the herd.

728 (March–June 1888)

. . . A society that definitely and *instinctively* gives up war and conquest is in decline: it is ripe for democracy and the rule of shopkeepers—In most cases, to be sure, assurances of peace are merely narcotics.

751 (March–June 1888)

"The will to power" is so hated in democratic ages that their entire psychology seems directed toward belittling and defaming it. . . .

752 (1884)

. . . Democracy represents the disbelief in great human beings and an elite society: "Everyone is equal to everyone else." "At bottom we are one and all self-seeking cattle and mob."

753 (1885)

I am opposed to 1. socialism, because it dreams quite naively of "the good, true, and beautiful" and of "equal rights" (—anarchism also desires the same ideal, but in a more brutal fashion); 2. parliamentary government and the press, because these are the means by which the herd animal becomes master.

Excerpt(s) from THE WILL TO POWER by Friedrich Nietzsche, translated by Walter Kaufmann and R.J. Hollingdale; edited, with commentary, by Walter Kaufmann, translation copyright © 1967 by Walter Kaufmann. Used by permission of Random House, an imprint and division of Penguin Random House LLC. All rights reserved.

762 (1885)

European democracy represents a release of forces only to a very small degree. It is above all a release of laziness, of weariness, of *weakness.*

765 (Jan.–Fall 1888)

. . . Another Christian concept, no less crazy, has passed even more deeply into the tissue of modernity: the concept of the "equality of souls before God." This concept furnishes the prototype of all theories of equal rights: mankind was first taught to stammer the proposition of equality in a religious context, and only later was it made into morality: no wonder that man ended by taking it seriously, taking it practically!—that is to say, politically, democratically, socialistically, in the spirit of the pessimism of indignation.

854 (1884)

In the age of *suffrage universel*, i. e., when everyone may sit in judgment on everyone and everything, I feel impelled to reestablish *order of rank.*

855 (Spring–Fall 1887)

What determines rank, sets off rank, is only quanta of power, and nothing else.

857 (Jan.–Fall 1888)

I distinguish between a type of ascending life and another type of decay, disintegration, weakness. Is it credible that the question of the relative rank of these two types still needs to be posed?

858 (Nov. 1887–March 1888)

What determines your rank is the quantum of power you are: the rest is cowardice.

861 (1884)

A declaration of war on the masses by *higher men* is needed! Everywhere the mediocre are combining in order to make themselves master! Everything that makes soft and effeminate, that serves the ends of the "people" or the "feminine," works in favor of *suffrage universel*, i. e., the dominion of *inferior* men. But we should take reprisal and bring this whole affair (which in Europe commenced with Christianity) to light and to the bar of judgment.

862 (1884)

A doctrine is needed powerful enough to work as a breeding agent: strengthening the strong, paralyzing and destructive for the world-weary.

The annihilation of the decaying races. Decay of Europe.—The annihilation of slavish evaluations.—Dominion over the earth as a means of producing a higher type.—The annihilation of the tartuffery [hypocrisy] called "morality." . . . The annihilation of *suffrage universel*; i. e., the system through which the lowest natures prescribe themselves as laws for the higher.

870 (1884)

The root of all evil: that the slavish morality of meekness, chastity, selflessness, absolute obedience, has triumphed—ruling natures were thus condemned (1) to hypocrisy, (2) to torments of conscience—creative natures felt like rebels against God, uncertain and inhibited by eternal values. . . .

In summa: the best things have been slandered because the weak or the immoderate swine have cast a bad light on them—and the best men have remained hidden—and have often misunderstood themselves.

814 (1884)

The degeneration of the rulers and the ruling classes has been the cause of the greatest mischief in history! Without the Roman Caesars and Roman society, the insanity of Christianity would never have come to power.

When lesser men begin to doubt whether higher men exist, then the danger is great! And one ends by discovering that there is *virtue* also among the lowly and subjugated, the poor in spirit, and that *before God* men are equal—which has so far been the . . . [height] of nonsense on earth! For ultimately, the higher men measured themselves according to the standard of virtue of slaves—found they were "proud," etc., found all their higher qualities reprehensible.

997 (1884)

I teach: that there are higher and lower men, and that a single individual can under certain circumstances justify the existence of whole millennia—that is, a full, rich, great, whole human being in relation to countless incomplete fragmentary men.

1001 (1884)

Not "mankind" but *overman* is the goal!

Nietzsche regarded Christianity as a life-denying religion that appeals to the masses. Fearful and resentful of their betters, he said, the masses espouse a faith that preaches equality and compassion. He maintained that Christianity has "waged a war to the death against (the) higher type of man." The following passages are from *The Antichrist*, written in 1888.

THE ANTICHRIST

2. What is good?—All that heightens the feeling of power, the will to power, power itself in man.

What is bad?—All that proceeds from weakness.

What is happiness?—The feeling that power *increases*—that a resistance is overcome.

Not contentment, but more power; *not* peace at all, but war; *not* virtue, but proficiency (virtue in the Renaissance style, *virtù,* virtue free of moralic acid).

The weak and ill-constituted shall perish: first principle of *our* philanthropy. And one shall help them to do so.

What is more harmful than any vice?— Active sympathy for the ill-constituted and weak—Christianity. . . .

3. The problem I raise here is not what ought to succeed mankind in the sequence of species (—the human being is an *end*—): but what type of human being one ought to *breed,* ought to *will,* as more valuable, more worthy of life, more certain of the future.

This more valuable type has existed often enough already: but as a lucky accident, as an exception, never as *willed.* He has rather been the most feared, he has hitherto been virtually *the* thing to be feared—and out of fear the reverse type has been willed, bred, *achieved*: the domestic animal, the herd animal, the sick animal man—the Christian. . . .

5. One should not embellish or dress up Christianity: it has waged *a war to the death* against this *higher* type of man, it has excommunicated all the fundamental instincts of this type, it has distilled evil, the *Evil One,* out of these instincts—the strong human being as the type of reprehensibility, as the "outcast." Christianity has taken the side of everything weak, base, ill-constituted, it has made an ideal out of *opposition* to the preservative instincts of strong life; it has depraved the reason even of the intellectually strongest natures by teaching men to feel the supreme values of intellectuality as sinful, as misleading, as *temptations.* . . .

7. Christianity is called the religion of *pity.*— Pity stands in antithesis to the tonic emotions which enhance the energy of the feeling of life: it has a depressive effect. One loses force when one pities. . . .

18. The Christian conception of God— God as God of the sick, God as spider, God as spirit—is one of the most corrupt conceptions of God arrived at on earth: perhaps it even represents the low-water mark in the descending development of the God type. God degenerated to the *contradiction of life,* instead of being its

transfiguration and eternal *Yes!* In God a declaration of hostility towards life, nature, the will to life! God the formula for every calumny of "this world," for every lie about "the next world"! In God, nothingness deified, the will to nothingness sanctified! . . .

21. In Christianity the instincts of the subjugated and oppressed come into the foreground: it is the lowest classes which seek their salvation in it . . . .

43. The poison of the doctrine *"equal* rights for all"—this has been more thoroughly sowed by Christianity than by anything else; from the most secret recesses of base instincts, Christianity has waged a war to the death against every feeling of reverence and distance between man and man, against, that is, the *precondition* of every elevation, every increase in culture—it has forged out of the [resentment] of the masses its *chief weapon* against *us,* against everything noble, joyful, high-spirited on earth, against our happiness on earth. . . . "Immortality" granted to every Peter and Paul has been the greatest and most malicious outrage on *noble* mankind ever committed.—*And* let us not underestimate the fatality that has crept out of Christianity even into politics! No one any longer possesses today the courage to claim special privileges or the right to rule, the courage to feel a sense of reverence towards himself and towards his equals—the courage for a *pathos of distance* . . . . Our politics is *morbid* from this lack of courage!— The aristocratic outlook has been undermined most deeply by the lie of equality of souls; and if the belief in the "prerogative of the majority" makes revolutions and *will continue to make them*— it is Christianity, let there be no doubt about it, *Christian* value judgement which translates every revolution into mere blood and crime! Christianity is a revolt of everything that crawls along the ground directed against that which is *elevated*: the Gospel of the "lowly" *makes* low. . . .

———————
From *Twilight of the Idols: or, How to Philosophize With a Hammer; The Anti-Christ* by Friedrich Nietzsche, translated by R. J. Hollingdale (Penguin Classics, 1968), pp. 115–118, 125, 128, 131, 133, 156–157. Copyright © R. J. Hollingdale, 1968. Reproduced by permission of Penguin Books Ltd.

REVIEW QUESTIONS

1. Do you agree with Friedrich Nietzsche that the pursuit of power is a human being's most elemental desire?
2. Why did Nietzsche attack democracy and socialism? How do you respond to his attack?
3. What were Nietzsche's criticisms of Christianity? How do you respond to this attack?
4. How does Nietzsche's philosophy stand in relation to the Enlightenment?

---

2 The Unconscious

After graduating from medical school in Vienna, Sigmund Freud (1856–1939), the founder of psychoanalysis, specialized in the treatment of nervous disorders. By encouraging his patients to speak to him about their troubles, Freud was able to probe more deeply into their minds. These investigations led him to conclude that childhood fears and experiences, often sexual in nature, accounted for neuroses—hysteria, anxiety, depression, obsessions, and so on. So threatening and painful were these childhood emotions and experiences that his patients banished them from conscious memory to the realm of the unconscious. To understand and treat neurotic behavior, Freud said it is necessary to look behind overt symptoms and bring to the surface emotionally charged experiences and fears—childhood traumas—that lie buried in the unconscious.

"The term *unconscious*" said Freud, "designates . . . ideas with a certain dynamic character, ideas keeping apart from consciousness in spite of their intensity and activity." Freud probed the unconscious by urging his patients to say whatever came to their minds. This procedure, called free association, rests on the premise that spontaneous and uninhibited talk reveals a person's underlying preoccupations, his or her inner world. A second avenue to the unconscious is the analysis of dreams; an individual's dreams, said Freud, reveal his or her secret wishes.

Freud's investigation of psychic developments led him to conclude that powerful mental processes hidden from consciousness govern human behavior more than reason does. His exploration of the unconscious produced a new image of the human being that has had a profound impact on twentieth-century thought and beyond.

Sigmund Freud
CIVILIZATION AND ITS DISCONTENTS

In the tradition of the Enlightenment philosophes, Freud valued reason and science, but he did not share the philosophes' confidence in human goodness and humanity's capacity for future progress. In *Civilization and Its Discontents* (1930), Freud posited the frightening theory that human beings are driven by an inherent aggressiveness that threatens civilized life—that civilization is fighting a losing battle with our aggressive instincts. Although Freud's pessimism was no doubt influenced by the tragedy of World War I, many ideas expressed in *Civilization and Its Discontents* derived from views that he had formulated decades earlier.

The element of truth behind all this, which people are ready to disavow, is that men are not gentle creatures who want to be loved and who at most can defend themselves if they are attacked: they are on the contrary, creatures among whose instinctual endowments is to be reckoned a powerful share of aggressiveness. As a result, their neighbor is for them not only a potential helper or sexual object but also someone who tempts them to satisfy their aggressiveness on him, to exploit his capacity for work without compensation, to use him sexually without his consent, to seize his possessions, to humiliate him, to cause him pain, to torture and to kill him. *Homo homini lupus* [Man is wolf to man]. Who in the face of all his experiences of life and to history, will have the courage to dispute this assertion. . . . [W]hen the mental counterforces which ordinarily inhibit [aggression] are out of action, it also manifests itself spontaneously and reveals man as a savage beast to whom consideration towards his own kind is something alien. Anyone who calls to mind the atrocities committed during . . . the invasions of the Huns, or by . . . the Mongols, . . . or at the capture of Jerusalem by the pious Crusaders, or even, indeed, the horrors of the recent World War . . . will have to bow humbly before the truth of this view. . . .

In consequence of this primary mutual hostility of human beings, civilized society is perpetually threatened with disintegration. The interest of work in common would not hold it together; instinctual passions are stronger than reasonable interests. Civilization has to use its utmost efforts in order to set limits to man's aggressive instincts and to hold the manifestations of them in check. . . . [Hence] the ideal's commandment to love one's neighbor as oneself—a commandment which is really justified by the fact that nothing else runs so strongly counter to the original nature of man. In spite of every effort, these endeavours of civilization have not so far achieved very much. . . . The time comes when each one of us has to give up as illusions the expectations which in his youth, he pinned upon his fellowmen, and when he may learn how much difficulty and pain has been added to his life by their ill-will. . . .

It is clearly not easy for men to give up the satisfaction of this inclination to aggression. They do not feel comfortable without it. . . .

If civilization imposes such great sacrifices not only on man's sexuality but on his aggressivity, we can understand better why it is hard for him to be happy in that civilization . . .

In all that follows I adopt the standpoint, therefore, that the inclination to aggression is an original, self-subsisting instinctual disposition in man, and I return to my view that it constitutes the greatest impediment to civilization.

Sigmund Freud, *Civilization and Its Discontents*, trans. James Strachey, copyright by James Strachey (New York: W. W. Norton, 1961) pp. 58–59, 61–62, 69.

REVIEW QUESTIONS

1. What did Freud consider the "greatest impediment to civilization"? Why?
2. How would Freud react to the Marxist view that private property is the source of evil?
3. Compare Freud's view of human nature and reason to that of Enlightenment philosophes.
4. Point out instances that would support Freud's view of human nature, that would oppose this view.

---

3 The Political Potential of the Irrational

The new insights into the irrational side of human nature and the growing assault on reason had immense implications for political life. In succeeding decades, these currents of irrationalism would be ideologized and politicized by unscrupulous demagogues, who sought to mobilize and manipulate the masses. The popularity after World War I of Fascist movements, which openly denigrated reason and exalted race, blood, action, and will, demonstrated the naiveté of nineteenth-century liberals, who believed that reason had triumphed in human affairs.

Among the late nineteenth- and early twentieth-century social theorists who focused on the implications of the nonrational for political life were Gustave Le Bon and Vilfredo Pareto. Twentieth-century dictators would employ Le Bon's insights into groups and mass psychology for the purpose of gaining and maintaining power.

Gustave Le Bon
MASS PSYCHOLOGY

Gustave Le Bon (1841–1931), a French social psychologist with strong conservative leanings, examined mass psychology as demonstrated in crowd behavior, a phenomenon of considerable importance in an age of accelerating industrialization and democratization. "The substitution of the unconscious action of crowds for the conscious activity of individuals is one of the principal characteristics of the present age," Le Bon declared in the preface to *The Crowd* (1895), excerpts from which follow.

Thousands of isolated individuals may acquire at certain moments, and under the influence of certain violent emotions—such, for example, as a great national event—the characteristics of a psychological crowd. . . .

The most striking peculiarity presented by a psychological crowd is the following: Whoever be the individuals that compose it, however like or unlike be their mode of life, their occupations, their character, or their intelligence, the fact that they have been transformed into a crowd puts them in possession of a sort of collective mind which makes them feel, think, and act in a manner quite different from that in which each individual of them would feel, think, and act were he in a state of isolation. . . .

To obtain [an understanding of crowds] it is necessary in the first place to call to mind the truth established by modern psychology, that unconscious phenomena play an altogether preponderating part not only in organic life, but also in the operations of the intelligence. The conscious life of the mind is of small importance in comparison with its unconscious life. . . . Behind the avowed causes of our acts there undoubtedly lie secret causes that we do not avow, but behind these secret causes there are many others more secret still which we ourselves ignore. The greater part of our daily actions are the result of hidden motives which escape our observation. . . .

. . . In the collective mind the intellectual aptitudes of the individuals, and in consequence their individuality, are weakened . . . and the unconscious qualities obtain the upper hand. . . .

. . . In a crowd every sentiment and act is contagious, and contagious to such a degree that an individual readily sacrifices his personal interest to the collective interest. This is an aptitude very contrary to his nature, and of which a man is scarcely capable, except when he [is] part of a crowd. . . .

. . . [An] individual [immersed] for some length of time in a crowd in action soon finds himself . . . in a special state, which much resembles the state of fascination in which the hypnotised individual finds himself in the hands of the hypnotiser. The activity of the brain being paralysed in the case of the hypnotised subject, the latter becomes the slave of all the unconscious activities of his spinal cord, which the hypnotiser directs at will. The conscious personality has entirely vanished; will and discernment are lost. All feelings and thoughts are bent in the direction determined by the hypnotiser.

Such also is approximately the state of the individual forming part of a psychological crowd. He is no longer conscious of his acts. In his case, as in the case of the hypnotised subject, at the same time that certain faculties are destroyed, others may be brought to a high degree of exaltation. Under the influence of a suggestion, he will undertake the accomplishment of certain acts with irresistible impetuosity. . . . He is no longer himself, but has become an automaton who has ceased to be guided by his will.

Moreover, by the mere fact that he forms part of an organised crowd, a man descends several rungs in the ladder of civilisation. Isolated, he may be a cultivated individual; in a crowd, he is a barbarian—that is, a creature acting by instinct. He possesses the spontaneity, the violence, the ferocity, and also the enthusiasm and heroism of primitive beings, whom he further tends to resemble by the facility with which he allows himself to be impressed by words and images—which would be entirely without action on each of the isolated individuals composing the crowd—and to be induced to commit acts contrary to his most obvious interests and his best-known habits. . . .

In consequence, a crowd perpetually hovering on the borderland of unconsciousness, readily yielding to all suggestions, having all the violence of feeling peculiar to beings who cannot appeal to the influence of reason, deprived of all critical faculty, cannot be otherwise than excessively credulous. The improbable does not exist for a crowd, and it is necessary to bear this circumstance well in mind to understand the facility with which are created and propagated the most improbable legends and stories. . . . A crowd thinks in images, and the image itself immediately calls up a series of other images, having no logical connection with the first. . . .

Gustave Le Bon, *The Crowd: A Study of the Popular Mind* (New York: Macmillan Co., 1896), pp. 3, 6–13, 22–24, 49, 55–57, 59, 63–65, 112–113, 118–119, 126–128.

Our reason shows us the incoherence there is in these images, but a crowd is almost blind to this truth, and confuses with the real event what the deforming action of its imagination has superimposed thereon. A crowd scarcely distinguishes between the subjective and the objective. It accepts as real the images evoked in its mind. . . .

Whatever be the ideas suggested to crowds they can only exercise effective influence on condition that they assume a very absolute, uncompromising, and simple shape. They present themselves then in the guise of images, and are only accessible to the masses under this form. These imagelike ideas are not connected by any logical bond of analogy or succession. . . .

. . . A chain of logical argumentation is totally incomprehensible to crowds, and for this reason it is permissible to say that they do not reason or that they reason falsely and are not to be influenced by reasoning. . . . An orator in intimate communication with a crowd can evoke images by which it will be seduced. . . .

. . . [The] powerlessness of crowds to reason aright prevents them [from] displaying any trace of the critical spirit, prevents them, that is, from being capable of discerning truth from error, or of forming a precise judgment on any matter. Judgments accepted by crowds are merely judgments forced upon them and never judgments adopted after discussion. . . .

. . . Crowds are to some extent in the position of the sleeper whose reason, suspended for the time being, allows the arousing in his mind of images of extreme intensity which would quickly be dissipated could they be submitted to the action of reflection. Crowds, being incapable both of reflection and of reasoning, are devoid of the notion of improbability; and it is to be noted that in a general way it is the most improbable things that are the most striking.

This is why it happens that it is always the marvellous and legendary side of events that more specially strike crowds. . . .

Crowds being only capable of thinking in images are only to be impressed by images. It is only images that terrify or attract them and become motives of action. . . .

How is the imagination of crowds to be impressed?. . . [The] feat is never to be achieved by attempting to work upon the intelligence or reasoning faculty, that is to say, by way of demonstration. . . .

Whatever strikes the imagination of crowds presents itself under the shape of a startling and very clear image, freed from all accessory explanation . . . examples in point are a great victory, a great miracle, a great crime, or a great hope. . . .

When [the convictions of crowds] are closely examined, whether at epochs marked by fervent religious faith, or by great political upheavals such as those of the last century, it is apparent that they always assume a peculiar form which I cannot better define than by giving it the name of a religious sentiment. . . .

A person is not religious solely when he worships a divinity, but when he puts all the resources of his mind, the complete submission of his will, and the whole-souled ardour of fanaticism at the service of a cause or an individual who becomes the goal and guide of his thoughts and actions.

Intolerance and fanaticism are the necessary accompaniments of the religious sentiment. . . .

All founders of religious or political creeds have established them solely because they were successful in inspiring crowds with those fanatical sentiments which have as result that men find their happiness in worship and obedience and are ready to lay down their lives for their idol. This has been the case at all epochs . . . .

We have already shown that crowds are not to be influenced by reasoning, and can only comprehend rough-and-ready associations of ideas. The orators who know how to make an impression upon them always appeal in consequence to their sentiments and never to their reason. The laws of logic have no action on crowds. To bring home conviction to crowds it is necessary first of all to thoroughly comprehend the sentiments by which they are animated, to pretend to share these sentiments. . . .

As soon as a certain number of living beings are gathered together, whether they be animals or men, they place themselves instinctively under the authority of a chief.

In the case of human crowds the chief is often nothing more than a ringleader or agitator, but as such he plays a considerable part. His will is the nucleus around which the opinions of the crowd are grouped and attain to identity. . . . A crowd is a servile flock that is incapable of ever doing without a master.

The leader has most often started as one of the led. He has himself been hypnotised by the idea, whose apostle he has since become. It has taken possession of him to such a degree that everything outside it vanishes, and that every contrary opinion appears to him an error or a superstition. An example in point is Robespierre, hypnotised by the philosophical ideas of Rousseau [an opponent of monarchy and supporter of democracy], and employing the methods of the Inquisition to propagate them.

The leaders we speak of are more frequently men of action than thinkers. . . . The multitude is always ready to listen to the strong-willed man, who knows how to impose himself upon it. Men gathered in a crowd lose all force of will, and turn instinctively to the person who possesses the quality they lack. . . .

When . . . it is proposed to imbue the mind of a crowd with ideas and beliefs . . . the leaders have recourse to different expedients. The principal of them are three in number and dearly defined—affirmation, repetition, and contagion. . . .

Affirmation pure and simple, kept free of all reasoning and all proof, is one of the surest means of making an idea enter the mind of crowds. The conciser an affirmation is, the more destitute of every appearance of proof and demonstration, the more weight it carries. . . .

Affirmation, however, has no real influence unless it be constantly repeated, and so far as possible in the same terms. It was Napoleon, I believe, who said that there is only one figure in rhetoric of serious importance, namely, repetition. The thing affirmed comes by repetition to fix itself in the mind in such a way that it is accepted in the end as a demonstrated truth.

The influence of repetition on crowds is comprehensible when the power is seen which it exercises on the most enlightened minds. This power is due to the fact that the repeated statement is embedded in the long run in those profound regions of our unconscious selves in which the motives of our actions are forged. At the end of a certain time we have forgotten who is the author of the repeated assertion, and we finish by believing it.

When an affirmation has been sufficiently repeated and there is unanimity in this repetition . . . what is called a current of opinion is formed and the powerful mechanism of contagion intervenes. Ideas, sentiments, emotions, and beliefs possess in crowds a contagious power as intense as that of microbes.

Vilfredo Pareto
POLITICS AND THE NONRATIONAL

Vilfredo Pareto (1848–1923), an economist and sociologist, focused on "elites" and the persistence of the nonrational in politics. Democracy, argued Pareto, was a fraud, particularly when it came to realizing equality. All societies, he said,

were governed by a powerful ruling elite considerably smarter, shrewder, and richer than the great mass of people. Regarding the nonrational, Pareto concluded that social behavior does not rest primarily on reason but on nonrational instincts and sentiments. These deeply rooted and essentially changeless feelings are the fundamental elements in human behavior. Whoever aims to lead and to influence people must appeal not to logic but to elemental feelings.

Much of Pareto's work was devoted to studying the nonrational elements of human consciousness and the various beliefs invented to give the appearance of rationality to behavior that derives from feeling and instinct.

The sources of men's illusions about the motives determining their behaviour are manifold. A main one lies in the fact that a very large number of human actions are not the outcome of reasoning. They are purely instinctive actions, although the man performing them experiences a feeling of pleasure in giving them, quite arbitrarily, logical causes. He is, generally speaking, not very exacting as to the soundness of this logic, and is very easily satisfied by a semblance of rationality. Nevertheless, he would feel very uncomfortable if there were lacking a smattering of logic. . . .

. . . When they feel drawn by certain religious, moral or humanitarian movements, human beings believe—and almost all of them entirely in good faith—that their convictions have been formed by a series of strict syllogisms deriving from real and incontestable facts. We shall guard against falling prey to this illusion, and shall make every effort to reveal its origins. . . .

Human beings habitually make all their actions dependent on a small number of rules of conduct in which they have a religious faith. It is inevitable that this should be so, for the great mass of men possess neither the character nor the intelligence necessary for them to be capable of relating these actions to their real causes. Indeed, even the most intelligent men

are obliged to condense their rules of conduct into a few axioms for, when one has to act, there really is not time for indulging in long and theoretical deliberations. . . .

. . . A hollow phraseology, empty, high-sounding, emotional formulas, abstract and repetitive phrases, vague and airy expressions with never a firm meaning—this is all that men ask for when they are looking, not for truth, which they wouldn't know what to do with, but only for a justification of actions which are advantageous or simply agreeable to them. . . .

Human beings follow their sentiments and their interests, but they like to think they follow reason. They also look for—and never fail to find—a theory which *a posteriori* gives a certain colour of logic to their behaviour. If this theory could be reduced scientifically to nil, the only outcome would be the substitution of another theory for the first in order to achieve the same aim. It would have a new form, but the pattern of behaviour would remain the same. Hence when it is desired to get men to act in a particular way and follow a prescribed path, the main appeal is to sentiments and interests. Very little is known as yet of the theory of these phenomena, and we cannot here go further into the question.

History shows us that the governing classes have always endeavoured to speak to the people, not in the language which they believe most truly reflects reality, but in that which they believe best suits the ends they have in mind. And this is the case even in the most advanced democracies. . . .

Vilfredo Pareto, *sociological Writings*, selected by S. E. Finer and translated by derick Mirfin (New York: Frederick a. Praeger Publishers, 1966), pp. 124–127, 141, 151, 155, 157, 159.

Human society is not homogeneous; it is made up of elements which differ to a greater or lesser degree, not only in respect to very obvious characteristics—like sex, age, physical strength, health, etc.—but also in respect to less obvious but no less important characteristics—like intellectual and moral qualities, energy, courage, etc. The assertion that men are objectively equal is so patently absurd that it is not worth refuting. On the other hand, the subjective idea of human equality is a fact of great importance and one which has a powerful influence in determining the changes which occur in society.

Just as one can distinguish the rich and the poor in a society, even though incomes may show an almost imperceptible increase as one traces them upwards from the very lowest to the very highest, so one can distinguish the elite in a society—the aristocratic groups (in the etymological sense of the word, i. e., "best")—and the commonalty. But it must always be remembered that these groups imperceptibly merge into one another.

The notion of an elite is governed by the qualities which are looked for in it. There can be an aristocracy of saints or an aristocracy of brigands, an aristocracy of the learned, an aristocracy of the criminal and so on. The totality of qualities promoting the well-being and domination of a class in society constitutes something which we will call simply *the elite.*

This elite exists in all societies and governs them even in cases where the regime in appearance is highly democratic. In conformity with a law which is of great importance and is the principal explanation of many social and historical factors, these aristocracies do not last but are continually renewed. This phenomenon may be called *the circulation of elites.* . . .

The great error of the present age is of believing that men can be governed by pure reasoning, without resort to force. Yet force is the foundation of all social organisation. It is interesting to note that the antipathy of the contemporary bourgeoisie to force results in giving a free hand to violence. Criminals and rioters, their impunity assured, do more or less as they like. . . .

As we have already pointed out, . . . society has the appearance of a heterogeneous mass with a hierarchic organisation. This hierarchy always exists, save perhaps among very primitive peoples who live in dispersed units like animals. It follows from this that a community is always governed by a small number of men, by an *elite,* even when it seems to have an absolutely democratic character. . . .

REVIEW QUESTIONS

1. According to Gustave Le Bon, how are individuals transformed once they become part of a crowd? How does the leader sway the crowd?
2. Point out instances in recent and contemporary history that support Le Bon's insights.
3. What are the implications of Vilfredo Pareto's theory of human nature and society for contemporary political life?

4 Human Irrationality in the Modernist Novel

At the same time that Nietzsche, Freud, and other thinkers were breaking with the Enlightenment view of human nature and society, artists and writers were rebelling against traditional forms of artistic and literary expression that had governed European cultural life since the Renaissance. Rejecting both classical and realist models, they subordinated form and objective reality to the inner life—to feelings, imagination, and the creative process. These avant-garde writers and artists found new and creative ways to express those explosive forces within the human psyche that increasingly had become the subject of contemporary thinkers. Their experimentations produced a great cultural revolution called *modernism,* which still profoundly influences the arts. In some ways, modernism was a continuation of the Romantic Movement, which had dominated European culture in the early nineteenth century. Both movements subjected to searching criticism cultural styles that had been formulated during the Renaissance and had roots in ancient Greece.

Even more than Romanticism, modernism aspired to an intense introspection—a heightened awareness of self—and saw the intellect as a barrier to the free expression of elemental human emotions. Modernist artists and writers abandoned conventional literary and artistic models and experimented with new modes of expression. They liberated the imagination from the restrictions of conventional forms and enabled their audience, readers, and viewers alike to share in the process of creation, often unconscious, and to discover fresh insights into objects, sounds, people, and social conditions. They believed that there were further discoveries to be made in the arts, further possibilities of expression, that past masters had not realized.

Like Freud, modernist artists and writers probed beyond surface appearances for a more profound reality—impulses, instincts, and drives—hidden in the human psyche. Writers such as Marcel Proust, August Strindburg, D. H. Lawrence, and Franz Kafka explored the inner life of the individual and the psychopathology of human relations in order to lay bare the self. They dealt with the predicament of men and women who rejected the values and customs of their day, and they depicted the anguish of people burdened by guilt, torn by internal conflicts, and driven by an inner self-destructiveness. Besides showing the overwhelming might of the irrational and the seductive power of the primitive, they also broke the silence about sex that had prevailed in Victorian literature.

Joseph Conrad
HEART OF DARKNESS

Behavior driven by the unconscious and by the human capacity to act irrationally and cruelly—the dark side of human nature, which was the subject of Freud's investigations—intrigued many modernist writers, including British novelist Joseph Conrad (1857–1924), born Józef Teodor Konrad Korzeniowski in what is now Ukraine. In 1862, when Conrad was not yet five years old, his father, who had participated in an insurrection to liberate Poland from Russian rule, was exiled to northern Russia. In this harsh environment, his mother died of tuberculosis in 1865. His father, who translated the works of French and English authors into Polish, which the precocious young Conrad read voraciously, made the difficult decision to place his only child in the care of Joseph's maternal uncle in Poland, where he attended school. Joseph lost his father when he was twelve, and five years later, he left his school in Poland to become an apprentice seaman on a French merchant ship. In 1878, speaking only a few words of English, he joined the British merchant navy.

During his twenty years at sea, Conrad visited exotic lands and experienced danger. These adventures found literary expression in Conrad's novels and short stories, including *An Outcast of the Islands* (1896), *Heart of Darkness* (1899), *Lord Jim* (1900), *Nostromo* (1904), and *The Secret Agent* (1907). But Conrad was far more than a masterful tenderer of adventure stories. His reputation as one of England's finest novelists derives from both his compelling prose and his creative exploration of human depravity, a phenomenon to which he seemed irresistibly drawn. In 1891, after a four-month stay in the Congo Free State, a land notoriously exploited and brutalized by agents of the Belgian King Leopold II (see page 237), Conrad suffered psychological trauma. His experiences in the heart of Africa led him to write his most compelling work, *Heart of Darkness.*

The two principal characters in the work are Kurtz, a company agent who runs a very successful ivory trading post deep in the Congo, and Marlow, a riverboat pilot, who is repelled by the cruelty inflicted on Africans by the company's agents. Marlow, who narrates his experiences, pilots a steamer upriver to Kurtz's station, Slowly he learns about Kurtz from the other agents of the company, including those accompanying him, and from a young Russian devoted to Kurtz, whom Marlow spots on the shore near Kurtz's post. Marlow finds out that Kurtz is a poet, musician, and painter with politically progressive views and that when he first came to Africa, Kurtz was imbued with humanitarian sentiments. One company employee describes him as "an emissary of pity and science and progress" who intended to bring enlightenment to "savage" Africans. But Kurtz's other self, long repressed by European values, comes to the fore. Kurtz becomes a depraved tyrant who decorates the fence poles around his house with human heads. The charismatic Kurtz has made disciples of the villagers, who view him as a godlike figure; they heed his every word and, at his command, launch murderous raids against nearby villages for more ivory. Kurtz engages in mysterious ceremonies—Conrad leaves the nature of these ceremonies to the reader's imagination, but it is likely that they are human sacrifices—which contribute to this uncanny power over the Africans.

Although shriveled by disease, Kurtz is reluctant to return with Marlow, but eventually relents. As the ship travels down the river, Marlow engages Kurtz in long conversations. During one of these talks, Kurtz senses that death is imminent and, suddenly gripped by "craven terror," he blurts out: "The horror! The horror!" He dies later that evening. Conrad relies on the reader to determine the meaning of Kurtz's agonizing cry.

There now exists a rich body of commentary analyzing the layers of meaning in Conrad's work. One obvious interpretation is that Conrad intended to write an indictment of imperialism, for *Heart of Darkness* expressed his revulsion for avaricious European imperialists who, in their quest for riches, plundered and destroyed African villages and impressed the natives into forced labor. Their greed, callousness, and brutality belied the altruism that they claimed was their motivation for coming to Africa.

Most commentators also regard *Heart of Darkness* as a tale of moral deterioration: The forbidding jungle environment, far from the restraints of European civilization, and the repulsive scramble for riches disfigure Kurtz, who is transformed into a sadist driven by dark urges no longer buried within his unconscious. The wilderness "whispered to him things about himself which he did not know, things of which he had no conception till he took counsel with this great solitude—and the whisper had proved irresistibly fascinating." When the dying Kurtz cries out: "The horror! The horror!" in "that supreme moment of complete knowledge," is he referring to his own moral collapse? Thus "darkness" refers not only to the jungle interior, but also to the destructive tendencies that are at the core of human nature. Marlow's travels into the dark interior of Africa in search of Kurtz can be seen as a descent into the dark interior of the unconscious. Civilization, as Freud maintained, is very fragile; only a thin barrier separates it from barbarism. Given the right circumstances, all human beings are capable of the moral disfigurement experienced by Kurtz.

In the following excerpt from *Heart of Darkness,* Marlow, an experienced seaman, sets out upstream on a steamer in order to relieve Kurtz at the Inner Station. The journey is filled with symbolic meaning. Marlowe is not only penetrating a primeval forest, but also returning to humanity's primitive, barbaric past, particularly the inner darkness of the human heart which is capable of savage behavior. Marlow, like Freud, understands the importance of resisting this descent to savagery.

It is this lure of savage reversion, symbolized by the wilderness, which has overwhelmed Kurtz, far from the restraints of European civilization. The manager of the Central Station, who is on board the steamer, fills Marlowe in on Kurtz's background and actions.

" . . . The wilderness had patted him on the head, and, behold, it was like a ball—an ivory ball; it had caressed him, and—lo!—he had withered; it had taken him, loved him, embraced him, got into his veins, consumed his flesh, and sealed his soul to its own by the inconceivable ceremonies of some devilish initiation. He was its spoiled and pampered favorite. Ivory? I should think so. Heaps of it, stacks of it. The old mud shanty was bursting with it. You would think there was not a single tusk left either above or below the ground in the whole country, 'Mostly fossil,' the manager had remarked, disparagingly. It was no more fossil than I am; but they call it fossil when it is dug up. It appears these niggers do

bury the tusks sometimes—but evidently they couldn't bury this parcel deep enough to save the gifted Mr. Kurtz from his fate. We filled the steamboat with it, and had to pile a lot on the deck. Thus he could see and enjoy as long as he could see, because the appreciation of his favor had remained with him to the last. You should have heard him say, 'My ivory.' Oh yes, I heard him. 'My Intended, my ivory, my station, my river, my—' everything belonged to him. It made me hold my breath in expectation of hearing the wilderness burst into a prodigious peal of laughter that would shake the fixed stars in their places. Everything belonged to him—but that was a trifle. The thing was to know what he belonged to, how many powers of darkness claimed him for their own. That was the reflection that made you creepy all over. It was impossible—it was not good for

Joseph Conrad, *Youth and Two Other Stories* (New York: McClure, Phillips & Co., 1903), pp. 131–135, 147–150.

one either—trying to imagine. He had taken a high seat amongst the devils of the land—I mean literally. You can't understand. How could you?—with solid pavement under your feet, surrounded by kind neighbors ready to cheer you or to fall on you, stepping delicately between the butcher and the policeman, in the holy terror of scandal and gallows and lunatic asylums—how can you imagine what particular region of the first ages a man's untrammeled feet may take him into by the way of solitude—utter solitude without a policeman—by the way of silence—utter silence, where no warning voice of a kind neighbor can be heard whispering of public opinion? These little things make all the great difference. When they are gone you must fall back upon your own innate strength, upon your own capacity for faithfulness. . . .

". . . The original Kurtz had been educated partly in England, and—as he was good enough to say himself—his sympathies were in the right place. His mother was half-English, his father was half-French. All Europe contributed to the making of Kurtz; and by and by I learned that, most appropriately, the International Society for the Suppression of Savage Customs had intrusted him with the making of a report, for its future guidance. And he had written it, too. I've seen it. I've read it. It was eloquent, vibrating with eloquence, but too high-strung, I think. Seventeen pages of close writing he had found time for! But this must have been before his—let us say—nerves, went wrong, and caused him to preside at certain midnight dances ending with unspeakable rites, which—as far as I reluctantly gathered from what I heard at various times—were offered up to him—do you understand?—to Mr. Kurtz himself. But it was a beautiful piece of writing. The opening paragraph, however, in the light of later information, strikes me now as ominous. He began with the argument that we whites, from the point of development we had arrived at, 'must necessarily appear to them [savages] in the nature of supernatural beings—we approach them with the might as of a deity,' and so on, and

so on. 'By the simple exercise of our will we can exert a power for good practically unbounded,' etc., etc. From that point he soared and took me with him. The peroration was magnificent, though difficult to remember, you know. It gave me the notion of an exotic Immensity ruled by an august Benevolence. It made me tingle with enthusiasm. This was the unbounded power of eloquence—of words—of burning noble words. There were no practical hints to interrupt the magic current of phrases, unless a kind of note at the foot of the last page, scrawled evidently much later, in an unsteady hand, may be regarded as the exposition of a method. It was very simple, and at the end of that moving appeal to every altruistic sentiment it blazed at you, luminous and terrifying, like a flash of lightning in a serene sky: 'Exterminate all the brutes!'" . . .

As the steamer approaches the Inner Station, Marlow spots a white man on the shore who greets them. He turns out to be a young and strange Russian adventurer very much devoted to Kurtz. Accompanied by the Russian, Marlow heads for Kurtz's house. When he is within distance, he peers into his field glasses.

" . . . I directed my glass to the house. There were no signs of life, but there was the ruined roof, the long mud wall peeping above the grass, with three little square window holes, no two of the same size; all this brought within reach of my hand, as it were. And then I made a brusque movement, and one of the remaining posts of that vanished fence leaped up in the field of my glass. You remember I told you I had been struck at the distance by certain attempts at ornamentation, rather remarkable in the ruinous aspect of the place. Now I had suddenly a nearer view, and its first result was to make me throw my head back as if before a blow. Then I went carefully from post to post with my glass, and I saw my mistake. These round knobs were not ornamental but symbolic; they were expressive and puzzling, striking and disturbing—food for thought and also for the vultures if there had been any looking down from the sky; but at all events for such ants as were industrious enough to ascend the pole. They would have been even more impressive, those heads on the stakes, if their faces had not been turned to the house. Only one, the first I had made out, was facing my way. I was not so shocked as you may think. The start back I had given was really nothing but a movement of surprise. I had expected to see a knob of wood there, you know. I returned deliberately to the first I had seen—and there it was, black, dried, sunken, with closed eyelids, a head that seemed to sleep at the top of that pole, and, with the shrunken dry lips showing a narrow white line of the teeth, was smiling, too, smiling continuously at some endless and jocose [humorous] dream of that eternal slumber.

"I am not disclosing any trade secrets. In fact, the manager said afterwards that Mr. Kurtz's methods had ruined the district. I have no opinion on that point, but I want you clearly to understand that there was nothing exactly profitable in these heads being there. They only showed that Mr. Kurtz lacked restraint in the gratification of his various lusts, that there was something wanting in him—some small matter which, when the pressing need arose, could not be found under his magnificent eloquence. Whether he knew of this deficiency himself I can't say. I think the knowledge came to him at last—only at the very last. But the wilderness had found him out early, and had taken on him a terrible vengeance for the fantastic invasion. I think it had whispered to him things about himself which he did not know, things of which he had no conception till he took counsel with this great solitude—and the whisper had proved irresistibly fascinating. It echoed loudly within him because he was hollow at the core. . . .

I put down the glass, and the head that had appeared near enough to be spoken to seemed at once to have leaped away from me into inaccessible distance.

"The admirer of Mr. Kurtz was a bit crestfallen. In a hurried, indistinct voice he began to assure me he had not dared to take these—say, symbols—down. He was not afraid of the natives; they would not stir till Mr. Kurtz gave the word. His ascendancy was extraordinary. The camps of these people surrounded the place, and the chiefs came every day to see him. They would crawl. . . . 'I don't want to know anything of the ceremonies used when approaching Mr. Kurtz,' I shouted. Curious, this feeling that came over me that such details would be more intolerable than those heads drying on the stakes under Mr. Kurtz's windows. After all, that was only a savage sight, while I seemed at one bound to have been transported into some lightless region of subtle horrors, where pure, uncomplicated savagery was a positive relief, being something that had a right to exist—obviously—in the sunshine. The young man looked at me with surprise. I suppose it did not occur to him that Mr. Kurtz was no idol of mine. He forgot I hadn't heard any of these splendid monologues on, what was it? On love, justice, conduct of life—or whatnot. If it had come to crawling before Mr. Kurtz, he crawled as much as the veriest savage of them all. I had no idea of the conditions, he said: these heads were the heads of rebels. I shocked him excessively by laughing. Rebels! What would be the next definition I was to hear? There had been enemies, criminals, workers—and these were rebels. Those rebellious heads looked very subdued to me on their sticks. 'You don't know how such a life tries a man like Kurtz,' cried Kurtz's last disciple."

REVIEW QUESTION

How does Joseph Conrad's *Heart of Darkness* show the power of the irrational? In what way is it a commentary on modern Western Civilization?

CHAPTER 11

World War I

CELEBRATING THE BEGINNING OF WORLD WAR I, 1914. For many people, the declaration of war was a cause for celebration. Few Europeans realized what a horror the war would turn out to be. *(Archives Larousse, Paris, France/Bridgeman Images)*

To many Europeans, the opening years of the twentieth century seemed full of promise. Advances in science and technology, the rising standard of living, the expansion of education, and the absence of wars between the Great Powers since the Franco-Prussian War (1870–1871) all contributed to a general feeling of optimism. Yet these accomplishments hid disruptive forces that were propelling Europe toward a cataclysm. On June 28, 1914, Archduke Franz Ferdinand, heir to the throne of Austria-Hungary, was assassinated by Gavrilo Princip, a young Serbian nationalist (and Austrian subject), at Sarajevo in the Austrian province of Bosnia, which was inhabited largely by South Slavs. The assassination triggered those explosive forces that lay below the surface of European life, and six weeks later, Europe was engulfed in a general war that altered the course of Western civilization.

Belligerent, irrational, and extreme nationalism was a principal cause of World War I. Placing homeland above all else, nationalists in various countries fomented hatred of other nationalities and called for the expansion of their own nation's borders—attitudes that fostered belligerence in foreign relations. Wedded to nationalism was a militaristic view that regarded war as heroic and as the highest expression of individual and national life.

Yet Europe might have avoided the world war had the nations not been divided into hostile alliance systems. By 1907, the Triple Alliance of Germany, Austria-Hungary, and Italy confronted the loosely organized Triple Entente of France, Russia, and Great Britain. What German chancellor Otto von Bismarck said in 1879 was just as true in 1914: "The great powers of our time are like travellers, unknown to one another, whom chance has brought together in a carriage. They watch each other, and when one of them puts his hand into his pocket, his neighbor gets ready his own revolver in order to be able to fire the first shot."

A danger inherent in an alliance is that a country, knowing that it has the support of allies, may pursue an aggressive foreign policy and may be less likely to compromise during a crisis; also, a war between two states may well draw in the other allied powers. These dangers materialized in 1914.

In the diplomatic furor of July and early August 1914, following the assassination of Franz Ferdinand, several patterns emerged. Austria-Hungary, a multinational empire dominated by Germans and Hungarians, feared the nationalist aspirations of its Slavic minorities. The nationalist yearnings of neighboring Serbia aggravated Austria-Hungary's problems, because the Serbs, a South Slav people, wanted to create a Greater Serbia by uniting with South Slavs of Austria-Hungary. If Slavic nationalism gained in intensity, the Austro-Hungarian (or Hapsburg) Empire would be broken into states based on nationality. Austria-Hungary decided to use the assassination as justification for crushing Serbia.

The system of alliances escalated the tensions between Austria-Hungary and Serbia into a general European war. Germany saw itself threatened by the Triple Entente (a conviction based more on paranoia than on objective fact) and regarded Austria-Hungary as its only reliable ally. Holding that at all costs its ally must be kept strong, German officials supported Austria-Hungary's decision to crush Serbia. Fearing that Germany and Austria-Hungary aimed to extend their power into southeastern Europe, Russia would not permit the destruction of Serbia. With the support of France, Russia began to mobilize, and when it moved to full mobilization, Germany declared war. As German battle plans, drawn up years before, called for a war with both France and Russia, France was drawn into the conflict; Germany's invasion of neutral Belgium brought Great Britain into the war.

Most European statesmen and military men believed the war would be over in a few months. Virtually no one anticipated that it would last more than four years and that the casualties would number in the millions.

World War I was a turning point in Western history. In Russia, it led to the downfall of the tsarist autocracy and the rise of the Soviet state. The war created unsettling conditions that led to the emergence of Fascist movements in Italy and Germany, and it shattered, perhaps forever, the Enlightenment belief in the inevitable and perpetual progress of Western civilization.

1 Militarism

Historians regard a surging militarism as an underlying cause of World War I. One sign of militarism was the rapid increase in expenditures for armaments in the years prior to 1914. Between 1910 and 1914, both Austria-Hungary and Germany, for example, doubled their military budgets. The arms race intensified suspicion among the Great Powers. A second danger was the increased power of the military in policymaking, particularly in Austria-Hungary and Germany. In the crisis following the assassination, generals tended to press for a military solution. The few dissenting voices raised against militarism were all but drowned out in this martial atmosphere.

Heinrich von Treitschke
THE GREATNESS OF WAR

Coupled with the military's influence on state decisions was a romantic glorification of the nation and war, an attitude shared by both the elite and the masses. Although militarism generally pervaded Europe, it was particularly strong in

Germany. In the following reading from *Politics* (1899–1900), the influential German historian Heinrich von Treitschke (1834–1896) glorified warfare.

War is regenerative + progress

. . . One must say with the greatest determination: War is for an afflicted people the only remedy. When the State exclaims: My very existence is at stake! then social self-seeking must disappear and all party hatred be silent. The individual must forget his own *ego* and feel himself a member of the whole, he must recognize how negligible is his life compared with the good of the whole. Therein lies the greatness of war that the little man completely vanishes before the great thought of the State. The sacrifice of nationalities for one another is nowhere invested with such beauty as in war. At such a time the corn is separated from the chaff. All who lived through 1870 will understand the saying of Niebuhr[1] with regard to the year 1813, that he then experienced the "bliss of sharing with all his fellow citizens, with the scholar and the ignorant, the one common feeling—no man who enjoyed this experience will to his dying day forget how loving, friendly and strong he felt."

By only the needs of the whole.

Distorted idea of war.

It is indeed political idealism which fosters war, whereas materialism rejects it. What a perversion of morality to want to banish heroism from human life. The heroes of a people are the personalities who fill the youthful souls with

delight and enthusiasm, and amongst authors we as boys and youths admire most those whose words sound like a flourish of trumpets. He who cannot take pleasure therein, is too cowardly to take up arms himself for his fatherland. All appeal to Christianity in this matter is perverted. The Bible states expressly that the man in authority shall wield the sword; it states likewise that: "Greater love hath no man than this that he giveth his life for his friend." Those who preach the nonsense about everlasting peace do not understand the life of the Aryan race (see chapter 8), the Aryans are before all brave. They have always been men enough to protect by the sword what they had won by the intellect. . . .

Anti-pacifist

To the historian who lives in the realms of the Will, it is quite clear that the furtherance of an everlasting peace is fundamentally reactionary. He sees that to banish war from history would be to banish all progress and becoming. It is only the periods of exhaustion, weariness and mental stagnation that have dallied with the dream of everlasting peace. . . . The living God will see to it that war returns again and again as a terrible medicine for humanity.

Heinrich von Treitschke, *Die Politik*, excerpted in *Germany's War Mania* (New York: Dodd, Mead, 1915), pp. 221–223.

[1]Barthold G. Niebuhr (1776–1831) was a Prussian historian. The passage refers to the Franco-Prussian War (1870–1871) and the German War of Liberation against Napoleon (1813), which German patriots regarded as a glorious episode in their national history.—Eds.

Friedrich von Bernhardi
GERMANY AND THE NEXT WAR

Friedrich von Bernhardi (1849–1930), a German general and influential military writer, considered war "a biological necessity of the first importance." The following excerpt comes from his work *Germany and the Next War* (1911), which was immensely popular in his country.

. . . War is a biological necessity of the first importance, a regulative element in the life of mankind which cannot be dispensed with, since without it an unhealthy development will follow, which excludes every advancement of the race, and therefore all real civilization. "War is the father of all things." The sages of antiquity long before Darwin recognized this.[1]

The struggle for existence is, in the life of Nature, the basis of all healthy development. . . . The law of the stronger holds good everywhere. Those forms survive which are able to procure themselves the most favourable conditions of life, and to assert themselves in the universal economy of Nature. The weaker succumb. . . .

Struggle is, therefore, a universal law of Nature, and the instinct of self-preservation which leads to struggle is acknowledged to be a natural condition of existence.

Strong, healthy, and flourishing nations increase in numbers. From a given moment they require a continual expansion of their frontiers, they require new territory for the accommodation of their surplus population. Since almost every part of the globe is inhabited, new territory must, as a rule, be obtained at the cost of its possessors—that is to say, by conquest, which thus becomes a law of necessity.

The right of conquest is universally acknowledged.

. . . Vast territories inhabited by uncivilized masses are occupied by more highly civilized States, and made subject to their rule. Higher civilization and the correspondingly greater power are the foundations of the right to annexation. . . .

Lastly, in all times the right of conquest by war has been admitted. It may be that a growing people cannot win colonies from civilized races, and yet the State wishes to retain the surplus population which the mother-country can no longer feed. Then the only course left is to acquire the necessary territory by war. Thus the instinct of self-preservation leads inevitably to war, and the conquest of foreign soil. It is not the possessor, but the victor, who then has the right. . . .

In such cases might gives the right to occupy or to conquer. Might is at once the supreme right, and the dispute as to what is right is decided by the arbitrament of war. War gives a biologically just decision, since its decisions rest on the very nature of things. . . .

The knowledge, therefore, that war depends on biological laws leads to the conclusion that every attempt to exclude it from international relations must be demonstrably untenable.

_____

Friedrich von Bernhardi, *Germany and the Next War*, translated by Allan H. Fowles (New York: Longmans, Green and Co., 1914), pp. 18, 22–24.

[1]Social Darwinists—those who transferred Darwin's scientific theories to the social world—insisted that races and nations were engaged in a struggle for survival in which only the fittest survive and deserve to survive. In their view, war was nature's way of eliminating the unfit.—Eds.

Henri Massis and Alfred de Tarde
THE YOUNG PEOPLE OF TODAY

War fever was not limited to Germany. A few years prior to the war, two French journalists, Henri Massis and Alfred de Tarde, undertook a survey of Parisian students enrolled at various elite educational institutions. The survey, which first appeared as a newspaper article in 1912 and then as a book in 1913, seemed to demonstrate that many young French males between the ages of eighteen and twenty-five had abandoned the Enlightenment humanitarianism of the older generation for a militant Catholicism, fervent nationalism, and romantic militarism. Excerpts from the survey follow.

The sentiment which is at the heart of youthful consciousness, the one that is in complete accord with the depth of their thought, is the patriotic faith. There is no possible equivocation or denial that the young are possessed by this faith. Optimism, that state of the soul which defines the attitude of the youth of today, is clearly shown from the beginning by the confidence they place in the future of France: there they find their primary reason for acting, what determines, directs, and predicts their action.

The young men of today have read the word of their destiny in this French soul, which has dictated for them a clear and imperious duty. . . .

And here is something even more significant. Students of advanced rhetoric in Paris, that is the most cultured elite of youth, declare that they find in war an aesthetic ideal of energy and strength. They believe that "France needs heroism in order to live." "Such is the faith that burns in modern youth," says Monsieur Tourelle.

How many times in the last two years have we not heard repeatedly "Rather war than this endless waiting." No bitterness in this wish, but a secret hope. . . .

War! The word has once again assumed a sudden prestige. It is a young word, quite new, adorned with that seduction which the eternal bellicose instinct has revived in the hearts of men. These young men fill it with all the beauty with which they are smitten and of which they are deprived by ordinary life. In their eyes it is above all an occasion for the most noble human virtues, for those that they place highest: energy, mastery, sacrifice for a cause that transcends us. And they think like William James that life "would become contemptible if it no longer offered either risks or rewards for the courageous man."

A professor of philosophy at the lycée Henri IV confided in us, "I told them that there are unjust wars, wars caused by anger, that it is necessary to rationally justify war-like feelings. The class, obviously unmoved, resisted this distinction."

Read this passage that a young student of rhetoric, of Alsatian origin, has written to us: "The existence which we lead doesn't satisfy us completely because if we possess all the elements of a beautiful life, we cannot organize them in a direct practical action that would seize us body and soul and would thrust us outside of ourselves. A single event will make this action possible: war. Also, we desire it. . . . It is in the life of the camps, it is under fire that we will experience the French powers that are within us. Our mind will no longer be troubled before the unknowable, since it will be able to concentrate entirely on a present duty from which all uncertainty and hesitation will be excluded."

How can we fail to understand the success of the stories of our colonialists, even, and perhaps especially, with the intellectual youth that we are considering here? The expeditions of Moll, Lenfant, and Baratier [three colonialists] arouse their enthusiasm; they seek in their safe existence a moral equivalent for these bold actions; they make an effort to absorb in their interior life these courageous values.

Some go even further: having completed their studies, they satisfy their taste for action

Agathon (Henri Massis—Alfred de Tarde), *Les jeunes gens d'aujourd'hui; le goût de l'action, la foi patriotique, une renaissance catholique, le réalisme politique*, deuxième édition (Paris: Librairie Plon-Nourrit et cie, 1919), pp. 21, 31–34. Translated by Howard E. Negrin.

in colonial adventures. It's no longer enough to learn history; they make it. A young graduate of the École Normale, Monsieur Klipfell, who received his advanced teaching diploma in literature in July 1912, asked to see action in Morocco when he enlisted in the expeditionary corps. And we can cite many similar examples. Consider Jacques Violet, a 28-year-old officer, who died heroically at Ksar-Teuchon in Adrar. He was killed leading his men, at a moment of victory, in a palm grove. In his bag, they found a pair of white gloves and a copy of *Military Servitude and Grandeur*.[1] That was how he went into combat. . . .

For such young men, moved by a patriotic faith and the cult of military virtues, all that is necessary is an opportunity for heroism.

———————

[1] Written by Alfred de Vigny (1797–1863), poet, novelist, and playwright, this book is difficult to categorize. It is in part an autobiographical account of de Vigny's life as an army officer and of his views on military service, and it also has several short stories that draw material from the author's military experience.—Eds.

REVIEW QUESTIONS

1. Why did Heinrich von Treitschke regard war as a far more desirable condition than peace?
2. According to Treitschke, what is the individual's highest responsibility?
3. According to Treitschke, what function does the hero serve in national life?
4. What conclusions did Friedrich von Bernhardi draw from his premise that war was "a biological necessity"?
5. Why were French students so attracted to war?

2 Pan-Serbism: Nationalism and Terrorism

The conspiracy to assassinate Archduke Franz Ferdinand was organized by a secret Serbian society called Union or Death, more popularly known as the Black Hand. Founded in 1911, the Black Hand aspired to create a Greater Serbia by uniting with their kinsmen, the South Slavs dwelling in Austria-Hungary. Thus, Austrian officials regarded the aspirations of Pan-Serbs as a significant threat to the Hapsburg Empire.

THE BLACK HAND

In 1914, the Black Hand had some 2,500 members, most of them army officers. The society indoctrinated members with a fanatic nationalism and trained them in terrorist methods. The initiation ceremony, designed to strengthen a new member's commitment to the cause and to foster obedience to the society's leaders, had the appearance of a sacred rite. The candidate entered a dark room in which a table stood covered with a black cloth; resting on the table were a dagger, a revolver, and a crucifix. When the candidate declared his readiness to take the oath of allegiance, a masked member of the society's elite entered the room and stood in silence. After the initiate pronounced the oath, the masked man shook his hand and departed without uttering a word. Excerpts of the Black Hand's bylaws, including the oath of allegiance, follow.

BY-LAWS OF THE ORGANIZATION UNION OR DEATH

Article 1. This organization is created for the purpose of realizing the national ideal: the union of all Serbs. Membership is open to every Serb, without distinction of sex, religion, or place of birth, and to all those who are sincerely devoted to this cause.

Article 2. This organization prefers terrorist action to intellectual propaganda, and for this reason it must remain absolutely secret.

Article 3. The organization bears the name *Ujedinjenje ili Smirt* (Union or Death).

Article 4. To fulfill its purpose, the organization will do the following:

1. Exercise influence on government circles, on the various social classes, and on the entire social life of the kingdom of Serbia, which is considered the Piedmont[1] of the Serbian nation;
2. Organize revolutionary action in all territories inhabited by Serbs;
3. Beyond the frontiers of Serbia, fight with all means the enemies of the Serbian national idea;
4. Maintain amicable relations with all states, peoples, organizations, and individuals who support Serbia and the Serbian element;
5. Assist those nations and organizations that are fighting for their own national liberation and unification. . . .

Article 24. Every member has a duty to recruit new members, but the member shall guarantee with his life those whom he introduces into the organization.

Article 25. Members of the organization are forbidden to know each other personally. Only members of the central committee are known to each other.

Article 26. In the organization itself, the members are designated by numbers. Only the central committee in Belgrade knows their names.

Article 27. Members of the organization must obey absolutely the commands given to them by their superiors.

Article 28. Each member has a duty to communicate to the central committee at Belgrade all information that may be of interest to the organization.

Article 29. The interests of the organization stand above all other interests.

Article 30. On entering the organization, each member must know that he loses his own personality, that he can expect neither personal glory nor personal profit, material or moral. Consequently, any member who endeavors to exploit the organization for personal, social, or party motives, will be punished. If by his acts he harms the organization itself, his punishment will be death.

Article 31. Those who enter the organization may never leave it, and no one has the authority to accept a member's resignation.

Article 32. Each member must aid the organization, with weekly contributions. If need be, the organization may procure funds through coercion. . . .

Article 33. When the central committee of Belgrade pronounces a death sentence the only thing that matters is that the execution is carried out unfailingly. The method of execution is of little importance.

"The Black Hand," from M. Boghitchevitch, *Le Proces de Salonique, Juin 1917*, Andre Delpeuch, ed., 1927, pp. 41–42, 46–48. Translation © Marvin Perry.

[1]The Piedmont was the Italian state that served as the nucleus for the unification of Italy.—Eds.

Article 34. The organization's seal is composed as follows. On the center of the seal a powerful arm holds in its hand an unfurled flag. On the flag, as a coat of arms, are a skull and crossed bones; by the side of the flag are a knife, a bomb, and poison. Around, in a circle, are inscribed the following words reading from left to right: "Union or Death," and at the base "The Supreme Central Directorate."

Article 35. On joining the organization, the recruit takes the following oath:

"I (name), in becoming a member of the organization, 'Union or Death,' do swear by the sun that shines on me, by the earth that nourishes me, by God, by the blood of my ancestors, on my honor and my life that from this moment until my death, I shall be faithful to the regulations of the organization and that I will be prepared to make any sacrifice for it. I swear before God, on my honor and on my life, that I shall carry with me to the grave the organization's secrets. May God condemn me and my comrades judge me if I violate or do not respect, consciously or not, my oath."

Article 36. These regulations come into force immediately.

Article 37. These regulations must not be changed.

Belgrade, 9 May 1911.

Baron von Giesl
AUSTRIAN RESPONSE TO THE ASSASSINATION

Austrian officials who wanted to use the assassination as a pretext to crush Serbia feared that Pan-Serbism would lead to revolts among Slavs living in the Hapsburg Empire. This attitude was expressed in a memorandum written on July 21, 1914, three weeks after the assassination, by Baron von Giesl, the Austrian ambassador to Serbia, to foreign minister Count Leopold von Berchtold.

Belgrade, July 21, 1914.

After the lamentable crime of June 28th, I have now been back at my post for some time, and I am able to give some judgment as to the tone which prevails here.

After the annexation crisis[1] the relations between the Monarchy and Servia [Serbia] were poisoned on the Servian side by national chauvinism, animosity and an effective propaganda of Great-Servian aspirations carried on in that part of our territory where there is a Servian population; since the last two Balkan Wars [in 1912 and 1913], the success of Servia has increased this chauvinism to a paroxysm, the expression of which in some cases bears the mark of insanity.

Reprinted from Great Britain, Foreign Office, *Collected Diplomatic Documents Relating to the Outbreak of the European War* (London: His Majesty's Stationary Office, 1915), The Austro-Hungarian Red Book, document no. 6, pp. 450–452.

[1]Since 1878, Austria-Hungary had administered the provinces of Bosnia and Herzegovina, which were officially a part of the Ottoman Empire. The population of these lands consisted mainly of South Slavs, ethnic cousins of the Serbs. When Austria-Hungary annexed Bosnia and Herzegovina in 1908, Serbia was enraged.—Eds.

I may be excused from bringing proof and evidence of this; they can be had easily everywhere among all parties, in political circles as well as among the lower classes. I put it forward as a well-known axiom that the policy of Servia is built up on the separation of the territories inhabited by Southern Slavs, and as a corollary to this on the abolition of the [Hapsburg] Monarchy as a Great Power; this is its only object.

No one who has taken the trouble to move and take part in political circles here for a week can be blind to this truth, . . .

The crime at Serajevo [the assassination of Franz Ferdinand] has aroused among the Servians an expectation that in the immediate future the Hapsburg States will fall to pieces; it was this on which they had set their hopes.

Austria-Hungary, hated as she is, now appears to the Servians as powerless, and as scarcely worthy of waging war with; contempt is mingled with hatred; she is ripe for destruction, and she is to fall without trouble into the lap of the Great-Servian Empire, which is to be realised in the immediate future.

Newspapers, not among the most extreme, discuss the powerlessness and decrepitude of the neighbouring Monarchy in daily articles, and insult its officials without reserve and without fear of reprimand. They do not even stop short of the exalted person of our ruler. Even the official organ refers to the internal condition of Austria-Hungary as the true cause of this wicked crime. There is no longer any fear of being called to account, For decades the people of Servia has been educated by the press, and the policy at any given time is dependent on the party press; the Great-Servian propaganda and its monstrous offspring the crime of June 28th, are a fruit of this education. . . .

. . . The electoral campaign has united all parties on a platform of hostility against Austria-Hungary. None of the parties which aspire to office will incur the suspicion of being held capable of weak compliance towards the Monarchy. The campaign, therefore, is conducted under the catchword of hostility towards Austria-Hungary.

For both internal and external reasons the Monarchy is held to be powerless and incapable of any energetic action, and it is believed that the serious words which were spoken by leading men among us are only "bluff." . . .

I have allowed myself to trespass too long on the patience of Your Excellency, not because I thought that in what I have said I could tell you anything new, but because I considered this picture led up to the conclusion which forces itself upon me that a reckoning with Servia, a war for the position of the Monarchy as a Great Power, even for its existence as such, cannot be permanently avoided.

If we delay in clearing up out relations with Servia, we shall share the responsibility for the difficulties and the unfavourable situation in any future war which must, however, sooner or later be carried through.

For any observer on the spot, and for the representative of Austro-Hungarian interests in Servia, the question takes the form that we cannot any longer put up with any further injury to our prestige. . . .

Half measures, the presentation of demands, followed by long discussions and ending only in an unsound compromise, would be the hardest blow which could be directed against Austria-Hungary's reputation in Servia and her position in Europe.

REVIEW QUESTIONS

1. How did the Black Hand seek to accomplish its goal of uniting all Serbs?
2. What type of people do you think were attracted to the objectives and methods of the Black Hand?
3. According to Baron von Giesl, how did Serbia view the Hapsburg monarchy? What policy toward Serbia did he advocate?

---

3 War as Celebration: The Mood in European Capitals

An outpouring of patriotism greeted the proclamation of war. Huge crowds thronged the avenues and squares of capital cities to express their devotion to their nations and their willingness to bear arms. Many Europeans regarded war as a sacred moment that held the promise of adventure and an escape from a humdrum and purposeless daily existence. Going to war seemed to satisfy a yearning to surrender oneself to a noble cause: the greatness of the nation. The image of the nation united in a spirit of fraternity and self-sacrifice was immensely appealing.

Roland Dorgelès
PARIS: "THAT FABULOUS DAY"

In his essay "After Fifty Years," Roland Dorgelès (1885–1973), a distinguished French writer, recalls the mood in Paris at the outbreak of the war.

"It's come[1] It's posted at the district mayor's office," a passerby shouted to me as he ran.

I reached the Rue Drouot in one leap and shouldered through the mob that already filled the courtyard to approach the fascinating white sheet pasted to the door. I read the message at a glance, then reread it slowly, word for word, to convince myself that it was true:

THE FIRST DAY OF
MOBILIZATION WILL BE
SUNDAY, AUGUST 2

Only three lines, written hastily by a hand that trembled. It was an announcement to a million and a half Frenchmen.

The people who had read it moved away, stunned, while others crowded in, but this silent numbness did not last. Suddenly a heroic wind lifted their heads. What? War, was it? Well, then, let's go! Without any signal, the "Marseillaise" poured from thousands of throats, sheafs of flags appeared at windows, and howling processions rolled out on the boulevards. Each column brandished a placard: ALSACE VOLUNTEERS, JEWISH VOLUNTEERS, POLISH VOLUNTEERS. They hailed one another above the bravos of

---

Roland Dorgelès, "After Fifty Years," in George A. Panichas, ed., *Promise of Greatness* (New York: The John Day Company, 1968), pp. 13–15. Used by kind permission of the Estate of George A. Panichas.

[1]Translated from the French by Sally Abeles.

the crowd, and this human torrent, swelling at every corner, moved on to circle around the Place de la Concorde, before the statue of Strasbourg banked with flowers, then flowed toward the Place de la République, where mobs from Belleville and the Faubourg St. Antoine yelled themselves hoarse on the refrain from the great days, *"Aux armes, citoyens!"* (To arms, citizens!) But this time it was better than a song.

To gather the news for my paper, I ran around the city in every direction. At the Cours la Reine I saw the fabled cuirassiers [cavalry] in their horsetail plumes march by, and at the Rue La Fayette footsoldiers in battle garb with women throwing flowers and kisses to them. In a marshaling yard I saw guns being loaded, their long, thin barrels twined around with branches and laurel leaves, while troops in red breeches piled gaily into delivery vans they were scrawling with challenges and caricatures. Young and old, civilians and military men burned with the same excitement. It was like a Brotherhood Day.

Dead tired but still exhilarated, I got back to *L'Homme libre* and burst into the office of Georges Clemenceau, our chief.[2]

"What is Paris saying?" he asked me.

"It's singing, sir!"

"Then everything will be all right. . . ."

His old patriot's heart was not wrong; no cloud marred that fabulous day. . . .

Less than twenty-four hours later, seeing their old dreams of peace crumble [socialist workers] would stream out into the boulevards . . . [but] they would break into the "Marseillaise," not the "Internationale"; they would cry, "To Berlin!," not "Down with war!"

What did they have to defend, these black-nailed patriots? Not even a shack, an acre to till, indeed hardly a patch of ground reserved at the Pantin Cemetery; yet they would depart, like their rivals of yesterday, a heroic song on their lips and a flower in their guns. No more poor or rich, proletarians or bourgeois, right-wingers or militant leftists; there were only Frenchmen.

Beginning the next day, thousands of men eager to fight would jostle one another outside recruiting offices, waiting to join up. Men who could have stayed home, with their wives and children or an imploring mama. But no. The word "duty" had a meaning for them, and the word "country" had regained its splendor.

I close my eyes, and they appear to me, those volunteers on the great day; then I see them again in the old kepi [military cap] or blue helmet, shouting, "Here!" when somebody called for men for a raid, or hurling themselves into an attack with fixed bayonets, and I wonder, and I question their bloody [ghosts].

Tell me, comrades in eternal silence, would you have besieged the enlistment offices with the same enthusiasm, would you have fought such a courageous fight had you known that fifty years later those men in gray knit caps or steel helmets you were ordered to kill would no longer be enemies and that we would have to open our arms to them? Wouldn't the heroic "Let's go!" you shouted as you cleared the parapets have stuck in your throats? Deep in the grave where you dwell, don't you regret your sacrifice? "Why did we fight? Why did we let ourselves get killed?" This is the murmur of a million and a half voices rising from the bowels of the earth, and we, the survivors, do not know what to answer. . . .

---

[2]*L'Homme libre* (The Free Man) was but one of several periodicals Clemenceau founded and directed during his long political career.—Trans.

Stefan Zweig
VIENNA: "THE RUSHING FEELING OF FRATERNITY"

Some intellectuals viewed the war as a way of regenerating the nation; nobility and fraternity would triumph over life's petty concerns. In the following reading, Stefan Zweig (1881–1942), a prominent Austrian literary figure, recalled the scene in Vienna, the capital of the Austro-Hungarian Empire, at the outbreak of World War I. This passage comes from Zweig's autobiography, *The World of Yesterday*, written in 1941.

The trains were filled with fresh recruits, banners were flying, music sounded, and in Vienna I found the entire city in a tumult. The first shock at the news of war—the war that no one, people or government, had wanted. . . had suddenly been transformed into enthusiasm. There were parades in the street, flags, ribbons, and music burst forth everywhere, young recruits were marching triumphantly, their faces lighting up at the cheering—they, the John Does . . . who usually go unnoticed and uncelebrated.

And to be truthful, I must acknowledge that there was a majestic, rapturous, and even seductive something in this first outbreak of the people from which one could escape only with difficulty. And in spite of all my hatred and aversion for war, I should not like to have missed the memory of those first days. As never before, hundreds of thousands felt . . . that they belonged together. A city of two million, a country of nearly fifty million, in that hour felt that they were participating . . . in a moment which would never recur . . . . All differences of class, rank, and language were flooded over at that

moment by the rushing feeling of fraternity. . . . Each individual experienced an exaltation of his ego, he was no longer the isolated person of former times, he had been incorporated into the mass, and . . . his hitherto unnoticed person had been given meaning. The petty mail clerk, . . . the cobbler, had suddenly achieved a romantic possibility in life: he could become a hero, and everyone who wore a uniform was already being cheered by the women. . . . But it is quite possible that a deeper, more secret power was at work in this frenzy. So deeply, so quickly did the tide break over humanity that, foaming over the surface, it churned up the depths, the subconscious primitive instincts of the human animal—that which Freud so meaningfully calls "the revulsion from culture," the desire to break out of the conventional bourgeois world of codes and statutes, and to permit the primitive instincts of the blood to rage at will. It is also possible that these powers of darkness had their share in the wild frenzy into which everything was thrown—self-sacrifice and alcohol, the spirit of adventure and the spirit of pure faith, the old magic of flags and patriotic slogans, that mysterious frenzy of the millions . . . which, for the moment, gave a wild and almost rapturous impetus to the greatest crime of our time. . . .

Stefan Zweig, *The World of Yesterday*, trans. Helmut Ripperger, pp. 222–224, 226–227.

A rapid excursion into the romantic, a wild, manly adventure—that is how the war of 1914 was painted in the imagination of the simple man, and the young people were honestly afraid that they might miss this most wonderful and exciting experience of their lives; that is why they hurried and thronged to the colors, and that is why they shouted and sang in the trains that carried them to the slaughter; wildly and feverishly the red wave of blood coursed through the veins of the entire nation.

Philipp Scheidemann
BERLIN: "THE HOUR WE YEARNED FOR"

Philipp Scheidemann (1865–1939), one of the founding fathers of the Weimar Republic, described Berlin's martial mood in his memoirs, published in 1929.

At express speed I had returned to Berlin. Everywhere a word could be heard the conversation was of war and rumours of war. There was only one topic of conversation—war. The supporters of war seemed to be in a great majority. Were these pugnacious fellows, young and old, bereft of their senses? Were they so ignorant of the horrors of war? . . . Vast crowds of demonstrators paraded. . . . Schoolboys and students were there in their thousands; their bearded seniors, with their Iron Crosses of 1870–71 on their breasts, were there too in huge numbers.

Treitschke and Bernhardi[1] (to say nothing of the National Liberal beer-swilling heroes) seemed to have multiplied a thousandfold. Patriotic demonstrations had an intoxicating effect and excited the war-mongers to excess. "A call like the voice of thunder." Cheers! "In triumph we will smite France to the ground." "All hail to thee in victor's crown." Cheers! Hurrah!

The counter-demonstrations immediately organized by the Berlin Social Democrats were imposing, and certainly more disciplined than the Jingo [extremely nationalistic] processions, but could not outdo the shouts of the fire-eaters. "Good luck to him who cares for truth and right. Stand firmly round the flag." "Long live peace!" "Socialists, close up your ranks." The Socialist International cheer. The patriots were sometimes silenced by the Proletarians; then they came out on top again. This choral contest . . . went on for days.

"It is the hour we yearned for—our friends know that," so the Pan-German[2] papers shouted, that had for years been shouting for war. The *Post*, conducted by von Stumm, the Independent Conservative leader and big Industrial, had thus moaned in all its columns in 1910, at the fortieth celebration of the Franco-German War: "Another forty years of peace would be a national misfortune for Germany." Now these firebrands saw the seeds they had

---

The Making of New Germany: The Memoirs of Philipp Scheidemann, translated by James Edward Mitchell, vol. 11, pp. 310–312, 316–317, 319.

---

[1] Both Heinrich von Treitschke and General von Bernhardi glorified war (see pages 275–276).—Eds.
[2] The Pan-German League, whose membership included professors, schoolteachers, journalists, lawyers, and aristocrats, spread nationalist and racial theories and glorified war as an expression of national vitality (see page 217). —Eds.

planted ripening. Perhaps in the heads of many who had been called upon to make every effort to keep the peace Bernhardi's words, that "the preservation of peace can and never shall be the aim of politics," had done mischief. These words are infernally like the secret instructions given by Baron von Holstein to the German delegates to the first Peace Conference at The Hague:

"For the State there is no higher aim than the preservation of its own interests; among the Great Powers these will not necessarily coincide with the maintenance of peace, but rather with the hostile policy of enemies and rivals."

✳ Bertrand Russell
LONDON: "AVERAGE MEN AND WOMEN WERE DELIGHTED AT THE PROSPECT OF WAR"

Bertrand Russell (1872–1970), the distinguished mathematician and philosopher, was dismayed by the war fever that gripped English men and women. During the war Russell was fined and imprisoned for his pacifistic activities. The following account is from his autobiography published in 1968.

I spent the evening walking round the streets, especially in the neighbourhood of Trafalgar Square, noticing cheering crowds, and making myself sensitive to the emotions of passers-by. During this and the following days I discovered to my amazement that average men and women were delighted at the prospect of war. I had fondly imagined what most pacifists contended, that wars were forced upon a reluctant population by despotic and Machiavellian governments. . . .

The first days of the war were to me utterly amazing. My best friends, such as the Whiteheads, were savagely warlike. Men like J. L. Hammond, who had been writing for years against participation in a European war, were swept off their feet by [Germany's invasion of] Belgium. . . .

The prospect [of the impending disaster] filled me with horror, but what filled me with even more horror was the fact that the anticipation of carnage was delightful to something like ninety percent of the population. I had to revise my views on human nature. . . .

. . . As a lover of truth, the national propaganda of all the belligerent nations sickened me. As a lover of civilization, the return to barbarism appalled me. As a man of thwarted parental feeling, the massacre of the young wrung my heart. . . .

Others see war as essential to civilization.

On August 15, 1914, the London *Nation* published a letter written by Russell, part of which follows.

. . . Those who saw the London crowds, during the nights leading up to the Declaration of War saw a whole population, hitherto peaceable and humane, precipitated in a few days

Excerpted from *The Autobiography of Bertrand Russell*, 1914–1944, pp. 3–7, 41.

down the steep slope to <u>primitive barbarism</u>, letting loose, in a moment, the instincts of hatred and blood lust against which the whole fabric of society has been raised. "Patriots" in all countries acclaim this brutal orgy as a noble determination to vindicate the right; reason and mercy are swept away in one great flood of hatred; dim abstractions of unimaginable wickedness—Germany to us and the French, Russia to the Germans—conceal the simple fact that <u>the enemy are men, like ourselves</u>, neither better nor worse—<u>men who love their homes and the sunshine, and all the simple pleasures of common lives.</u>

REVIEW QUESTIONS

1. Why was war welcomed as a positive event by so many different peoples?
2. Do you think human beings are aggressive by nature? Explain your answer.
3. Why did the events of July and August 1914 cause Bertrand Russell to revise his views of human nature? Do you agree with his assessment?

 # 4 The Horror of Trench Warfare

In 1914 the young men of European nations marched off to war believing that they were embarking on a glorious and chivalrous adventure. They were eager to serve their country, to demonstrate personal valor, and to experience life at its most intense moments. But in the trenches, where unseen enemies fired machine guns and artillery that killed indiscriminately and relentlessly, for many this romantic illusion about combat disintegrated.

In the trenches, soldiers were reduced to a primitive existence. Sometimes they stood knee-deep in freezing water or slimy mud; the stench from human waste, rotting corpses, pieces of flesh and bone, and unwashed bodies overwhelmed the senses; rats, made more fecund and larger by easy access to food, including decaying flesh, swarmed over the dead and scampered across the wounded and the sleeping; and ubiquitous lice caused intense discomfort and disease, which frequently required hospitalization for several weeks. After days of uninterrupted, fearsome, earsplitting bombardment by artillery, even the most stouthearted were reduced to shivering, whimpering creatures. Unless the dugouts were fortified with concrete, soldiers rarely survived a direct hit; sometimes they were simply burned alive or torn apart and made unrecognizable by exploding shells. Fired from a distance, artillery, which had been made more lethal in recent decades, accounted for about 70 percent of casualties. Between the opposing armies lay "no man's land," a wasteland of mud, shattered trees, torn earth, shell-cratered ground, and broken bodies. The agonizing cries and pleas of the wounded, left to die on the battlefield because it was too dangerous to attempt a rescue, shattered the nerves of the men in the trenches.

British and German Combatants
THE BATTLE OF THE SOMME

At the end of June 1916, the British, assisted by the French, attempted a break-through at the Somme River. For seven days British artillery relentlessly bombarded German defenses, but the British had insufficient heavy guns and many of them were operated by inexperienced gunners. Despite the unprecedented bombardment, German positions, including the barbed wire protecting the trenches from attackers and the artillery batteries, remained largely undamaged. On July 1 at 7:30 A.M., British soldiers climbed out of their trenches—with machine-gun bullets whistling over and all around them, some never made it "over the top"—and ventured into no man's land. Emerging from their deep dugouts reinforced by concrete, German machine gunners, ready for the attack, fired repeatedly at the British who had been ordered to advance in rows. So tightly packed were the advancing British infantry that German machine gunners hardly had to aim. British lines marched into this maelstrom of concentrated machine-gun fire and continuous artillery barrages. Pinned-down British soldiers desperately searched for ways to get through still-intact German wire in which many were entangled. The Germans killed these helpless men with rifle fire and bayonets. Few British troops reached the German trenches that day. For days, the wounded, some of them losing consciousness, lay in no man's land, begging for rescue, their horrifying shrieks unheeded, because attempts to search them out and carry them back to the trenches would only end in more deaths. Out of 110,000 who attacked on July 1, some 57,000 fell dead or wounded—mostly in the first hour of the assault—a tragedy that the British continue to memorialize.

Following are brief accounts of British and German combatants who survived that ghastly day.

A BRITISH PRIVATE:

The first line all lay down and I thought they'd had different orders because we'd all been told to walk. It appears they lay down because they'd been shot and either killed or wounded. They were just mown down like corn. Our line simply went forward and the same thing happened. You were just trying to find your way in amongst the shell holes.

You can imagine, walking through shell-pitted ground with holes all over the place, trying to walk like that. You couldn't even see where you were walking! When you got to the line you saw that a lot of the first line were stuck on the wire, trying to get through. We didn't get to the German wire, I didn't get as far as our wire. Nobody did, except just a few odd ones who got through and got as far as the German wire. The machine-gun fire was all trained on our wire. Only a few crept along. I lay down. We weren't getting any orders at all; there was nobody to give any orders, because the officers were shot down.

Peter Hart, *The Somme: The Darkest Hour on the Western Front*, New York: Pegasus Books, 2008, pp. 137–138. Reprinted with permission from Pegasus Books.

A BRITISH CORPORAL

At half past seven, Mr Morris—the officer with the lisp—pulled out his revolver, blew his whistle, and said, "Over!" As he said it, a bullet hit him straight between the eyes and killed him. I went over with all the other boys. The barbed wire that was supposed to have been demolished had only been cut in places. Just a gap here, a gap there, and everyone made for the gaps in order to get through. There were supposed to be no Germans at all in the front line—but they were down in the ground in their concrete shelters. They just fired at the breeches in the wire and mowed us down. It seemed to me, eventually, I was the only man left. I couldn't see anybody at all. All I could see were men lying dead, men screaming, men on the barbed wire with their bowels hanging down, shrieking, and I thought, "What can I do?" I was alone in a hell of fire and smoke and stink.

A RETREATING BRITISH SERGEANT:

I was walking along, and a bullet blew all my teeth out. I fell forward and spat all my teeth out. I collapsed and, hours later, I came round. My left eye was closed. I couldn't talk. I could breathe, that was all. I got my field dressing out and wound it round my face and left eye. I could see through my right eye and I saw one of my corporals who'd been shot through the foot. I took his boot off, bandaged it up, put his boot on again and he used his rifle as a crutch and together we went back. There was nobody around. Just the dead.

We saw a man. A shell had come over and hit him and knocked off his left arm and his left leg. His left eye was hanging on his cheek, and he was calling out, "Annie!" I shot him. I

had to. Put him out of his misery. It hurt me. It hurt me.

A GERMAN OFFICER:

"The British keep charging forward. Despite the fact that hundreds are already lying dead in the shell holes to our front, fresh waves keep emerging from the assault trenches over there. We have got to fire! . . .

"The British have closed to grenade throwing range and hand grenades fly backwards and forwards. . . .

"High pillars of steam rise from all the machine guns. Most of the steam hoses have been torn off or shot away. Skin hangs in ribbons from the fingers of the burnt hands of the gunners and gun commanders! Constant pressure by their left thumbs on the triggers has turned them into swollen, shapeless lumps of flesh. Their hands rest, as though cramped, on the vibrating weapons.

"18,000 rounds! The other platoon weapon has a stoppage. Gunner Schwarz falls shot through the head, over the belt he is feeding. The belt twist, feeds rounds into the gun crookedly and they jam! Next man forward! The dead man is removed. The gunner strips the feed mechanism, removes the rounds and reloads. Fire; pause; barrel change; fetch ammunition; lay the dead and wounded on the floor of the crater. That is the hard, unrelenting tempo of the morning of 1st July 1916. The sound of machine gun fire can be heard right across the divisional front. The youth of England . . . bled to death in front of Serre. The weapon which was commanded by Unteroffizier Koch from Pforzheim and which was stationed directly on the Serre-Mailly road fires off a last belt! It has fired no fewer 20,000 rounds at the British!"

From *Forgotten Voices of the Somme* by Joshua Levine, Published by Ebury Press. Reprinted by permission of The Random House Group Limited. © 2008.

Jack Sheldon, *The German Army on the Somme* 1914–1916 (South Yorkshire, Pen & Sword Military, 2005), pp. 142–143.

Siegfried Sassoon
"BASE DETAILS"

Front-line soldiers often looked with contempt on generals who, from a safe distance, ordered massive assaults against enemy lines protected by barbed wire and machine guns. Such attacks could cost the lives of tens of thousands of soldiers in just a few days. Siegfried Sassoon (1886–1967), a British poet who served at the front for much of the war and earned a Military Cross for bravery, showed his disdain for coldhearted officers in the following poem, composed in 1917.

If I were fierce, and bald, and short of breath,
   I'd live with scarlet Majors at the Base,
And speed glum heroes up the line to death.
   You'd see me with my puffy petulant face,

Guzzling and gulping in the best hotel,
   Reading the Roll of Honour, "Poor young chap,"
I'd say—"I used to know his father well;
   Yes, we've lost heavily in this last scrap."
And when the war is done and youth stone dead,
I'd toddle safely home and die—in bed.

"Base Details," from Siegfried Sassoon, *Counter-Attack: And Other Poems* (New York: E. P. Dutton & Company, 1947), p. 25.

Wilfred Owen
"DISABLED"

Wilfred Owen (1893–1918), another British poet, volunteered for duty in 1915. At the Battle of the Somme he sustained shell shock, and he was sent to a hospital in Britain. In 1918 he returned to the front and was awarded the Military Cross; he died one week before the Armistice. In the following poem, "Disabled," Owen portrays the enduring misery of war.

He sat in a wheeled chair, waiting for dark,
And shivered in his ghastly suit of gray,
Legless, sewn short at elbow. Through the park
Voices of boys rang saddening like a hymn,
Voices of play and pleasure after day,
Till gathering sleep mothered them from him.

About this time Town used to swing so gay
When glow-lamps budded in the light blue trees,
And girls glanced lovelier as the air grew dim,—
In the old times, before he threw away his knees. . . .

He asked to join. He didn't have to beg;
Smiling they wrote his lie: aged nineteen years.
Germans he scarcely thought of; all their guilt,

Wilfred Owen, *Poems* (London: Chatto and Windus, Ltd., 1920, 1963), p. 32.

And Austria's, did not move him. And no fears
Of Fear came yet. He thought of jeweled hilts
For daggers in plaid socks; of smart salutes;
And care of arms; and leave; and pay arrears;
Esprit de corps [group spirit], and hints for
    young recruits.
And soon, he was drafted out with drums and
    cheers. . . .

Now, he will spend a few sick years in Institutes,
And do what things the rules consider wise,
And take whatever pity they may dole.
Tonight he noticed how the women's eyes
Passed from him to the strong men that were
    whole,
How cold and late it is! Why don't they come
And put him into bed? Why don't they come?

REVIEW QUESTIONS

1. Why was trench warfare so cruel?
2. What mistakes did British generals make in their planning for the Somme offensive?
3. Which lines in either Siegfried Sassoon's or Wilfred Owen's poem do you consider the most powerful?

---

5 Women at War

In order to release men for military service, women in England, France, and Germany responded to their countries' wartime needs and replaced men in all branches of civilian life. They took jobs in munitions factories, worked on farms, were trained for commercial work and in the nursing service. They drove ambulances, mail trucks, and buses. They worked as laboratory assistants, plumbers' helpers, and bank clerks. By performing effectively in jobs formerly occupied by men, women demonstrated that they had an essential role to play in their countries' economic life. By the end of the war, little opposition remained to granting women political rights.

Naomi Loughnan
GENTEEL WOMEN IN THE FACTORIES

Naomi Loughnan was one of millions of women who replaced men in all branches of civilian life, in allied and enemy countries alike, during World War I. She was a young, upper-middle-class woman who lived with her family in London and had never had to work for her living. In her job in a munitions plant, she had to adjust to close association with women from the London slums, to hostel life, and to twelve-hour shifts doing heavy and sometimes dangerous work. The chief motivation for British women of her class was their desire to aid the war effort, not the opportunity to earn substantial wages.

We little thought when we first put on our overalls and caps and enlisted in the Munition Army how much more inspiring our life was to be than we had dared to hope. Though we munition workers sacrifice our ease we gain a life worth living. Our long days are filled with interest, and with the zest of doing work for our country in the grand cause of Freedom. As we handle the weapons of war we are learning great lessons of life. In the busy, noisy workshops we come face to face with every kind of class, and each one of these classes has something to learn from the others. Our muscles may be aching, and the brightness fading a little from our eyes, but our minds are expanding, our very souls are growing stronger. And excellent, too, is the discipline for our bodies, though we do not always recognize this. . . .

The day is long, the atmosphere is breathed and rebreathed, and the oil smells. Our hands are black with warm, thick oozings from the machines, which coat the work and, incidentally, the workers. We regard our horrible, begrimed members [limbs] with disgust and secret pride. . . .

. . . The genteel among us wear gloves. We vie with each other in finding the most up-to-date grease-removers, just as we used to vie about hats. Our hands are not alone in suffering from dirt. . . . [D]ust-clouds, filled with unwelcome life, find a resting-place in our lungs and noses.

The work is hard. It may be, perhaps, from sheer lifting and carrying and weighing, or merely because of those long dragging hours that keep us sitting on little stools in front of whirring, clattering machines that are all too easy to work. We wish sometimes they were not quite so "fool-proof," for monotony is painful. Or life may appear hard to us by reason of those same creeping hours spent on our feet, up and

down, to and fro, and up and down again, hour after hour, until something altogether queer takes place in the muscles of our legs. But we go on. . . . It is amazing what we can do when there is no way of escape but desertion. . . .

. . . The first thing that strikes the new-comer, as the shop door opens, is the great wall of noise that seems to rise and confront one like a tangible substance. The crashing, tearing, rattling whirr of machinery is deafening. And yet, though this may seem almost impossible, the workers get so accustomed to it after a little time that they do not notice it until it stops. . . .

The twelve-hour shift at night, though taking greater toll of nerve and energy, has distinct charms of its own. . . . The first hours seem to go more quickly than the corresponding ones on day work, until at last two o'clock is reached. Then begins a hand-to-hand struggle with Morpheus [Greek god of dreams]. . . . A stern sense of duty, growing feebler as the moments pass, is our only weapon of defence, whereas the crafty god has a veritable armoury of leaden eyelids, weakening pulses, sleep-weighted heads, and slackening wills. He even leads the foremen away to their offices and softens the hearts of languid over-lookers. Some of us succumb, but there are those among us who will not give in. An unbecoming greyness alters our faces, however young and fresh by day, a strange wilting process that steals all youth and beauty from us—until the morning. . . .

Engineering mankind is possessed of the unshakable opinion that no woman can have the mechanical sense. If one of us asks humbly why such and such an alteration is not made to prevent this or that drawback to a machine, she is told, with a superior smile, that a man has worked her machine before her for years, and that therefore if there were any improvement possible it would have been made. As long as we do exactly what we are told and do not attempt to use our brains, we give entire satisfaction, and are treated as nice, good children. Any swerving from the easy path prepared for us by our males

Naomi Loughnan, "Munition Work," in *Women War Workers*, edited by Gilbert Stone (London: George Harrap & Company, 1917), pp. 25, 28–33, 35–38, 40–41.

arouses the most scathing contempt in their manly bosoms. The exceptions are as delightful to meet as they are rare. Women have, however, proved that their entry into the munition world has increased the output. Employers who forget things personal in their patriotic desire for large results are enthusiastic over the success of women in the shops. But their workmen have to be handled with the utmost tenderness and caution lest they should actually imagine it was being suggested that women could do their work equally well, given equal conditions of training—at least where muscle is not the driving force. This undercurrent of jealousy rises to the surface rather often, but as a general rule the men behave with much kindness, and are ready to help with muscle and advice whenever called upon. If eyes are very bright and hair inclined to curl, the muscle and advice do not even wait for a call.

The coming of the mixed classes of women into the factory is slowly but surely having an educative effect upon the men. "Language" is almost unconsciously becoming subdued. There are fiery exceptions who make our hair stand up on end under our close-fitting caps, but a sharp rebuke or a look of horror will often [straighten out] the most truculent. He will at the moment, perhaps, sneer at the "blooming milksop fools of women," but he will be more careful next time. It is grievous to hear the girls also swearing and using disgusting language. Shoulder to shoulder with the children of the slums, the upper classes are having their eyes prised open at last to the awful conditions among which their sisters have dwelt. Foul language, immorality, and many other evils are but the natural outcome of overcrowding and bitter poverty. If some of us, still blind and ignorant of our responsibilities, shrink horrified and repelled from the rougher set, the compliment is returned with open derision and ribald laughter. There is something, too, about the prim prudery of the "genteel" that tickles the East-Ender's [a lower-class person] sharp wit. On the other hand, attempts at friendliness from the more understanding are treated with the utmost suspicion, though once that suspicion is overcome and friendship is established, it is unshakable. Our working hours are highly flavoured by our neighbours' treatment of ourselves and of each other. Laughter, anger, acute confusion, and laughter again, are constantly changing our immediate outlook on life. Sometimes disgust will overcome us, but we are learning with painful clarity that the fault is not theirs whose actions disgust us, but must be placed to the discredit of those other classes who have allowed the continued existence of conditions which generate the things from which we shrink appalled. . . .

Whatever sacrifice we make of wearied bodies, brains dulled by interminable night-shifts, of roughened hands, and faces robbed of their soft curves, it is, after all, so small a thing. We live in safety, we have shelter, and food whenever necessary, and we are even earning quite a lot of money. What is ours beside the great sacrifice? Men in their prime, on the verge of ambition realized, surrounded by the benefits won by their earlier struggles, are offering up their very lives. And those boys with Life, all glorious and untried, spread before them at their feet, are turning a smiling face to Death.

Magda Trott
OPPOSITION TO FEMALE EMPLOYMENT

In the second year of the war a German woman described the hostility faced by women in the work force.

With the outbreak of war men were drawn away from the management of numerous organizations and, gradually, the lack of experienced personnel made itself felt. Women working in offices were therefore urged not to waste the opportunities offered them by the war, and to continue their education so that they would be prepared to take on the position once held by a male colleague, should the occasion arise.

Such occasions have indeed arisen much sooner than anticipated. The demand for educated women has risen phenomenally during the six months since the war began. Women have been employed in banks, in large commercial businesses, in urban offices—everywhere, in fact, where up till now only men had been employed. They are to be tested in order to see whether they can perform with equal success.

All those who were certain that women would be completely successful substitutes for men were painfully disappointed to discover that many women who had worked for years in a firm and were invited to step up to a higher level, now that the men were absent, suddenly handed in their resignations. An enquiry revealed that, especially in recent days, these notices were coming with great frequency and, strange as it may seem, applied mostly to women who had been working in the same company from four to seven years and had now been offered a better and even better-paid job. They said "no" and since there was no possibility for them to remain in their old jobs, they resigned.

The enemies of women's employment were delighted. Here was their proof that women are incapable of holding down responsible positions. Female workers were quite successful as clerks, stenographers, and typists, in fact, in all those positions that require no independent

activity—but as soon as more serious duties were demanded of them, they failed.

Naturally, we enquired of these women why they had given up so quickly, and then the truth of the matter became plain. All women were quite ready, if with some trepidation, to accept the new positions, particularly since the boss made it clear that one of the gentlemen would carefully explain the new assignments to them. Certainly the work was almost entirely new to the young ladies since till now they had only been concerned with their stenography, their books, and so forth. However, they entered their new duties with enthusiasm.

But even on the first day it was noticeable that not everything would proceed as had been supposed. Male colleagues looked askance at the "intruder" who dared to usurp the position and bread of a colleague now fighting for the Fatherland, and who would, it was fervently hoped, return in good health. Moreover, the lady who came as a substitute received exactly half of the salary of the gentleman colleague who had previously occupied the same position. A dangerous implication, since if the lady made good, the boss might continue to draw on female personnel; the saving on salaries would clearly be substantial. It became essential to use all means to show the boss that female help was no substitute for men's work, and a united male front was organized.

It was hardly surprising that all the lady's questions were answered quite vaguely. If she asked again or even a third time, irritated remarks were passed concerning her inadequacy in comprehension, and very soon the male teacher lost patience. Naturally, most of his colleagues supported him and the lady found it difficult, if not impossible, to receive any instruction and was finally forced to resign.

This is what happened in most known cases. We must, however, also admit that occasionally the fault does lie with the lady, who simply did not have sufficient preparation to fill a difficult position. There may be male colleagues who would gladly share information with women; however, these women are unable to understand, because they have too little business experience. In order to prevent this sort of thing, we would counsel all women who are seeking a position in which they hope to advance, to educate themselves as much as possible. All those women who were forced to leave their jobs of long standing might not have been obliged to do so, had they been more concerned in previous years with understanding the overall nature of the business in which they were employed. Their colleagues would surely and generously have answered their questions and given them valuable advice, which would have offered them an overview and thereby avoided the total ignorance with which they entered these advanced positions when they were offered. At least they would have had an inkling and saved themselves the questions that betrayed their great ignorance to their colleagues. They might even have found their way through all the confusion and succeeded in the new position.

Therefore, once again: all you women who want to advance yourselves and create an independent existence, use this time of war as a learning experience and keep your eyes open.

Russian Women in Combat

From 1915 onwards accounts began to appear in American magazines of Russian women disguising themselves as men and joining up with male soldiers, or fighting as all-female units in the Russian army. The first women's unit was called "The Battalion of Death," and its valor on the Russian front inspired a movement for a women's army. By the winter of 1917, five thousand women were in training throughout Russia.

No official statistics of women volunteers in the regular Russian army were kept, but judging by the frequent reports of women soldiers awarded the St. George's Cross for bravery at the front, their numbers were considerable. They came from all classes of Russian society and assumed male names and attire, as the following account relates. It was originally published in a Russian newspaper and was reprinted in *The New York Times* in 1916.

Stories are filtering in from the various belligerent countries telling of actual fighting in the ranks by women. . . . A correspondent of the *Novoe Vremya* tells an interesting story of the experiences of twelve young Russian girls who fought in the ranks as soldiers of the line. The story, as related by one of their number, was also authenticated by the Petrograd correspondent of *The London Times*, who wrote as follows:

"She was called Zoya Smirnov. She came to our staff straight from the advanced positions, where she had spent fourteen months wearing soldier's clothes and fighting with the foe on even terms with the men.

"Zoya Smirnov was only 16 years old. Closely cropped hair gave her the appearance of a boy, and only a thin girlish voice involuntarily betrayed her sex.

"At the beginning Zoya was somewhat shy; she carefully chose her words and replied confusedly to our questions; but later she recovered and told us her entire history, which brought

Current History: A Monthly Magazine of the New York Times, May 1916, pp. 365–367.

tears to the eyes of many a case-hardened veteran who heard it.

"She and her friends decided to go to the war on the eighth day of mobilization—i.e., at the end of July, 1914; and early in August they succeeded in realizing their dream.

"Exactly twelve of them assembled; and they were all nearly the same age and from the same high school. Almost all were natives of Moscow, belonging to the most diversified classes of society, but firmly united in the camaraderie of school life.

"We decided to run away to the war at all costs, said Zoya. It was impossible to run away from Moscow, because we might have been stopped at the station. It was therefore necessary to hire izvozchiks [carriages] and ride out to one of the suburban stations through which the military echelons were continually passing. We left home early in the morning without saying a word to our parents and departed. It was a bit terrible at first; we were very sorry for our fathers and mothers, but the desire to see the war and ourselves kill the Germans overcame all other sentiments.

"And so they attained the desired object. The soldiers treated the little patriots quite paternally and properly, and having concealed them in the cars took them off to the war. A military uniform was obtained for each; they donned these and unobstructed arrived at the Austrian frontier, where they had to detrain and on foot proceed to Lemberg. Here the regimental authorities found out what had happened, but not being able to persuade the young patriots to return home allowed them to march with the regiment.

"The regiment traversed the whole of Galicia; scaled the Carpathians,[1] incessantly participating in battle, and the girls never fell back from it a step, but shared with the men all the privations and horrors of the march and discharged the duties of ordinary privates, since they were taught to shoot and were given rifles.

"Days and months passed.

"The girls almost forgot their past, they hardly responded to their feminine names, for each of them had received a masculine surname, and completely mingled with the men. The soldiers themselves mutually guarded the girls and observed each other's conduct.

"The battles in which the regiment engaged were fierce and sanguinary, particularly in the Spring, when the Germans brought up their heavy artillery to the Carpathians and began to advance upon us with their celebrated phalanx. Our troops underwent a perfect hell and the young volunteers endured it with them."

"Was it terrible?" an officer asked Zoya. "Were you afraid?"

"I should say so! Who wouldn't be afraid? When for the first time they began to fire with their heavy guns, several of us couldn't stand it and began to cry out."

"What did you cry out?"

"We began to call 'Mamma.' Shura was the first to cry, then Lida. They were both 14 years old, and they remembered their mothers all the time. Besides, it seems that I also cried out as well. We all cried. Well, it was frightful even for the men."

"During one of the Carpathian engagements, at night, one of the twelve friends, the sixteen-year-old Zina Morozov, was killed outright by a shell. It struck immediately at her feet, and the entire small body of the girl was torn into fragments." . . .

"After the death of Zina other of her friends were frequently wounded in turn—Nadya, Zhena, and the fourteen-year-old Shura. Zoya herself was wounded twice—the first time in the leg, and the second time in the side. Both wounds were so serious that Zoya was left unconscious on the battlefield, and the stretcher-bearers subsequently discovered her

---

[1]Galicia was an Austrian province in east central Europe, which is today divided between Poland and Ukraine. Lemberg was the capital of Galicia. The Carpathians are a range of mountains stretching through eastern Europe, where many battles were fought in World War I.

only by accident. After the second wound she was obliged to lie at a base hospital for over a month. On being discharged she again proceeded to the positions, endeavoring to find her regiment, but on reaching the familiar trenches she could no longer find a single regimental comrade, not a single fellow-volunteer; they had all gone to another front, and in the trenches sat absolute strangers. The girl lost her presence of mind, and for the first time during the entire campaign began to weep, thus unexpectedly betraying her age and sex. Her unfamiliar fellow-countrymen gazed with amazement upon the strange young noncommissioned officer with the Cross of St. George and medal on her breast, who resembled a stripling and finally proved to be a girl. But the girl had with her all necessary documents, not excepting a certificate giving her the right to wear the St. George's Cross

received for a brave and dashing reconnoissance, and distrustful glances promptly gave place to others full of respect.

"Zoya was finally induced to abandon the trenches, at least for the time being, and to try to engage in nursing at one of the advanced hospitals. She is now working at the divisional hospital of the N—division, in the village of K., ten versts from the Austrian town of Z.

"From her remaining friends whom she left with the regiment which went to another front Zoya has no news whatever.

"What has befallen them? Do these amazing Russian girls continue their disinterested and heroic service to the country, or do graves already hold them, similar to that which was dug for the remnants of poor little Zina, who perished so gloriously in the distant Carpathians?"

REVIEW QUESTIONS

1. How was Naomi Loughnan's life transformed by her job as a munitions worker?
2. What insights into gender and class distinctions at the time of World War I does Loughnan provide?
3. Why, according to Magda Trott, did German women have difficulty gaining acceptance in the work force?
4. How were the Russian women soldiers treated by their male comrades?
5. Would you consider the experiences of the women soldiers in the war a good reason for involving women in battle?

6 The Ethnic Cleansing of Turkey's Armenian Minority

The Armenians in the Ottoman Empire were but one of several minority populations. However, many Armenians had achieved a degree of material prosperity through trade or modest manufacturing enterprises, and this led to growing resentment within the broader Turkish and other Ottoman ethnic communities. Moreover, the Armenian population's strong sense of identity—both as a distinct ethnic group and as a Christian religious community—lent it a sense of confidence that the Ottoman authorities perceived as subversive, particularly since Armenians in Eastern Turkey began more intently to seek a degree of local autonomy within the Ottoman state, but security was not the only issue. Many Turks wanted the government to rid the land of economic competitors. Others believed that Muslims had a religious duty to slaughter the infidels living in their land.

The measures taken against Armenians beginning in 1915 correspond with what we have come to know as ethnic cleansing, and can be characterized as mass murder at the very least. Armenian intellectuals, religious leaders, and political figures found themselves arrested and deported from population centers into Eastern Anatolia, where they and local Armenian men were murdered. Armenian conscripts in the Turkish army, usually segregated into unarmed labor battalions, were executed en masse. Turkish gendarmes marched women, children, and elderly men into the mountains and deserts and ensured their deaths from lack of water and food. Others suffered robbery, rape, or murder at the hands of hostile Turkish or Kurdish villagers. Armenian children were often taken from their families and raised as Turks—another form of ethnic cleansing designed to eliminate every possible trace of "Armenianness." Precise figures vary for Armenian fatalities. Between the most vicious measures in 1915 and the displacements and murders that subsided in 1923, estimates have ranged between 500,000 and perhaps 750,000 at the lower end, and as high as approximately 1.5 million at the higher end.

The Turkish position has long been that the events took place under conditions of bitter warfare, that there were casualties on both sides, and the deaths resulted from the necessity of relocating the Armenian population for strategic reasons (i.e., concern for pro-Russian sympathies among Turkish Armenians and solidarity with their brethren across the hostile border). Both the scale of death and the regime's intentionality have been denied since the 1920s, and the subject has become a taboo in modern Turkish society.

Takhoui Levonian and Yevnig Adrouni
THE SURVIVORS REMEMBER

Takhoui Levonian was fifteen years old when she experienced the violent population transfer of Armenians from her town into southeastern Anatolia. Her account of flight, the violence Armenians experienced, and her abduction at the hands of marauding Turks is consistent with the accounts of many other survivors. She eventually settled in Los Angeles and shared her story in 1981.

We were the first caravan [ordered] to leave with much tears and anguish since it meant separation for so many. They assigned a few soldiers to us and thus we began. We used to travel by day, and in the evenings we stopped to eat and rest. In five to six days we reached Palu. There, while we were washing up, I will never,

Samuel Totten and Williams S. Parsons, eds., *Century of Genocide: Critical Essays and Eyewitness Accounts* (New York: Routledge, 1997), pp. 83–85.

never forget, they took my father away, along with all the men down to 12 years of age. The next day our camp was filled with the Turks and Kurds of Palu, looting, dragging away whatever they could, both possessions and young women. They knocked the mules down to kill them. I was grabbing onto my six-year-old brother; my sister was holding her baby, and my two young sisters were grabbing her skirt; my mother was holding the basket of bread. There was so much confusion, and the noise of bullets shooting by us. Some people were getting shot, and the rest of us were running in the field, not knowing where to go. . . .

Then I saw with my own eyes the Turks beating a fellow name Sahag, who had hid under his wife's dress. They were beating him with hammers, axes right in front of me and his wife. He yelled to her to run away, that we were all going to die a "donkey death." And then I saw the husband of my aunt, who was too old to have been taken previously, and he was being beaten in the head with an ax. They then threw him in the river. It finally calmed down. The Turks left some dead, took some with them, and the rest of us found each other.

At this time it was announced that anyone who would become a Turk could remain here. Otherwise, we must continue on. Many stayed. So we took off again. [We felt] much loss, that was not material loss only, but human loss. We were in tears and anguish as we left.

From Palu to Dikranagerd they tormented us a great deal. We suffered a lot. These was no water or food. Whatever my mom had in her bag, she gave us a little at a time. We walked the whole day, 10 to 15 days. No shoes remained on our feet. We finally reached Dikranagerd. There, by the water, we washed, and whatever little dry bread we had we wetted it and ate it.

Word came that the *vali* [governor] wanted from the Armenians a very pretty 12-year-old girl. . . . So by night, they came with their lamps looking for such a girl. They found one, dragged her from the mother, saying to the weeping mother that they will return her. Later, they returned the child, in horrible condition, almost dead, and left her at her mother's knees.

The mother was weeping so badly, and, of course, the child could not make it and died. The women could not comfort her. Finally, several of the women tried to dig a hole, and with the help of one of the *gendarme's* guns, they buried the girl and covered her. Dikranagerd had a large wall around it, so my mother and a few other women wrote on it, "Shushan buried here."

We remained under the walls [where Shushan was buried] for two to three days. Then they made us leave again. This time they assigned to us an elderly *gendarme.* He had tied to his horse a large container of water and the whole way he kept giving it to children and never himself rode the horse, but allowed old women to take turns on it. We went to Mardin. He also always took us near the villages so we could buy some food, and he would not allow the villagers to sell food at expensive prices. A lot of people either died on the way or stayed behind, because they could not keep up. So by the time we reached Mardin we were a lot less in number although still a lot. They deposited us in a large field. There they gave us food. . . . At this point my mother was not with us.

A Kurd woman came and told my sister that two horsemen were going to kidnap me. She panicked and started looking for my mom, but she was not around. So she thought of giving the baby, who was in her arms, to the Kurd woman, so that she would help me. So she disguised me, but when we turned around, the woman was gone with the baby.

Turks used to pay high prices for babies, probably the woman sold him. My poor sister, Zarouhi, went crazy. I, too, was going crazy, feeling that I was the cause. I cried and cried. We remained in Mardin for five days and never found the baby. My poor sister was lactating, and her milk was full but there was no baby to nurse . . . .

It came time to leave, and we had to leave the baby behind with uncontrollable tears. The journey was dreadful. With no shoes on our feet, it was so painful to walk on the paths they took us on. We used to wrap cloth on them to ease the pain, but it didn't really help much. There was no water. In fact, at one stretch, for three full days, we had no water at all. The children would cry: "Water, water, water." One of the children died.

Then toward morning one day, my sister and another woman crawled out of camp to a far place and brought some water in a tin can. Finally, they dumped us next to a small river. There my mother took me to the river to wash my face which was always covered up, except for my eyes. But one of the *gendarmes*, having spotted my eyes, showed up and grabbed me.

My mother fainted, and, acting bravely, I shook his hand loose and ran, mingling among the people. I could hear the women yelling to my mother to wake up, that I got away. As the caravan moved again, I kept watching that man, always trying to stay behind him. . . .

REVIEW QUESTIONS

1. Why is ethnic cleansing almost always accompanied by cruelty?
2. Working with your instructor, draw up a list of places where ethnic cleansing has taken place since the end of World War I.

7 The Paris Peace Conference

The most terrible war the world had experienced ended in November 1918; in January 1919, representatives of the victorious powers assembled in Paris to draw up a peace settlement. The principal figures at the Paris Peace Conference were Woodrow Wilson (1856–1924), president of the United States; David Lloyd George (1863–1945), prime minister of Great Britain; Georges Clemenceau (1841–1929), premier of France; and Vittorio Orlando (1860–1952), premier of Italy. Disillusioned intellectuals and the war-weary masses turned to Wilson as the prince of peace who would fashion a new and better world.

Woodrow Wilson
THE IDEALISTIC VIEW

Wilson sought a peace of justice and reconciliation, one based on democratic and Christian ideals, as the following excerpts from his speeches illustrate.

(May 26, 1917)

We are fighting for the liberty, the self-government, and the undictated development of all peoples, and every feature of the settlement that concludes this war must be conceived and executed for that purpose. Wrongs must first

The Public Papers of Woodrow Wilson: War and Peace, part 3, vol. 1 (New York: Harper, 1927), p. 50–51.

be righted and then adequate safeguards must be created to prevent their being committed again. . . .

. . . No people must be forced under sovereignty under which it does not wish to live. No territory must change hands except for the purpose of securing those who inhabit it a fair chance of life and liberty. No indemnities must be insisted on except those that constitute payment for manifest wrongs done. No readjustments of power must be made except such as will tend to secure the future peace of the world and the future welfare and happiness of its peoples.

And then the free peoples of the world must draw together in some common covenant, some genuine and practical co-operation that will in effect combine their force to secure peace and justice in the dealings of nations with one another.

The following are excerpts from the Fourteen Points, the plan for peace that Wilson announced on January 8, 1918.

IV. Adequate guarantees given and taken that national armaments will be reduced to the lowest point consistent with domestic safety.

V. A free, open-minded, and absolutely impartial adjustment of all colonial claims, based upon a strict observance of the principle that in determining all such questions of sovereignty the interests of the populations concerned must have equal weight with the equitable claims of the government whose title is to be determined. . . .

VIII. All French territory should be freed and the invaded portions restored, and the wrong done to France by Prussia in 1871 in the matter of Alsace-Lorraine, which has unsettled the peace of the world for nearly fifty years, should be righted, in order that peace may once more be made secure in the interest of all.

IX. A readjustment of the frontiers of Italy should be effected along clearly recognizable lines of nationality.

X. The peoples of Austria-Hungary, whose place among the nations we wish to see safeguarded and assured, should be accorded the freest opportunity of autonomous development. . . .

XII. The Turkish portions of the present Ottoman Empire should be assured a secure sovereignty, but the other nationalities which are now under Turkish rule should be assured an undoubted security of life and an absolutely

unmolested opportunity of autonomous development, and the Dardanelles should be permanently opened as a free passage to the ships and commerce of all nations under international guarantees.

XIII. An independent Polish state should be erected which should include the territories inhabited by indisputably Polish populations, which should be assured a free and secure access to the sea, and whose political and economic independence and territorial integrity should be guaranteed by international covenant.

XIV. A general association of nations must be formed under specific covenants for the purpose of affording mutual guarantees of political independence and territorial integrity to great and small states alike.

(February 11, 1918)

. . . The principles to be applied [in the peace settlement] are these:

First, that each part of the final settlement must be based upon the essential justice of that particular case and upon such adjustments as are most likely to bring a peace that will be permanent;

Second, that peoples and provinces are not to be bartered about from sovereignty to sovereignty as if they were mere chattels and pawns in a game, even the great game, now forever discredited, of the balance of power; but that

Third, every territorial settlement involved in this war must be made in the interest and for the benefit of the populations concerned, and not as a part of any mere adjustment or compromise of claims amongst rival states; and

Fourth, that all well-defined national aspiration shall be accorded the utmost satisfaction that can be accorded them without introducing new or perpetuating old elements of discord and antagonism that would be likely in time to break the peace of Europe and consequently of the world.

(April 6, 1918)

. . . We are ready, whenever the final reckoning is made, to be just to the German people, deal fairly with the German power, as with all others. There can be no difference between peoples in the final judgment, if it is indeed to be a righteous judgment. To propose anything but justice, even-handed and dispassionate justice, to Germany at any time, whatever the outcome of the war, would be to renounce and dishonor our own cause. For we ask nothing that we are not willing to accord.

———

(December 16, 1918)

. . . The war through which we have just passed has illustrated in a way which never can be forgotten the extraordinary wrongs which can be perpetrated by arbitrary and irresponsible power.

It is not possible to secure the happiness and prosperity of the world, to establish an enduring peace, unless the repetition of such wrongs is rendered impossible. This has indeed been a people's war. It has been waged against absolutism and militarism, and these enemies of liberty must from this time forth be shut out from the possibility of working their cruel will upon mankind.

———

(January 3, 1919)

. . . Our task at Paris is to organize the friendship of the world, to see to it that all the moral forces that make for right and justice and liberty are united and are given a vital organization to which the peoples of the world will readily and gladly respond. In other words, our task is no less colossal than this, to set up a new international psychology, to have a new atmosphere.

———

(January 25, 1919)

. . . We are . . . here to see that every people in the world shall choose its own masters and govern its own destinies, not as we wish, but as it wishes. We are here to see, in short, that the very foundations of this war are swept away.

Those foundations were the private choice of small coteries of civil rulers and military staffs. Those foundations were the aggression of great powers upon the small. Those foundations were the holding together of empires of unwilling subjects by the duress of arms. Those foundations were the power of small bodies of men to work their will upon mankind and use them as pawns in a game. And nothing less than the emancipation of the world from these things will accomplish peace.

Georges Clemenceau
FRENCH DEMANDS FOR SECURITY AND REVENGE

Wilson's promised new world clashed with French demands for security and revenge. Almost all the fighting on the war's Western Front had taken place in France; its industries and farmlands lay in ruins, and many of its young men had perished. France had been invaded by Germany in 1870 as well as in 1914, so the French believed that only by crippling Germany could they gain security. Premier Georges Clemenceau, who was called "the Tiger," dismissed Wilson's vision of a new world as mere noble sentiment divorced from reality, and he fought tenaciously to gain security for France. Clemenceau's profound hatred and mistrust of Germany are revealed in his book *The Grandeur and Misery of Victory* (1930), written a decade after the Paris Peace Conference.

For the catastrophe of 1914 the Germans are responsible. Only a professional liar would deny this. . . .

What after all is this war, prepared, undertaken, and waged by the German people, who flung aside every scruple of conscience to let it loose, hoping for a peace of enslavement under the yoke of a militarism destructive of all human dignity? It is simply the continuance, the recrudescence, of those never-ending acts of violence by which the first savage tribes carried out their depredations with all the resources of barbarism. The means improve with the ages. The ends remain the same. . . .

Germany, in this matter, was unfortunate enough to allow herself (in spite of her skill at dissimulation) to be betrayed into an excess of candour by her characteristic tendency to go to extremes. *Deutschland über alles. Germany above everything!* That, and nothing less, is what she asks, and when once her demand is satisfied she will let you enjoy a peace under the yoke. . . .

And what is this "Germanic civilization," this monstrous explosion of the will to power, which threatens openly to . . . [impose] the implacable mastery of a race . . . ? [The historian Heinrich von Trieitschke asserts that Germany] finds herself condemned, by her very greatness, either to

absorb all nations in herself or to return to nothingness. . . . Ought we not all to feel menaced in our very vitals by this mad doctrine of universal Germanic supremacy over England, France, America, and every other country? . . .

What document more suitable to reveal the direction of "German culture" than the famous manifesto of the ninety-three super-intellectuals of Germany,[1] issued to justify the bloodiest and the least excusable of military aggressions against the great centres of civilization? At the moment . . . violated Belgium lay beneath the heel of the malefactor (October 1914) . . . [and German troops were] razing . . . great historical buildings to the ground [and] burning down . . . libraries. . . .

Professor Ostwald had already written, *"Germany has reached a higher stage of civilization than the other peoples, and the result of the War will be an organization of Europe under German leadership."* Professor Haeckel had demanded *"the conquest of London, the division of Belgium between Germany and Holland, the annexation of North-east France, of Poland, the Baltic Provinces, the Congo, and a great part of the English colonies. . ."*

Coming from duly hallmarked professors, such statements explain all German warfare by alleging that Germany's destiny is universal domination.

Georges Clemenceau, *The Grandeur and Misery of Victory*, trans. F. M. Atkinson (New York: Harcourt Brace, 1930), pp. 105, 107–108, 115–117, 273–274

---

[1]Shortly after the outbreak of war, ninety-three leading German scholars and scientists addressed a letter to the world, defending Germany's actions.—Eds.

REVIEW QUESTIONS

1. What principles did Woodrow Wilson want to serve as the basis of the peace settlement?
2. According to Wilson, what were the principal reasons for the outbreak of war in 1914?
3. What accusations did Georges Clemenceau make against the German national character?
4. How did Clemenceau respond to the manifesto of the German intellectuals?
5. Why, more than a decade after the war, did Clemenceau believe that Germany should still be feared?

8 The Bolshevik Revolution

In March 1917, in the middle of World War I, Russians were demoralized. The army, poorly trained, inadequately equipped, and incompetently led, had suffered staggering losses; everywhere soldiers were deserting. Food shortages and low wages drove workers to desperation; the loss of fathers and sons at the front embittered peasants. Discontent was keenest in Petrograd, (now St. Petersberg), where on March 9, two hundred thousand striking workers shouting "Down with autocracy!" packed the streets. After some bloodshed, government troops refused to fire on them. Faced with a broad and debilitating crisis—violence and anarchy in the capital, breakdown of transport, uncertain food and fuel supplies, and general disorder—Tsar Nicholas II was forced to turn over authority to a provisional government, thereby ending three centuries of tsarist rule under the Romanov dynasty.

The Provisional Government, after July 1917 guided by Aleksandr Kerensky (1881–1970), sought to transform Russia into a Western-style liberal state, but the government failed to comprehend the urgency with which the Russian peasants wanted the landlords' lands, and soldiers and the masses wanted peace. Resentment spiraled. Kerensky's increasing unpopularity and the magnitude of popular unrest seemed to the Bolsheviks' leader, Vladimir Ilyich Lenin (1870–1924), then in hiding, to offer the long-expected opportunity for the Bolsheviks to seize power and bring about a socialist revolution.

V. I. Lenin
WHAT IS TO BE DONE?

The most dynamic leader of the Russian Marxist movement, Lenin believed that on its own the working class could never achieve a successful revolution; workers without the right leadership could not rise above petty trade unionism. A seminal document of Marxism-Leninism was Lenin's pamphlet *What Is to Be Done?* published in 1902, fifteen years before the tsar's overthrow. In this tract, Lenin argued that given the ignorance of the working class, revolutionary leadership had to come from a close-knit vanguard of dedicated and disciplined professional revolutionaries who comprehended what is required for building a successful revolutionary movement. Following are excerpts from Lenin's pamphlet.

Without revolutionary theory there can be no revolutionary movement. This idea cannot be insisted upon too strongly. . . .

. . . I assert: (1) that no revolutionary movement can endure without a stable organisation of leaders maintaining continuity; (2) that the broader the popular mass drawn spontaneously into the struggle, which forms the basis of the movement and participates in it, the more urgent the need for such an organisation, and the more solid this organisation must be (for it is much easier for all sorts of demagogues to sidetrack the more backward sections of the masses); (3) that such an organisation must consist chiefly of people professionally engaged in revolutionary activity; (4) that in an autocratic state, the more we *confine* the membership of such an organisation to people who are professionally engaged in revolutionary activity and who have been professionally trained in the art of combating the political police, the more difficult will it be to unearth the organisation; and (5) the *greater* will be the number of people from the working class and from the other social classes who will be able to join the movement and perform active work in it . . .

. . . The only serious organisational principle for the active workers of our movement should be the strictest secrecy, the strictest selection of members, and the training of professional revolutionaries. Given these qualities something

even more than "democratism" would be guaranteed to us, namely, complete, comradely, mutual confidence among revolutionaries. . . . They have a lively sense of their *responsibility*, knowing as they do from experience that an organisation of real revolutionaries will stop at nothing to rid itself of an unworthy member. . . .

. . . Our worst sin with regard to organisation consists in the fact that *by our primitiveness we have lowered the prestige of revolutionary in Russia.* A person who is flabby and shaky on questions of theory, who has a narrow outlook, who pleads the spontaneity of the masses as an excuse for his own sluggishness, who resembles a trade-union secretary more than a spokesman of the people, who is unable to conceive of a broad and bold plan that would command the respect even of opponents, and who is inexperienced and clumsy in his own professional art—the art of combating the political police—such a man is not a revolutionary, but a wretched amateur!

V. I. Lenin
THE CALL TO POWER

On November 6 (October 24 by the old-style calendar then in use in Russia), Lenin urged immediate action, as the following document reveals.

. . . The situation is critical in the extreme. In fact it is now absolutely clear that to delay the uprising would be fatal.

With all my might I urge comrades to realise that everything now hangs by a thread; that we are confronted by problems which are not to be solved by conferences or congresses (even congresses of Soviets), but exclusively by peoples, by the masses, by the struggle of the armed people. The bourgeois onslaught of the

Kornilovites [followers of General Kornilov, who tried to establish a military dictatorship] show that we must not wait. We must at all costs, this very evening, this very night, arrest the government, having first disarmed the officer cadets (defeating them, if they resist), and so on.

We must not wait! We may lose everything!

Who must take power?

That is not important at present. Let the Revolutionary Military Committee [Bolshevik organization working within the army and navy] do it, or "some other institution" which

Collected Works of V. I. Lenin, vol. 26 (Moscow: Progress Publishers, 1964), pp. 234–235.

will declare that it will relinquish power only to the true representatives of the interests of the people, the interests of the army (the immediate proposal of peace), the interests of the peasants (the land to be taken immediately and private property abolished), the interests of the starving.

All districts, all regiments, all forces must be mobilised at once and must immediately send their delegations to the Revolutionary Military Committee and to the Central Committee of the Bolsheviks [governing organization of the Bolshevik party] with the insistent demand that under no circumstances should power be left in the hands of Kerensky and Co. . . . not under any circumstances; the matter must be decided without fail this very evening, or this very night.

History will not forgive revolutionaries for procrastinating when they could be victorious today (and they certainly will be victorious today), while they risk losing much tomorrow, in fact, they risk losing everything.

If we seize power today, we seize it not in opposition to the Soviets but on their behalf.

The seizure of power is the business of the uprising; its political purpose will become clear after the seizure. . . .

. . . It would be an infinite crime on the part of the revolutionaries were they to let the chance slip, knowing that the *salvation of the revolution,* the offer of peace, the salvation of Petrograd, salvation from famine, the transfer of the land to the peasants depend upon them.

The government is tottering. It must be *given the death-blow* at all costs.

To delay action is fatal.

In the prevailing anarchy following the Bolshevik seizure of power, Russia lay open to the German armies. To consolidate Bolshevik power, Lenin signed an agreement that ended the war with Germany, who imposed a punishing peace treaty. With Russia out of the war and eager to emerge victorious before the Americans could significantly bolster the French and British, the Germans launched powerful offensives on the Western Front that ultimately failed.

REVIEW QUESTIONS

1. According to V. I. Lenin, what were the requirements of a revolutionary organization and a revolutionary elite?
2. What promises did V. I. Lenin hold out to his supporters should the revolution succeed?
3. How would you define, from the evidence here offered, a revolutionary situation? What factors create it?

---

9 The War and European Consciousness

World War I was a great turning point in the history of the West. The war left many with the gnawing feeling that Western civilization had lost its vitality and was caught in a rhythm of breakdown. It seemed that Western civilization was fragile and perishable, that Western people, despite their extraordinary accomplishments, were never more than a step or two away from barbarism. Surely, any civilization that could allow such senseless slaughter to last four years had entered its decline and could look forward to only the darkest of futures.

Now only the naive could believe in continuous progress, a principal dogma of nineteenth-century liberal culture. Western civilization had entered an age of violence, anxiety, and doubt.

The Enlightenment worldview, weakened in the nineteenth century by the assault of Romantics, Social Darwinists, extreme nationalists, race mystics, and glorifiers of the irrational, was now disintegrating. The enormity of the war had shattered faith in the capacity of reason to deal with crucial social and political questions. It appeared that civilization was fighting an unending and seemingly hopeless battle against the irrational elements in human nature. Six months after the outbreak of war, Freud described the conflict as the resurgence of primitive, aggressive, and destructive instincts that civilization seeks to suppress. Freed from civilization's restraints, said Freud, man has reverted to his primal nature. Thinking people feared that war would be a continuous phenomenon in the twentieth century.

The war produced a generation of young people who had reached their maturity in combat. Violence had become a way of life for millions of soldiers hardened by battle, and for millions of civilians aroused by four years of war stories. The relentless massacre of Europe's young men had a brutalizing effect. For many, violence, cruelty, suffering, and even wholesale death seemed to be natural and acceptable components of human existence. The sanctity of the individual seemed to be liberal and Christian claptrap. The fascination with, if not worship of, violence and contempt for life fueled radical movements. Particularly in Germany, the veterans who aspired to recapture the exhilaration experienced in combat and men who had been too young to fight but were inspired by the heroic deeds of their elders made ideal recruits for extremist political movements that glorified action and brutality and promised to rescue society from a decadent liberalism.

D. H. Lawrence
DISILLUSIONMENT

World War I caused many intellectuals to have grave doubts about the Enlightenment tradition and the future of Western civilization. More than ever, the belief in human goodness, reason, and the progress of humanity seemed an illusion. Despite its many accomplishments, some intellectuals contended that Western civilization was flawed and perishable. The British novelist D. H. Lawrence (1885–1930) understood that the brutality and hate unleashed by the war had ruined old Europe and would give rise to even greater evils. On the day the armistice was signed, he warned prophetically:

I suppose you think the war is over and that we shall go back to the kind of world you lived in before it. But the war isn't over. The hate and evil is greater now than ever. Very soon war will break out again and overwhelm you. . . . The crowd outside thinks that Germany is crushed forever. But the Germans will soon rise again.

Quoted in Samuel Hynes, *A War Imagined* (New York: Atheneum, 1991), p. 266.

Europe is done for. . . . The war isn't over. Even if the fighting should stop, the evil will be worse because the hate will be dammed up in men's hearts and will show itself in all sorts of ways which will be worse than war. Whatever happens there can be no Peace on Earth.

Ernst von Salomon
BRUTALIZATION OF THE INDIVIDUAL

Many returned veterans, their whole being enveloped by the war, continued to yearn for the excitement of battle and the fellowship of the trenches. Brutalized by the war, these men became ideal recruits for Fascist parties that relished violence and sought the destruction of the liberal state.

Immediately after the war ended, thousands of soldiers and adventurers joined the Free Corps—volunteer brigades that fought Communists in Poland, Latvia, and Estonia and Communist revolutionaries in Germany. Many of these freebooters later became members of Hitler's movement. Ernst von Salomon, a leading spokesman of the Free Corps movement, was a sixteen-year-old student in Berlin when the defeated German army marched home. In the passage that follows, taken from his book *Die Geächteten* (The Outlaws), published in 1930, he describes the soldiers who "will always carry the trenches in their blood."

The soldiers walked quickly, pressed closely to each other. Suddenly the first four came into sight, looking lifeless. They had stony, rigid faces. . . .

Then came the others. Their eyes lay deep in dark, gray, sharp-edged hollows under the shadow of their helmets. They looked neither right nor left, but straight ahead, as if under the power of a terrifying target in front of them; as if they peered from a mud hole or a trench over torn-up earth. In front of them lay emptiness. They spoke not a word. . . .

O God, how these men looked, as they came nearer—those utterly exhausted, immobile faces under their steel helmets, those bony limbs, those ragged dusty uniforms! And around them an infinite void. It was as if they had drawn a magic circle around themselves, in which dangerous forces, invisible to outsiders, worked their secret spell. Did they still carry in their minds the madness of a thousand battles compressed into whirling visions, as they carried in their uniforms the dirt and the dust of shell-torn fields? The sight was unbearable. They marched like envoys of death, of dread, of the most deadly and solitary coldness. And here was their homeland, warmth, and happiness. Why were they so silent? Why did they not smile?

. . . When I saw these deadly determined faces, these faces as hard as if hacked out of wood, these eyes that glanced past the onlookers, unresponsive, hostile—yes, hostile indeed—then I knew—it suddenly came over me in a fright—that everything had been utterly different from what we had thought, all of us who stood here watching. . . . What did we know about these men? About the war in the trenches? About our soldiers? Oh God, it was terrible: What we had

From *Die Geächteten* (Berlin: Ernst Rowohlt Verlag, 1931), pp. 28–30, 34–35. Excerpt translated by Theodore H. Von Laue. Reprinted by permission of Angela Von Laue.

been told was all untrue. We had been told lies. These were not our beloved heroes, the protectors of our homes—these were men who did not belong to us, gathered here to meet them. They did not want to belong to us; they came from other worlds with other laws and other friendships. And all of a sudden everything that I had hoped and wished for, that had inspired me, turned shallow and empty. . . . What an abysmal error it had been to believe for four years that these men belonged to us. Now that misunderstanding vanished. . . .

Then I suddenly understood. These were not workers, peasants, students; no, these were not mechanics, white-collar employees, businessmen, officials—these were soldiers. . . . These were men who had responded to the secret call of blood, of spirit, volunteers one way or the other, men who had experienced exacting comradeship and the things behind things— who had found a home in war, a fatherland, a community, and a nation. . . .

The homeland belonged to them; the nation belonged to them. What we had blabbered like marketwomen, they had actually lived. . . . The trenches were their home, their fatherland, their nation. And they had never used these words; they never believed in them; they believed in themselves. The war held them in its grip and dominated them; the war will never discharge them; they will never return home; they will always carry the trenches in their blood, the closeness of death, the dread, the intoxication, the iron. And suddenly they were to become peaceful citizens, set again in solid every-day routines? Never! That would mean a counterfeit that was bound to fail. The war is over; the warriors are still marching, . . . dissatisfied when they are demobilized, explosive when they stay together. The war had not given them answers; it had achieved no decision. The soldiers continue to march. . . .

Appeals were posted on the street corners for volunteer units to defend Germany's eastern borders. The day after the troops marched into our town, I volunteered. I was accepted and outfitted. Now I too was a soldier.

Friedrich Wilhelm Heinz
THE PERSISTENT WAR SPIRIT

The brutalizing effect of the war is evident in this statement by Friedrich Wilhelm, a veteran who fought with the Free Corps and subsequently became a high ranking official in the S. A., a Nazi paramilitary force that intimidated and assaulted Jews and opponents of Hitler.

People told us that the War was over. That made us laugh. We ourselves are the War. Its flame burns strongly in us. It envelops our whole being and fascinates us with the enticing urge to destroy. We obeyed and marched onto the battlefields of the postwar world just as we had gone into battle on the Western Front: singing, reckless, and filled with the joy of adventure as we marched to the attack; silent, deadly, remorseless in battle.

Robert G. L. Waite, *Vanguard of Nazism: The Free Corps Movement in Postwar Germany, 1918–1923* (New York: W. W. Norton, 1969), p. 42.

Erich Maria Remarque
THE LOST GENERATION

Although the war stirred militarism and violent passions, many people—including veterans—were repelled by the slaughter and abandoned the popular romantic view that war was glorious and heroic. These veterans saw themselves as part of a lost generation decimated physically and emotionally by the war. In Erich Maria Remarque's *All Quiet on the Western Front* (1929), the most famous literary work to emerge from World War I, a wounded German soldier observing the dying and mutilated in the hospital reflects on the war and his future. There is no fascination for war here.

A man cannot realize that above such shattered bodies there are still human faces in which life goes its daily round. And this is only one hospital, one single station; there are hundreds of thousands in Germany, hundreds of thousands in France, hundreds of thousands in Russia. How senseless is everything that can ever be written, done, or thought, when such things are possible. It must be all lies and of no account when the culture of a thousand years could not prevent this stream of blood being poured out, these torture-chambers in their hundreds of thousands. A hospital alone shows what war is.

I am young, I am twenty years old; yet I know nothing of life but despair, death, fear, and fatuous superficiality cast over an abyss of sorrow. I see how peoples are set against one another, and in silence, unknowingly, foolishly, obediently, innocently slay one another. I see that the keenest brains of the world invent weapons and words to make it yet more refined and enduring. And all men of my age, here and over there, throughout the whole world see these things; all my generation is experiencing these things with me. What would our fathers do if we suddenly stood up and came before them and [put forward] our account? What do they expect of us if a time ever comes when the war is over? Through the years our business has been killing;—it was our first calling in life. Our knowledge of life is limited to death. What will happen afterwards? And what shall come out of us?

Erich Maria Remarque, *All Quiet on the Western Front* (New York: Little Brown, 1929) pp. 268–271.

REVIEW QUESTIONS

1. In what ways were D. H. Lawrence's words prophetic?
2. How did World War I contribute to the rise of radicalism in Germany?
3. Why do you think many veterans felt part of a lost generation?

CHAPTER 12

Era of Totalitarianism

ADOLF HITLER BEFORE HIS LABOR ARMY AT NUREMBERG, Germany September 1938 in a scene designed to display Hitler's power. (*Bettmann/Getty Images*)

Following World War I, Fascist movements arose in Italy, Germany, and many other European countries. Although these movements differed—each a product of separate national histories and the outlook of its leader—they shared a hatred of liberalism, democracy, and Communism; a commitment to aggressive nationalism; and a glorification of the party leader. Fascist leaders cleverly utilized myths, rituals, and pageantry to mobilize and manipulate the masses.

Several conditions fostered the rise of Fascism. One factor was the fear of Communism among the middle and upper classes. Inspired by the success of the Bolsheviks in Russia, Communists in other lands were calling for the establishment of Soviet-style republics. Increasingly afraid of a Communist takeover, industrialists, landowners, government officials, army leaders, prominent clergy, professionals, and shopkeepers were attracted to Fascist movements that promised to protect their nations from this threat. A second factor contributing to the growth of Fascism was the disillusionment of World War I veterans and the mood of violence bred by the war. The thousands of veterans facing unemployment and poverty made ideal recruits for Fascist parties that glorified combat and organized private armies. A third contributing factor was the inability of democratic parliamentary governments to cope with the problems that burdened postwar Europe. Having lost confidence in the procedures and values of democracy, many people joined Fascist movements that promised strong leadership, an end to party conflicts, and a unified national will.

Fascism's appeal to nationalist feelings also drew people into the movement. In a sense, Fascism expressed the aggressive racial nationalism that had emerged in the late nineteenth century. Fascists saw themselves as dedicated idealists engaged in a heroic struggle to rescue their nations from domestic and foreign enemies; they aspired to regain lands lost by their countries in World War I or to acquire lands denied them by the Paris Peace Conference.

Fascists glorified instinct, will, and blood as the true forces of life; they openly attacked the ideals of reason, liberty, and equality—the legacies of the Enlightenment and the French Revolution. At the center of German Fascism (National Socialism, or Nazism) was a bizarre racial mythology that preached the superiority of the German race and the inferiority of others, particularly Jews and Slavs.

Benito Mussolini, founder of the Italian Fascist Party, came to power in 1922. Although he established a one-party state, he was less successful than Adolf Hitler, the leader of the German National Socialists, in controlling the state and the minds of the people. After gaining power as chancellor of the German government in 1933, Hitler moved to establish a totalitarian state.

In the 1930s, the term *totalitarianism* was commonly used to describe the Fascist regime in Italy, the National Socialist regime in Germany, and the Communist regime in the Soviet Union. To a degree that far exceeds the ancient tyrannies and early modern autocratic states, these dictatorships aspired to and, with varying degrees of success, did attain control over the individual's consciousness and behavior and all phases of political, social, and cultural life. To many people it seemed that a crises-riddled democracy was dying and that the future belonged to these dynamic totalitarian movements.

Totalitarianism was a twentieth-century phenomenon, for such all-embracing control over the individual and society could have been achieved only in an age of modern ideology, technology, and bureaucracy. The ideological aims and social and economic policies of Hitler and Stalin differed fundamentally. However, both Communist Russia and Nazi Germany shared the totalitarian goal of monolithic unity and total domination, and both employed similar methods to achieve it. Mussolini's Italy is more accurately called *authoritarian*, for the party-state either did not intend to control all phases of life or lacked the means to do so. Moreover, Mussolini hesitated to use the ruthless methods that Hitler and Stalin employed so readily.

Striving for total unity, control, and obedience, the totalitarian dictatorship is the antithesis of liberal democracy. It abolishes all competing political parties, suppresses individual liberty, eliminates or regulates private institutions, and utilizes the modern state's bureaucracy and technology to impose its ideology and enforce its commands. The party-state determines what people should believe—what values they should hold. There is no room for individual thinking, private moral judgment, or individual conscience. The individual possesses no natural rights that the state must respect.

Unlike previous dictatorial regimes, the dictatorships of both the Left and the Right sought to legitimatize their rule by gaining the masses' approval. They claimed that their governments were higher and truer expressions of the people's will. The Soviet and Nazi dictatorships established their rule in the name of the people—the German Volk or the Soviet proletariat.

A distinctive feature of totalitarianism is the overriding importance of the leader, who is seen as infallible and invincible. The masses' slavish adulation of the leader and their uncritical acceptance of the dogma that the leader or the party is always right promote loyalty, dedication, and obedience and distort rational thinking.

Totalitarian leaders want more than power for its own sake; in the last analysis, they seek to transform the world according to an all-embracing ideology, a set of convictions and beliefs, which, says Hannah Arendt, "pretend[s] to know the mysteries of the whole historical process—the secrets of the past, the intricacies of the present, the uncertainties of the future." The ideology constitutes a higher and exclusive truth, based on a law of history, and it contains a dazzling vision of the future—a secular New Jerusalem—that strengthens the will of the faithful and attracts converts.

Like a religion, the totalitarian ideology provides its adherents with beliefs that make society and history intelligible, that explain all of existence in an emotionally gratifying way. Again like a religion, it creates true believers, who feel that they are participating in a great cause—a heroic fight against evil—that gives meaning to their lives.

Not only did the totalitarian religion-ideology supply followers with a cause that claimed absolute goodness, it also provided a devil. For the Soviets, the source of evil and the cause of all the people's hardships were the degenerate capitalists, the traitorous Trotskyites, or the saboteurs and foreign agents, who impeded the realization of the socialist society. For the Nazis, the devil was the conspirator Jew. These "evil" ones must be eliminated in order to realize the totalitarian movement's vision of the future. Thus, totalitarian regimes liquidate large segments of the population designated as "enemies of the people." Historical necessity or a higher purpose demands and justifies their liquidation. The appeal to historical necessity has all the power of a great myth. Presented as a world-historical struggle between the forces of good and the forces of evil, the myth incites fanaticism and numbs the conscience. Seemingly decent people engage in terrible acts of brutality with no remorse, convinced that they are waging a righteous war.

Unlike earlier autocratic regimes, the totalitarian dictatorship is not satisfied with its subjects' outward obedience; it demands the masses' unconditional loyalty and enthusiastic support. It strives to control the inner person: to shape thoughts, feelings, and attitudes in accordance with the party ideology, which becomes an official creed. It seeks to create a "new man," one who dedicates himself body and soul to the party and its ideology. Such unquestioning, faithful subjects can be manipulated by the party.

The totalitarian dictatorship deliberately politicizes all areas of human activity. Ideology pervades works of literature, history, philosophy, art, and even science. It dominates the school curriculum and influences everyday speech and social relations. The state is concerned with everything its citizens do: there is no distinction between public and private life, and every institution comes under the party-state's authority. If voluntary support for the regime cannot be generated by indoctrination, then the state unhesitatingly resorts to terror and violence to compel obedience.

1 Socialist Condemnation of the Bolsheviks

The Bolshevik Revolution's call for a new society free of exploitation made a profound impression around the world. Yet its reliance on force and compulsion, entailing gross disregard for human life and dignity, also aroused strong protest within the socialist camp.

PROCLAMATION OF THE KRONSTADT REBELS

In March 1921 the sailors at the Kronstadt naval base, in league with the workers of nearby Petrograd (St. Petersberg)—all ardent allies of the Bolsheviks in 1917–1918—revolted against the repressive Communist government. The high expectations created by the revolution clashed brutally with Lenin's ruthless determination to restore order to a country utterly defeated in World War I and threatened with anarchy and dissolution. In their disillusionment the Kronstadt sailors and their working-class allies reaffirmed their revolutionary ideals (expressed in the document below) by taking up arms against "the dictatorship of the proletariat."

Their rebellion, a profound embarrassment to the Communist regime, was quickly crushed by Red troops; a large number of the Kronstadt rebels were executed. Yet it also persuaded Lenin, now that the White Army had been defeated in the civil war, to relax the grip of the Communist party and restore a measure of private enterprise under the New Economic Policy (NEP), which lasted until the Stalin revolution of 1929. Under USSR President Gorbachev (1990–1991), the idealism of the Kronstadt sailors was recognized; and in January 1994, Russian Federation President Yeltsin declared their repression "illegal and in violation of basic human rights." He decreed that a monument be erected in honor of the victims.

With the October Revolution the working class had hoped to achieve its emancipation. But there resulted an even greater enslavement of human personality.

The power of the police and gendarme monarchy fell into the hands of usurpers—the Communists—who, instead of giving the people liberty, have instilled in them only the constant fear of the Tcheka [secret police], which by its horrors surpasses even the gendarme regime of

Alexander Berkman, "The Kronstadt Rebellion," from *Russian Revolution* Series, No. 3 (Berlin—printed for Der Syndikalist, 1922), pp. 26–28.

Tsarism. . . . Worst and most criminal of all is the spiritual cabal of the Communists: they have laid their hand also on the internal world of the laboring masses, compelling everyone to think according to Communist prescription.

. . . Russia of the toilers, the first to raise the red banner of labor's emancipation, is drenched with the blood of those martyred for the greater glory of Communist dominion. In that sea of blood the Communists are drowning all the bright promises and possibilities of the workers' revolution. It has now become clear that the Russian Communist Party is not the defender of the laboring masses, as it pretends to be. The interests of the working people are foreign to it. Having gained power it is now fearful only of losing it, and therefore it considers all means permissible: defamation, deceit, violence, murder, and vengeance upon the families of the rebels.

There is an end to long-suffering patience. Here and there the land is lit up by the fires of rebellion in a struggle against oppression and violence. Strikes of workers have multiplied, but the Bolshevik police regime has taken every precaution against the outbreak of the inevitable Third Revolution.

But in spite of it all it has come, and it is made by the hands of the laboring masses. The Generals of Communism see clearly that it is the people who have risen, the people who have become convinced that the Communists have betrayed the ideas of Socialism. Fearing for

their safety and knowing that there is no place they can hide in from the wrath of the workers, the Communists still try to terrorise the rebels with prison, shooting, and other barbarities. But life under the Communist dictatorship is more terrible than death. . . .

There is no middle road. To conquer or to die! The example is being set by Kronstadt. . . . Here has taken place the great revolutionary deed. Here is raised the banner of rebellion against the three-year-old tyranny and oppression of Communist autocracy, which has put in the shade the three-hundred-year-old despotism of monarchism. Here, in Kronstadt, has been laid the cornerstone of the Third Revolution which is to break the last chains of the worker and open the new, broad road to Socialist creativeness.

Karl Kautsky
"SOCIALISM HAS ALREADY SUFFERED A DEFEAT"

Karl Kautsky (1854–1938), a leading German Social Democrat, denounced the Bolshevik regime for its terrorism, repression, and authoritarianism. Kautsky viewed the course of the Russian Revolution from the humanitarian perspectives of democratic German socialists. Eager to safeguard what he regarded as the moral purity of the Marxist creed, he deplored the Bolsheviks' brutality. The following reflections, written in 1919, spell out his reactions to the course of the revolution in Russia.

[When the Bolsheviks came] into power they threw overboard all their democratic principles. In order to keep themselves in power they have had to let their Socialist principles go the way of the democratic. They have . . . sacrificed their principles, and have proved themselves to be thoroughgoing opportunists. . . .

Among the phenomena for which Bolshevism has been responsible, Terrorism, which begins with the abolition of every form of freedom of the Press, and ends in a system of wholesale execution, is certainly the most striking and the most repellant of all. It is that which gave rise to the greatest hatred against the Bolsheviks. . . .

The instruments of terrorism were the revolutionary tribunals and the extraordinary commissions. . . . Both have carried on fearful work, quite apart from the so-called military punitive expeditions, the victims of which are incalculable. . . .

Karl Kautsky, *Terrorism and Communism: A Contribution to the Natural History of Revolution*, trans. by W. H. Kerridge (Westport, CT: Hyperion Press, 1913), 198–199, 208–210, 215–217, 221.

[The Bolsheviks] thus become unfaithful to the principles of the sanctity of human life, which they themselves openly proclaimed. . . .

Originally [the Bolsheviks] were. . . . fiery upholders of democracy within the proletariat, but they are repressing this democracy more and more by means of their personal dictatorship. . . .

. . . The hereditary sin of Bolshevism has been its suppression of democracy through a form of government, namely, the dictatorship, which has no meaning unless it represents the unlimited and despotic power, either of one, single person or of a small organisation intimately bound together. . . .

. . . The Bolsheviks are prepared, in order to maintain their position, to make all sorts of possible concessions to bureaucracy, to militarism, and to capitalism, whereas any concession to democracy seems to them to be sheer suicide.

REVIEW QUESTIONS

1. How, according to the Kronstadt rebels, had the Communists betrayed the ideas of socialism?
2. Where, according to Karl Kautsky, had the Bolsheviks strayed from the true spirit of socialism?

---

2 Modernize or Perish

Lenin died in 1924, and the task of achieving the goal he had set was taken up by Joseph Stalin (1879–1953). The "man of steel" was crude and vulgar, toughened by the revolutionary underground and tsarist prisons. Relentlessly energetic but relatively inconspicuous among key Bolsheviks, Stalin had been given, in 1922, the unwanted and seemingly routine task of general secretary of the party. He used this position to build up a reliable party cadre. When he was challenged, particularly by Leon Trotsky and his associates in the protracted struggles for the succession to Lenin, none of his rivals could match Stalin's skill in party infighting. More powerful and ruthless than Lenin, Stalin was determined to force his country to overcome the economic and political weakness that had led to defeat and ruin in World War I.

Joseph Stalin
THE HARD LINE

Firmly entrenched in power by 1929, Stalin mobilized at top speed the economic potential of the country whatever the human price. The alternative, he was sure, was foreign domination that would totally destroy his country's independence. In this spirit, he addressed a gathering of industrial managers in 1931, talking to them not in Marxist-Leninist jargon, but in terms of hard-line Russian nationalism.

It is sometimes asked whether it is not possible to slow down the tempo a bit, to put a check on the movement. No, comrades, it is not possible! The tempo must not be reduced! On the contrary, we must increase it as much as is within our powers and possibilities. This is dictated to us by our obligations to the workers and peasants of the U.S.S.R. This is dictated to us by our obligations to the working class of the whole world.

To slacken the tempo would mean falling behind. And those who fall behind get beaten. But we do not want to be beaten. No, we refuse to be beaten! One feature of the history of old Russia was the continual beatings she suffered for falling behind, for her backwardness. She was beaten by the Mongol Khans. She was beaten by the Turkish beys. She was beaten by the Swedish feudal lords. She was beaten by the Polish and Lithuanian gentry. She was beaten by the British and French capitalists. She was beaten by the Japanese barons. All beat her—for her backwardness: for military backwardness, for cultural backwardness, for political backwardness, for industrial backwardness, for agricultural backwardness. She was beaten because to do so was profitable and could be done with impunity. Do you remember the words of the pre-revolutionary poet [Nikolai Nekrassov]: "You are poor and abundant, mighty and impotent, Mother Russia." These words of the old poet were well learned by those gentlemen. They beat her, saying: "You are abundant," so one can enrich oneself at your expense. They beat her, saying: "You are poor and impotent," so you can be beaten and plundered with impunity. Such is the law of the exploiters—to beat the backward and the weak. It is the jungle law of capitalism. You are backward, you are weak—therefore you are wrong; hence, you can be beaten and enslaved. You are mighty—therefore you are right; hence, we must be wary of you.

That is why we must no longer lag behind.

In the past we had no fatherland, nor could we have one. But now that we have overthrown capitalism and power is in the hands of the working class, we have a fatherland, and we will defend its independence. Do you want our socialist fatherland to be beaten and to lose its independence? If you do not want this you must put an end to its backwardness in the shortest possible time and develop [a] genuine Bolshevik tempo in building up its socialist system of economy. There is no other way. That is why Lenin said during the October Revolution: "Either perish, or overtake and outstrip the advanced capitalist countries."

We are fifty or a hundred years behind the advanced countries. We must make good this distance in ten years. Either we do it, or they crush us.

This is what our obligations to the workers and peasants of the U.S.S.R. dictate to us.

Joseph Stalin, *Leninism: Selected Writings* (New York: International Publishers, 1942), pp. 199–200.

REVIEW QUESTIONS

1. Why did Joseph Stalin argue that the tempo of industrialization could not be slowed down?
2. How important is the idea of "fatherland" to Stalin?

---

3 Forced Collectivization

The forced collectivization of agriculture from 1929 to 1933 was an integral part of the Stalin revolution. His argument in favor of it was simple: an economy divided against itself cannot stand—planned industrial mobilization was incompatible with small-scale private agriculture in the traditional manner. Collectivization meant combining many small peasant holdings into a single large unit run in theory by the peasants (now called collective farmers), but run in practice by the collective farm chairman and guided by the government's Five-Year Plan, which was designed to industrialize the country rapidly.

Collectivization, not surprisingly, met with fierce resistance, especially from the more successful peasants called kulaks, who were averse to surrendering their private plots and their freedom in running their households. Their resistance therefore had to be broken, and the Communist Party fomented a rural class struggle, seeking help from the poorer peasants. Sometimes, however, even the poorest peasants sided with the local kulaks. Under these conditions, Stalin did not shrink from unleashing violence in the countryside aimed at the "liquidation of the kulaks as a class." For Stalin the collectivization drive meant an all-out war on what was for him the citadel of backwardness: the peasant tradition and rebelliousness so prominent under the tsars.

Lev Kopelev
TERROR IN THE COUNTRYSIDE

Here a militant participant in the collectivization drive, Lev Kopelev, recalls some of his experiences. These passages are from his memoirs published in 1978. Kopelev (1912–1997), raised in a Ukrainian middle-class Jewish family, evolved from a youthful Stalinist into a tolerant, gentle person in later years. After trying to keep Russian soldiers from raping and pillaging in German territory in 1945, he was given a ten-year sentence for antistate crimes. Subsequently out of favor because of his literary protests against the inhumanities of the Soviet system, he was exiled from the Soviet Union to West Germany in 1980.

In *The Education of a True Believer*, Kopelev details the coercion employed by teams of young collective farmers and government agents against the kulaks. They confiscated the kulaks' livestock and food, clothing, and valuables, leaving them destitute. Kopelev watched and even participated in the plundering and searching for hidden grain in the belief that he was aiding international communism, which he then considered the noblest ideal, that he was overcoming the ignorance of peasants and transforming them into productive labor based on socialist principles. Even in the great famine of 1933 when he saw emaciated women and children, deprived of grain, dying of hunger and skeleton-thin men being driven into the fields in order to meet Soviet quotas, Kopelev remained a true believer, a decision that tormented him in later years. He said that, like many of his generation, he believed that Communism's goals were good for all humanity, and that achieving these goals justified destroying hundreds of thousands of people, in this case peasants too ignorant to realize that their opposition to collectivization hindered progress.

In the following passages, Kopelev discusses the terrible plundering of peasant homes and his own motivation and state of mind as a participant in Stalin's drive for total collectivization.

The women howled hysterically, clinging to the bags.

"Oy, that's the last thing we have! That was for the children's kasha [cereal]! Honest to God, the children will starve!"

They wailed, falling on their trunks:

"Oy, that's a keepsake from my dead mama! People, come to my aid, this is my trousseau, never e'en put on!"

I heard the children echoing them with screams, choking, coughing with screams. And I saw the looks of the men: frightened, pleading, hateful, dully impassive, extinguished with despair or flaring up with half-mad, daring ferocity.

"Take it. Take it away. Take everything away. There's still a pot of borscht on the stove. It's plain, got no meat. But still it's got beets, taters 'n' cabbage. And it's salted! Better take it, comrade citizens! Here, hang on, I'll take off my shoes. They're patched and re-patched, but maybe they'll have some use for the proletariat, for our dear Soviet power."

It was excruciating to see and hear all this. And even worse to take part in it. . . . And I persuaded myself, explained to myself. I mustn't give in to debilitating pity. We were realizing historical necessity. We were performing our revolutionary duty. We were obtaining grain for the socialist fatherland. For the five-year plan. . . .

I have always remembered the winter of the last grain collections, the weeks of the great famine. . . .

Who was guilty of the famine which destroyed millions of lives?

How could I have participated in it? . . .

We were raised as the fanatical [believers] of a new creed, the only true *religion* of scientific socialism. The party became our church militant, bequeathing to all mankind eternal salvation, eternal peace and the bliss of an earthly paradise. It victoriously surmounted all other churches, schisms and heresies. The works of Marx, Engels and Lenin were accepted as holy writ, and Stalin was the infallible high priest. . . .

And we believed him unconditionally. . . .

With the rest of my generation I firmly believed that the ends justified the means. Our great goal was the universal triumph of Communism, and for the sake of that goal everything was permissible—to lie, to steal, to destroy hundreds of thousands and even millions of people, all those who were hindering our work or could hinder it, everyone who stood in the way. And to hesitate or doubt about all this was to give in to "intellectual squeamishness" and "stupid liberalism," the attributes of people who "could not see the forest for the trees."

Lev Kopelev, *The Education of a True Believer*, trans. Gary Kern (New York: Harper & Row, 1980), pp. 234–235, 248–250.

Miron Dolot
FAMINE IN UKRAINE

Collectivization was most cruel in Ukraine, as the following eye-witness account attests, where famine killed approximately three million people. Stalin deliberately starved the peasants in order to export food to raise cash needed to buy industrial equipment and to punish Ukrainians for their resistance to collectivization.

EXECUTION BY HUNGER

The liquidation of the kulaks began in late 1929, extending through the length and breadth of the country during the winter. The confiscation of kulak property, the deportations, and the killing rose to a brutal climax in the following spring and continued for another two years, by which time the bulk of the private farms had been eliminated. Some kulaks were driven from their huts, deprived of all possessions, and left destitute in the dead of winter. Some two million were deported to special settlements in distant wastelands or to forced labor camps in the far north where many ultimately perished from hunger, cold, and abuse.

The upheaval destroyed agricultural production in these years: farm animals died or were killed in huge numbers; fields lay barren. In 1932 and 1933, famine stalked the south and southeast, killing additional millions. The vast tragedy caused by collectivization did not deter Stalin from pursuing his goals: the establishment of state farms run like factories and the subordination of the rebellious and willful peasantry to state authority.

Miron Dolot witnessed the horrors of state-induced famine in Ukraine and later emigrated to the West. In *Execution by Hunger: The Hidden Holocaust* (1985), excerpted below, Dolot recounts his experiences.

Around this time the plight of the villagers became desperate. This was the memorable spring of 1932 when the famine broke out, and the first deaths from hunger began to occur. I remember the endless procession of beggars on roads and paths, going from house to house. They were in different stages of starvation, dirty and ragged. With outstretched hands, they begged for food, any food: a potato, a beet, or at least a kernel of corn. Those were the first victims of starvation: destitute men and women; poor widows and orphaned children who had no chance of surviving the terrible ordeal.

Some starving farmers still tried to earn their food by doing chores in or outside the village. One could see these sullen, emaciated men walking from house to house with an ax, or a shovel, in search of work. Perhaps someone might hire them to dig up the garden, or chop some firewood. They would do it for a couple of potatoes. But not many of us had a couple of potatoes to spare.

Crowds of starving wretches could be seen scattered all over the potato fields. They were looking for potatoes left over from last year's harvest. No matter what shape the potatoes were in, whether frozen or rotten, they were still edible. . . .

But the majority of those who looked for help would go to the cities as they used to do before. It was always easier to find some work there, either gardening, cleaning backyards, or sweeping streets. But now, times had changed. It was illegal to hire farmers for any work. The purpose of the prohibition was twofold: it was done not only to stop the flow of labor from the collective farms, but also, and primarily, to prevent the farmers from receiving food rations in the cities. . . .

. . . Now starving, we were facing the spring of 1932 with great anxiety for there was no hope of relief from the outside. Deaths from starvation became daily occurrences. There was always some burial in the village cemetery. One could see strange funeral processions: children pulling homemade hand-wagons with the bodies of their dead parents in them or the parents carting the bodies of their children. There were no coffins; no burial ceremonies performed by priests. The bodies of the starved were just deposited in a large common grave, one upon the other; that was all there was to it. . . .

4 Shaping a New Society and a "New Man"

Stalin aimed to mold a new type of suitably motivated and disciplined citizen, one dedicated to hard work, social cooperation, and the Communist ideal of shaping a new society. Moreover, he believed that only Communist regimentation and monolithic control by the party over state and society could liberate Russia from its historic inferiority. The Five-Year Plans obliterated private enterprise; virtually every worker and peasant was now an employee of the state. The totalitarian state accorded with his desire to exercise total control over the party and the nation. Stalin's totalitarianism aimed at a complete reconstruction of state and society, down to the innermost recesses of human consciousness. It called for a "new man," devoted to Soviet Communism and to Stalin, the wise and righteous leader.

Stalin's totalitarianism encompassed all cultural activity. Religion, which offered an alternative worldview, came under attack. Priests were jailed, organized worship was discouraged, and churches were converted into barns. All means of communication—literature, the arts, music, the stage—were forced into subservience to the Five-Year Plan and Soviet ideology. In literature, as in all art, an official style was promulgated. Called *socialist realism*, it was expected to describe the world as the party saw it or hoped to shape it. Novels in the social realist manner told how the romances of tractor drivers and milkmaids or of lathe operators and office secretaries led to new victories of production under the Five-Year Plan. Composers found their music examined for remnants of bourgeois spirit; they were to write simple tunes suitable for heroic times. Everywhere huge, high-color posters showed men and women hard at work with radiant faces, calling others to join them; often Stalin, the wise father and leader, was shown among them. In this way, artistic creativity was locked into a dull, utilitarian straitjacket of official cheerfulness; creativity was allowed only to boost industrial productivity. Behind the scenes, all artists were disciplined to conform to the will of the party or be crushed.

A. O. Avdienko
THE CULT OF STALIN

Among a people so deeply divided by ethnicity and petty localism and limited by a pervasive narrowness of perspective, building countrywide unity and consensus was a crucial challenge for the government. In the Russian past, the worship of saints and the veneration of the tsar had served that purpose. The political mobilization of the masses during the revolution required an intensification of that tradition. It led to the "cult of personality," the deliberate fixation of individual dedication and loyalty on the all-powerful leader, whose personality exemplified the challenge of extraordinary times. The following selection illustrates by what emotional bonds the individual was tied to Stalin, and through Stalin to the prodigious transformation of Russian state and society that he was attempting.

Thank you, Stalin. Thank you because I am joyful. Thank you because I am well. No matter how old I become, I shall never forget how we received Stalin two days ago. Centuries will pass, and the generations still to come will regard us as the happiest of mortals, as the most fortunate of men, because we lived in the century of centuries, because we were privileged to see Stalin, our inspired leader. Yes, and we regard ourselves as the happiest of mortals because we are the contemporaries of a man who never had an equal in world history.

The men of all ages will call on thy name, which is strong, beautiful, wise and marvellous. Thy name is engraven on every factory, every machine, every place on the earth, and in the hearts of all men.

Every time I have found myself in his presence I have been subjugated by his strength, his charm, his grandeur. I have experienced a great desire to sing, to cry out, to shout with joy and happiness. And now see me—me!—on the same platform where the Great Stalin stood a year ago. In what country, in what part of the world could such a thing happen.

I write books. I am an author. All thanks to thee, O great educator, Stalin. I love a young woman with a renewed love and shall perpetuate myself in my children—all thanks to thee, great educator, Stalin. I shall be eternally happy and joyous, all thanks to thee, great educator, Stalin. Everything belongs to thee, chief of our great country. And when the woman I love presents me with a child the first word it shall utter will be: Stalin.

O great Stalin, O leader of the peoples,
Thou who broughtest man to birth.
Thou who fructifiest the earth,
Thou who restorest the centuries,
Thou who makest bloom the spring,
Thou who makest vibrate the musical chords . . .
Thou, splendour of my spring, O Thou,
Sun reflected by millions of hearts . . .

Stalin: Great Lives Observed, edited by T. H. Rigby, pp. 111–112.

Yevgeny Yevtushenko
LITERATURE AS PROPAGANDA

After Stalin's death in 1953, Soviet intellectuals breathed more freely, and they protested against the rigid Stalinist controls. In the following extract from his *Precocious Autobiography*, Russian poet Yevgeny Yevtushenko (1933–2017) looks back to the raw days of intellectual repression and the stifling of artistic creativity under Stalin.

Blankly smiling workers and collective farmers looked out from the covers of books. Almost every novel and short story had a happy ending. Painters more and more often took as their subject state-banquets, weddings, solemn public meetings, and parades.

The apotheosis of this trend was a movie which in its grand finale showed thousands of collective farmers having a gargantuan feast against the background of a new power station.

Recently I had a talk with its producer, a gifted and intelligent man.

"How could you produce such a film?" I asked. "It is true that I also once wrote verses in that vein, but I was still wet behind the ears, whereas you were adult and mature."

The producer smiled a sad smile. "You know, the strangest thing to me is that I was absolutely sincere. I thought all this was a necessary part of building communism. And then I believed Stalin." . . .

Yevgeny Yevtushenko, *A Precocious Autobiography*, trans. Andrew R. MacAndrew (New York: E. P. Dutton, 1963) pp. 73–76, 81.

How was it possible for even gifted and intelligent people to be deceived?

To begin with, Stalin was a strong and vivid personality. When he wanted to, Stalin knew how to charm people. He charmed Gorky and Barbusse. In 1937, the cruelest year of the purges, he managed to charm that tough and experienced observer, Lion Feuchtwanger.[1]

In the second place, in the minds of the Soviet people, Stalin's name was indissolubly linked with Lenin's. Stalin knew how popular Lenin was and saw to it that history was rewritten in such a way as to make his own relations with Lenin seem much more friendly than they had been in fact. . . .

---

[1]Gorky was a prominent Russian writer; Barbusse and Feuchtwanger were well-known Western European writers.—Eds.

Stalin's theory that people were the little cogwheels of communism was put into practice and with horrifying results. . . . Russian poets, who had produced some fine works during the war, turned dull again. . . .

Poets visited factories and construction sites but wrote more about machines than about the men who made them work. . . .

The generation of poets that had been spawned by the war and that had raised so many hopes had petered out. Life in peacetime turned out to be more complicated than life at the front. Two of the greatest Russian poets, Zabolotsky and Smelyakov, were in concentration camps. The young poet Mandel (Korzhavin) had been deported. . . .

. . . Now that ten years have gone by, I realize that Stalin's greatest crime was not the arrests and the shootings he ordered. His greatest crime was the corruption of the human spirit.

REVIEW QUESTIONS

1. In light of the A. O. Avdienko reading, how would you say Communists were supposed to feel about Stalin?
2. Soviet propaganda was designed to create a politically united industrial society out of backward peasants. Can you think of alternative ways to accomplish that task?

5 Stalin's Terror

To break stubborn wills and compel conformity, Stalin—calculating, cunning, cold, cruel, and cynical—unleashed raw terror. Terror had been used as a tool of government ever since the Bolsheviks seized power. Lenin, who had provided theoretical justification for terror in the struggle against tsarism, employed it after the Revolution (and the tsars had also used it intermittently). Stalin used terror to herd the peasants onto collective farms, to crush opposition (often imagined), and to instill abject fear in the ranks of the party and in Russian society at large.

Terror became an instrument of Stalin's drive for unchallenged personal power. His paranoia, which defied all logic and morality, led him to see threats to his rule everywhere and more and more enemies to be exterminated in ever-increasing numbers. Included among the millions that Stalin consigned to death were close friends and comrades in the Bolshevik Revolution. Almost half of the country's 70,000 officers were either shot or sent to labor camps, for which the country paid a heavy price when Germany attacked in 1941. Stalin also decimated the cultural elite that had survived the Lenin revolution. Thousands of engineers, scientists, industrial managers, scholars, and artists disappeared; accused of counterrevolutionary crimes, they were shot or sent to forced-labor camps, where many of them perished. Their relatives also suffered, often fired from their jobs, evicted from their apartments, exiled to remote regions, and even sentenced to labor camps. No one was safe. To frighten the common people in all walks of life, men, women, and even children were dragged into the net of Stalin's secret police, leaving the survivors with a soul-killing reminder: submit or else. "In the years of the terror," recalled one victim, "there was not a house in the country where people did not sit trembling at night."

The bloodletting was ghastly; however, Stalin was untroubled by the waste of life. By showing party officials and the Russian masses how vulnerable they were, how dependent they were on his will, he frightened them into servility. No doubt the terror was also an expression of his craving for personal power and of his cruel, vengeful, and suspicious, some say clinically paranoid, nature. He saw enemies everywhere, took pleasure in selecting victims, and revelled in his omnipotence. Although it might take decades for some to realize it, Stalin's criminal rule blackened the ideal of a humane socialist society.

Lev Razgon
TRUE STORIES

In 1988, Lev Razgon, a survivor of Stalin's camps, published an account of his experiences, which appeared in English under the tide *True Stories* in 1997. Razgon was a journalist who married the daughter of a high-ranking member of the Soviet secret police. Gaining access to the Soviet elite, in 1934 he attended the Seventeenth Party Congress. In 1937, his father-in-law was arrested for "counterrevolutionary" activities, along with many family friends; the following year the police came for Razgon and his wife. She perished in a transit prison en route to a northern camp, and Razgon spent the next seven years in a labor camp. Released in 1945, he was confined to various provincial towns; in 1949, he was rearrested and returned to the camps. Finally, he was released again in 1956 after Stalin's death.

Over the years Razgon began to write down his prison experiences—but only for his desk drawer, with the specific intent of preserving the memory of fellow prisoners who did not survive. As the Soviet Union began to crumble, Razgon was able to publish his stories. In the following extract from *True Stories*, Razgon reproduces a discussion he had with a former prison guard, whom he met by chance in a hospital ward in 1977. The guard described to Razgon his role as an executioner of political prisoners, revealing the brutality and irrationality of the Soviet prison system under Stalin.

"How did they behave, once they were in the van?"

"The men, well, they kept quiet. But the women would start crying, they'd say: 'What are you doing, we're not guilty of anything, comrades, what are you doing?' and things like that.". . .

"Were the women young? Were there a lot of them?"

"Not so many, about two vanloads a week. No very young ones but there were some about twenty five or thirty. Most were older, and some even elderly."

"Did you drive them far?"

"Twelve kilometers or so, to the hill. The Distant Hill, it was called. There were hills all around and that's where we unloaded them."

"So you would unload them, and then tell them their sentence?"

"What was there to tell them?! No, we yelled, 'Out! Stand still!' They scrambled down and there was already a trench dug in front of them. They clambered down, clung together and right away we got to work. . . ."

"They didn't make any noise?"

"Some didn't, others began shouting, 'We're Communists, we are being wrongly executed,' that type of thing. But the women would only cry and cling to each other. So we just got on with it. . . ."

"Did you have a doctor with you?"

"What for? We would shoot them, and those still wriggling got another bullet and then we were off back to the van. The work team from

the Dalag camps was already nearby, waiting [to fill in the pits].". . .

"We would arrive back at the camp, hand in our weapons at the guardhouse and then we could have as much to drink as we wanted. The others used to lap it up—it didn't cost them a kopeck. I always had my shot, went off to the canteen for a hot meal, and then back to sleep in the barracks."

"And did you sleep well? Didn't you feel bad or anything?"

"Why should I?"

"Well, that you had just killed other people. Didn't you feel sorry for them?"

"No, not at all. I didn't give it a thought. No, I slept well and then I'd go for a walk outside the camp. . . ."

"Grigory Ivanovich, did you know that the people you were shooting were not guilty at all, that they hadn't done anything wrong?"

"Well, we didn't think about that then. Later, yes. We were summoned to the procurators [officials] and they asked us questions. They explained that those had been innocent people. There had been mistakes, they said, and—what was the word?—excesses. But they told us that it was nothing to do with us, we were not guilty of anything."

"Well, I understand, then you were under orders and you shot people. But when you learned that you had been killing men and women who were not guilty at all, didn't your conscience begin to bother you?"

"Conscience? No. . . . it didn't bother me. I never think about all that now, and when I do remember something, [it is] as if nothing had happened. . . ."

Lev Razgon, *True Stories*, translated by John Crowfoot (New York: Overlook Press, Ardis, 1997), pp. 25–26.

Anatoly Zhigulin
A "CANNIBALISTIC SPORT"

Often cruel guards added to the misery of the inmates. Anatoly Zhigulin, a poet who was released from the gulag after Stalin's death, describes a particularly sadistic game played by the guards.

This cannibalistic sport was especially popular with the guard details and sentries at Camp No. 031. But it flourished everywhere throughout the Gulag given the right conditions: small groups of convicts out in the woods, in the field; automatic weapons; close range; someone easy to shoot.

There was a system of incentives for guards who prevented or interrupted escapes. Shoot a runner—get a new stripe on your uniform, home leave, a bonus, a medal. No doubt biology was at work here as well—the aggression that comes naturally to young males. Moreover, hatred for the prisoners was inculcated in them from the start. The prisoners were *vlasovlsy*,[1] they were S.S., they were traitors and spies.

Anne Applebaum, ed., *Gulag Voices: An Anthology* (New Haven: Yale University Press, 2011), pp. 64–65.
[1]Soviet soldiers who collaborated with German forces during World War II.

Guards were perverted both by the absolute power they were given and by the weapons they so longed to use. Convicts were generally shot down either by very young soldiers or by hardened sadists and murderers. . . . One of the convoy detail would pick a victim and begin to stalk him. The guard would wheedle, persuade, try to lure the victim over the line. Unless a smart and savvy crew both had warned the victim ahead of time, the deception worked The soldier would say, "Hey! You! Go get me that little log to sit on!"

"But sir, it's off limits!"

"Not a problem. You have my permission. Move, go!"

The prisoner steps over the line. One quick burst of fire and he's dead. Typical. Banal.

Sometimes the guards and sentries would actually order their victims to step over the line, or just shove or chase them out, the better to shoot them. A guard was authorized to order a convict to cross the cordon. He was also authorized to mow that same man down.

REVIEW QUESTION

How do you explain the cruelty of the prison guards and the bureaucrats who supervised them?

---

6   The Rise of Italian Fascism

Benito Mussolini (1883–1945) started his political life as a socialist and in 1912 was appointed editor of *Avanti*, the leading Italian socialist newspaper. During World War I, Mussolini was expelled from the Socialist Party for advocating Italy's entry into the conflict. Immediately after the war, he organized the National Fascist Party. Exploiting labor unrest, fear of Communism, and thwarted nationalist hopes, Mussolini gained followers among veterans and the middle class. Powerful industrialists and landowners, viewing the Fascists as a bulwark against Communism, helped to finance the young movement. An opportunist, Mussolini organized a march on Rome in 1922 to bring down the government. King Victor Emmanuel, fearful of civil war, appointed the Fascist leader prime minister. Had Italian liberals and the king taken a firm stand, the government could have easily crushed the 20,000 lightly armed marchers.

Benito Mussolini
FASCIST DOCTRINES

Ten years after he seized power, Mussolini, assisted by philosopher Giovanni Gentile (1875–1944), contributed an article to the *Italian Encyclopedia* in which he discussed Fascist political and social doctrines. In this piece, Mussolini lauded violence as a positive experience; attacked Marxism for denying idealism by subjecting human beings to economic laws and for dividing the nation into warring classes; and denounced liberal democracy for promoting individual selfishness at the expense of the national community and for being unable to solve the nation's problems. The Fascist state, he said, required unity and power, not individual freedom. The following excerpts are from Mussolini's article.

. . . Above all, Fascism, the more it considers and observes the future and the development of humanity quite apart from political considerations of the moment, believes neither in the possibility nor the utility of perpetual peace. It thus repudiates the doctrine of Pacifism— born of a renunciation of the struggle and an act of cowardice in the face of sacrifice. War alone brings up to its highest tension all human energy and puts the stamp of nobility upon the peoples who have the courage to meet it. All other trials are substitutes, which never really put men into the position where they have to make the great decision—the alternative of life or death. Thus a doctrine which is founded upon this harmful postulate of peace is hostile to Fascism. And thus hostile to the spirit of Fascism, though accepted for what use they can be in dealing with particular political situations, are all the international leagues and societies which, as history will show, can be scattered to the winds when once strong national feeling is aroused by any motive—sentimental, ideal, or practical. This anti-pacifist spirit is carried by Fascism even into the life of the individual; the proud motto of the *Squadrista*, "Me ne frego" [It doesn't matter], written on the bandage of the

wound, is an act of philosophy not only stoic, the summary of a doctrine not only political— it is the education to combat, the acceptation of the risks which combat implies, and a new way of life for Italy. Thus the Fascist accepts life and loves it, knowing nothing of and despising suicide: he rather conceives of life as duty and struggle and conquest, life which should be high and full, lived for oneself, but above all for others—those who are at hand and those who are far distant, contemporaries, and those who will come after. . . .

. . , Fascism [is] the complete opposite of . . . Marxian Socialism, the materialist conception of history; according to which the history of human civilization can be explained simply through the conflict of interests among the various social groups and by the change and development in the means and instruments of production. That the changes in the economic field—new discoveries of raw materials, new methods of working them, and the inventions of science—have their importance no one can deny; but that these factors are sufficient to explain the history of humanity excluding all others is an absurd delusion. Fascism, now and always, believes in holiness and in heroism; that is to say, in actions influenced by no economic motive, direct or indirect. And if the economic conception of history be denied, according to which theory men are no more than puppets,

---

Benito Mussolini, *The Political and Social Doctrine of Fascism* (New York: Carnegie Endowment for International Conciliation, 1935), pp. 7–10, 12–13, 15–17.

carried to and fro by the waves of chance, while the real directing forces are quite out of their control, it follows that the existence of an unchangeable and unchanging class-war is also denied—the natural progeny of the economic conception of history. And above all Fascism denies that class-war can be the preponderant force in the transformation of society. . . .

After Socialism, Fascism combats the whole complex system of democratic ideology, and repudiates it, whether in its theoretical premises or in its practical application. Fascism denies that the majority, by the simple fact that it is a majority, can direct human society; it denies that numbers alone can govern by means of a periodical consultation, and it affirms the immutable, beneficial, and fruitful inequality of mankind, which can never be permanently leveled through the mere operation of a mechanical process such as universal suffrage. . . .

. . . Fascism denies, in democracy, the absurd conventional untruth of political equality dressed out in the garb of collective irresponsibility, and the myth of "happiness" and indefinite progress. . . .

. . . Given that the nineteenth century was the century of Socialism, of Liberalism, and of Democracy, it does not necessarily follow that the twentieth century must also be a century of Socialism, Liberalism, and Democracy: political doctrines pass, but humanity remains; and it may rather be expected that this will be a century of authority, . . . a century of Fascism. For if the nineteenth century was a century of individualism (Liberalism always signifying individualism) it may be expected that this will be the century of collectivism, and hence the century of the State. . . .

The foundation of Fascism is the conception of the State, its character, its duty, and its aim. Fascism conceives of the State as an absolute, in comparison with which all individuals or groups are relative, only to be conceived of in their relation to the State. The conception of the Liberal State is not that of a directing force, guiding the play and development, both material and spiritual, of a collective body, but merely a force limited to the function of recording results: on the other hand, the Fascist State is itself conscious and has itself a will and a personality—thus it may be called the "ethic" State. . . .

. . . The Fascist State organizes the nation, but leaves a sufficient margin of liberty to the individual; the latter is deprived of all useless and possibly harmful freedom, but retains what is essential; the deciding power in this question cannot be the individual, but the State alone. . . .

. . . For Fascism, the growth of empire, that is to say the expansion of the nation, is an essential manifestation of vitality, and its opposite a sign of decadence. Peoples which are rising, or rising again after a period of decadence, are always imperialist; any renunciation is a sign of decay and of death. Fascism is the doctrine best adapted to represent the tendencies and the aspirations of a people, like the people of Italy, who are rising again after many centuries of abasement and foreign servitude. But empire demands discipline, the coordination of all forces and a deeply felt sense of duty and sacrifice: this fact explains many aspects of the practical working of the regime, the character of many forces in the State, and the necessarily severe measures which must be taken against those who would oppose this spontaneous and inevitable movement of Italy in the twentieth century, and would oppose it by recalling the outworn ideology of the nineteenth century—repudiated wheresoever there has been the courage to undertake great experiments of social and political transformation; for never before has the nation stood more in need of authority, of direction, and of order. If every age has its own characteristic doctrine, there are a thousand signs which point to Fascism as the characteristic doctrine of our time. For if a doctrine must be a living thing, this is proved by the fact that Fascism has created a living faith; and that this faith is very powerful in the minds of men is demonstrated by those who have suffered and died for it.

REVIEW QUESTIONS

1. Why did Benito Mussolini consider pacifism to be the enemy of Fascism?
2. Why did Mussolini attack Marxism?
3. How did Mussolini view majority rule and equality?
4. What relationship did Mussolini see between the individual and the state?

7 The Fledgling Weimar Republic

In the last days of World War I, a revolution—the "November Revolution"—brought down the German government, a semiauthoritarian monarchy, and led to the creation of a democratic republic. The new government, headed by Chancellor Friedrich Ebert (1871–1925), a Social Democrat, signed the armistice agreement ending the war. Many Germans blamed the new democratic leadership for the defeat—a baseless accusation, for the German generals, knowing that the war was lost, had sought an armistice. In February 1919, the recently elected National Assembly met at Weimar and proceeded to draw up a constitution for the new state. The Weimar Republic—born in revolution, which most Germans detested, and military defeat, which many attributed to the new government—faced an uncertain future. The legend that traitors, principally Jews and Social Democrats, cheated Germany of victory was created and propagated by the conservative Right—generals, high-ranking bureaucrats, university professors, and nationalists, who wanted to preserve the army's reputation and bring down the new and hated democratic Weimar Republic.

Dominated by moderate socialists, the infant Republic faced internal threats from both the radical Left and the radical Right. In January 1919, the newly established German Communist Party, or Spartacists, disregarding the advice of their leaders Rosa Luxemburg and Karl Liebknecht, took to the streets of Berlin and declared Ebert's government deposed. To crush the revolution, Ebert turned to the Free Corps: volunteer brigades of ex-soldiers and adventurers, led by officers loyal to the emperor, who had been fighting to protect the eastern borders from encroachments by the new states of Poland, Estonia, and Latvia. The men of the Free Corps relished action and despised Bolshevism; many of them would later become prominent in Hitler's party. The Free Corps suppressed the revolution and murdered Luxemburg and Liebknecht on January 15.

The Spartacist revolt and the short-lived "soviet" republic in Munich (and others in Baden and Brunswick) had a profound effect on the German psyche. The Communists had been easily subdued, but fear of a Communist insurrection remained deeply embedded in the middle and upper classes—a fear that drove many of their members into the ranks of the Weimar Republic's right-wing opponents.

Refusing to disband as the government ordered, detachments of the right-wing Free Corps marched into Berlin and declared a new government, headed by Wolfgang Kapp, a staunch German nationalist. Insisting that it could not fire on fellow soldiers, the German army, the *Reichswehr*, made no move to defend the Republic. A general strike called by the labor unions prevented Kapp from governing, and the coup collapsed. However, the Kapp Putsch (*putsch* is a violent attempt to overthrow the government) demonstrated that the loyalty of the army to the Republic was doubtful and that important segments of German society supported the overthrow, by violence if necessary, of the Weimar Republic and its replacement by an authoritarian government driven by a nationalist credo.

Friedrich Jünger
ANTIDEMOCRATIC THOUGHT IN THE WEIMAR REPUBLIC

The rightist attack on the Weimar Republic was multifaceted. Traditional conservatives—aristocrats, army leaders, and industrialists—were contemptuous of democracy and sought a strong government that would protect the nation from Communism and check the power of the working class. In a peculiar twist of logic, radical right-wing nationalists blamed Germany's defeat in World War 1 and the humiliation of the Versailles Treaty on the Republic.

The constitution of the Weimar Republic, premised intellectually and emotionally on the liberal-rational tradition, had strong opposition from German conservatives who valued the authoritarian state promoted by Bismarck and the kaisers. In expressing their hostility to the Weimar Republic, radical rightists attacked liberal democracy and reason, and embraced an ultranationalist philosophy of blood, soil, and action. In the brittle disunity and disorientation of German society, conservative nationalists searched for community and certainty in the special qualities of the German soul. Their antirationalism, hostility to democracy, and ultranationalism undermined the Weimar Republic and contributed to the triumph of Nazism.

The selection below is freely adapted from a small book, *The Rise of the New Nationalism* (1926), written by Friedrich Georg Jünger, the brother of Ernst Jünger, who is well known for his literary glorification of the war experience.

The new nationalism envisages a state elevated by popular enthusiasm and gathering in itself the fullness of power as the sole guarantor of Germany's collective future. It is both armor and sword, preserving indigenous culture and

destroying the alien elements that arrogantly push against it.

The new nationalism in its formative state throbs with revolutionary excitement. It lives unrestrained in our gut feeling, seething in our blood, although still full of confusion.

The November revolution that overthrew the monarchy was the result of a moral collapse promoted by external pressures. It happened at a time when the frightful struggle of the war

Translated and adapted by Theodore H. Von Laue from Priedrich Georg Jünger, *Aufmarsch des Nationalismus* (The Rise of the New Nationalism) (Leipzig, 1926), pp. 5–65 passim. Reprinted by permission of Angela Von Laue.

should have demanded the concentration of all energies. Rightly it was called a stab in the back, because it was led by Germans against Germans, provocatively and from the rear. The revolution proved the shallowness of its promoters They could not radiate youth, warmth, energy, or greatness. There were deputies, but no leaders. There was no man among them who stood out by his exceptional qualities. We saw the feeble liberals and heard for the hundredth time the promulgation of human rights. One might say, a dusty storeroom was thrown open from which emerged human rights, freedom, toleration, parliament, suffrage, and popular representation. Finally they wrote a Liberalist novel: the Weimar constitution.

But the Weimar regime was a body in which there flowed no blood. You could talk about it only in empty phrases. What an overabundance of phrases and phrasemakers! They had plastered the last available fence, the last walls, with their babble.

The new nationalism wants to awaken a sense of the greatness of the German past. Life must be evaluated according to the will to power, which reveals the warlike character of all life, The value of the individual is assessed according to his military value for the state, and the state is recognized as the most creative and toughest source of power. . . .

It is necessary to look at the conditions that have preceded and created the new nationalism. The recent past has destroyed our inherited collective sense of tender intimacy by trying to subvert and weaken all close bonds of community. It has denied all values that create cohesion in the community. Everything conspired to speed the disintegration of human ties in state, church, marriage, family, and many other institutions. A mad urge for throwing off all restraints, for dissolution, for unbridled liberty, dissolved society into driftwood. This urge shaped the flighty masses, depriving them of all convictions of meaningfulness. These excesses finally aroused disgust and a counter movement arose. A new consolidation of purpose began.

From it arises the future success of the new nationalism, its resistance to the atomistic liberty and to the freedom of soulless decadence. Social life is never free. A mighty mysterious bond of blood links the lives of individuals and subsumes them in a fateful wholeness. Blood, as it were, sings the song of destiny.

Life is deeply bonded. And only as it remains true to these bonds and is rooted in them, can it fulfill itself. Life withers if these roots are cut or if it seeks nourishment from alien roots. It is tied to the blood; at its core it is part of a community of blood. The intellect enjoys freedom only to the degree to which it is loyal to the blood. The new nationalism is born of the new awareness of blood-bonded community; it wants to make the promptings of the blood prevail. Escaping from the boundlessness of contemporary life, it is driven forward by the yearning for the bonds of blood.

The new nationalism wants to strengthen the blood bonds and form them into a new state. Those who are part of an alien blood community, or those internationalists who feel joined to a transcendent community, are excluded. They have to be driven out, because they weaken the rich and fertile body of the nation that nourishes everything of significance.

The awareness of these blood bonds demands the fight against all movements weakening the spiritual bonds that affirm the community of blood. It judges all values according to that principle. It wants life to be whole, lived in a new intoxicating abundance, responsibly restricted, and not dissipated or fatigued by the intellect. In every nationalism there is something intoxicating, a wild and lusty pride, a mighty heroic vitality. It has no critical or analytic inclinations, which weaken life. It wants no tolerance, because life docs not know tolerance. It is fanatical, because the promptings of the blood are fanatical and unjust. It does not care for scientific justification.

Nationalism must apply its force to the masses and try to set them afire by means peculiar to itself. These means are neither parliaments nor parties, but rather military units mobilized by a fierce loyalty to a leader. These units alone are called to carry out the will of the new nationalism. They will be the more powerful and successful the more they act in an organized and disciplined manner, the more unconditionally they subject themselves to the ideal of the nationalist state. The intensity of their discipline is the decisive factor. Next comes the urgent task to create a mighty organization covering all of Germany and to seize the reins of government. The community of blood is given the highest priority. It is defined race-like by the nationalist sentiment. It recognizes no European community, no common humanity. For us, mingling races and wiping out the difference between masters and slaves among the peoples of the world are an abomination. We want the sharpest separation of races.

The new state, obviously, will be authoritarian. The new nationalism is determined to make that authoritarianism absolute, all surpassing, consolidating the state as the new steel-like instrument of power. It values the state as the highest historic fact and the most important vehicle for attaining the nationalist aims. That state shall be the mold for the nation's blood-bound will to power. For that reason the nationalist movement urges the annihilation of all political forms of liberalism. No more parties, parliaments, elections! No more hailshowers of prattle or the bustle of the senile parliamentary intrigues that burden the country! No more packs of petty politicians and literati poking fun at the state! Tremendous energies ate wasted in the labyrinth of parliamentary procedure.

The madhouse of parliamentary activity in which every event is dragged out unconscionably without providing a sense of a great future, without consideration for the nation's dignity, reveals the foul sickness of liberalism. Masculine earnestness is dirtied by empty phrases: everything is befogged by the dense steam of corruption. . . .

While these people debate, vote, and slander each other in the battle of slogans, the new nationalism prepares for the crucial blow. The nationalist revolution proceeds on course; its thunderstorms loom over the horizon. And we can only wish that the explosion will be terrifying. May the elementary liberation of blood sweep away all the debris that burdens the times. The new nationalism is not given to compromise. Every institution needs to be examined whether it responsibly serves the nation or whether it is ripe to be smashed.

The nationalist state makes no claim to be the freest and most just state—that smacks of liberalism and negates its authoritarian character. The nationalist state aims at creating the most disciplined government devoid of any feeling of justice for its enemies. It wants a state permeated by a leader's personality. The personal element, inherent in all contemporary nationalist striving, belongs among the foundations of the new nationalism and of the state it wants to create. The will of the dictator is essential for the future. The craving for the blood-bond concentration of power raises the hope for an absolute leader even higher.

. . . The concentration of power in one man gives the state incredible strength and vitality. Decisions gain in strength and correctness; the choice of means becomes more effective; the frictions lessen; and the thrust of policy becomes more unified. The state must be prepared for something extraordinary, ready to jump. That this condition be achieved as soon as possible is the anxious yearning rising from our blood.

The great war has not ended. It has been the prelude to a brutal age of armed conflict. According to the deepest insight of the new nationalism, it is the beginning of a terrible, all-demanding struggle. Everything points to the fact that a new age of great violence is in the offing. Our blood is not deceived by the exhausted masses and the intellectual trends that passionately proclaim the dawn of freedom, human brotherhood, and sweet peace for all mankind. Nobody can prevent the war that arises from fateful depths and perhaps tomorrow will blanket the earth with corpses.

The savagery and corruption in the present world prepare mighty upheavals for the future. Then everything incapable and exhausted will be eliminated, and only he who carries within himself an unbounded fighting spirit and is armed to the teeth will be found worthy for the final decision. . . . At stake is the question: which people will finish the fight and administer the world and its resources in their own name? The convictions of the new nationalism are by necessity imperialist. The rule is: either domination or submission. Domination means being imperialist, having the will to exercise power and achieve superiority. Top priority, therefore, goes to mobilizing human wills. That is best done by the nationalist state. It guarantees total mobilization down to the last derail. The development of technology parallels the trends of political imperialism. It conveys a sense of the coming conflicts. The state, the economy, science all are slowly geared to imperialist expansion, proving the fatefulness of the trend. Should we avoid it because it demands great sacrifices and the submission of the individual, or because the awesome aims make life cheap? "Never!" cries the nationalist, because he aims at domination and not submission. He does not want to reject fate. He will not retreat even before the prospect of getting wiped out. He looks forward to the great and mighty Germany of the future, the irresistible strength of a hundred million Germans at the core of Europe!

Konrad Heiden
THE RUINOUS INFLATION, 1923

Economic developments also weakened Weimar. Inflation plagued Germany throughout the first years of the Republic, brought on by financing of the war through bonds instead of direct taxes and round-the-clock printing of paper money by German banks. The situation came to a head early in 1923, when French forces occupied the Ruhr to make Germany comply with the steep reparations demands of the Versailles Treaty. The government declared a state of passive resistance, and the inflation accelerated into hyperinflation. By autumn, the currency was valued at 4.2 billion German marks to the American dollar; workers were being paid twice a day and carting home their wages in wheelbarrows. Finally, in November, Chancellor Gustav Stresemann (1878–1929) called off passive resistance, launching a period of reconciliation with Germany's former enemies and of increasing economic stability and prosperity. The hyperinflation had ended, but those who had seen their savings wiped out would hold Weimar responsible.

The following description of the inflation comes from Konrad Heiden's early biography of Adolf Hitler. Heiden (1901–1966) was an author and journalist affiliated with the liberal *Frankfurter Zeitung*. He fled Germany during the 1930s.

On Friday afternoons in 1923, long lines of manual and white-collar workers waited outside the pay-windows of the big German factories, department stores, banks, offices: dead-tired workingmen in grimy shifts open at the neck; gentlemen in shiny blue suits, saved from before the war, in mended white collars, too big for their shrunken necks; young girls, some of them with the new bobbed heads; young men in puttees and gray jackets, from which the tailor had removed the red seams and regimentals, embittered against the girls who had taken their jobs. They all stood in lines outside the pay-windows, staring impatiently at the electric wall clock, slowly advancing until at last they reached the window and received a bag full of paper notes. According to the figures inscribed on them, the paper notes amounted to seven hundred thousand or five hundred million, or three hundred and eighty billion, or eighteen trillion marks—the figures rose from month to month, then from week to week,

finally from day to day. With their bags the people moved quickly to the doors, all in haste, the younger ones running. They dashed to the nearest food store, where a line had already formed. Again they moved slowly, oh, how slowly, forward. When you reached the store, a pound of sugar might have been obtainable for two millions; but, by the time you came to the counter, all you could get for two millions was half a pound, and the saleswoman said the dollar had just gone up again. With the millions or billions you bought sardines, sausages, sugar, perhaps even a little butter, but as a rule the cheaper margarine—always things that would keep for a week, until next pay-day, until the next stage in the fall of the mark.

For money could not keep, the most secure of all values had become the most insecure. The mark wasn't just low, it was slipping steadily downward. Goods were still available, but there was no money; there was still labor and consumption, but no economy; you could provide for the moment, but you couldn't plan for the future. It was the end of money. It was the end of the old shining hope that everyone would be rich. The secular religion of the nineteenth century was crumbling amid the profanation of holy property.

Heinrich Hauser
"WITH GERMANY'S UNEMPLOYED"

The Great Depression started in the United States in 1929 and quickly spread throughout the world. In the 1920s, hundreds of thousands of Americans had bought stock on credit; this buying spree sent stock prices soaring well beyond what the stocks were actually worth. In late October 1929, the stock market was hit by a wave of panic selling; prices plummeted. Within a few weeks, the value of stocks listed on the New York Stock Exchange fell by some $26 billion. A terrible chain reaction followed. Businesses cut production and fired their employees; farmers unable to meet mortgage payments lost their land; banks that had made poor investments closed down. American investors withdrew the capital they had invested in Europe, causing European banks and businesses to fail. Throughout the world, trade declined and unemployment soared.

The following article excerpted from the periodical *Die Tat* {The Deed} describes the loss of dignity suffered by the unemployed wandering Germany's roads and taking shelter in municipal lodging houses. The author, a German writer, experienced conditions in a public shelter firsthand. Conditions in 1932 as described in the article radicalized millions of Germans, particularly young people, and led them to embrace Hitler's leadership.

An almost unbroken chain of homeless men extends the whole length of the great Hamburg-Berlin highway.

There are so many of them moving in both directions, impelled by the wind or making their way against it, that they could shout a message from Hamburg to Berlin by word of mouth.

It is the same scene for the entire two hundred miles, and the same scene repeats itself between Hamburg and Bremen, between Bremen and Kassel, between Kassel and Würzburg, between Würzburg and Munich. All the highways in Germany over which I traveled this year presented the same aspects. . . .

. . . Most of the hikers paid no attention to me. They walked separately or in small groups, with their eyes on the ground. And they had the queer, stumbling gait of barefooted people, for their shoes were slung over their shoulders. Some of them were guild members—carpenters with embroidered wallets, knee breeches, and broad felt hats; milkmen with striped red shirts, and bricklayers with tall black hats—but they were in a minority. Far more numerous were those whom one could assign to no special profession or craft—unskilled young people, for the most part, who had been unable to find a place for themselves in any city or town in Germany, and who had never had a job and never expected to have one. There was something else that had never been seen before—whole families that

had piled all their goods into baby carriages and wheelbarrows that they were pushing along as they plodded forward in dumb despair. It was a whole nation on the march.

I saw them—and this was the strongest impression that the year 1932 left with me—I saw them, gathered into groups of fifty or a hundred men, attacking fields of potatoes. I saw them digging up the potatoes and throwing them into sacks while the farmer who owned the field watched them in despair and the local policeman looked on gloomily from the distance. I saw them staggering toward the lights of the city as night fell, with their sacks on their backs. What did it remind me of? Of the War, of the worst periods of starvation in 1917 and 1918, but even then people paid for the potatoes. . . .

I saw that the individual can know what is happening only by personal experience. I know what it is to be a tramp. I know what cold and hunger are, I know what it is to spend the night outdoors or behind the thin walls of a shack through which the wind whistles. I have slept in holes such as hunters hide in, in hayricks, under bridges, against the warm walls of boiler houses, under cattle shelters in pastures, on a heap of fir-tree boughs in the forest. But there are two things that I have only recently experienced—begging and spending the night in a municipal lodging house.

I entered the huge Berlin municipal lodging house in a northern quarter of the city. . . .

. . . There was an entrance arched by a brick vaulting, and a watchman sat in a little wooden sentry box. His white coat made him look like

Heinrich Hauser, "With Germany's Unemployed," *Living Age* [trans. from *Die Tat*], vol. 344, no. 4398 (March 1933), pp. 27–41, 34–38.

a doctor. We stood waiting in the corridor. Heavy steam rose from the men's clothes. Some of them sat down on the floor, pulled off their shoes, and unwound the rags that were bound around their feet. More people were constantly pouring in the door, and we stood closely packed together. Then another door opened. The crowd pushed forward, and people began forcing their way almost eagerly through this door, for it was warm in there. Without knowing it I had already caught the rhythm of the municipal lodging house. It means waiting, waiting, standing around, and then suddenly jumping up.

We now stand in a long hall, down the length of which runs a bar dividing the hall into a narrow and a wide space. All the light is on the narrow side. There under yellow lamps that hang from the ceiling on long wires sit men in white smocks. We arrange ourselves in long lines, each leading up to one of these men, and the mill begins to grind. . . .

. . . As the line passes in single file the official does not look up at each new person to appear. He only looks at the paper that is handed to him. These papers are for the most part invalid cards or unemployment certificates. The very fact that the official does not look up robs the homeless applicant of self-respect, although he may look too beaten down to feel any. . . .

. . . Now it is my turn and the questions and answers flow as smoothly as if I were an old hand. But finally I am asked, "Have you ever been here before?"

"No."

"No?" The question reverberates through the whole room. The clerk refuses to believe me and looks through his card catalogue. But no, my name is not there. The clerk thinks this strange, for he cannot have made a mistake, and the terrible thing that one notices in all these clerks is that they expect you to lie. They do not believe what you say. They do not regard you as a human being but as an infection, something foul that one keeps at a

distance. He goes on. "How did you come here from Hamburg?"

"By truck."

"Where have you spent the last three nights?"

I lie coolly.

"Have you begged?"

I feel a warm blush spreading over my face. It is welling up from the bourgeois world that I have come from. "No."

A course peal of laughter rises from the line, and a loud, piercing voice grips me as if someone had seized me by the throat: "Never mind. The day will come, comrade, when there's nothing else to do." And the line breaks into laughter again, the bitterest laughter I have ever heard, the laughter of damnation and despair.

Again the crowd pushes back in the kind of rhythm that is so typical of a lodging house, and we are all herded into the undressing room. It is like all the other rooms except that it is divided by benches and shelves like a fourth-class railway carriage. I cling to the man who spoke to me. He is a Saxon with a friendly manner and he has noticed that I am a stranger here. A certain sensitiveness, an almost perverse, spiritual alertness makes me like him very much.

Out of a big iron chest each of us takes a coat hanger that would serve admirably to hit somebody over the head with. As we undress the room becomes filled with the heavy breath of poverty. We are so close together that we brush against each other every time we move. Anyone who has been a soldier, anyone who has been to a public bath is perfectly accustomed to the look of naked bodies. But I have never seen anything quite so repulsive as all these hundreds of withered human frames. For in the homeless army the majority are men who have already been defeated in the struggle of life, the crippled, old, and sick. There is no repulsive disease of which traces are not to be seen here. There is no form of mutilation or degeneracy that is not represented, and the naked bodies of the old men are in a disgusting state of decline. . . .

It is superfluous to describe what follows. Towels are handed out by the same methods described above. Then nightgowns—long, sack-like affairs made of plain unbleached cotton but freshly washed. Then slippers. All at once a new sound goes up from the moving mass that has been walking silently on bare feet. The shuffling and rattling of the hard soles of the slippers ring through the corridor.

Distribution of spoons, distribution of enameledware bowls with the words "Property of the City of Berlin" written on their sides. Then the meal itself. A big kettle is carried in. Men with yellow smocks have brought it and men with yellow smocks ladle out the food. These men, too, are homeless and they have been expressly picked by the establishment and given free food and lodging and a little pocket money in exchange for their work about the house.

. . . Now the men are standing in a long row, dressed in their plain nightshirts that reach to the ground, and the noise of their shuffling feet is like the noise of big wild animals walking up and down the stone floor of their cages before feeding time. The men lean far over the kettle so that the warm steam from the food envelops them and they hold out their bowls as if begging and whisper to the attendant. "Give me a real helping. Give me a little more." A piece of bread is handed out with every bowl.

My next recollection is sitting at table in another room on a crowded bench that is like a seat in a fourth-class railway carriage. Hundreds of hungry mouths make an enormous noise eating their food. The men sit bent over their food like animals who feel that someone is going to take it away from them. They hold their bowl with their left arm part way around it, so that nobody can take it away, and they also protect it with their other elbow and with their head and mouth, while they move the spoon as fast as they can between their mouth and the bowl. . . .

We shuffle into the sleeping room, where each bed has a number painted in big letters on the wall over it. You must find the number that you have around your neck, and there is your bed, your home for one night. It stands in a row with fifty others and across the room there are fifty more in a row. . . .

I curl up in a ball for a few minutes and then see that the Saxon is lying the same way, curled up in the next bed. We look at each other with eyes that understand everything. . . .

. . . Only a few people, very few, move around at all. The others lie awake and still, staring at their blankets, wrapped up in themselves but not sleeping. Only an almost soldierly sense of comradeship, an inner self-control engendered by the presence of so many people, prevents the despair that is written on all these faces from expressing itself. The few who are moving about do so with the tormenting consciousness of men who merely want to kill time. They do not believe in what they are doing.

Going to sleep means passing into the unconscious, eliminating the intelligence. And one can read deeply into a man's life by watching the way he goes to sleep. For we have not always slept in municipal lodgings. There are men among us who still move as if they were in a bourgeois bedchamber. . . .

. . . The air is poisoned with the breath of men who have stuffed too much food into empty stomachs. There is also a sickening smell of lysol. It seems completely terrible to me, and I am not merely pitying myself. It is painful just to look at the scene. Life is no longer human here. Today, when I am experiencing this for the first time, I think that I should prefer to do away with myself, to take gas, to jump into the river, or leap from some high place, if I were ever reduced to such straits that I had to live here in the lodging house. But I have had too much experience not to mistrust even myself. If I ever were reduced so low, would I really come to such a decision? I do not know. Animals die, plants wither, but men always go on living.

REVIEW QUESTIONS

1. What is the significance of the leader principle, military discipline, imperial conquest, war, peace, and the blood-bonded community for Friedrich Jünger?
2. Why did Jünger attack liberalism?
3. What political implications do you see in Jünger's statement that there is in nationalism "something intoxicating, a wild and lusty pride, a mighty heroic vitality"?
4. What was the psychological impact on Germans victimized by the inflation? The Great Depression?

---

8   The Rise of Nazism

Many extreme racist-nationalist and paramilitary organizations sprang up in postwar Germany. Adolf Hitler (1889–1945), a veteran of World War I, joined one of these organizations, which became known as the National Socialist German Worker's Party (commonly called the Nazi Party). Hitler's uncanny insight into the state of mind of postwar Germans, along with his extraordinary oratorical gifts, enabled him to gain control of the party. Had it not been for the Great Depression that began in late 1929, the National Socialists might have remained a relatively small and insignificant party, a minor irritant outside the mainstream of German politics. In 1928 the Nazis had 810,000 votes; in 1930, during the Depression, their share of votes soared to 6,400,000. To many Germans, the Depression was final evidence that the Weimar Republic had failed. Hitler and the National Socialists would come to power in 1933.

Adolf Hitler
MEIN KAMPF

In the "Beer Hall Putsch" of November 1923, Hitler attempted to overthrow the state government in Bavaria as the first step in bringing down the Weimar Republic. But the Nazis quickly scattered when the Bavarian police opened fire. Hitler was arrested and sentenced to five years' imprisonment—he served only nine months. While in prison, Hitler wrote *Mein Kampf (My* Struggle) (1925–1926), in which he presented his views. The book came to be regarded as an authoritative expression of the Nazi worldview and served as a kind of sacred writing for the Nazi movement.

Hitler's thought—a patchwork of nineteenth-century anti-Semitic, Volkish, Social Darwinist, and anti-Marxist ideas—contrasted sharply with the core values of both the Judeo-Christian and the Enlightenment traditions. Central to Hitler's worldview was racial mythology: a heroic Germanic race that was descended from the ancient Aryans, who once swept across Europe, and was battling for survival against racial inferiors. Hitler's aim was to gain power and establish a personal dictatorship which eradicated freedom, molded Germans to embrace wholeheartedly Nazi nationalistic, racist, and militaristic ideology, and legitimized brutality and terror against Nazi enemies. In the following passages, Hitler presents his views of race, of propaganda, and of National Socialist territorial goals.

THE PRIMACY OF RACE

Nature does not want a pairing of weaker individuals with stronger ones; it wants even less a mating of a higher race with a weaker one. Otherwise its routine labors of promoting a higher breed lasting perhaps over hundreds of thousands of years would be wiped out.

History offers much evidence for this process. It proves with terrifying clarity that any generic mixture of Aryan blood with people of a lower quality undermines the culturally superior people. The population of North America consists to a large extent of Germanic elements, which have mixed very little with inferior people of color. Central and South America shows a different humanity and culture; here Latin immigrants mixed with the aborigines, sometimes on a large scale. This example alone allows a clear recognition of the effects of racial mixtures. Remaining racially pure the Germans of North America rose to be masters of their continent; they will remain masters as long as they do not defile their blood.

The result of mixing races in short is: a) lowering the cultural level of the higher race; b) physical and spiritual retrogression and thus the beginning of a slow but progressive decline.

To promote such a development means no less than committing sin against the will of the eternal creator. . . .

Everything that we admire on earth—science, technology, invention—is the creative product of only a few people, and perhaps originally of only one race; our whole culture depends upon them. If they perish, the beauties of the earth will be buried. . . .

All great cultures of the past perished because the original creative race was destroyed by the poisoning of its blood.

Such collapse always happened because people forgot that all cultures depend on human beings. In order to preserve a given culture it is necessary to preserve the human beings who created it. Cultural preservation in this world is tied to the iron law of necessity and the right to victory of the stronger and better. . . .

If we divide humanity into three categories: into founders of culture, bearers of culture, and destroyers of culture, the Aryan would undoubtedly rate first. He established the foundations and walls of all human progress. . . .

The mixing of blood and the resulting lowering of racial cohesion is the sole reason why cultures perish. People do not perish by defeat in war, but by losing the power of resistance inherent in pure blood.

All that is not pure race in this world is chaff.
. . .

A state which in the age of racial poisoning dedicates itself to the cultivation of its best racial elements will one day become master of the world.

Excerpts translated by T. H. Von Laue from Adolf Hitler, *Mein Kampf*, Central Publisher of the NSDAP, Franz Eher Nachf, Munich. Copyright vol. I 1925, vol. II 1927, by Franz Eher Nachf. Verlag Gambit, Munich. All rights reserved. Reprinted by permission of Angela Von Laue.

Modern anti-Semitism was a powerful legacy of the Middle Ages and the unsettling changes brought about by rapid industrialization; it was linked to racist doctrines that asserted the Jews were inherently wicked and bore dangerous racial qualities. Hitler grasped the political potential of anti-Semitism: by concentrating all evil in one enemy, he could provide non-Jews with an emotionally satisfying explanation for all their misfortunes and thus manipulate and unify the German people.

ANTI-SEMITISM

The Jew offers the most powerful contrast to the Aryan. . . . Despite all their seemingly intellectual qualities the Jewish people are without true culture, and especially without a culture of their own. What Jews seem to possess as culture is the property of others, for the most part corrupted in their hands.

In judging the Jewish position in regard to human culture, we have to keep in mind their essential characteristics. There never was—and still is no—Jewish art. The Jewish people made no original contribution to the two queen goddesses of all arts: architecture and music. What they have contributed is bowdlerization or spiritual theft. Which proves that Jews lack the very qualities distinguishing creative and culturally blessed races. . . .

The first and biggest lie of Jews is that Jewishness is not a matter of race but of religion, from which inevitably follow even more lies. One of them refers to the language of Jews. It is not a means of expressing their thoughts, but of hiding them. While speaking French a Jew thinks Jewish, and while he cobbles together some German verse, he merely expresses the mentality of his people.

As long as the Jew is not master of other peoples, he must for better or worse speak their languages. Yet as soon as the others have become his servants, then all should learn a universal language (Esperanto for instance), so that by these means the Jews can rule more easily. . . .

For hours the blackhaired Jewish boy lies in wait, with satanic joy on his face, for the unsuspecting girl whom he disgraces with his blood and thereby robs her from her people. He tries by all means possible to destroy the racial foundations of the people he wants to subjugate.

But a people of pure race conscious of its blood can never be enslaved by the Jew; he remains forever a ruler of bastards.

Thus he systematically attempts to lower racial purity by racially poisoning individuals.

In politics he begins to replace the idea of democracy with the idea of the dictatorship of the proletariat.

He found his weapon in the organized Marxist masses, which avoid democracy and instead help him to subjugate and govern people dictatorially with his brutal fists.

Systematically he works toward a double revolution, in economics and politics.

With the help of his international contacts he enmeshes people who effectively resist his attacks from within in a net of external enemies whom he incites to war, and, if necessary, goes on to unfurling the red [Communist] flag of revolution over the battlefield.

He batters the national economies until the ruined state enterprises are privatized and subject to his financial control.

In politics he refuses to give the state the means for its self-preservation, destroys the bases of any national self-determination and defense, wipes out the faith in leadership, denigrates the historic past, and pulls everything truly great into the gutter.

In cultural affairs he pollutes art, literature, theatre, befuddles national sentiment, subverts all concepts of beauty and grandeur, of nobleness and goodness, and reduces people to their lowest nature.

Religion is made ridiculous, custom and morals are declared outdated, until the last props of national character in the battle for survival have collapsed. . . .

Thus the Jew is the big rabble-rouser for the complete destruction of Germany. Wherever in the world we read about attacks on Germany, Jews are the source, just as in peace and during the war the newspapers of both the Jewish stock market and the Marxists systematically incited hatred against Germany. Country after country gave up its neutrality and joined the world war coalition in disregard of the true interest of the people.

Jewish thinking in all this is clear. The Bolshevization of Germany, i.e., the destruction of the German national people-oriented intelligentsia and thereby the exploitation of German labor under the yoke of Jewish global finance are but the prelude for the expansion of the Jewish tendency to conquer the world. As so often in history, Germany is the turning point in this mighty struggle. If our people and our state become the victims of blood-thirsty and money-thirsty Jewish tyrants, the whole world will be enmeshed in the tentacles of this octopus. If, however, Germany liberates itself from this yoke, we can be sure that the greatest threat to all humanity has been broken. . . .

Hitler was a master propagandist and advanced his ideas on propaganda techniques in *Mein Kampf*. He mocked the learned and book-oriented German liberals and socialists who he felt were entirely unsuited for modern mass politics. The successful leader, he said, must win over the masses through the use of simple ideas and images, constantly repeated to evoke primitive feelings that weaken thinking, enabling the leader to gain control of the mind. Hitler contended that mass meetings were the most effective means of winning followers. What counted most at these demonstrations, he said, were willpower, strength, and unflagging determination radiating from the speaker to every single individual in the crowd.

PROPAGANDA AND MASS RALLIES

The task of propaganda does not lie in the scientific training of individuals, but in directing the masses toward certain facts, events, necessities, etc., whose significance is to be brought to their attention.

The essential skill consists in doing this so well that you convince people about the reality of a fact, about the necessity of an event, about the correctness of something necessary, etc. . . . You always have to appeal to the emotions and far less to the so-called intellect. . . .

The art of propaganda lies in sensing the emotional temper of the broad masses, so that you, in psychologically effective form, can catch their attention and move their hearts. . . .

The attention span of the masses is very short, their understanding limited; they easily forget. For that reason all effective propaganda has to concentrate on very few points and drive them home through simple slogans, until even the simplest can grasp what you have in mind. As soon as you give up this principle and become too complex, you will lose your effectiveness, because the masses cannot digest and retain what you have offered. You thereby weaken your case and in the end lose it altogether.

The larger the scope of your case, the more psychologically correct must be the method of your presentation. . . .

The task of propaganda lies not in weighing right and wrong, but in driving home your own point of view. You cannot objectively explore the facts that favor others and present them in doctrinaire sincerity to the masses. You have to push relentlessly your own case. . . .

Even the most brilliant propaganda will not produce the desired results unless it follows this fundamental rule: You must stick to limiting yourself to essentials and repeat them endlessly. Persistence on this point, as in so many other cases in the world, is the first and most important precondition for success. . . .

Propaganda does not exist to furnish interesting diversions to blasé young dandies, but to convince above all the masses. In their clumsiness they always require a long lead before they are ready to take notice. Only by thousandfold repetition will the simplest concepts stick in their memories.

No variation of your presentation should change the content of your propaganda; you always have to come to the same conclusion. You may want to highlight your slogans from various sides, but at the end you always have to reaffirm them. Only consistent and uniform propaganda will succeed. . . .

Every advertisement, whether in business or politics, derives its success from its persistence and uniformity. . . .

The mass meeting is . . . necessary because an incipient supporter of a new political movement will feel lonely and anxiously isolated. He needs at the start a sense of a larger community which among most people produces vitality and courage. The same man as member of a military company or battalion and surrounded by his comrades will more lightheartedly join an attack than if he were all by himself. In a crowd he feels more sheltered, even if reality were a thousandfold against him.

The sense of community in a mass demonstration not only empowers the individual, but also promotes an esprit de corps. The person who in his business or workshop is the first to represent a new political creed is likely to be exposed to heavy discrimination. He needs the reassurance that comes from the conviction of being a member and a fighter in a large comprehensive organization. The sense of this organization comes first to him in a mass demonstration. When he for the first time goes from a petty workshop or from a large factory, where he feels insignificant, to a mass demonstration surrounded by thousands and thousands of like-minded fellows—when he as a seeker is gripped by the intoxicating surge of enthusiasm among three or four thousand others—when the visible success and the consensus of thousands of others prove the correctness of his new political creed and for the first time arouse doubts about his previous political convictions—then he submits to the miraculous influence of what we call "mass suggestion." The will, the yearning, and also the power of thousands of fellow citizens now fill every individual. The man who full of doubts and uncertain enters such a gathering, leaves it inwardly strengthened; he has become a member of a community. . . .

Hitler wanted a reawakened, racially unite Germany to achieve *Lebensraum*—living space—by expanding eastward at the expense of the Slavs, whom he viewed as racially inferior.

LEBENSRAUM

A people gains its freedom of existence only by occupying a sufficiently large space on earth. . . .

If the National Socialist movement really wants to achieve a hallowed mission in history for our people, it must, in painful awareness of its position in the world, boldly and methodically fight against the aimlessness and incapacity which have hitherto guided the foreign policy of the German people. It must then, without respect for "tradition" and prejudice, find the courage to rally the German people to a forceful advance on the road which leads from their present cramped living space to new territories. In this manner they will be liberated from the danger of perishing or being enslaved in service to others.

The National Socialist movement must try to end the disproportion between our numerous population and its limited living space, the source of our food as well as the base of our power—between our historic past and the hopelessness of our present impotence. . . .

The demand for restoring the boundaries of 1914 is a political nonsense with consequences so huge as to make it appear a crime—quite apart from the fact that our pre-war boundaries were anything but logical. They neither united all people of German nationality nor served strategic-political necessity. . . .

In the light of this fact we National Socialists must resolutely stick to our foreign policy goals, namely *to secure for the German people the territorial base to which they are entitled.* This is the only goal which before God and our German posterity justifies shedding our blood. . . .

Just as our forebears did not receive the soil on which we live as a gift from heaven—they had to risk their lives for it—so in future we will not secure the living space for our people by divine grace, but by the might of the victorious sword.

However much all of us recognize the necessity of a reckoning with France, it would remain ineffectual if we thereby limited the scope of our foreign policy. It makes sense only if we consider it as a rear-guard action for expanding our living space elsewhere in Europe. . . .

If we speak today about gaining territory in Europe, we think primarily of Russia and its border states. . . .

Kurt G. W. Ludecke
THE DEMAGOGIC ORATOR

Nazi popularity grew partly due to Hitler's power as an orator to play on the dissatisfactions of postwar Germans with the Weimar Republic. In the following selection from *I Knew Hitler—The Story of a Nazi Who Escaped the Blood Purge* (1937), Kurt G. W. Ludecke, an early supporter of Hitler who later broke with the Nazis, describes Hitler's ability to mesmerize his audience. Ludecke's observations support the analysis of Thomas Mann, the distinguished German writer. Two years before Hitler took power, Mann described Nazism as an inhumane and frenzied orgiastic cult in which "fanaticism turns into a means of salvation, enthusiasm into epileptic ecstasy, politics becomes an opiate for the masses . . . and reason veils her face." Placed in a concentration camp shortly after Hitler came to power, Ludecke escaped and fled to the United States. The fortunate Ludecke eluded the blood purge that Hitler instituted against people considered a threat to his rule.

. . . [W]hen the Nazis marched into the Koenigsplatz with banners flying, their bands playing stirring German marches, they were greeted with tremendous cheers. An excited, expectant crowd was now filling the beautiful square to the last inch and overflowing into surrounding streets. They were well over a hundred thousand. . . . I was close enough to see Hitler's face, watch every change in his expression, hear every word he said.

When the man stepped forward on the platform, there was almost no applause. He stood silent for a moment. Then he began to speak, quietly and ingratiatingly at first. Before long his voice had risen to a hoarse shriek that gave an extraordinary effect of an intensity of feeling. There were many high-pitched, rasping notes. . . .

Critically I studied this slight, pale man, his brown hair parted on one side and falling again and again over his sweating brow. Threatening and beseeching, with small, pleading hands and flaming, steel-blue eyes, he had the look of a fanatic.

Presently my critical faculty was swept away. Leaning from the tribune as if he were trying to impel his inner self into the consciousness of all these thousands, he was holding the masses, and me with them, under a hypnotic spell by the sheer force of his conviction.

He urged the revival of German honor and manhood with a blast of words that seemed to cleanse. "Bavaria is now the most German land in Germany!" he shouted, to roaring applause. Then, plunging into sarcasm, he indicted the leaders in Berlin as "November Criminals," [founders of the Weimar Republic] daring to put into words thoughts that Germans were now almost afraid to think and certainly to voice.

It was clear that Hitler was feeling the exaltation of the emotional response now surging up toward him from his thousands of hearers.

His voice rising to passionate climaxes, he finished his speech with an anthem of hate against the "Novemberlings" and a pledge of undying love for the Fatherland. "Germany must be free!" was his final defiant slogan. Then two last words that were like the sting of a lash: *"Deutschland Erwache!"*

Kurt G.W. Ludecke, *I Knew Hitler—The Story of a Nazi Who Escaped the Blood Purge* (1937). Used by permission of AMS Press.

Awake, Germany! There was thunderous applause, then the masses took a solemn oath "to save Germany in Bavaria from Bolshevism."

I do not know how to describe the emotions that swept over me as I heard this man. His words were like a scourge. When he spoke of the disgrace of Germany, I felt ready to spring on any enemy. His appeal to German manhood was like a call to arms, the gospel he preached a sacred truth. He seemed another Luther. I forgot everything but the man; then, glancing round, I saw that his magnetism was holding these thousands as one.

Of course I was ripe for this experience. I was a man of thirty-two, weary of disgust and disillusionment, a wanderer seeking a cause; a patriot without a channel for his patriotism, a yearner after the heroic without a hero. The intense will of the man, the passion of his sincerity seemed to flow from him into me. I experienced an exaltation that could be likened only to religious conversion.

I felt sure that no one who had heard Hitler that afternoon could doubt that he was the man of destiny, the vitalizing force in the future of Germany. The masses who had streamed into the Koenigsplatz with a stern sense of national humiliation seemed to be going forth renewed.

The bands struck up, the thousands began to move away. I knew my search was ended. I had found myself, my leader, and my cause.

REVIEW QUESTIONS

1. How did Adolf Hitler account for cultural greatness? Cultural decline?
2. What comparisons did Hitler draw between Aryans and Jews?
3. What kind of evidence did Hitler offer for his anti-Semitic arguments?
4. Theodor Mommsen, a nineteenth-century German historian, said that anti-Semites do not listen to "logic and ethical arguments. . . . They listen only to their own envy and hatred, to the meanest instincts." Discuss this statement.
5. What insights did Hitler have into mass psychology and propaganda?
6. What foreign policy goals did Hitler have for Germany? How did he expect them to be achieved?
7. According to Kurt G. W. Ludecke, how did Hitler mesmerize his audience?

---

9   The Leader-State

Adolf Hitler came to power by legal means, appointed chancellor by President Paul von Hindenburg on January 30, 1933, according to the constitution of the Weimar Republic. Thereafter, however, he proceeded to dismantle the legal structure of the Weimar system and replace it with an inflexible dictatorship that revolved around his person. Quickly reacting to the popular confusion caused by the suspicious Reichstag (German Parliament) fire, Hitler issued a decree on February 28, 1933, that suspended all guarantees of civil and individual freedom. In March, the Reichstag adopted the Enabling Act, which vested all legislative powers in Hitler's hands. Then Hitler proceeded to destroy the autonomy of the federal states, dissolve the trade unions, outlaw other political parties, and end freedom of the press. By the time he eliminated party rivals in a blood purge on June 30, 1934, the consolidation of power was complete. Meanwhile, much of Germany's public and institutional life fell under Nazi Party control in a process known as the *Gleichschaltung*, or coordination. The Third Reich was organized as a leader-state, in which Hitler the *Führer* (leader) embodied and expressed the real will of the German people, commanded the supreme loyalty of the nation, and had unlimited authority.

Ernst Rudolf Huber
"THE AUTHORITY OF THE FÜHRER IS . . . ALL-INCLUSIVE AND UNLIMITED"

In *Verfassungsrecht des grossdeutschen Reiches* (Constitutional Law of the Greater German Reich) (1939), legal scholar Ernst Rudolf Huber (1903–1990) offered a classic explication of the basic principles of National Socialism. The following excerpts from that work describe the nature of Hitler's political authority.

The Führer-Reich of the [German] people is founded on the recognition that the true will of the people cannot be disclosed through parliamentary votes and plebiscites but that the will of the people in its pure and uncorrupted form can only be expressed through the Führer. Thus a distinction must be drawn between the supposed will of the people in a parliamentary democracy, which merely reflects the conflict of the various social interests, and the true will of the people in the Führer-state, in which the collective will of the real political unit is manifested. . . .

It would be impossible for a law to be introduced and acted upon in the Reichstag which had not originated with the Führer or, at least, received his approval. The procedure is similar to that of the plebiscite: The lawgiving power does not rest in the Reichstag; it merely proclaims through its decision its agreement with the will of the Führer, who is the lawgiver of the German people.

The Führer unites in himself all the sovereign authority of the Reich; all public authority in the state as well as in the movement is derived from the authority of the Führer. We must speak not of the state's authority but of the Führer's authority if we wish to designate the character of the political authority within the Reich correctly. The state does not hold political authority as an impersonal unit but receives it from the Führer as the executor of the national will. The authority of the Führer is complete and all-embracing; it unites in itself all the means of political direction; it extends into all fields of national life; it embraces the entire people, which is bound to the Führer in loyalty and obedience. The authority of the Führer is not limited by checks and controls, by special autonomous bodies or individual rights, but it is free and independent, all-inclusive and unlimited. It is not, however, self-seeking or arbitrary and its ties are within itself. It is derived from the people; that is, it is entrusted to the Führer by the people. It exists for the people and has its justification in the people; it is free of all outward ties because it is in its innermost nature firmly bound up with the fate, the welfare, the mission, and the honor of the people.

Ernst Rudolf Huber, *Constitutional Law of the German Reich* (1939), (Washington D..C.: Government Printing Office, 1943), pp. 34, 36–38.

REVIEW QUESTION

REVIEW QUESTION

Point out several ways that Ernst Rudolf Huber's views represent a rejection of the
  Western liberal-democratic tradition.

---

10 The Nazification of Culture and Society

The Nazis aspired to more than political power; they also wanted to have the
German people view the world in accordance with National Socialist ideology.
Toward this end, the Nazis strictly regulated cultural life. Believing that the
struggle of racial forces occupied the center of world history, Nazi ideologists
tried to strengthen the racial consciousness of the German people. Numerous
courses in "race science" introduced in schools and universities emphasized the
superiority of the Nordic soul as well as the worthlessness of Jews and their
threat to the nation.

Jakob Graf
HEREDITY AND RACIAL BIOLOGY
FOR STUDENTS

The following assignments from a textbook entitled *Heredity and Racial Biology
for Students* (1935), written by a Nazi ideologist, show how young people were
indoctrinated with racist teachings.

HOW WE CAN LEARN TO RECOGNIZE A PERSON'S RACE
Assignments

1. Summarize the spiritual characteristics of
the individual races.

2. Collect from stories, essays, and poems
examples of ethnological illustrations. Under-
line those terms which describe the type and
mode of the expression of the soul.

3. What are the expressions, gestures, and
movements which allow us to make conclusions
as to the attitude of the racial soul?

4. Determine also the physical features which
go hand in hand with the specific racial soul
characteristics of the individual figures.

5. Try to discover the intrinsic nature of the
racial soul through the characters in stories and
poetical works in terms of their inner attitude.
Apply this mode of observation to persons in
your own environment.

6. Collect propaganda posters and caricatures
for your race book and arrange them according to a racial scheme. What image of beauty
is emphasized by the artist (a) in posters publicizing sports and travel? (b) in publicity for

George L. Mosse, ed., *Nazi Culture: Intellectual, Cultural,
and Social Life in the Third Reich* (New York: Grosset &
Dunlap, 1966), p. 80.

cosmetics? How are hunters, mountain climbers, and shepherds drawn?

7. Collect from illustrated magazines, newspapers, etc., pictures of great scholars, statesmen, artists, and others who distinguish themselves by their special accomplishments (for example, in economic life, politics, sports). Determine the preponderant race and admixture, according to physical characteristics. Repeat this exercise with the pictures of great men of all nations and times.

8. When viewing monuments, busts, etc.,, be sure to pay attention to the race of the person portrayed with respect to figure, bearing, and physical characteristics. Try to harmonize these determinations with the features of the racial soul.

9. Observe people whose special racial features have drawn your attention, also with respect to their bearing when moving or when speaking. Observe their expressions and gestures.

10. Observe the Jew: his way of walking, his bearing, gestures, and movements when talking.

11. What strikes you about the way a Jew talks and sings?

Louis P. Lochner
BOOK BURNING

The anti-intellectualism of the Nazis was demonstrated on May 10, 1933, when the principal German student body organized students for a book-burning festival. In university towns, students consigned to the flames books that were considered a threat to the Germanic spirit, many of them written by prominent Jewish authors. Louis P. Lochner (1887–1975), head of the Associated Press Bureau in Berlin, provided an eyewitness account of the scene in the German capital.

The whole civilized world was shocked when on the evening of May 10, 1933, the books of authors displeasing to the Nazis, including even those of our own Helen Keller, were solemnly burned on the immense Franz Joseph Platz between the University of Berlin and the State Opera on Unter den Linden. I was a witness to the scene.

All afternoon Nazi raiding parties had gone into public and private libraries, throwing onto the streets such books as Dr. [Joseph] Goebbels [Nazi Progaganda Minister] in his supreme wisdom had decided were unfit for Nazi Germany.

From the streets Nazi columns of beerhall fighters had picked up these discarded volumes and taken them to the square above referred to.

Here the heap grew higher and higher, and every few minutes another howling mob arrived, adding more books to the impressive pyre. Then, as night fell, students from the university, mobilized by the little doctor, performed veritable Indian dances and incantations as the flames began to soar skyward.

When the orgy was at its height, a cavalcade of cars drove into sight. It was the Propaganda Minister himself, accompanied by his bodyguard and a number of fellow torch bearers of the new Nazi *Kultur.*

"Fellow students, German men and women!" he said as he stepped before a

Louis P. Lochner, ed., *The Goebbels Diaries, 1942–43* (Garden City, NY: Doubleday, 1948), pp. 17–18.

microphone for all Germany to hear him. "The age of extreme Jewish intellectualism has now ended, and the success of the German revolution has again given the right of way to the German spirit. . . .

"You are doing the right thing in committing the evil spirit of the past to the flames at this late hour of the night. It is a strong, great, and symbolic act—an act that is to bear witness before all the world to the fact that the spiritual foundation of the November [Weimar] Republic has disappeared. From the ashes there will rise the phoenix of the spirit. . . .

"The past is lying in flames. The future will rise from the flames within our own hearts. . . . Brightened by these flames our vow shall be: The Reich and the Nation and our Fuehrer Adolf Hitler: *Heil! Heil! Heil!*"

The few foreign correspondents who had taken the trouble to view this "symbolic act" were stunned. What had happened to the "Land of Thinkers and Poets?" they wondered.

Stephen H. Roberts
THE NUREMBERG RALLY, 1936

Symbolic of the Nazi regime were the monster rallies staged at Nuremberg. Scores of thousands roared, marched, and worshiped at their leader's feet. These true believers, the end product of Nazi indoctrination, celebrated Hitler's achievements and demonstrated their loyalty to their savior. Everything was brilliantly orchestrated to impress Germans and the world with the irresistible power, determination, and unity of the Nazi movement and the greatness of the Führer. Armies of youths waving flags, storm troopers bearing weapons, and workers shouldering long-handled spades paraded past Hitler, who stood at attention, his arm extended in the Nazi salute. The endless columns of marchers, the stirring martial music played by huge bands, the forest of flags, the chanting and cheering of spectators, and the burning torches and beaming spotlights united the participants into a racial community. "Wherever Hitler leads we follow," thundered thousands of Germans in a giant chorus. The Nuremberg rallies were among the greatest theatrical performances of the twentieth century.

Stephen H. Roberts, an Australian professor of history who was in Germany from November 1935 to March 1937, observed firsthand the 1936 party rally at Nuremberg. His description of the event, first published in 1938, follows.

The Rally opened in the huge Congress Hall, where 60,000 people gathered to listen to Hitler's proclamation on his achievements of the last three years. Hundreds of swastika banners filed in, to the impressive music of the *Song of the Standards*, and formed a solid mass of red and gold at the back of the stage. Every device of music and coloured light was used to keep the atmosphere tense, and the spotlight that played on the giant swastika behind the banners exerted an influence that was almost hypnotic. . . .

The atmosphere was most strained and unreal. The speakers deliberately played on the feelings of

Stephen H. Roberts, *The House That Hitler Built* (New York: Harper & Brothers Publishers, 1938), pp. 138–142.

the people. At intervals, when something particularly impressive was read out, a curious tremor swept the crowd, and all around me individuals uttered a strange cry, a kind of emotional sigh that invariably changed into a shout of *"Heil Hitler"*. It was a definite struggle to remain rational in a horde so surcharged with tense emotionalism. . . .

The rest of the week consisted either of lavish displays or of meetings at which Party leaders spoke. The German excels in mass meetings. Not an hour of the day or night was quiet, and, when the official functions ended, zealous Nazis formed impromptu torchlight processions of their own. One day 160,000 men of the popular Labour Service Corps filed past, with their dark-brown uniforms and bright-polished shovels, and, on a bitterly cold morning, many thousands of them stood stripped to the waist for hours, listening to official speeches. On another day, a still larger number of Hitler Youth and Maidens and groups of the sea-scouts crowded a huge arena to listen to Hitler and von Schirach.[1] On still another day, the Brownshirts and Black Guards [SS] formed a solid mass of humanity in the Leopold Arena—160,000 of them. One of the most striking ceremonies took place. Before addressing them, Hitler solemnly marched up to the sacrificial fires that paid homage to those who had died for the movement. It was the only moment of quietness in the whole week. For what seemed an interminable time, three men—Hitler, Himmler, and Lutze[2]—strode up the wide path that clove the brown mass in twain and, after saluting the fire, as solemnly matched back. It was a superbly arranged gesture. Those three men represented individualism as against the solid anonymity of the massed Brownshirts; they stood for leadership as against the blind obedience of the people.

The silence became almost unendurable, and it was a relief when Hitler returned to the presidential stand and broke into one of his impassioned speeches that "the Brown Army must march again, as it has marched in the past, if Bolshevism raises its challenging head in Germany or on Germany's frontiers.". . .

That Sunday afternoon every Brownshirt and every Black Guard in Nuremberg filed past Hitler in the central square of the town. For five and a half hours they marched in columns of twelve, and the whole time Hitler stood erect, punctiliously acknowledging every salute and never showing fatigue. Göring[3] obtained relief by leaning against the side of Hitler's car, and the standard-bearers had to be relieved every half-hour, but Hitler went on to the end—and then dashed away to other lectures and a round of committee meetings. Anybody doubting his physical strength need only look at his list of engagements that day. . . .

So the week closed of a triumph of organization and showmanship. A million and a quarter visitors were crammed into a town of 400,000 people, and every man—indeed, every guest—was moved about as if he were under orders. In fact, it was said that, amongst its many purposes, the Party Rally was a miniature mobilization. As a display of mass organization and as a colourful spectacle, the Rally could scarcely be surpassed; but, as one left Nuremberg with Hitler's closing speech against the Bolsheviks tinging in one's ears, one wondered about many things. One felt deadened by the endless reiteration of a few simple motives. Everything was hammered in at a relentless pace, until one craved for solitude and quietness. Undoubtedly this was a new Germany one was seeing, with a new kind of patriotism; but the values, clad with mysticism and pseudo-religious ceremonies though they were, made one conscious of an impassable mental gulf between Nazi Germany and the outside democracies.

---

[1]Baldur von Schirach (b. 1907) was Hitler's appointee as head of all youth organizations in the Third Reich.—Eds.

[2]Heinrich Himmler (1900–1945) wielded enormous power in Nazi Germany by virtue of his position as head of the security police (the *Schutzstaffeln*, or SS); Viktor Lutze headed the Nazi storm troopers (the *Sturmabteilung*, or SA), a paramilitary group, also known as the "brownshirts."—Eds.

---

[3]Hermann Göring (1893–1946) was the founder of the Nazi air force (the *Luftwaffe*), director of economic planning, originator of the Gestapo and the concentration camps, and second in command to Hitler.—Eds.

REVIEW QUESTIONS

1. What was Jakob Graf's purpose in teaching students how to recognize a person's race?
2. Why do you think the Nazis made the burning of books a public event? Why does book burning have such potent symbolism?
3. Why did Hitler give such great importance to giant rallies?

---

11 Persecution of the Jews

The Nazis deprived Jews of their German citizenship and instituted many anti-Jewish measures designed to make them outcasts. Thousands of Jewish doctors, lawyers, musicians, artists, and professors were barred from practicing their professions, and Jewish members of the civil service were dismissed. A series of laws tightened the screws of humiliation and persecution. Marriages or sexual encounters between Germans and Jews were forbidden. Universities, schools, restaurants, pharmacies, hospitals, theaters, museums, and athletic fields were gradually closed to Jews.

Subjected to economic strangulation, frequent racial slurs by neighbors and strangers, random assaults and vandalizing of their homes by Nazi thugs, deserted by old Christian friends who had either embraced Nazi racial ideology or feared for their safety if they consorted with Jews, and constantly worrying about arrest, life for German Jews had become a nightmare. This was a heart-wrenching tragedy for the small Jewish minority—some 523,000 out of a population of more than 60 million—who loved Germany and had made enormous contributions to German culture. When Hitler took power, Jews, who constituted less than 1 percent of the population, had won 32 percent of the country's Nobel Prizes, mainly in science and medicine.

In November 1938, using as a pretext the assassination of a German official in Paris by a seventeen-year-old Jewish youth whose family had been mistreated by the Nazis, the Nazis organized an extensive pogrom. Nazi gangs murdered scores of Jews and burned and looted thousands of Jewish businesses, homes, and synagogues all over Germany—an event that became known as Night of the Broken Glass (*Kristallnacht*). Thirty thousand Jews were thrown into concentration camps. The Reich then imposed on the Jewish community a fine of one billion marks. By the outbreak of the war in September 1939, approximately one-half of Germany's 600,000 Jews had fled the country. Those who stayed behind would fall victim to the last stage of the Nazi anti-Jewish campaign—the Final Solution.

THE NUREMBERG LAWS: DEPRIVING JEWS OF CIVIL LIBERTIES

Introduced in 1935, the Law for the Protection of German Blood and German Honor, known as the Nuremberg Laws, played a major role in excluding Jews from German society and crippling them economically. In expressing support for the Nuremberg Laws, two high German officials showed their contempt for the Western liberal tradition and their support for the Nazi goal of transforming Germany into a racial state:

> National Socialism opposes to the theories of the equality of all men and of the fundamentally unlimited freedom of the individual vis-a-vis the State, the harsh but necessary recognition of the inequality of men and of the differences between them based on the laws of nature. Inevitably, differences in the rights and duties of the individual derive from differences between races, nations and peoples.

Following are the Nuremberg Laws.

Moved by the understanding that purity of German blood is the essential condition for the continued existence of the German people, and inspired by the inflexible determination to ensure the existence of the German nation for all time, the Reichstag has unanimously adopted the following law, which is promulgated herewith;

ARTICLE 1

1. Marriages between Jews and subjects of the state of German or related blood are forbidden. Marriages nevertheless concluded are invalid, even if concluded abroad to circumvent this law.

2. Annulment proceedings can be initiated only by the state prosecutor.

ARTICLE 2

Extramarital relations between Jews and subjects of the state of German or related blood are forbidden.

ARTICLE 3

Jews may not employ in their households female subjects of the state of German or related blood who are under 45 years old.

ARTICLE 4

1. Jews are forbidden to fly the Reich or national flag or display Reich colors.

2. They are, on the other hand, permitted to display the Jewish colors. The exercise of this right is protected by the state.

ARTICLE 5

1. Any person who violates the prohibition under Article 1 will be punished with prison or with prison with hard labor.

2. A male who violates the prohibition under Article 2 will be punished with prison or prison with hard labor.

3. Any person violating the provisions under Articles 3 or 4 will be punished with prison with hard labor for up to one year and a fine, or with one or the other of these penalties.

ARTICLE 6

The Reich Minister of the Interior, in coordination with the Deputy of the Führer and the Reich Minister of Justice, will issue the legal and administrative regulations required to implement and complete this law.

ARTICLE 7

The law takes effect on the day following promulgation, except for Article 3, which goes into force on 1 January 1936.

Ernst Heimer
JEW-HATRED IN SCHOOL BOOKS

School, while they were still not yet barred, was often agony for young Jews. In addition to being tormented by classmates who often called them "Jewish pig," Jewish children faced the taunts of Nazi teachers who, in front of the class, denounced Jews as wicked and a danger to the nation. At times teachers wore Nazi uniforms in school. School textbooks on "race science" taught students that Jews were racially inferior to Germans and cruel exploiters by nature.

From an early age students were assigned anti-Semitic writings that labeled Jews a vile and dangerous people. In 1938, Ernst Hiemer, a notorious Nazi and former school teacher, published *The Poisonous Mushroom,* which was designed to shape the minds of young children with fear and hatred of Jews.

The book opens with Franz and his mother looking in the forest for mushrooms. Reaching into her son's basket, the mother discovers some poisonous mushrooms mixed in with the good mushrooms. She then draws a lesson for Franz. Just as there are good and bad mushrooms, so it is with people, and Jews are bad people.

[The mother says] "They are poisonous for our folk."

"Like the poisonous mushrooms!" says Franz.

"Yes, my child! Just like a single poisonous mushroom can kill an entire family, so can a single Jew destroy an entire village, an entire city, yes, even an entire folk!"

Franz has understood his mother.

"Mother, do all non-Jews know that the Jew is as dangerous as the poisonous mushroom?"

The mother shakes her head.

"Unfortunately not, my child. There are many millions of non-Jews who have not yet become acquainted with the Jews. And therefore we must enlighten the people and must warn them against the Jew. But we must also warn our youth against the Jew. Our boys and girls must become acquainted with the

Jew. They must learn that the Jew is the most dangerous poisonous mushroom that there is. Just like poisonous mushrooms sprout from the earth everywhere, so is the Jew to be found in all the lands of the world. Just like poisonous mushrooms often bring along the most terrible misfortune, so is the Jew the cause of misery and distress, of sickness and death."

The German youth must become acquainted with the Jewish poisonous mushroom. It must know what danger the Jew means for the German folk and the whole world. It must know that the Jewish question is a fate question for all of us.

The following stories proclaim the truth about the Jewish poisonous mushroom. They show us the most diverse guises under which the Jew appears. They show us the depravity and baseness of the Jewish race. They show as the Jew as that, which he is in reality, **as devil in human form.**

Ernst Hiemer, *The Poisonous Mushroom* (Lincoln, NE: Third Reich Books, 2006), pp. 6–7.

David H. Buffum
NIGHT OF THE BROKEN GLASS
(KRISTALLNACHT)

The Nazi press depicted the terrible events of *Kristallnacht*—the burning and vandalizing of thousands of Jewish synagogues, homes, and businesses throughout Germany and the killing and maiming of Jews—as a "spontaneous wave of righteous indignation" directed at enemies of Germany. In reality the violence was planned and coordinated by the Nazi government. While many Germans were horrified by the destruction of property and the abuse inflicted on helpless people, often neighbors and respected merchants, there were others who rejoiced at the Jews' misfortune and relished the violence in which they participated. The following account of the vicious onslaught in Leipzig was prepared by David H. Buffum, the American consul.

At 3 A.M. November 10, 1938, was unleashed a barrage of Nazi ferocity as had had no equal hitherto in Germany, or very likely anywhere else in the world since savagery, if ever. Jewish dwellings were smashed into and contents demolished or looted. In one of the Jewish sections an eighteen year old boy was hurled from a three story window to land with both legs broken on a street littered with burning beds and other household furniture and effects from his family's and other apartments. This information was supplied by an attending physician. It is reported from another quarter that among domestic effects thrown out of a Jewish dwelling, a small dog descended four flights to a broken spine on a cluttered street. Although apparently centered in poor districts, the raid was not confined to the humble classes. One apartment of exceptionally refined occupants known to this office, was violently ransacked, presumably in a search for valuables that was not in vain, and one of the marauders thrust a cane through a priceless medieval painting portraying a biblical scene. Another apartment of

the same category is known to have been turned upside down in the frenzied course of whatever the invaders were after. Reported loss of looting of cash, silver, jewelry, and otherwise easily convertible articles, have been frequent.

Jewish shop windows by the hundreds were systematically and wantonly smashed throughout the entire city at a loss estimated at several millions of marks. There are reports that substantial losses have been sustained on the famous Leipzig "Bruhl," as many of the shop windows at the time of the demolition were filled with costly furs that were seized before the windows could be boarded up. In proportion to the general destruction of real estate, however, losses of goods are felt to have been relatively small. The spectators who viewed the wreckage when daylight had arrived were mostly in such a bewildered mood, that there was no danger of impulsive acts, and the perpetrators probably were too busy in carrying out their schedule to take off a whole lot of time for personal profit. At all events, the main streets of the city were a positive litter of shattered plate glass. According to reliable testimony, the debacle was executed by S. S. men and Storm Troopers not in uniform, each group

Nazi Conspiracy and Aggression, vol. 7 (Washington, D.C.: Government Printing Office, 1946), pp. 1037–1041.

having been provided with hammers, axes, crowbars and incendiary bombs.

Three synagogues in Leipzig were fired simultaneously by incendiary bombs and all sacred objects and records desecrated or destroyed, in most instances hurled through the windows and burned in the streets. No attempts whatsoever were made to quench the fires, functions of the fire brigade having been confined to playing water on adjoining buildings. All of the synagogues were irreparably gutted by flames, and the walls of the two that are in the close proximity of the consulate are now being razed. The blackened frames have been centers of attraction during the past week of terror for eloquently silent and bewildered crowds. One of the largest clothing stores in the heart of the city was destroyed by flames from incendiary bombs, only the charred walls and gutted roof having been left standing. As was the case with the synagogues, no attempts on the part of the fire brigade were made to extinguish the fire, although apparently there was a certain amount of apprehension for adjacent property, for the walls of a coffee house next door were covered with asbestos and sprayed by the doughty firemen. It is extremely difficult to believe, but the owners of the clothing store were actually charged with setting the fire and on that basis were dragged from their beds at 6 A.M. and clapped into prison.

Tactics which closely approached the ghoulish took place at the Jewish cemetery where the temple was fired together with a building occupied by caretakers, tombstones uprooted and graves violated. Eye witnesses considered reliable report that ten corpses were left unburied at this cemetery for a week's time because all grave diggers and cemetery attendants had been arrested.

Ferocious as was the violation of property, the most hideous phase of the so-called "spontaneous" action, has been the wholesale arrest and transportation to concentration camps of male German Jews between the ages of sixteen and sixty, as well as Jewish men without citizenship. This has been taking place daily since the night of horror. This office has no way of accurately checking the numbers of such arrests, but there is very little question that they have gone into several thousands in Leipzig alone. Having demolished dwellings and hurled most of the moveable effects to the streets, the insatiably sadistic perpetrators threw many of the trembling inmates into a small stream that flows through the Zoological Park, commanding horrified spectators to spit at them, defile them with mud and jeer at their plight. The latter incident has been repeatedly corroborated by German witnesses who were nauseated in telling the tale. The slightest manifestation of sympathy evoked a positive fury on the part of the perpetrators, and the crowd was powerless to do anything but turn horror-stricken eyes from the scene of abuse, or leave the vicinity. These tactics were carried out the entire morning of November 10th without police intervention and they were applied to men, women and children.

There is much evidence of physical violence, including several deaths. At least half a dozen cases have been personally observed, victims with bloody, badly bruised faces having fled to this office, believing that as refugees their desire to emigrate could be expedited here. As a matter of fact this consulate has been a bedlam of humanity.

REVIEW QUESTIONS

1. What was the purpose of the Nuremberg Laws?
2. How did Nazi children's books demonstrate the power of mythical thinking?
3. What evidence does David H. Buffum provide to show that many Germans did not approve of the events of *Kristallnacht*? Why do you think that many Germans did approve?

12 The Anguish of the Intellectuals

A somber mood gripped European intellectuals in the interwar period. The memory of World War I and the hypernationalism behind it, the rise of totalitarianism, and the Great Depression caused intellectuals to have grave doubts about the nature and destiny of Western civilization. To many European liberals, it seemed that the sun was setting on the Enlightenment tradition, that the ideals of reason and freedom, already gravely weakened by World War I, could not endure the threats posed by surging chauvinism, economic collapse, and totalitarian ideologies.

Johan Huizinga
IN THE SHADOW OF TOMORROW

Dutch historian Johan Huizinga (1872–1945) wrote that European civilization was at the breaking point in his book *In the Shadow of Tomorrow* (1936).

We are living in a demented world. And we know it. It would not come as a surprise to anyone if tomorrow the madness gave way to a frenzy which would leave our poor Europe in a state of distracted stupor . . . with the spirit gone.

Everywhere there are doubts as to the solidity of our social structure, vague fears of the imminent future, a feeling that our civilization is on the way to ruin. . . . How to avoid the recognition that almost all things which once seemed sacred and immutable have now become unsettled, truth and humanity, justice and reason? We see forms of government no longer capable of functioning, production systems on the verge of collapse, social-forces gone wild with power. The roaring engine of this tremendous time seems to be heading for a breakdown. . . .

If, then, this civilization is to be saved, if it is not to be submerged by centuries of barbarism

but to secure the treasures of its inheritance on new and more stable foundations, there is indeed need for those now living fully to realise how far the decay has already progressed. . . .

How naïve the glad and confident hope of a century ago, that the advance of science and the general extension of education assured the progressive perfection of society, seems to us today! Who can still seriously believe that the translation of scientific triumphs into still more marvelous technical achievements is enough to save civilization, or that the eradication of illiteracy means the end of barbarism! . . .

Delusion and misconception flourish everywhere. . . . The world is filled with hate and misunderstanding. . . . For the shallow, semi-educated person the beneficial restraints of respect for tradition, form and cult are gradually falling away. Worst of all is that widely prevalent indifference to truth which reaches its peak in the open advocacy of the political lie.

Barbarisation sets in when, in an old culture which once, in the course of many centuries, had raised itself to purity and clarity of thought and

Johan Huizinga, *In the Shadow of Tomorrow* (London: Heinemann, 1936), pp. 1–3, 51, 194–195.

understanding, the vapours of the magic and fantastic rise up again from the seething brew of passions to cloud the understanding: when the *muthos* [myth] supplants the *logos* [reason].

Again and again the new creed of the heroic will to power, with its exaltation of life over understanding, is seen to embody the very tendencies which to the believer in the Spirit spell the drift towards barbarism. For the "life-philosophy" does exactly this: it extols *muthos* over *logos*. To the prophets of the life-philosophy barbarism has no deprecatory implications. The term itself loses its meaning. The new rulers desire nothing else.

Nicolas Berdyaev
MODERN IDEOLOGIES AT VARIANCE WITH CHRISTIANITY

To Nicolas Berdyaev, a Russian Christian philosopher who fled the Soviet Union, Communism and Nazism were modern forms of idolatry in opposition to the core values of Christianity. Nationalism, he said, "dehumanizes ethics" and provokes hatred among peoples. Nazi racism, which demonizes Jews because of their genes, is "unworthy of a Christian." Only by a return to Christian piety, maintained Berdyaev, can we overcome the "collective demoniac possession" that was destroying European civilization. By Christian piety, he meant an active struggle for human dignity and social justice. Berdyaev expressed these views in *The Fate of Man in the Modern World* (1935), which is excerpted below.

We are witnessing the process of dehumanization in all phases of culture and of social life. Above all, moral consciousness is being dehumanized, Man has ceased to be the supreme value: he has ceased to have any value at all. The youth of the whole world, communist, fascist, national-socialist or those simply carried away by technics or sport—this youth is not only anti-humanistic in its attitudes, but often anti-human. . . .

. . . A bestial cruelty toward man is characteristic of our age, and this is more astonishing since it is displayed at the very peak of human refinement, where modern conceptions of sympathy, it would seem, have made impossible the old, barbaric forms of cruelty. Bestialism is something quite different from the old, national, healthy barbarism; it is barbarism within a refined civilization . . . Here the atavistic, barbaric instincts are filtered through the prism of civilization, and hence they have a pathological character. . . . The bestialism of our time is a continuation of the war, it has poisoned mankind with the blood of war. The morals of war-time have become those of "peaceful" life, which is actually the continuation of war, a war of all against all. According to this morality, everything is permissible: man may be used in any way desired for the attainment of inhuman or anti-human aims. Bestialism is a denial

Nicolas Berdyaev, The Fate of Man in the Modern World (Ann Arbor, MI: The University of Michigan Press, 1961), pp. 25, 27–29, 83–84, 87–88, 90, 100–102.

of the value of the human person, of every human personality; it is a denial of all sympathy with the fate of any man. The new humanism is closing; this is inescapable. . . .

We are entering an inhuman world, a world of inhumanness, inhuman not merely in fact, but in principle as well. Inhumanity has begun to be presented as something noble, surrounded with an aureole of heroism. Over against man there rises a class or a race, a deified collective or state. Modern nationalism bears marks of bestial inhumanity. No longer is every man held to be a man, a value, the image and likeness of God. . . .

. . . The new world which is taking form is moved by other values than the value of man or of human personality, or the value of truth: it is moved by such values as power, technics, race-purity, nationality, the state, the class, the collective. The will to justice is overcome by the will to power. . . .

. . . National passion is tearing the world and threatening the destruction of European culture. This is one more proof of the strength of atavism in human society, of how much stronger than the conscious is the subconscious, of how superficial has been the humanizing process of past centuries. . . . [M]odern nationalism means the dehumanization and bestialization of human societies. It is a reversion from the category of culture and history to that of zoology. . . .

. . . The results of the Christian-humanistic process of unifying humanity seem to be disappearing. We are witnessing the paganization of Christian society. Nationalism is polytheism: it is incompatible with monotheism.

This process of paganization takes shocking forms in Germany, which wishes no longer to be a Christian nation, has exchanged the swastika for the cross and demands of Christians that they should renounce the very fundamentals of the Christian revelation and the Christian faith, and cast aside the moral teaching of the Gospels. . . .

Nationalism turns nationality into a supreme and absolute value to which all life is subordinated. This is idolatry. The nation replaces God. Thus Nationalism cannot but come into conflict with Christian universalism, with the Christian revelation that there is neither Greek nor Jew, and that every man has absolute value. Nationalism uses everything as its own instrument, as an instrument of national power and prosperity. . . .

. . . Nationalism has no Christian roots and it is always in conflict with Christianity. . . .

. . . Nationalism involves not only love of one's own, but hatred of other nations, and hatred is usually a stronger motive than Love. Nationalism preaches either seclusion, isolation, blindness to other nations and cultures, self-satisfaction and particularism, or else expansion at the expense of others, conquest, subjection, imperialism. And in both cases it denies Christian conscience, contraverts the principle and the habits of the brotherhood of man. Nationalism is in complete contradiction to a personal ethic and denies the supreme value of human personality. Modern Nationalism dehumanizes ethics, it demands of man that he renounce humanity. It is all one and the same process, in Communism as in Nationalism. Man's inner world is completely at the mercy of collectivism, national or social. . . .

[R]acialism . . . has no basis at all in Christianity. . . . Racialist anti-Semitism inevitably leads to anti-Christianity, as we see in Germany to-day. That Germano-Aryan Christianity now being promoted is a denial of the Gospels and of Christ Himself. . . .

[R]acialist anti-Semitism . . . inevitably turns into anti-Christianity, for the human origins of Christianity are Hebrew.

. . . [I]t is impossible, it is forbidden, for a true Christian to be a racialist and to hate the Jews. . . .

. . . According to the race theory there is no hope of salvation, whatever: if you were born a Jew or a negro, no change of consciousness or belief or conviction can save you, you are doomed. A Jew may become a Christian: that does him no good. Even if he becomes a national-socialist, he cannot be saved.

REVIEW QUESTIONS'

1. What contrasts did Johan Huizinga draw between Europe at the turn of the century and the Europe of his day?
2. According to Nicolas Berdyaev, how is nationalism contradictory to Christian values?
3. Berdyaev is obviously talking about extreme nationalism. What distinctions would you draw between extreme and moderate nationalism?

CHAPTER 13

World War II

ROUNDING UP JEWS, 1943. The Nazis herded the Jews of Poland into walled ghettos, where they were starved, beaten, and humiliated prior to being deported to death camps. This picture from 1943 shows Jews being rounded up, probably for deportation and the gas chambers. *(Serge Plantureux/Corbis Premium Historical/Getty Images)*

From the early days of his political career, Hitler dreamed of forging a vast German empire in central and eastern Europe. He believed that only by waging a war of conquest against Russia could the German nation gain the living space and security it required and, as a superior race, deserved. War was an essential component of National Socialist ideology; it also accorded with Hitler's temperament. For the former corporal from the trenches, the Great War had never ended. Hitler aspired to political power because he wanted to mobilize the material and human resources of the German nation for war and conquest. Whereas historians may debate the question of responsibility for World War I, few would disagree with French historian Pierre Renouvin that World War II was Hitler's war:

> It appears to be an almost incontrovertible fact that the Second World War was brought on by the actions of the Hitler government, that these actions were the expression of a policy laid down well in advance in Mein Kampf, and that this war could have been averted up until the last moment if the German government had so wished.

Western statesmen had sufficient warning that Hitler was a threat to peace and the essential values of Western civilization, but they failed to rally their people and take a stand until Germany had greatly increased its capacity to wage aggressive war.

World War II was the most destructive war in history. Estimates of the number of dead range as high as fifty million, including twenty-five million Russians, who sacrificed more than the other participants in both population and material resources. The consciousness of Europe, already profoundly damaged by World War I, was again grievously wounded. Nazi racial theories showed that even in an age of sophisticated science the mind remains attracted to irrational beliefs and mythical imagery. Nazi atrocities proved that people will torture and kill with religious zeal and machinelike indifference. The Nazi assault on reason and freedom demonstrated anew the precariousness of Western civilization. This assault would forever cast doubt on the Enlightenment conception of human goodness, secular rationality, and the progress of civilization through advances in science and technology.

1 Prescient Observers of Nazi Germany

After Hitler took power in January 1933, many Western officials hoped that his radicalism would be tamed by the responsibilities of leadership; these officials either had never read *Mein Kampf* or did not take it seriously. But there were also astute observers who, within months of Hitler becoming chancellor, warned that Nazi Germany constituted a threat to the European peace. They maintained that Hitler, who believed that a Darwinian struggle for existence governed relations between nations and races, would eventually launch a war in order to realize the territorial aims of Nazi ideology.

Horace Rumbold
"PACIFISM IS THE DEADLIEST OF SINS"

On April 26, 1933, Horace Rumbold (1869–1941), Britain's ambassador to Germany, sent the following dispatch to London. It is clear that Rumbold had read and correctly assessed the meaning of *Mein Kampf.*

The outlook for Europe is far from peaceful if the speeches of Nazi leaders, especially of the Chancellor, are borne in mind. The Chancellor's account of his political career in *Mein Kampf* contains not only the principles which have guided him during the last fourteen years, but explains how he arrived at these fundamental principles. Stripped of the verbiage in which he has clothed it, Hitler's thesis is extremely simple. He starts with the assertions that man is a fighting animal, therefore the nation is, he concludes, a fighting unit, being a community of fighters. Any living organism which ceases to fight for its existence is, he asserts, doomed to extinction. A country or a race which ceases to fight is equally doomed. The fighting capacity of a race depends on its purity. Hence the necessity for ridding it of foreign impurities. The Jewish race, owing to its universality, is of necessity pacifist and internationalist. Pacifism is the deadliest sin, for pacifism means the surrender of the race in the fight for existence. The first duty of every country is, therefore, to nationalise the masses; intelligence is of secondary importance in the case of the individual; will and determination are of higher importance. The

individual who is born to command is more valuable than countless thousands of subordinate natures. Only brute force can ensure the survival of the race. Hence the necessity for military forms. The race must fight; a race that rests must rust and perish. The German race, had it been united in time, would now be master of the globe today. The new Reich must gather within its fold all the scattered German elements in Europe. A race which has suffered defeat can be rescued by restoring its self-confidence. Above all things, the army must be taught to believe in its own invincibility. To restore the German nation again, it is only necessary to convince the people that the recovery of freedom by force of arms is a possibility.

Hitler describes at great length in his turgid style the task which the new Germany must therefore set itself. Intellectualism is undesirable. The ultimate aim of education is to produce a German who can be converted with the minimum of training into a soldier. The idea that there is something reprehensible in chauvinism [extreme nationalism] is entirely mistaken. Indeed, the greatest upheavals in history would have been unthinkable had it not been for the driving force of fanatical and hysterical passions. Nothing could have been effected by the *bourgeois* virtues of peace and order. The world is now moving towards such an upheaval, and the new (German) State must see to it that

---

Horace Rumbold in *Documents in British Foreign Policy, 1919–1939,* 2nd Series, vol. V (1933), ed. by E. L. Woodward and Rohan Butler, 1956, pp. 47–51, 53.

the race is ready for the last and greatest decisions on this earth. . . . Again and again he proclaims that fanatical conviction and uncompromising resolution are indispensable qualities in a leader.

The climax of education is military service . . . but unless he is a soldier [a man] will fail in the great crises of life. . . . An army is indispensable to ensure the maintenance and expansion of the race. The recovery of lost provinces has never been effected by protest and without the use of force. To forge the necessary weapons is the task of the internal political leaders of the people.

. . . Germany's lost provinces cannot be gained by solemn appeals to Heaven or by pious hopes in the League of Nations, but only by force of arms. Germany must not repeat the mistake of fighting all her enemies at once. She must single out the most dangerous in turn and attack him with all her forces. . . . It is the business of the Government to implant in the people feelings of manly courage and passionate hatred. The world will only cease to be anti-German when Germany recovers equality of rights and resumes her place in the sun. . . .

Still more disquieting is the fact that though Germany remains nominally a member of the League of Nations the official policy of the country so far as it has been translated into action or expounded by members of the Government is fundamentally hostile to the principles on which the League is founded. Not only is it a crime to preach pacifism or condemn militarism but it is equally objectionable to preach international understanding, and while politicians and writers who have been guilty of the one have actually been arrested and incarcerated, those guilty of the other have at any rate been removed from public life and of course from official employment. . . .

[Germany has] to rearm on land, and, as Herr Hitler explains in his memoirs, they have to lull their adversaries into such a state of coma that they will allow themselves to be engaged one by one. Here Hitler has been as cautious and discreet as he was formerly blunt and frank. He declares that he is anxious that peace should be maintained for a ten-year period. What he probably means can be more accurately expressed by the [following] formula: Germany needs peace until she has recovered such strength that no country can challenge her without serious and irksome preparations. I fear that it would be misleading to base any hopes on a return to sanity or a serious modification of the views of the Chancellor and his entourage.

George S. Messersmith
"THE NAZIS WERE AFTER . . . UNLIMITED TERRITORIAL EXPANSION"

Two months after Rumbold's dispatch, George S. Messersmith, American consul general at Berlin, reported to the State Department on the "dangerous situation" developing in Germany. Appointed minister to Austria in 1934, he continued to warn that the Nazis were serious about expanding Germany's territory. Following is the State Department's Summary of Messersmith's reports.

CONSUL GENERAL MESSERSMITH'S REPORT FROM BERLIN

The United States Consul General at Berlin, George S. Messersmith, who had been at that post since 1930, reported frequently to the Department of State during this period on the menace inherent in the Nazi regime. Mr. Messersmith expressed the view, in a letter of June 26, 1933, to Under Secretary of State Phillips, that the United States must be exceedingly careful in its dealings with Germany as long as the existing Government was in power, as that Government had no spokesmen who could really be depended upon and those who held the highest positions were "capable of actions which really outlaw them from ordinary intercourse." He reported that some of the men who were running the German Government were "psychopathic cases"; that others were in a state of exaltation and in a frame of mind that knew no reason; and that those men in the party and in responsible positions who were really worthwhile were powerless because they had to follow the orders of superiors who were suffering from the "abnormal psychology" prevailing in Germany. "There is a real revolution here and a dangerous situation," he said.

Consul General Messersmith reported further that a martial spirit was being developed in Germany; that everywhere people were seen drilling, including children from the age of five or six to persons well into middle age; that a psychology was being developed that the whole world was against Germany, which was defenseless before the world; that people were being trained against gas and airplane attacks; and that the idea of war from neighboring countries was constantly harped upon. He emphasized that Germany was headed in directions which could only carry ruin to it and create a situation "dangerous to world peace." He said

we must recognize that while Germany at that time wanted peace, it was by no means a peaceful country or one looking forward to a long period of peace; that the German Government and its adherents desired peace ardently for the time being because they needed peace to carry through the changes in Germany which they wanted to bring about. What they wanted to do was to make Germany "the most capable instrument of war that there has ever existed."

Consul General Messersmith reported from Berlin five months later, in a letter of November 23, 1933, to Under Secretary Phillips, that the military spirit in Germany was constantly growing and that innumerable measures were being taken to develop the German people into a hardy, sturdy race which would "be able to meet all comers." He said that the leaders of Germany had no desire for peace unless it was a peace in complete compliance with German ambitions; that Hitler and his associates really wanted peace for the moment, but only to have a chance to prepare for the use of force if it were found essential; and that they were preparing their way so carefully that the German people would be with them when they wanted to use force and when they felt that they had the "necessary means to carry through their objects." . . .

Mr. Messersmith, who had been appointed Minister to Austria in 1934, continued to send to the Department of State reports on the situation in Germany. In February 1935 he reported that the Nazis had their eyes on Memel, Alsace-Lorraine, and the eastern frontier; that they nourished just as strongly the hope to get the Ukraine for the surplus German population; that Austria was a definite objective; and that absorption or hegemony over the whole of southeastern Europe was a definite policy. A few weeks later he reported a conversation with William E. Dodd, United States Ambassador to Germany, in which they had agreed that no faith whatsoever could be placed in the Nazi regime and its promises, that what the Nazis were after was "unlimited territorial expansion."

From *Peace and War: United States Foreign Policy*, 1931–1941, (Washington, D.C.: U.S. Government Printing Office, 1942) pp. 15–16.

REVIEW QUESTIONS

1. According to Rumbold, what was the basic thesis underlying Hitler's political philosophy?
2. Why, according to Rumbold, did Hitler want to maintain peace for a ten-year period? How did the events of the 1930s prove Rumbold's assertions correct?
3. What indications did George Messersmith provide that Germany was preparing for war?

---

2 Remilitarization of the Rhineland

In the Locarno Pact (1925)—signed by Germany, France, and Belgium—Germany, in effect, had accepted both the return of Alsace and Lorraine to France and the demilitarization of the Rhineland—two provisions of the Treaty of Versailles. On March 7, 1936, Hitler marched troops into the Rhineland, violating both the Versailles Treaty and the Locarno Pact. German generals had cautioned Hitler that such a move would provoke a French invasion of Germany and reoccupation of the Rhineland[1]—which the German army, still in the first stages of rearmament, could not repulse. But Hitler gambled that France and Britain, lacking the will to fight, would take no action. He had assessed the Anglo-French mood correctly. British statesmen in particular championed a policy of appeasement: giving in to Hitler in the hope that Europe would not be dragged through another world war.

William L. Shirer
BERLIN DIARY

Immediately after the German army occupied the demilitarized zone, Hitler addressed the Reichstag. William L. Shirer, an American correspondent in Germany, witnessed the speech and recorded his observations, reproduced below, in his diary.

The Reichstag, more tense then I have ever felt it (apparently the hand-picked deputies on the main floor had not yet been told what had happened, though they knew something was afoot), began promptly at noon. . . . Hitler began with a long harangue which he has often given before, but never tires of repeating, about the injustices of the Versailles Treaty and the peacefulness of Germans. Then his voice, which had been low and hoarse at the beginning, rose to a shrill, hysterical scream as he raged against Bolshevism.

William L. Shirer, *Berlin Diary: The Journal of a Foreign Correspondent, 1934–1941* (New York: A. A. Knopf, 1941), pp. 51–53.

---

[1]From 1919 to 1930 French troops occupied the Rhineland in accordance with the Versailles Treaty. Right-wing German nationalists were incensed that many were black colonial soldiers. Some German women married these black soldiers or had children out of wedlock.

"I will not have the gruesome Communist international dictatorship of hate descend upon the German people! This destructive Asiatic *Weltanschauung* [worldview] strikes at all values! . . . "

Then . . . "Germany no longer feels bound by the Locarno Treaty. In the interest of the primitive rights of its people to the security of their frontier and the safeguarding of their defense, the German Government has re-established, as from today, the absolute and unrestricted sovereignty of the Reich in the demilitarized zone!"

Now the six hundred deputies, personal appointees all of Hitler, little men with big bodies and bulging necks and cropped hair and pouched bellies and brown uniforms and heavy boots, little men of clay in his fine hands, leap their feet like automatons, their right arms upstretched in the Nazi salute, and scream *"Heil's,"* the first two or three wildly, the next twenty-five in unison, like a college yell. Hitler raises his hand for silence. It comes slowly. Slowly the automatons sit down. Hitler now has them in his claws. He appears to sense it.

He says in a deep, resonant voice: "Men of the German Reichstag!" The silence is utter. "In this historic hour, when in the Reich's western provinces German troops are at this minute marching into their future peace-time garrisons, we all unite in two sacred vows."

He can go no further. It is news to this hysterical "parliamentary" mob that German soldiers are already on the move into the Rhineland. All the militarism in their German blood surges to their heads. They spring, yelling and crying, to their feet. The audience in the galleries does the same, all except a few diplomats and about fifty of us correspondents. Their hands are raised in slavish salute, their faces now contorted with hysteria, their mouths wide open, shouting, shouting, their eyes, burning with fanaticism, glued on the new god, the Messiah. The Messiah plays his role superbly. His head lowered as if in all humbleness, he waits patiently for silence. Then, his voice still low, but choking with emotion, utters the two vows:

"First, we swear to yield to no force whatever in the restoration of the honour of our people, preferring to succumb with honour to the severest hardships rather than to capitulate, Secondly, we pledge that now, more than ever we shall strive for an understanding between European peoples . . . . We have no territorial demands to make in Europe! . . . Germany will never break the peace."

It was a long time before the cheering stopped. . . .

Shirer recorded that Hitler could not survive if the French responded forcefully to his blatant challenge and railed at their "stupidity" for failing to do so.

REVIEW QUESTION

What did William L. Shirer think of the Nazis?

---

3 The Anschluss, March 1938

One of Hitler's aims was the *Anschluss*, or the incorporation of Austria into the Third Reich. The Treaty of Versailles had expressly prohibited the union of the two countries, but in *Mein Kampf,* Hitler had insisted that an Anschluss was necessary for German living space. In February 1938, under intense pressure from Hitler, Austrian chancellor Kurt von Schuschnigg promised to accept Austrian Nazis in his cabinet and agreed to closer relations with Germany. Austrian independence was slipping away, and increasingly, Austrian Nazis undermined Schuschnigg's authority. Seeking to gain his people's support, Schuschnigg made plans for a plebiscite on the issue of preserving Austrian independence. An enraged Hitler ordered his generals to draw up plans for an invasion of Austria. Hitler then demanded Schuschnigg's resignation and the formation of a new government headed by Arthur Seyss-Inquart, an Austrian Nazi.

Believing that Austria was not worth a war, Britain and France informed the embattled chancellor that they would not help in the event of a German invasion. Schuschnigg then resigned, and Austrian Nazis began to take control of the government. Under the pretext of preventing violence, Hitler ordered his troops to cross into Austria, and on March 13, 1938, Austrian leaders, with the overwhelming support of the Austrian people, declared that Austria was a province of the German Reich.

In the first days after the Anschluss, anti-Nazis, particularly Social Democrats, were incarcerated; a wave of dissidents, politicians, and intellectuals fled the country; and Jews were subjected to torment and humiliation. Austrian Nazis, often with the approval of their fellow citizens, plundered Jewish shops, pulled elderly Orthodox Jews around by their beards, and made Jews scour pro-Schuschnigg slogans off the streets with toothbrushes or their bare hands. One eyewitness recalled years later: "I saw in the crowd a well-dressed woman . . . holding up a little girl, a blond lovely little girl with these curls, so that the girl could see better how a . . . Nazi Storm Trooper kicked an old Jew who fell down because he wasn't allowed to kneel. He had to scrub and just bend down sort of, and he fell and he kicked him. And they all laughed and she laughed as well—it was wonderful entertainment—and that shook me."

Stefan Zweig
THE WORLD OF YESTERDAY

One of modern, German-speaking Europe's most important authors, Stefan Zweig (see page 285) was born into a well-to-do Viennese Jewish household in 1881, came of age during the waning years of the monarchy, and witnessed both the devastation of World War I and the chaos of the interwar years. A passionate European and a convinced Austrian patriot, Zweig was disgusted by national chauvinisms, particularly the virulent German nationalism clearly discernible in Austria after the collapse of the Habsburg monarchy. His autobiographical *World of Yesterday*, posthumously published in 1943, both laments the loss of European cosmopolitanism and offers biting criticism of the inability, or unwillingness, of many Austrians to come to terms with the violent intolerance in their own society and the spreading danger of Nazism. Zweig's despair was all-consuming; he took his own life in South American exile in 1942, unable to reconcile himself to the changes in his beloved Europe and his Austrian homeland.

In the following selection from his autobiography, Zweig describes the orgy of hate that engulfed Vienna immediately after the Anschluss.

. . . University professors were obliged to scrub the streets with their naked hands, pious white-bearded Jews were dragged into the synagogue by hooting youths and forced to do knee-exercises and to shout "Heil Hitler" in chorus. Innocent people in the streets were trapped like rabbits and herded off to clean the latrines in the S. A. barracks. . . .

Breaking into homes and tearing earrings from trembling women may well have happened in the looting of cities, hundreds of years ago during medieval wars; what was new, however, was the shameless delight in public tortures, . . . in the refinements of humiliation. . . .

[In the future, people] will shudder to read what a single hate-crazed man perpetrated in that city of culture in the twentieth century. For amidst his military and political victories Hitler's most diabolic triumph was that he succeeded through progressive excesses in blunting every sense of law and order. . . .

In 1938, after Austria, our universe had become accustomed to inhumanity, to lawlessness, and brutality as never in centuries before. . . .

Those days, marked by daily cries for help from the homeland when one knew close friends to be kidnapped and humiliated and one trembled helplessly for every loved one, were among the most terrible of my life. . . . Hitler had not been master of the city for a week when the bestial order forbidding Jews to sit on public benches was issued—one of those orders obviously thought up only for the sadistic purpose of malicious torture. There was logic and reason in robbing Jews for with the booty from [their] factories, the home furnishings, the villas, and the jobs compulsorily vacated they could feather their followers' nests, reward their satellites; after all, Goering's picture-gallery owes its splendor mainly to this generously exercised practice. But to deny an aged woman or an exhausted old man a few minutes on a park bench to catch his breath—this remained reserved to the twentieth century and to the man whom millions worshipped as the greatest in our day. . . .

Zweig reports an event involving his dying mother a few months after the invasion. His Jewish cousin, sixty years old, intended to spend the night with the woman now on her deathbed. The nurse informed him that National Socialist laws, intended to guard against race defilement, forbade her to stay under the same roof with a Jewish man.

Stefan Zweig, *The World of Yesterday,* trans. Helmut Ripperger, pp. 405–408. Translation copyright 1943 by the Viking Press, Inc.

REVIEW QUESTIONS

1. What was the underlying purpose of the various anti-Jewish ordinances in Vienna that Stefan Zweig refers to? How might they have paved the way for even harsher actions?

2. Zweig accurately predicted that people in "a more peaceful day" would later "shudder to read what a single hate-crazed man perpetrated in that city of culture in the twentieth century." Why do you think so many of Zweig's contemporaries failed to feel the same dismay and horror as these events unfolded?

4   The Munich Agreement

Hitler sought power to build a great German empire in Europe, a goal that he revealed in *Mein Kampf.* In 1935, Hitler declared that Germany was no longer bound by the Versailles Treaty and would restore military conscription. Germany remilitarized the Rhineland in 1936 and incorporated Austria into the Third Reich in 1938. Although these actions violated the Versailles Treaty, Britain and France offered no resistance.

In 1938, Hitler also threatened war if Czechoslovakia did not cede to Germany the Sudetenland with its large German population—of the 3.5 million people living in the Czech Sudetenland, some 2.8 million were Germans. In September 1938, Hitler met with other European leaders at Munich. Prime Minister Neville Chamberlain (1869–1940) of Great Britain and Prime Minister Édouard Daladier (1884–1970) of France agreed to Hitler's demands, despite France's mutual assistance pact with Czechoslovakia and the Czechs' expressed determination to resist the dismemberment of their country. Both Chamberlain and Daladier were praised by their compatriots for ensuring, as Chamberlain said, "peace in our time."

Neville Chamberlain
IN DEFENSE OF APPEASEMENT

Britain and France pursued a policy of appeasement—giving in to Germany in the hope that a satisfied Hitler would not drag Europe into another war. Appeasement expressed the widespread British desire to heal the wounds of World War I and to correct what many British officials regarded as the injustices of the Versailles Treaty. Some officials, lauding Hitler's anti-Communism, regarded a powerful Germany as a bulwark against the Soviet Union. Britain's lack of military preparedness was another compelling reason for not resisting Hitler. On September 27, 1938, when negotiations between Hitler and Chamberlain reached a tense moment, the British prime minister addressed his nation. Excerpts of this speech before the House of Commons, which appeared in his *In Search of Peace* (1939), follows.

First of all I must say something to those who have written to my wife or myself in these last weeks to tell us of their gratitude for my efforts and to assure us of their prayers for my success. Most of these letters have come from women— mothers or sisters of our own countrymen.

But there are countless others besides—from France, from Belgium, from Italy, even from Germany, and it has been heartbreaking to read of the growing anxiety they reveal and their intense relief when they thought, too soon, that the danger of war was past.

If I felt my responsibility heavy before, to read such letters has made it seem almost overwhelming. How horrible, fantastic, incredible it is that we should be digging trenches and

Neville Chamberlain, *In Search of Peace* (London: Hutchinson, 1939), pp. 173–175.

trying on gas masks here because of a quarrel in a far-away country between people of whom we know nothing. It seems still more impossible that a quarrel which has already been settled in principle should be the subject of war.

I can well understand the reasons why the Czech Government have felt unable to accept the terms which have been put before them in the German memorandum. Yet I believe after my talks with Herr Hitler that, if only time were allowed, it ought to be possible for the arrangements for transferring the territory that the Czech Government has agreed to give to Germany to be settled by agreement under conditions which would assure fair treatment to the population concerned. . . .

However much we may sympathies with a small nation confronted by a big and powerful neighbour, we cannot in all circumstances undertake to involve the whole British Empire in war simply on her account. If we have to fight it must be on larger issues than that. I am myself a man of peace to the depths of my soul. Armed conflict between nations is a nightmare to me; but if I were convinced that any nation had made up its mind to dominate the world by fear of its force, I should feel that it must be resisted. Under such a domination life for people who believe in liberty would not be worth living; but war is a fearful thing, and we must be very clear, before we embark on it, that it is really the great issues that are at stake, and that the call to risk everything in their defence, when all the consequences are weighed, is irresistible.

For the present I ask you to await as calmly as you can the events of the next few days. As long as war has not begun, there is always hope that it may be prevented, and you know that I am going to work for peace to the last moment. Good night. . . .

On October 6, 1938, in a speech to Britain's House of Commons, Chamberlain defended the Munich Agreement signed on September 30.

Since I first went to Berchtesgaden [to confer with Hitler in Germany] more than 20,000 letters and telegrams have come to No. 10, Downing Street [British prime minister's residence]. Of course, I have only been able to look at a tiny fraction of them, but I have seen enough to know that the people who wrote did not feel that they had such a cause for which to fight, if they were asked to go to war in order that the Sudeten Germans might not join the Reich. That is how they are feeling. That is my answer to those who say that we should have told Germany weeks ago that, if her army crossed the border of Czechoslovakia, we should be at war with her. We had no treaty obligations and no legal obligations to Czechoslovakia and if we had said that, we feel that we should have received no support from the people of this country. . . .

. . . When we were convinced, as we became convinced, that nothing any longer would keep the Sudetenland within the Czechoslovakian State, we urged the Czech Government as strongly as we could to agree to the cession of territory, and to agree promptly. The Czech Government, through the wisdom and courage of President Benes, accepted the advice of the French Government and ourselves. It was a hard decision for anyone who loved his country to take, but to accuse us of having by that advice betrayed the Czechoslovakian State is simply preposterous. What we did was to save her from annihilation and give her a chance of new life as a new State, which involves the loss of territory and fortifications, but may perhaps enable her to enjoy in the future and develop a national existence under a neutrality and security comparable to that which we see in Switzerland today. Therefore, I think the Government deserve the approval of this House for their conduct of affairs in this recent crisis which has saved Czechoslovakia from destruction and Europe from Armageddon.

Does the experience of the Great War and of the years that followed it give us reasonable hope that, if some new war started, that would end war any more than the last one did? . . .

One good thing, at any rate, has come out of this emergency through which we have passed. It has thrown a vivid light upon our preparations for defence, on their strength and on their weakness. I should not think we were doing our duty if we had not already ordered that a prompt and thorough inquiry should be made to cover the whole of our preparations, military and civil, in order to see, in the light of what has happened during these hectic days, what further steps may be necessary to make good our deficiencies in the shortest possible time.

Winston Churchill
"A DISASTER OF THE FIRST MAGNITUDE"

On October 5, 1938, Britain's elder statesman Winston Churchill (1874–1965) delivered a speech in the House of Commons attacking the Munich Agreement and British policy toward Nazi Germany.

. . . I will begin by saying what everybody would like to ignore or forget but which must nevertheless be stated, namely, that we have sustained a total and unmitigated defeat, and that France has suffered even more than we have. . . .

All is over. Silent, mournful, abandoned, broken, Czechoslovakia recedes into the darkness. She has suffered in every respect by her association with the Western democracies and with the League of Nations, of which she has always been an obedient servant. She has suffered in particular from her association with France, under whose guidance and policy she has been actuated for so long. . . .

We in this country, as in other Liberal and democratic countries, have a perfect right to exalt the principle of self-determination, but it comes ill out of the mouths of those in totalitarian States who deny even the smallest element of toleration to every section and creed within their bounds. . . .

What is the remaining position of Czechoslovakia? Not only are they politically mutilated, but, economically and financially, they are in complete confusion. Their banking, their railway arrangements, are severed and broken, their industries are curtailed, and the movement of their population is most cruel. The Sudeten miners, who are all Czechs and whose families have lived in that area for centuries, must now flee into an area where there are hardly any mines left for them to work. It is a tragedy which has occurred. . . .

I venture to think that in future the Czechoslovak State cannot be maintained as an independent entity. You will find that in a period of time which may be measured by years, but may be measured only by months, Czechoslovakia will be engulfed in the Nazi regime. . . . But we cannot consider the abandonment and ruin of Czechoslovakia in the

Winston Churchill, *Parliamentary Debates,* House of Commons V339, 12th vol. of session, 1937–1938, 1938, pp. 361–369, 373.

light only of what happened only last month. It is the most grievous consequence which we have yet experienced of what we have done and of what we have left undone in the last five years—five years of futile good intention, five years of eager search for the line of least resistance, five years of uninterrupted retreat of British power, five years of neglect of our air defences. Those are the features which I stand here to declare and which marked an improvident stewardship for which Great Britain and France have dearly to pay. We have been reduced in those five years from a position of security so overwhelming and so unchallengeable that we never cared to think about it. We have been reduced from a position where the very word "war" was considered one which would be used only by persons qualifying for a lunatic asylum. We have been reduced from a position of safety and power—power to do good, power to be generous to a beaten foe, power to make terms with Germany, power to give her proper redress for her grievances, power to stop her arming if we chose, power to take any step in strength or mercy or justice which we thought right—reduced in five years from a position safe and unchallenged to where we stand now.

When I think of the fair hopes of a long peace which still lay before Europe at the beginning of 1933 when Herr Hitler first obtained power, and of all the opportunities of arresting the growth of the Nazi power which have been thrown away, when I think of the immense combinations and resources which have been neglected or squandered, I cannot believe that a parallel exists in the whole course of history. So far as this country is concerned the responsibility must rest with those who have the undisputed control of our political affairs. They neither prevented Germany from rearming, nor did they rearm ourselves in time. . . . They neglected to make alliances and combinations which might have repaired previous errors, and thus they left us in the hour of trial without adequate national defence or effective international security. . . .

We are in the presence of a disaster of the first magnitude which has befallen Great Britain and France. Do not let us blind ourselves to that. It must now be accepted that all the countries of Central and Eastern Europe will make the best terms they can with the triumphant Nazi Power. The system of alliances in Central Europe upon which France has relied for her safety has been swept away, and I can see no means by which it can be reconstituted. . . .

. . . If the Nazi dictator should choose to look westward, as he may, bitterly will France and England regret the loss of that fine army of ancient Bohemia [Czechoslovakia] which was estimated last week to require not fewer than 30 German divisions for its destruction. . . .

. . . Many people, no doubt, honestly believe that they are only giving away the interests of Czechoslovakia, whereas I fear we shall find that we have deeply compromised, and perhaps fatally endangered, the safety and even the independence of Great Britain and France. . . . [T]here can never be friendship between the British democracy and the Nazi Power, that Power which spurns Christian ethics, which cheers its onward course by a barbarous paganism, which vaunts the spirit of aggression and conquest, which derives strength and perverted pleasure from persecution, and uses, as we have seen, with pitiless brutality the threat of murderous force. That Power cannot ever be the trusted friend of the British democracy. . . .

. . . [O]ur loyal, brave people . . . should know the truth. They should know that there has been gross neglect and deficiency in our defences; they should know that we have sustained a defeat without a war, the consequences of which will travel far with us along our road; they should know that we have passed an awful milestone in our history, when the whole equilibrium of Europe has been deranged, and that the terrible words have for the time being been pronounced against the Western democracies:

Thou art weighed in the balance and found wanting.

And do not suppose that this is the end. This is only the beginning of the reckoning.

This is only the first sip, the first foretaste of a bitter cup which will be proffered to us year by year unless by a supreme recovery of moral health and martial vigour, we arise again and take our stand for freedom as in the olden time.

REVIEW QUESTIONS

1. In Neville Chamberlain's view, how did the British people regard a war with Germany over the Sudetenland?
2. How did Chamberlain respond to the accusation that Britain and France had betrayed Czechoslovakia?
3. What did Chamberlain consider to be the "one good thing" to come out of the Sudetenland crisis?
4. Why did Winston Churchill believe that "there [could] never be friendship between the British democracy and the Nazi Power"?
5. Why did Churchill believe that the Munich Agreement was "a disaster of the first magnitude" for Britain and France?
6. What policy toward Nazi Germany did Churchill advocate?

5 World War II Begins

After Czechoslovakia, Hitler turned to Poland. In the middle of June 1939, the army presented him with a battle plan for an invasion of Poland; and on August 22, Hitler informed his leading generals that war with Poland was necessary. The following day, Nazi Germany signed a nonaggression pact with Communist Russia, which blocked Britain and France from duplicating their World War I alliance against Germany. The Nazi–Soviet Pact was the green light for an attack on Poland. At dawn on September 1, 1939, German forces, striking with coordinated speed and power, invaded Poland, starting World War II.

Adolf Hitler
"POLAND WILL BE DEPOPULATED AND SETTLED WITH GERMANS"

An American journalist was given a copy of Hitler's speech to his generals at the August 22 conference. Probably the supplier was an official close to Admiral Canaris, an opponent of Hitler who had attended the conference. The journalist then gave it to the British ambassador. The speech follows.

Decision to attack Poland was arrived at in spring. Originally there was fear that because of the political constellation we would have to strike at the same time against England, France, Russia and Poland. This risk too we should have had to take. Göring had demonstrated to us that his Four-Year Plan is a failure and that we are at the end of our strength, if we do not achieve victory in a coming war.

Since the autumn of 1938 and since I have realised that Japan will not go with us unconditionally and that Mussolini is endangered by that nitwit of a King and the treacherous scoundrel of a Crown Prince, I decided to go with Stalin. After all there are only three great statesmen in the world, Stalin, I and Mussolini. Mussolini is the weakest, for he has been able to break the power neither of the crown nor of the Church. Stalin and I are the only ones who visualise the future. So in a few weeks hence I shall stretch out my hand to Stalin at the common German-Russian frontier and with him undertake to re-distribute the world.

Our strength lies in our quickness and in our brutality; Genghis Khan has sent millions of women and children into death knowingly and with a light heart. History sees in him only the great founder of States. As to what the weak Western European civilisation asserts about me, that is of no account. I have given the command and I shall shoot everyone who utters one word of criticism, for the goal to be obtained in the war is not that of reaching certain lines but of physically demolishing the opponent. And so for the present only in the East I have put my death-head formations[1] in place with the command relentlessly and without compassion to send into death many women and children of Polish origin and language. Only thus we can gain the living space that we need. Who after all is today speaking about the destruction of the Armenians?

Colonel-General von Brauchitsch has promised me to bring the war against Poland to a close within a few weeks. Had he reported to me that he needs two years or even only one year, I should not have given the command to march and should have allied myself temporarily with England instead of Russia for we cannot conduct a long war. To be sure a situation has risen. I experienced those poor worms Daladier and Chamberlain in Munich. They will be too cowardly to attack. They won't go beyond a blockade. Against that we have our autarchy [economic self-sufficiency] and the Russian raw materials.

Poland will be depopulated and settled with Germans. My pact with the Poles was merely conceived of as a gaining of time. As for the rest, gentlemen, the fate of Russia will be exactly the same as I am now going through with in the case of Poland. After Stalin's death—he is a very sick man—we will break the Soviet Union. Then there will begin the dawn of the German rule of the earth. . . .

The opportunity is as favourable as never before. I have but one worry, namely that Chamberlain or some other such pig of a fellow ("Saukerl") will come at the last moment with proposals or with ratting ("Umfall"). He will fly down the stairs, even if I shall personally have to trample on his belly in the eyes of the photographers.

No, it is too late for this. The attack upon and the destruction of Poland begins Saturday [August 26] early. I shall let a few companies in Polish uniform attack in Upper Silesia or in the Protectorate. Whether the world believes it is quite indifferent ("Scheissegal"). The world believes only in success.

For you, gentlemen, fame and honour are beginning as they have not since centuries. Be hard, be without mercy, act more quickly and

---

Documents on British Foreign Policy, 1919–1939, 2nd series, vol. 7, 1939, pp. 258–260.

---

[1]The SS Death's Head formations were principally employed in peacetime in guarding concentration camps. When war started they became part of the Waffen SS combat units.—Eds.

brutally than the others. The citizens of Western Europe must tremble with horror. That is the most human way of conducting a war. For it scares the others off.

The new method of conducting war corresponds to the new drawing of the frontiers. A war extending from Reval, Lublin, Kaschau to the mouth of the Danube. The rest will be given to the Russians. Ribbentrop has orders to make every offer and to accept every demand. In the West I reserve to myself the right to determine the strategically best line. Here one will be able to work with Protectorate regions, such as Holland, Belgium and French Lorraine.

And now, on to the enemy, in Warsaw we will celebrate our reunion.

The speech was received with enthusiasm. Göring jumped on a table, thanked blood-thirstily and made bloodthirsty promises. He danced like a wild man. The few that had misgivings remained quiet. (Here a line of the memorandum is missing in order no doubt to protect the source of information.)[2]

During the meal which followed Hitler said he must act this year as he was not likely to live very long. His successor however would no longer be able to carry this out. Besides, the situation would be a hopeless one in two years at the most.

-----

[2]This sentence in parentheses forms part of the original typescript.—Eds.

REVIEW QUESTIONS

1. What were the decisive reasons that led Hitler to launch the war against Poland?
2. What type of warfare did Hitler want his generals to wage?

-----

6 The Fall of France

On May 10, 1940, Hitler launched his offensive in the west with an invasion of neutral Belgium, Holland, and Luxembourg. French troops rushed to Belgium to prevent a breakthrough, but the greater menace lay to the south, on the French frontier. Meeting almost no resistance, German panzer (tank) divisions had moved through the narrow mountain passes of Luxembourg and the dense Forest of the Ardennes in southern Belgium. On May 12, German units were on French soil near Sedan. Thinking that the Forest of the Ardennes could not be penetrated by a major German force, the French had only lightly fortified the western extension of the Maginot Line, the immense fortifications designed to hold back a German invasion.

The battle for France turned into a rout. Whole French divisions were cut off or in retreat. At the end of May and beginning of June, in a heroic effort, the British Expeditionary Force (BEF) escaped to England from the port of Dunkirk. On June 10, Mussolini also declared war on France. With authority breaking down and resistance dying, the French cabinet appealed for an armistice, which was signed on June 22 in the same railway car in which Germany had agreed to the armistice ending World War I.

Several reasons explain the collapse of France. France had somewhat fewer planes, particularly bombers, than Germany, but, what is still a mystery, many French planes never left the airfields. And because French airfields lacked early warning systems and sufficient antiaircraft guns, many were destroyed on the ground. Nor did the French High Command deploy their airforce properly. Unlike the Germans, the French were not proponents of a tactical airforce in close support of infantry and tanks. As for tanks, the French had as many as the Germans, and some were superior. Nor was German manpower overwhelming. France met disaster largely because its military leaders, unlike the Germans, had not mastered the psychology and technology of motorized warfare. "The French commanders, trained in the slow-motion methods of 1918, were mentally unfitted to cope with {the pace of German panzers}, and it produced a spreading paralysis among them," says British military expert Sir Basil Liddell Hart. One also senses a loss of will among the French people: a consequence of internal political disputes dividing the nation, poor leadership, the years of appeasement and lost opportunities, and German propaganda, which depicted Nazism as irresistible and the Führer as a man of destiny. It was France's darkest hour.

Heinz Guderian
"FRENCH LEADERSHIP . . . COULD NOT GRASP THE SIGNIFICANCE OF THE TANK IN MOBILE WARFARE"

After the war, German general Heinz Guderian (1888–1954), whose panzer divisions formed the vanguard of the attack through the Ardennes into France, analyzed the reasons for France's collapse in *Panzer Leader* (1952).

. . . Despite the tank weapons to which our enemies owed in large measure their 1918 victory, they were preoccupied with the concepts of positional warfare. . . .

. . . Despite possessing the strongest forces for mobile warfare the French had also built the strongest line of fortifications in the world, the Maginot Line. Why was the money spent on the construction of those fortifications not used for the modernisation and strengthening of France's mobile forces?

It must be concluded that the highest French leadership either would not or could not grasp the significance of the tank in mobile warfare. . . . Only a fraction of the French armour was organised for operational employment.

So far as the French were concerned the German leadership could safely rely on the defence of France being systematically based on fortification and carried out according to a rigid doctrine: this doctrine was the result of the lessons that the French had learned from the First World War, their experience of positional warfare, of the high value they attached to fire power, and of their underestimation of movement. . . .

Heinz Guderian, *Panzer Leader*, trans. Constantine Fitzgibbon (New York: Da Capo Preis, 1996), pp. 94, 96–97.

We knew and respected the French soldier from the First World War as a brave and tough fighter who had defended his country with stubborn energy. We did not doubt that he would show the same spirit this time. But so far as the French leaders were concerned, we were amazed that they had not taken advantage of their favourable situation during the autumn of 1939 to attack, while the bulk of the German forces, including the entire armoured force, was engaged in Poland. Their reasons for such restraint were at the time hard to see. We could only guess. Be that as it may, the caution shown by the French leaders led us to believe that our adversaries hoped somehow to avoid a serious clash of arms. The rather inactive behavior of the French during the winter of 1939–40 seemed to indicate a limited enthusiasm for the war on their part.

From all this I concluded that a determined and forcibly led attack by strong armoured forces through Sedan and Amiens, with the Atlantic coast as its objective, would hit the enemy deep in the flank of his forces advancing into Belgium [thinking that Germany would take the same route it took in World War I]; I did not think that he disposed of sufficient reserves to parry this thrust; and I therefore believed it had a great chance of succeeding and, if the initial success were fully exploited, might lead to the cutting off of all the main enemy forces moving up into Belgium.

REVIEW QUESTION

What mistaken lessons did the French draw from their experience in World War I?

---

7   Battle of Britain

Hitler expected that after his stunning victories in the West, Britain would make peace. The British, however, continued to reject Hitler's overtures, for they envisioned a bleak future if Nazi Germany dominated the Continent. With Britain unwilling to come to terms, Hitler proceeded in earnest with invasion plans. A successful crossing of the English Channel and the establishment of beachheads on the English coast depended on control of the skies. In early August 1940, the Luftwaffe (air force) began massive attacks on British air and naval installations. Virtually every day during the Battle of Britain, hundreds of planes fought in the sky above Britain as British pilots rose to the challenge. On September 15, 1940, the Royal Air Force (RAF) shot down sixty aircraft; two days later Hitler postponed the invasion of Britain "until further notice." The development of radar by British scientists, the skill and courage of British fighter pilots, and the inability of Germany to make up its losses in planes saved Britain in its struggle for survival. With the invasion of Britain called off, the Luftwaffe concentrated on bombing English cities, industrial centers, and ports. Almost every night for months, the inhabitants of London sought shelter in subways and cellars to escape German bombs, while British planes rose time after time to make the Luftwaffe pay the price. British morale never broke during the "Blitz."

Winston Churchill
"BLOOD, TOIL, TEARS, AND SWEAT"

Churchill, at the age of sixty-six, proved to be an undaunted leader, sharing the perils faced by all, and able by example and by speeches to rally British morale. When he first addressed Parliament as prime minister on May 13, 1940, he left no doubt about the grim realities that lay ahead. Excerpts from his speeches in 1940 follow.

May 13, 1940

I would say to the House, as I said to those who have joined this Government: "I have nothing to offer but blood, toil, tears, and sweat." We have before us an ordeal of the most grievous kind. We have before us many, many long months of struggle and suffering. You ask: "What is our policy?" I will say: "It is to wage war by sea, land, and air with all our might, and with all the strength that God can give us; to wage war against a monstrous tyranny, never surpassed in the dark lamentable catalogue of human crime." That is our policy.

You ask: "What is our aim?" I can answer in one word: "Victory!" Victory at all costs, victory in spite of all terror, victory however long and hard the road may be; for without victory there is no survival.

When Churchill spoke next, on May 19, the Dutch had surrendered to the Germans, and the French and British armies were in retreat. Still, Churchill promised that "conquer we shall."

May 19, 1940

This is one of the most awe-striking periods in the long history of France and Britain. It is also beyond doubt the most sublime. Side by

---

side, unaided except by their kith and kin in the great Dominions and by the wide Empires which rest beneath their shield—side by side, the British and French peoples have advanced to rescue not only Europe but mankind from the foulest and most soul-destroying tyranny which has ever darkened and stained the pages of history. Behind them—behind us—behind the armies and fleets of Britain and France—gather a group of shattered states and bludgeoned races: the Czechs, the Poles, the Norwegians, the Danes, the Dutch, the Belgians—upon all of whom the long night of barbarism will descend unbroken even by a star of hope, unless we conquer, as conquer we must; as conquer we shall.

By early June the Belgians had surrendered to the Germans, and the last units of the British Expeditionary Force in France had been evacuated from Dunkirk; the French armies were in full flight. Again Churchill spoke out in defiance of events across the Channel.

June 4, 1940

We shall not flag or fail. We shall go on to the end. We shall fight in France, we shall fight on the seas and oceans, we shall fight with growing confidence and growing strength in the air. We shall defend our island, whatever the cost may be. We shall fight on the beaches, we shall fight on the landing-grounds, we shall fight in the fields and in the streets, we shall fight in the hills. We shall never surrender; and even if, which I do not for a moment believe, this island or a large part of it were subjugated and starving, then our Empire beyond the seas, armed and guarded by the British Fleet, would carry on the struggle, until, in God's good time, the New World, with all its power and might, steps forth to the rescue and liberation of the Old.

By June 18 the battle of France was lost; on June 22 France surrendered. Now Britain itself was under siege. Churchill again found the right words to sustain his people:

June 18, 1940

What General [Maxime] Weygand [commander of the French army] called the Battle of France is over. . . . The Battle of Britain is about to begin. Upon this battle depends the survival of Christian civilization. Upon it depends our own British life and the long continuity of our institutions and our Empire. The whole fury and might of the enemy must very soon be turned upon us. Hitler knows that he will have to break us in this island or lose the war.

If we can stand up to him, all Europe may be free and the life of the world may move forward into broad sunlit uplands. But if we fail, then

the whole world, including the United States, including all that we have known and cared for, will sink into the abyss of a new Dark Age made more sinister and perhaps more prolonged by the lights of a perverted science.

Let us therefore brace ourselves to our duty and so bear ourselves that if the British Empire and Commonwealth last for a thousand years, men will still say, "This was their finest hour."

While the Battle of Britain raged, Churchill lauded the courage of British airmen who rose to the challenge.

August 20, 1940

The gratitude of every home in our island, in our Empire, and indeed throughout the world, except in the abodes of the guilty, goes out to the British airmen who, undaunted by odds, unwearied in their constant challenge and mortal danger, are turning the tide of world war by their prowess and by their devotion. Never in the field of human conflict was so much owed by so many to so few. All hearts go out to the fighter pilots whose brilliant actions we see with our own eyes day after day.

REVIEW QUESTIONS

1. According to Winston Churchill, what would a Nazi victory mean for Europe?
2. On whose help did Churchill ultimately count for the liberation of Europe?
3. Both Hitler and Churchill were gifted orators. Compare their styles.

---

8 Nazi Ideology and the German Military: The Indoctrination of the German Soldier

After World War II, Germans maintained that the Wehrmacht (the German army) was an apolitical professional fighting force that remained free of Nazi ideology and was uninvolved in criminal acts perpetrated by Heinrich Himmler's SS, the elite units responsible for the extermination of Jews. It is now known that units of the German army assisted the SS in the rounding up of Jews and at times participated in mass murder. Recently historians have also argued that the regular army, far from being apolitical, was imbued with Nazi ideology, and that many German officers and soldiers, succumbing to Nazi indoctrination, viewed the war, particularly against the Soviet Union (which the Nazis invaded in June 1941), as a titanic struggle against evil and "subhuman" Jewish-led Bolsheviks who threatened the very existence of the German Volk.

Wehrmacht troops were provided with news sheets, newspapers, and leaflets replete with Nazi propaganda. Many junior officers who had direct contact with the soldiers considered it their duty to raise morale by indoctrinating the men with Nazi racial ideology.

Nazi Tracts, Generals' Memorandums, Letters Home
BOLSHEVIKS AND JEWS AS DEVILS

Nazi racial ideology destined for the troops declared that Russians were a lower form of humanity governed by Jewish-Bolshevism, for Jews supposedly controlled the Soviet Union. Most commanders accepted without question Hitler's equating Bolshevism with Jews and Judaism. Jewish-Bolshevism was another absurd anti-Semitic myth that defied the facts. Jews as an organized body exercised no power in the Soviet Union, and by 1939 there were virtually no Jews in the ruling circles of the Communist Party. Moreover, many Communists, Russians, and ethnic minorities harbored a traditional anti-Semitism. During the war the Soviet Union gave no recognition to Jewish concerns or even revealed Nazi war crimes directed specifically at Jews. But the association of Jews with Communism and the labeling of Jews as an existential threat to the nation, staples of Nazi propaganda, were deeply embedded in the psyche of both the SS and the Wehrmacht as the following excerpts reveal.

German propaganda described Jews and Russian Communists in racial and religious terms, calling them a morally depraved form of humanity in the service of Satan. A tract from SS headquarters illustrates the mythical nature of Nazi ideology.

Just as night rises up against the day, just as light and darkness are eternal enemies, so the greatest enemy of world-dominating man is man himself. The sub-man—that creature which looks as though biologically it were of absolutely the same kind, endowed by Nature with hands, feet and a sort of brain, with eyes and mouth—is nevertheless a totally different, a fearful creature, is only an attempt at a human being, with a quasi-human face, yet in mind and spirit lower than any animal. Inside this being a cruel chaos of wild, unchecked passions: a nameless will to destruction, the most primitive lusts, the most undisguised vileness. A sub-man— nothing else! . . . Never has the sub-man granted peace, never has he permitted rest. . . .

To preserve himself he needed mud, he needed hell, but not the sun. And this underworld of sub-men found its leader: the eternal Jew!

Hitler ordered that Soviet commissars, political officials attached to the Red Army, were to be immediately liquidated. A propaganda tract distributed to German soldiers described the commissars as mostly Jewish men (of course most were not Jews) and as beasts.

Anyone who has ever looked at the face of a red commissar knows what the Bolsheviks are like. Here there is no need for theoretical expressions. We would be insulting the animals if we were to describe these men, who are mostly Jewish, as beasts. They are the embodiment of the Satanic and insane hatred against the whole of noble humanity. The shape of these commissars reveals to us the rebellion of the *Untermenschen* [subhuman] against noble blood. The masses, whom they have sent to their deaths by making use of all means at their disposal such as ice-cold terror and insane incitement, would have brought an end to all meaningful life, had this eruption not been dammed at the last moment.

In October 1941, Walter Reichenau, a fervent Nazi and commander of the German Sixth Army, appealed to his men in the language of Nazi ideology.

The most essential aim of war against the Jewish-Bolshevistic system is a complete destruction of Asiatic influence from the European culture. . . .

The soldier in the Eastern territories is not merely a fighter according to the rules of the art of war, but also a bearer of ruthless national ideology and the avenger of bestialities which have been inflicted upon German and racially related nations.

Therefore, the soldier must have full understanding for the necessity of a severe but just revenge on subhuman Jewry. . . .

The soldier has to fulfill two tasks:

1. Complete annihilation of the false Bolshevistic doctrine of the Soviet state and its armed forces.

2. The pitiless extermination of alien treachery and cruelty and thus the protection of the lives of German military personnel in Russia.

This is the only way to fulfill our historic task to liberate the German people once and for ever from the Asiatic-Jewish danger.

In October 1941, Major General von Bechtolsheim ordered that "the Jews must disappear from the countryside." In two other reports a few days later, he told his men

---

to make every effort to remove Jews entirely from the villages. In case after case, it is clear that these are the sole support the partisans find in order survive. . . . Their annihilation is therefore to be carried out in whatever manner. . . . The Jews . . . are our mortal enemies. These enemies are, however, no longer human beings in the sense of our European culture; rather they

Norman Cohn, *Warrant for Genocide* (New York: Harper Torchbooks, 1967), p. 188.
Omer Bartov, *The Eastern Front 1941–45: German Troops and the Barbarization of Warfare* (New York: Palgrave, second edition, 2001), p. 83.

Whitney R. Harris, *Tyranny on Trial: The Evidence at Nuremberg* (Dallas: Southern Methodist University Press, 1954; the 1995 edition was published by Barnes & Noble), p. 186.
Hanes Heer, "Killing Fields: The Wehrmacht and the Holocaust in Belorussia, 1941–43," in Hanes Heer and Klaus Naumann, eds., *War of Extermination: The German Military in World War II, 1941–1944* (New York: Berghahn Books, 2000), pp. 63–64.

are raised to be criminals from their childhood on and are as criminally schooled beasts. Beasts must be destroyed.

Nazi newspapers, radio broadcasts, orders and reports from generals, and the proliferation of propaganda by junior officers convinced many soldiers that they were fighting a defensive war to protect Germany from a Soviet invasion and had a duty to destroy "Jewish-Bolshevism," which threatened European civilization, and to decimate the evil subhuman Jews. In September 1941, a notorious Jew-hating newspaper that was widely circulated among the troops, published these words: "The source of the world's disaster will be done away with forever only when Jewry in its entirety has been annihilated." The impact of Nazi propaganda can be seen in the soldiers' letters home.

One soldier

The great task that has placed us in battle against Bolshevism lies in the destruction of eternal Judaism. When you see what the Jew has brought about here in Russia, only then can you begin to understand why the führer began this struggle against Judaism. What sort of misfortune would have been visited upon our Fatherland, if this bestial people had gotten the upper hand.

Another soldier

The political doctrine of Bolshevism . . . is but a purely political act of world Jewry. And just as the Talmud teaches nothing except murder and destruction, so Bolshevism knows [only] cruel and barbaric murder.

Stephen G. Fritz, *Frontsoldaten: The German Soldier in World War II* (Lexington, KY: The University Press of Kentucky, 1995), pp. 195, 197.

The following letters home from tank gunner Karl Fuchs, an idealistic young German, also illustrate the hold that Nazi propaganda had on the Wehrmacht. Fuchs was killed in a tank battle in November 1941.

3 August 1941

All you have to do is look at the Russian prisoners. Hardly ever do you see the face of a person who seems rational and intelligent. They all look emaciated and the wild, half-crazy look in their eyes makes them appear like imbeciles. And these scoundrels, led by Jews and criminals, wanted to imprint their stamp on Europe, indeed on the world. Thank God that our Führer, Adolf Hitler, is preventing this from happening!

4 August 1941

Having encountered these Bolshevik hordes and having seen how they live has made a lasting impression on me. Everyone, even the last doubter, knows today that the battle against these subhumans, who've been whipped into a frenzy by the Jews, was not only necessary but came in the nick of time. Our Führer has saved Europe from certain chaos.

15 October 1941

Our duty has been to fight and to free the world from this Communist disease. One day, many years hence, the world will thank the Germans and our beloved Führer for our victories here in Russia. Those of us who took part in this liberation battle can look back on those days with pride and infinite joy. That's all for today. I send you my greetings.

Your Loyal and Loving Son: The Letters of Tank Gunner Karl Fuchs, 1937–1941, edited and translated by Horst Fuchs Richardson (Washington, D.C.: Brasseys, 1987, 2003), pp. 118, 120, 139.

Heinrich Himmler
THE RACIAL EMPIRE

The Nazi leadership intended the German master race to rule over and exploit people viewed as racial inferiors. A principal proponent of this thinking was Heinrich Himmler, head of the SS and a key architect of the Holocaust. As the following documents show, he envisioned a vast German empire in the East in which the local population had an overriding duty to serve their German masters.

During the war, millions of people, most of them seized and deported to Germany, toiled as slave laborers. In a memorandum issued in May 1941, Himmler defined how the subjugated Poles should be treated.

There must not be a more advanced education for the non-German population of the east than four years of primary school.

This primary education has the following objective only; doing simple arithmetic up to 500, writing one's name, learning that it was God's command that the Germans must be obeyed, and that one had to be honest, diligent, and obedient. I don't consider reading skills necessary. Except for this school, no other kind of school must be allowed in the east. . . .

The population will be at our call as a slave people without leaders, and each year will provide Germany with migrant workers and workers for special projects.

Hannah Vogt, *The Burden of German Guilt*, trans. Herbert Strauss (New York: Oxford University Press, 1964), p. 263.

In an address given to SS generals in October 1943, Himmler maintained that Germans should regard conquered peoples as slaves.

"What happens to the Russians, to the Czechs, does not interest me in the slightest. What the nations can offer in the way of good blood of our type we will take, if necessary, by kidnapping their children and raising them here with us. Whether the other nations live in prosperity or starve to death interests me only insofar as we need them as slaves for our culture; otherwise, it is of no interest to me. Whether 10,000 Russian females fall down from exhaustion while digging an anti-tank ditch or not interests me only insofar as the anti-tank ditch for Germany is finished."

Trial of the Major War Criminals (Nuremberg International Military Tribunal, 1947–49), vol. 3, p. 406.

REVIEW QUESTIONS

1. How did Nazi propaganda depict Hitler? Germans? Jews? Russians?
2. Why was such propaganda effective?
3. On the basis of Heinrich Himmler's words, what would a Nazi victory have meant for the Slavs of Eastern Europe?

9 Stalingrad: A Turning Point

In July 1942, the Germans resumed their advance into the U.S.S.R. that had begun the previous summer, seeking to conquer Stalingrad (now Volgograd), a vital transportation center located on the Volga River. Germans and Russians battled with dogged ferocity over every part of the city; 99 percent of Stalingrad was reduced to rubble. A Russian counteroffensive in November trapped the German Sixth Army. Realizing that the Sixth Army, exhausted and short of weapons, ammunition, food, and medical supplies, faced annihilation, German generals pleaded in vain with Hitler to permit withdrawal before the Russians closed the ring. On February 2, 1943, the remnants of the Sixth Army surrendered. More than a million people—Russian civilians and soldiers, Germans and their Italian, Hungarian, and Romanian allies—perished in the epic struggle for Stalingrad. The Russian victory was a major turning point in the war.

Anton Kuzmich Dragan
A SOVIET VETERAN RECALLS

Anton Kuzmich Dragan, a Russian soldier, describes the vicious street fighting in Stalingrad during late September 1942.

The Germans had cut us off from our neighbours. The supply of ammunition had been cut off; every bullet was worth its weight in gold. I gave the order to economize on ammunition, to collect the cartridge-pouches of the dead and all captured weapons. In the evening the enemy again tried to break our resistance, coming up close to our positions. As our numbers grew smaller, we shortened our line of defence. We began to move back slowly towards the Volga, drawing the enemy after us, and the ground we occupied was invariably too small for the Germans to be able easily to use artillery and aircraft.

We moved back, occupying one building after another, turning them into strongholds. A soldier would crawl out of an occupied position only when the ground was on fire under him and his clothes were smouldering. During the day the Germans managed to occupy only two blocks.

At the crossroads of Krasnopiterskaya and Komsomolskaya Streets we occupied a three-storey building on the corner. This was a good position from which to fire on all corners and it became our last defence. I ordered all entrances to be barricaded, and windows and embrasures to be adapted so that we could fire through them with all our remaining weapons.

At a narrow window of the semi-basement we placed the heavy machine-gun with our emergency supply of ammunition—the last belt of cartridges. I had decided to use it at the most critical moment.

Two groups, six in each, went up to the third floor and the garret. Their job was to break down walls, and prepare lumps of stone and beams to throw at the Germans when they came up close. A place for the seriously wounded

Vasili I. Chuikov, *The Battle for Stalingrad,* trans. Harold Silver (New York: Holt, Rinehart and Winston, 1964), pp. 125–129.

was set aside in the basement. Our garrison consisted of forty men. Difficult days began. Attack after attack broke unendingly like waves against us. After each attack was beaten off we felt it was impossible to hold off the onslaught any longer, but when the Germans launched a fresh attack, we managed to find means and strength. This lasted five days and nights.

The basement was full of wounded; only twelve men were still able to fight. There was no water. All we had left in the way of food was a few pounds of scorched grain; the Germans decided to beat us with starvation. Their attacks stopped, but they kept up the fire from their heavy-calibre machine-guns all the time.

We did not think about escape, but only about how to sell our lives most dearly—we had no other way out. . . .

The Germans attacked again. I ran upstairs with my men and could see their thin, blackened and strained faces, the bandages on their wounds, dirty and clotted with blood, their guns held firmly in their hands. There was no fear in their eyes. Lyuba Nesterenko, a nurse, was dying, with blood flowing from a wound in her chest. She had a bandage in her hand. Before she died she wanted to help to bind someone's wound, but she failed. . . .

The German attack was beaten off. In the silence that gathered around us we could hear the bitter fighting going on for Mameyev Kurgan and in the factory area of the city.

How could we help the men defending the city? How could we divert from over there even a part of the enemy forces, which had stopped attacking our building?

We decided to raise a red flag over the building, so that the Nazis would not think we had given up. But we had no red material. Understanding what we wanted to do, one of the men who was severely wounded took off his bloody vest and, after wiping the blood off his wound with it, handed it over to me.

The Germans shouted through a megaphone: "Russians! Surrender! You'll die just the same!"

At that moment a red flag rose over our building.

"Bark, you dogs! We've still got a long time to live!" shouted my orderly, Kozhushko.

We beat off the next attack with stones, firing occasionally and throwing our last grenades. Suddenly from behind a blank wall, from the rear, came the grind of a tank's caterpillar tracks. We had no anti-tank grenades. All we had left was one anti-tank rifle with three rounds. I handed this rifle to an anti-tank man, Berdyshev, and sent him out through the back to fire at the tank point-blank. But before he could get into position he was captured by German tommy-gunners. What Berdyshev told the Germans I don't know, but I can guess that he led them up the garden path, because an hour later they started to attack at precisely that point where I had put my machine-gun with its emergency belt of cartridges.

This time, reckoning that we had run out of ammunition, they came impudently out of their shelter, standing up and shouting. They came down the street in a column.

I put the last belt in the heavy machine-gun at the semi-basement window and sent the whole of the 250 bullets into the yelling, dirty-grey Nazi mob. I was wounded in the hand but did not leave go of the machine-gun. Heaps of bodies littered the ground. The Germans still alive ran for cover in panic. An hour later they led our anti-tank rifleman on to a heap of ruins and shot him in front of our eyes, for having shown them the way to my machine-gun.

There were no more attacks. An avalanche of shells fell on the building. The Germans stormed at us with every possible kind of weapon. We couldn't raise our heads.

Again we heard the ominous sound of tanks. From behind a neighbouring block stocky German tanks began to crawl out. This, clearly, was the end. The guardsmen said good-bye to one another. With a dagger my orderly scratched on a brick wall: "Rodimtsev's guardsmen fought and died for their country here." The battalion's documents and a map case containing the Party and Komsomol cards of the defenders of the building had been put in a hole in a corner of the basement.

The first salvo shattered the silence. There were a series of blows, and the building rocked and collapsed. How much later it was when I opened my eyes, I don't know. It was dark. The air was full of acrid brickdust. I could hear muffled groans around me. Kozhushko, the orderly, was pulling at me:

"You're alive. . . ."

On the floor of the basement lay a number of other stunned and injured soldiers. We had been buried alive under the ruins of the three-storey building. We could scarcely breathe. We had no thought for food or water—it was air that had become most important for survival. I spoke to the soldiers;

"Men! We did not flinch in battle, we fought even when resistance seemed impossible, and we have to get out of this tomb so that we can live and avenge the death of our comrades!" Even in pitch darkness you can see somebody else's face, feel other people close to you.

With great difficulty we began to pick our way out of the tomb. We worked in silence, our bodies covered with cold, clammy sweat, our badly-bound wounds ached, our teeth were covered with brickdust, it became more and more difficult to breathe, but there were no groans or complaints.

A few hours later, through the hole we had made, we could see the stars and breathe the fresh September air.

Utterly exhausted, the men crowded round the hole, greedily gulping in the autumn air. Soon the opening was wide enough for a man to crawl through. Kozhushko, being only relatively slightly injured, went off to reconnoitre. An hour later he came back and reported: "Comrade Lieutenant, there are Germans all round us; along the Volga they are mining the bank; there are German patrols nearby. . . ."

We took the decision to fight our way through to our own lines.

Joachim Wieder
MEMORIES AND REASSESSMENTS

In 1962, Joachim Wieder, a German officer who had survived Stalingrad and Russian captivity, wrote *Stalingrad: Memories and Reassessments,* in which he described his feelings as the Russians closed the ring on the trapped German Sixth Army. Wieder recalled his outrage at Hitler's refusal to allow the Sixth Army to break out when it still had a chance. As the German army faced decimation, he reflected on the misery and death the invading German forces had inflicted on other people and the terrible retribution Germany would suffer.

A foreboding I had long held grew into a terrible certainty. What was happening here in Stalingrad was a tragic, senseless self-sacrifice, a scarcely credible betrayal of the final commitment and devotion of brave soldiers. Our innocent trust had been misused in the most

Joachim Wieder and Heinrich Graf von Einsiedel, *Stalingrad: Memories and Reassessments,* translated by Helmut Bogler (1993), pp. 112–113, 117–118, 120, 131. Copyright © 2002, Cassell Military Paperbacks. Reprinted by permission of F.A. Herbig Verlagsbuchhandllung.

despicable manner by those responsible for the catastrophe. We had been betrayed, led astray and condemned. The men of Stalingrad were dying in betrayed belief and in betrayed trust. In my heart the bitter feeling of ". . . and all for nothing" became ever more torturing.

In my soul arose again the whole abysmal disaster of the war itself. More clearly than ever before I appreciated the full measure of misery and wretchedness of the other countries in Europe to which German soldiers and German arms had brought boundless misfortune. Had not we, so far the victors, been all too prone to close our eyes and our hearts and to forget that always and everywhere, the issues were living human beings their possessions and their happiness?

Probably only a few among us had entertained the thought that the suffering and dying being caused by our sorry profession of war would one day be inflicted upon us. We had carried our total war into one region of Europe after another and thereby destructively interfered in the destinies of foreign nations. Far too little had we asked the reason why, the necessities and the justifications for what was happening, or reflected on the immeasurability of our political responsibility that these entailed. Misery and death had been initiated by us and now they were inexorably coming home to roost. The steppe on the Don and the Volga had drunk streams of precious human blood. Here in their hundreds of thousands had Germans, Roumanians, Italians, Russians and members of other Soviet peoples found their common grave.

The Russians were certainly also making cruelly high blood sacrifices in the murderous battle of Stalingrad. But they, who were defending their country against a foreign aggressor, knew better than we why they were risking their lives.

Several thousand Red Army prisoners suffering hunger and misery behind barbed wire at Voroponovo and doomed to share our downfall were particularly to be pitied. In my broodings which constantly haunted and tortured me, I began to realise just how much our feelings had atrophied towards the continual boundless disregard and violation of human dignity and human life. At the same time my horror and revulsion of the Moloch[1] of war, to whom ethical-religious conscience had stood in irreconcilable opposition from the very beginning, grew.

And so as the last days of our army were drawing to a close, a deep moral misery gnawed

at the hearts of the men helplessly doomed to destruction. Added to their indescribable external suffering were the violent internal conflicts caused by the voice of conscience, and not only with regard to the question of the unconditional duty to obey. Wherever I went and observed I saw the same picture. And what I learned about the matter later on only confirmed the impressions I had gained. Whoever was still unclear about the contexts and reasons for the catastrophe sensed them in dark despair.

Many officers and commanders now began to oppose the insane orders emanating from Führer Headquarters and being passed on by Army Command. By this time they began to reject the long eroded military concepts of honour and discipline to which the Army leadership had clung until the end. In the unconditional obedience, such as was fatally being upheld here at Stalingrad, they no longer saw a soldierly stance but rather a lack of responsibility. . . .

How shocked had we been then at the very outset of the eastern campaign, about two inhumane orders of the day that had been in open breach of international law and of true, decent German soldiery itself! These were the unethical "commissar order" that required the physical extermination of the regulators of the Bolshevik ideology in the Red Army, and the "Barbarossa order" dealing with military tribunals, that abolished mandatory prosecution of crimes by German soldiers against civilians in the eastern theatre. Even if these orders had only been acknowledged by our staffs on the front and evaded as far as possible, was it not guilt enough to have accepted and tolerated them in silence like so much else?

And what had gone on in the rear of the fighting troops? Many an ugly rumour had come to one's ears, many an ugly picture had come before one's eyes. I had heard of brutal acts of retribution which had struck the innocent with the guilty. On a drive through the occupied area I had on one occasion seen in Minsk, with its dozens of public gallows, scenes

---

[1] In the Old Testament Moloch was the god of the Ammonites and the Phoenicians to whom children were sacrificed.—Eds.

of shameful inhumanity. Were all these excesses and evils not bound to rebound on us sooner or later? . . .

Now, faced with the imminently impending final catastrophe, the question about the sense of what was happening that had plagued me so often during the war seized me again with cruel force. Hundreds of thousands of flowering human lives were suddenly being senselessly snuffed out here in Stalingrad. What an immeasurable wealth of human happiness, human plans, hopes, talents, fertile possibilities for the future were thereby being destroyed for ever! The criminal insanity of an irresponsible war management with its superstitious belief in technology and its utter lack of feeling for the life, value and dignity of man, had here prepared a hell on earth for us. Of what importance was the individual in his uniqueness and distinctiveness? He felt himself as if extinguished and used up as raw material in a demonic machine of destruction. Here war showed itself in its unmasked brutality. Stalingrad appeared to me as an unsurpassed violation and degeneration of

the human essence. I felt myself to be locked into a gigantic, inhuman mechanism that was running on with deadly precision to its own dissolution and destruction. . . .

In the sad events on the Volga I saw not only the military turning-point of the war. In the experiences behind me I felt and apprehended something else as well; the anticipation of the final catastrophe towards which the whole nation was reeling. In my mind's eye I suddenly saw a second Stalingrad, a repetition of the tragedy just lived through, but of much greater, more terrible proportions. It was a vast pocket battle on German soil with the whole German nation fighting for life or death inside. And were the issues not the same as those of the final months of our Sixth Army? In the sacrifice thus already ordained, would insight, the power of decision and the strength either to break out or to surrender be able to mature?

In our helpless abandonment, to feel our own fate and destruction breaking in on our country, was a crushing mental burden that was to become virtually unbearable in the times ahead.

REVIEW QUESTIONS

1. What does Anton Kuzmich Dragan's account reveal about the resolve of the Russian soldiers at Stalingrad?
2. What kinds of doubts attacked Joachim Wieder when the Sixth Army was trapped at Stalingrad?

10 The Holocaust

Over conquered Europe the Nazis imposed a "New Order" marked by exploitation, torture, and mass murder. The Germans took some 5.5 million Russian prisoners of war, of whom more than 3.5 million perished; many of these prisoners were deliberately starved to death by the Wehrmacht—not the SS—that ran the camps. The Germans imprisoned and executed many Polish intellectuals and priests and slaughtered vast numbers of Roma (Gypsies). Using the modern state's organizational capacities and the instruments of modern technology, the Nazis murdered six million Jews, including one and a half million children—two-thirds of the Jewish population of Europe. Gripped by the mythical, perverted worldview of Nazism, the SS, Hitler's elite guard, carried out these murders with dedication and idealism; they believed that they were exterminating subhumans who threatened the German nation.

Hermann Graebe
SLAUGHTER OF JEWS IN UKRAINE

While the regular German army penetrated deeply into Russia, special SS units, the *Einsatzgruppen*, rounded up Jews for mass executions. Aided by Ukrainian, Lithuanian, and Latvian auxiliaries, and contingents from the Romanian army, the Einsatzgruppen massacred 1 to 1.4 million Jews. Hermann Graebe, a German construction engineer, saw such a mass slaughter in Dubno in Ukraine. He gave a sworn affidavit before the Nuremberg tribunal, a court at which the Allies tried Nazi war criminals after the end of World War II.

Graebe had joined the Nazi Party in 1931 but later renounced his membership, and during the war he rescued Jews from the SS. Graebe was the only German citizen to volunteer to testify at the Nuremberg trials, an act that earned him the enmity of his compatriots. Socially ostracized, Graebe emigrated to the United States, where he died in 1986 at the age of eighty-five.

On October 5, 1942, when I visited the building office at Dubno, my foreman told me that in the vicinity of the site, Jews from Dubno had been shot in three large pits, each about 30 metres long and 3 metres deep. About 1,500 persons had been killed daily. All the 5,000 Jews who had still been living in Dubno before the pogrom were to be liquidated. As the shooting had taken place in his presence, he was still much upset.

Thereupon, I drove to the site accompanied by my foreman and saw near it great mounds of earth, about 30 metres long and 2 metres high. Several trucks stood in front of the mounds. Armed Ukrainian militia drove the people off the trucks under the supervision of an S.S. man. The militiamen acted as guards on the trucks

and drove them to and from the pit. All these people had the regulation yellow patches on the front and back of their clothes, and thus could be recognized as Jews.

My foreman and I went directly to the pits. Nobody bothered us. Now I heard rifle shots in quick succession from behind one of the earth mounds. The people who had got off the trucks—men, women and children of all ages—had to undress upon the orders of an S.S. man, who carried a riding or dog whip. They had to put down their clothes in fixed places, sorted according to shoes, top clothing and underclothing. I saw a heap of shoes of about 800 to 1,000 pairs, great piles of underlinen and clothing.

Without screaming or weeping, these people undressed, stood around in family groups, kissed each other, said farewells, and waited for a sign from another S.S. man, who stood near the pit, also with a whip in his hand.

Nazi Conspiracy and Aggression, vol. 5 (Washington, D.C.: Government Printing Office, 1946), pp. 696–699, document PS2992.

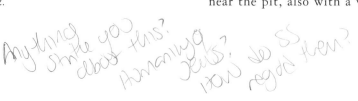

During the fifteen minutes that I stood near I heard no complaint or plea for mercy. I watched a family of about eight persons, a man and a woman both about fifty with their children of about one, eight and ten, and two grown-up daughters of about twenty to twenty-nine. An old woman with snow-white hair was holding the one-year-old child in her arms and singing to it and tickling it. The child was cooing with delight. The couple were looking on with tears in their eyes. The father was holding the hand of a boy about ten years old and speaking to him softly; the boy was fighting his tears. The father pointed to the sky, stroked his head, and seemed to explain something to him.

At that moment the S.S. man at the pit shouted something to his comrade. The latter counted off about twenty persons and instructed them to go behind the earth mound. Among them was the family which I have mentioned. I well remember a girl, slim and with black hair, who, as she passed close to me, pointed to herself and said "[age] 23." I walked around the mound and found myself confronted by a tremendous grave. People were closely wedged together and lying on top of each other so that only their heads were visible. Nearly all had blood running over their shoulders from their heads. Some of the people shot were still moving. Some were lifting their arms and turning their heads to show that they were still alive. The pit was already two-thirds full. I estimated that it already contained about 1,000 people.

I looked for the man who did the shooting. He was an S.S. man, who sat at the edge of the narrow end of the pit, his feet dangling into the pit. He had a tommy-gun on his knees and was smoking a cigarette. The people, completely naked, went down some steps which were cut in the clay wall of the pit and clambered over the heads of the people lying there, to the place to which the S.S. man directed them. They lay down in front of the dead or injured people; some caressed those who were still alive and spoke to them in a low voice.

Then I heard a series of shots. I looked into the pit and saw that the bodies were twitching or the heads lying motionless on top of the bodies which lay before them. Blood was running from their necks. I was surprised that I was not ordered away, but I saw that there were two or three postmen in uniform nearby. The next batch was approaching already. They went down into the pit, lined themselves up against the previous victims and were shot.

When I walked back round the mound, I noticed another truckload of people which had just arrived. This time it included sick and infirm persons. An old, very thin woman with terribly thin legs was undressed by others who were already naked, while two people held her up. The woman appeared to be paralyzed. The naked people carried the woman around the mound. I left with my foreman and drove in my car back to Dubno.

On the morning of the next day, when I again visited the site, I saw about thirty naked people lying near the pit—about 30 to 50 metres away from it. Some of them were still alive; they looked straight in front of them with a fixed stare and seemed to notice neither the chilliness of the morning nor the workers of my firm who stood around. A girl of about twenty spoke to me and asked me to give her clothes and help her escape. At that moment we heard a fast car approach and I noticed that it was an S.S. detail. I moved away to my site. Ten minutes later we heard shots from the vicinity of the pit. The Jews alive had been ordered to throw the corpses into the pit, then they had themselves to lie down in it to be shot in the neck.

zero humanity

Can you see any problems with this method from the nazis POV?

Rudolf Hoess
COMMANDANT OF AUSCHWITZ

To speed up the "final solution of the Jewish problem," the SS established death camps in Poland. Jews from all over Europe were crammed into cattle cars and shipped to these camps to be gassed or worked to death. At Auschwitz, the most notorious of the concentration camps, the SS used five gas chambers to kill as many as 9,000 people a day. At times, wrote a survivor of Auschwitz, "children were taken away, crying and screaming, with wild terror in their eyes, to be undressed, thrown into the waiting graves, drenched with some inflammable material and burned alive." Special squads of Jewish prisoners, called *Sonderkommandos*, were forced to pick over the corpses for gold teeth, jewelry, and anything else of value for the German war effort. Some 1.3 million Jews perished at Auschwitz. Rudolf Hoess (1900–1947), commandant of Auschwitz, described the murder process in a deposition at the trial in Nuremberg of major Nazi war criminals. He was executed by Polish authorities in 1947. An excerpt from Hoess's account follows.

In the spring of 1942 the first transports of Jews, all earmarked for extermination, arrived from Upper Silesia.

They were taken from the detraining platform to the "cottage"—to bunker I—across the meadows where later building site II was located. The transport was conducted by Aumeier and Palitzsch and some of the block leaders. They talked with the Jews about general topics, inquiring concerning their qualifications and trades, with a view to misleading them. On arrival at the "cottage," they were told to undress. At first they went calmly into the rooms where they were supposed to be disinfected. But some of them showed signs of alarm, and spoke of death by suffocation and of annihilation. A sort of panic set in at once. Immediately all the Jews still outside were pushed into the chambers, and the doors were screwed shut. With subsequent transports the difficult individuals were picked out early and most carefully supervised. At the first signs

of unrest, those responsible were unobtrusively led behind the building and killed with a small-caliber gun, that was inaudible to the others. The presence and calm behavior of the Special Detachment [of *Sonderkommandos*] served to reassure those who were worried or who suspected what was about to happen. A further calming effect was obtained by members of the Special Detachment accompanying them into the rooms and remaining with them until the last moment, while an SS man also stood in the doorway until the end.

It was most important that the whole business of arriving and undressing should take place in an atmosphere of the greatest possible calm. People reluctant to take off their clothes had to be helped by those of their companions who had already undressed, or by men of the Special Detachment.

The refractory ones were calmed down and encouraged to undress. The prisoners of the Special Detachment also saw to it that the process of undressing was carried out quickly, so that the victims would have little time to wonder what was happening. . . .

Nazi Conspiracy and Aggression, vol. 6 (Washington, D.C.: Government Printing Office, 1946), pp. 788–789.

Many of the women hid their babies among the piles of clothing. The men of the Special Detachment were particularly on the lookout for this, and would speak words of encouragement to the woman until they had persuaded her to take the child with her. The women believed that the disinfectant might be bad for their smaller children, hence their efforts to conceal them.

The smaller children usually cried because of the strangeness of being undressed in this fashion, but when their mothers or members of the Special Detachment comforted them, they became calm and entered the gas chambers, playing or joking with one another and carrying their toys.

I noticed that women who either guessed or knew what awaited them nevertheless found the courage to joke with the children to encourage them, despite the mortal terror visible in their own eyes.

One woman approached me as she walked past and, pointing to her four children who were manfully helping the smallest ones over the rough ground, whispered:

"How can you bring yourself to kill such beautiful, darling children? Have you no heart at all?"

One old man, as he passed by me, hissed:

"Germany will pay a heavy penance for this mass murder of the Jews."

His eyes glowed with hatred as he said this. Nevertheless he walked calmly into the gas chamber, without worrying about the others.

One young woman caught my attention particularly as she ran busily hither and thither, helping the smallest children and the old women to undress. During the selection she had had two small children with her, and her agitated behavior and appearance had brought her to my notice at once. She did not look in the least like a Jewess. Now her children were no longer with her. She waited until the end, helping the women who were not undressed and who had several children with them, encouraging them and calming the children. She went with the very last ones into the gas chamber. Standing in the doorway, she said:

"I knew all the time that we were being brought to Auschwitz to be gassed. When the selection took place I avoided being put with the able-bodied ones, as I wished to look after the children. I wanted to go through it all, fully conscious of what was happening. I hope that it will be quick. Goodbye!"

From time to time women would suddenly give the most terrible shrieks while undressing, or tear their hair, or scream like maniacs. These were immediately led away behind the building and shot in the back of the neck with a small-caliber weapon.

It sometimes happened that, as the men of the Special Detachment left the gas chamber, the women would suddenly realize what was happening, and would call down every imaginable curse upon our heads.

I remember, too, a woman who tried to throw her children out of the gas chamber, just as the door was closing. Weeping, she called out:

"At least let my precious children live."

There were many such shattering scenes, which affected all who witnessed them.

During the spring of 1942 hundreds of vigorous men and women walked all unsuspecting to their death in the gas chambers, under the blossom-laden fruit trees of the "cottage" orchard. This picture of death in the midst of life remains with me to this day.

The process of selection, which took place on the unloading platforms, was in itself rich in incident.

The breaking up of families, and the separation of the men from the women and children, caused much agitation and spread anxiety throughout the whole transport. This was increased by the further separation from the others of those capable of work. Families wished at all costs to remain together. Those who had been selected ran back to rejoin their relations. Mothers with children tried to join their husbands, or old people attempted to find those of their children who had been selected for work, and who had been led away.

Often the confusion was so great that the selections had to be begun all over again. The limited area of standing room did not permit better sorting arrangements. All attempts to pacify these agitated mobs were useless. It was often necessary to use force to restore order.

As I have already frequently said, the Jews have strongly developed family feelings. They stick together like limpets. . . .

Then the bodies had to be taken from the gas chambers, and after the gold teeth had been extracted, and the hair cut off, they had to be dragged to the pits or to the crematoria. Then

the fires in the pits had to be stoked, the surplus fat drained off, and the mountain of burning corpses constantly turned over so that the draught might fan the flames. . . .

It happened repeatedly that Jews of the Special Detachment would come upon the bodies of close relatives among the corpses, and even among the living as they entered the gas chambers. They were obviously affected by this, but it never led to any incident.[1]

_____

[1]On October 7, 1944, the *Sonderkommandos* attacked the SS. Some SS guards were killed, and one crematorium was burned. Most of the prisoners who escaped were caught and killed.—Eds.

Survivors
CONCENTRATION CAMP LIFE AND DEATH

Jews not immediately selected for extermination faced a living death in the concentration camps, which also imprisoned non-Jewish inmates, many of them opponents of the Nazi regime. The SS, who ran the camps, took sadistic pleasure in humiliating and brutalizing their helpless Jewish victims. In the various camps, SS men entertained themselves by hurling prisoners to their deaths from high walls—they called the doomed victims parachutists—killing them in target practice, repeatedly and severely kicking them with heavy boots, and turning them into punching bags, breaking their noses, knocking out their teeth, and leaving them drenched in blood; the whole time, another Jewish inmate would be forced to keep the pounded Jew from collapsing to the ground. The prisoners had to watch the cruel torture and listen to the victims' cries of pain, some of whom died in horrible agony.

The following accounts by Jewish survivors depict the treatment of Jewish prisoners by brutal SS guards. The first account, by a Jewish physician imprisoned at Auschwitz, reveals the SS deriving ghoulish humor from their treatment of pregnant Jewish women.

A few days after the arrival of a new transport, one of the S.S. chiefs would address the women, encouraging the pregnant ones to step forward, because they would be taken to another camp

where living conditions were better. He also promised them double bread rations so as to be strong and healthy when the hour of delivery came. Group after group of pregnant women left

Camp C. Even I was naive enough, at that time, to believe the Germans, until one day I happened to have an errand near the crematories and saw with my own eyes what was done to these women.

They were surrounded by a group of S.S. men and women, who amused themselves by giving these helpless creatures a taste of hell, after which death was a welcome friend. They were beaten with clubs and whips, torn by dogs, dragged around by the hair and kicked in the stomach with heavy German boots. Then, when they collapsed, they were thrown into the crematory—alive.

Guards devised perverted ways of humiliating and brutalizing their helpless charges. Every morning at roll-call, often in horrendous weather, prisoners had to stand at attention for hours, and anyone who dared to move was severely dealt with. Guards amused themselves by compelling prisoners to "play" depraved games, as one survivor reports.

Gisella Perl, *I was a Doctor in Auschwitz* (reprint edition; North Stratford, NH: Ayer Company Publishers, Inc., 2003). Original copyright 1946, p. 80.

The Germans devised ways of punishment that amused them. . . . The prisoners are lined up in two long rows facing each other. . . . Every prisoner has a cudgel with which he must beat the prisoner chosen to compete in the race that is run between the two rows. These wretches run as fast as they can while their fellow prisoners beat them over their bodies without ceasing. Should anyone out of pity not strike with all his force then he himself is made to do the running in which death is almost certain since few succeed in reaching the end of the line. . . . One of the veteran prisoners told us that he had seen another game in which the participants did not have to beat one another but took part in a contest with trained dogs. . . . A group of completely naked prisoners were put into a fenced tennis court, followed by half the number of great dogs. The dogs were trained not to kill, but to bite arms, legs, or private parts. The prisoners ran about from one end of the small enclosure to the other, with the dogs hunting and savaging them. Some tried to jump over the fence, but there stood Germans who beat them back.

Moshe Sandberg, *My Longest Year: In the Hungarian Labor Service and in Nazi Camps*, edited with an historical introduction by Livia Rothkirchen, trans., S. C. Hyman (Jerusalem: Yad Vashem, 1968), pp. 60–61.

Joseph Freeman
THE DEATH MARCH

In the closing months of the war, Nazi Germany, wanting to conceal their horrific crimes from invading Allied armies, dismantled concentration camps in occupied territory and force-marched hundreds of thousands of inmates—Jews and non-Jews—to facilities in Germany. The SS brutalized the emaciated and sick prisoners, who were often fed just a piece of bread for the day. Marching for miles each day unprotected from the cold, starving, and constantly being tormented by cruel guards who beat and killed stragglers, some 250,000 perished in the Nazi Death March. In the following account, excerpted from *The Road to Hell: Recollections of the Nazi Death March*, Joseph Freeman, a survivor of the heinous ordeal, depicts the suffering of the victims and the inhumanity of the SS.

The moment someone slowed down or fell, these monsters would command specially-trained German shepherds to attack. The dogs grabbed the fallen inmates by the legs. With razor-like teeth they ripped out pieces of flesh. The agonizing screams from the victims made the dogs even more aggressive. But this was only the beginning of the torture. As the wounded prisoners lay on the ground, the SS called off the dogs and they took over, smashing the crying inmates with the butts of their guns, shouting, *"Aufstehen schmutzige Jude!"* ("Get up, dirty Jew!"). The blood spurting from open wounds did not deter the SS from their murderous work. The cries of the tortured still ring in my ears. I can never erase that moment of pain and inhumanity. Once the crying stopped, the SS finished off the victim with a gunshot to the head. Pools of blood spread around the bodies lying on the road.

The guards forced us to watch the atrocity and warned us that this would be our fate if we stumbled on the march. We stood silent, biting our lips. We did not react; in shock, we were incapable of crying—the pain, the terror, and the hunger having robbed us of much of our human emotion. The road was covered with blood, evidence of the monstrous brutality of the SS.

We were convinced the end was near, that none of us would survive. Worse, most of us were transformed into unfeeling robots who no longer cared whether we lived or died. However, a handful of us miraculously retained the will and the hope of survival. But that spark was dying as we passed the bodies of friends lying on the road. I held onto Chaim, silently saying Kaddish [prayer for the dead] for our murdered companions.

Joseph Freeman, *The Road to Hell: Recollections of the Nazi Death March* (St. Paul, MN: Paragon House, 1998), pp. 69–71.

REVIEW QUESTIONS

1. How did the SS view their Jewish victims?
2. What do these Holocaust accounts reveal about the capacity of human beings to commit evil?
3. How should Germans today view the Holocaust? How should Jews?

11 Resistance in Warsaw

Each occupied country had its collaborators who welcomed the demise of democracy, saw Hitler as Europe's best defense against Communism, and profited from the sale of war material. Each country also produced a resistance movement that grew stronger as Nazi barbarism became more visible and prospects of a German defeat more likely. The Nazis retaliated by torturing and executing captured resistance fighters and killing hostages—generally fifty for every German killed. Two historic episodes of resistance occurred in Warsaw.

Marek Edelman
THE WARSAW GHETTO UPRISING, 1943

Three million Jews lived in Poland at the time of the Nazi invasion in 1939. In 1940, the Nazis began herding Jews from all over the country into densely packed ghettos—six or seven to a room in Warsaw—located in a number of cities. There the Jews worked as slave laborers for the German war effort. Many died of beatings, shootings, disease, and starvation before being transported to death camps. The largest of the ghettos was in Warsaw, the Polish capital, where 450,000 Jews were confined behind a ten-foot wall, sealing them off from the rest of the Polish population, which the Nazis referred to as the "Aryan side." The Germans killed anyone they found trying to escape from the ghetto, including starving children desperate to smuggle food in from beyond the wall. Between July and October 1942, the Germans deported some 300,000 Jews in freight cars from the Warsaw Ghetto to be gassed in the death camp at Treblinka.

By the beginning of 1943, a remnant of 60,000 Jews remained in the Warsaw Ghetto. Jewish underground organizations now resolved to resist the final deportations to the gas chambers. They knew they had no chance to succeed; their hope was stated in the Jewish Combat Organization's (ZOB) "Manifesto to the Poles": "We, as well as you, are burning with the desire to punish the enemy for all his crimes, with a desire for vengeance. It is a fight for our freedom, as well as yours; for our human dignity and national honour, as well as yours." Armed with a few pistols, rifles, automatic firearms, and several hundred homemade bottled explosives, the insurgents battled the German troops and their Ukrainian and Latvian auxiliaries from April 19 to May 16. From their hiding places in buildings, the Jews rained grenades and bullets on Nazi patrols. Unable to dislodge the Jews from their positions, the Nazis block-by-block systematically set fire to and blew up the buildings in the ghetto. In this ghastly inferno, the Jewish partisans continued their desperate struggle until resistance was no longer possible. Some 14,000 Jews perished in the uprising; many of them were burned alive or perished from smoke inhalation. The Germans rounded up surviving Jews, executed large numbers on the spot, and transported the remaining Jews mainly to Treblinka, where most were exterminated. A few Jews escaped to the "Aryan side" through the sewers and continued their struggle in the forests. Some were imprisoned in a concentration camp in the ghetto and, when liberated by Polish forces in the Warsaw Uprising of the following year, fought alongside their fellow Poles (see the next selection). News of the Jewish revolt in the Warsaw Ghetto quickly spread throughout Poland and occupied Europe, inspiring Jews and non-Jews alike to resist their Nazi overlords.

The following selection is from *The Ghetto Fights*, first published in Warsaw in 1945. The author, Marek Edelman, who died in 2009, was the last surviving leader of the Warsaw Ghetto Uprising. After the war Edelman became a prominent cardiologist; in the 1980s he was a leading supporter of Solidarity, the independent trade union movement that helped bring down Poland's Communist regime.

Finally, the Germans decided to liquidate the Warsaw Ghetto completely, regardless of cost. On 19 April, 1943, at 2 A.M., the first messages concerning the Germans' approach arrived from our outermost observation posts. These reports made it clear that German gendarmes, aided by Polish "navy-blue" policemen, were encircling the outer Ghetto walls at 30-yard intervals. An emergency alarm to all our battle groups was immediately ordered, and at 2.15 A.M., that is 15 minutes later, all the groups were already at their battle stations. We also informed the entire population of the imminent danger, and most of the Ghetto inhabitants moved instantly to previously prepared shelters and hide-outs in the cellars and attics of buildings. A deathly silence enveloped the Ghetto. The ZOB was on the alert.

At 4 A.M. the Germans, in groups of threes, fours, or fives, so as not to arouse the ZOB's or the population's suspicion, began penetrating into the "inter-Ghetto" areas. Here they formed into platoons and companies. At seven o'clock motorised detachments, including a number of tanks and armoured vehicles, entered the Ghetto. Artillery pieces were placed outside the walls. Now the SS men were ready to attack. In closed formations, stepping haughtily and loudly, they marched into the seemingly dead streets of the Central Ghetto. Their triumph appeared to be complete. It looked as if this superbly equipped modern army had scared off the handful of bravado-drunk men. . . .

But no, they did not scare us and we were not taken by surprise. We were only awaiting an opportune moment. Such a moment presently arrived. The Germans chose the intersection at Mila and Zamenhofa Streets for their bivouac area, and battle groups barricaded at the four corners of the street opened concentric fire on them. Strange projectiles began

exploding everywhere (the hand grenades of our own make), the lone machine pistol sent shots through the air now and then (ammunition had to be conserved carefully), rifles started firing a bit further away. Such was the beginning.

The Germans attempted a retreat, but their path was cut. German dead soon littered the street. The remainder tried to find cover in the neighbouring stores and house entrances, but this shelter proved insufficient. The "glorious" SS, therefore, called tanks into action under the cover of which the remaining men of two companies were to commence a "victorious" retreat. But even the tanks seemed to be affected by the Germans' bad luck. The first was burned out by one of our incendiary bottles, the rest did not approach our positions. The fate of the Germans caught in the Mila Street–Zamenhofa Street trap was settled. Not a single German left this area alive. . . .

Simultaneously, fights were going on at the intersection of Nalewki and Gesia Streets. Two battle groups kept the Germans from entering the Ghetto area at this point. The fighting lasted more than seven hours. The Germans found some mattresses and used them as cover, but the partisans' well-aimed fire forced them to several successive withdrawals. German blood flooded the street. German ambulances continuously transported their wounded to the small square near the Community buildings. Here the wounded lay in rows on the sidewalk awaiting their turn to be admitted to the hospital. At the corner of Gesia Street a German air liaison observation post signalled the partisans' positions and the required bombing targets to the planes. But from the air as well as on the ground the partisans appeared to be invincible. The Gesia Street–Nalewki Street battle ended in the complete withdrawal of the Germans. . . .

The following day there was silence until 2 P.M. At that time the Germans, again in closed formation, arrived at the brushmakers' gate. They did not suspect that at that very moment an observer lifted an electric plug.

The Ghetto Fights: The Warsaw Ghetto Uprising by Marek Edelman. Copyright © 1990. Reprinted with permission from Bookmarks Publications.

A German factory guard walked toward the gate wanting to open it. At precisely the same moment the plug was placed in the socket and a mine, waiting for the Germans for a long time, exploded under the SS men's feet. Over one hundred SS men were killed [probably an exaggeration] in the explosion. The rest, fired on by the partisans, withdrew. . . .

The Germans tried again. They attempted to enter the Ghetto at several other points, and everywhere they encountered determined opposition. Every house was a fortress. . . .

The partisans' stand was so determined that the Germans were finally forced to abandon all ordinary fighting methods and to try new, apparently infallible tactics. Their new idea was to set fire to the entire brushmakers' block from the outside, on all sides simultaneously. In an instant fires were raging over the entire block, black smoke choked one's throat, burned one's eyes. The partisans, naturally, did not intend to be burnt alive in the flames. We decided to gamble for our lives and attempt to reach the Central Ghetto area regardless of consequences. . . .

The flames cling to our clothes, which now start smouldering. The pavement melts under our feet into a black, gooey substance. Broken glass, littering every inch of the streets, is transformed into a sticky liquid in which our feet are caught. Our soles begin to burn from the heat of the stone pavement. One after another we stagger through the conflagration. From house to house, from courtyard to courtyard, with no air to breathe, with a hundred hammers clanging in our heads, with burning rafters continuously falling over us, we finally reach the end of the area under fire. We feel lucky just to stand here, to be out of the inferno. . . .

The omnipotent flames were now able to accomplish what the Germans could not do. Thousands of people perished in the conflagration. The stench of burning bodies was everywhere. Charred corpses lay around on balconies, in window recesses, on unburned steps. The flames chased the people out from their shelters, made them leave the previously prepared safe hideouts in attics and cellars. Thousands staggered about in the courtyards where they were easy prey for the Germans who imprisoned them or killed them outright. Tired beyond all endurance, they would fail asleep in driveways, entrances, standing, sitting, lying and were caught asleep by a passing German's bullet. Nobody would even notice that an old man sleeping in a corner would never again wake up, that a mother feeding her baby had been cold and dead for three days, that a baby's crying and sucking was futile since its mother's arms were cold and her breast dead. Hundreds committed suicide jumping from fourth or fifth stories of apartment houses. Mothers would thus save their children from terrible death in flames. The Polish population saw these scenes from Sto Jerska Street and from Krasinskich Square. . . .

The Germans now tried to locate all inhabited shelters by means of sensitive sound-detecting devices and police dogs. On 3 May they located the shelter on 30 Franciszkanska Street, where the operation base of those of our groups who had formerly forced their way from the brushmakers' area was at the time located. Here one of the most brilliant battles was fought. The fighting lasted for two days and half of all our men were killed in its course. . . .

On 8 May detachments of Germans and Ukrainians surrounded the Headquarters of the ZOB Command. The fighting lasted two hours, and when the Germans convinced themselves that they would be unable to take the bunker by storm, they tossed in a gas-bomb. Whoever survived the German bullets, whoever was not gassed, committed suicide, for it was quite clear that from here there was no way out, and nobody even considered being taken alive by the Germans. Jurek Wilner called upon all partisans to commit suicide together. Lutek Rotblat shot his mother, his sister, then himself. Ruth fired at herself seven times.

Thus 80 per cent of the remaining partisans perished, among them the ZOB Commander, Mordchaj Anilewicz.

At night the remnants, who had miraculously escaped death, joined the remaining few of the brushmakers' detachments now deployed at 22 Franciszkanska Street.

That very same night two of our liaison men (S Ratajzer—"Kazik," and Franek) arrived from the "Aryan side."

Ten days previously the ZOB Command had dispatched Kazik and Zygmunt Frydrych to our representative on the "Aryan side," Icchak Cukierman ("Antek"), to arrange the withdrawal of the fighting groups through the sewer mains. Now these liaison men arrived. . . .

All night we walked through the sewers, crawling through numerous entanglements built by the Germans for just such an emergency. The entrance traps were buried under heaps of rubble, the throughways booby-trapped with hand-grenades exploding at a touch. Every once in a while the Germans would let gas into the mains. In similar conditions, in a sewer 28 inches high, where it was impossible to stand up straight and where the water reached our lips, we waited 48 hours for the time to get out. Every minute someone else lost consciousness.

Thirst was the worst handicap. Some even drank the thick slimy sewer water. Every second seemed like months.

On 10 May, at 10 A.M., two trucks halted at the trap door on the Prosta Street–Twarda Street intersection. In broad daylight, with almost no cover whatsoever (the promised Home Army [Polish resistance] cover failed and only three of our liaison men and Comrade Krzaczek—a People's Army representative specially detailed for this assignment—patrolled the street), the trap door opened and one after another, with the stunned crowd looking on, armed Jews appeared from the depths of the dark hole (at this time the sight of *any* Jew was already a sensational occurrence). Not all were able to get out. Violently, heavily the trapdoor snapped shut, the trucks took off at full speed.

Two battle groups remained in the Ghetto. We were in contact with them until the middle of June. From then on every trace of them disappeared.

Those who had gone over to the "Aryan side" continued the partisan fight in the woods. The majority perished eventually. The small group that was still alive at the time took an active part in the 1944 Warsaw Uprising as the "ZOB Group."

Tadeusz Bor-Komorowski
THE WARSAW UPRISING, 1944

Nazi policy toward defeated Poland was especially harsh. To counter this brutality and maintain their national identity, the Poles created an underground, alternative society. Perhaps their most notable institution was the Home Army, an amalgamation of all of the resistance units in Poland. With 380,000 members at its height, the Home Army represented the fourth-largest Allied army, after the Soviet, American, and British. It carried out numerous intelligence and guerrilla operations against the German occupiers while awaiting the proper moment for a general revolt. That moment seemed to have arrived in the summer of 1944. Nazi armies were in flight throughout Europe, and the Red Army stood just across the Vistula. Fearful of Stalin's intention to install a puppet government in Poland after the war, the Home Army decided to take matters into its own hands and rid Warsaw of the Nazis, in effect declaring themselves masters in their own house.

The Warsaw Uprising began August 1, 1944. In the opening days of the battle, the Home Army, which numbered about 40,000 fighters in Warsaw, defeated the Germans in several bloody skirmishes, and the citizens of Warsaw were jubilant when the Polish national flag was unfurled. Several other partisan groups and volunteers, including Jews in hiding on the "Aryan side" and recently freed by Polish insurgents from a concentration camp standing in the ruins of the Warsaw Ghetto, fought with the Home Army. Reinforced German troops counterattacked, and, true to Heinrich Himmler's orders, special murder squads went house to house massacring some 40,000 civilians, including women and children, in the Wola district alone. Despite these and other German atrocities—using civilians as human shields for tanks and killing outright captured insurgents—the Poles continued their heroic resistance. However, defying the expectations of the insurgents' leaders, the Red Army provided no support. Seeing an opportunity to rid himself of political opponents, Stalin prevented Soviet troops from assisting the Poles. Shortages of food, water, and ammunition and the great loss of life—some 2,000 a day were perishing—forced the capitulation of the Home Army on October 2, 1944. An enraged Hitler ordered the total destruction of the city, particularly its historic religious and cultural centers. The Nazis evacuated the remainder of Warsaw's population and then, street by street, special detonation squads reduced the once beautiful Polish capital to rubble and ruins. It is estimated that more than 200,000 Poles died in the uprising and many survivors were sent to concentration camps; some 25,000 Germans were also killed.

After the war, the Communist leadership imposed by Stalin deported to Siberia or executed many of the leaders of the uprising; and until the demise of Communism in Poland, it was prohibited to honor the insurgents. Today the Poles commemorate the sixty-three-day uprising as a symbol of national pride and inspiration.

Tadeusz Bor-Komorowski was one of the organizers of the Home Army and, from 1943 until its disbandment late in 1944, its commander. His history of this underground military organization, *The Secret Army,* was published in 1950 while he was living in exile in Britain. The following excerpts from that work provide a thumbnail sketch of the Warsaw Uprising.

. . . Warsaw by now was fully aware that the battle would not pass it by. The hope that it would be fought for the dignity, freedom, and sovereignty of the Polish nation gave the inhabitants a strength of spirit capable of the greatest valour and sacrifice. The general lust of revenge for the years of tragedy and humiliation suffered under the Germans was overwhelming and practically impossible to check. The whole town was waiting breathlessly for a call to arms, and the vast majority of the population would have considered a passive attitude as a betrayal of the Polish cause . . . .

Having decided to fight, we faced a situation without precedent in the carrying out of full mobilisation in a town occupied by an enemy. For the first time a revolution was worked out as a military operation, according to a prearranged plan. Our strength amounted to nearly 40,000 Underground soldiers and about 4,200 women. The majority were workers, railwaymen, artisans, students and clerks in factories, railways and offices. These men had to be informed verbally of the place, date and hour to muster. It was only after many rehearsals and thanks to a continuously improved system of warning that we achieved the rate at which an order given by me reached the lower ranks in two hours. This enabled us to decide the rising no more than twenty-four hours before it was to start. But the task of informing 40,000 men, of giving them the code word and fixing hours and places of assembly was not the whole work. There was also liaison between the fighting groups to be established. Commanders of all ranks had to be constantly furnished with information and orders, and thousands of instructions had to be distributed throughout the city. All these tasks were carried out by girl messengers. From dawn till dusk they covered the length and breadth of the city, climbed numberless stairs and repeated orders and reports, mostly by word of mouth. . . .

. . . Thirty minutes before zero hour, all preparations were completed. The soldiers brought out their arms and put on white-and-red arm-bands, the first open sign of a Polish army on Polish soil since the occupation. For five years they had all awaited this moment. Now the last seconds seemed an eternity. At five o'clock they would cease to be an underground resistance movement and would become once more Regular soldiers fighting in the open.

At exactly five o'clock thousands of windows flashed as they were flung open. From all sides a hail of bullets struck passing Germans, riddling their buildings and their marching formations. In the twinkling of an eye, the remaining civilians disappeared from the streets. From the entrances of houses, our men streamed out and rushed to the attack. In fifteen minutes an entire city of a million inhabitants was engulfed in the fight. . . .

My first message to the soldiers in the capital read:

Soldiers of the capital!

I have to-day issued the order which you desire, for open warfare against Poland's age-old enemy, the German invader. After nearly five years of ceaseless and determined struggle, carried on in secret, you stand to-day openly with arms in hand, to restore freedom to our country and to mete out fitting punishment to the German criminals for the terror and crimes committed by them in Polish soil.

Bor.
Comnander-in-Chief, Home Army.

. . . People in the streets reacted with shouts and applause at the sight of the Polish eagle or the uniform which they had not seen for five years and when they saw German prisoners or captured arms. In this case, a window was flung open and a loud-speaker started up the song "Warszawianka," the Polish revolutionary song composed 114 years before. Everyone in the street, whether passing by or busy at the barricades, stood to attention and joined in the song. I was deeply affected by the fervour of the crowd. I think those moments were my happiest of the whole war. Unfortunately, they were short-lived.

On my return to the Kammler Factory, I found reports awaiting me on the incredible bestialities being practised by the Germans on civilians. This cruelty affected all the civilians in districts and buildings still in German hands. At the beginning, the Germans had set fire to most of the houses in these districts. The city was covered by a smoky glow. In many cases the inhabitants were not allowed to leave their houses or else not given sufficient time to do so. Thousands of people were burned alive. . . .

. . . Actually, there was not a single place in Warsaw which was out of range of artillery fire, incendiaries and mines, or grenades and bombs. Raid followed raid in such quick succession that from dawn to dusk the whole city lived in a state of continual alert. Every day, in nearly every street, more houses fell victim to the Luftwaffe . . . .

Meanwhile, the prolongation of the fight in the city forced us to more intensive use of the sewers for communication purposes. These dark, underground tunnels, mysterious and forbidding, stretching for miles, were the scene of a human effort of the greatest self-sacrifice—an effort to link up the torn shreds of fighting Warsaw so that all our isolated battles could form one whole and united operation fought in common. The network of sewers carried water and sewage to the Vistula. Built sixty years before, they formed a complicated labyrinth under the houses and streets of the city.

They had previously been used when fighting was going on in the Ghetto, which the Germans had surrounded by a wall and a cordon of police. By this route food, arms and ammunition had been smuggled in. Special organisations were formed at the time and provided with a suitable means of transport to ensure the supply of food for the Jewish population over a period of several months. Handcarts on rubber wheels, built to a width which would allow them to be pushed along the tunnels, were used. During the massacre of the Ghetto, many young Jews managed to flee by the same route.

When the Ghetto had been liquidated and destroyed, the sewers were forgotten, but now that our present fight was continuing, we were obliged once more to use these underground lines of communication. . . .

The tunnels were pitch dark, because for security reasons lights were either severely restricted or completely banned. The acrid air was asphyxiating and brought tears to the eyes. The size of passages varied. The smallest which could be negotiated were 3 feet high and 2 wide. Sharp debris, such as broken glass, strewed the semicircular floor of the passages, making hand support impossible when crawling. The most superficial scratch would have caused septicæmia. Two sticks had to be used as supports and progress was made in short jumps, rather like the motion of a kangaroo. It was extremely tiring and slow. To give an example, one of the routes leading from Stare Miasto to the centre of the city through one of the narrowest tunnels took as long as nine hours to negotiate, although the distance was no more than a mile. To advance along a narrow passage of this sort in pitch darkness, with mud up to the shoulders, often caused stark terror. I knew many men, in no way lacking courage, who would never have hesitated to attack enemy tanks with a bottle of petrol, who nevertheless lost their nerve and were overcome by complete exhaustion after only a few hundred yards in one of these narrow passages. The feeling of panic was increased by the difficulty of breathing in the fetid atmosphere and by the fact that it was impossible to turn round. If an immovable obstacle was encountered, the only course was to back out.

Great help was given to the traffic now moving along the sewers by women's units. The women who volunteered for it were known as *Kanalarki (kanal,* in Polish, is a sewer). They carried messages and orders, reconnoitred new passages and removed obstacles.

In September the tunnels became the route of withdrawal for units being evacuated from overrun positions. Even wounded were transported underground, a proof of the greatest self-sacrifice and devotion on the part of the soldiers who refused to allow their officers and comrades to be left to fall into enemy hands. . . .

REVIEW QUESTIONS

1. What motivated the fighters in the Warsaw Ghetto and the Polish Home Army?
2. How did these uprisings demonstrate both Jewish and Polish heroism and Nazi cruelty?

12 D-Day, June 6, 1944

On June 6, 1944, the Allied forces launched their invasion of Nazi-occupied France. The invasion, called Operation Overlord, had been planned with meticulous care. Under the supreme command of General Dwight D. Eisenhower (1890–1969), the Allies organized the biggest amphibious operation of the war. It involved 5,000 ships of all kinds, 11,000 aircraft, and 2 million soldiers, 1.5 million of them Americans, all equipped with the latest military gear. Two artificial harbors and several oil pipelines stood ready to supply the troops once the invasion was under way.

Historical Division, U.S. War Department
OMAHA BEACHHEAD

Allied control of the air was an important factor in the success of D-Day. A second factor was the fact that the Germans were caught by surprise. Although expecting an invasion, they did not believe that it would take place in the Normandy area of France, and they dismissed June 6 as a possible date because weather conditions were unfavorable.

Ultimately the invasion's success depended on what happened during the first few hours. If the Allies had failed to secure beachheads, the operation would have ended in disaster. As the following reading illustrates, some of the hardest fighting took place on Omaha Beach, which was attacked by the Americans. The extract, published in 1945, comes from a study prepared in the field by the 2nd Information and Historical Service, attached to the U.S. First Army, and by the Historical Section, European Theater of Operations.

As expected, few of the LCVP's and LCA's [amphibious landing craft] carrying assault infantry were able to make dry landings. Most of them grounded on sandbars 50 to 100 yards

out, and in some cases the water was neck deep. Under fire as they came within a quarter-mile of the shore, the infantry met their worst experiences of the day and suffered their heaviest casualties just after touchdown. Small-arms fire, mortars, and artillery concentrated on the landing area, but the worst hazard was produced by

Omaha Beachhead (Washington, D.C.: War Department Historical Division, 1945, 1984), pp. 43–47, 56–59, 71.

converging fires from automatic weapons. Survivors from some craft report hearing the fire beat on the ramps before they were lowered, and then seeing the hail of bullets whip the surf just in front of the lowered ramps. Some men dove under water or went over the side to escape the beaten zone of the machine guns. Stiff, weakened from seasickness, and often heavily loaded, the debarking troops had little chance of moving fast in water that was knee deep or higher, and their progress was made more difficult by uneven footing in the runnels crossing the tidal flat. Many men were exhausted before they reached shore, where they faced 200 yards or more of open sand to cross before reaching cover at the sea wall or shingle bank. Most men who reached that cover made it by walking, and under increasing enemy fire. Troops who stopped to organize, rest, or take shelter behind obstacles or tanks merely prolonged their difficulties and suffered heavier losses. . . .

Perhaps the worst area on the beach was Dog Green, directly in front of strongpoints guarding the Vierville draw [gully] and under heavy flanking fire from emplacements to the west, near Pointe de la Percée. Company A of the 116th was due to land on this sector with Company C of the 2d Rangers on its right flank, and both units came in on their targets. One of the six LCA's carrying Company A foundered about a thousand yards off shore, and passing Rangers saw men jumping overboard and being dragged down by their loads. At H+6[1] minutes the remaining craft grounded in water 4 to 6 feet deep, about 30 yards short of the outward band of obstacles. Starting off the craft in three files, center file first and the flank files peeling right and left, the men were enveloped in accurate and intense fire from automatic weapons. Order was quickly lost as the troops attempted to dive under water or dropped over the sides into surf over their heads. Mortar fire scored four direct hits on one LCA, which "disintegrated." Casualties were suffered all the way to the sand, but when the survivors

got there, some found they could not hold and came back into the water for cover, while others took refuge behind the neatest obstacles. Remnants of one boat team on the right flank organized a small firing line on the first yards of sand, in full exposure to the enemy. In short order every officer of the company, including Capt. Taylor N. Fellers, was a casualty, and most of the sergeants were killed or wounded. The leaderless men gave up any attempt to move forward and confined their efforts to saving the wounded, many of whom drowned in the rising tide. Some troops were later able to make the sea wall by staying in the edge of the water and going up the beach with the tide. Fifteen minutes after landing, Company A was out of action for the day. Estimates of its casualties range as high as two-thirds. . . .

As headquarters groups arrived from 0730 on, they found much the same picture at whatever sector they landed. Along 6,000 yards of beach, behind sea wall or shingle embankment, elements of the assault force were immobilized in what might well appear to be hopeless confusion. As a result of mislandings, many companies were so scattered that they could not be organized as tactical units. At some places, notably in front of the German strongpoints guarding draws, losses in officers and noncommissioned officers were so high that remnants of units were practically leaderless. . . .

There was, definitely, a problem of morale. The survivors of the beach crossing, many of whom were experiencing their first enemy fire, had seen heavy losses among their comrades or in neighboring units. No action could be fought in circumstances more calculated to heighten the moral effects of such losses. Behind them, the tide was drowning wounded men who had been cut down on the sands and was carrying bodies ashore just below the shingle. Disasters to the later landing waves were still occurring, to remind of the potency of enemy fire. . . .

---

[1]H indicates the start of an operation.—Eds.

At 0800, German observers on the bluff sizing up the grim picture below them might well have felt that the invasion was stopped at the edge of the water. Actually, at three or four places on the four-mile beachfront, U.S. troops were already breaking through the shallow crust of enemy defenses.

The outstanding fact about these first two hours of action is that despite heavy casualties, loss of equipment, disorganization, and all the other discouraging features of the landings, the assault troops did not stay pinned down behind the sea wall and embankment. At half-a-dozen or more points on the long stretch, they found the necessary drive to leave their cover and move out over the open beach flat toward the bluffs. Prevented by circumstance of mislandings from using carefully rehearsed tactics, they improvised assault methods to deal with what defenses they found before them. In nearly every case where advance was attempted, it carried through the enemy beach defenses. . . .

Various factors, some of them difficult to evaluate, played a part in the success of these advances. . . . But the decisive factor was leadership. Wherever an advance was made, it depended on the presence of some few individuals, officers and noncommissioned officers, who inspired, encouraged, or bullied their men forward, often by making the first forward moves. On Easy Red a lieutenant and a wounded sergeant of divisional engineers stood up under fire and walked over to inspect the wire obstacles just beyond the embankment. The lieutenant came back and, hands on hips, looked down disgustedly at the men lying behind the shingle bank. "Are you going to lay there and get killed, or get up and do something about it?" Nobody stirred, so the sergeant and the officer got the materials and blew the wire. On the same sector, where a group advancing across the flat was held up by a marshy area suspected of being mined, it was a lieutenant of engineers who crawled ahead through the mud on his belly, probing for mines with a hunting knife in the absence of other equipment. When remnants of an isolated boat section of Company B, 116th Infantry, were stopped by fire from a well-concealed emplacement, the lieutenant in charge went after it single-handed. In trying to grenade the rifle pit he was hit by three rifle bullets and eight grenade fragments, including some from his own grenade. He turned his map and compass over to a sergeant and ordered his group to press on inland. . . .

. . . Col. George A. Taylor arrived in the second section at 0815 and found plenty to do on the beach. Men were still hugging the embankment, disorganized, and suffering casualties from mortar and artillery fire. Colonel Taylor summed up the situation in terse phrase: "Two kinds of people are staying on this beach, the dead and those who are going to die—now let's get the hell out of here." Small groups of men were collected without regard to units, put under charge of the nearest non-commissioned officer, and sent on through the wire and across the flat, while engineers worked hard to widen gaps in the wire and to mark lanes through the minefields.

REVIEW QUESTIONS

1. What difficulties did American troops face while attempting the amphibious landing at Omaha Beach? Why were casualties so heavy?
2. According to the Historical Division publication, many of the American soldiers at Omaha Beach were experiencing their first enemy fire. How did the officers who survived manage to rally these shaken and demoralized soldiers?

13 The End of the Third Reich

In January 1945, the Russians launched a major offensive, which ultimately brought them into Berlin. In February, American and British forces were battling the Germans in the Rhineland, and in March they crossed the Rhine into the interior of Germany. In April, the Russians encircled Berlin. After heavy artillery and rocket-launchers inflicted severe damage on the besieged city, Russian infantry attacked and engaged in vicious street fighting. From his underground bunker near the chancellery in Berlin, a physically exhausted and emotionally unhinged Hitler engaged in wild fantasies about new German victories.

The last weeks of the war were chaotic and murderous. Many German soldiers fought desperately against the invaders of the Fatherland, particularly the Russians, who had been depicted by Nazi propaganda as Asiatic barbarians. SS crews, still loyal to Hitler and National Socialism, hunted down and executed reluctant fighters as a warning to others. The misery of the Jews never abated. As the Russians neared the concentration camps, the SS marched the inmates, many of them, human skeletons, in a death march (see page 395).

As Russian troops advanced into Germany, many terrified German civilians fled westward, and not without reason. The invading Russians, many seeking vengeance for the suffering and ruin the Nazis had inflicted on their homeland and kinfolk, committed numerous atrocities against the conquered enemy, including the rape of more than a million women. It quickly became official Soviet policy to prevent the perpetration of such personal acts of revenge and mayhem.

Nerin E. Gun
THE LIBERATION OF DACHAU

In the closing weeks of the war, the Allies liberated German concentration camps, revealing the full horror of Nazi atrocities to a shocked world. On April 29, 1945, American soldiers entered Dachau. One of the liberated prisoners was Nerin E. Gun, a Turkish Catholic journalist, who had been imprisoned by the Nazis during the war for his reports about the Warsaw Ghetto and his prediction that the German armies would meet defeat in Russia. Gun described the liberation of Dachau in *The Day of the Americans* (1966), from which the following selection is taken.

The first wave of Americans had been followed by a second, which must have broken into the camp either through the crematorium or through the marshaling-yard, where the

Nerin E. Gun, *The Day of the Americans* (New York: Fleet Publishing Corp., 1966), pp. 23, 62–64.

boxcars loaded with thousands of corpses had been parked. For, as soon as they saw the SS men standing there with their hands on their heads, these Americans, without any other semblance of trial, without even saying a warning word, turned their fire on them. Most of the inmates applauded this summary justice, and those who had been able to get over the ditch rushed out to strip the corpses of the Germans. Some even hacked their feet off, the more quickly to be able to get their boots. . . .

The detachment under the command of the American major had not come directly to the [entrance]. It had made a detour by way of the marshaling yard, where the convoys of deportees normally arrived and departed. There they found some fifty-odd cattle cars parked on the tracks. The cars were not empty.

"At first sight," said [Lieutenant Colonel Will] Cowling, ' they seemed to be filled with rags, discarded clothing. Then we caught sight of hands, stiff fingers, faces. . . ."

The train was full of corpses, piled one on the other, 2,310 of them, to be exact. The train had come from Birkenau, and the dead were Hungarian and Polish Jews, children among them. Their journey had lasted perhaps thirty or forty days. They had died of hunger, of thirst, of suffocation, of being crushed, or of being beaten by the guards. There were even evidences of cannibalism. They were all practically dead when they arrived at Dachau Station. The SS men did not take the trouble to unload them. They simply decided to stand guard and shoot down any with enough strength left to emerge from the cattle cars. The corpses were strewn everywhere—on the rails, the steps, the platforms.

The men of the 45th Division had just made contact with the 42nd, here in the station. They too found themselves unable to breathe at what they saw. One soldier yelled: "Look, Bud, it's moving!" He pointed to something in motion among the cadavers. A louse-infested prisoner was crawling like a worm, trying to attract attention. He was the only survivor.

"I never saw anything like it in my life," said Lieutenant Harold Mayer. "Everyone of my men became raving mad. We turned off toward the

east, going around the compound, without even taking the trouble to reconnoiter first. We were out to avenge them." . . .

The ire of the men of the First Battalion, 157th Regiment, was to mount even higher as they got closer to the Lager [camp] of the deportees. The dead were everywhere—in the ditches, along the side streets, in the garden before a small building with chimneys—and there was a huge mountain of corpses inside the yard of this building, which they now understood to be the crematorium. And finally there was the ultimate horror—the infernal sight of those thousands and thousands of living skeletons, screaming like banshees, on the other side of the placid poplars.

When some of the SS men on the watchtowers started to shoot into the mobs of prisoners, the Americans threw all caution to the winds. They opened fire on the towers with healthy salvos. The SS men promptly came down the ladders, their hands reaching high. But now the American GI saw red. He shot the Germans down with a telling blast, and to make doubly sure sent a final shot into their fallen bodies. Then the hunt started for any other Germans in SS uniforms [a number of whom—the exact number is uncertain—were killed by enraged Americans and revengeful camp inmates].

In the SS refectory, one soldier had been killed while eating a plate of beans. He still held a spoonful in his hand. At the signal center, the SS man in charge of the switchboard was slumped over his panel, blood running down to the receiver, the busy signal from Munich still ringing in his unheeding ear. At the power plant, the SS foreman had been beaten to death with shovels by a Polish prisoner and his Czech assistant. After that, they had been able to cut the high-voltage current from the barbed-wire fences around the camp.

Margaret Freyer
THE FIRE BOMBING OF DRESDEN

In an attempt to shatter German morale and to support the Russians who were advancing west into Germany, in early 1945 the Allies planned to mass bomb several large cities in East Germany. They believed that such attacks, particularly if they destroyed railyards, would hinder the movement of German reinforcements to the Russian front. On February 13–14, Allied planes dropped tons of high explosive bombs and incendiaries packed with highly combustible chemicals on the relatively defenseless city of Dresden. The bombings created a firestorm that turned the city into an inferno. A landmark cultural center, famous for its splendid architecture, was devastated. Some 30,000 inhabitants, many of them refugees fleeing the advancing Russians, perished, and thousands of others suffered horrific wounds.

The massive destruction of Dresden has aroused a historical controversy regarding the morality of terror-bombing civilians. The German Far Right has maintained that the firebombings of German cities, particularly Dresden, were war crimes that equaled or exceeded what the Nazis had done, and that the Allied leadership should be labeled war criminals. And some British and American commentators have called the bombing a criminal act. Dresden, they argue, was of no military importance, and with the war nearly won its destruction was totally unnecessary. Defenders of the raid point out that Dresden was a major railway junction that could be used for transporting troops to fight the Russians; its factories produced military gunsights, radar equipment, gas masks, parts for the German air force, and fuses for antiaircraft shells; and, with the Germans offering strong resistance on both fronts, there was no certainty that the war would end shortly. Moreover, maintain its defenders, Allied bombing of German cities was the price Germany paid for initiating this policy of destroying civilian targets— Guernica (1937) during the Spanish Civil War, Warsaw (1939), Rotterdam (1940), London (1940), Stalingrad (1942)—in order to terrorize the population.

Margaret Freyer (born 1920), who barely escaped being sent to a concentration camp by the Gestapo for telling political jokes, took shelter in a cellar during the first wave of the attack. During a lull in the bombing, she left the damaged building and went to her friend Cenci's apartment. When the sirens sounded again, she and Cenci, thirty-nine other women, and Cenci's husband fled to the building's cellar. In the following excerpt, Freyer describes the horror of the fire-bombing.

I made a last attempt to convince everyone in the cellar to leave, because they would suffocate

---

Alexander McKee, *Dresden 1945: The Devil's Tinderbox* (London: Souvenir Press, 1982), pp. 171–173, 175.

if they did not; but they didn't want to. And so I left alone—and all the people in that cellar suffocated. . . .

A witches' cauldron was waiting for me out there: no street, only rubble nearly a metre high, glass, girders, stones, craters. . . .

To my left I suddenly see a woman. I can see her to this day and shall never forget it. She carries a bundle in her arms. It is a baby. She runs, she falls, and the child flies in an arc into the fire. . . . The fire-storm is incredible, there are calls for help and screams from somewhere but all around is one single inferno. I hold another wet handkerchief in front of my mouth, my hands and my face are burning; it feels as if the skin is hanging down in strips . . . .

In front of me is something that might be a street, filled with a hellish rain of sparks which look like enormous rings of fire when they hit the ground. I have no choice. I must go through. I press another wet handkerchief to my mouth and almost get through, but I fall and am convinced that I cannot go on. It's hot. Hot! My hands are burning like fire. . . .

I stumbled on towards where it was dark. Suddenly, I saw people again, right in front of me. They scream and gesticulate with their hands, and then—to my utter horror and amazement—I see how one after the other they simply seem to let themselves drop to the ground. . . .

Today I know that these unfortunate people were the victims of lack of oxygen. They fainted and then burnt to cinders . . . Once more I fall down and feel that I am not going to be able to get up again, but the fear of being burnt pulls me to my feet. Crawling, stumbling, my last handkerchief pressed to my mouth . . . I do not know how many people I fell over. I knew only one feeling: that I must not burn. . . .

I try once more to get up on my feet, but I can only manage to crawl forward on all fours. I can still feel my body, I know I'm still alive. . . . I was suffering from lack of oxygen. I must have stumbled forwards roughly ten paces when I all at once inhaled fresh air.

[The next day I searched for my fiancé] amongst the dead, because hardly any living beings were to be seen anywhere. What I saw is so horrific that I shall hardly be able to describe it. Dead, dead, dead everywhere. Some completely black like charcoal. Others completely untouched, lying as if they were asleep. . . . Some clinging to each other in groups as if they were clawing at each other.

From some of the debris poked arms, heads, legs, shattered skulls. The static water-tanks were filled up to the top with dead, human beings. . . .

Adolf Hitler
POLITICAL TESTAMENT

On April 30, 1945, with the Russians only blocks away, Hitler took his own life. In his political testament, which is printed below, he again resorted to his delusions and pathological obsessions, blaming the war on Jews.

More than thirty years have now passed since I in 1914 made my modest contribution as a volunteer in the first world-war that was forced upon the Reich.

In these three decades I have been actuated solely by love and loyalty to my people in all my thoughts, acts, and life. They gave me the strength to make the most difficult decisions which have ever confronted mortal man. I have spent my time, my working strength, and my health in these three decades.

Nazi Conspiracy and Aggression, vol. 7 (Washington, D.C.: Government Printing Office, 1946), pp. 260–263.

It is untrue that I or anyone else in Germany wanted the war in 1939. It was desired and instigated exclusively by those international statesmen who were either of Jewish descent or worked for Jewish interests. I have made too many offers for the control and limitation of armaments, which posterity will not for all time be able to disregard for the responsibility for the outbreak of this war to be laid on me. I have further never wished that after the first fatal world war a second against England, or even against America, should break out. Centuries will pass away, but out of the ruins of our towns and monuments the hatred against those finally responsible whom we have to thank for everything, International Jewry and its helpers, will grow.

Three days before the outbreak of the German-Polish war I again proposed to the British ambassador in Berlin a solution to the German-Polish problem—similar to that in the case of the Saar district, under international control. This offer also cannot be denied. It was only rejected because the leading circles in English politics wanted the war, partly on account of the business hoped for and partly under influence of propaganda organized by international Jewry.

I also made it quite plain that, if the nations of Europe are again to be regarded as mere shares to be bought and sold by these international conspirators in money and finance, then that race, Jewry, which is the real criminal of this murderous struggle, will be saddled with the responsibility. I further left no one in doubt that this time not only would millions of children of Europe's Aryan peoples die of hunger, not only would millions of grown men suffer death, and not only hundreds of thousands of women and children be burnt and bombed to death in the towns, without the real criminal having to atone for this guilt, even if by more humane means.

After six years of war, which in spite of all set-backs, will go down one day in history as the most glorious and valiant demonstration of a nation's life purpose, I cannot forsake the city which is the capital of this Reich. As the forces are too small to make any further stand against the enemy attack at this place and our resistance is gradually being weakened by men who are as deluded as they are lacking in initiative, I should like, by remaining in this town, to share my fate with those, the millions of others, who have also taken upon themselves to do so. Moreover I do not wish to fall into the hands of an enemy who requires a new spectacle organized by the Jews for the amusement of their hysterical masses.

I have decided therefore to remain in Berlin and there of my own free will to choose death at the moment when I believe the position of the Fuehrer and Chancellor itself can no longer be held.

I die with a happy heart, aware of the immeasurable deeds and achievements of our soldiers at the front, our women at home, the achievements of our farmers and workers and the work, unique in history, of our youth who bear my name.

That from the bottom of my heart I express my thanks to you all, is just as self-evident as my wish that you should, because of that, on no account give up the struggle, but rather continue it against the enemies of the Fatherland, no matter where. . . . From the sacrifice of our soldiers and from my own unity with them unto death, will in any case spring up in the history of Germany, the seed of a radiant renaissance of the National Socialist movement and thus of the realization of a true community of nations. . . .

May it, at some future time, become part of the code of honour of the German officer—as is already the case in our Navy—that the surrender of a district or of a town is impossible, and that above all the leaders here must march ahead as shining examples, faithfully fulfilling their duty unto death. . . .

Hitler then expelled Goering and Himmler from the party and made several appointments to govern the nation after his death. And he left instructions for the new leaders.

. . . Let them be hard, but never unjust, above all let them never allow fear to influence their actions, and set the honour of the nation above everything in the world. Finally, let them be conscious of the fact that our task, that of continuing the building of a National Socialist State, represents the work of the coming centuries, which places every single person under an obligation always to serve the common interest and to subordinate his own advantage to this end. I demand of all Germans, all National Socialists, men, women and all the men of the Armed Forces, that they be faithful and obedient unto death to the new government and its President.

Above all I charge the leaders of the nation and those under them to scrupulous observance of the laws of race and to merciless opposition to the universal poisoner of all peoples, international Jewry.

Given in Berlin, this 29th day of April 1945. 4:00 A.M.

Adolf Hitler.

Witnessed by
Dr. Josef Fuhr.   Martin Bormann.
Wilhelm Buergdorf.   Hans Krebs.

REVIEW QUESTIONS

1. According to Nerin E. Gun, how did the American soldiers react when they discovered conditions at Dachau?
2. What do you think was the reaction of Germans to the mass bombings of their cities and towns?
3. Compare Hitler's final testament with his speech to his generals in 1939 (see page 394). Had his views and expectations changed by the end of the war?

14 The Defeat of Japan

By the spring of 1942, the Japanese had conquered the coast of China, Indochina (Vietnam, Cambodia, and Laos), Thailand, Burma, Malaya, the Dutch East Indies (Indonesia), and several Pacific islands, including the Philippines. But in June 1942 Japan suffered a major reversal at Midway when American carrier-based planes destroyed 4 aircraft carriers and 322 Japanese planes. American forces then attacked strategic islands held by Japan. American troops had to battle their way up beaches and through tropical jungles tenaciously defended by Japanese soldiers who believed that death was preferable to the disgrace of surrender. By early 1945, Japan's navy had been decimated and key islands lost. American submarines blockaded Japanese ports, greatly reducing the food supply, and American planes regularly bombed Japanese cities, causing great damage and loss of life. With little chance of victory, Japan hoped to engage the United States in a war of attrition that would inflict many casualties on the Americans, thereby making them reluctant to invade the Japanese mainland and more amenable to a negotiated settlement that would permit Japan to retain parts of its empire.

Veterans
THE BATTLE OF IWO JIMA

In February 1945 American marines invaded the Japanese island of Iwo Jima, which is only 5.5 miles long and 2 miles wide. The U.S. wanted to capture the island's two airfields that would serve as staging areas for American planes. For five weeks the marines, many of them boys with little or no combat experience, battled the entrenched and determined Japanese defenders in what is often called the deadliest and bloodiest campaign in the history of the Marine Corps. In thirty-six days of unrelenting conflict and death, the Americans suffered 6,800 dead and more than 19,000 wounded. Of the 22,600 Japanese fighters, 18,844 perished, a number of them suicides.

The marines scrambled to get off the unprotected beach now littered with corpses and body parts. Displaying great discipline and bravery, they advanced across terrain devoid of cover while facing intense Japanese artillery, mortar, and machine gun fire. The Japanese, who awaited the enemy in fortified positions, often caves, tunnels, and blockhouses, proved to be ferocious warriors; considering surrender a loss of honor, they fought to the end and often took their own lives to avoid the disgrace of capture. Utilizing flame-throwing tanks and explosives, marine units cleared each stronghold one by one, often with considerable bloodletting. Many Japanese soldiers were incinerated; others were pulverized or trapped by collapsing cave walls and ceilings.

Marines approached Japanese dead cautiously, for they could be booby-trapped or feigning death while concealing a gun or grenade. Few prisoners were taken by either side. Marine corpses that showed signs of torture and mutilation were a horrific sight. Following are graphic accounts by veterans of the campaign.

Day One[1]

The first night on Iwo Jima can only be described as a nightmare in hell. About the beach in the morning lay the dead. They died with the greatest possible violence. Nowhere in the Pacific have I seen such badly mangled bodies. Many were cut squarely in half. Legs and arms lay 50 feet away from any body. All through the bitter night, the Japs rained heavy mortars and rockets and artillery on the entire area between the beach and the airfield. Twice they hit casualty stations on the beach. Many men who had been only wounded were killed.

Attacking the Caves (as told to the author by his uncle)[2]

There seemed to be no end in sight. One day blurred into the next as they attacked and eliminated one enemy position after another. Eliminating one position meant that they were only that much closer to the next. When they could see the caves, they appeared as black eye sockets peering malevolently down on them.

Unaware of the overall grand strategy for defeating the enemy, Jim's war was confined to that part of the battlefield immediately in front of him, the next cave or fortified-position

---

[1]Robert Sherrod, quoted in George W. Garand and Truman R. Strobridge, *Western Pacific Operations*, vol. 4, *History of U.S. Marine Corps Operations in World War II* (Washington, D.C.: USMC, 1971), p. 527.

[2]John C. Shively, *The Last Lieutenant: A Foxhole View of the Epic Battle for Iwo Jima* (New York: New American Library, 2006), p. 109.

bristling with machine guns, mortars, and hidden snipers. For the men of the 1st Platoon, the cave war was a microcosm of the entire operation, if not the entire war. His strategy was simple: take out this cave or that bunker, then move on to the next one, all the while trying, to stay alive. They would eliminate one position, then move forward until the next one began firing on them. They would dive for cover and laboriously crawl along the parched, sulfurous ground to flush out the enemy and then repeat the process. It was monotonous and terrifying. He never knew when or where the next shot would come from.

Hand-to-Hand Combat[3]

There was no room to use rifles. One Marine made a flying tackle at the nearest Jap and, when felled, twisted the Jap's neck and broke it. Another plunged feet first on a Japanese lieutenant, catching him in the groin. The third Marine leapt Tarzan-like from atop the cave, his jungle knife flashing. The Jap he landed on was stabbed in the heart before they hit the ground. There were no rules, no quarter, no surrender.

Caves and Canyons[4]

Each cave and pillbox, once silenced by flame tanks and infantry, had to be sealed by the engineers before we could move deeper into that deadly canyon. The contorted terrain made it impossible for tanks to operate effectively until armored bulldozers had cleared a road for their advance. We were too close to the enemy to use artillery, naval gunfire, or air support, so the infantry advanced warily to draw fire, thereby identifying enemy positions. Then, armored bulldozers under cover of infantry had to clear the broken ground of rocks, ditches, and mines, allowing flame tanks to roll in and to burn out the caves.

Demolition squads armed with bazookas and shaped charges followed closely. Engineers closed the larger caves {burying alive the defenders]. Only flame tanks seemed to scare the Japanese into fleeing their fighting positions inside the gorge and its approaches. All other forms of attack were met with fierce resistance until the defenders had been silenced. Where it was impossible to bring flame tanks to bear, the only heavy fire support for the infantry and demolitions squads were 37mm antitank guns, manhandled into position in the cliffs by teams of weary, struggling Marines. It was tough going all the way.

Misery of the Japanese[5]

"There was no natural water on the island, and we were quite lucky because our Navy made water aboard ship. The Japanese only had what little they could catch, and it didn't rain very much. By the time we were about a third of the way up the island, they were getting a hard biscuit a day and about a cup of water, terrible water. In my judgment, the Japanese officers were criminal in continuing this battle; they tortured their own men. These poor bastards got a biscuit and a cup of water a day, and they had to work underground in temperatures of one hundred ten to one hundred twenty degrees. As letters from [Lieutenant General Tadamichi] Kuribayashi pointed out, they'd work maybe ten or fifteen minutes, and then they'd have to get out. Otherwise they'd collapse from heat exhaustion.

"They were going to die anyhow, and he told them, 'Look, guys, I want you to kill ten Americans before you die.' That was the order. And it looked like for a little while like they might be able to do that. It was the only battle in which we lost more than they did. They lost about twenty-one thousand and we had more than six thousand dead, nineteen thousand wounded.

---

[3]Alvin T. Josephy Jr. et al., "Iwo: The Red Hot Rock," in *Semper Fidelis: The U.S. Marines in the Pacific, 1942–1945*, eds. Patrick O'Sheet and Gene Cook (New York: William Shoane Associates, 1947), pp. 93–94.
[4]Fred Haynes and James A. Warren, *The Lions of Iwo Jima* (New York: Henry Holt, 2008), pp. 211–212.

[5]Larry Smith, *Iwo Jima World War II Veterans Remember the Greatest Battle of The Pacific* (New York: W.W. Norton, 2008), p. 49.

The Enemy As Human[6]

One Marine reached over and plucked his wallet out [of a Japanese corpse], giving it to me saying, "What the hell. He won't be using it anymore." There were some bills neatly folded, which I removed and pocketed. It was then that I saw a small photo which had been pasted on the inside flap. It showed a small Jap soldier sitting with what appeared to be his bride, who stood partly behind him. She was wearing what must have been her wedding dress with all the bows and stuff that only made her look smaller. Her round white face showed no expression. This hit hard. It gave this ghastly corpse a soul. "They" also had loved ones back home who would never see them again or know how they died. . . . The enemy had just taken on a new face for me. Why don't they make the Tojos[7] of this world fight their own wars.

---

[6]Fred Haynes and James A. Warren, *The Lions of Iwo Jima* (New York: Henry Holt, 2008), pp. 220–221.

---

[7]Hideki Tojo, a Japanese general and later prime minister, who held strong militarist and nationalist views. After the war, he was tried by an international military court and found guilty of waging wars of aggression, including ordering the attack on Pearl Harbor and permitting the inhumane treatment of prisoners of war. He was sentenced to execution.

REVIEW QUESTION

What was particularly difficult for American marines in the Battle of Iwo Jima? For Japanese defenders?

CHAPTER 14

Europe: A New Era

THE END OF THE THIRD REICH, 1945. Hitler promised the German people a "Thousand-Year Reich." Here, two forlorn old men sit among the ruins of Berlin in May 1945. *(Everett Historical/Shutterstock.com)*

At the end of World War II, Winston Churchill lamented: "What is Europe now? A rubble heap, a charnel house, a breeding ground for pestilence and hate." Everywhere the survivors counted their dead. War casualties were relatively light in Western Europe: Britain and the Commonwealth suffered 460,000 casualties; France, 570,000; and Italy, 450,000. War casualties were heavier in Central and Eastern Europe: 5 million people in Germany, 6 million in Poland (including 3 million Jews), 1 million in Yugoslavia, and more than 25 million in the Soviet Union. The material destruction had been unprecedentedly heavy in the battle zones of northwestern Europe, northern Italy, and Germany, growing worse farther east, where Hitler's and Stalin's armies had fought without mercy. Industry, transportation, and communication had come to a virtual standstill. Yet Europe did recover from this blight, and with astonishing speed.

The term displaced persons (DPs) was coined at the end of World War II to describe the millions of people who were uprooted by almost six years of war. DP camps were established by the Allies to feed and house these refugees until they could move on.

The situation was particularly onerous for Jewish survivors of Nazi genocide. The end of the war did not end their misery. Of the Jewish concentration camp survivors, 40 percent died within a month or two after liberation, so dreadful was their physical condition. Most of the Jews languishing in DP camps in hated Germany wanted to leave Europe, which was soaked with Jewish blood.

The war also produced a shift in power arrangements. The United States and the Soviet Union emerged as the two most powerful states in the world. The traditional Great Powers—Britain, France, and Germany—were now dwarfed by these superpowers. The United States had the atomic bomb and immense industrial might; the Soviet Union had the largest army in the world and was extending its dominion over Eastern Europe. With Germany defeated, the principal incentive for Soviet-American cooperation had evaporated.

After World War I, divisive nationalist passions intensified. After World War II, Western Europeans progressed toward unity. The Hitler years convinced many Europeans of the dangers inherent in extreme nationalism, and fear of the Soviet Union prodded them toward greater cooperation.

Some intellectuals, shocked by the irrationality and horrors of the Hitler era, drifted into despair. To these thinkers, life was absurd, without meaning; human beings could neither comprehend nor control it. In 1945, only the naive could have faith in continuous progress or believe in the essential goodness of the individual. The future envisioned by the Enlightenment philosophes seemed more distant than ever. Nevertheless, this profound disillusionment was tempered by hope. Democracy had, in fact, prevailed over Nazi totalitarianism and terror. Moreover, fewer intellectuals were now attracted to antidemocratic thought. The Nazi dictatorship convinced many of them, even some who had wavered in previous decades, that freedom and human dignity were precious ideals and that liberal constitutional government, despite its imperfections, was the best means of preserving these ideals.

To be sure, immediately after the war, many Europeans gravitated to the Left, believing that Communists, who had been very active in resistance movements against the Nazis and Fascists, would overcome social injustice. However, in the decades to come, more disclosures of Communist oppression and ineptitude would greatly weaken Marxism's appeal. The future for Western civilization belonged to liberal and social democracy, its institutions and values for which the West had fought and sacrificed in World War II.

1   The Aftermath in Germany

In 1945 European cities everywhere were in rubble; bridges, railway systems, waterways, and harbors destroyed; farmlands laid waste; livestock killed; coal mines wrecked. Homeless and hungry people wandered the streets and roads. Europe faced the gigantic task of rebuilding.

Theodore H. White
GERMANY IN RUINS

American political journalist Theodore H. White (1915–1986) covered postwar reconstruction and European politics during a more than five-year residence on the Continent in the late 1940s and early 1950s. In the following account, White describes circumstances in Germany during the initial postwar years with an eye to the transformation he witnessed by 1951–1952.

[T]he roads that ran from village to town, from town to city were torn and ruptured by the passage of war; tanks had disemboweled the roadbeds, artillery and planes had shattered the bridges. And the roads led to cities, one more

From *Fire in the Ashes: Europe in Mid-Century* by Theodore H. White. (Toronto: George J. McLeod Limited, 1953), pp. 134–136.

appalling than the other—rubble heaps of stone and brick, rank with the smell of sewage and filth, dirty with the dust of destruction working its way into clothes, linen, skin and soul.

The forlorn people who lived in the ruins in those Winter Years could feel little beyond hunger. The clear German skin . . . shrunk sallow over shriveled bodies, or puffed over the unhealthy putty of children bloated by hunger edema. . . . White-faced men and women collapsed at their jobs for lack of food. Dignified people sought jobs as clerics or servants in the office of the occupying armies because in the barracks of the conquerors they got one hot meal of stew a day, which kept them alive. The United States government appropriated money to give every German school child one hot meal a day in his classroom. . . . The search for shelter was a nightmare; for this country, forty per cent of whose homes had been smashed, was being forced to absorb and shelter eight million refugees thrust back into it. For a German the perspective of ambition was the search to find for his family two rooms with a toilet and running water, . . .

Values withered: Girls roamed the streets, sleeping with the conquering soldiers for a candy bar, a cake of soap, a tin of Quaker Oats, coming home to once-chaste beds dirty with disease. Money was meaningless, cigarettes were currency; two cartons of American cigarettes bought a set of Meissen china, three cartons bought a Leica camera, two cigarettes were a tip. Businessmen became pirates. Families dissolved.

By an enormous, instinctive act of national resolution Germans put thinking out of their minds and concentrated on simple things: how to find a job, and how to work, For only by working could one find food, find clothes, find a roof. Even work was difficult; Germany could make only a strictly limited quantity of steel, of aluminum, of sulfur, of copper. She was forbidden to make again the vast range of intricate machinery in which lay her commercial strength; she could not build airplanes, could not fly airplanes, could not synthesize rubber or gasoline. One worked at what came to hand. In the Ruhr [the center of German industry] workmen stood in sullen silence and watched the dismantlers surveying for removal of generators, rolling mills and steel ovens. Krupp[1] sat in his prison and British engineers carefully paced the jungle of his Essen works marking with white chalk the machine tools, the drop forges, the presses to be taken away. At the Bochumer Verein, which had made both submarine assemblies and the finest crucible steels, the newest and most efficient shops were dismanteled.

---

[1]Alfred Krupp was a leading industrialist and supporter of Nazism whose factory empire in Germany and occupied Europe brutalized slave laborers. Convicted by an Allied court of crimes against humanity, he was sentenced to twelve years in prison.—Eds.

A German Expellee from Czechoslovakia
"GERMANS WERE DRIVEN OUT OF THEIR HOMELAND LIKE DOGS"

Millions of Germans were expelled from Poland, Czechoslovakia, Yugoslavia, Romania, and Hungary, places where their ancestors had lived for centuries, by vengeful Eastern Europeans. Leaders in these countries, driven by nationalist aspirations, welcomed an opportunity to rid their nations of an ethnic minority, particularly since many of these Germans had aided the Nazi occupiers. In 1945–1946, some 12 million to 13 million Germans were driven westward, either fleeing the invading Russians or in a massive campaign of ethnic cleansing. Expelled from their homes, often with only a few minutes' warning, they had to leave virtually all their property and possessions behind; the Nazis had done exactly the same to Jews and Poles. Herded into internment camps they were brutalized by Polish and Czech guards who relished the opportunity to torment Germans. Tens of thousands of expellees died from malnutrition, disease, exposure, and mistreatment; thousands more committed suicide. Estimates for the number of refugees who perished before reaching their destination in Germany range from 500,000 to 1.7 million. The following selection describes the suffering endured by Germans expelled from Czechoslovakia.

In August 1945, the first Germans were driven out of their homeland like dogs. Individual family members were chosen at will and driven off to the railway station, where cattle cars stood ready. The cars had no roofs, and they were literally stuffed full of people. Old people as well as small children were forced into these cars, getting nothing to eat or drink. In these first days of expulsion the temperature averaged 30 degrees Centigrade [86 degrees Fahrenheit]. We were standing some 10 to 15 meters from these cattle cars but were not allowed to even once bring water or food to our relatives and friends. . . . Even a priest, whose parents were part of the transport, was denied permission to bring something to his folks. He cried bitterly because he couldn't give his suffering parents so much as a drink of water. No one can imagine the pain and suffering that reigned over these families at such a sight, and as a consequence of these events. Probably because of protests from abroad these humiliating expulsions were stopped for a while. In any case, a second wave of expulsions began in January 1946. . . . My wife, her parents and I were expelled on March 1, 1946. First we were all assembled in a

camp where our baggage was inspected, weighed and anything over 50 kg confiscated. . . . After this first check we were body searched. Had they found the money, I would have been whipped, for it had been strictly forbidden to take more than 500 Reichsmarks. On March 3, 1946, like the others before us, we were loaded onto cattle cars. . . .

Regarding confiscation of homes and businesses, I personally witnessed this as well. As already noted, my wife's parents owned a bakery and a store for groceries and shoes. . . It was the last German business in the area. On the evening of October 21, 1945, around 6 P.M., a group of soldiers came in, locked us in a room, posted a guard at the door and kept us prisoner until 10 P.M. During that time two men ransacked the bakery, the other business and the apartment. . . . The next day we were taken to jail, where I was beaten. The reason for the beating was not that I had broken some law, it was because I was German. That was also the reason for our imprisonment. Moreover, as we discovered later, during the time we were in jail our home and business had been completely looted. Since they couldn't prove [Nazi] Party membership or any other transgressions on our part, we were released. . . . [but] we were not permitted to return to our own house. Thus, overnight, our property and possessions were gone.

Alfred-Maurice de Zayas, *A Terrible Revenge: The Ethnic Cleaning of the East European Germans, 1944–1950*, pp. 94–96. Published 2006 by Palgrave Macmillan.

The Nuremberg Trials of Nazi War Criminals

After the war, many German war criminals went into hiding, changed their identity, lied about their wartime record, or fled to other countries, particularly in South America. Only a small percentage of Nazi war criminals were prosecuted, and many of the convicted served ridiculously short sentences. Thousands of Germans who shot hostages, rounded up Jews for deportation to the gas chambers, staffed the concentration camps, were part of units that massacred Jews, and brutalized slave laborers never faced punishment. With the Cold War looming, Nazi war criminals escaped justice by working for British, American, and Soviet intelligence services that protected them. For example, Britain recruited Friedrich Buchardt, an Einsatzgruppen commander who oversaw the murder of some one hundred thousand Jews. Using a pseudonym or hiding their past, some Nazis criminals launched successful careers in postwar Germany.

Nevertheless, a significant number of German war criminals were indicted, and their trials provided a detailed record of the Nazi regime and its criminal behavior. In 1945–1946, twenty-two leading Nazis stood trial before the International Military Tribunal (IMT), comprised of representatives of the United States, Great Britain, the Soviet Union, and France, for conspiracy to wage war and for crimes against humanity. They were tried at Nuremberg, the scene of Hitler's giant rallies prior to the war.

The accused were shown horrifying documentaries of German atrocities, including of the concentration camps at the time when American, British, and Soviet troops entered them. They also heard equally horrifying accounts from survivors. Particularly distressing for the war criminals were pictures of young children with skulls bashed in and descriptions of Jewish children thrown alive into the furnaces. In denying responsibility for war crimes, the defendants offered a variety of specious defenses: they were not anti-Semitic and had no knowledge of the murder of Jews; they tried to save Jews; they did not personally kill anyone; they were obeying orders. In response to these claims, the newly founded anti-Nazi *Berliner Zeitung* commented sarcastically:

> Having now heard the testimony of more than half of the defendants, one could get the impression from their words that the inmates of the concentration camp had themselves carried out the selections for the gas chambers, ordered themselves to march into the chambers, themselves turned on the gas and obediently choked to death or had . . . beaten and bestially mistreated themselves, . . . and shot themselves. All these villainous organizers of mass extermination claim to not have been there at all, in fact they were practically benefactors of the inmates.

Rejecting the defendants' arguments that they did not personally participate in the atrocities committed against Jews and others or that they were only obeying orders forced on them in wartime against their will, the court sentenced twelve to death by hanging and one in absentia; seven were given jail sentences from ten years to life; and three were acquitted.

Nuremberg: International Military Tribunal, 1948, Vol. XIX, pp. 397, 418–419 426–427.

Justice Robert H. Jackson
CLOSING ARGUMENTS FOR CONVICTING NAZI WAR CRIMINALS

Serving as United States Chief of Counsel at the tribunal was Robert H. Jackson, whose closing arguments for conviction of the Nazi war criminals is regarded as a memorable historic document. Justice Jackson insisted that German crimes of aggression, "war crimes and the crimes against humanity [were not] unplanned, isolated, or spontaneous offenses . . . [but] fitted into the general scheme of the government." The wars of aggression, the extermination of Jews, the enslavement of five million laborers, the plundering of Europe, and the building of concentration camps were components of an integrated master plan in which the defendants played evil roles. Jackson mocked the defendants' argument that they were either ignorant of the crimes of the Third Reich until after the war or that not they, but Hitler, Himmler, and Goebbels, all now conveniently dead, were to blame for the crimes of the Third Reich. Justice Jackson reminded them of their devotion to Hitler and Nazi ideology and that the regime depended on their zealous and effective support.

Following are excerpts from Justice Jackson's closing arguments.

It is common to think of our own time standing at the apex of civilization, from which the deficiencies of preceding ages may patronizingly be viewed in the light of what is assumed to be "progress." The reality is that in the long perspective of history the present century will not hold an admirable position, unless its second half is to redeem its first. These two-score years in this Twentieth Century will be recorded in the book of years as one of the most bloody in all annals. Two World Wars have left a legacy of dead which number more than all the armies engaged in any war that made ancient or medieval history. No half-century ever witnessed slaughter on such a scale, such cruelties and inhumanities, such wholesale deportations of peoples into slavery, such annihilations of minorities. The Terror of [the Spanish Inquisition] pales before the Nazi Inquisition. These

deeds are the overshadowing historical facts by which generations to come will remember this decade. If we cannot eliminate the causes and prevent the repetition of these barbaric events, it is not an irresponsible prophecy to say that this Twentieth Century may yet succeed in bringing the doom of civilization.

The dominant fact which stands out from all the thousands of pages of the record of this trial is that the central crime of the whole group of Nazi crimes—the attack on the peace of the world—was *clearly and deliberately planned*. The beginning of these wars of aggression was *not* an unprepared and spontaneous springing to arms by a population excited by some current indignation. A week before the invasion of Poland Hitler told his military commanders:

"I shall give a propagandist cause for starting war—never mind whether it be plausible or not. The victor shall not be asked later on whether we told

(International Military Tribunal Nuremberg (1948)), Vol. XIX, pp. 397, 418–419 426–427.

the truth or not. In starting and making a war, not the right is what matters, but victory."

The propagandist incident was duly provided by dressing concentration camp inmates in Polish uniform, in order to create the appearance of a Polish attack on a German frontier radio station. The plan to occupy Belgium, Holland and Luxembourg first appeared as early as August 1938 in connection with the plan for attack on Czechoslovakia. The intention to attack became a program in May 1939, when Hitler told his commanders that

> "The Dutch and Belgian air bases must be occupied by armed forces. Declarations of neutrality must be ignored."

Thus, the follow-up wars were planned before the first was launched. These were the most carefully plotted wars in all history. Scarcely a step in their terrifying succession and progress failed to move according to the master blueprint or the subsidiary schedules and timetables until long after the crimes of aggression were consummated.

Nor were the war crimes and the crimes against humanity unplanned, isolated, or spontaneous offenses. Aside from our undeniable evidence of their plotting, it is sufficient to ask whether six million people could be separated from the population of several nations on the basis of their blood and birth, could be destroyed and their bodies disposed of, except that the operation fitted into the general scheme of government.

Could the enslavement of five millions of laborers, their impressment into service, their transportation to Germany, their allocation to work where they would be most useful, their maintenance, if slow starvation can be called maintenance, and their guarding have been accomplished if it did not fit into the common plan?

Could hundreds of concentration camps located throughout Germany, built to accommodate hundreds and thousands of victims, and each requiring labor and materials for construction, manpower to operate and supervise, and close gearing into the economy—could such efforts have been expended under German autocracy if they had not suited the plan?

Has the Teutonic passion for organization become famous for its toleration of nonconforming activity?

Each part of the plan fitted into every other. The slave labor program meshed with the needs of industry and agriculture, and these in turn synchronized with the military machine. The elaborate propaganda apparatus geared with the program to dominate the people and incite them to a war their sons would have to fight. The armament industries were fed by the concentration camps. The concentration camps were fed by the Gestapo. The Gestapo was fed by the spy systems of the Nazi Party. Nothing was permitted under the Nazi iron rule that was not in accordance with the program. Everything of consequence that took place in this regimented society was but a manifestation of a premeditated and unfolding purpose to secure the Nazi state a place in the sun by casting all others into darkness. . . .

In the testimony of each defendant, at some point there was reached the familiar blank wall: nobody knew anything about what was going on. Time after time we have heard the chorus from the dock.

"I only heard about these things here for the first time."

These men saw no evil, spoke none, and none was uttered in their presence. This claim might sound very plausible if made by one defendant. But when we put all their stories together, the impression which emerges of the Third Reich, which was to last a thousand years, is ludicrous. If we combine only the stories from the front bench, this is the ridiculous composite picture of Hitler's government that emerges. It was composed of:

A No. 2 man who knew nothing of the excesses of the Gestapo which he created, and never suspected the Jewish extermination program although he was the signer of over a score of decrees which instituted the persecutions of that race;

A No. 3 man who was merely an innocent middleman transmitting Hitler's orders without even reading them, like a postman or delivery boy;

A Foreign Minister who knew little of foreign affairs and nothing of foreign policy;

A Field Marshal who issued orders to the armed forces but had no idea of the results they would have in practice;

A security chief who was of the impression that the policing functions of his Gestapo and SB were somewhat on the order of directing traffic;

A Party philosopher who was interested in historical research, and had no idea of the violence which his philosophy was inciting in the Twentieth Century;

A Governor General of Poland who reigned but did not rule;

A Gauleiter of Franconia whose occupation was to pour forth filthy writings about the Jews, but had no idea that anybody would read them;

A Minister of the Interior who knew not even what went on in the interior of his own office, much less the interior of his own department, and nothing at all about the interior of Germany;

A Reichsbank President who was totally ignorant of what went in and out of the vaults of his bank;

And a Plenipotentiary for the War Economy who secretly marshaled the entire economy for armament, but had no idea it had anything to do with war.

This may seem like a fantastic exaggeration, but this is what you would actually be obliged to conclude if you were to acquit these defendants.

They do protest too much. They deny knowing what was common knowledge. They deny knowing plans and programs that were as public as "Mein Kampf" and the Party program. They deny even knowing the contents of documents they received and acted upon.

REVIEW QUESTIONS

1. What problems did Germany face immediately after the war?
2. Why were the Czechs so hard on Germans living in Czechoslovakia?
3. How did Justice Jackson regard the defendants' claim that they were not responsible for Nazi aggression or war crimes?

---

2 The Cold War

After World War II the first Western statesman to express his alarm over Soviet expansionism was Winston Churchill, the doughty and articulate wartime leader of Great Britain. In a famous speech at Fulton, Missouri, on March 5, 1946, when he was no longer in office, Churchill articulated his views on the duty of Western democracies in the face of Soviet expansion.

He declared that an "iron curtain" had descended across the states of Central and Eastern Europe. The people of these countries were now subject to increasing control by the Soviet Union. And the Communist parties in these countries, traditionally small, had been elevated to power and were seeking totalitarian control. Prompted by the failure of attempts to appease Hitler and by the war experience, he urged military strength and political cooperation between Western Europe and the United States in order to stem the Communist advance.

In the United States, George Kennan (1904–2005), a foreign service officer with extensive experience in Eastern Europe and Moscow soon followed Churchill's lead, advocating the thwarting of Soviet ambitions by a policy of containment. Churchill and Kennan formulated the Western outlook in what came to be called the "Cold War."

George F. Kennan
THE POLICY OF CONTAINMENT

In the July 1947 issue of the prestigious journal *Foreign Affairs*, an article appeared signed with the pseudonym "X" that is considered one of the most important and influential policy statements of the Cold War period. It soon emerged that the author was George F. Kennan, a diplomat and Russian expert who had previously held several positions in the American embassy in Moscow. Kennan advised that the United States should respond to the Soviet threat through a policy of "containment, designed to confront the Russians with an unalterable counter-force at every point where they show signs of encroaching upon the interests of a peaceful and stable world." Kennan also argued that the inherent weaknesses in the Soviet system must lead eventually "either to the breakup or the gradual mellowing of Soviet power." He believed that if the United States pursued successful and responsible policies both domestically and internationally, while retaining a "spiritual vitality," it could contribute to the weakening of both Soviet power and the international Communist movement.

Below is an excerpt from the concluding section of the article.

It is clear that the United States cannot expect in the foreseeable future to enjoy political intimacy with the Soviet régime. It must continue to regard the Soviet Union as a rival, not a partner, in the political arena. It must continue to expect that Soviet policies will reflect no abstract love of peace and stability, no real faith in the possibility of a permanent happy coexistence of the Socialist and capitalist worlds, but rather a cautious, persistent pressure toward the disruption and weakening of all rival influence and rival power.

Balanced against this are the facts that Russia, as opposed to the Western world in general, is still by far the weaker party, that Soviet policy is highly flexible, and that Soviet society may well contain deficiencies which will eventually weaken its own total potential. This would of itself warrant the United States entering with reasonable confidence upon a policy of firm containment, designed to confront the Russians with unalterable counter-force at every point where they show signs of encroaching upon the interests of a peaceful and stable world.

But in actuality the possibilities for American policy are by no means limited to holding the line and hoping for the best. It is entirely possible for the United States to influence by its actions the internal developments, both within Russia and throughout the international Communist movement, by which Russian policy is largely determined. This is not only a question of the modest measure of informational activity which this government can conduct in the Soviet Union and elsewhere, although that, too, is important. It is rather a question of the degree to which the United States can create among the peoples of the world generally the impression of a country which knows what it wants, which is coping successfully with the problems of its internal life and with the responsibilities of a World Power, and which has a spiritual vitality capable of holding its own among the major ideological currents of the time. To the extent that such an impression can be created and maintained, the aims of Russian Communism must appear sterile and quixotic, the hopes and enthusiasm of Moscow's supporters must wane, and added strain must be imposed on the Kremlin's foreign policies. For the palsied decrepitude of the capitalist world is the keystone of Communist philosophy. Even the failure of the United States to experience the early economic depression which the ravens of the Red Square have been predicting with such complacent confidence since hostilities ceased would have deep and important repercussions throughout the Communist world.

By the same token, exhibitions of indecision, disunity and internal disintegration within this country have an exhilarating effect on the whole Communist movement. At each evidence of these tendencies, a thrill of hope and excitement goes through the Communist world; a new jauntiness can be noted in the Moscow tread; new groups of foreign supporters climb on to what they can only view as the band wagon of international politics; and Russian pressure increases all along the line in international affairs.

It would be an exaggeration to say that American behavior unassisted and alone could exercise a power of life and death over the Communist movement and bring about the early fall of Soviet power in Russia. But the United States has it in its power to increase enormously the strains under which Soviet policy must operate, to force upon the Kremlin a far greater degree of moderation and circumspection than it has had to observe in recent years, and in this way to promote tendencies which must eventually find their outlet in either the break-up or the gradual mellowing of Soviet power. For no mystical, Messianic movement—and particularly not that of the Kremlin—can face frustration indefinitely without eventually adjusting itself in one way or another to the logic of that state of affairs.

Thus the decision will really fall in large measure in this country itself. The issue of Soviet-American relations is in essence a test of the overall worth of the United States as a nation among nations. To avoid destruction the United States need only measure up to its own best traditions and prove itself worthy of preservation as a great nation.

REVIEW QUESTION

How did George F. Kennan hope to weaken the Soviet Union and international Communism?

3 Communist Oppression

In imposing an ideological belief system, Communist regimes throughout the world committed massive crimes. It is estimated that their criminal acts caused 20 million deaths in the Soviet Union, 65 million in China, 2 million in Cambodia, and several million more in other lands. The stage was set by Lenin and his Bolsheviks who branded ideological political opponents—liberals, moderate socialists, tsarists—and social groups—nobility, bourgeoisie, the intelligentsia, clergy—as enemies of the Bolshevik regime who had to be eliminated. The system of terror instituted by Lenin was magnified by Stalin, who ordered the elimination of the kulaks (the better-off peasantry), imposed a deadly famine in the Ukraine, instituted the Great Purge, and sent millions to the gulag. Communist leaders in China and Cambodia perpetuated the Soviet Union's murderous policies.

Communist leaders believed that terror and mass murder were necessary to secure their power from real or imagined ideological enemies; sometimes these enemies were leading fellow Communists who were perceived as rivals. Moreover, the leaders who instituted terror and those who implemented it believed that they were participating in a historic effort to remodel society; to establish a socialist utopia it was necessary to eliminate, if not exterminate, those who impeded the realization of this noble goal. They were certain that Communist ideology, which they were fulfilling for the good of humanity, was a higher and infallible truth discovered by Marx that explained the essential meaning and direction of history. Those who opposed the party were deemed "enemies of the people" who impeded the realization of the new society. Communist action—deportations, enslavement, torture, mass murder—paralleled the behavior of the Nazis. Also like the Nazis, Communist officials dehumanized their victims, viewing them as the Other—repugnant and wicked people unworthy of life.

Communist parties did not rule by brute force alone, but also sought to create a "new man," one who dedicates himself body and soul to the party and its ideology. Communists, like the Nazis, were not satisfied with their subjects' outward obedience; they demanded the masses' unconditional loyalty and enthusiastic support. Through a planned system of indoctrination, they strove to control the inner person: to shape thoughts, feelings, and attitudes in accordance with the party's ideology. Thus works of literature, history, philosophy, art, and even science were pervaded with Communist ideology, which also governed the school curriculum from elementary school through college. The party permitted no ideological deviation.

Fens Jicai
CHINA'S CULTURAL REVOLUTION: COMMUNIST FANATICISM

After a civil war between the Communists led by Mao Zedong and the Nationalists led by Chiang Kai-shek, the Communists gained control of the entire Chinese mainland in 1949, leaving Chiang Kai-shek in control of only the large island of Taiwan and several small offshore islands. Mao set about socializing agriculture, industry, and commerce in the new Communist state. By 1958, he became determined to rapidly make China into a major world industrial power and he introduced a program labeled "The Great Leap Forward." As part of his strategy to make agriculture more efficient so that it could support an increased urban population and workers who were shifted to industrial production, Mao abolished private holdings and forced peasants into huge state-operated communes, each containing some 5,000 households. Poor management and terrible weather greatly reduced yields, creating what has been characterized as the greatest famine in history. Estimates as to the number of people who died during the Great Leap Forward vary greatly, but numbers ranging from 20 to 30 million are commonly cited. The Great Leap Forward also failed dismally in its aim of making China a major world industrial power. That would come later in Chinese history.

Faced with stark evidence of the failure of his policies and opposition within the Communist Party hierarchy, Mao signaled an end to the Great Leap Forward in 1962. By 1966, Mao, growing old and sensing a loss of revolutionary fervor even within the cadres of the Communist Party, unleashed the Cultural Revolution, a movement designed to combat the type of "revisionism" he saw in the Soviet Union with its efforts to seek some sort of accommodation with the West. The Cultural Revolution sought to root out "bourgeois" and "capitalist" elements within the party and the country, and it aimed at destroying the cultural, artistic, and religious traditions of China's past. Mao mobilized the young, who were organized into Red Guard units that quickly spread to include elements of the military, workers, and members of the Communist Party itself.

The Red Guards physically attacked and humiliated all suspected of deviationist tendencies. Teachers and academic administrators were beaten, forced to kneel and wear dunce caps, and to confess errors; party officials were attacked; large numbers of people were tortured, executed, imprisoned under harsh conditions, or sent to re-education camps; and works of art, religious centers, and sacred texts were destroyed.

The rampage left both the economy and the educational system in shambles. By 1968, Mao, seeing the damage being done, dispersed the Red Guards by sending them to the countryside and the factories to work with the people. This signaled an end to the worst phase of the Cultural. Revolution, but trouble and conflict continued within the Communist Party. One of the leaders in the latter phase of the Cultural Revolution was Mao's wife, Jiang Qing, and three of her associates, the so-called "Gang of Four." It was only in 1976, the year of Mao's death, that the Cultural Revolution finally ended, when Mao's hand-picked successor arrested the Gang of Four, who were ultimately sentenced to long terms in prison. Under Deng Xiaoping, who emerged as leader in the period following Mao's death, China entered a new path that resulted in the country becoming a dominant world economic power.

Fens Jicai, a well-known Chinese writer, collected oral histories of victims of the Cultural Revolution ten years after it ended. However, even in the changed atmosphere of China, he felt it necessary to conceal the identities of his subjects. The following selection is drawn from one of the accounts.

. . .Suddenly some men from the Revolutionary Committee of the Public Security Bureau came and carted me off to prison. This time I was scared. I hadn't committed any crime, so why'd they nab me and throw me in jail? Could it be that they've got the wrong man, I wondered. But I didn't dare ask, because in those days there was no such thing as getting the wrong man. Back then, men weren't much different from chickens or cats. How could you grab the "wrong" one? . . .

I was interrogated six separate times. Each interrogation was conducted in the middle of the night. They asked me very strange questions. They kept asking me over and over again to turn in my pistol. I thought they must have got it wrong, that it was not me they wanted. I told them, even if you wanted me to go out right now and get a pistol. I wouldn't know where to go to get one. I've spent my whole life in school. When I graduated I got a job teaching. Except for in the movies, I've never even seen a gun.

After the six interrogation sessions, they suddenly stopped. It was as if it had been an episode too weird even for a dream.

Fens Jicai, "I've Become a Different Person," trans. Cathy Clayton, in *Ten Years of Madness: Oral Histories of China's Cultural Revolution* (san Francisco: China Books & Periodicals, 1996), pp. 66–70. Reprinted with permission from the publisher.

While in prison, I was ordered to study political propaganda materials every day. The furnishings in this prison were pretty unusual. In the middle of each cell was a string of long, low benches. During the daytime, prisoners would sit on these benches reading Mao's works and other revolutionary propaganda; in the evenings, they spread wide wooden planks on top of the benches and slept there. On the door were a couple of palm-sized little windows that could slide open and shut—they were the observation holes for the guards. As soon as one of the little windows slid open, all the prisoners would immediately sit up straight and act serious. Then the little sliding windows were replaced with mercury mirrors. The mirrors were scored with lines, the mirror side facing in, so the guards could see into the room, but the prisoners couldn't see out. Pretty slick, huh? Once they did that, none of the prisoners dared to slack off, ever. . . .

One day, they suddenly brought me up again for interrogation. Again came the questions about the pistol.

This time I got aggravated. I said, "I have absolutely nothing to do with any pistol."

This was the first time in my whole life that I had ever dared talk back to the authorities. Who'd have thought it. Instead of getting pissed off, the interrogator mellowed a little. He said, "Don't be too quick to dismiss this matter. Let me give you a little hint; start thinking about toys."

Well I thought that was really weird in such a serious, life-and-death kind of situation, what's he doing talking about toys? I said, "I've seen toy pistols, yeah, but think about it, I'm a teacher, I can't carry a toy gun around with me all day!"

The interrogator was really patient that day. He said, "Calm down. Think a little harder. What else do you carry around with you."

I thought again, and then I remembered I'd had a little pistol-shaped ornament on my keychain, about two centimeters long. A friend had given it to me. It was made in France. It was copper inlaid with silver, really pretty. I said, "There was one. A little pendant on my keychain."

The interrogator said, "Exactly. Why didn't you confess to that earlier?"

I was stunned. Had they really thrown me in prison on account of a keychain? Did they really think I could have used such a little thing to commit a crime? I mean, every house has a kitchen cleaver, so should the whole country be thrown in jail? I stared at him with my mouth agape, speechless.

He said, "I just want you to write about this problem."

Problem? My sky went black with clouds; my brain spun. But I wrote down all the information I could think of about who had given me the little keychain, which years I carried it, and when it was confiscated during a house search. He also told me to draw a little sketch of it. He read the "account of the problem" that I had just finished writing, nodded, and praised me, "What a good attitude your are demonstrating!"

From the time I was arrested until my sentencing, they had asked only about this pistol. They never asked about anything else. I'd been locked up already for eight or nine months.

At first I thought, when this matter was cleared up, they would let me out. As the days drew on, I became puzzled as to why I hadn't been released. After some more time, I felt sure that something wasn't right. I had a sense of impending disaster. I felt as if I had been gripped by some strange magic hand. Whose hand it was I had no idea. It was just a feeling. I couldn't escape it.

Sure enough, on November 26th—it was snowing lightly that day—someone called, "Number 171!" As soon as I left my cell, a bunch of armed police officers in full uniform appeared. They tied me up with a rope and threw me in the back of a big truck. On board the truck were a number of other prisoners. We were all being taken to a big theater for a public sentencing. When we got to the theater, I was ordered to stand at the head of the line. This was the position reserved for prisoners with the heaviest sentences, usually the death sentence. I thought, that's it, it's all over for me. Nothing I could say or scream would help me now. I was a chicken on the chopping block. . . .

The court pronounced me guilty on three counts: extremely reactionary thought; attacking the command of the proletariat and the policies of the cultural Revolution; and using my home as a base to receive enemy radio broadcasts, voice grievances on behalf of Liu Shaoqi,[1] and plot to organize a counterrevolutionary clique.

Any one of these three crimes was punishable by death. As I drifted in a space of nothingness, I heard them yelling from the stage. "Sentenced to twenty years in prison!"

Only twenty years? Ah, my life was given back to me, I was going to be OK. At that point, twenty years in prison didn't seem like much. [He was released after serving ten years.]

---

[1]Liu Shaoqi was a close associate of Mao when the Cultural Revolution began. Mao turned against him and denounced him as a "traitor" who supported capitalist policies. He was arrested, persecuted, and died in disgrace in 1969.

Teeda Butt Mam
GENOCIDE IN CAMBODIA: "IT TAKES A RIVER OF INK TO WRITE OUR STORIES"

In the wake of the collapse of Cambodia's American-supported government in 1975, Cambodian Communists—the Khmer Rouge—seized power under their leader, Pol Pot, who aspired to establish a new Communist agrarian utopia devoid of modern technology, urban and financial institutions, religion, higher education, and an intelligentsia. To create instantly this new society of ideologically regimented rural communes, the Khmer Rouge forcibly drove more than two million people from the capital city of Phnom Penh and other cites to the countryside. The Khmer Rouge compelled the transplanted city people to toil fourteen or more hours a day with very little food to sustain them and systematically tortured and killed people designated as subversives and traitors; they particularly targeted educated middle-class Cambodians. From 1975 to 1979, nearly two million people perished in this barbarous act of genocide.

Teeda Butt Mam, an educated girl from a middle-class family, was fifteen years old when the Khmer Rouge came to power. She survived the genocide and is now a U.S. citizen. In the following selection, she describes her horrific ordeal under the Khmer Rouge.

[The Khmer Rouge] forced millions of residents of Phnom Penh and other cities out of their homes. . . . They ripped off our homes and our possessions. They did this intentionally, without mercy.

They were willing to pay any cost, any lost lives for their mission. Innocent children, old women, and sick patients from hospital beds were included. Along the way, many innocent Cambodians were dying of starvation, disease, loss of loved ones, confusion, and execution. . . .

They took my father. They told my family that my father needed to be reeducated. Brainwashed. But my father's fate is unknown to this day. . . .

Later the Khmer Rouge killed the wives and children of the executed men in order to avoid revenge. They encouraged children to find fault with their own parents and spy on them. They openly showed their intention to destroy the family structure that once held love, faith, comfort, happiness, and companionship. They took young children from their homes to live in a commune so that they could indoctrinate them.

Parents lost their children. Families were separated. We were not allowed to cry or show any grief when they took away our loved ones. A man would be killed if he lost an ox he was assigned to tend. A woman would be killed if she was too tired to work. Human life wasn't even worth a bullet. They clubbed the back of our necks and pushed us down to smother us and let us die in a deep hole with hundreds of other bodies.

They told us we were VOID. We were less than a grain of rice in a large pile. . . .

The people on the Khmer Rouge death list were the group called the city people. . . .

Dith Pran, ed., *Children of Cambodia's Killing Fields* (New Haven, CT.: Yale University Press, 1997), pp. 11–16. Reprinted with the permission of Yale University Press.

. . . The merchants, the capitalists, and the businessmen. Their crime was exploiting the poor. The rich farmers and the landlords. Their crime was exploring the peasants. The intellectuals, the doctors, the lawyers the monks, the teachers, and the civil servants. These people thought, and their memories were tainted by the evil Westerners. Students were getting education to exploit the poor. Former celebrities, the poets. These people carried bad memories of the old, corrupted Cambodia. . . .

I was always hungry. I woke up hungry before sunrise and walked many kilometers to the worksite with no breakfast. . . . Every night I went to sleep dirty and hungry. I was sad because I missed my mom. I was fearful that this might be the night I'd be taken away tortured, raped, and killed.

I wanted to commit suicide but I couldn't. If I did, I would be labeled "the enemy" because I dared to show my unhappiness with their regime. My death would be followed by my family's death because they were the family of the enemy. . . .

. . . We were cold because we had so few clothes and blankets. We had no shoes. We were "volunteered" to work fifteen hours or more a day in the rain or in the moonlight with no holidays. . . .

The Khmer Rouge said they were creating a utopian nation where everyone would be equal. . . . But while the entire population was dying of starvation, disease, and hopelessness, the Khmer Rouge was creating a new upper class. Their soldiers and the Communist party members were able to choose any woman or man they wanted to marry. In addition to boundless food, they were crazed with gold jewelry, perfume, imported watches. Western medicine, cars, motorcycles, bicycles, silk, and other imported goods. . . .

In January 1979 I was called to join a district meeting. The district leader told us that it was time to get rid of "all the wheat that grows among the rice plant." The city people were the wheat. The city people were to be eliminated. My life was saved because the Vietnamese invasion came just two weeks later.

When the Vietnamese invasion happened, I cried. I was crying with joy that my life was saved. . . . I stood on Cambodian soil feeling that I no longer belonged to it. I wanted freedom. I decided to escape to the free world.

I traveled with my family from the heart of the country to the border of Thailand. It was devastating to witness the destruction of my homeland that had occurred in only four years. Buddhist temples were turned into prisons. Statues of Buddha and artwork were vandalized. Schools were turned into Khmer Rouge headquarters where people were interrogated, tortured, killed, and buried. School yards were turned into killing fields. Old marketplaces were empty. Books were burned. Factories were left to rust. Plantations were without tending and bore no fruit.

This destruction was tolerable compared to the human conditions. Each highway was filled with refugees. We were refugees of our own country. With our skinny bodies, bloated stomachs, and hollow eyes, we carried our few possessions and looked for our separated family members. We asked who lived and didn't want to mention who died. We gathered to share our horrifying stories. Stories about people being pushed into deep wells and ponds and suffocating to death. People were baked alive in a local tile oven. One woman was forced to cook her husband's liver, which was cut out while he was still alive. Women were raped before execution. One old man said, "It takes a river of ink to write our stories."

REVIEW QUESTIONS

1. What was the purpose of imprisoning people during the Cultural Revolution?
2. What was the attitude of the Communist interrogators towards prisoners?
3. What were the aims of the Khmer Rouge?
4. What kind of people staffed Khmer Rouge prisons and labor camps?

4 Resistance and Dissidence in the Communist World

Opportunities to oppose the Communist regimes in the Soviet satellites were virtually nonexistent during Stalin's lifetime. Control was thorough and punishments severe. But discontent with Communist rule was deeply felt, and in the years following Stalin's death in 1953 it assumed an organized form in Hungary in 1956 and in Czechoslovakia in 1968. But fearing that the move toward reform would reduce the Soviet Union's control over political life in both countries and threaten Soviet mastery of Eastern Europe, the Kremlin used force to crush the Hungarian Revolution and the Czech experiment to humanize and democratize socialism—to create "socialism with a human face" as they called it.

Milovan Djilas
THE NEW CLASS: AN ANALYSIS OF THE COMMUNIST SYSTEM

Milovan Djilas' book *The New Class: An Analysis of the Communist System* (1957), from which the following excerpts are taken, provides astute insights into the explosion of discontent in Hungary, Czechoslovakia, and Poland under Soviet control. Djilas (1911–1995), a Yugoslav author and political commentator, became a Communist after finishing his studies in 1933. Although he began as a close friend of Marshal Tito, the all-powerful leader of Yugoslavia, in 1953 he turned critic, not only of his friend, but also of Communist practice and ideology. Jailed for his heresies in 1956, he wrote his assessment of the Communist system, showing its connection to the unprecedented new class of political bureaucrats dominating state and society. Under Communism the state did not wither away, as early theorists had expected. On the contrary, it grew more powerful, thanks to that highly privileged "exploiting and governing class." Aware of the dynamics of nationalism at work underneath each Communist regime, Djilas pointed to the weaknesses of Communist rule and the growing desire for national self-assertion among the peoples of the Soviet satellite states.

Earlier revolutions, particularly the so-called bourgeois ones, attached considerable significance to the establishment of individual

freedoms immediately following cessation of the revolutionary terror . . . The final results of earlier revolutions were often greater legal security and greater civil rights. This cannot be said of the Communist revolution . . .

In contrast to earlier revolutions, the Communist revolution, conducted in the name of doing away with classes, has resulted in the most complete authority of any single new class. Everything else is sham and an illusion. . . .

The new class may be said to be made up of those who have special privileges and economic preference because of the administrative monopoly they hold. . . .

The mechanism of Communist power . . . leads to the most refined tyranny and the moat brutal exploitation. The simplicity of this mechanism originates from the fact that one party alone, the Communist Party, is the backbone of the entire political, economic, and ideological activity. The entire public life is at a standstill or moves ahead, falls behind or turns around according to what happens in the party forums. . . .

. . . Communist control of the social machine . . . restricts certain government posts to party members. These jobs, which are essential in any government but especially in a Communist one, include assignments with police, especially the secret police; and the diplomatic and officers corps, especially positions in the information and political services. In the judiciary only top positions have until now been in the hands of Communists. . . .

Only in a Communist state are a number of both specified and unspecified positions reserved for members of the party. The Communist government, although a class structure, is a party government; the Communist army is a party army; and the state is a party state. More precisely, Communists tend to treat the army and the state as their exclusive weapons.

The exclusive, if unwritten, law that only party members can become policemen, officers, diplomats, and hold similar positions, or that only they can exercise actual authority, creates a special privileged group of bureaucrats. . . .

A citizen in the Communist system lives oppressed by the constant pangs of his conscience, and the fear that he has transgressed. He is always fearful that he will have to demonstrate that he is not an enemy of socialism, just as in the Middle Ages a man constantly had to show his devotion to the Church. . . .

. . . Tyranny over the mind is the most complete and most brutal type of tyranny; every other tyranny begins and ends with it. . . .

History will pardon Communists for much, establishing that they were forced into many brutal acts because of circumstances and the need to defend their existence. But the stifling of every divergent thought, the exclusive monopoly over thinking for the purpose of defending their personal interests, will nail the Communists to a cross of shame in history. . . .

Andor Heller
THE HUNGARIAN REVOLUTION, 1956

After Stalin's death in 1953, the rigid political controls in Hungary were relaxed, leading to an unstable balance between Soviet-oriented hardliners and patriotic reformers willing to grant greater freedom to the spirit of nationalism and individual enterprise stirring among the people. In 1956, the Hungarian yearning for escape from Soviet domination exploded. On October 23 a student demonstration in Budapest, the capital, provided the spark. Throughout the country, Communist officials were ousted and the Soviet troops forced to withdraw. A coalition government under Imre Nagy was formed to restore Hungary's independence; it even appeared that the country would withdraw from the newly formed Warsaw Pact controlled by Moscow. In Budapest especially, the popular excitement over the country's liberation from the Soviet yoke knew no bounds, as is described in the eyewitness account that follows. The author, Andor Heller, was a Hungarian news photographer. On November 4, 1956, Soviet forces invaded Hungary to end the Hungarian uprising. Andor fled to Western Europe with photographs of the invasion and published them in his book *No More Comrades* (1957).

Deep dejection followed the anger caused by the Soviet counterattack, which killed thousands of people and drove 200,000 into exile. A new "peasant-worker government" under János Kádár cynically boasted of having saved the country from "Fascist counter-revolution." Subsequently, however, Kádár transformed his country's economy. Dubbed "goulash Communism" for its mixture of state and private enterprise, it became the freest in the Soviet bloc and a model for Gorbachev's *perestroika* (restructuring) in the Soviet Union in the late 1980s.

I saw freedom rise from the ashes of Communism in Hungary: a freedom that flickered and then blazed before it was beaten down—but not extinguished—by masses of Russian tanks and troops.

I saw young students, who had known nothing but a life under Communist and Russian control, die for a freedom about which they had only heard from others or from their own hearts.

I saw workers, who had been pushed to the limit of endurance by their hopeless existence under Communism, lay down their tools and take up arms in a desperate bid to win back freedom for our country.

I saw a girl of fourteen blow up a Russian tank, and grandmothers walk up to Russian cannons.

I watched a whole nation—old and young, men and women, artists and engineers and doctors, clerks and peasants and factory workers—become heroes overnight as they rose up in history's first successful revolt against Communism.

Tuesday, October 23, 1956

No Hungarian will forget this day. . . . .

. . . In spite of the cold and fog, students are on the streets early in the morning, marching and singing. No one shows up for classes at the universities. After a decade of Communist control over our country, we are going to show our feelings spontaneously, in our own way—something never allowed under Communist rules.

The students carry signs with slogans that until now we have never dared express except to members of our own family—and not in every family. The slogans read:

RUSSIANS GO HOME!
LET HUNGARY BE INDEPENDENT!
BRING RAKOSI[1] TO JUSTICE!
WE WANT A NEW LEADERSHIP!. . . .

The walls of Budapest are plastered with leaflets put up by the students during the night. They list . . . demands adopted at the stormy meetings held at the universities:

1. Withdrawal of all Soviet troops from Hungary.
2. Complete economic and political equality with the Soviet Union, with no interference in Hungary's internal affairs. . . .
8. A secret general multi-party election. . . .
13. Restoration of Hungary's traditional national emblem and the traditional Hungarian army uniforms.
14. Destruction of the giant statue of Stalin.

Andor Heller, *No More Comrades* (Chicago: H. Regnery, 1957), pp. 10–13, 15, 18, 23–24, 156–157, 160–162.

[1]Matyas Rakosi, like Minaly Farkos (mentioned subsequently), was a notorious Hungarian Stalinist.—Eds.

During the morning a radio announcement from the Ministry of Interior bans all public meetings and demonstrations "until further notice," and word is sent to the universities that the student demonstrations cannot be held. At that moment the students decide that the will to freedom is greater than the fear of the A.V.H.—the Russian-controlled Hungarian secret police. The meeting will be held! . . .

At 3 P.M. there are 25,000 of us at the Petofi Monument. We weep as Imre Sinkovits, a young actor, declaims the *Nemzeti Dal* ("National Song"), Sandor Petofi's[2] ode to Hungary and our 1848 "freedom revolution." With tears in our eyes, we repeat the refrain with Sinkovits: . . .

"We swear, we swear, we will no longer remain slaves.". . .

. . . [W]e have swelled to some 60,000. Someone grabs a Hungarian flag and cuts out the hated hammer and sickle that the Communists had placed at its center.

One after another of the purified Hungarian flags appear. Suddenly someone remembers to put the old Kossuth[3] coat-of-arms on the flag, in place of the Communist emblem.

We have created a new flag of freedom!

Meantime we all sing the . . . *Appeal to the Nation*, and the *Hungarian National Hymn* that begins "God Bless the Magyar"—both of which had been banned under the Communist rule. . . .

The day is ending. We begin to march toward the Parliament Building. The crowds are peaceful, marching in orderly lines. We carry the new Hungarian flag.

As we march we are joined by workers leaving their jobs. By the time we arrive in Kossuth Lajos Square there are at least 150,000 of us, in front of the Parliament Building. On the square, the traffic stops. . . .

Suddenly everyone makes torches of newspapers, and lights them. It is a marvelous spectacle—ten thousand torches burning in the Square before the Parliament Building. . . .

But finally, Imre Nagy appears on the balcony. "Comrades!" he begins, but the crowd interrupts him with a roar: "There are no more comrades! We are all Hungarians!" . . .

The crowd grows still bigger, and we head for the Stalin statue. Now the demonstration has spread so large that it is going on simultaneously in three places: at the Parliament Building; in Stalin Square, where the crowd is trying to pull down the huge Stalin statue with tractors and ropes; and at the building of Radio Budapest, where part of the crowd has gone to demand the right of patriots to be heard over the air. . . .

I go with the group that heads for Stalin Square. Some of the workers have got hold of acetylene torches. They and the students are trying to cut down the dictator's twenty-five-foot metal figure. At the edge of the crowd the first Russian tanks appear, but at the moment they are only onlookers. The crowd pulls hard at the cables that have been attached to the Stalin statue. It leans forward, but is still held by its boots—a symbol, we feel. The cables are now being pulled by tractors, and the men with the torches work feverishly. The statue, though still in one piece, begins to bend at the knees. The crowds burst into cheers. . . .

. . . [W]e watch the Stalin statue, cut off at the knees, fall to the ground with a thunderous crash. . . .

Suddenly shooting breaks out from all sides. The security police—the A.V.H.—are firing into the crowds. In minutes the streets are strewn with the dying and wounded. News of the A.V.H. attack spreads. All over Budapest the workers and students are battling the hated A.V.H.

The peaceful demonstrations of the youth and the workers have been turned by Communist guns into a revolution for national freedom.

---

[2]Petofi was a Hungarian poet and revolutionary hero in the anti-Austrian rebellion of 1848–1849.—Eds.
[3]Lajos Kossuth was the leader of the Hungarian uprising of 1848–1849.—Eds.

For four days—from October 31 to November 3, 1956—Hungary was free. Although the Russian forces were still in our country, they had withdrawn from the cities and the fighting had stopped. The whole nation recognized the Imre Nagy government, which, knowing it had no other alternative, was ready to carry out the will of the people. . . .

On November 3, Radio Free Kossuth summed up: "The overwhelming weight of Hungarian public opinion sees the result of the revolution as the establishment of a neutral, independent and democratic country, and just as it was ready to sweep out Stalinist tyranny, so it will protect with the same determination and firmness its regained democratic achievement." . . .

In those four days of freedom, political liberty came quickly to life. . . .

Before October 23 there had been only five newspapers in Budapest, all under complete Communist control. On November 4 there were twenty-five. Neither news nor opinions could be suppressed any longer.

Plans for a free general election were speeded.

Religious freedom, like political freedom, came back to strong life in those four days. . . .

In the countryside, the peasants and their spokesmen were mapping the changes of the farm laws and regulations. All were agreed on the goal of a free farm economy based on the individual working farmers and peasants. Peasants would be free to join or leave the farm collectives. . . .

The factory committees and workers' groups were putting forward the needs and demands of the workers, not the government. The right to strike—a criminal act under the Communists—was upheld. Wages, prices, pension rights, working conditions were eagerly discussed and debated.

The economy was slowly getting on its feet. Everyone wanted to be on the streets together. . . .

Return of the Russians

At dawn on November 4, 1956, Soviet Russia attacked Hungary with 6,000 tanks, thousands of guns and armored cars, squadrons of light bombers, 200,000 soldiers—and a tidal wave of lies.

REVIEW QUESTIONS

1. How did Milovan Djilas characterize the "new class"? What were its qualities? How did it wield its power?
2. What would you say was the climax of the Budapest demonstration on October 23?
3. What was at stake for the workers and farmers of Hungary in the anti-Soviet uprising?
4. How did the Hungarians in those crucial October days assert their freedom? What evidence of nationalism did you observe in the anti-Soviet demonstrations?

5 The New Germany: Confronting the Past

May 1945 has long been referred to in Germany as *Stunde Null*, or "zero hour." This designation would suggest that everything prior to the end of the war had been eliminated by the defeat of the Third Reich—that the terrible destruction visited upon Germany as a result of the war launched by the Nazi government had wiped the slate clean, that Germans could go only forward, not backward.

Most Germans had little inclination to reflect upon the meaning of Nazi aggression and crimes against humanity. Their priorities included clearing rubble, restoring economic life, and creating a sense of normalcy.

During the mid-and late 1950s, the West German economy began to grow steadily as a manufacturing and consumer-based economy with a strong agricultural sector, soon becoming the most dynamic economy in Western Europe.

As of the early 1960s, the Federal Republic's "economic miracle," became an object of admiration for its neighbors. West German economic success, like that of Japan, helped to ensure social stability; this, in turn, worked against any potential embrace of Communism or a return to violent, intolerant nationalism. West Germany had undergone a transformation that no one would have dared imagine possible in the spring of 1945.

Hannah Vogt
THE BURDEN OF GUILT

In the years immediately following World War II, Germans were too preoccupied with rebuilding their devastated country to reflect on the horrific crimes committed by the Third Reich and bring the criminals to justice. Indeed, many Germans either failed to comprehend the enormity of these crimes or found the subject uncomfortable, for only a few years earlier they had faithfully served the Nazi regime and embraced its ideology. They simply wanted to sweep the extermination of European Jewry from memory. However, the public trials of war criminals starting in the 1960s and the greater attention given to the topic in books and the media, including an American television miniseries that dramatized and personalized the Jewish tragedy, stimulated open discussion and reflection within Germany.

Until the 1960s, German secondary school history courses generally ended with the beginning of the twentieth century. Few teachers discussed the Nazi regime, and appropriate books about Nazism and the Holocaust were lacking. Moreover, teachers who had previously endorsed Hitler were not eager to discuss the Holocaust with their students. Distressed by a sudden outburst of anti-Semitic incidents that afflicted Germany in 1959, notably desecrated cemeteries and swastikas smeared on the walls of synagogues, German educational authorities made a concerted effort to teach young people about the Nazi past. These same anti-Semitic outrages moved Hannah Vogt, a civil servant concerned principally with education, to write a book for students about the Nazi past. Published in 1961, *The Burden of Guilt* became a widely used text in secondary schools. In the preface, Vogt stated the book's purpose:

> [S]elf-examination and a repudiation of false political principles are the only means we have of winning new trust among those peoples who were forced to suffer fearful things under Hitler's brutal policy of force. . . . Only if we draw the right conclusions from the mistakes of the past and apply them to our thought and action can we win new trust. . . . Anyone who

makes an effort to understand recent political history will learn that in politics not every means is just [and] that law and the dignity of man are not empty phrases.

The book's conclusion, excerpted below, showed a sincere effort of German schools to come to grips with the darkest period in German history.

. . . The past cannot be erased, but the future is free. It is not predetermined. We have the power to re-examine our decisions and mend our wrong ways; we can renounce force and place our trust in peaceful and gradual progress; we can reject racial pride. Instead of impressing the world with war and aggression, we can strive for world prestige through the peaceful solution of conflicts, as the Swiss and the Scandinavians have done for centuries to their national glory. For us, the choice is open to condemn Hitler's deluded destructiveness and to embrace Albert Schweitzer's message—respect for life.

If we are really serious about this new respect for life, it must also extend to the victims of the unspeakable policy of extermination. . . . Everywhere it is the duty of the living to preserve the memory of the dead. Should we listen to insinuations that the time has come to forget crimes and victims because nobody must incriminate himself? Is it not, rather, cowardly, mean, and miserable to deny even now the dead the honor they deserve, and to forget them as quickly as possible?

We owe it to ourselves to examine our consciences sincerely and to face the naked truth, instead of minimizing it or glossing over it. This is also the only way we can regain respect in the world. Covering up or minimizing crimes will suggest that we secretly approve of them. Who will believe that we want to respect all that is human if we treat the death of nearly six million Jews as a "small error" to be forgotten after a few years?

The test of our change of heart should be not only the dead but the living. There are 30,000 Jewish fellow-citizens living among us. Many of them have returned only recently from emigration, overwhelmed with a desire for their old homeland. It is up to all of us to make sure that they live among us in peace and without being abused, that their new trust in us, won after much effort, is not destroyed by desecrated cemeteries, gutter slogans, or hate songs. Those who will never learn must not be allowed to take refuge in the freedom of opinion. A higher value is at stake here, the honor of the dead, and respect for the living. But it is not up to the public prosecutor to imbue our lives with new and more humane principles. This is everybody's business. It concerns us all! It will determine our future.

The Burden of Guilt: A Short History of Germany 1914-1945 by Vogtm, translated by Strauss (1966) 936w from pp. 285–286 © 1964 by Oxford University Press, Inc. By permission of Oxford University Press, USA.

Richard von Weizsäcker
"WE SEEK RECONCILIATION"

In recent decades there has been an open and frank discussion among Germans of the nation's crimes against the Jews during World War II. In a speech during a commemorative ceremony on May 8, 1985, the fortieth anniversary of the end of World War II in Europe, Richard von Weizsäcker (b. 1920), president of the Federal Republic of Germany from 1984 to 1994, reflected on the Holocaust and the need for remembrance.

May 8th is a day of remembrance. Remembering means recalling an occurrence honestly and undistortedly so that it becomes a part of our very beings. This places high demands on our truthfulness.

Today we mourn all the dead of the war and tyranny. In particular we commemorate the six million Jews who were murdered in German concentration camps. . . .

At the root of the tyranny was Hitler's immeasurable hatred of our Jewish compatriots. Hitler had never concealed this hatred from the public, and made the entire nation a tool of it. Only a day before his death, on April 30, 1945, he concluded his so-called "will" with the words: "Above all, I call upon the leaders of the nation and their followers to observe painstakingly the race laws and to oppose ruthlessly the poisoners of all nations: international Jewry." Hardly any country has in its history always remained free from blame for war or violence. The genocide of the Jews is, however, unparalleled in history.

The perpetration of this crime was in the hands of a few people. It was concealed from the eyes of the public, but every German was able to experience what his Jewish compatriots had to suffer, ranging from plain apathy and hidden intolerance to outright hatred. Who could remain unsuspecting after the burning of the synagogues, the plundering, the stigmatization with the Star of David, the deprivation of rights, the ceaseless violation of human dignity? Whoever opened his eyes and ears and sought information could not fail to notice that Jews were being deported. The nature and scope of the destruction may have exceeded human imagination, but in reality there was, apart from the crime itself, the attempt by too many people, including those of my generation, who were young and, were not involved in planning the events and carrying them out, not to take note of what was happening. There were many ways of not burdening one's conscience, of shunning responsibility, looking away, keeping mum. When the unspeakable truth of the Holocaust then became known at the end of the war, all too many of us claimed that they had not known anything about it or even suspected anything.

There is no such thing as the guilt or innocence of an entire nation. Guilt is, like innocence, not collective, but personal. There is discovered or concealed individual guilt. There is guilt which people acknowledge or deny. Everyone who directly experienced that era should today quietly ask himself about his involvement then.

The vast majority of today's population were either children then or had not been born. They cannot profess a guilt of their own for crimes that they did not commit. No discerning person can expect them to wear a penitential robe simply because they are Germans. But their forefathers have left them a grave legacy. All of us, whether guilty or not, whether old of young, must accept the past. We are all affected by its consequences and liable for it. The young and old generations must and can help each other to understand why it is vital to keep alive the memories. It is not a case of coming to terms with the past. That is not possible. It cannot be subsequently modified or made undone. However, anyone who closes his eyes to the past is blind to the present. Whoever refuses to remember the inhumanity is prone to new risks of infection.

Remembrance, Sorrow and Reconciliation: Speeches and Declarations in Connection with the 40th Anniversary of the End of the Second World War in Europe (Bonn: Press and Information Office of the Government of the Federal Republic of Germany, 1985), pp. 59–63.

The Jewish nation remembers and will always remember. We seek reconciliation. Precisely for this reason we must understand that there can be no reconciliation without remembrance. The experience of millionfold death is part of the very being of every Jew in the world, not only because people cannot forget such atrocities, but also because remembrance is part of the Jewish faith.

"Seeking to forget makes exile all the longer; the secret of redemption lies in remembrance." This oft quoted Jewish adage surely expresses the idea that faith in God is faith in the work of God in history. Remembrance is experience of the work of God in history. It is the source of faith in redemption. This experience creates hope, creates faith in redemption, in reunification of the divided, in reconciliation. Whoever forgets this experience loses his faith.

If we for our part sought to forget what has occurred, instead of remembering it, this would not only be inhuman, we would also impinge upon the faith of the Jews who survived and destroy the basis of reconciliation. We must erect a memorial to thoughts and feelings in our own hearts.

REVIEW QUESTIONS

1. How did Hannah Vogt suggest that Germans now confront the Holocaust?
2. What did Richard von Weizsäcker have to say about collective guilt, about the implications of forgetfulness and remembrance, and about the possibility of redemption, reconciliation, and salvation?
3. In your opinion what is the meaning of the Holocaust for Western civilization? For Jews? For Christians? For Germans?

6 The Twilight of Imperialism

The leading European imperialist countries emerged greatly weakened from World War II as they faced the enormous challenge of repairing the destruction and economic dislocation caused by the war. Power had shifted east to the Soviet Union and west to the United States, leaving Britain and France in much-reduced positions, no longer the great powers that they seemed to be before the war. The weakness of the European rulers had been brought home clearly to their colonies during the war when Germany conquered and occupied France, Belgium, and The Netherlands. Moreover, the Axis powers, especially Japan, seized and temporarily occupied British, French, and Dutch colonies. Colonial troops had fought loyally alongside their masters in a war whose slogans spoke of freedom and self-determination, and many among the native populations were not prepared to tolerate the continuing control of their lands by foreign powers with their attitudes of racial and cultural superiority.

Independence movements gained strength even during the war, and the end of the era of European imperialism came relatively quickly after the war. During a fifty-year period framed by the granting of independence to India by Great Britain in 1947 and the return to Chinese sovereignty of the British Crown

Colony of Hong Kong in 1997, almost all European colonies gained their inde-pendence, leaving only some scattered and generally small overseas possessions in European hands. Much of this decolonization occurred within an even shorter period in the 1960s. A total of thirty-four newly independent nations emerged between 1960 and 1968, with most of the colonies in Sub-Sahara Africa having obtained independence between 1960 and 1963.

In some cases, independence was granted without a violent struggle, as in the Gold Coast (Ghana), where the British turned over power in 1957; in others, it came only after years of bitter warfare, as in the French possessions of Algeria and Indochina (Vietnam, Cambodia, and Laos). Once independence came, the new nations often faced serious internal conflicts created by ethnic, religious, and/or political differences, as was the case in India and the Congo.

MAHATMA GANDHI
THE PARTITION OF INDIA

The subcontinent of India with its large multi-ethnic and multi-religious pop-ulation was the "Jewel in the Crown" of the British Empire. The Indians, heirs to a proud civilization, had long struggled for greater self-rule and ultimately independence. The struggle was led from 1885 by the Indian National Congress, which as the Congress Party today continues to play a central role in Indian politics. However, as early as 1906, the large Muslim minority, feeling that the National Congress was dominated by the Hindu majority, formed an indepen-dent organization, the Muslim League. In the years prior to independence, the League—led by Muhammad Ali Jinnah, who is considered the father of Pakistan—forcefully embraced the concept of a division of India to create a separate state for the Muslims. Great Britain acceded to this demand and in the sum-mer of 1947 granted independence to two new states, a Muslim Pakistan, and a now-truncated India with a Hindu majority.

Intercommunal violence broke out immediately as the new borders left mil-lions of Muslims in India and millions of Hindus in Pakistan. People fled homes their families had occupied for generations for the relative safety of the coun-try dominated by their coreligionists, greatly straining the facilities of the newly independent nations. In what has been characterized as one of the greatest pop-ulation transfers in history, more than 7 million people fled to India from Paki-stan, and a roughly equivalent number fled to Pakistan from India. Estimates of the number of lives lost in the violent outbreaks following independence range from 200,000 to one million.

Mohandas K. Gandhi, whose followers conferred upon him the honorific of Mahatma (Great Soul), was the long-term leader of the Indian independence movement. A figure of world-historical importance, whose philosophy of non-violent resistance has inspired many, including Martin Luther King Jr., Gandhi championed an approach that focused on the techniques of passive resistance, non-cooperation, and boycott in the struggle with the British. He opposed the division of India into two states and envisioned a united India with equal rights for all religions.

Warning against sectarian violence, he reminded Muslims that the meaning of the word "Islam" is peace, that Islam cannot be sustained by the sword. And he told fellow Hindus that "by killing and loot and arson they are destroying their own religion." His message of peace, unity, and tolerance failed to convince, and he was deeply disheartened by the violence that broke out upon independence. In January 1948, he was assassinated by a Hindu nationalist angered by his accommodative attitude toward Muslims.

In the following excerpts from his speeches, delivered shortly after the partition, Gandhi urged equality and toleration.

[12 September 1947]

Anger breeds revenge and the spirit of revenge is today responsible for all the horrible happenings here and elsewhere. What good will it do the Muslims to avenge the happenings in Delhi or for the Sikhs and the Hindus to avenge cruelties on our co-religionists in the Frontier and West Punjab?[1] If a man or a group of men go mad should everyone follow suit? I warn the Hindus and Sikhs that by killing and loot and arson they are destroying their own religions. I claim to be a student of religion and I know that no religion teaches madness. Islam is no exception. I implore you all to stop your insane actions at once. Let not future generations say that we lost the sweet bread of freedom because we could not digest it. Remember that unless we stop this madness the name of India will be mud in the eyes the world.

[26 September 1947]

Some [Muslims] dream of converting the whole of India to Islam. That will never happen through war. Pakistan can never destroy Hinduism. The Hindus alone can destroy themselves and their faith. Similarly, if Islam is destroyed,

it will be destroyed by the Muslims in Pakistan, not by the Hindus in Hindustan.

[13 November 1947]

Freedom without equality for all, irrespective of race or religion, is not worth having for the Congress. In other words, the Congress and any government representative of the Congress must remain a purely democratic, popular body, leaving every individual to follow that form of religion which best appeals to him without any interference from the State. There is so much in common between people living in the same State under the same flag owing undivided allegiance to it. There is so much in common between man and man that it is a marvel that there can be any quarrel on the ground of religion. Any creed or dogma which coerces others into following one uniform practice is a religion only in name, for a religion worth the name does not admit of any coercion. Anything that is done under coercion has only a short lease of life. It is bound to die. . . .

When I think of the plight of the Muslims in the Union, how in many places life has become difficult for them and how there is a continuing exodus of the Muslims from the

---

Rudrangshu Mukherjee, ed., The Penguin Gandhi Reader (New York: Penguin Books, 1996), pp. 278–280.

[1]There was a concentration of Sikhs in some regions that became part of Pakistan, and they, along with the Hindus, were exposed to the rioting and violence that broke out after independence. Many fled to the new Indian state.—Eds.

Union, I wonder whether the people who are responsible for creating such a state of things could ever become a credit to the Congress. I therefore hope that during the year which has just commenced, the Hindus and Sikhs will so behave as to enable every Muslim, whether a boy or a girl, to feel that he or she is as safe and free as the tallest Hindu or Sikh.

PATRICE LUMUMBA
CONGO INDEPENDENCE DAY

After control of the Congo was transferred from King Leopold II to the Belgian government in 1908 (see p. 238), treatment of the native population, which had suffered under the cruel and repressive policies of Leopold, improved. The Belgians built roads, railroads, schools, and hospitals, but did little to prepare the country for independence. Pressured by the moves towards independence in other European colonies, growing international support for decolonization, and internal demands and unrest among the Congolese, Belgium formally granted independence to the Congo on June 30, 1960. At independence, there were fewer than twenty university graduates in this vast country, the senior officers in the army were all Belgian, no Congolese held a rank above that of non-commissioned officer, and Belgians controlled the economy.

In the first election, no political party gained an absolute majority, and power was divided between two rival parties. The president was Joseph Kasavubu and the prime minister was Patrice Lumumba, a fiery, passionately anti-colonial orator. When Lumumba granted pay raises to all government employees except the military, he triggered a military mutiny that introduced a period of violent turmoil. For years the Congo was convulsed in personal, political, and ethnic rivalries. The Belgians, who hoped to continue to control the country after independence, were also involved, supporting the secessionist movement in the large mineral-rich province of Katanga, the most important of several secessionist movements.

The Congo also became immersed in Cold War rivalries. The Soviet Union saw in the Congo an opportunity to gain a strong foothold in Africa and supported Lumumba who, although probably not a Communist, sought and welcomed Soviet assistance. This led the United States to oppose Lumumba, and when he was arrested and ultimately executed in January 1961, there was widespread suspicion that United States was responsible. Although the CIA had hatched plots to assassinate Lumumba, his political rivals carried out the actual execution.

Another key player in the Congo at this time was the UN, which sent a peacekeeping force to establish order. The Secretary-General of the UN, Dag Hammarskjold, himself came to the Congo in an effort to mediate between the various factions. In September 1961, traveling to meet with Moise Tshombe, head of the secessionist Katanga government, he was killed in a plane crash. Although the initial investigation generally attributed the crash to pilot error, many thought that foul play was involved. The issue has never been resolved, and studies and investigations continue more than a half-century after the event.

In 1965, the army commander Joseph Mobotu seized power and within two years gained control over the entire country. Mobotu, who ruled for 30 years, established a repressive, corrupt dictatorship that ruined the economy and allowed the country's infrastructure to decay. While the country suffered, Mobutu amassed a large fortune and developed an extravagant life style. He owned luxurious residences in many countries, and he was known for such personal indulgences as chartering large passenger planes, including the supersonic Concorde, for extended vacations or shopping trips to Paris.

In the following selection drawn from a well-publicized speech given on Congo Independence Day, June 30, 1960, Patrice Lumumba expresses deep resentment over the suffering and indignities experienced by the Congolese under colonialism and offers an inspiring vision of the future of an independent Congo. Unfortunately, the events of the years following independence provided a cruel contrast with Lumumba's hopes and aspirations.

Ladies and gentleman of the Congo who have fought for the independence won today, I salute you in the name of the Congolese government. . . . No Congolese worthy of the name will ever forget that independence has been won by the struggle, an everyday struggle, an intense and idealistic struggle, a struggle in which we have spared neither our forces, our privations, our suffering, nor our blood.

This struggle of tears, fire, and blood makes us profoundly proud because it was a noble and just struggle, an indispensable struggle to put an end to the humiliating bondage imposed on us by force.

Our lot was 80 years of colonial rule; our wounds are still too fresh and painful to be driven from our memory.

We have known tiring labor exacted in exchange for salary which did not allow us to satisfy our hunger, to clothe and lodge ourselves decently or to raise our children like loved beings.

We have known ironies, insults, blows which we had to endure morning, noon and night because we were "Negroes." . . .

We have known that our lands were despoiled in the name of the supposedly legal texts which recognized only the law of the stronger.

We have known that the law was never the same depending on whether it concerned a white or a Negro: accommodating for one group, it was cruel and inhuman for other. . . .

We have known that there were magnificent houses for the white in the cities and tumble-down straw huts for the Negroes, that a Negro was not admitted in movie houses or restaurants or stores labeled "European," that a Negro traveled in the hulls of river boats at the feet of the white in his first class cabin.

Who will forget, finally, the fusillades [rapid shootings] where so many of our brothers perished or the prisons where all those were brutally flung who no longer wished to submit to the regime of a law of oppression and exploitation which the colonists had made a tool of their domination? . . .

The Congo Republic has been proclaimed and our beloved country is now in the hands of its own children.

Together, my brothers, we are going to begin a new struggle, a sublime struggle which is going to lead our country to peace, prosperity, and grandeur.

Patrick Thomas Madaldy, *The Revolution of Color* (New York: Hawthorne Books, 1966), pp. 173–177.

Together we are going to establish social justice and assure that everyone receives remuneration for his work.

We are going to show the world what the black man can do when he works in freedom, and we are going to make the Congo the center of radiance for the whole of Africa. . . .

We are not going to let a peace of guns and bayonets prevail, but rather a peace of courage and good will. . . .

The independence of the Congo marks a decisive step toward the liberation of the entire African continent.

Ho Chi Minh
DECLARATION OF INDEPENDENCE FOR THE REPUBLIC OF VIETNAM, SEPTEMBER 2, 1945

The French presence in Vietnam can be dated to the 1830s, when France intervened in the Nguyen dynasty's internal affairs to protect Christians implicated in a coup attempt. France gained possession of Saigon and the southern provinces by 1862, and extended colonial control northward to include the entire country by 1882. France's ostensible mission was to bring French culture and political values to Southeast Asia—in short, to "civilize" the Vietnamese—and the foreign ministry was aided in this task by a cadre of French-trained Vietnamese elites. In practice, French colonial rule meant the extraction of raw materials and exploitation of Vietnamese labor.

Between 1914 and 1918, almost 100,000 Vietnamese soldiers and workers helped to sustain the French war effort. It was expected that Vietnam would be rewarded with significant economic and political concessions after the conflict ended; however, the French government refused to deliver autonomy to Vietnam, eliciting bitter dissatisfaction among critical Vietnamese. Led by disaffected intellectuals, politicized Vietnamese embraced increasingly revolutionary strategies during the interwar years, and organized national liberation movements along the lines of the Chinese nationalist and Communist movements in order to expel the French colonial regime. The consolidation of Japanese control over Vietnam by mid-1942 temporarily solved the problem of French imperialism, yet replaced it with an occupation no more acceptable to nationalist activists. Determined resistance movements proved a source of steady annoyance to the Japanese and provided Vietnamese revolutionaries—Communist and non-Communist alike—with the opportunity to take decisive action for the cause of liberation when the French returned after Japan's defeat.

Ho Chi Minh, a Soviet-trained revolutionary, led the fight against the French while also attacking his non-Communist Vietnamese opponents. After years of conflict a peace treaty was signed in 1954 that divided the country into a Communist North Vietnam, headed by Ho Chi Minh, and a non-Communist Republic of Vietnam. As violence flared between the two Vietnams, the United States became increasingly involved in supporting the southern Republic of Vietnam, leading to a major commitment of U.S. forces in the long and bitter Vietnam War. In 1975, six years after the death of Ho Chi Minh, the North triumphed and unified the country under its rule.

The following document, signed by Ho Chi Minh, expressed Vietnamese aspirations for independence at the end of World War II in language resonant with American and French eighteenth-century revolutionary principles.

"All men are created equal. They are endowed by their Creator with certain inalienable rights, among these are Life, Liberty, and the Pursuit of Happiness."

This immortal statement was made in the Declaration of Independence of the United States of America in 1776. . . . The Declaration of the Rights of Man and the Citizen of the French Revolution in 1791 also states: "All men are born free and with equal rights, and must always be free and have equal rights." . . .

Nevertheless for more than eighty years, the French imperialists deceitfully raising the standard of Liberty, Equality, and Fraternity, have violated our fatherland and oppressed our fellow citizens. They have acted contrarily to the ideals of humanity and justice.

In the province of politics, they have deprived our people of every liberty.

They have enforced inhuman laws; to ruin our unity and national consciousness, they have carried out three different policies in the north, the center and the south of Vietnam.

They have founded more prisons than schools. They have mercilessly slain our patriots; they have deluged our revolutionary areas with innocent blood. They have fettered public opinion; they have promoted illiteracy.

To weaken our race they have forced us to use their manufactured opium and alcohol.

In the province of economics, they have stripped our fellow citizens of everything they

possessed, impoverishing the individual and devastating the land.

They have robbed us of our rice fields, our mines, our forests, our raw materials. They have monopolized the printing of banknotes, the import and export trade; they have invented numbers of unlawful taxes, reducing our people, especially our country folk, to a state of extreme poverty.

They have stood in the way of our businessmen and stifled all their undertakings; they have extorted our working classes in a most savage way.

In the autumn of the year 1940, when the Japanese fascists violated Indochina's territory to get one more foothold in their fight against the Allies, the French imperialists fell on their knees and surrendered, handing over our country to the Japanese, adding Japanese fetters to the French ones. From that day on, the Vietnamese people suffered hardships yet unknown in the history of mankind. The result of this double oppression was terrific: from Quangtri to the northern border two million people were starved to death in the early months of 1945.

On the 9th of March, 1945, the French troops were disarmed by the Japanese. Once more the French either fled, or surrendered unconditionally, showing thus that not only were they incapable of "protecting" us, but that they twice sold us to the Japanese.

Yet, many times before the month of March, the Vietminh had urged the French to ally with them against the Japanese. The French colonists never answered. On the contrary, they intensified their terrorizing policy. Before taking to

---

Ho Chi Mihn, *Selected Works* (Hanoi, 1960–1962), Vol. 3, pp. 17–21.

flight, they even killed a great number of our patriots who had been imprisoned at Yen-bay and Cao-bang.

Nevertheless, towards the French people our fellow citizens have always manifested an attitude pervaded with toleration and humanity. . . .

The whole population of Vietnam is united in common allegiance to the republican government and is linked by a common will, which is to annihilate the dark aims of the French imperialists.

We are convinced that the Allied nations which have acknowledged at Teheran and San Francisco the principles of self-determination and equality of status will not refuse to acknowledge the independence of Vietnam.

A people that has courageously opposed French domination for more than eighty years, a people that has fought by the Allies' side these last years against the fascists, such a people must be free, such a people must be independent.

For these reasons, we, members of the provisional government of Vietnam, declare to the world that Vietnam has the right to be free and independent, and has in fact become a free and independent country. We also declare that the Vietnamese people are determined to make the heaviest sacrifices to maintain its independence and its liberty.

REVIEW QUESTIONS

1. Account for Gandhi's enduring appeal.
2. What were Patrice Lumumba's critique of Belgian rule?
3. What were his expectations for the newly independent Congo?
4. What arguments did Ho Chi Minh use in presenting the case for the independence of Vietnam?

CHAPTER 15

The West in an Age of Globalism

MULTICULTURALISM OR ASSIMILATION? The niqab worn by this Muslim woman on a street in Brussels covers the body from head to toe, leaving only a slit for the eyes. Maintaining that such dress demeans women, Europeans are increasingly urging banning it outside the home. (© *Julien Warnand/AFP/Getty Images*)

The most important developments in recent European history have been the collapse of Communism as a viable political and economic model and the end of the Cold War. With the decline of Soviet power and the discrediting of Marxism, the countries of Eastern Europe, and Russia itself, struggled to adapt to Western democratic forms and the free market. The transition to free market capitalism proved particularly difficult in Russia, which remained plagued with corruption, organized crime, and a declining standard of living.

In late 1999, Vladimir Putin, a former Soviet KGB agent, became president of Russia. Putin, who felt that the dissolution of the Soviet Union was a historic tragedy, made clear that he wished to restore Russia as a great and respected world power. He engaged in conflict with several of the successor states of the Soviet Union. In 2008, Russian forces invaded Georgia in a dispute over several breakaway provinces that Georgia considered its territories. In 2014, Putin seized Crimea from Ukraine and supported a rebellion in the largely Russian-speaking eastern Ukraine with weapons and thinly disguised Russian military units. The European Union and the United States imposed a series of sanctions on Russia for its actions in Ukraine. Putin also intervened in the bloody Syrian civil war in support of the brutal Syrian dictator Bashar al-Assad. Some people fear that we are now entering a period of a new Cold War.

By the end of the twentieth century, the European nations, building on earlier agreements, had established a European Union (EU) which ultimately grew to include twenty-eight nations. However, by the second decade of the twenty-first century, serious problems had arisen. A resurgent nationalism, anti-EU populist movements in a number of countries, and continuing economic and cultural differences among member nations have left the future of the EU shrouded in uncertainty. The decision by Great Britain in 2016 to leave the EU, the so-called Brexit, dealt an especially severe blow.

In the closing decades of the twentieth century, ethnic conflicts grew more acute. Throughout Europe, it was not just right-wing parties that protested against immigration, particularly from African, Middle Eastern, and Asian lands, complaining that the essential character of their nations were being destroyed. At times, right-wing extremists, often neo-Nazis, employed violence against immigrants. Between 1991 and 2001, Yugoslavia was torn apart by the worst ethnic violence since World War II.

In the twenty-first century, globalization continues relentlessly; the world is being knit ever closer together by the spread of Western ideals, popular culture (particularly American), free-market capitalism, and technology. Government officials and business and professional people all over the world dress in Western clothes. Women follow Western fashions in dress and makeup. People line up to eat at McDonalds, see a Hollywood movie, or attend a rock concert. Everywhere people are eager to adopt the latest technology that originated in the West but is now also manufactured in other, particularly Asian, lands.

Advanced technology intensifies the means of communication, not only through television and radio, but also with e-mail, cellular phones, the Internet (Facebook), and smart-phone apps—all means of instantaneous individual communication that have become commonplace in the past two decades.

These developments promote shared interests among individuals and businesses, some of them multinational corporations, across the globe, reducing the importance of national frontiers. All these factors combined are reshaping non-Western societies in a relentless adjustment that causes both deep hardships and possibilities for a better life.

The ideals of freedom and democracy, historical accomplishments of Western civilization, exert a powerful influence worldwide; they are also part of the process of Westernization. Unlike technology, they cannot easily be put into practice outside the countries of their origin. However, they inspire human ambitions everywhere. They have even become part of the rhetoric of dictatorships.

At the same time, strong cultural traditions still divide the world. The hatred of radical Muslims for the West, which they see as a threat to traditional Islam, is a striking example of the clash of cultures. Muslim militants, organized in an international network—first al-Qaeda and then ISIS—were behind many appalling attacks in Africa, Asia, and Europe as well as the bombing of the World Trade Center and the Pentagon in 2001, the worst terrorist attack in history. Their ultimate aims are the destruction of Western civilization, which they see as immoral and an affront to God; the restoration of the Islamic empire that existed in the Middle Ages; and the imposition of strict Islamic law in all Islamic lands. Often fortified by a fundamentalist theology, these militants represent a radical attack on freedom and secularism, two hallmarks of modernity.

1 The Collapse of Communism

Throughout the 1970s and early 1980s the discrepancy between Soviet ambition and deteriorating economic conditions became apparent in the Soviet Union and the satellite countries of Eastern Europe. Economic productivity declined just when increasing contact with democratic and prosperous Western countries raised consumer expectations. In addition, loyalty toward the Soviet Union in the satellite countries had been steadily eroded by nationalist resentment against Communist repression.

The reforms instituted by Mikhail Gorbachev in 1986 led to a groundswell of support for liberation in Eastern Europe. Agitation for self-determination, democracy, and the end of Communist rule spread and was not suppressed as it had been in the past. During 1989, Soviet power crumbled as one by one the Eastern European countries declared their sovereignty and ousted their Communist governments. By the end of the year, all Communist regimes in Europe, except in Albania, had been overthrown. (Communist rule in Albania ended in 1991.) In the Soviet Union itself, the Communist empire collapsed at the end of 1991 as various non-Russian Soviet republics declared their independence. Within three years, the once-mighty superpower had disintegrated unexpectedly and in a remarkably peaceful manner. The Cold War seemed over.

Vaclav Havel
THE FAILURE OF COMMUNISM

Established as a sovereign state at the end of World War I, Czechoslovakia enjoyed two decades of independence until it fell under Hitler's rule in 1938–1939; in World War II it was brutally occupied by the German army. After Czechoslovakia's liberation by Soviet soldiers, Stalin ruthlessly turned it into a Communist state in 1948.

In 1968, enlightened party members, with the support of the Czech people, sought to loosen the oppressive restraints of the Communist order and reestablish ties with Western Europe. Under the leadership of Alexander Dubček the country was intoxicated with the air of freedom. Seeking a humane version of Marxism, the reformers rehabilitated the victims of the Stalinist past and stopped censorship.

Suddenly, on August 21, 1968, Soviet troops invaded the country. Although they avoided the bloodshed that had accompanied their suppression of the Hungarian uprising in 1956, the Soviet leaders stopped Dubček's reforms; liberalization in Czechoslovakia endangered the Soviet political system. "Socialism with a human face," as Dubček's program was called, came to an end.

Yet twenty years later, in December 1989, the Communist regime dissolved in the "Velvet Revolution." Vaclav Havel (1936–2011), a frequently imprisoned dissident playwright and a lively intellectual, was elected president. In his 1990 New Year's Day address, excerpted below, Havel told the Czech people how the Communist regime had abused its power.

THE TRUTH, UNVARNISHED

For 40 years you have heard on this day from the mouths of my predecessors, in a number of variations, the same thing: how our country is

Vaclav Havel, "New Year's Address to the Nation," Prague, January 1, 1990. Available online at: http://old.hrad.cz/president/Havel/speeches/1990/0101_uk.html.

flourishing, how many more millions of tons of steel we have produced, how we are all happy, how we believe in our Government and what beautiful prospects are opening ahead of us. I assume you have not named me to this office so that I, too, should lie to you.

Our country is not flourishing. The great creative and spiritual potential of our nation is not being applied meaningfully. Entire branches of industry are producing things for which there is no demand while we are short of things we need.

The state, which calls itself a state of workers, is humiliating and exploiting them instead. Our outmoded economy wastes energy, which we have in short supply. The country, which could once be proud of the education of its people, is spending so little on education that today, in that respect, we rank 72nd in the world. We have spoiled our land, rivers and forests, inherited from our ancestors, and we have, today, the worst environment in the whole of Europe. Adults die here earlier than in the majority of European countries. . . .

LEARNING TO BELIEVE AGAIN

The worst of it is that we live in a spoiled moral environment. We have become morally ill because we are used to saying one thing and thinking another. We have learned not to believe in anything, not to care about each other, to worry only about ourselves. The concepts of love, friendship, mercy, humility or forgiveness have lost their depths and dimension, and for many of us they represent only some sort of psychological curiosity or they appear as long-lost wanderers from faraway times, somewhat ludicrous in the era of computers and space ships. . . .

COGS NO LONGER

The previous regime, armed with a proud and intolerant ideology, reduced people into the means of production, and nature into its tools. So it attacked their very essence, and their mutual relations. . . . Out of talented and responsible people, ingeniously husbanding their land, it made cogs of some sort of great, monstrous, thudding, smelly machine, with an unclear purpose. All it can do is slowly but irresistibly, wear itself out, with all its cogs.

If I speak about a spoiled moral atmosphere I don't refer only to our masters. . . . I'm speaking about all of us. For all of us have grown used to the totalitarian system and accepted it as an immutable fact, and thereby actually helped keep it going. None of us are only its victims; we are all also responsible for it.

It would be very unwise to think of the sad heritage of the last 40 years only as something foreign; something inherited from a distant relative. On the contrary, we must accept this heritage as something we have inflicted on ourselves. If we accept it in such a way, we shall come to understand it is up to all of us to do something about it.

Let us make no mistake: even the best Government, the best Parliament and the best President cannot do much by themselves. Freedom and democracy, after all, mean joint participation and shared responsibility. If we realize this, then all the horrors that the new Czechoslovak democracy inherited cease to be so horrific. If we realize this, then hope will return to our hearts.

Everywhere in the world, people were surprised how these malleable, humiliated, cynical citizens of Czechoslovakia, who seemingly believed in nothing, found the tremendous strength within a few weeks to cast off the totalitarian system, in an entirely peaceful and dignified manner. We ourselves are surprised at it.

And we ask: Where did young people who had never known another system get their longing for truth, their love of freedom, their political imagination, their civic courage and civic responsibility? How did their parents, precisely the generation thought to have been lost, join them? How is it possible that so many people immediately understood what to do and that none of them needed any advice or instructions? . . .

RECALLING RUINED LIVES

Naturally we too had to pay for our present-day freedom. Many of our citizens died in prison in the 1950s. Many were executed. Thousands of human lives were destroyed. Hundreds of thousands of talented people were driven abroad. . . . Those who fought against totalitarianism during [World War II] were also persecuted. . . . Nobody who paid in one way or another for our freedom could be forgotten.

Independent courts should justly evaluate the possible guilt of those responsible, so that the full truth about our recent past should be exposed.

But we should also not forget that other nations paid an even harsher price for their present freedom, and paid indirectly for ours as well. All human suffering concerns each human being. . . . Without changes in the Soviet Union, Poland, Hungary, and the German Democratic Republic, what happened here could hardly have taken place, and certainly not in such a calm and peaceful way.

Now it depends only on us whether this hope will be fulfilled, whether our civic, national and political self-respect will be revived. Only a man or nation with self-respect, in the best sense of the word, is capable of listening to the voices of others, while accepting them as equals, of forgiving enemies and of expiating sins. . . .

A HUMANE REPUBLIC

Perhaps you are asking what kind of republic I am dreaming about. I will answer you: a republic that is independent, free, democratic, a republic with economic prosperity and also social justice, a humane republic that serves man and that for that reason also has the hope that man will serve it. . . .

THE PEOPLE HOLD SWAY

My most important predecessor started his first speech by quoting from Comenius.[1] Permit me to end my own first speech by my own paraphrase, Your Government, my people, has returned to you.

---

[1]Comenius was a Czech theologian and educator of the seventeenth century. The quotation was used by Tomáš Masatyk (1850–1937), the first president of Czechoslovakia, which was created after World War I. "I, too, believe before God that when the storms of wrath have passed, to thee shall return the rule over thine own things, O Czech people."—Eds.

REVIEW QUESTION

What did Vaclav Havel mean when he said the Czechs had lived in a "spoiled moral environment" for the past forty years?

---

2 Transplanting Western Democracy in Non-Western Lands

Western civilization, declared Arthur Schlessinger, Jr., is the "source—the *unique* source [of the] ideas of individual liberty, political democracy, the rule of law, human rights, and cultural freedom. . . . These are *European* ideas, not Asian nor African, nor Middle Eastern ideas except by adoption." These democratic principles and practices, which evolved from the history and traditions of Westerners, are difficult to transmit to non-Western nations, especially when they conflict with deeply ingrained cultural traditions, particularly religious beliefs, as John Agresto astutely explains in reference to Muslim lands:

Yet it is the character of a culture that shapes the aspirations of its citizens and the nature of its democracy. A culture in which there is little religious or intellectual freedom, where adherence to the commands of imam or religious scholars is sacrosanct, a culture that believes its duty before God is to punish dissent, kill apostates, and exterminate God's supposed enemies, a culture in which there is no deep acceptance of difference—such culture will produce illiberal souls who are hardly strong candidates to form a truly liberal and free democracy.

Many nations simply lack the historical and cultural preconditions to sustain democratic practices and ideals.

Fareed Zakaria
"DEMOCRACY HAS ITS DARK SIDES"

In the following selection from his book *The Future of Freedom* (2003), Fareed Zakaria, former editor of *Newsweek International* and current CNN host and *Washington Post* columnist, discusses the implications of the spread of democracy throughout much of the globe. In many countries, he observes, the adoption of democratic procedures—parliaments and the ballot—has enabled dictators to gain and retain power. Published in 2003, Zakaria's observations remain relevant today.

DEMOCRACY AND LIBERTY

"Suppose elections are free and fair and those elected are racists, fascists, separatists," said the American diplomat Richard Holbrooke about Yugoslavia in the 1990s. "That is the dilemma." Indeed it is, and not merely in Yugoslavia's past but in the world's present. Consider, for example, the challenge we face across the Islamic world. We recognize the need for democracy in those often-repressive countries. But what if democracy produces an Islamic theocracy or something like it? It is not an idle concern. Across the globe, democratically elected regimes, often ones that have been re-elected or reaffirmed through referenda, are routinely ignoring constitutional limits on their power and depriving

The Future of Freedom: Illiberal Democracy at Home and Abroad by Fareed Zakaria, pp. 17–18.

their citizens of basic rights. This disturbing phenomenon—visible from Peru to the Palestinian territories, from Ghana to Venezuela—could be called "illiberal democracy."

For people in the West, democracy means "liberal democracy": a political system marked not only by free and fair elections but also by the rule of law, a separation of powers, and the protection of basic liberties of speech, assembly, religion, and property. But this bundle of freedoms—what might be termed "constitutional liberalism"—has nothing intrinsically to do with democracy and the two have not always gone together, even in the West. After all, Adolf Hitler became chancellor of Germany via free elections. Over the last half-century in the West, democracy and liberty have merged. But today the two strands of liberal democracy, interwoven in the Western political fabric, are coming apart across the globe. Democracy is flourishing; liberty is not.

In some places, such as Central Asia, elections have paved the way for dictatorships. In others, they have exacerbated group conflict and ethnic tensions. Both Yugoslavia and Indonesia, for example, were far more tolerant and secular when they were ruled by strongmen (Tito and Suharto, respectively) than they are now as democracies. And in many nondemocracies, elections would not improve matters much. Across the Arab world elections held tomorrow would probably bring to power regimes that are more intolerant, reactionary, anti-Western, and anti-Semitic than the dictatorships currently in place. . . .

. . . [N]ewly democratic countries too often become sham democracies, which produces disenchantment, disarray, violence, and new forms of tyranny. Look at Iran and Venezuela. This is not a reason to stop holding elections, of course, but surely it should make us ask, What is at the root of this troubling development? Why do so many developing countries have so much difficulty creating stable, genuinely democratic societies? Were we to embark on the vast challenge of building democracy in Iraq, how would we make sure that we succeed?

REVIEW QUESTION

What does Fareed Zakaria mean when he says that throughout the world "democracy is flourishing; liberty is not"?

---

3 The Editors
The European Union: An Uncertain Future

One of the most important developments in the post–World War II West has been the evolving economic, political, and cultural integration of Europe. After centuries of warfare and shifting alliances, most European nations came together to form a single European Union (EU).

The EU can trace its origins to the signing of an agreement by six Western European countries in 1951 establishing a European Coal and Steel Community that pooled the coal and steel resources of members and gave considerable control over these resources to a central authority. This was followed by other landmark agreements that ultimately led to the establishment of the European Union by the Treaty of Maastricht in 1992. The original six countries were joined by others starting in 1973, and with the fall of the Berlin Wall and the end of the Cold War, the EU expanded into Central and Eastern Europe as countries formerly behind the Iron Curtain were now free to join. By 2013, the EU had twenty-eight member states.

The EU has open borders between member nations allowing for the free flow of people and goods. A large bureaucracy has developed, centered in Brussels, Belgium, which is considered the European capital. There is a European Parliament directly elected by the people of member nations, a European Commission that serves as an executive body, a European Central Bank, and other central bodies. The EU has considerable powers in some economic and political areas and shares authority with the member countries in others. In 1999, a new European currency, the euro, was introduced; by 2002, the euro became the official currency of a number of member states, but not all. By 2015, nineteen states were in the eurozone.

Despite these impressive achievements, the EU is faced with a series of serious problems that call into question its long-term future.

Economic problems loom large among the challenges faced by the EU. The Great Recession that struck both the United States and Europe starting in late 2007 highlighted the distinction between the weaker economies in southern Europe and the more successful ones in northern Europe. Countries such as Greece, Spain, and Portugal faced growing unemployment, banking crises, and high levels of debt. Even when the worst of the recession had passed, Europe seemed mired in chronic economic underperformance.

In 2013, Greece, crushed by the weight of a large, unmanageable public debt, seemed poised to create a European banking crisis when it appeared that the country might default on its debt and might even leave the EU. Other EU countries and the European Central Bank helped with several bailouts but imposed what many considered harsh conditions, demanding that Greece follow a policy of fiscal austerity that some economists felt could only exacerbate the severe economic problems. This controversial policy of fiscal austerity was central to the European Union's initial efforts to combat recession and continues to characterize the EU's approach to economic problems.

Although the Greek debt crisis passed, at least temporarily, it sharply indicated the serious problems relating to countries with disparate economies that are part of the eurozone and obliged to live under EU fiscal rules that limit budget deficits. Economists have pointed out that countries with their own currencies and unencumbered by EU fiscal policies can deal with depressed economies by devaluing their currencies and engaging in deficit spending. Currency devaluation can increase a nation's exports by making its products less expensive in other countries and can also effectively reduce public debt that is denominated in the devalued currency. Deficit spending occurs when a nation runs a larger than usual budget deficit in order to stimulate the economy by increased expenditures of public funds.

Moreover, the hybrid form of the EU—far more than free-trade bloc and far less than a federal republic—is brought into sharp relief by its failure to adopt reforms suggested by some economists, such as a common treasury that would promote greater economic integration and would enable the Union to respond more effectively to financial crises.

The EU bureaucracy centered in Brussels has drawn persistent fire from throughout Europe. It is pictured as remote and undemocratic and is accused of issuing constraining and picayune regulations. Members of the European Parliament that meets in Strasbourg, France, are chosen by popular vote, but the Parliament lacks the powers of a true legislative body. It votes on legislation proposed by the European Commission but cannot initiate legislation and has limited control over the Union's budget.

Although European integration may be the dominant theme since World War II, in recent years we have also witnessed the disintegration of multinational or binational states, including the Soviet Union, Yugoslavia, and Czechoslovakia, and heightened demands for autonomy or independence by minority groups in other states, such as the Basques and Catalans in Spain and the Scots in Great Britain. It seems clear that the forces of nationalism and ethnic rivalry remain powerful, and that the hopes of some that a European identity would replace traditional group loyalties failed to adequately account for the persistence of these long-term historic forces.

It is nevertheless notable that a number of successor nations that emerged from the dissolution of multinational states became members of the EU. These include the three Baltic republics that were formerly part of the Soviet Union, two of the former Yugoslav republics, and both the Czech Republic and Slovakia. Thus Europe in the last quarter of a century has witnessed a complex interplay of the forces of integration and disintegration.

The anti-immigrant sentiment in many European countries that has frequently targeted Islamic immigrants (see page 469) has also been directed at immigrants from within the EU who can legally live and work in any member country. People coming from countries with depressed economies to more prosperous members in search of employment have often been obliged to accept positions that are far below their skills level, to adapt to a different culture, and to face hostility from citizens of the host country. Many citizens of countries with stronger economies believe that the influx of people from the poorer EU countries has served to depress local wages. These are clear indications of the failure of the EU to create a binding sense of unity among its members.

The brutal civil war in Syria that began in 2011, as well as violence and poverty in other areas of the Middle East, Africa, and beyond, drove a wave of desperate refugees, who were overwhelmingly Muslim, to flee to Europe in 2015. When they arrived, they found a varying reception from EU member states.

Germany, under Chancellor Angela Merkel, accepted more than 900,000 refugees, whereas other countries, such as Hungary, greeted them with hostility and sought to block their entry. The effort by the EU to develop a quota system for allocating refugees to member nations has drawn strong opposition from some member countries, who are unwilling to accept them.

The series of problems faced by Europe have spawned a number of populist parties that have grown significantly and play increasingly prominent roles in the political life of their countries. Most of these are right-wing nationalist and traditionalist parties that have drawn strength from their opposition to immigrants, especially Muslim immigrants, and to the EU. Such parties as the Golden Dawn in Greece, the National Front in France, the Party for Freedom in The Netherlands, and the Jobbik Party in Hungary pose a serious challenge to more conventional political forces. In some cases these right-wing parties have shown disturbing fascist tendencies, casting a further shadow over Europe. In 2016, the candidate of the Freedom Party in Austria, which had been founded by former Nazis, came very close to winning the presidency of that country. In Hungary and Poland, government was captured by right-wing nationalist forces that have pursued undemocratic policies by, for example, imposing new restrictions on news media.

The EU has also faced new threats from Russia, led by Vladimir Putin, who became president at the end of 1999. Putin, who has called the breakup of the Soviet Union an historic tragedy, has adopted a nationalist policy designed to make Russia a strong and respected world power. Ruling at home in an authoritarian manner, he has engaged in conflicts with neighboring successor states of the old Soviet Union. In 2014, he seized Crimea from Ukraine and provided weaponry and thinly disguised Russian soldiers in support of a separatist movement in eastern Ukraine led by Russian-speakers. In response to this aggression, the EU joined the United States in imposing sanctions on Russia. Putin has reacted by taking actions designed to weaken European unity and to subvert democratic governments that offer a sharp contrast with his own. Russia has engaged in a disinformation program, has sent financial support to favored political parties and politicians, and has hacked important computer systems. Some European right-wing populist leaders have expressed considerable admiration for Putin as a strong nationalist, traditionalist leader. This is a troubling indication of the path they would wish to follow in their own countries.

Undoubtedly the EU suffered its most serious blow in June 2016 when a referendum in Great Britain resulted in a narrow majority voting to leave the union, the so-called Brexit. The impending loss of a major member that is a leading economic power, and whose capital, London, is one of the world's most important financial centers, raises questions as to whether the entire EU is poised to unravel. The British began negotiations in 2017 to determine the terms under which they will leave and the shape of their future relations with the EU, a process scheduled to last two years.

By early 2017, the future of the EU was clouded with uncertainty. Will Brexit be followed by other nations leaving the Union? Will the EU without Britain continue on its current path, perhaps with some modest reforms? Will it disintegrate into little more than a free-trade bloc? Or, will it somehow overcome what appear to be insuperable obstacles to create a stronger political and economic union?

REVIEW QUESTIONS

1. What are the achievements of the European Union?
2. What are the problems and challenges faced by the European Union?

4 The Editors
ISIS: Ideology, Appeal, Terrorism

A new jihadist force has emerged—ISIS (the Islamic State of Iraq and Syria)—more powerful, dangerous, and brutal than al-Qaeda, the perpetrator of 9/11. It began as a branch of al-Qaeda to wage an insurgency against the Americans who had invaded Iraq in 2003. Branching out into Syria during its civil war, it separated from al-Qaeda and took the name ISIS. ISIS attracted Iraqi Sunnis resentful of their elimination from key positions in the military and government by the Americans and of their general mistreatment by the new Shi'ite-led government. In late spring 2014, when ISIS was advancing in Iraq, the American-trained Iraqi army, which greatly outnumbered the insurgents, collapsed; fleeing troops left behind massive stores of American-supplied arms, including heavy equipment.

By mid-2015, ISIS—also called the Islamic State, ISIL (Islamic State of Iraq and the Levant), and Daesh (its Arabic-language acronym)—ruled an area in Iraq and Syria about the size of Great Britain. In June 2014, ISIS declared that the territory it commanded constituted a revived caliphate—the Islamic state that had theoretically ruled over Muslim lands for centuries. In ISIS's vision, the caliphate would eventually rule over all nations and purge them of infidels. The Islamic State hoped to realize Muhammad's vision of a global order in which the entire world would be subject to Islamic law and rule either as devotees of the true faith or as subject nations.

At the height of its power, ISIS called on all Muslims worldwide, including jihadist groups, to swear loyalty to Abu Bakr al-Baghdadi, its leader and the new caliph, and to recognize the caliphate's supreme authority. By the spring of 2015, a number of jihadist groups, including the especially violent and cruel Boko Haram in Nigeria, had committed to ISIS. ISIS ruled over several million people and had a centralized governing and military structure.

Ruling with Taliban-like rigor, ISIS enforced Sharia law: it banned soccer and music, instituted a strict dress code for women, and imposed extortionate taxes on Christians as a sign of submission, while destroying or vandalizing Christian churches, shrines, and cemeteries. To ensure obedience from their subjects, ISIS engaged in gruesome atrocities which were often videotaped in public and posted online—the mass execution of prisoners of war and Shi'ites, regarded by Sunni ISIS as apostates unworthy of life; the beheading of several Western journalists and aid workers, including Americans; the stoning to death of adulterers; the hurling of homosexuals to their death from tall buildings; the burning alive in a locked cage of a captured Jordanian pilot; and the killing of non-Muslims, including Christians. In early 2015, Libyan jihadists linked to ISIS beheaded twenty-one Egyptian Coptic Christians laboring in Libya. ISIS terror has spread to Europe and the United States where ISIS-trained jihadists or Muslims radicalized by ISIS have launched terrorist attacks, killing and maiming hundreds of civilians.

Particularly tragic was ISIS's treatment of the Yazidi minority,[1] a religious-ethnic people living principally in northern Iraq that ISIS views as devil worshippers. ISIS forces rounded up and massacred perhaps as many as 5,000 Yazidi men and boys; kidnapped hundreds, if not thousands, of Yazidi boys who were forced to convert and undergo military training; and abducted Yazidi women and girls as young as twelve, who were sold into sexual slavery to ISIS fighters or given as gifts to them as the spoils of war.

The Islamic State has become a magnet for thousands of young Muslims from all parts of the world, including some 5,000 from Europe and the United States who went to fight with ISIS. Analysts fear that these battle-hardened jihadists will engage in terrorism when they return home; some already have. But large numbers of Western recruits, killed or captured in 2017, and tightened border security in Europe, have somewhat reduced the threat.

In 2016–2017 the Islamic State suffered major reverses. Iraqi and Kurdish forces, aided by American-led coalition airstrikes and artillery bombardments and by American advisers, regained considerable territory from ISIS. In 2017, after a long and bloody struggle that caused the deaths or flight of hundreds of thousands of civilians and transformed the city into rubble and ruin, Iraqi forces captured Mosul, Iraq's second largest city. In October 2017, American-backed forces captured Raqqa, the self-declared capital of the Islamic State. In these and other liberated cities, civilians gave horrific accounts of ISIS torturing and publicly executing prisoners of war and civilians who were not totally adhering to ISIS's strict interpretation of Islamic law. Coalition forces have either captured or disabled the Islamic State's oil refineries and storage tanks, greatly curtailing ISIS's ability to smuggle oil, a significant source of its revenue. And the flow of foreign recruits into the Islamic State has greatly fallen. With only a few desert outposts remaining in Iraq, and with leaders fleeing, the Islamic State, which in 2014 controlled one-third of Iraq and had designs on ruling a global caliphate, was crumbling.

Nevertheless, with committed jihadists. including very likely sleeper cells, and self-radicalized zealots operating in several countries, the threat of terrorism will persist even if ISIS is stripped of its territory. Indeed, ISIS propaganda continues to entice extremists in Western lands and ISIS continues to coach and train operatives.

IDEOLOGY

Most Muslims condemn ISIS's barbaric behavior and both Muslim and Western commentators recognize that ISIS's worldview clashes with Western democratic ideals, particularly the commitment to human rights.[2] ISIS's ideology has caused controversy. Some Western government spokespersons, seeking not to exasperate anti-Western sentiments in the Muslim world, or to antagonize their own Muslim citizens, denied that ISIS is motivated by beliefs that have deep roots in Islam. These spokespersons regarded ISIS leaders as evil criminals

---

[1]The Yazidi religion has links to Christianity, Islam, Persian Zoroastrianism, and ancient Mesopotamian religions. Yazidis consider themselves monotheists.—Eds.

[2]Human rights abuse in much of the Muslim world goes beyond ISIS. While many Muslims, particularly among the educated, support many of the ideals and practices of the democratic West, large numbers of people cling to ancient traditions, which they see sanctioned by Islam, that violate human rights, and several governments openly suppress

and thugs who exploit Islam in their quest for personal power. Moreover, these officials pointed out basic truths—that ISIS represents only a small percentage of the Muslim world and that most Muslims do not support it and are repulsed by its brutality, which is directed principally at fellow Muslims who refuse to swear loyalty to the Islamic State. Indeed, ISIS has killed far more Muslims than Westerners.

Challenging ISIS's claim that it is a legitimate Muslim authority, numerous Muslim scholars, calling the Islamic State un-Islamic, have denounced ISIS for violating Islamic law and morality and corrupting Muhammad's teachings. They say that ISIS is motivated, not by true Islam, but by a narrow and distorted interpretation of Islam that totally neglects Muhammad's commands that mercy is a religious duty and killing civilian noncombatants a grave sin. Violent passages in the Koran, they point out, are subject to interpretation and are not to be accepted literally, and most Muslims do not accept them literally. The earlier condemnation of al-Qaeda and other Islamic fanatics by Abdurrahman Wahid, a former president of largely Muslim Indonesia, also applies to ISIS. Wahid denounced Muslim

fanatics for their "highly selective reading of the Koran" and urged Muslims to focus on the holy book's teachings, of which there are many, that promote a higher morality. In 2005, he wrote that humanity is threatened by

an extreme ideology perverted in the minds of fanatics. "They justify their brutality with slogans such as 'Islam is above everything else.' They seek to intimidate and subdue anyone else who does not share their extremist views, regardless of nationality or religion." Extremists are quick to drape themselves in the mantle of Islam and declare their opponents kafir, or infidels, and thus smooth the way for slaughtering nonfundamentalist Muslims. Their theology rests upon a simplistic, literal, and highly selective reading of the Koran and Sunnah (prophetic traditions), through which they seek to entrap the worldwide Muslim community in the confines of their narrow ideological grasp.

After terrorist attacks against civilians in Paris (see page 466), Muslim clerics and scholars throughout the globe denounced ISIS terrorists, calling them "criminals," "barbarians," "immoral," "madmen," "enemies of humanity."

Many Western analysts, however, reject the notion that ISIS's radicalism is simply un-Islamic; rather they hold that there is a connection between historic Islamic doctrine and both the attacks of 9/11 and the ideology and practices of ISIS. These analysts hold that ISIS's worldview has a substantial theological base, that jihadist terror and persecution—in several Muslim lands, Christians have been executed, persecuted, and forced to flee—find credibility and legitimacy in historic Islam, that in essence ISIS has politicized religious extremism. These analysts view ISIS as an expression of Islam's dark side. While ISIS's thinking does not represent mainstream Islam, say these analysts, it is fallacious to pretend that the Islamic State's professed aims and deliberate brutality have

intellectual and personal freedom. The cultural preconditions for liberal democracy, for free and just societies, are largely absent in Muslim societies. In a recent poll, more than 80 percent of Egyptians and Jordanians favored the death penalty for apostates and 80 percent of Egyptians approved stoning adulterers—historic religious punishments. Throughout the Muslim world and beyond, Saudi Arabia finances schools (madrassas) that teach young people an extremist form of Islam that can and has produced jihadists. In Saudi Arabia people can be given hundreds of whiplashes and imprisoned for years for "insulting Islam"; women are not permitted to leave their home without a male escort; school textbooks describe Christians as enemies of Islam, whom Muslims should hate; and Christians living in the country, mainly Asian workers, are barred from constructing churches. In Iran homosexuals are hanged. In Pakistan, a person accused of criticizing Muhammad or Islam can be executed (at times these "blasphemers" are beaten to death by an enraged mob) and about 1,000 Pakistani females a year are murdered, usually by family members, in so-called "honor killings." Attempting to terminate this brutality, the government has met resistance from Islamic hard-liners.—Eds.

nothing to do with Islam. The radical fundamentalist underpinning of ISIS terrorism must be heeded rather than ignored, minimized, or denied. These commentators argue that ISIS leaders are Islamic zealots who believe they have an uncompromising duty to return to "Pure Muhammadan Islam," that is, to medieval Islam when Allah's word, as revealed by Muhammad, governed the lives of Muslims. They maintain that ISIS identifies with Jihadi-Salafism, an ideological movement within Sunni Islam propagated by hardline scholars and religious authorities that is based on pre-modern theology. Its teachings, widely disseminated on websites, in the media, and in numerous writings, sponsor radical interpretations of Islamic scripture that urge strict adherence to Islamic law, including jihad. Supported by current scholarly authorities in its camp, ISIS sees itself as fighting unbelievers and infidels. It sees Arab lands as under attack by Western "crusader" states and considers it justifiable to kill anyone who aids the "crusader" occupiers in any way or rejects jihad. For ISIS, after disbelief in God, no sin is greater than forbidding jihad against unbelievers.

The early followers of Muhammad, says Bernard Lewis, professor emeritus of Near Eastern Studies at Princeton University, divided the world "into two houses: the House of Islam, in which a Muslim government ruled and Muslim law prevailed, and the House of War, the rest of the world . . . ruled by infidels. Between the two, there was to be a perpetual state of war until the entire world either embraced Islam or submitted to the rule of the Muslim state." Like al-Qaeda, ISIS sees itself resuming the war that began with Muhammad for religious dominance of the world. ISIS jihadists consider themselves true Muslims whose ideology and behavior accord with legitimate Muslim beliefs and practices. When jihadists insist that they are on the true path, some analysts suggest, they refer specifically to Muhammad, the Koran, the rulings and opinions of classic Muslim jurists, and centuries of commentary by prominent thinkers

and clerics. These authorities, maintain ISIS jihadists, considered the killing of apostates and hostile infidels proper and praiseworthy, a way of purifying the faith, and they regarded the enslavement of captives as a reward justified by Allah. (While Muhammad himself had slaves, he did tell his followers not to mistreat slaves and that it was a blessing to free a slave.)

ISIS leaders and fighters, who consistently and rigorously confirm their religious dedication, believe they have a historic mission to shape a caliphate powerful enough to efface modern infidel values, namely secularism and democratic principles and practices. To them, human rights and individual freedom are sinful, for they lead people to question God's laws; also sinful is the democratic belief that citizens can enact laws for their society. A legitimate legal system comes not from the people but from God only. Seeing democracy as antithetical to Islamic law, ISIS wants to extirpate it throughout the world. They insist that Islamic law is perfectly suitable for the contemporary world.

ISIS's dismissal of human rights is seen in its restoration of slavery and the crucifying and beheading of people designated as enemies of Islam—all practices approved in medieval Islamic texts, which contemporary jihadists interpret literally and with great seriousness. For example, the following passage from a recent ISIS publication justifies enslavement, which was practiced by Muhammad himself, and is authorized by Sharia law.

After capture, the Yazidi women and children were then divided according to the Sharia amongst the fighters of the Islamic State. The enslaved Yazidi families are now sold by the Islamic State. . . . Enslaving the families of the [infidel] and taking their women as concubines is a firmly established aspect of the Sharia that if one were to deny or mock, he would be denying or mocking the verses of the Quran and the narratives of the Prophet [Muhammad], and thereby apostatizing from Islam.

A particularly barbaric procedure organized and condoned by ISIS is the continuous and systematic rape of Yazidi women and girls. ISIS has developed a bureaucracy to handle this sex slavery of more than 3,000 Yazidi females. These unfortunates are used to please ISIS fighters and to lure recruits, all of whom feel that this behavior is sanctified by God.

Analysts who stress the link between Islam and ISIS refer to passages in Islam's sacred texts that provide theological justification for intolerance and brutality. While several verses in the Koran speak of peace, there are others that praise the sword. And while the greatly revered Muhammad performed acts of kindness and praised peace, unlike Jesus, he was also a warrior and conqueror. And these analysts maintain that the thousands of ISIS volunteers from several lands take seriously their Islamic identity; they see themselves as Islamic warriors devoted to Allah and his teachings, particularly the duty to participate in jihad. And, continue these commentators, when ISIS suicide bombers blow themselves up in market places crowded with civilians perceived to be enemies, they derive a sense of profound satisfaction; they believe that they are serving Allah and gaining the rewards of paradise. And there is no shortage of volunteers who seek this path to paradise. These analysts view ISIS not just as a perversion of Islam but as a sign that Islam has not broken with practices and teachings inherited from the Middle Ages that conflict with modern democratic values.

APPEAL

Some 30,000 recruits from many nations, including 5,000 from European countries and some from the United States, have gone to Syria to fight alongside ISIS. Numerous reasons account for ISIS's magnetism, particularly for the young. In Arab lands, ISIS appeals to disaffected youth repulsed by the failure of their countries to provide a better life. Seeing themselves with no future, they believe that ISIS will give them some stature and power. Some European youth and sympathizers come from the most marginalized among the Muslim populations—drifters, petty criminals, lost souls who see in ISIS a way of giving meaning to their lives. A large number of volunteers drawn to ISIS's message have been educated in the West and hold degrees from Western colleges and universities. Some recruits with an adventurous spirit are excited by the opportunity to do battle in a foreign land and to participate in ISIS's successful military campaigns of which they are proud. And, no doubt, some are psychopaths impelled by evil instincts who relish the chance to engage in slaughter and torture, all actions that they see as justified by Islam.

Skillful preachers in mosques and on the Internet remind Muslims that both the Koran and the hadith—the sayings attributed to Muhammad—explicitly prescribe jihad as an obligation for both the individual and the collective community. Potential recruits are told that Muhammad glorified jihad and criticized those who did not participate in it, calling them "hypocrites" and "sick at heart." Jihadist websites, numbering in the thousands, feature images of dead Americans killed by "glorious" jihadists and videos of suicide bombers giving their farewell speeches. They also provide instructions for making explosive devices. The Internet has shaped a community bonded by a hatred of those perceived as enemies of Islam. These words have particular appeal to those recruits who have recently turned to their ancestral religion, becoming true believers dedicated to serving a higher cause. As true believers, they abhor Western institutions, ideals, and practices that comprise modernity and see themselves as victims seeking vengeance against the West for its behavior toward Muslims. Many recruits, both in the Middle East and in Western countries, consider it an honor to serve the restored caliphate, which is dedicated to making Islam the central force in public life throughout the globe. They view the caliphate as a symbol of past greatness and the appropriate agent to unite the world's Muslims into one community capable of serving the faith and rectifying the years of humiliation suffered by Muslims at the hands of the West. For these recruits, defending the caliphate—whose leaders, they believe, convey God's will—is a sacred mission, and some devotees, particularly suicide bombers, relish the opportunity for martyrdom, which they are certain Allah will reward. They also regard martyrdom as their legacy to the Muslim community, a legacy that gives their life an overarching meaning. The rise of militant Islam demonstrates the immense difficulty of transplanting Western democratic principles to regions whose history and cultural traditions, particularly religious traditions, do not easily mesh with democracy.

EXPORTING TERRORISM TO WESTERN LANDS

The loss of considerable territory in Syria and Iraq and the killing of many ISIS leaders, often by American planes and drones, has weakened the Islamic State and diminished its appeal among radical Muslims. But, say some analysts, there is the danger that fighters returning home from the battlefield in Syria and Iraq will worsen Islamist terrorism in Europe and the United States. ISIS has also encouraged freelancers to kill civilians in their adopted Western countries, and it has built a network of trained jihadists and support groups that provide terrorists with financing, safe houses, and documents needed to escape the authorities. From bases in Syria, ISIS handlers, using the Internet expertly and discretely, have recruited terrorists and, in operations on three continents, have guided the attackers up to the last minute. Suicide bombings, which have

long been common in the Middle East, have now spread to Western lands. ISIS believes that attacks that kill civilians, preferably in large numbers, promote insecurity within the population, cause a significant loss of revenue from tourism, and provoke a backlash against Muslims living in the country; such a hoped-for backlash would radicalize more Muslims, abetting jihadist recruitment. Complicating the matter for authorities is that the terrorists and their supporters are often citizens, some born and raised in the lands where they are launching murderous jihadist attacks.

Several deadly terrorist attacks in Europe and the United States since the rise of ISIS have increased fear and anger in the Western world. Following is a sampling of major Islamist terrorist attacks in Europe and the United States from 2015 to 2017. There were other deadly operations and authorities thwarted a significant number of planned attacks. (In 2016, French authorities uncovered seventeen terrorist plots.) While ISIS was not directly responsible for all these attacks, it shaped a climate of opinion that inspired and justified terrorism against civilians; moreover, when news of the killings broke, ISIS gave its approval and glorified the dead terrorists as martyrs.

EUROPE

- In January 2015, two heavily armed Islamist militants affiliated with al-Qaeda stormed into the office of satirical newspaper *Charlie Hebdo* in Paris, killing twelve people and critically wounding three others. The terrorists sought to punish the newspaper staff for publishing articles and cartoons mocking Islamist terrorism and the Prophet Muhammad. (The magazine also lampooned other religions, including Christianity.) At the same time, another terrorist linked to the *Hebdo* assassins, but seeking Jewish targets, killed four men in a nearby kosher supermarket.

- In November 2015, nine Islamist terrorists divided into three teams, launched a sophisticated, synchronized, and deadly assault in Paris. The teams that shot up cafés and the concert hall created a blood bath—129 dead and 352 injured. All eight terrorists perished, seven in suicide blasts; one was shot by the police, triggering the explosive device on his suicide vest. The Islamic State claimed responsibility for the attack, calling Paris the "capital of prostitution and obscenity."

- On March 22, 2016, in a coordinated operation, Islamist suicide bombers attacked the Brussels Airport (Belgium) and a major metro station in Brussels. ISIS claimed responsibility for the bombings, which killed 32 civilians and injured more than 300. The three perpetrators died when they exploded their bombs.

- On March 22, 2017, a terrorist rammed his car into people on Westminster Bridge in London and then killed a policeman with a kitchen knife before he was shot. In all, the terrorist killed three and injured around forty, several critically.

- On May 22, 2017, a terrorist detonated a homemade bomb packed with nuts and bolts as the audience in a concert hall in Manchester, England, was leaving a performance by the popular American singer, Ariana Grande. The suicide bomber killed 23 people, 10 under twenty years of age, and injured another 59 before blowing himself up. It appears that the terrorist deliberately targeted young people, knowing that they would attend the concert in large numbers.

- On June 3, 2017, terrorists drove their van into pedestrians on London Bridge and then stabbed people in restaurants and pubs in nearby Borough Market. Eight people perished and dozens more were injured before the police killed the terrorists.

UNITED STATES

- An example of terrorism by freelancers that shocked the American people occurred during the running of the famed Boston Marathon in April 2013. Two brothers, refugees from the region where Russia is battling Muslim Chechen separatists, had lived for many years in the United States, which had granted their family political asylum (and welfare for a time); one brother had become a naturalized citizen. After embracing Islamic extremism, they planted explosives near the finish line of the race, crowded with spectators. The attack left three people dead and some 260 injured, sixteen of whom, including children, lost legs or feet. One of the brothers died after a fierce gun battle with the police and the other was put on trial and found guilty.

- In December 2015, a married Muslim couple, the husband an American-born citizen of Pakistani descent and his Pakistan-born, Saudi-raised wife, herself a legal resident of the United States, engaged in a murderous terrorist act. Inspired by jihadi propaganda, much of it found on the Internet, the couple committed themselves to jihadism and martyrdom. They targeted a function organized by the San Bernadino health department where the husband, Syed Rizwan Farook, was employed. Armed with semi-automatic weapons and wearing ski masks and black gear, the couple fired at the people seated around tables. Responding immediately, the police located the terrorists fleeing by car and killed both in a gunfight. In all, the terrorists killed 14 people and seriously injured 22.

- In June 2016, Omar Mateen, an American citizen born in New York who proclaimed allegiance to ISIS, fired an assault rifle in a gay night club in Orlando, Florida. Moments after the patrons had been joyously dancing to Latin rhythms, the nightclub was drenched with blood and piled with bodies. Fifty people perished and 53 were wounded in this attack, at the time, the largest mass shooting of civilians in American history.

- At the end of October, 2017, a terrorist drove a rental truck into pedestrians on a bike path in lower Manhattan, killing eight and injuring several others. Getting out of his car, and carrying two realistic looking guns, he raced down the street screaming in Arabic "Allahu Akbar" God is great, before being wounded by a policeman.

ISIS is actively promoting truck attacks on civilians, even providing guidelines on the Internet for killing the maximum number of people.

CONCLUSION

Widely promoted and circulated by ISIS is the conviction that the world is divided into good believers and evil infidels who do not deserve to live unless they convert to the one true faith or accept the status of obedient subjects. For ISIS the only legitimate government is one based on God-given Sharia. Jihadists loathe Western civilization, which they view as materialistic, hedonistic, and sacrilegious; they are repelled by secular democracies that promote freedom of thought and female equality and tolerate homosexuality—all principles they regard as anathema to true Islam.

ISIS, despite its well-documented barbarism, repressive worldview, and territorial losses, continues to retain the loyalty of many of its fighters and to sustain a worldwide following, although small in overall numbers. And while polls tell us that most Muslims reject murderous terrorism against civilians, the minority that considers these atrocities wholly justifiable, according to the polls, is not negligible—if extrapolated, perhaps as many as 300 million. These facts lead many analysts, some of them Muslims, to press for significant changes in Islam's message to its devotees. It is imperative, say these analysts, for Islamic clerics, scholars, and political leaders to harness the humane elements within Islam, particularly those teachings that promote compassion and mercy and prohibit indiscriminate slaughter of civilians. It is hoped that this effort at humaneness, widely taught and disseminated, might neutralize the

religious extremism and obscurantism that underpins ISIS.

Some critics go further. While it is laudable that Muslims throughout the world have condemned ISIS's brutality, they say, it is necessary for Muslim thinkers to examine and specifically repudiate religious texts that underlie this brutality. They urge a broad reformation within Islam, which unlike the West did not experience the Enlightenment of the eighteenth century that attacked the historic abuses of the Christian churches—support for burning heretics and witches, endorsing sectarian warfare between Catholics and Protestants, and the suppression of free thought. Enlightenment thinkers challenged Christian doctrines that stifled reason and seemed harmful to society, and called for religious toleration and the elimination of censorship by churches. They denounced torture—accepted by both churches and the state—advocated governments that protected individual rights, including freedom of speech, the press, and religion, and called for the separation of church and state, which they saw as a necessary prerequisite for preserving freedom.

Christian thinkers and clerics now dismiss historic religious dogmas that promote intolerance and violence. There are Muslims who want to break the stranglehold that rigid fundamentalists have over their faith and to suffuse Islam with modern values which challenge medieval religious dogmas and traditions that promote violence, stifle freedom, and subjugate women. But to voice such sentiments can be very dangerous in several Muslim lands, for hard-line Muslim clerics tenaciously resist Western liberal democratic principles which they regard as an attack on the ultimate truths transmitted by Muhammad. In their view, believers must not question these truths but always submit to them. Such unquestioning religious tenacity has helped to create states in the Muslim world that are incompatible with both the spirit and practice of democracy. It also nurtures extremist movements like ISIS.

REVIEW QUESTIONS

1. Do you agree with those Western statesmen who refuse to see Islamic roots for ISIS's ideology. Why? Why not?
2. Why are some Muslims eager to join ISIS? How can they be persuaded not to by Muslim moderates?
3. In your opinion, how dangerous is ISIS and what should the United States do to combat it?

---

5 The Editors
Islam in Europe: Failure of Assimilation

Muslim immigration has become a major concern for many Europeans. The conflicts in the Middle East, particularly in Syria, have led hundreds of thousands of Muslims to escape the killing fields and seek asylum in Europe. No doubt many Muslims from the Middle East claiming to seek asylum are really hoping for economic betterment. Joining them are Muslim migrants from African lands, also dreaming of escaping debilitating poverty. Some migrants traveled great distances to reach the coastal regions where they were crammed into small unfit boats that were always in danger of sinking. In 2015 more than 3,600 migrants either drowned or were lost at sea attempting to cross the Mediterranean. In 2016 over 5,000 migrants perished.

These new arrivals, often paying smugglers extortionist fees, and at times enduring life-threatening transit often do not find Europe a welcoming haven. In 2015, at the height of the crisis, many Europeans, motivated by humanitarian sentiments, rushed to aid the asylum seekers. But after being traumatized by several major terrorist attacks (see pages 465–467) and resenting having to provide large social welfare benefits for hundreds of thousands of poor refugees, many Europeans have grown bitter about Muslim immigration. Fearing that the Muslim influx is changing the face of their countries, an increasing number of Europeans are becoming attracted to far-Right nationalist parties that propagate anti-immigrant sentiments. Warning that jihadists are posing as refugees in order to establish terrorist cells in Europe and that increased Muslim migration combined with a declining European birth rate will lead to the Islamization of major European cities, these parties demand strict limits on Muslim immigration. Often their rhetoric is ugly, xenophobic, and racist.

In the 1950s and 1960s, Western Europe's booming economy created a demand for cheap labor that was met by an influx of Muslims into several European countries, notably France, Germany, Britain, Belgium, Holland, Sweden, and Spain, which now have substantial Muslim populations. (Some cities have as many if not more mosques than churches.) In past decades European countries have essentially tried two approaches to absorbing Muslim immigrants—multiculturalism and assimilation. Practiced in Britain, Holland, and Germany, multiculturalism treats Muslims as members of a separate community with a distinct religious and cultural identity; this approach assumes that the Muslims' way of life could exist side by side with the cultural norms of the host country. Assimilation, the integration model adopted in France, does not grant Muslims a special status but encourages individual Muslims to embrace the nation's culture and values, to think of themselves as proud and loyal French citizens. Both approaches are now perceived as largely failures, for many Muslims remain profoundly alienated from European society and at odds with its values. European liberal democracy, which espouses religious freedom, equal rights for women, separation of church and state, and freedom of expression, conflicts with many facets of Muslim tradition.

In describing the failure of the multicultural approach in Britain, analysts refer to terrorist acts and plots by Muslims who were not foreign jihadists but were born and educated in Britain. The attack in 2005 on London's transit system that killed more than 50 people and injured some 700 was planned and executed by British Muslims. In 2006, British security foiled a terrorist plot to blow up several transatlantic flights departing Heathrow airport that would have killed more people than had perished on 9/11. The main terrorists were British-born Muslims, some of Pakistani descent.

In addition to terrorism, analysts in Britain and other countries refer to the behavior patterns and values evidenced by Muslims living among them that threaten to change the face of the nation. Muslims cluster in densely populated ghettos in which police do not feel safe, have a high percentage of unemployment due to limited technical and language skills, and receive a disproportionate share of welfare benefits.

Exacerbating the conflict with native citizens is the demand of Islamic radicals that largely Muslim communities be governed by Sharia (religious law), based on God's revelations in the Koran, and not the law of the land. Indeed, in some European communities, for all intents and purposes, this has taken effect. In many respects these Muslim ghettos have become a society within a society. People in the host country resent the perpetuation by some Muslims of cultural conventions that sanction polygamy, forced marriages between young girls and much older men, and wife-beating; that also permit so-called honor killings of "wayward" females, often by immediate family members; and that require women to keep their bodies and faces hidden from view when in public. European authorities find it difficult to contain and prosecute Muslim bigotry and violence against women.

There are serious educational problems among Muslims living in Europe: a high dropout rate and the emergence of Muslim schools where students concentrate on studying the Koran at the expense of secular subjects that would prepare them for employment and for understanding the history and culture of the people amid whom they now reside. In 2014, Britain published a report on the impact of conservative Muslims on schools in Birmingham, which has a large Muslim population. The report concluded that some Muslim teachers and school board governors promoted anti-Semitism and homophobia, expressed support for al-Qaeda, invited speakers who called for countries to be governed by Islamic law, advocated segregation of girls, and discriminated against female teachers.

Promoting fear and distrust is the high crime rate among Muslims, particularly male youth involved in gangs and drug dealing. Numbering about 10 percent of France, Muslims may comprise as much as 70 percent of prison inmates. While Muslims constitute 4.7 percent of Britain's population, they account for 14 percent of prison inmates.

Assaults and robberies by young Muslim men—combined with murderous terrorist attacks by jihadists—have fueled European fear and resentment of Muslim immigration. For example, the disdain felt by Germans, particularly on the political Right, for the influx of Muslims to their country soared when on December 31, 2015, New Year's Eve, rampaging Muslim youth, many of them recent arrivals, robbed and sexually assaulted hundreds of women and girls in Cologne. This outrage provoked numerous arson attacks directed at refugee housing in Germany.

Faced with what is perceived as a rapidly growing, inassimilable Muslim minority, Europe is experiencing a backlash against Muslim immigrants and multiculturalism. British commentators have raised a difficult question. In the past, they say, immigrant Jews and, more recently, Indian Sikhs and Hindus have thrived in Britain, even when confronted with prejudice. Why they ask, is the integration of Muslim immigrants in Western society so fraught with problems?

An increasing number of Europeans now say that assigning equal value to and tolerating Islamic traditions that are hostile to Western values was a mistake, for several of these traditions undermine democracy and fragment the nation. The sentiments of Jan Wolter, a Dutch judge, are shared by many native Europeans: "We demand a new social contract. We no longer accept that people don't learn our language, we require that they send their daughters to school, and we demand they stop bringing in young brides from the desert and locking them up in third floor apartments." Increasingly, governments are introducing tighter immigration laws, are deporting Muslim radicals, and have attempted to counteract the jihadist poison flooding the Internet.

Governments have established programs to de-radicalize young Muslims and to encourage the Muslim community to inform the authorities of potential terrorists. They are trying to work with moderate Muslim leaders who support integration into European society and value Europe's liberal-democratic tradition. However, successful integration, say some commentators, is a two-way street. It is necessary for European society to address the socioeconomic problems confronting Muslims. Muslim immigrants are usually grateful to those countries that granted them sanctuary, but burdened with unemployment and bigotry, they come under the influence of radicals and criminals Achieving beneficial integration requires Europeans to overcome racist attitudes toward immigrants, not to give the impression that Islam as a religion is being attacked and insulted, and to recognize the fact that numerous Muslims, particularly second-generation Muslims, do work—a number have achieved success in business and academia—and pay taxes, respect the laws of their adopted country, and reject extremism. In

The Myth of the Muslim Tide: Do Immigrants Threaten the West? published in 2012, Doug Saunders, a respected Canadian journalist, draws conclusions markedly different from critics who see only failure and danger. He maintains that many Muslims in Europe, like Christians and Jews, do not practice their faith or are selective regarding those beliefs and practices which they choose to follow, and in polls express an affinity for the country in which they are living.

Europe is wracked with an ethical crisis. Not to respond with compassion and generosity to the suffering of human beings fleeing savage conflicts and crushing poverty can be seen as morally callous, a turning away from Europe's noble Christian and liberal principles. But many Europeans feel that protecting fellow citizens from jihadists and criminals and aspiring to preserve a nation's historic values is a moral imperative that their government must not circumvent. And those critical of Muslim immigration ask: Why doesn't the Muslim world solve its own problems instead of dumping them on us? Why do prosperous Saudi Arabia and the Gulf States refuse to take in fellow Arab refugees while we are expected to provide them with housing and welfare? For many years to come, Europeans will be confronted with—or tormented by—the question of the place of Muslims in their countries.

REVIEW QUESTIONS

1. What prevents more Muslim migrants from integrating into European society?
2. What can be done by European governments and Muslim moderates to foster successful integration?

---

6 Female Oppression

"The two biggest threats to women today are Islamic fundamentalism and the trafficking and normalization of prostitution," says Donna Hughes, professor of women's studies at the University of Rhode Island and an expert on the trafficking of women. As Southeast Asia opened to the West and the Soviet Union collapsed, trafficking (that is, illegal commercial trading) in women and young girls for prostitution became a major international issue. Conservative evangelical Christians in the United States had pushed the Bush administration to pressure foreign governments to curb trafficking or face sanctions. This has had some success, particularly where countries have been able to abolish the use of underage girls in brothels.

Trafficking is only one facet of the larger problem of the oppression of women. The resurgence of Islamic fundamentalism among 1.8 billion Muslims has had a marked effect on the social position of Muslim women. While women in Western-influenced Islamic countries have made progress in gaining rights and freedoms, the more conservative Islamic states have maintained traditional Islamic law (Sharia) that relegates women to a subordinate position in society, governing their conduct and the way they dress, and consigning them to a domestic role in a male-dominated society.

The revolution of 1979 in Iran changed a| modernizing country into an Islamic republic with repressive laws governing women. The worst excesses of female oppression occurred in Afghanistan under the fundamentalist Taliban regime (1996–2001) that imposed rules for women, permitting beatings by male relatives, prohibiting females from working, barring them from schools, restricting medical treatment, and demanding that they wear the burqa—a garment that covered them from head to foot. Violators could be severely beaten, imprisoned, or executed.

U.N. Secretary-General
ENDING VIOLENCE AGAINST WOMEN: "THE SYSTEMATIC DOMINATION OF WOMEN BY MEN"

In October 2006 the United Nations released the Secretary-General's in-depth study of violence against women, *Ending Violence against Women,* which concluded that "the pervasiveness of violence against women across the boundaries of nation, culture, race, class and religion points to its roots in patriarchy—the systematic domination of women by men." Excerpts from the study, many of whose findings still apply, follow.

INTRODUCTION

. . . The central premise of the analysis of violence against women within the human rights framework is that the specific causes of such violence and the factors that increase the risk of its occurrence are grounded in the broader context of systemic gender-based discrimination against women and other forms of subordination. Such violence is a manifestation of the historically unequal power relations between women and men reflected in both public and private life .
. . . Vulnerability to violence is understood as a condition created by the absence or denial of rights.

Excerpted from *Ending Violence against Women: From Words to Action; Study of the Secretary-General,* October 9, 2006, pp. 27–32, 37–43. Available online at: http://www.un.org/womenwatch/daw/vaw/v-sg-ov.htm. Reprinted with permission from the United Nations Publications Board.

Intimate Partner Violence

112. The most common form of violence experienced by women globally is intimate partner violence. The pervasiveness of different forms of violence against women within intimate relationships, commonly referred to as domestic violence or spousal abuse, is now well established.

113. Intimate partner violence includes a range of sexually, psychologically and physically coercive acts used against adult and adolescent women by a current or former intimate partner, without her consent. Physical violence involves intentionally using physical force, strength or a weapon to harm or injure the woman. Sexual violence includes abusive sexual contact, making a woman engage in a sexual act without her consent, and attempted or completed sex acts with a woman who is ill, disabled, under pressure or under the influence of alcohol or

other drugs. Psychological violence includes controlling or isolating the women, and humiliating or embarrassing her. Economic violence includes denying a woman access to and control over basic resources.

Harmful Traditional Practices

118. Female infanticide and prenatal sex selection, early marriage, dowry-related violence, female genital mutilation/cutting[1], crimes against women committed in the name of "honour," and maltreatment of widows, including inciting widows to commit suicide, are forms of violence against women that are considered harmful traditional practices, and may involve both family and community.

119. The most extensive body of research concerns female genital mutilation/cutting. It is estimated that more than 130 million girls and women alive today have undergone female genital mutilation/cutting, mainly in Africa and some countries in the Middle East. The practice is also prevalent among immigrant communities in Europe, North America and Australia. Surveys revealed significant geographic variations in the prevalence rates in 19 countries: 99 percent in Guinea, 97 percent in Egypt, 80 percent in Ethiopia, 17 percent in Benin, and 5 percent in Ghana and Niger. They also show that the practice may be slowly declining even in high prevalence countries because of increasing opposition from women's groups. Higher female educational levels, female access to and control over economic resources, ethnicity and women's own female genital mutilation/cutting status have been found to be significantly associated with their support for or opposition to female genital mutilation/cutting.

120. Practices of son preference, expressed in manifestations such as female infanticide, prenatal sex selection and systematic neglect of girls,

have resulted in adverse female-male sex ratios and high rates of female infant mortality in South and East Asia, North Africa, and the Middle East. A study in India estimated that prenatal sex selection and infanticide have accounted for half a million missing girls per year for the past two decades. In the Republic of Korea, among pregnancies having sex-identification tests, more than 90 percent of pregnancies with male foetuses resulted in normal births, whereas more than 30 percent of those with female foetuses were terminated, according to the National Fertility and Family Health Survey.

121. Early marriages involve the marriage of a child, i.e., a person below the age of 18. Minor girls have not achieved full maturity and capacity to act and lack ability to control their sexuality. When they marry and have children, their health can be adversely affected, their education impeded and economic autonomy restricted. Early marriage also increases the risk of HIV infection. Such marriages take place all over the world, but are most common in sub-Saharan Africa and South Asia, where more than 30 percent of girls aged 15 to 19 are married. In Ethiopia, it was found that 19 percent of girls were married by the age of 15 and in some regions such as Amhara, the proportion was as high as 50 percent. In Nepal, 7 percent of girls were married before the age of 10 and 40 percent by the age of 15. A UNICEF global assessment found that in Latin America and the Caribbean, 29 percent of women aged 15 to 24 were married before the age of 18.

122. A forced marriage is one lacking the free and valid consent of at least one of the parties. In its most extreme form, forced marriage can involve threatening behaviour, abduction, imprisonment, physical violence, rape and, in some cases, murder. . . . One study of 1,322 marriages across six villages in Kyrgyzstan found that one half of ethnic Kyrgyz marriages were the result of kidnappings, and that as many as two thirds of these marriages were non-consensual. In the United Kingdom of Great Britain

---

[1]Removing a young girl's clitoris so she would not derive pleasure from sexual intercourse.—Eds.

and Northern Ireland, a Forced Marriage Unit established by the Government intervenes in 300 cases of forced marriage a year.

123. Violence related to demands for dowry—which is the payment of cash or goods by the bride's family to the groom's family—may lead to women being killed in dowry-related femicide. According to official crime statistics in India, approximately 6,822 women were killed in 2002 as a result of such violence. Small community studies have also indicated that dowry demands have played an important role in women being burned to death and in deaths of women labelled as suicides.

124. Crimes against women committed in the name of "honour" may occur within the family or within the community. These crimes are receiving increased attention, but remain underreported and under-documented. The most severe manifestation is murder—so-called "honour killings." UNFPA [United Nations Population Fund] estimated that 5,000 women are murdered by family members each year in "honour killings" around the world. A government report noted that "karo-kari" ("honour killings") claimed the lives of 4,000 men and women between 1998 and 2003 in Pakistan, and that the number of women killed was more than double the number of men.

125. Older women, including in particular widows, are subject to harmful practices in a number of countries, which can involve both the family and the community. A study conducted in Ghana, based on data collected from news reports and interviews, found that many poor, often elderly women were accused of witchcraft. Some were murdered by male relatives and those who survived were subjected to a range of physical, sexual and economic abuses. Violence directed against widows, including sexual abuse and harassment and property-related violence at the hands of relatives, mainly in-laws, has been reported from a number of countries including India, but information remains scarce.

Femicide: The Gender-Based Murder of a Woman

127. Femicide occurs everywhere, but the scale of some cases of femicide within community contexts—for example, in Ciudad Juárez, Mexico and Guatemala—has drawn attention to this aspect of violence against women. Most official sources agree that more than 320 women have been murdered in Ciudad Juárez, one third of whom were brutally raped. In Guatemala, according to National Civil Police statistics, 1,467 women were murdered between 2001 and the beginning of December 2004. Other sources claim the figure is higher, with 2,070 women murdered, mostly aged 14 to 35. The killings have been concentrated in areas where the economies are dominated by *maquilas*, assembly plants for export products owned and operated in tax-free zones by multinational companies. Impunity for these crimes is seen as a key factor in these occurrences, and in the case of Guatemala, the legacy of the internal armed conflict that ended in 1996 is also seen as a contributing factor.

REVIEW QUESTIONS

1. List examples of violence against females discussed in the U.N. study.
2. What traditional practices did the study find particularly harmful?

7 The Taliban's War on Women

After taking over much of Afghanistan in the mid-1990s, the Taliban imposed rigid restrictions on women, which they insisted accorded with Islamic law and protected the dignity of women. They limited medical care for women and forced almost all women to quit their jobs, a hardship particularly for widows who had no other source of income, and banned girls above the age of eight from attending school. Some expelled teachers conducted secret classes in their homes for both children and women; if discovered by the Taliban these women were beaten and threatened with death. The Taliban required women and girls to wear the burqa, a tent-like garment that covered them from head to toe, and religious police roaming the streets beat women, sometimes with whips, who showed any skin on their feet or arms or wore lipstick or nail polish. Women were not permitted to leave the house unaccompanied by a close male relative. Nor could they be photographed or filmed, and pictures of females could not be shown in newspapers and books or displayed on walls in homes and shops. Women were also banned from talking to a male who was not a relative.

Regarding female education as symbol of the West's moral depravity, Taliban militants in northwestern Pakistan (which now also has an ISIS presence), bombed more than 800 girls' schools. On October 9, 2012, Taliban gunmen in Pakistan boarded a school bus in an attempt to assassinate Malala Yousafzai, a fifteen-year-old girl who was active in promoting women's rights and female education. Although shot in the head, she survived. A chief spokesman for the Pakistani Taliban claimed religious justification for the shooting and warned that it would try again. This obscene display of bigotry aroused worldwide disgust.

With good reason, Afghan women fear the return of the Taliban to power.

A Persecuted Afghan Woman
"YOU COME FROM A FAMILY OF INFIDELS"

Behind the Burqa: Our Life in Afghanistan and How We Escaped to Freedom is an account by two sisters about the torment suffered by women in Afghanistan. At different times, each sister fled the country. Fearing reprisal, they do not reveal their true identities. In the following excerpt, one sister describes what happened almost five months after she opened a clandestine school in her home.

Three members of the Religious Police started banging at the door.

Only when I heard someone banging hard and shouting did I put on my burqa and answer the door. When I saw who was standing there, I nearly fainted. My knees turned to water. My stomach leaped into my throat and I wanted to throw up. There was no mistaking the white uniform, beard, turban, gun, and unyielding facial expression. I was staring at three members of the Religious Police.

The tallest man scowled at me. "Are you the teacher?"

"Teacher? I don't know what you are talking about."

In my mind, I spoke to the children. I pleaded with them. Please, please stay quiet. Don't move. Don't laugh. And then to God, but without words. A silent prayer for my life. Please.

"I heard there was a school here." The same man was talking.

"You heard the wrong information," I said. "There has been some mistake."

"Are you sure?" The man tried to peer into the house behind me, but I deliberately stood in the door, blocking his view.

"Really." Could he tell from my voice that I was lying? Well, here was one advantage of the burqa. They could not see my face. . . .

He stared at me long and hard. I waited for him to say something. I waited for a child to make some noise that would give us all away. Those moments of waiting seemed to last forever.

"I hope you are telling the truth," he finally said. "Because if you're not, we will punish you severely."

Behind the Burqa: Our Life in Afghanistan and How We Escaped to Freedom, by "Sulima" and "Hala" as told to Batya Swift Yasgur (Hoboken, NJ: John Wiley & Sons, 2002), pp. 213–215.

The second man spoke up. "We will come back and kill you."

The first man motioned to the others and they left. . . .

I was sitting in the room where we handed out assignments to the children. I looked out the window onto the courtyard, and there they were. Four of them this time. All with guns.

Today they didn't knock. They pushed against the door and stormed through the house. Two of them grabbed my hair and pulled me down the stairs and into the courtyard.

"You lied to us!" It was yesterday's man speaking.

"What are you talking about?" I barely recognized my own voice. He pulled my hair harder and the other man slapped me. "We know who you are. You come from a family of infidels. Your sister was a Communist. Now she's a Christian. You're a Christian too. Lying and heresy run in your blood." The other man slapped me again, shouting about Christianity and teaching English, a language of the corrupt West.

I do not remember all the rest. I remember the pain. I remember the blows. I remember the feeling of fists against my cheek. Of hair being wrenched from my scalp. The sound of a woman crying. The sound of children shrieking. The sound of the men shouting. "Children, go home. If we ever catch any one of you in this house again, we will burn down the house with you in it."

The next thing I knew, I was being pulled to my feet by my hair. "You deserve to die," one of the men said.

"And we will come back for you," the other added. "We will make an example of you. Everyone who finds out what you have done and how you have been punished will learn not to sin against God."

He pushed me and I fell. "We'll be back for you tomorrow!" he called, waving his gun at me.

REVIEW QUESTIONS

1. What motivated the Religious Police?
2. In what ways would the Religious Police denounce the movement for female equality in many parts of the world?

---

8 U.S. Department of State
Human Trafficking

Often called modern slavery, trafficking in human beings who are recruited and transported, usually to other countries, and subjected to forced labor without pay or to prostitution, has become a worldwide phenomenon. Recruiters entice impoverished young people with the promise of well-paying jobs and educational opportunities and arrange for their transportation. Once they reach their destinations, the young persons' hopes are quickly dashed. Faced with beatings, they are forced to work incredibly long hours at various tasks, including prostitution, and have no freedom of movement. The U.S. Department of State has published elaborate reports on human trafficking throughout the world. These reports contain testimonies of the suffering endured by the victims of trafficking. Following are testimonies included in the reports for 2015 and 2016.

2015

United Kingdom / Greece. . . .

When she was 14 years old, Cara met Max while on vacation in Greece with her mother. She fell in love with him and, after only a few weeks, Max persuaded her to move in with him, rather than return to England. He soon broke his promise to take care of her and forced Cara to have sex with strangers. Max first convinced her that the money she made was helping to keep them together; he later threatened to kill her mother if she tried to stop. Max gave Cara to another trafficker who forced her to send postcards to her mother depicting a happy life in Athens. Cara eventually suffered an emotional breakdown and, once hospitalized, was able to ask for help.

United States

Tanya was only 11 years old when her mother traded her to a drug dealer for sex in exchange for heroin. Both Tanya's mother and the drug dealer have been indicted on multiple charges, including sex trafficking. In addition the drug dealer was accused of rape as well as videotaping his sex crimes. At the end of the school year, after four months of such abuse and being forced to take heroin, Tanya went to live with her father and stepmother and confided in them about what had happened. Both her mother and the drug dealer face the possibility of life in prison if convicted on all accounts.

Ghana / United States

At 13 years old, Effia moved to the United States with family friends, excited to learn English an go to school—something her parents in Ghana could not afford. When she arrived, these so-called friends forbade her from attending school and forced her to clean, cook, and watch their children for up to 18 hours a day. The father physically and sexually abused her. Effia received no payment and could not use the telephone. Six years later, after a particularly severe beating, she escaped the house and a neighbor called the police.

Democratic Republic of the Congo

Ruth's grandmother could not afford her tuition, and Ruth, due to physical disabilities, had a difficult time finding employment. When a family friend offered to both take care of Ruth and pay for her studies if she worked for him, the grandmother eagerly accepted. But the friend did not follow through on his promises. He never allowed Ruth to attend school, he forced her to work as a domestic servant and as an agricultural laborer for third parties, and he confiscated all her earnings. The man also raped Ruth repeatedly and abandoned her when she became pregnant.

Iraq

The Islamic State of Iraq and the Levant (ISIL) overran Tariq's town and kidnapped his daughter, along with the wives and daughters of many others. [Gaining access to a telephone, the daughter called Tariq] to tell him that she was going to be sold for $10. In the past year ISIL has abducted and exploited thousands of women and children, sold them in markets and sexually enslaved them, forced them into marriages, or subjected them to forced labor.

Nigeria

Aisha was at a friend's wedding when she was abducted by Boko Haram along with her sister, the bride, and the bride's sister. They were taken to a camp where her friends were forcibly married to Boko Haram fighters. Aisha, at 19 years old, had to learn how to fight; she was trained how to shoot and kill, detonate bombs, and execute attacks on villages. She was forced to participate in armed operations, including against her own village; those that refused were buried in a mass grave. Aisha saw more than 50 people killed, including her sister, before she managed to escape.

Ukraine / United States

Over a period of several years, five Ukrainian brothers fraudulently promised 70 Ukrainians well-paying janitorial jobs at retail stores in the United States. They further lured workers with promises to pay for their room and board and all their travel expenses. Once the workers arrived in the United States, however, the traffickers exacted reimbursement for $10,000–$50,000 in travel debts, making them work 10 to 12 hours per day, seven days a week to repay the debt, almost never providing compensation. The brothers abused the workers physically, psychologically, and sexually, and threatened to hurt the workers' families if they disobeyed. The brothers brought many of the workers into the United States illegally through Mexico. Over time, several new recruits were detained at the border and other victims bravely came forward exposing the trafficking ring. Four of the brother were convicted on charges of human trafficking; one remains a fugitive and is thought to be in Ukraine.

2016

Vietnam / China

When Ping was 12 years old, an acquaintance offered her and a friend jobs in a different city in Vietnam. Ping and her friend accepted the offer. The recruiter took them to a local bus station and placed them on a bus with their "caretaker." When they disembarked, the caretaker revealed they were in China and had been sold into prostitution with 20 other girls. When one of the girls refused to do as she was told, the owners beat her severely. Ping suffered in the brothel for almost a year before authorities raided the establishment, rescued the girls, and returned them to Vietnam.

Nigeria / United Kingdom

When a British-Nigerian couple offered to take Paul, 14 years old, from Nigeria to the UK, enroll him in school, and pay him to perform

---

Department of State U.S.A., *Trafficking in Persons Report* (July 2015), pp. 25, 31, 33–34, 37, 39, 48.
Department of State U.S.A., *Trafficking in Persons Report* (June 2016), pp. 8, 15–16, 21, 23, 39.

housework, he accepted. Once in Britain, however, the family changed his name and added him to their family passport as an adopted son. They forced him to clean their homes for as many as 17 hours each day for no pay and did not allow him to go to school. They took his passport, set up cameras to monitor his movements, and limited his contact with the outside world. Paul tried several times to escape; once he contacted the police, who told him they did not handle family matters. Eight years after that, Paul heard a radio report about modern slavery and bravely reached out to an NGO (a nongovernment organization associated with the United Nations). The NGO helped, and the couple was arrested a few months later after having exploited Paul for 24 years. They each received 10-year sentences.

Guatemala / Belize

When Janine was 13 years old, she met a woman in Guatemala who promised her a well-paying babysitting job in Belize, where the woman lived. Janine accepted and was willingly smuggled from Guatemala to Belize. Instead of a babysitting job, the woman coerced Janine to work at a bar in a small village, and also subjected her to sex trafficking. Janine was never paid and was threatened with detention for having entered the country illegally. Janine was also afraid of a complicit law enforcement official who sexually exploited her. Janine escaped a year later and received assistance from local villagers and other law enforcement visitors.

Syria / Lebanon

Recruiters came to Angela's town in Syria offering paid work in restaurants or hotels in Lebanon, and Angela accepted the opportunity to leave her war torn country. Once in Lebanon, she was subjected to sex trafficking along with more than 7-other women and girls, many of whom were also Syrian. The traffickers locked the girls in hotels and barred their windows. They subjected the women to sex trafficking for more than two months, sometime forcing them to see 20 clients each day. The traffickers also raped and tortured the girls into submission. One day Angela and three others took advantage of a momentary lapse in security and escaped. They boarded a bus and confided in the driver. He reported the incident to the police, who raided the premises, helped release the other victims, and arrested 18 suspected traffickers.

Uganda / United Arab Emirates

When Sanyu's friend moved from Uganda to UAE, she told Sanyu she had found her a job that would cover her travel expenses. Sanyu agreed to join her friend. Only a few days after arriving in Dubai, her friend disappeared and Sanyu's situation changed drastically. A woman came to Sanyu's house and demanded Sanyu repay her for covering her travel expenses. The woman explained Sanyu would need to sell herself for sex. When Sanyu resisted, the traffickers tortured her, denied her food, and made her sleep outside for three weeks. She was trapped in a house with 14 other girls from Uganda and forced to have sex for money. Sanyu and two other girls escaped and returned to Uganda.

A Sex Trafficker

Matthew, convicted sex trafficker: I had girls from the whole country. I had a guy in a nearby village, and he was looking for the girls for me. He was asking 500 euros [about $750 at the time] per girl. . . . In the worst night, a woman would make you 300 Euros. There were some nights when a woman made 1,500 to 2,000 euros.

REVIEW QUESTION

What can be done to curtail human trafficking?

9 Resurgence of Anti-Semitism

In the decades following the Holocaust, overt anti-Semitism appeared to have receded in Western Europe. The outbursts of the traditionally anti-Semitic Far Right—nationalists, racists, Fascists, and opponents of democracy—did not greatly affect the surviving Jews and their descendants who represented a model of successful integration. In recent years, however, there has been a significant upsurge of anti-Semitic incidents in European lands, including physical assaults, the firebombing of Jewish synagogues, schools, and homes, and the desecration of Jewish cemeteries with Nazi symbols—much of it, but not all, initiated by the growing number of Muslims residing in Western Europe. Labor MP Denis MacShane, who, in 2007, chaired a committee of British parliamentarians that studied anti-Semitism in Britain concluded that hatred of Jews has reached new heights in Europe. Similar conclusions were reached by the U.S. State Department and the Parliamentary Assembly of the Council of Europe.

In the past few years in France, radical Muslims have harassed Jews in the streets, engaged in physical attacks on Jews, including the murder of school children, desecrated Jewish cemeteries, and firebombed synagogues. At the time of Israel's conflict with Hamas in Gaza, Muslim mobs attempted to raid or burn several Jewish synagogues in Paris. In one incident, a mob wielding weapons and crying "Death to the Jews," tried to break through a barricaded door and attack some two hundred congregants inside. In January 2015, a Muslim extremist killed four Jewish hostages in a Parisian kosher grocery. The French government immediately deployed some 20,000 soldiers to guard Jewish schools and institutions across the country. Reacting to repellent anti-Semitic incidents, some 7,000 Jews left France in 2014 and the number was expected to grow.

Reaching epidemic proportions, anti-Semitism has become a principal theme in Middle Eastern media and motivation for attacks on Jews by Muslims living in Europe. As Cardinal Tucci, the director of Vatican Radio, stated in November 2003; "Now in the whole Muslim world, in the media, the radio, television, in schools, a whole system inciting to anti-Semitism exists. It is the worst anti-Semitism that can be imagined after Nazi anti-Semitism, if not its equal."

Contemporary Muslim anti-Semitism borrows considerably from traditional European anti-Semitism—Christian, nationalist, and Nazi. Like the Nazis, much of the Muslim world perceives Jews as a criminal people that threatens all humanity. As in Nazi Germany, the media in the Arab/Muslim world are often filled with repulsive caricatures of Jews—dark, stooped, sinister, hook-nosed, devil-like creatures—many of them taken from Nazi works. In Arab sermons, classrooms, schoolbooks, and on the Internet, Jews are often referred to as "accursed," "descendants of apes and pigs," "the scum of the human race," "the rats of the world," "bacteria," "vampires," "usurers," and "whoremongers."

The Arab media have even revived the medieval European myth of blood libel, that Jews are required to murder non-Jewish children to obtain their blood for making unleavened bread for Passover. Holocaust denial is widespread in the Middle East; so too is celebrating Hitler's mass murder of Jews. A columnist for

Al Akhbar, considered a moderate newspaper sponsored by the Egyptian government, gives "thanks to Hitler of blessed memory," for taking revenge against Jews—although Muslims "do have a complaint against him for his revenge on them was not enough." And Dr. Ahmed Abu Halabiyah, rector of advanced studies at the Islamic University of Gaza expresses similar genocidal thoughts: "The Jews must be butchered and must be killed. . . . It is forbidden to have mercy in your hearts for the Jews in any place and in any land, make war on them anywhere that you find yourself. Any place that you meet them, kill them."

Propagated over the Internet and by radical imams in mosques throughout Europe, this demonization of the Jews—together with scenes of violent conflict between Israelis and Palestinians and Hezbollah frequently depicted on television—has incited Muslim youth in Europe to acts of intimidation, physical assault, and vandalism against Jews; it has also led to organized campaigns of vilification of Jews in universities. On a positive note, in some European lands Muslim and Jewish organizations |are engaged in interfaith dialogue, and some Muslim intellectuals and religious leaders have condemned anti-Semitic outbursts.

In addition to the anti-Semitic incidents initiated by Muslims residing in various European lands, analysts have pointed to the ongoing Jew-hatred of the Far Right and a rather new phenomenon—a growing and insidious anti-Semitism afflicting the Left, which is strongly anti-Israel and pro-Palestinian.

As in the past, European anti-Semitism remains a bulwark of the Far Right, who propagate Holocaust denial and Jewish conspiracy theories—that Jews invented a "Holocaust hoax" to extract compensation from Germany; Jews control the world's media and finances and are conspiring to dominate the planet; Jews are the real power behind the U.S. government; Jews are a threat to the nation.

During the Nazi era and for decades before, the Left—liberals, socialists, trade unionists, and intellectuals, including many academics—had been the strongest defenders of Jews against their detractors and oppressors. But now the distinguishing feature of the "new anti-Semitism" is its adoption by many on the Left who employ anti-Semitic language and imagery—linking the Star of David with the swastika—to express their support of the Palestinians and to delegitimize Israel; for them, Israelis are today's Nazis, and Israel is a criminal state that should disappear.

Many Europeans are concerned about the revival of anti-Semitism. They recognize that Jew-hatred and the irrational myths associated with it, which undermine rational thinking and incite barbaric violence, transcend a purely Jewish concern. They threaten the core values of Western civilization as Nazism so painfully demonstrated.

U.S. State Department
CONTEMPORARY GLOBAL ANTI-SEMITISM

The following brief passages are drawn from a comprehensive study, *Contemporary Global Anti-Semitism: A Report Provided to the United States Congress*, prepared in 2008 by the U.S. State Department.

Over the last decade, U.S. embassies and consulates have reported an upsurge in anti-Semitism . . . .

This same trend has been reported with concern by other governments, multilateral institutions, and world leaders. . . .

In the United Kingdom, an All-Party Parliamentary Inquiry into anti-Semitism launched an investigation into anti-Semitism. The Inquiry produced a September 2006 report, which states, "It is clear that violence, desecration of property, and intimidation directed towards Jews is on the rise."

In June 2007, the Parliamentary Assembly of the Council of the Europe issued Resolution 1563, which notes "the persistence and escalation of anti-Semitic phenomena . . . [and that] far from having been eliminated, anti-Semitism is today on the rise in Europe. It appears in a variety of forms and is becoming relatively commonplace.". . .

CONTEMPORARY FORMS OF ANTI-SEMITISM

Contemporary anti-Semitism manifests itself in overt and subtle ways, both in places where sizeable Jewish communities are located and where few Jews live. Anti-Semitic crimes range from acts of violence, including terrorist attacks against Jews, to the desecration and destruction of Jewish property such as synagogues and cemeteries. Anti-Semitic rhetoric, conspiracy theories, and other propaganda circulate widely and rapidly by satellite television, radio, and the Internet.

Traditional forms of anti-Semitism persist and can be found across the globe. Classic anti-Semitic writings, such as *The Protocols of the Learned Elders of Zion* and *Mein Kampf*, remain

commonplace. Jews continue to be accused of blood libel, dual loyalty, and undue influence on government policy and the media, and the symbols and images associated with age-old forms of anti-Semitism endure. These blatant forms of anti-Semitism, often linked with Nazism and Fascism, are considered unacceptable by the mainstream in the democratic nations of Western Europe, North America, and beyond, but they are embraced and employed by the extreme fringe.

Anti-Semitism has proven to be an adaptive phenomenon. New forms of anti-Semitism have evolved. They often incorporate elements of traditional anti-Semitism. However, the distinguishing feature of the new anti-Semitism is criticism of Zionism or Israeli policy that—whether intentionally or unintentionally—has the effect of promoting prejudice against all Jews by demonizing Israel and Israelis and attributing Israel's perceived faults to its Jewish character.

This new anti-Semitism is common throughout the Middle East and in Muslim communities in Europe, but it is not confined to these populations. For example, various United Nations bodies are asked each year on multiple occasions to commission investigations of what often are sensationalized reports of alleged atrocities and other violations of human rights by Israel. Various bodies have been set up within the UN system with the sole purpose of reporting on what is assumed to be ongoing, abusive Israeli behavior. The motive for such actions may be to defuse an immediate crisis, to show others in the Middle East that there are credible means of addressing their concerns other than resorting to violence, or to pursue other legitimate ends. But the collective effect of unremitting criticism of Israel, coupled with a failure to pay attention to regimes that are demonstrably guilty of grave violations, has the effect of reinforcing the notion that the Jewish state is one of the sources, if not the greatest source, of abuse of the rights of others, and thus intentionally or not encourages anti-Semitism.

Contemporary Global Anti-Semitism: A Report Provided by the United States Congress, prepared in 2008 by the United States State Department, pp. 3–7, 19, 21–24.

Comparing contemporary Israeli policy to that of the Nazis is increasingly commonplace. Anti-Semitism couched as criticism of Zionism or Israel often escapes condemnation since it can be more subtle than traditional forms of anti-Semitism, and promoting anti-Semitic attitudes may not be the conscious intent of the purveyor. Israel's policies and practices must be subject to responsible criticism and scrutiny to the same degree as those of any other country. At the same time, those criticizing Israel have a responsibility to consider the effect their actions may have in prompting hatred of Jews. At times hostility toward Israel has translated into physical violence directed at Jews in general. There was, for example, a sharp upsurge in anti-Semitic incidents worldwide during the conflict between Hezbollah and Israel in the summer of 2006.[1]

Governments are increasingly recognized as having a responsibility to work against societal anti-Semitism. But instead of taking action to fight the fires of anti-Semitism, some irresponsible leaders and governments fan the flames of anti-Semitic hatred within their own societies and even beyond their borders. Iran's President Mahmoud Ahmadinejad has actively promoted Holocaust denial, Iran's Jewish population faces official discrimination, and the official media outlets regularly produce anti-Semitic propaganda. The Syrian government routinely demonizes Jews through public statements and official propaganda. In Belarus, state enterprises freely produce and distribute anti-Semitic material. And in Venezuela, President Hugo Chavez has publicly demonized Israel and utilized stereotypes about Jewish financial influence and control, while Venezuela's government-sponsored mass media have become vehicles for anti-Semitic discourse, as have government news media in Saudi Arabia and Egypt.

Elsewhere, *despite* official condemnation and efforts to combat the problem, societal anti-Semitism continues to exist. In Poland, the conservative Catholic radio station *Radio Maryja* is one of Europe's most blatantly anti-Semitic media venues. The Interregional Academy of Personnel Management, a private institution in Ukraine commonly known by the acronym MAUP, is one of the most persistent anti-Semitic institutions in Eastern Europe. In Russia and other countries where xenophobia is widespread, such as some in Central and Eastern Europe, traditional anti-Semitism remains a problem. In France, Germany, the United Kingdom, and elsewhere, anti-Semitic violence remains a significant concern. Recent increases in anti-Semitic incidents have been documented in Argentina, Australia, Canada, South Africa, and beyond.

Today, more than 60 years after the Holocaust, anti-Semitism is not just a fact of history, it is a current event. Around the globe, responsible governments, intergovernmental organizations, non-governmental groups, religious leaders, other respected figures, and ordinary men and women are working to reverse the disturbing trends documented in this report. Much more remains to be done in key areas of education, tolerance promotion, legislation, and law enforcement before anti-Semitism, in all its ugly forms, finally is consigned to the past. . . .

The European Monitoring Center on Racism and Xenophobia (EUMC) [drafted] *A Working Definition of Anti-Semitism.* The EUMC's working definition provides a useful framework for identifying and understanding the problem and is adopted for the purposes of this report. . . .

The EUMC provides explanatory text that discusses the kinds of acts that could be considered anti-Semitic. . . .

---

[1]This upsurge was documented in the U.S. Department of State's 2006 annual *Country Report on Human Rights Practices*, as well as its annual *Report on International Religious Freedom.* These reports can be found at www.state.gov/g/drl.—Eds.

- Calling for, aiding, or justifying the killing or harming of Jews in the name of a radical ideology or an extremist view of religion.

- Making mendacious, dehumanizing, demonizing, or stereotypical allegations about Jews as such or the power of Jews as a collective—such as, especially but not exclusively, the myth about a world Jewish conspiracy or of Jews controlling the media, economy, government or other societal institutions.

- Accusing Jews as a people of being responsible for real or imagined wrongdoing committed by a single Jewish person or group, or even for acts committed by non-Jews.

- Denying the fact, scope, mechanisms (e.g., gas chambers) or intentionality of the genocide of the Jewish people at the hands of National Socialist Germany and its supporters and accomplices during "World War II (the Holocaust).

- Accusing the Jews as a people, or Israel as a state, of inventing or exaggerating the Holocaust.

- Accusing Jewish citizens of being more loyal to Israel, or to the alleged priorities of Jews worldwide, than to the interests of their own nations.

Examples of the ways in which anti-Semitism manifests itself with regard to the state of Israel taking into account the overall context could include:

- Denying the Jewish people their right to self-determination. . . .

- Applying double standards by requiring of it a behavior not expected or demanded of any other democratic nation.

- Using the symbols and images associated with classic anti-Semitism (e.g., claims of Jews killing Jesus or blood libel) to characterize Israel or Israelis.

- Drawing comparisons of contemporary Israeli policy to that of the Nazis.

- Holding Jews collectively responsible for actions of the state of Israel.

The EUMC makes clear, however, that criticism of Israel similar to that leveled against any other country cannot be regarded in itself as anti-Semitic.

CONSPIRACY THEORIES

As noted in the EUMC *Working Definition of Anti-Semitism*, "anti-Semitism frequently charges Jews with conspiring to harm humanity, and it often is used to blame Jews for 'why things go wrong.'" The EUMC includes as contemporary examples of anti-Semitism, "Making mendacious, dehumanizing, or stereotypical allegations about Jews as such or the power of Jews as a collective—such as . . . the myth about a world Jewish conspiracy or of Jews controlling the media, economy, government or other societal institutions."

Anti-Semitism is at the root of numerous contemporary conspiracy theories, including the following examples of false claims.

- Four thousand Jews were falsely accused of not reporting to work at the World Trade Center on September 11, 2001, supposedly because they had been warned not to do so by those who had advance knowledge of the attack.

- The October 2002 terrorist bombing of a nightclub in Bali, Indonesia was falsely rumored to have been caused by an Israeli "mini-nuclear weapon."

- The December 2004 South and Southeast Asian tsunami, caused by an earthquake, was falsely rumored to have been caused by a joint U.S.-Israeli underground nuclear test.

- The United States and Israel are falsely accused of having created an "American Quran"—a document that does not exist.

- U.S. founding father Benjamin Franklin is falsely alleged to have said that Jews were a "great danger" to the United States and should be "excluded by the Constitution." Anti-Semitic conspiracy theories play to widespread hatreds and suspicions. The examples above did not arise spontaneously. In many cases, they had been deliberately concocted. [Thus a Syrian diplomat stated five weeks after 9/11:]

Syria has documented proof of the Zionist regime's involvement in the September 11 terror attacks on the United States . . . [That] 4,000 Jews employed at the World Trade Center did not show up for work before the attack clearly attests to Zionist involvement in these attacks.

The canards reviewed above appear to be 20th and 21st century variations on the classic conspiracy myth of *The Protocols of the Learned Elders of Zion*, which asserts that Jews are inherently evil, manipulate world events for their own purposes, and dominate the world. This century-old Czarist forgery was exposed in 1921 as a fabrication, but it continues to be widely popular and influential around the world, including in bookstores throughout the Middle East, parts of Europe, and beyond.[2] . . .

In fact, long passages of the *Protocols* were plagiarized, word-for-word, from a book published in 1864 titled, *Dialogues in Hell between Machiavelli and Montesquieu*, a work of political satire that did not have an anti-Semitic theme but was written to discredit Emperor Napoleon III of France. Conspiracy theories about alleged predominant Jewish power can have tremendous influence. . . .

HOLOCAUST DENIAL AND TRIVIALIZATION

Efforts to deny or minimize the Nazi genocide against the Jews have become one of the most prevalent forms of anti-Semitic discourse. At its core, Holocaust denial relies upon—and furthers—the traditional anti-Semitic myth of a world Jewish conspiracy.

Holocaust deniers explicitly or implicitly reject that the Nazi government and its allies had a systematic policy of exterminating the Jews, killing between five and seven million Jews, and that genocide was carried out at extermination camps using tools of mass murder such as gas chambers. . . .

Initially, Holocaust deniers primarily were neo-Nazis interested in rehabilitating Fascism and restoring the image of Nazi Germany; for such groups, Holocaust denial has an obvious appeal. The neo-Nazis then were joined by other right-wing groups, such as white supremacists, who were drawn to both Fascism and anti-Semitism. The neo-Nazis and white supremacists share a belief that Jews invented the Holocaust for financial gain (reparations) and spread this "myth" of the Holocaust via their alleged control of the media.

In addition to outright Holocaust deniers, others trivialize the Holocaust and accuse the Jewish people of exaggerating it as justification for the creation of the state of Israel.

A number of deniers have published articles or books trying to discredit well documented facts, historical research, and eye witness accounts, all

---

[2]*The Protocols of the Learned Elder of Zion* has been a recent best seller in Turkey and Syria and once was a best seller in Lebanon. There are at least nine different Arabic translations of the *Protocols* and more editions in Arabic than in any other language. Arabic translations are prominently displayed in bookstores throughout North Africa and the Middle East, as well as Arabic-language bookstores in Western Europe. The *Protocols* also have been prominently displayed at international book fairs (e.g., by the government of Iran at the 2005 Frankfurt International Book Fair). In addition, the *Protocols* are so popular that they have inspired television broadcasts in Egypt, Syria, and other Arab states. In the past, Saudi textbooks reprinted sections and presented them as facts. Hamas and Hezbollah also teach the *Protocols* as fact. Since 2003, new editions of *The Protocols of the Learned Elders of Zion* have been printed in English, Ukrainian, Indonesian, Japanese, Spanish, Italian, Portuguese, Greek, Russian, and Serbian.

the while casting themselves as martyrs standing up to public opprobrium and censorship. . . .

While Holocaust denial began in the 20th century with neo-Nazis and white supremacists in Europe and the United States, in the 21st century it also is found in the Middle East. The potent anti-Semitic assumptions upon which Holocaust denial is founded—primarily the myth of a world Jewish conspiracy—make it an attractive weapon for those seeking to demonize Jews and de-legitimize a major basis for the founding of the state of Israel. . . . [For example:]

"I agree wholeheartedly with [Iranian] President Ahmadinejad. There was no such a [sic] thing as the 'Holocaust.' The so-called 'Holocaust' is nothing but Jewish/Zionist propaganda. There is no proof whatsoever that any living Jew was ever gassed or burned in Nazi Germany or in any of the territories that Nazi Germany occupied during World War II. The Holocaust propaganda was started by the Zionist Jews in order to acquire worldwide sympathy for the creation of Israel after World War II."

—Saudi professor Dr. Abdullah Muhammad Sindi, interview with the *Iranian Mehr News Agency*, December 26, 2005.

REVIEW QUESTION

How does the resurgence of anti-Semitism reveal both the persistence of traditional forms of anti-Semitism and a new adaptive anti-Semitism? Give examples of both.

---

10 In Defense of European Values

In recent years, modern Western civilization, whose core values were articulated during the Enlightenment, has come under severe attack. Some religious thinkers deplore the modern age for its secularism that removes God from life and fosters a soulless materialism. And radical Muslims view Western civilization as fundamentally evil—a satanic foe of God. Some intellectuals have argued that the Western tradition, which has been valued as a great and creative human achievement, is fraught with gender, class, and racial bias, and that its vaunted ideals are really a cloak of hypocrisy intended to conceal, rationalize, and legitimize the power, privileges, and preferences of white European male elites. They condemn the West for continuing to marginalize the poor and people of color and for arrogantly exalting Western values and achievements while belittling other cultures.

Nevertheless, the traditional values that have underlain and inspired European achievements in the modern age—and that represent Europe's legacy to America—continue to find their advocates. At times they have extolled European civilization in the face of critics inclined to belittle its significance. Others call for Europe to embrace its historic roots. To all such commentators, European civilization in the twenty-first century remains vital and enduring.

Jacques Ellul
THE BETRAYAL OF THE WEST

Jacques Ellul (1912–1994), a French sociologist with a pronounced moralist bent, is known for his study of the impact of technology and bureaucracy on the modern world. Ellul wrote *The Betrayal of the West* (1978), excerpts from which follow, to defend Western civilization from its many detractors. His ideas remain pertinent more than forty years after the book's appearance.

I am not criticizing or rejecting other civilisation and societies. . . .

The thing, then that I am protesting against is the silly attitude of western intellectuals in hating their own world and then illogically exalting all other civilizations. Ask yourself . . . Who invented the "rights of man"? . . .

. . . [T]he essential, central, undeniable fact is that the West was the first civilization in history to focus attention on the individual and on freedom. Nothing can rob us of the praise due us for that. We have been guilty of denials and betrayals, . . . we have committed crimes, but we have also caused the whole of mankind to take a gigantic step forward and to leave its childhood behind. . . .

Today men point the finger of outrage at slavery and torture. Where did that kind of indignation originate? What civilization or culture cried out that slavery was unacceptable and torture scandalous? Not Islam, or Buddhism, or Confucius, or Zen, or the religions and moral codes of Africa and India! The West alone has defended the inalienable rights of the human person, the dignity of the individual, . . . [T]he whole European world has certainly not lived up to its own ideal all the time, but to say that it has never lived up to it would be completely false.

. . . The point is that the West originated values and goals that spread throughout the world . . . and inspired man to demand his freedom . . . and affirm his value as an individual. . . .

. . . [T]he West has given the world a certain number of values, movements, and orientations that no one else has provided. No one else has done quite what the West has done. . . . The whole world is living, and living almost exclusively, by these values, ideas, and stimuli . . .

It was not economic power or sudden technological advances that made the West what it is. These played a role, no doubt, but a negligible one in comparison with the great change—the discovery of freedom and the individual. . . .

. . . Communication is the highest expression of freedom, but it has little meaning unless there is a content which, in the last analysis, is supplied by reason. . . . Here precisely we have the magnificent discovery made by the West: that the individual's whole life can be, and even is, the subtle, infinitely delicate interplay of reason and freedom. . . .

. . . No other culture made this discovery. We of the West have the most rounded and self-conscious type of man. . . .

Let me return to my main argument. It was the West that established the splendid interplay of freedom [and] reason, . . . It thus produced a type of human being that is unique in history: true western man. . . . I see no other satisfactory model that can replace what the West has produced.

Excerpted from *The Betrayal of the West* by Jacques Ellul, translated by Matthew J. O'Connell pp. 16–21, 23–24, 28–30, 44–45.

REVIEW QUESTION

From your knowledge of the history of Western civilization, point out historical periods and events that contributed to the traditions of reason and freedom.